Exploring Technology for Writing and Writing Instruction

Kristine E. Pytash
Kent State University, USA

Richard E. Ferdig
Kent State University, USA

A volume in the Advances in Educational
Technologies and Instructional Design
(AETID) Book Series

Information Science REFERENCE

An Imprint of IGI Global

Managing Director:	Lindsay Johnston
Editorial Director:	Joel Gamon
Production Manager:	Jennifer Yoder
Publishing Systems Analyst:	Adrienne Freeland
Development Editor:	Austin DeMarco
Assistant Acquisitions Editor:	Kayla Wolfe
Typesetter:	Christina Barkanic
Cover Design:	Jason Mull

Published in the United States of America by
Information Science Reference (an imprint of IGI Global)
701 E. Chocolate Avenue
Hershey PA 17033
Tel: 717-533-8845
Fax: 717-533-8661
E-mail: cust@igi-global.com
Web site: http://www.igi-global.com

Library of Congress Cataloging-in-Publication Data

Exploring technology for writing and writing instruction / Kristine E. Pytash and Richard E. Ferdig, editors. pages cm
Includes bibliographical references and index.
Summary: "This book examines the use of writing technologies in early childhood, elementary, secondary, and post-secondary classrooms, as well as in professional development contexts"--Provided by publisher.
ISBN 978-1-4666-4341-3 (hardcover) -- ISBN 978-1-4666-4342-0 (ebook) -- ISBN 978-1-4666-4343-7 (print & perpetual access) 1. English language--Rhetoric--Study and teaching--Computer-assisted instruction. 2. Educational technology. 3. English language--Composition and exercises--Study and teaching--Computer-assisted instruction. I. Pytash, Kristine E., 1979- II. Ferdig, Richard E. (Richard Eugene)
  PE1404.E97 2013
  808'.04207--dc23
2013012270

This book is published in the IGI Global book series Advances in Educational Technologies and Instructional Design (AETID) (ISSN: 2326-8905; eISSN: 2326-8913)

British Cataloguing in Publication Data
A Cataloguing in Publication record for this book is available from the British Library.

All work contributed to this book is new, previously-unpublished material. The views expressed in this book are those of the authors, but not necessarily of the publisher.

Advances in Educational Technologies and Instructional Design (AETID) Book Series

Lawrence A. Tomei
Robert Morris University, USA

ISSN: 2326-8905
EISSN: 2326-8913

Mission

Education has undergone, and continues to undergo, immense changes in the way it is enacted and distributed to both child and adult learners. From distance education, Massive-Open-Online-Courses (MOOCs), and electronic tablets in the classroom, technology is now an integral part of the educational experience and is also affecting the way educators communicate information to students.

The **Advances in Educational Technologies & Instructional Design (AETID) Book Series** is a resource where researchers, students, administrators, and educators alike can find the most updated research and theories regarding technology's integration within education and its effect on teaching as a practice.

COVERAGE
Adaptive Learning
Collaboration Tools
Curriculum Development
Digital Divide in Education
E-Learning
Game-Based Learning
Hybrid Learning
Instructional Design
Social Media Effects on Education
Web 2.0 and Education

IGI Global is currently accepting manuscripts for publication within this series. To submit a proposal for a volume in this series, please contact our Acquisition Editors at Acquisitions@igi-global.com or visit: http://www.igi-global.com/publish/.

Titles in this Series

For a list of additional titles in this series, please visit: www.igi-global.com

Pedagogical Considerations and Opportunities for Teaching and Learning on the Web
Michael Thomas (University of Central Lancashire, UK)
Information Science Reference • copyright 2014 • 357pp • H/C (ISBN: 9781466646117) • US $175.00 (our price)

Technology Platform Innovations and Forthcoming Trends in Ubiquitous Learning
Francisco Milton Mendes Neto (Rural Federal University of Semi-Arid, Brazil)
Information Science Reference • copyright 2014 • 317pp • H/C (ISBN: 9781466645424) • US $175.00 (our price)

Advancing Technology and Educational Development through Blended Learning in Emerging Economies
Nwachukwu Prince Ololube (University of Education Port Harcourt, Nigeria)
Information Science Reference • copyright 2014 • 329pp • H/C (ISBN: 9781466645745) • US $175.00 (our price)

Packaging Digital Information for Enhanced Learning and Analysis Data Visualization, Spatialization, and Multidimensionality
Shalin Hai-Jew (Kansas State University, U.S.A)
Information Science Reference • copyright 2014 • 349pp • H/C (ISBN: 9781466644625) • US $175.00 (our price)

Cases on Communication Technology for Second Language Acquisition and Cultural Learning
Joan E. Aitken (Park University, USA)
Information Science Reference • copyright 2014 • 358pp • H/C (ISBN: 9781466644823) • US $175.00 (our price)

Exploring Technology for Writing and Writing Instruction
Kristine E. Pytash (Kent State University, USA) and Richard E. Ferdig (Research Center for Educational Technology - Kent State University, USA)
Information Science Reference • copyright 2014 • 368pp • H/C (ISBN: 9781466643413) • US $175.00 (our price)

Cases on Educational Technology Planning, Design, and Implementation A Project Management Perspective
Angela D. Benson (University of Alabama, USA) Joi L. Moore (University of Missouri, USA) and Shahron Williams van Rooij (George Mason University, USA)
Information Science Reference • copyright 2013 • 328pp • H/C (ISBN: 9781466642379) • US $175.00 (our price)

Common Core Mathematics Standards and Implementing Digital Technologies
Drew Polly (University of North Carolina at Charlotte, USA)
Information Science Reference • copyright 2013 • 364pp • H/C (ISBN: 9781466640863) • US $175.00 (our price)

DISSEMINATOR OF KNOWLEDGE

www.igi-global.com

701 E. Chocolate Ave., Hershey, PA 17033
Order online at www.igi-global.com or call 717-533-8845 x100
To place a standing order for titles released in this series, contact: cust@igi-global.com
Mon-Fri 8:00 am - 5:00 pm (est) or fax 24 hours a day 717-533-8661

JJ & Ryan
Owen & Ethan

"that is, that you and I may be mutually encouraged by each other's faith" (Romans 1:12, NIV)

Editorial Advisory Board

Table of Contents

Section 1
New Tools and Theories

Section 5
Writing and Identity

Detailed Table of Contents

Section 1
New Tools and Theories

As educators consider and learn about ways to teach writing with technology, new tools are being developed. What tools have been developed and found to be empirically sound in the teaching of writing? How do teachers and students learn to use these tools and what does it mean for their instruction and learning? As teachers embed these tools into their teaching practices, how does this change their instructional approaches and goals? How do these tools develop students' writing abilities and perceptions about themselves as writers? These new technological tools are fundamentally changing the physical act of writing and the linguistic structures of language. The last two chapters featured in this section examine new and emerging theories. The first explores how technological tools have changed how people engage in the physical nature of writing and the final chapter analyze how technological tools are producing shifts in discourse and speech communication.

Rod D. Roscoe, Arizona State University, USA
Russell D. Brandon, Arizona State University, USA
Erica L. Snow, Arizona State University, USA
Danielle S. McNamara, Arizona State University, USA

In this chapter, the authors consider the value of educational games to support students' writing strategy acquisition and practice. Sixty-five high school students participated in a summer program using the Writing Pal, an intelligent tutoring system designed to support adolescents' persuasive writing across multiple phases of the writing process. Overall, students who interacted with the full W-Pal intelligent tutoring system (i.e., animated strategy lessons, game-based practice, and essay-based practice with feedback) were better able to articulate new writing strategies than students who engaged in intensive essay-based practice by writing and revising twice as many essays with feedback. Importantly, performance within several educational games was found to be a significant predictor of strategy acquisition. The authors argue that these strategy benefits arise from the ways in which strategy-specific, game-based practice activities support the decomposition of task goals, clear operations for achieving those goals, compensation for individual differences, and motivation to practice.

Chapter 2

Youngmin Park, University of California – Irvine, USA

Mark Warschauer, University of California – Irvine, USA

Penelope Collins, University of California – Irvine, USA

Jin Kyoung Hwang, University of California – Irvine, USA

Charles Vogel, Eagle Valley Schools, USA

The recently adopted Common Core State Standards emphasize the importance of language forms and structure in learning to write. Yet most language arts teachers have either downplayed the linguistic structure of writing in favor of process approaches or emphasized the teaching of grammatical structures outside of the context of authentic writing. Technology-supported writing activities tend to mimic these two approaches, with teachers using technology for either process-based writing or for grammar drills. Most teachers are not well prepared to teach linguistic structures in context or to deploy technology for that purpose. This chapter introduces a new tool called Visual-Syntactic Text Formatting (VSTF) that has powerful affordances for teaching linguistic and textual structures in the context of authentic written genres. Drawing on an empirical study and an action research project conducted by the authors, they share evidence for the value of using VSTF and point to ways that it can be used in the classroom to help students master language structures and employ them in their composition.

Chapter 3

Brian Kissel, University of North Carolina – Charlotte, USA

S. Michael Putman, University of North Carolina – Charlotte, USA

Katie Stover, Furman University, USA

There is a clear consensus that students need to be proficient in the use of digital technologies to help them become knowledgeable participants in an era of global information sharing (International Reading Association, 2009). Acknowledging this, the current study was situated in the belief that writers, when engaged in online composition and the creation of digital portfolios, engage in processes that differ from traditional pencil-paper types of writing. A qualitative approach was utilized to examine student writing samples and reflections over a two-year timeframe as the students transitioned from traditional writing portfolios to those created and maintained digitally on a wiki. The results demonstrated that digital portfolios provide a platform for students to communicate, express their ideas, share their understandings, and collaboratively construct meaning with an authentic audience. Correspondingly, it also demonstrates the necessity of adjusting teaching practices to accommodate for conditions that arise from the unique opportunities presented by the digital environment.

Chapter 4

Ewa McGrail, Georgia State University, USA

J. Patrick McGrail, Jacksonville State University, USA

Twenty-first century technologies, in particular the Internet and Web 2.0 applications, have transformed the practice of writing and exposed it to interactivity. One interactive method that has received a lot of critical attention is blogging. The authors sought to understand more fully whom young bloggers both invoked in their blogging (their idealized, intentional audience) and whom they addressed (whom they actually blogged to, following interactive posts). They studied the complete, yearlong blog histories of fifteen fifth-graders, with an eye toward understanding how these students constructed audiences and modified them, according to feedback they received from teachers as well as peers and adults from around the world. The authors found that these students, who had rarely or never blogged before, were much more likely to respond to distant teachers, pre-service teachers, and graduate students than to their own classroom teachers or peers from their immediate classroom. The bloggers invoked/addressed their audiences differently too, depending on the roles that they had created for their audiences and themselves. The authors explore how and why this came to be the case with young writers.

Chapter 5

"The Internet is the most appealing and expressive technology that humanity has ever encountered; the point for teachers is not to push that round peg into our square hole, but to make the Internet a productive technology for what people inherently want to do, make sense with each other."-Fred Kemp. This chapter invites writing instructors to consider integrating blogging practices as a writing exercise that both supports the 21st Century Google-aged learner and the contemplative writing classroom. The author suggests that blogging mirrors traditional personal voice writing and, if supported by a mindful practice such as freewriting, can assist students in bringing all of their faculties into the classroom, thus providing a more holistic and meaningful learning experience.

Chapter 6

Due to increasing digitization, more and more of our writing is done by tapping on keyboards rather than by putting pen to paper. As handwriting is increasingly marginalized both inside and outside of schools, and children learn to write by typing "ready-mades" on different kinds of keyboards rather than by shaping each letter from scratch, we ought to acknowledge the physical and sensorimotor aspect of writing, in addition to the more typically studied cognitive and linguistic aspects. The shaping of letters and words in handwriting involve distinct kinesthetic processes that differ markedly from the kinesthesia involved in tapping keys on a keyboard. The ways in which we use our fingers and hands play an important role in perceptual and cognitive processing; hence, the shift from handwriting to typewriting might entail far-reaching cognitive as well as educational implications. This chapter reflects on some largely neglected aspects of the ongoing shift from handwriting to typewriting, focusing in particular on potential cognitive and phenomenological implications of the increasing abstraction of inscription entailed in typing on a keyboard, and the intangibility of the resulting text on screen compared to that produced by handwriting with pen on a material substrate such as paper.

Chapter 7

A study by the Pew Internet and American Life Project has indicated that teens are writing more than ever and that much of this writing is done in digital spaces. However, digitalk, the informal language used, often breaks from Standard English, and adults are concerned about the effects of digitalk on literacy skills in general. This chapter reports research that focuses on what language teens use in their digitalk and why they make the choices they do. With analysis of digital writing from 81 adolescents, researchers identified 18 conventions of digitalk. In a second phase of research, teens were surveyed and interviewed about their linguistic choices. Findings indicate that adolescents attend to audience, and they consider personal voice in their digital writing. Teens develop these competencies in a community of writers – outside of school.

Section 2
New Tools for Revision and Feedback

How can writing instructors provide feedback that nurtures and develops students' growth as writers? How do educators teach students to effectively respond to others' writing during peer-review opportunities in the classroom? Issues surrounding how to provide effective feedback and engage students in the feedback and revision process have been a long-standing research questions in the field of writing. Providing writers with specific feedback can be a challenging task for teachers and students alike. New online environments and tools have prompted researchers to examine specific platforms that teachers and students might use to respond to writing during instruction. The chapters in this section explore specific tools and research with specific online platforms in classroom settings.

Chapter 8

Using the method of a formative experiment, this investigation examines how the use of peer revision and collaboration in an online environment, specifically a social network, could be implemented in a middle school classroom to increase revision over multiple drafts and improve the quality of student expository writing. Thirty-six students in two sections of a seventh-grade English language arts class participated in the study. Quantitative and qualitative data were collected prior to, during, and after the intervention to establish baseline data, as well as determine progress toward the pedagogical goal. Analyses reveal improvement in the amount of student revision and quality of student writing, as well as improved peer feedback using an online community for peer revision and collaboration. The enhancing and inhibiting effects of technology in this intervention is examined, as well as the unanticipated effects of the intervention.

Chapter 9

In this chapter, the authors present a case study of one writer, Tom, to uncover how his writing was mediated by school-level and individual factors. The online writing environment had three major affordances for Tom in this 8th grade classroom: the online writing environment increased Tom's access to peer response, motivated him write to a higher standard for an audience, and both scaffolded and increased his response repertoire. However, the larger policy context in which Tom's writing was embedded placed constraints on the classroom and school. Other constraints included Tom's lack of access to a computer at home, the teacher's highly structured task, and the online tool's assignment of random reviewers that forced Tom to continually write to a new audience of peers who lacked the previous context. In light of the situated nature of Tom's writing and responses in this classroom, the authors make recommendations for policy, research, and instruction.

Chapter 10

Sarah-Beth Hopton, University of South Florida, USA

In the past decade, digital feedback tools to review and revise student writing have proliferated. Scholarship in rhetoric, composition, and professional writing has yet to consider how digital feedback systems might offer a promising alternative to traditional and arguably broken feedback practices. This chapter offers a review of the latest scholarship on the digital feedback and revision practices of students and professors, and demonstrates the use of a heuristic customized to college writing applications and programs, which can help professors review and assess new digital tools used to manage an electronic feedback and assessment protocol.

Section 3
Online Spaces for Writing

There are many conversations about how young people spend a significant amount of time writing in online spaces, but what does it mean to write "online" or in a "digital environment"? What affordances do these new spaces provide writers? How do teachers use online spaces for writing instruction? The chapters in this section examine online spaces for writing and how these are being used by writers both in and out of the classroom. These chapters specifically examine how young adults writing in these online spaces have more opportunities for collaboration and engaging in a writerly community.

Chapter 11

Jayne C. Lammers, University of Rochester, USA
Alecia Marie Magnifico, University of Illinois – Urbana-Champaign, USA
Jen Scott Curwood, University of Sydney, Australia

This chapter explores how writers respond to interactions with readers and audience members in two technology-mediated writing contexts: a *Hunger Games* fan's use of FanFiction.net and a classroom using *Scholar* to write original narrative texts. The authors look across the two spaces to analyze similarities in how the technology is used to foster interaction with readers and develop writers' craft through these interactions. In particular, they analyze how writing functions in each space as a tool, a place, and a way of being. By considering the affordances of these two contexts, the authors argue that technology is changing how we write and learn to write, in and out-of-school, by connecting writers with an audience that can significantly shape their goals, skills, and processes.

Chapter 12

Bernadette Dwyer, St. Patrick's College, Dublin City University, Ireland
Lotta Larson, Kansas State University, USA

Digital reading environments are redefining the relationship between reader, text, activity, and sociocultural context. This chapter explores the nature of engagement, collaboration, and reader/writer response, as sixth-grade students from Ireland and the United States read and responded to electronic books within the context of an online global literature circle. In response to the readings, students composed digital thinkmarks, which served as springboards for subsequent written asynchronous message board discussions. Findings from this qualitative case study suggest that peer collaboration in an online literature discussion forum enabled the construction of social identity, community building, and a sociocultural situated response and engendered immersion in, involvement with, and interpretation of texts.

Chapter 13

Michelle A. Honeyford, University of Manitoba, Canada

This chapter addresses the disconnect between in- and out-of-school writing spaces. Drawing from a larger study of the writing of bilingual Latino immigrant youth in a middle school English language class, the author examines the epistolary community created through an exchange of emails with a group of first-generation Latino university students. The author draws on an ecologies of writing framework to explore writing and place-based identities and the notion of writing across digital and cultural communities in order to analyze the relational, locational, and collective work the students were engaged in. The chapter suggests implications for creating new spaces for writing in school, drawing on social and digital media to participate in imaginative and intellectual literacy work.

Section 4
Writing Instruction

Teachers' instructional practices must be guided by a strong conceptual framework that includes knowledge of writing and the pedagogical approaches effective for the teaching of writing. Technology has influenced our conceptions of what it means to write as students are now engaged in multimodal compositions and digital writing. What does this shift in writing mean for the pedagogical strategies used to teach writing? The chapters in this section explore how instruction is changing to meet the new demands of writing with technology. How should teachers teach writing with technology? The chapters in this section address these important questions.

Chapter 14

Jennifer Higgs, University of California – Berkeley, USA
Catherine Anne Miller, University of California – Berkeley, USA
P. David Pearson, University of California – Berkeley, USA

As Computer-Mediated Communication (CMC) is increasingly adopted for literacy instruction in K-12 classrooms, careful attention should be paid to its instructional benefits and challenges. In this chapter, the authors take a careful look at how the metaphors of social interaction guiding teacher translation of CMC into their lessons mask the full range of affordances and limitations of CMC. Using a linguistic lens, they analyze teacher interviews and student online discussion data to make a case that using Classroom Digital Interaction (CDI) as a pedagogical tool requires a close look at the aims of literacy instruction and the constraints and affordances of computer mediated discussion.

In this chapter, the authors review literature describing how reading processes appear to work in online and other digital environments. In particular, the nature of reading, writing, and the academic utility of new literacies is explored and applied to the digital environments of secondary school students. Writing is described as an ill-defined domain and situated theoretically in classical discourse theories as well as cognitive-linguistic approaches that explain reading and writing interactions in digital environments. Specific considerations for using digital texts as sources for written work are explained, including the role of search engine optimization techniques on reading and how access to multiple varied sources changes what students can learn. Implications and suggestions for future research are provided.

Chapter 16

It is increasingly clear that this generation of adolescents is almost always connected to online information (Horrigan, 2010; Pew Research Center, 2010). Indeed, the Internet has quickly become this generation's defining technology for literacy, in part due to facilitating access to an unlimited amount of online information and media (Rideout, Foehr, & Roberts, 2010). Yet it is a paradox that history's first generation of "always connected" individuals (Pew Research Center, 2010) is not taught how to effectively and authentically use the digital texts and tools that permeate society. As society has incorporated dynamic and new media in everyday life, educators are required to expand traditional understandings of text and literacy that have replaced many of the ways that we communicate, create, and socialize (Sutherland-Smith, 2002; Alvermann, 2002). Put simply, there is a need to value and construct different kinds of texts, learning, and interactions within the classroom (Beach & Myers, 2001). To achieve this goal, this chapter presents a synthesis of theoretical perspectives and research into a new instructional model known as Online Content Construction (OCC). OCC is defined as the skills, strategies, and dispositions necessary as students construct, redesign, or reinvent online texts by actively encoding and decoding meaning through the use of digital texts and tools.

Chapter 17

This chapter aims to synthesize research on technology and second language writing through the lenses of three common and broad discourses surrounding literacy and technology: achievement, change, and power (modified from Warschauer & Ware, 2008). The authors discuss the meaning and relationship of each perspective to the field of technology and second language writing as well as provide an overview of recent research under each category. This framework-based analysis sheds new light on current research, offering researchers and teachers an opportunity to consider the weaknesses and strengths of each research focus as well as the gaps in the literature. Through examining the interwoven relationship between technology and second language writing under different perspectives, the authors ultimately aim to explore the ways we can maximize the educational benefits of technology use for non-native speakers of English.

Section 5
Writing and Identity

If technology is influencing the way people write, what does this mean for how students and teachers perceive themselves as writers and writing instructors? Having a writerly identity is important, but what does it mean to have a writerly identity in an online space? Similarly, when teachers use technology to teach writing in the classroom, what does this mean for not only their pedagogical approaches, but also about their belief structures about writing instruction.

Chapter 18
"The More I Write…The More my Mind Evolves into Something Outstanding": Composing

Mary Beth Hines, Indiana University – Bloomington, USA

Jennifer M. Conner-Zachocki, Indiana University – Columbus, USA

Becky Rupert, Graduation High School, USA

This chapter draws from a one-year qualitative investigation of a ninth-grade English classroom in a new technology-rich high school. The study explores the question, What identities did students compose as they alternately resisted and embraced the use of digital media in the writing classroom? Presenting a case study of one student, Shane, the chapter traces the ways in which he responded to the teacher's invitations to use digital media, thereby discursively crafting particular identity performances in on-site and online communities. Analysis identifies a number of tensions specific to the use of authentic audiences and purposes in the 21st century digital writing classroom and reveals three identity performance categories: Shane the comedian, Shane the subversive and Shane the artist. In analyzing the ways in which social networking tools, literacy practices, and identity performances converge in the classroom, the chapter challenges dominant pedagogical assumptions about using new technologies in the schools to engage learners.

Chapter 19
"What Up" and "TQM": English Learners Writing on Facebook to Acquire English and Express

Mary Amanda Stewart, Texas Woman's University, USA

Previous scholarship demonstrates that immigrant students are using digital technologies for unique purposes in their out-of-school writing. This study explores the writing on Facebook of four Latina/o immigrant youth who are English Learners. The findings show that the participants write on Facebook to further their English acquisition and express their Latina/o identities in ways not accessible to them in school. Their purposes for writing demonstrate there is much academic potential in leveraging social networking for in-school writing instruction for immigrant students.

Chapter 20

Adding the "Digital Layer": Examining One Teacher's Growth as a Digital Writer Through an

Troy Hicks, Central Michigan University, USA

Opportunities for teachers to engage in professional development that leads to substantive change in their instructional practice are few, yet the National Writing Project (NWP) provides one such "transformational" experience through their summer institutes (Whitney, 2008). Also, despite recent moves in the field of English education to integrate digital writing into teacher education and K-12 schools (NWP, et al., 2010), professional development models that support teachers' "technological pedagogical content knowledge" (Mishra & Koehler, 2008) related to teaching digital writing are few. This case study documents the experience of one teacher who participated in an NWP summer institute with the author, himself a teacher educator and site director interested in technology and writing. Relying on evidence from her 2010 summer experience, subsequent work with the writing project, and an interview from the winter of 2013, the author argues that an integrative, immersive model of teaching and learning digital writing in the summer institute led to substantive changes in her classroom practice and work as a teacher leader. Implications for teacher educators, researchers, and educational policy are discussed.

Foreword

Once upon a time, the act of entering text into a computer was unknown to most and challenging for a select few. A decade later, as it became more commonplace, many were delighted to discover the wonderful feature of word processing that meant never having to copy over just because some change was needed. By the 1970s word processing had entered the business world, and soon after, the classroom. Some educators began to say that writing, not mathematics, might be the signature feature of the computer. In the 1980s, I worked with *Quill*, which provided early versions of organization tools, email, and collaboration tools, but those were primitive by today's standards. More typically, writing with computers meant little more than a means to facilitate revision, if that happened at all, or to make student work look neater than it would if written by hand.

How things have changed! As the chapters in *Exploring Technology for Writing and Writing Instruction* attest, writing with new technologies has blossomed into a garden of creative activities. We now see blogging, remixing, rating, portfolio building, and the use of online information. The computer serves to guide revision, display text features, and provide sources for writers, not just to enable text production. The authors in this volume are exploring how to build writing and response communities. They are examining the implications for developing writers and for English Language Learners.

Kristine Pytash and Rick Ferdig have brought together an outstanding group of authors whose explorations show us that the space for technology for writing is more varied and more challenging than some had imagined. Rather than having a tool that simply facilitates some aspects of pedagogy, we have a set of tools, or new media, as some would prefer, which transform possibilities for inquiry, communication, creation, and expression. Technology for writing enters the pedagogical world in three important ways, each of which are well represented in this book.

First, we need to *learn the technologies*. Young people today are often viewed as being digital natives, able to miraculously manipulate any device with an "e-" or "i-" in front of its name. They walk around with ear buds and smart phones, operating two, three, or more instruments at once. They Google the world and post incessantly, but this picture is incomplete at best. Many young people have limited access to these new tools. Multitasking is more an illusion than a fact. Perhaps, most importantly, the very facility that some young people demonstrate belies (the) misconceptions and limited awareness they have of the very tools that are supposed to represent their generation. The chapters here address the need to learn the (these) technologies. They show what learners can do with blogs, glogs, wikis, computer-mediated communication, social media, affinity spaces, and other media, but also, where they can learn more. By implication, they also serve to show what teachers can learn, both for their own facility and for teaching others.

Second, we need to *learn through the technologies*. New media offers opportunities to learn language, science, history, indeed, every aspect of the curriculum. They are thinking tools, which help us develop and extend our general problem-solving abilities. At the same time, they can limit our understanding, as, for example, when an online search leads to inaccurate information, or a collaboration (collaborative?) space results in a hurtful or unhelpful response. Thus, there is a need for developing critical engagement and understanding the perspectives of others (maybe a bit more? or maybe not). The chapters describe explorations of this learning through technology, demonstrating what is possible, as well as what is needed to facilitate that learning.

Third, we need to *learn about the technologies*—what they mean for our individual lives and our collective endeavors. This is crucial for both students in the classroom and for teachers. Questions that might seem to be reserved for a linguist, a literary critic, or a philosopher are ones that the beginning student needs to engage with at some level: What is a text? What is an audience? How do I assess validity of a claim? What is an online identity? How does community relate to writing and learning to write? The chapters here offer a powerful resource for understanding what the technologies are, what they facilitate or hinder, and what they mean for ourselves and our futures.

Bertram Bruce
University of Illinois – Urbana-Champaign, USA

Bertram (Chip) Bruce *is a Professor Emeritus in Library & Information Science at the University of Illinois at Urbana-Champaign. He also had appointments in Curriculum & Instruction, Bioengineering, the Center for Writing Studies, and the Center for East Asian & Pacific Studies. During 2007-08, he held a Fulbright Distinguished Chair at the National College of Ireland in Dublin. Professor Bruce's research goals include contributing to a conception of democratic education, meaning both the development of critical, socially-engaged citizens and of learning environments (formal and informal learning centers, home and work, and online), which are themselves democratic. Aspects of this work include research on community inquiry through collaborative community-based work, inquiry-based learning, drawing especially upon scholarship of the American pragmatists and the history of Progressive Education, and technology-enhanced learning, including research on the affordances and constraints of new media for learning.*

Preface

The Oriental Institute of the University of Chicago featured an exhibit, *Visible Language: Inventions of Writing in the Ancient Middle East*, which displayed the origins of written language: the hieroglyphs of ancient Egypt that often told the narrative of a Pharoh's life and the cuneiform tablets of Ancient Summarian and Phoenicans that recorded business transactions, land titles, and the king's expenditures. The exhibit curator, Christopher Woods (2010) said, "In the eyes of many, writing represents a defining quality of civilization" (p. 3).

These early texts reflected aspects of the culture of societies. Each written record had a form, a graphic representation, and a particular function. Written language captured unique histories and stories that reflected the times. Written words ignited revolutions, spread religions, and established and enforced judicial systems. When analyzing and examining writing from a historical perspective, Olson (1994) posited, "new ways of reading gave rise to new ways of writing texts and both gave rise to new ways of thinking about the world and about the mind" (p. 143).

Today we are witnessing another great writing revolution as technology is fundamentally changing how we physically write, the spaces where we produce writing, the ways writing is disseminated, and the amount of people who have access to that writing. Technology and writing have always influenced each other. For example, the radical shift in information and schooling was due to the Gutenberg printing press—books could be available to everyone, ideas could be widely disseminated. However, these recent, rapid changes in technology have prompted new questions about writing and its role in society, education, policy, and culture.

- How has digital writing (including text, tweets, blogs, social media, etc.) changed both the forms and functions of writing in our current society?
- What is the relevance of writing in our digital and technological age?
- What is the function of writing and does digital writing change our thinking? Our culture?
- If technology is changing the form and function of writing, what does this change mean for how we educate members of our society?
- How have digital tools in classrooms created new affordances for students learning to write?
- How do writing in online spaces teach students about the many nuances of writing?
- How do technological tools continue to develop what writing researchers know are effective methods for teaching writing?
- How are researchers and educators using new tools to conceptualize new instructional models for effective instruction?
- Do technological tools and online spaces further divide students' in-school and out-of-school writing practices? Or do technological tools and online spaces provide a bridge to increase teachers' abilities to create culturally relevant pedagogies surrounding writing instruction?
- New assessments, with significant components devoted to writing, are being developed. What do these standards mandate about a technological component of writing instruction? How might technology be used to create platforms for new assessments?

One volume will not be able to answer all of these questions. However, one goal of this book is to promote and disseminate current research exploring technology for writing and writing instruction—research that begins to examine and provide evidence to answer or provide further insight into many of these questions. A second goal is to bring together voices of influential researchers and educators in the fields of writing and technology, as well as, the work of promising up-and-coming researchers. A third goal is to thoughtfully represent the most current research related to technology and writing instruction. Having a sense of the current research landscape strengthens future work in both the research conducted and the practices implemented in classrooms. However, we acknowledge technology is rapidly changing and developing, and so this book is not necessarily intended to highlight specific tools that should be used during writing instruction. Rather, we hope these chapters initiate more general conversations about the affordances of using technological tools in writing classrooms.

The curriculum being enacted in classrooms and the instructional approaches being practiced are heavily influenced by educational policies. Thus, a final goal is that this book can be used by those designing policies to consider the various affordances and constraints of technology for writing instruction.

THE PROCESS OF EDITING THIS BOOK

We are fortunate to work at a university that encourages collaboration amongst faculty members. In March of 2011, we both attended a meeting facilitated by the college Dean with the goal of facilitating interdisciplinary conversations and work. This initial meeting led to subsequent discussions about the intersections of technology and literacy. Our appreciation for each others' work allowed us to engage in many conversations surrounding the issues, challenges, and current research in our respective fields. We shared the articles and books we were currently reading, provided feedback on each others' work, and began collaborating on research and writing projects. This work prompted us to ask how technology was influencing the way people conceptualize writing, how people write, and how we teach writing. The idea for this book evolved from these many and extensive discussions about the intersections between technology, writing, and writing instruction.

It is important to note that we did not select authors to write particular chapters. In the early fall of 2012, we distributed an open call for proposals. We asked for theoretical and empirical chapters focused on topics, such as digital assessments, online writing communities, technology-facilitated feedback and revision, online education, and social media. These are just a few of the many topics featured in the proposals we received. The call for proposals was distributed in multiple venues.

1. We worked with our graduate assistant to gather the names and email addresses of researchers and educators who received funding for work on writing and technology in the last 10 years, as evidenced by a search in the *National Science Foundation* and *Institute of Education Sciences* databases. Using various academic search engines, we found authors who published on this topic within the same timeframe. This information was collected, and authors were emailed the call for proposals.
2. We sent the call using major professional organizations' listservs. This included the ITForum, the LRA listserv, the NCTE discussion forum, the ALER listserv (thanks to Kristine Still), the AERA Writing and Literacies SIG (thanks to Heather Pleasants), and the IRA TILE-SIG (thanks to Julie Coiro).

3.   The Editorial Review Board was created. They were asked to share the call for proposals to their network of colleagues.

4.   We created a Website that contained pertinent information for potential authors.

Proposals were submitted at the end of September 2012. While we were obviously aware of the growing number of researchers and educators interested in this topic and working in this field of study, we were surprised to receive over 100 proposals. We reviewed each proposal and accepted ones based mainly on their content and appropriateness for the book and the quality of the theoretical or empirical research presented. Authors were notified of the acceptance of their proposal and were given until December 31, 2012 to write their full chapter. Chapters were then sent through a double-blind peer review process with our Editorial Review Board. The Editorial Review Board provided guidance as we selected chapters for acceptance and also provided extensive feedback and insight to authors about their work. Authors whose chapters were accepted had until March 1, 2013 to submit their final chapters.

THE ORGANIZATION OF THIS BOOK

This book is divided into five sections:

New Tools and Theories: The chapters in this section examine technological tools to teach writing. Researchers examine tools used in classrooms for instruction and the affordances they create for students. This section also includes chapters focused on new theories about how these tools change the physical act of writing and the linguistic structures of language.

New Tools for Revision and Feedback: This section analyzes tools specifically used for revision and feedback. While this section might seem similar to the chapters in the previous section, it is interesting to note that educators are looking to technology to assist with teaching a particular aspect of the writing process.

Online Spaces for Writing: The chapters in this section highlight online spaces for writing. These chapters examine how writing is changing because of the places where people compose and produce texts.

Writing Instruction: This section includes chapters that examine how the inclusion of technology in the classroom requires educators to reflect on and reconsider instructional practices. These authors provide pedagogical models for effectively teaching writing using technology.

Writing and Identity: The final section of the book examines how it is not only technology, tools, and spaces that are changing because of technology but also the influence of technology on writerly identities. These chapters analyze the ways students and teachers perceive themselves as digital writers and teachers of digital writers.

In order to organize the book, we divided the chapters into sections by asking ourselves about the main goals of each chapter. We asked ourselves, "What is this chapter intending to examine and what contribution is it making to the field?" These sections are not mutually exclusive. There are chapters that represent multiple themes and could have been placed in multiple sections. For example, Stewart's chapter on the Facebook writings of four Latina/o immigrant youth was placed in the section "Writing and Identity." This decision was made as one of the main findings was the divide between the youth's in-school writing and writing on Facebook, which they used to express their Latina/o identities. However, because Facebook is an online space where people write, it could have also been placed in the section, "Online Spaces."

We used overarching themes to place the chapter in the section that best represented the overall findings and objectives of the chapter. We also used the headings to highlight key topics being researched in the field as evidenced by the chapters. Regardless of placement in specific sections, we hope readers examine each chapter while considering the following questions:

- How have digital tools in classrooms created new affordances for students just learning to write?
- How does writing in online spaces teach students about the many nuances of writing?
- How is technology changing the way we talk and write?
- How do technological tools continue to develop what writing researchers know are effective methods for teaching writing?
- What new models and frameworks are being conceptualized to teach writing?

CONCLUSION

We proudly offer this collected work as a way to support the importance of technology for writing and writing instruction. The chapters in this book represent the diverse and exciting work taking place in our field. This book is offered for discussion about and reflection on the changing nature of writing, the influence of technology, and the research being done in the field. We believe a comprehensive examination of the research surrounding technology and writing will strengthen future work in this important area of study. We encourage educators to continue the exploration of the implications of using technological tools in writing classrooms, and we hope research in this area will influence conversations of policy surrounding technology, writing, and writing instruction.

Respectfully,

Kristine E. Pytash
Kent State University, USA

Richard E. Ferdig
Kent State University, USA

REFERENCES

Olson, D. (1994). *World on paper*. New York, NY: Cambridge University Press.

Woods, C. (2010). *Visible language: Inventions of writing in the ancient Middle East*. Retrieved March 20, 2013 from http://oi.uchicago.edu/museum/special/writing/

Section 1
New Tools and Theories

As educators consider and learn about ways to teach writing with technology, new tools are being developed. What tools have been developed and found to be empirically sound in the teaching of writing? How do teachers and students learn to use these tools and what does it mean for their instruction and learning? As teachers embed these tools into their teaching practices, how does this change their instructional approaches and goals? How do these tools develop students' writing abilities and perceptions about themselves as writers?

How are these technological tools fundamentally changing the physical act of writing and the linguistic structures of language.

In the first chapter, Roscoe, Brandon, Snow, and McNamara describe Writing Pal, an intelligent, gamed-based tutoring system used during the teaching of persuasive writing. Students are exposed to writing strategies with opportunities to practice the writing strategies through Writing Pal. This chapter reports the findings from a study with 65 high school students who participated in a lab-based summer program using Writing Pal. They found students were able to acquire new writing strategies and students' reported the games as enjoyable and helpful.

The second chapter by Park, Warschauer, Collins, Kyoung Hwang, and Vogel highlights how the teaching of grammar is often decontextualized from writing instruction. They present the Visual-Syntactic Text Formatting (VSTF) for the teaching of language and textual structures. The authors report the findings of two studies that found the VSTF improved students' ability to write more sophisticated sentences and assisted in the revision process.

Researchers highlight that one of the main benefits of technological tools is the ability to have students write for a wider audience, beyond the teacher evaluating their writing. Three chapters examine how specific tools provided environments, which contributed to students' growth as writers. The third chapter, authored by Putman, Kissel, and Stover is a two year study that examined students transition from traditional writing portfolios to digital writing portfolios. Results found the digital portfolios allowed students to communicate, express their ideas, and share collaboratively with an authentic audience. The study also highlights the need to adjust instructional practices to support digital writing.

Two chapters in this section specifically examine blogging. While these research studies took place in different settings with learners from different demographic backgrounds, the authors found blogging to be an effective tool for writing instruction. McGrail and McGrail examined the yearlong blog histories of 15 fifth-graders. The researchers recruited retired teachers and graduate students to be the students' audience. The study focused on students' intended audience and whom the students actually addressed during their interactive posts. They found students were aware of audience and made changes to their writing based on audience. Bryant penned the final chapter in this section by articulating the relationship between freewriting and blogging. She describes an action research in which she had college-age students create blogs. She found blogs provided her students many affordances, particularly the students felt engaged in a personal and meaningful writing experience.

The last two chapters featured in this section examine new and emerging theories. The first explores how technological tools have changed how people engage in the physical nature of writing and the final chapter analyzes how technological tools are producing shifts in discourse and speech communication. The sixth chapter explores the different kinesthetic processes between the physical nature of handwriting and typing on a keyboard. Mangen argues that our use of the hand influences cognitive processes; therefore, the shift from handwriting to digitally typing texts has cognitive implications influencing educational policy and practice.

Whereas Mangen's chapter examines how the physical nature of writing has changed and how those shifts influence education, the final chapter in this section examines functions of language, discourse, and communication. Turner explores the concept of "digitalk" by analyzing the linguistic decisions of 81 adolescents. This chapter examines not only what language teens use but why they make those choices. Turner posits that digitalk allows adolescents to consider their audience, as well as develop their personal voices.

This section provides an in-depth examination of the new technological tools and theories surrounding writing and writing instruction.

Chapter 1
Game–Based Writing Strategy Practice with the Writing Pal

Rod D. Roscoe
Arizona State University, USA

Russell D. Brandon
Arizona State University, USA

Erica L. Snow
Arizona State University, USA

Danielle S. McNamara
Arizona State University, USA

ABSTRACT

In this chapter, the authors consider the value of educational games to support students' writing strategy acquisition and practice. Sixty-five high school students participated in a summer program using the Writing Pal, an intelligent tutoring system designed to support adolescents' persuasive writing across multiple phases of the writing process. Overall, students who interacted with the full W-Pal intelligent tutoring system (i.e., animated strategy lessons, game-based practice, and essay-based practice with feedback) were better able to articulate new writing strategies than students who engaged in intensive essay-based practice by writing and revising twice as many essays with feedback. Importantly, performance within several educational games was found to be a significant predictor of strategy acquisition. The authors argue that these strategy benefits arise from the ways in which strategy-specific, game-based practice activities support the decomposition of task goals, clear operations for achieving those goals, compensation for individual differences, and motivation to practice.

DOI: 10.4018/978-1-4666-4341-3.ch001

GAME-BASED WRITING STRATEGY PRACTICE WITH THE WRITING PAL

Writing is a difficult process that involves the coordination of complex cognitive tasks and goals, and a central aim of writing instruction is to enable students to meet these myriad challenges (Breetvelt, van den Bergh, & Rijlaarsdam, 1994; Deane et al., 2008; Flower & Hayes, 1981). Increasingly, and as communicated by the contributors in this volume, researchers are exploring ways to enhance such instruction via technology. For example, automated essay scoring and automated writing evaluation systems (Grimes & Warschauer, 2010; Warschauer & Grimes, 2008) have become popular tools that allow teachers to assign more essays to students while providing feedback to the students on key problems and errors. Prior research has also explored how technology can support specific writing skills, such as summarization (Kintsch, Caccamise, Franzke, Johnson, & Dooley, 2007) and argumentation (Wolfe, Britt, Petrovich, Albrecht, & Kopp, 2009).

In this chapter, we consider the value of *educational games* to support the acquisition and practice of writing strategies. This research occurs within the context of the Writing Pal (W-Pal), an intelligent tutoring system (ITS) designed to support adolescent students' persuasive writing and strategy development across multiple phases and aspects of the writing process (McNamara et al., 2012; Roscoe, Varner, Weston, Crossley, & McNamara, in press). We first briefly describe the strategy instruction framework that informs W-Pal pedagogy and game-based practice. Subsequently, we examine changes in students' articulation of writing strategies after learning with W-Pal, and how such changes are related to students' performance within a suite of educational games.

Benefits of Strategy Instruction and Practice

Strategies are effortful and purposeful procedures that a person can apply to achieve a goal or facilitate the accomplishment of a task (Alexander, Graham, & Harris, 1998; Healy, Schneider, & Bourne, 2012). Consistently, decades of research on writing education have identified *explicit strategy instruction* as a fundamental means of improving student writing across age levels (Graham, McKeown, Kiuhara, & Harris, 2012; Graham & Perin, 2007). In such instruction, students are provided background information about the processes and goals of writing, and then are taught concrete strategies for enacting those processes and goals. For example, de la Paz and Graham (2002) taught middle-school writers to use a PLAN and WRITE strategy. The *PLAN* mnemonic teaches students to consider the prompt, generate main and supporting ideas, and organize these ideas. The *WRITE* mnemonic instructs students to implement these plans and to vary their sentence structure and vocabulary. de la Paz and Graham found that students who were taught the PLAN and WRITE strategies generated more plans of higher quality ($d = 1.17$), wrote longer essays ($d = .82$), used more sophisticated vocabulary ($d = 1.13$), and wrote better essays ($d = 1.71$) compared to a control condition that received traditional writing instruction (i.e., grammar, spelling, vocabulary, idea generation, and organization). Thus, explicit strategy instruction facilitated adolescent students' development of writing proficiency.

We summarize the benefits of strategy instruction using three general principles. First, strategy instruction benefits learning and performance by *decomposing complex or challenging processes into manageable sub-goals* (Healy et al., 2012).

The writing process is multifaceted and involves several interactive, iterative stages (Deane et al., 2008; Flower & Hayes, 1981) such as *prewriting* (i.e., generating and organizing ideas prior to writing), *drafting* (i.e., translating initial thoughts and plans into coherent text), and *revising* (i.e., elaborating and restructuring an essay to improve overall quality). Strategy instruction makes the purposes and procedures of these writing processes more visible and tractable. Thus, students can develop mastery of individual steps and tasks before having to enact the entire writing process. Second, strategy instruction *explicates the operations and actions needed to accomplish writing goals*. Strategy instruction provides the concrete "how to" information and heuristics that enable students to complete tasks, solve problems, and evaluate outcomes (Alexander et al., 1998). Finally, strategy instruction can help to *compensate for students' individual limitations and challenges* (e.g., Graham, Harris, & Mason, 2005). For example, some developing writers lack broad world knowledge or topic knowledge, leading to essays with unsupported claims and insufficient elaboration. Other students may have a less-developed vocabulary, resulting in text that is highly repetitive. However, strategies can help students leverage their available resources to overcome such limitations. Brainstorming strategies can help students probe their prior knowledge more deeply, and certain rhetorical strategies can help students leverage their personal experiences as evidence in lieu of objective or quantitative data. Indeed, research has shown that strategy instruction is especially important for less-skilled writers (Graham et al., 2005).

The decomposition of tasks and goals, clear operations, and compensation for individual differences contribute to the educational potential of strategy instruction. However, to fully realize this potential, students must also be given opportunities for *sustained and deliberate practice* to internalize the newly-acquired strategies (Kellogg, 2008; Kellogg & Whiteford, 2009), and *individualized*

feedback to guide them in effective and appropriate strategy use (McGarrell & Verbeem, 2007; Shute, 2008; Sommers, 1982). During the initial stages of acquisition, strategy implementation may be slow and error-prone because the steps are misapplied or forgotten. Students might even experience a decrement in performance as they struggle to use the new strategy. However, through deliberate practice in which learners purposefully seek to improve their skills, students can internalize key operations and understand how to apply specific strategies effectively (Ericcson, Krampe, & Tesch-Romer, 1993; Plant, Ericcson, Hill, & Asberg, 2005). Sustained practice over time is also crucial because knowledge and understanding of the newly learned strategies may decay without reinforcement (Carpenter, Pashler, Wixted, & Vul, 2008; Rohrer & Pashler, 2010). Finally, further support for students' strategy acquisition and development is provided by feedback (Hattie & Temperley, 2007; Shute, 2008). Feedback helps to focus attention on key aspects of the learning task, outcomes, and the relationship between those factors and strategy use. Summative feedback helps students gauge their performance and recognize when they have implemented a strategy incorrectly during practice. Formative feedback provides concrete guidance for how to improve in future practice. Both types of feedback can help students to optimize their strategy acquisition and practice.

Writing Pal and Game-Based Practice

The W-Pal writing tutor provides strategy instruction and writing practice that is aligned with the strategy framework outlined above. W-Pal provides comprehensive strategy instruction across major phases of writing and provides diverse practice opportunities with feedback. Direct strategy instruction is provided via eight writing strategy modules, which teach strategies for prewriting, drafting, and revising (Table 1). Students are introduced to specific strategies via

Table 1. Summary of writing strategy module content and practice games

Module	Strategy Content	Practice Games
Prologue	Introduces W-Pal, the animated characters, and discusses the importance of writing	
Prewriting Phase		
Freewriting (FW)	Covers *freewriting* strategies for quickly generating essay ideas, arguments, and evidence prior to writing (*FAST mnemonic*)	Freewrite Flash
Planning (PL)	Covers *outlining* and *graphic organizer* strategies for organizing arguments and evidence in an essay	Mastermind Outline Planning Passage
Drafting Phase		
Introduction Building (IB)	Covers strategies for writing introduction paragraph *thesis statements*, *argument previews*, and *attention-grabbing techniques* (*TAG mnemonic*)	Essay Launcher Dungeon Escape Fix It
Body Building (BB)	Covers strategies for writing *topic sentences* and providing objective *supporting evidence* (*CASE mnemonic*)	RoBoCo Fix It
Conclusion Building (CB)	Covers strategies for restating the thesis, summarizing arguments, closing an essay, and maintain reader interest in conclusion paragraphs (*RECAP mnemonic*)	Lockdown Dungeon Escape Fix It
Revising Phase		
Paraphrasing (PA)	Covers strategies for expressing ideas with more *precise and varied wording*, *sentence structure*, *splitting* run-ons, and *condensing* choppy sentences	Adventurer's Loot Map Conquest
Cohesion Building (CH)	Covers strategies for adding cohesive cues to text, such as *connective phrases*, *clarifying undefined referents*, and *threading ideas* throughout the text	CON-Artist Undefined & Mined
Revising (RE)	Covers strategies for reviewing an essay for completeness and clarity, and strategies for how to improve an essay by adding, removing, moving, or substituting ideas (*ARMS mnemonic*)	Speech Writer

short animated videos narrated by pedagogical agents. These videos decompose the goals and operations for each strategy, such as explaining how to preview one's arguments in the introduction of an essay (see Figure 1).

Essay-based practice is common among technologies for computer-based writing instruction (e.g., Kellogg, Whiteford, & Quinlan, 2010; Warschauer & Grimes, 2008), and W-Pal similarly allows students to compose timed, persuasive essays based on a variety of SAT-style prompts. Essays are typed using a straightforward word processor interface and then submitted for automated assessment. This scoring is powered by natural language algorithms utilizing Coh-Metrix and other text analysis tools (McNamara, Crossley, & Roscoe, 2012). Submitted essays initially receive a holistic rating from "Poor" to "Great" (6-point scale), and then receive formative feedback that addresses specific writing goals and strategies (Figure 2). This feedback is implemented as a scaffolded series of thresholds as-

Figure 1. Screenshot from the argument previews lesson within the Introduction Building module

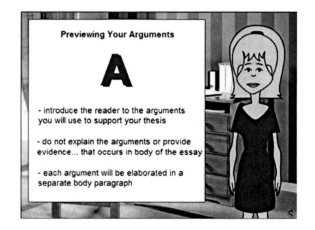

Figure 2. Screenshot of automated essay feedback report within W-Pal

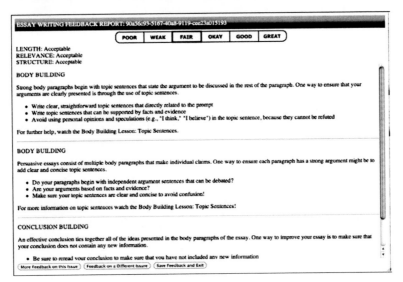

sessing *Legitimacy*, *Length*, *Relevance*, *Structure*, *Introduction*, *Body*, *Conclusion*, and overall *Revising*. To avoid overwhelming users (Grimes & Warschauer, 2010), W-Pal gives feedback on only one *Initial Topic* (i.e., first problem detected in the hierarchical series of checks). Students can then request more feedback on that topic or feedback on one additional *Next Topic* (i.e., next problem detected).

One of the challenges of essay-based practice, however, is that students must enact the entire writing process (Braaksma, Rijlaarsdam, van den Bergh, & van Hout-Wolters, 2004; Breetvelt et al., 1994). Consequently, essay-based practice may not help students focus their efforts on mastering specific strategies. Given the goals of W-Pal, it was important to develop practice opportunities that better supported the principles of decomposition, operations, and compensation. Thus, we selected strategies covered in the lessons and constructed strategy-specific identification or generative practice tasks for each module. In *identification practice* tasks, students examine brief texts to label the strategies used or identify strategies that could be applied to improve the text. For example, students might identify the

undefined referents in a short text or identify the attention-grabbing technique used in an introductory paragraph. In *generative practice* tasks, students authored short texts while applying one or more strategies. For instance, students might freewrite for several minutes on a given prompt or write a conclusion paragraph that summarizes an essay outline.

A further barrier to practice may be motivation or fatigue, which decreases the likelihood of sustained or deliberate practice. For many learning technologies, such as ITSs that require significant training time, student disengagement is a common problem (McNamara, Jackson, & Graesser, 2009). Although computer-based learning tools often initially benefit from novelty effects, such newness can wear thin (e.g., Clark, 1983). Importantly, students also frequently report negative attitudes toward writing, describing the experience as boring, unpleasant, or impossible (Bruning & Horn, 2000; Hidi, Berndorff, & Ainley, 2002; Pajares, 2003). For these reasons, we chose to support strategy practice within W-Pal using *educational games,* which are argued to leverage students' enjoyment of gaming to promote deeper engagement (Dondlinger, 2007; Malone & Lepper,

1987; Ryan, Rigby, & Przybylski, 2006; Young et al., 2012). Researchers have proposed various frameworks describing players' goals for gaming, such as earning points, collecting treasures, exploring worlds, discovering game mechanics, or defeating other players (Quick, Atkinson, & Lin, 2012). Other taxonomies describe generalized game features that players may find enjoyable, such as fantasy, narrative, challenge, discovery, and competition (Hunicke, LeBlanc, & Zubek, 2004). Together, such design elements may stimulate students' continued interest in playing the game and thereby continuing to practice the strategies.

W-Pal uniquely offers game-based practice via a suite of 16 educational games (Table 2). Identification and generative practice tasks were embedded in diverse game features and narratives, including elements of competition, puzzle-solving, role-play, and adventure. To exemplify W-Pal practice, we briefly describe two games. In *Adventurer's Loot*, students practice identifying paraphrasing strategies by taking on the role of a treasure hunter (Figure 3). Paraphrasing strategies include the *Synonym Strategy* (using more varied and precise words), *Structure Strategy* (reorganizing sentences), *Condensing Strategy* (combining choppy sentences), and *Splitting Strategy* (fixing run-on sentences). Students begin by choosing a site, which sends them to an exotic location such as an underground lake. "Clues" are given in the form of an original sentence along with a target paraphrasing strategy. To "decipher" the clue, players must identify which of four answer sentences implements the given strategy. Correct answers earn treasures (score increase) and incorrect answers cause a monster to appear (score decrease). Importantly, students need only consider only a few sentences at a time, which allows them to

Table 2. Brief descriptions of Writing Pal practice games

Game	Description
Freewrite Flash	Fill the Idea Meter and earn Idea Flash Cards by freewriting on a prompt.
Mastermind Outline	Repair the Mastermind Mainframe by assembling an outline from given argument and evidence statements.
Planning Passage	Travel to various destinations and earn souvenirs by selecting appropriate arguments and evidence.
Dungeon Escape	Escape by avoiding the guard and rising waters. Select doors by labeling attention-grabbing techniques.
Essay Launcher	Rescue spaceships by selecting thesis statements and attention-grabbers for sample introduction paragraphs.
Fix It	Evaluate paragraphs for missing key elements, such as thesis statements and evidence. Fix the broken circuit board.
RoBoCo	Build robots by writing topic and evidence sentences for a given thesis.
Lockdown	Stop computer hackers by writing conclusions based on a given outline.
Adventurer's Loot	Explore different locations and obtain treasure by correctly identifying use of paraphrasing strategies.
Map Conquest	Earn flags by identifying paraphrasing strategies, and then use those flags to conquer the game board.
Undefined & Mined	Disarm mines by identifying undefined referents in short texts.
CON-Artist	Catch a thief by following clues. The clues are solved by selecting transition words to link given sentences.
Speech Writer	Help a friend on the debate team revise a speech. Identify the major problems and then edit the speech to improve it.

Figure 3. Screenshot of Adventurer's Loot game within the Paraphrasing module

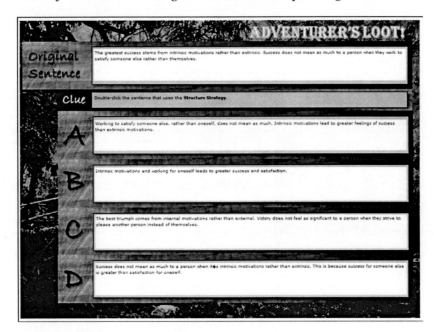

focus on key features of each paraphrase type. In addition, the best treasures are earned when players answer correctly on their first attempt. Thus, this game rewards thoughtful analysis of the potential answers rather than guesswork.

RoBoCo is a generative practice game in which students write topic sentences and evidence for body paragraphs (Figure 4). Students take on the role of a robot designer at the Robot Body Company who must design new robots. Students read a SAT-style writing prompt and then write a topic sentence and several evidence sentences to support that claim. Importantly, these two tasks are somewhat distinct. The topic and evidence sentences are typed into separate interfaces that further decompose the task of writing a body paragraph while maintaining the overall context. After students submit their text, natural language algorithms assess whether the topic sentence is on-topic and contains an argument, and whether evidence sentences are on-topic and contain objective details (e.g., specific names and dates) rather than subjective or hypothetical details (e.g., what-if statements). Students can request strategy

hints throughout the game. Across two rounds, students can earn up to four robot "heads" for good topic sentences and four robot "bodies" for good evidence. Thus, the number of parts earned is an indicator of how well the student is performing. Subsequently, students can use these earned robot parts (if any) to assemble robots that are displayed at the Annual Show. The final score is based on performance of the task and the number of robots built, which is expressed as financial profit that the student has earned for the company.

In sum, educational games within W-Pal serve an important and unique role in strategy acquisition and practice. Students are initially exposed to the strategies via the strategy lessons. However, rather than immediately requiring students to implement new strategies within essay compositions, W-Pal allows students to further master each strategy in isolation. Moreover, by embedding such practice in games, some of the affective obstacles of strategy acquisition may be offset. Game-based practice may encourage more delib-

Figure 4. Screenshot of RoBoCo game within the Body Building module

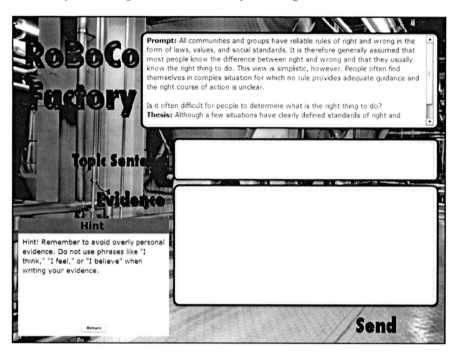

erate and sustained practice as students strive to earn better scores or compete with others.

To explore the potential of game-based strategy practice, we describe a study that contrasts two modes of writing instruction and practice. One mode follows a typical approach for computer-based writing instruction wherein students write and revise many practice essays with automated feedback. In this case, students are exposed to writing strategies via the feedback received and have ample opportunities to explore these strategies through essay writing. An alternative mode provides direct strategy instruction along with game-based practice, but at the cost of writing practice essays. In this mode, students write half as many essays with feedback, but can practice explicitly-taught strategies via educational games. We hypothesize that the latter mode will better support students' acquisition of new writing strategies.

METHOD

Participants

High school students ($n = 65$) from a large, urban area in the southwestern United States participated in a lab-based summer program using W-Pal. The average age of students was 16 years old, with 70.8% female students. With regards to ethnicity, 6.2% of students identified as African-American, 15.4% as Asian, 24.6% as Caucasian, and 44.6% as Hispanic. Average grade level was 10.2 with 35.4% of students reporting a GPA of 3.0 or below. Most students self-identified as native speakers of English ($n = 38$) although many self-identified as English Language Learners (ELL, $n = 27$). However, an analysis of prior writing ability (e.g., pre-study essay scores) found no difference between native speakers and ELLs, $t(62) = 1.05$, $p = .30$.

Procedures

Students attended 10 sessions over 2-4 weeks. A test of writing strategy knowledge was given in the first and final sessions, along measures of writing proficiency, reading comprehension, vocabulary, and writing attitudes. Sessions 2-9 were devoted to training. Students in the *W-Pal Condition* (*n* = 33) used the full W-Pal, including essay writing, lessons, and games. In each session, these students wrote and revised one essay and completed one module. Students rated each game immediately after playing. Students in the *Essay Condition* interacted only with the essay and feedback tools (*n* = 32). These students wrote and revised two essays per session with feedback. Due to a data logging error, the post-study materials of one Essay condition student were lost, resulting in a final sample of 31 students.

Measures

Strategy Knowledge Test

Students responded to six open-ended questions regarding strategies "good writers use" when 1) preparing to write, 2) writing introductory paragraphs, 3) writing body paragraphs, 4) writing concluding paragraphs, 5) making an essay more understandable, and 6) revising an essay (see Appendix). Students' responses were content-coded to identify the presence of relevant *strategy concepts*. For example, in response to Question 1 (preparation), a student wrote, "They can brainstorm ideas about what their writing like a list or brainstorm web." This response contains three strategy concepts: *brainstorming*, *lists*, and *webs*. Another student answered, "In order to prepare, I pre-write or organize my prior knowledge before writing an essay." This response exhibits three different concepts: *prewriting*, *organization*, and *use of prior knowledge*. Strategy concept scores were computed for each question by tabulating valid strategy concepts. Thus, students' responses

could earn similar scores by articulating different, yet valid, conceptions of writing strategies.

To develop this coding scheme, the entire corpus of responses was reviewed and a standardized template of acceptable strategy concepts was constructed for each question. The resulting templates were detailed, ranging from 26 to 47 strategy concepts per question. To establish reliability, two raters (blind to condition and test phase) independently applied the coding scheme to approximately one-third of the corpus. Initial inter-rater agreement was high or acceptable for all questions: Question 1 (97.7%), Question 2 (94.1%), Question 3 (88.6%), Question 4 (87.3%), Question 5 (78.9%), and Question 6 (86.1%). Subsequently, the complete corpus was coded by the first author and reviewed by coauthors. All disagreements were resolved through collaborative discussion.

Game Perception Surveys and Log Data

Embedded within the system were surveys soliciting students' game perceptions. W-Pal students used a 4-point scale to rate games on *enjoyment*, *helpfulness for learning*, *ease of gameplay*, and *graphics*. Higher ratings indicated a more positive response. Two additional questions were asked as a check to make sure the games were playable. These usability questions showed that students considered game instructions to be understandable ($M = 3.4$, $SD = 0.4$) and game controls to be clear ($M = 3.5$, $SD = 0.4$). Students' game scores were automatically logged by the W-Pal system.

RESULTS

Strategy Knowledge

We first examined students' raw strategy concept scores prior to the study and after the study (Table 3). There were no pretest differences for any of the questions (all $Fs < 2.50$). To assess

Table 3. Pretest and posttest strategy concept scores

Question	Writing Pal		Essay		Gain	
	Pretest	Posttest	Pretest	Posttest	$F(1,62)$	p
1 – Preparation	2.4 (1.4)	2.5 (1.7)	2.4 (1.4)	2.2 (1.2)	< 1	.810
2 – Introduction	2.2 (1.5)	2.6 (2.0)	1.9 (1.3)	2.0 (1.2)	1.52	.223
3 – Body	2.5 (1.4)	3.0 (2.2)	2.1 (1.3)	2.2 (1.2)	1.46	.231
4 – Conclusion	1.9 (1.0)	2.7 (1.7)	1.8 (1.0)	1.9 (1.0)	7.09	.010
5 – Understandable	1.9 (1.2)	2.4 (2.2)	1.9 (1.1)	2.0 (1.3)	2.31	.134
6 – Revising	2.7 (1.2)	2.9 (1.6)	2.2 (1.4)	2.6 (1.6)	2.24	.140

changes in strategy concept scores over time, a 2 (test) x 2 (condition) mixed model ANOVA was conducted for each question. With the exception of Question 4 (conclusion-building strategies), there were no main effects of test (all Fs < 2.50). Thus, students articulated approximately the same number of valid strategy concepts at pretest and posttest for the majority of the questions. For Question 4 (conclusion-building strategies), students articulated significantly more strategy concepts at posttest, $F(1,62) = 7.09$, $p \leq .01$. There were no significant test by condition interactions for any of the questions (all Fs ≤ 1). Thus, neither condition expressed more strategy concepts over time than the other.

The raw strategy concept scores indicate the overall quantity of strategy knowledge students articulated before and after training. However, these scores do not take into account the *content* of students' responses. For example, in response to Question 3 (body building strategies) one student wrote at pretest, "Have a different paragraph for each idea, use good vocabulary." This response contained two concepts: *one argument per paragraph* and *vocabulary*. However, the student's posttest response was substantially different, stating "include topic sentences, connect ideas and sentences, use transition words when starting a new paragraph, be descriptive." This response contained three new concepts: *topic sentences*, *connectives and transitions*, and *descriptive details*. Thus, although the student's score on this

question increased by only 1 point, the content changed entirely. Whereas the student initially focused on word choice and paragraph structure, the posttest response reveals attention to the specific requirements of body paragraphs. This does not mean the student had forgotten previous, valid strategies for writing body paragraphs. Rather, interaction with W-Pal appeared to introduce new strategies or shift the student's focus to other salient strategies.

To assess articulation of *new* strategy concepts after instruction, we reexamined the strategy concepts articulated in students' pretest and posttest responses. We tabulated those responses which were *not* repeated from the pretest, and calculated the *proportion of new strategy concepts* articulated in the posttest for each question. These proportion scores indicate the extent to which instruction and practice in the study influenced or added to students' strategy knowledge (Table 4). ANOVAs were conducted to compare conditions across each question.

The results reveal benefits for the W-Pal condition. For four of the six questions, W-Pal condition students articulated a greater proportion of new strategy concepts than did Essay condition students, with strong effect sizes (i.e., Cohen's *d*). Students who used the full W-Pal system showed an advantage in strategy knowledge for questions about introduction building (Question 2), body building (Question 3), conclusion building (Question 4), and revising (Question 6) strategies. Al-

Table 4. Proportion of new posttest strategy concepts by condition

Question	Writing Pal	Essay	$F(1,62)$	p	d
1 – Preparation	.62 (.42)	.51 (.39)	1.29	.260	.28
2 – Introduction	.66 (.35)	.38 (.38)	9.52	.003	.77
3 – Body	.81 (.30)	.58 (.36)	7.80	.007	1.06
4 – Conclusion	.70 (.34)	.52 (.36)	4.33	.042	.80
5 – Understandable	.82 (.32)	.68 (.43)	2.34	.131	.38
6 – Revising	.84 (.30)	.59 (.42)	7.63	.008	.69

though not statistically significant, the same trend was observed for questions about preparing to writing (e.g., freewriting and planning) and making an essay more clear and understandable (e.g., paraphrasing and cohesion building).

Overall, neither mode of instruction and practice was particularly effective in inducing students to articulate *more* strategy concepts over time. That is, students' responses were not more detailed at posttest compared to pretest. However, instruction that utilized a blend of strategy instruction, game-based practice, essay-based practice, and formative feedback was more effective for strategy acquisition than instruction that focused on intensive writing practice. Although opportunities to write and revise essays are crucial for students' to improve their writing, that mode of practice was less efficient for helping students learn new strategies. Thus, computer-based writing instruction that reinforces decomposition of task goals, clear operations, and compensation may be more effective early in students' writing strategy development.

Strategy Acquisition and Games

Although W-Pal users articulated more new strategy concepts than did Essay-only students, these results could be explained by the fact that W-Pal users viewed explicit strategy instruction lessons. Indeed, we assume this to be the case. However, game-based practice is also hypothesized to motivate and reinforce strategy acquisition. To support this hypothesis, it is important to demonstrate that students perceived the games as enjoyable and helpful, and that game performance was related to strategy knowledge. The former issue speaks to the power of games to motivate students to continue playing, and thereby continue to practice their strategies. The second issue pertains to whether engaging in game-based practice is indeed beneficial.

With regards to game perceptions, students appeared to enjoy most of the games (i.e., most means were above 2.5 on a 4-point scale, with higher values indicating positive ratings). Similarly, ratings of helpfulness for learning, ease of gameplay, and graphics appeal were also positive. However, a few games seemed to stand out as somewhat less enjoyable than others: *RoBoCo*, *Speech Writer*, *Lockdown*, and *Essay Launcher*. These games also tended to receive somewhat lower ratings with regard to helpfulness and ease. Thus, not surprisingly, games that were viewed as more difficult were seen as less helpful or fun (see Table 5). Overall, these results suggest that W-Pal games were viewed as sufficiently enjoyable and valuable to students to warrant continued play. It is possible that ratings of more challenging games would improve as students mastered the strategies and game mechanics – the games would become less difficult and students might enjoy the feeling of "beating" a tough game – but such temporal patterns could not be assessed in this study.

Next, to assess the relationship between game performance and strategy knowledge, we con-

Table 5. Average student perception of Writing Pal games

Game	Enjoyment	Helpfulness	Ease of Play	Graphics
Freewrite Flash	3.1	3.2	2.6	3.2
Mastermind	3.3	3.4	2.8	3.2
Planning Passage	2.8	3.2	2.9	3.2
Essay Launcher	2.7	2.9	2.6	3.3
Dungeon Esc. (IB)	3.3	3.3	3.2	3.4
Fix It (IB)	3.2	3.2	3.1	3.3
RoBoCo	2.2	2.5	2.0	3.3
Fix It (BB)	3.2	3.3	3.3	3.4
Lockdown	2.7	2.8	2.4	3.3
Dungeon Esc. (CB)	2.9	2.9	2.7	3.3
Fix It (CB)	3.2	3.4	3.3	3.4
Adventurer's Loot	3.1	3.1	3.0	3.4
Map Conquest	3.2	3.3	2.8	3.4
Und. & Mined	3.2	3.2	2.9	3.3
CON-Artist	3.5	3.5	3.3	3.4
Speech Writer	2.5	2.8	2.4	3.3

ducted regression analyses to predict posttest strategy knowledge based on pretest knowledge and game scores. We extracted students' best scores for each game from the log data, which were represented as a proportion of the highest score obtained by any player. Proportions allowed us to standardize performance measures across games, which each used different scoring mechanics and values. For each test question, pretest strategy concept scores and relevant game scores were entered as predictors of new strategy concepts articulated on the posttest (Table 6).

The regression models for Question 2 (introductions) and Question 4 (conclusions) were not significant and there were no significant predictors (Table 6). Thus, students' pretest knowledge of introduction and conclusion strategies did not predict new strategy concepts at posttest, nor did students' interaction with practice games. For these questions, strategy acquisition was most likely determined by the explicit strategy lessons. Both the Introduction Building and Conclusion

Building modules present simple mnemonic devices for their respective tasks. Introduction Building teaches the *TAG mnemonic* (*T*hesis statements, *A*rgument preview, and *G*rab the reader's attention) and Conclusion Building teaches the *RECAP mnemonic* (*R*estate the thesis, *E*xplain how arguments supported the thesis, *C*lose the essay, *A*void adding new examples and evidence, and *P*resent the conclusion in an interesting manner). Such straightforward instruction may have been sufficient to convey these new strategies.

Regression models for Question 1 (preparation), Question 3 (body), Question 5 (making essays understandable), and Question 6 (revising) were significant or approaching significance (Table 6). Moreover, students' interactions with one or more specific games contributed to students' strategy acquisition. For Question 1, *Planning Passage* scores positively predicted new strategy concepts, and *Mastermind Outline* scores exhibited a similar trend. Both of these games emphasize the relationship between thesis statements,

Table 6. Regression analysis to predict new strategy concepts at posttest

Predictors	Overall Model			Contribution of Predictors		
	R^2	F	p	β	t	p
Question 1: Preparing to write	.51	2.50	.065			
Pretest				.050	0.286	**.777**
Freewrite Flash				-.011	-0.065	**.948**
Mastermind Outline				.288	1.629	**.114**
Planning Passage				**.349**	**1.980**	**.058**
Question 2: Introduction	.27	< 1.00	.72			
Pretest				-.158	-0.837	**.410**
Dungeon Escape (IB)				.016	0.082	**.935**
Essay Launcher				.185	0.951	**.350**
Fix It (IB)				.107	0.560	**.580**
Question 3: Body	.67	7.50	.001			
Pretest				.385	2.628	**.014**
Fix It (BB)				.099	0.641	**.527**
RoBoCo				**.405**	**2.607**	**.014**
Question 4: Conclusion	.27	< 1.00	.69			
Pretest				-.204	-1.062	**.297**
Dungeon Escape (CB)				.178	0.896	**.378**
Fix It (CB)				.073	0.367	**.716**
Lockdown				-.117	-0.601	**.553**
Question 5: Understandable	.72	5.78	.001			
Pretest				.409	2.995	**.006**
Adventurer's Loot				**.606**	**4.045**	**.000**
Map Conquest				-.252	-1.594	**.123**
CON-Artist				-.012	-0.079	**.938**
Undefined & Mined				**.379**	**2.374**	**.025**
Question 6: Revising	.41	3.04	.063			
Pretest				-.143	-.841	**.407**
Speech Writer				**.413**	**2.436**	**.021**

arguments, and evidence, and how these elements are strategically organized within an essay. For Question 3, *RoBoCo* scores positively predicted strategy acquisition of body building strategies. Interestingly students' knowledge of body-building strategies at pretest was also a predictor. Thus, W-Pal instruction and game-based practice likely helped students build upon prior strategy knowledge to understand this writing task in new ways. Likewise, for Question 5, pretest scores predicted strategy acquisition along with two games, *Adventurer's Loot* scores and *Undefined & Mined* scores. Adventurer's Loot, as a described above, was designed to help students learn paraphrasing strategies. Undefined & Mined appeared in the Cohesion Building module, and was designed to help students learn how to recognize and resolve undefined referents in text (e.g., words like *this* and *that*, which must be accompanied by a clear noun to provide clarity for the reader). Finally, for Question 6, *Speech Writer* scores positively predicted acquisition of revising strategies. In this complex game, students take on the role of helping a friend prepare for a debate team match. Students must read a "speech" (i.e., a persuasive essay) and identify key flaws, such as missing evidence or word repetition. Subsequently, students are given the opportunity to revise the essay to fix these flaws and generally improve the essay.

In sum, results suggest that educational games within W-Pal were plausible contributors to students' strategy acquisition across multiple phases of writing. Moreover, students perceived the games as overall enjoyable and helpful for learning, which speaks to their potential for motivating deliberate and sustained practice. Thus, these findings provide evidence that game-based practice is a valuable and meaningful instructional tool for intelligent writing tutors and computer-based writing instruction.

DISCUSSION

Developing writers benefit from explicit strategy instruction that renders the processes of writing transparent and tractable and equips students with clear actions and techniques for enacting those processes (Graham et al., 2012; Graham & Perin, 2007). In this study, we explored the value of game-based strategy practice to reinforce writing strategy acquisition in the context of the Writing Pal, an intelligent tutoring system that provides writing strategy instruction. This approach was contrasted with intensive essay-based practice, which is the dominant mode among computer-based writing instruction (Grimes & Warschauer, 2010).Overall, students who interacted with the full W-Pal system (i.e., strategy lessons, game-based practice, and essay-based practice) were more likely to learn new writing strategies than students who engaged in essay-based practice by writing and revising many essays with feedback. Although strategy acquisition for W-Pal users was almost certainly supported by the direct instruction provided by the lessons, performance within several educational games was also a significant predictor. We argue that these strategy benefits arise from the ways in which strategy-specific practice activities support the *decomposition* of task goals, clear *operations* for achieving those goals, and *compensation* for individual differences. Given that the students also perceived the games as enjoyable and helpful, we can conclude that game-based strategy practice is a worthwhile technology for supporting writing instruction.

One limitation of the current study was that we recruited a fairly small sample of high school students. This design was necessitated by the time-intensive nature of the study; each student participated in the program for approximately 15-17 hours over one month. The study also took place in a laboratory setting in which students traveled to a college campus to participate. Both of these factors could limit the generalizability of the current findings. In addition, we could not assess the effects of game-based practice over time. Students completed one module per session, which included playing each game associated with that module one to three times. However, in later sessions, students could not return to previously-played games. Although the games allowed students to practice the writing strategies, we could not examine the effects such games might have over multiple sessions, days, or weeks. As a result, current results may underestimate the benefits of truly sustained game-based practice.

To address these temporal questions, W-Pal will be deployed with close to 1,000 high school students within authentic high school English and Language Arts classes. W-Pal will be used for several months – up to a semester or entire school year in select schools. These data will allow us to explore temporal effects of practice and learning. For example, some data suggested that games perceived as "easier" were also viewed as more enjoyable or helpful than "harder" games. Not surprisingly, students who experienced increased difficulty or challenge in some games (e.g., *RoBoCo* and *Speech Writer*) probably felt more frustrated as they struggled to complete the task. However, over time and continued practice, we expect students' performance to improve. One might predict a reversal in game perceptions: initially "easy" and "fun" games might become boring once the task is mastered, but "hard" or "frustrating" games may become more enjoyable as students experience increased self-efficacy for overcoming a difficult task.

Implications for Instruction and Research

One implication of this research is that *writing strategy instruction and practice can be beneficially embedded within educational games*. With regards to motivation, digital games have become popular within educational technology due to their assumed potential to foster deeper engagement and enjoyment (Dondlinger, 2007; Young et al., 2012). Given students' anxieties and negative attitudes specifically toward writing and writing instruction (Bruning & Horn, 2000; Pajares, 2003), the affective benefits of educational games may be particularly helpful. Our data suggest that students viewed W-Pal games positively despite the fact that our games clearly focused on writing practice rather than action, adventure, or storytelling. Moreover, our games did not utilize high-end graphics, virtual worlds, sophisticated soundtracks, or other hallmarks of the lucrative gaming industry. Although more research is needed, our results imply that educational games for writing need not implement many of expensive bells and whistles common in commercial entertainment games. However, incorporating more game features may further enhance the appeal of educational games, which in turn may foster greater motivation.

A related consideration for educational games may be the potential cognitive parallels between game mastery and strategy acquisition. As with many learning tasks, digital games are also typically organized around a series of goals and objectives that require the synthesis of multiple skills and strategies (Charsky, 2010; Hunicke, LeBlanc, & Zubek, 2004; Shute, Rieber, & Van Eck, 2011). Initially, the required skills may be quite simple (e.g., jumping), but then gradually increase in difficulty or complexity (e.g., jumping while attacking and dodging enemies). Similarly, both learning tasks and games possess underlying rules that define allowable actions and their efficacy for success. Game designers and players often carefully consider the "learning curve" of games – the time and effort it takes to become proficient or expert in a game (e.g., Gee, 2004). For some games, a "tutorial mode" is available that helps new players understand and master the basic elements of game play before progressing on to harder challenges. Consequently, although games are usually designed for entertainment, and may foster engagement in learning settings, they are also incremental and strategic learning experiences. Players expect to be confronted with challenges that must be overcome through knowledge and skill, which are acquired through sustained and deliberate practice (Charsky, 2010). In educational games, the mechanisms for "winning" are defined by the learning tasks and goals. Instead of requiring virtual weapons or fast reflexes to succeed, students must apply their domain expertise and strategies. Such cognitive parallels may make game-based practice particularly well-suited to strategy instruction and acquisition.

A further implication of this work is that *essay-based practice alone may be inadequate for fostering students' deep and strategic understanding of writing*. The writing process is complex and requires coordination of diverse skills, tasks, and goals (Breetvelt et al., 1994). However, practice that targets specific strategies may help students understand and enact these writing processes more effectively. Students may benefit from opportunities to develop their writing strategy expertise before they are asked to synthesize these procedures within essay compositions, and our results contribute to the body of research emphasizing the importance of strategy instruction (e.g., Graham et al., 2005; Graham et al., 2012; Graham & Perin, 2007). Consequently, educators and instructional technology developers may need to evaluate how and whether current systems privilege essay-based practice over strategy-based practice, or perhaps ignore strategy instruction altogether. For example, popular commercial technologies such as *Criterion* and *MyAccess* strongly emphasize essay writing and automated scoring (Burstein, Chodorow, & Leacock, 2004; Grimes & Warschauer, 2010; Rudner, Garcia, & Welch, 2006; Warschauer & Grimes, 2008). Indeed, one of the fundamental motivations for most instructional writing technologies is to enable teachers to offer more essay writing assignments than may be otherwise feasible (e.g., Shermis & Burstein, 2003). The current study suggests that these kinds of systems may be improved or supplemented by the inclusion of targeted strategy instruction and practice activities.

Importantly, we are not arguing for the reduction of essay-based practice in favor of games. It remains crucial that students be given many opportunities to author essays, across different genres, and receive meaningful feedback from their mentors (Kellogg et al., 2010). Thus, a crucial question for writing instruction and technology pertains to the *optimal timing or balance of various computer-based writing supports.* On the one hand, game-based strategy practice might be helpful early in writing development to support both strategy acquisition and positive attitudes toward writing. Targeted strategy practice could then gradually give way to longer or more authentic writing assignments. In contrast, some instructors may wish to emphasize substantive writing assignments interspersed with strategy practice. For instance, strategy instruction (via animated lessons), strategy practice (via games), and essay-based practice were interwoven in this study. On each day of instruction, students in the W-Pal condition wrote and revised an essay, and then studied and practiced a new set of writing strategies. An alternative curriculum might have asked students to complete all of the lessons first, then play the practice games, and only then write practice essays. In the classroom, teachers could ask students to write practice essays as preparation for using W-Pal. Students would then have a corpus of their own work to reevaluate in the context of W-Pal lessons.

In W-Pal, the modular design the tutoring system purposefully enables a variety of curricular trajectories – the strategy lessons, practice games, and essay tools can be accessed in any order based on teachers' instructional needs (Roscoe et al., in press). Such modularity also allows educators and researchers to explore different W-Pal curricula experimentally, thus revealing how alternative instructional designs work best or meet the needs of individual students. At this time, the most effective weighting or ordering of strategy practice versus essay-based practice is not known. Thus, educators and developers may wish to adopt a similarly comprehensive and flexible approach in the use of technologies for writing, which affords both instructor freedom and opportunities for empirical research. That is, by incorporating tools for both strategy practice (including games) and essay writing, we may simultaneously increase the efficacy of instructional writing technologies and advance research on the methods, benefits, and impacts of digital writing.

ACKNOWLEDGMENT

The research reported here was supported by the Institute of Education Sciences, U.S. Department of Education, through Grant R305A080589 to Arizona State University. The opinions expressed are those of the authors and do not represent views of the Institute or the U.S. Department of Education.

REFERENCES

Alexander, P., Graham, S., & Harris, K. (1998). A perspective on strategy research: progress and prospects. *Educational Psychology Review*, *10*, 129–154. doi:10.1023/A:1022185502996.

Braaksma, M., Rijlaarsdam, G., van den Bergh, H., & van Hout-Wolters, B. (2004). Observational learning and its effects on the orchestration of writing processes. *Cognition and Instruction*, *22*, 1–36. doi:10.1207/s1532690Xci2201_1.

Breetvelt, I., van den Bergh, H., & Rijlaarsdam, G. (1994). Relations between writing processes and text quality: When and how? *Cognition and Instruction*, *12*, 103–123. doi:10.1207/s1532690xci1202_2.

Bruning, R., & Horn, C. (2000). Developing motivation to write. *Educational Psychologist*, *35*, 25–37. doi:10.1207/S15326985EP3501_4.

Burstein, J., Chodorow, M., & Leacock, C. (2004). Automated essay evaluation: The criterion online writing system. *AI Magazine*, *25*, 27–36.

Carpenter, S., Pashler, H., Wixted, J., & Vul, E. (2008). The effects of tests on learning and forgetting. *Memory & Cognition*, *36*, 438–448. doi:10.3758/MC.36.2.438 PMID:18426072.

Charsky, D. (2010). From edutainment to serious games: A change in the use of game characteristics. *Games and Culture*, *5*(2), 177–198. doi:10.1177/1555412009354727.

Clark, R. (1983). Reconsidering research on learning from media. *Review of Educational Research*, *53*, 445–459. doi:10.3102/00346543053004445.

de la Paz, S., & Graham, S. (2002). Explicitly teaching strategies, skills, and knowledge: Writing instruction in middle school classrooms. *Journal of Educational Psychology*, *94*, 687–698. doi:10.1037/0022-0663.94.4.687.

Deane, P., Odendahl, N., Quinlan, T., Fowles, M., Welsh, C., & Bivens-Tatum, J. (2008). *Cognitive models of writing: writing proficiency as a complex integrated skill* (Research Report No. RR-08-55). Princeton, NJ: Educational Testing Service.

Dondlinger, M. (2007). Educational video game design: a review of the literature. *Journal of Applied Educational Technology*, *4*, 21–31.

Ericcson, A., Krampe, R., & Tesch-Romer, C. (1993). The role of deliberate practice in the acquisition of expert performance. *Psychological Review*, *100*, 363–406. doi:10.1037/0033-295X.100.3.363.

Flower, L., & Hayes, J. (1981). A cognitive process theory of writing. *College Composition and Communication*, *32*, 365–387. doi:10.2307/356600.

Gee, J. (2004). Learning by design: Games as learning machines. *Interactive Educational Multimedia*, *8*, 15–23.

Graham, S., Harris, K., & Mason, L. (2005). Improving the writing performance, knowledge, and self-efficacy of struggling young writers: The effects of self-regulated strategy development. *Contemporary Educational Psychology*, *30*, 207–241. doi:10.1016/j.cedpsych.2004.08.001.

Graham, S., McKeown, D., Kiuhara, S., & Harris, K. (2012). A meta-analyses of writing instruction for students in the elementary grades. *Journal of Educational Psychology*, *104*, 879–896. doi:10.1037/a0029185.

Graham, S., & Perin, D. (2007). A meta-analysis of writing instruction for adolescent students. *Journal of Educational Psychology*, *99*, 445–476. doi:10.1037/0022-0663.99.3.445.

Grimes, D., & Warschauer, M. (2010). Utility in a fallible tool: A multi-site case study of automated writing evaluation. *Journal of Technology, Learning, and Assessment*, *8*, 4–43.

Habgood, J., & Ainsworth, S. (2011). Motivating children to learn effectively: exploring the value of intrinsic integration in educational games. *Journal of the Learning Sciences, 20,* 169–206. doi:10.1080/10508406.2010.508029.

Hattie, J., & Temperley, H. (2007). The power of feedback. *Review of Educational Research, 77,* 81–112. doi:10.3102/003465430298487.

Healy, A., Schneider, V., & Bourne, L. (2012). Empirically valid principles of training. In Healy, A., & Bourne, L. (Eds.), *Training cognition: Optimizing efficiency, durability, and generalizability* (pp. 13–39). New York: Psychology Press.

Hidi, S., Berndorff, D., & Ainley, M. (2002). Children's argument writing, interest and self-efficacy: An intervention study. *Learning and Instruction, 12,* 429–446. doi:10.1016/S0959-4752(01)00009-3.

Hunicke, R., LeBlanc, M., & Zubek, R. (2004). MDA: A formal approach to game design and game research. In *Proceedings of the Challenges in Games AI Workshop, 19th National Conference on Artificial Intelligence* (pp. 1-5). San Jose, CA: AAAI Press.

Kellogg, R. (2008). Training writing skills: a cognitive development perspective. *Journal of Writing Research, 1,* 1–26.

Kellogg, R., & Whiteford, A. (2009). Training advanced writing skills: the case for deliberate practice. *Educational Psychologist, 44,* 250–266. doi:10.1080/00461520903213600.

Kellogg, R. T., Whiteford, A. P., & Quinlan, T. (2010). Does automated feedback help students learn to write? *Journal of Educational Computing Research, 42*(2), 173–196. doi:10.2190/EC.42.2.c.

Kintsch, E., Caccamise, D., Franzke, M., Johnson, N., & Dooley, S. (2007). Summary Street ®: computer-guided summary writing. In T. K. Landauer, D. M., McNamara, S. Dennis, & W. Kintsch (Eds.), Latent Semantic Analysis (pp. 263-277). Mahwah, NJ: Erlbaum.

Malone, T., & Lepper, M. (1987). Making learning fun: a taxonomy of intrinsic motivations of learning. In R. Snow & M. Farr (Eds.), Aptitude, learning, and instruction: Vol. 3: Cognition and affective process analyses (pp. 223-253). Hillsdale, NJ: Lawrence Erlbaum.

McGarrell, H., & Verbeem, J. (2007). Motivating revision of drafts through formative feedback. *ELT Journal, 61,* 228–236. doi:10.1093/elt/ccm030.

McNamara, D., Crossley, S., & Roscoe, R. (2012). Natural language processing in an intelligent writing strategy tutoring system. *Behavior Research Methods.* doi: doi:10.3758/s13428-012-0258-1 PMID:23055164.

McNamara, D., Jackson, G., & Graesser, A. (2009). Intelligent tutoring and games (iTaG). In H. Lane, A. Ogan, & V. Shute (Eds.), *Proceedings of the Workshop on Intelligent Educational Games at the 14th Annual Conference on Artificial Intelligence in Education* (pp. 1-10). Brighton, UK: AIED.

McNamara, D., Raine, R., Roscoe, R., Crossley, S., Jackson, G., & Dai, J. … Graesser, A. (2012). The writing-pal: Natural language algorithms to support intelligent tutoring on writing strategies. In P. McCarthy & C. Boonthum-Denecke (Eds.), Applied natural language processing and content analysis: Identification, investigation, and resolution (pp. 298-311). Hershey, PA: IGI Global.

Pajares, F. (2003). Self-efficacy beliefs, motivation, and achievement in writing: A review of the literature. *Reading & Writing Quarterly, 19,* 139–158. doi:10.1080/10573560308222.

Plant, E., Ericcson, K., Hill, L., & Asberg, K. (2005). Why study time does not predict grade point average across college students: implications of deliberate practice for academic performance. *Contemporary Educational Psychology, 30,* 96–116. doi:10.1016/j.cedpsych.2004.06.001.

Quick, J., Atkinson, R., & Lin, L. (2012). Empirical taxonomies of gameplay enjoyment: Personality and video game preference. *International Journal of Game-Based Learning, 2*, 11–31. doi:10.4018/ijgbl.2012070102.

Rohrer, D., & Pashler, H. (2010). Recent research on human learning challenges conventional instructional strategies. *Educational Researcher, 39*, 406–412. doi:10.3102/0013189X10374770.

Roscoe, R., Varner, L., & Weston, J., Crossley, & McNamara, D. (in press). The writing pal intelligent tutoring system: Usability testing and development. *Computers and Composition.*

Rudner, L., Garcia, V., & Welch, C. (2006). An evaluation of the IntelliMetric essay scoring system. *Journal of Technology, Learning, and Assessment, 4*(4), 3–21.

Ryan, R., Rigby, C., & Przybylski, A. (2006). The motivational pull of video games: A self-determination theory approach. *Motivation and Emotion, 30*, 347–363. doi:10.1007/s11031-006-9051-8.

Shermis, M., & Burstein, J. (2003). *Automated essay scoring: A cross-disciplinary perspective.* Mahwah, NJ: Erlbaum.

Shute, V. (2008). Focus on formative feedback. *Review of Educational Research, 78*, 153–189. doi:10.3102/0034654307313795.

Shute, V., Rieber, L., & Van Eck, R. (2011). Games… and… learning. In Reiser, R., & Dempsey, J. (Eds.), *Trends and issues in instructional design and technology* (3rd ed., pp. 321–332). Upper Saddle River, NJ: Pearson Education Inc..

Sommers, N. (1982). Responding to student writing. *College Composition and Communication, 33*, 148–156. doi:10.2307/357622.

Warschauer, M., & Grimes, D. (2008). Automated writing assessment in the classroom. *Pedagogies. International Journal (Toronto, Ont.), 3*, 22–36.

Wolfe, C., Britt, M., Petrovic, M., Albrecht, M., & Kopp, K. (2009). The efficacy of a web-based counterargument tutor. *Behavior Research Methods, 41*, 691–698. doi:10.3758/BRM.41.3.691 PMID:19587180.

Young, M., Slota, S., Cutter, A., Jalette, G., Mullin, G., & Lai, B. et al. (2012). Our princess is in another castle: A review of trends in serious gaming for education. *Review of Educational Research, 82*, 61–89. doi:10.3102/0034654312436980.

APPENDIX: STRATEGY KNOWLEDGE TEST QUESTIONS

- **Question 1:** What strategies can good writers use to prepare to write an essay?
- **Question 2:** What strategies can good writers use to write the introduction of an essay?
- **Question 3:** What strategies can good writers use to write the body of an essay?
- **Question 4:** What strategies can good writers use to write the conclusion of an essay?
- **Question 5:** What strategies can good writers use to make an essay more understandable to the reader?
- **Question 6:** What strategies can good writers use to revise an essay?

Chapter 2
Building Awareness of Language Structures with Visual–Syntactic Text Formatting

Youngmin Park
University of California – Irvine, USA

Mark Warschauer
University of California – Irvine, USA

Penelope Collins
University of California – Irvine, USA

Jin Kyoung Hwang
University of California – Irvine, USA

Charles Vogel
Eagle Valley Schools, USA

ABSTRACT

The recently adopted Common Core State Standards emphasize the importance of language forms and structure in learning to write. Yet most language arts teachers have either downplayed the linguistic structure of writing in favor of process approaches or emphasized the teaching of grammatical structures outside of the context of authentic writing. Technology-supported writing activities tend to mimic these two approaches, with teachers using technology for either process-based writing or for grammar drills. Most teachers are not well prepared to teach linguistic structures in context or to deploy technology for that purpose. This chapter introduces a new tool called Visual-Syntactic Text Formatting (VSTF) that has powerful affordances for teaching linguistic and textual structures in the context of authentic written genres. Drawing on an empirical study and an action research project conducted by the authors, they share evidence for the value of using VSTF and point to ways that it can be used in the classroom to help students master language structures and employ them in their composition.

DOI: 10.4018/978-1-4666-4341-3.ch002

BUILDING AWARENESS OF LANGUAGE STRUCTURES WITH VISUAL-SYNTACTIC TEXT FORMATTING

On a recent nationwide writing assessment in the United States, only 25 percent of eighth and twelfth grade students performed at or above the proficient level (National Center for Education Statistics (NCES), 2012d). This statistic is disappointing compared to the percentage of students at or above proficient level on other subjects, such as reading, mathematics, or science, which ranges from 32 to 35 percent (NCES, 2012a, 2012b, 2012c). Potential causes for this phenomenon may lie in inadequate instructional time devoted to writing or low quality instruction. Even though more time is given to writing instruction now than decades ago, typical secondary students are asked to produce less than four pages a week for the main four subjects—English, science, social studies, and mathematics—combined (Applebee & Langer, 2011). Besides, most of writing instruction consists of writing without composing, such as filling in the blank or short answer exercises. A challenge to solving this problem in writing instruction is the complexity of the language structures required to be successful.

High quality writing instruction addresses the issues of writing structure, supporting the development of genre awareness, linguistic norms, and stylistic flexibility in order to help students effectively write for diverse purposes and audiences (Rijlaarsdam et al., 2012). Building structural awareness in writing instruction is consistent with the goals of the recently developed Common Core State Standards (CCSS). The CCSS not only aims to increase the emphasis on writing in schools, but also propose a shift from a heavy focus on narrative texts to a greater focus on informational texts (Common Core State Standards Initiative, 2010). According to the CCSS, students across all grade levels are expected to write for a variety of audiences and purposes, such as explaining a perspective or arguing a point of view. These changes in the curriculum standards have prompted a renewed emphasis on forms and structures of writing (Roberts, 2012) under the belief that attention to particular linguistic structures of academic genres is required for students to succeed in higher education and their careers.

However, current instructional practice does not seem to effectively address writing structures. The models frequently employed in classroom developed and modified by Flower and Hayes (1977, 1980, 2006) shifted the focus of teachers and researchers toward the processes by which good writers plan their tasks, translate their ideas, and review their texts. According to them, writing is a recursive process that incorporates mental operations throughout these processes. The planning phase includes goal-setting and idea generation. Writers translate their ideas into sentence generation in the translating phase. This phase is followed by the reviewing phase where writers monitor, evaluate, and revise texts. Writing instruction enlightened by Flower and Hayes' models has faciliated students' learning how to write. Similarly, technological advancements continue to enrich the writing process, as tools, such as word processing, discussion forums, wikis, Google docs, and blogs, are frequently used in classroom to provide students with more opportunities to engage in the iterative process of writing. While these writing models provide framework for understanding expert writers' processes and while technological scaffolding may facilitate these processes, these models and tools do not effectively provide students with guidance on how to craft the language or structure their text. This lack may explain in part why process writing is criticized (Scarcella, 2003) and why technology use does not necessarily enhance the quality of writing (Daiute, 1986; Grejda & Hannafin, 1992).

This chapter aims to explore potential conditions under which using technology in writing instruction may facilitate students' development of such structural expertise in terms of linguistic conventions, genres, and styles. To this end, Visual-Syntactic Text Formatting (VSTF) is introduced as a medium of writing and writing instruction with a focus on the structural characteristics of writing across different contexts. We will begin with a close look at the needs for knowledge of language structure within writing development continuum. This will be followed by a discussion of the language components that ought to be taught and how those components are effectively learned. These studies suggest several general principles underlying successful writing instruction with an emphasis on language structures, within which the specific features of VSTF as an instructional tool will be discussed. We will then turn to the potential of VSTF to facilitate teaching and learning language structures in light of the pedagogical stance we are taking by presenting an empirical study and an action research project conducted by the authors. The limited results of these studies will frame further discussion about what is needed to confirm the positive relationship between VSTF use and writing development, which was insufficiently provided by our studies. We will close by suggesting how further research using VSTF as an instructional and research tool enriches our knowledge about the student writing process, thereby contributing to the development of evidence-based practice.

LEARNING TO WRITE

Writing Development

Developmental stage models may allow us to better recognize what learners need for their writing development. Bereiter and Scardamalia (1987) proposed that the development of writing skill progresses through three major stages: knowledge telling, knowledge transforming, and knowledge crafting. Beginners use writing to tell what they know, which is commonly limited to idea retrieval. In the knowledge transforming stage sentence generation and handwriting have become automatized

and take up less cognitive capacity; writers increasingly learn to critically shape their texts in a way to reflect their purpose of writing. This shaping requires profound understanding and balancing of the writing processes—planning, transcribing, and reviewing—and knowledge about the language that writers use. The distinguished feature of the last stage is the recognition of a target audience. Skilled writers at this stage can review representations of author, text, and readers.

There is a more detailed model that covers a wide range of literacy growth levels. In attempting to propose a theoretical model of reciprocity between reading and writing, Fitzgerald and Shanahan (2000) specify critical cognitive markers that are significant for literacy proficiency in each of six stages. The first three stages place more emphasis on learning and developing graphophonics—letters and word identification and generation—than other linguistic knowledge or skills. Knowledge of language structures plays an important role in stages 4 and 5. As stage 4 is characterized by a marked increase in academic content, students encounter a greater emphasis on more complicated syntactic and organizational structures. Moreover, they are required to make connections between that which they learn and to create meaningful texts for a variety of purposes. While the critical features of stage 4 are further developed in the next stage, learners at stage 5 are also expected to deal with diverse perspectives. That is, comparing their goals in writing texts to their readers' expectations, writers can revise their written pieces to resolve potential disagreement between writers and readers. The pivotal knowledge in the last stage is metaknowledge about how readers and writers interact. In order to apply this knowledge to their writing, it is prerequisite to fully develop knowledge about language structures in the previous stages.

Despite the divergence in the number of stages in the two aforementioned models, there is an overlap between the two models, which highlights the fact that knowledge of language structures become increasingly important as learners progress.

What Needs to Be Taught?

Given that students need to master increasingly complex language structures as they develop as writers, writing instruction ought to help students understand and produce texts with complicated sentential and textual structures. Such instruction would help students develop mastery of these language structures and use them to craft knowledge in a manner appropriate for their audiences. The term language structure typically refers to three elements of language: phonology (patterns of sounds), morphology (patterns of sound sequence and words), and syntax (patterns of phrases and sentences). Morphology and syntax taken together are what is commonly known as grammar. Further, language structures may include higher level organization, such as rhetoric or genre. Such high level structures are also closely linked to language use that concerns how to effectively organize linguistic signals (words, sentences, and texts) in order to produce the intended effect on readers. In order to help writers select language structures for their purpose-driven writing, we argue that writing instruction be designed to increase both writers' knowledge about linguistic conventions and genre awareness.

Without explicit and direct effort, it is unlikely that students will acquire sophisticated features of the English language, such as low frequency words, embedded clauses, and substantial sentence variety (Scarcella, 2003). Children naturally pay attention to the meaning of texts rather than form or linguistic structures. Further, they are more familiar with the high frequency words and simple sentence structures that are more than commonly used in everyday communication. In this sense, Scarcella warns that writing instruction that places too much emphasis on meaningful communication or the content may be insufficient in building students' proficiency with the linguistic structures of academic English. She adds that instructors who give vague or no feedback on students' errors concerning language structures provide students with little chance to increase their academic proficiency. In sum, desirable writing instruction promotes mastery of complex language structures that are otherwise hard to learn, stimulates the development of skills to use these structures effectively and to revise already written texts with suitable structures.

How Are These Skills Typically Taught?

Explicit and Decontextualized Grammar Instruction

The explicit teaching of grammar and conventions that enjoyed its popularity in writing classes from ancient times is still widely used in schools for teaching linguistic norms. This type of teaching involves teaching the parts of speech and sentence structures. Whether or not teaching language structures works in writing education has been explored in a number of studies. Among experimental studies conducted between 1963 and 1982, Hillocks (1984) found five studies that focused on traditional grammar or mechanics, such as the study of parts of speech and punctuation, as the treatment. He found that this kind of instruction had no effect on the quality of student writing; rather, too much emphasis on correct grammar use had a harmful effect. More recent studies appear to confirm this deleterious outcome. Another meta-analysis by Graham and Perin (2007b) examined a great number of studies done over the last 40 years, out of which 11 studies investigated the effects of grammar instruction on student writing. Across these studies, grammar instruction had a significantly negative impact on writing quality. However, some studies suggest that grammar instruction has a positive effect, in the case of students with learning disabilities (Graham & Perin, 2007a). Therefore, explicit grammar instruction may benefit struggling writers.

Sentence Combining

As an alternative to traditional grammar instruction, sentence-combining activities, which involve teaching how to combine simple sentences into more sophisticated ones, have been used in writing class. Unlike explicit grammar teaching, this activity involves both explicit instruction and application to real writing tasks. Five studies in Hillocks' (1984) review included these activities as the treatment, showing a significantly greater effect on writing quality than grammar instruction. His review revealed that sentence combining was even more effective than free writing in enhancing student writing. The effectiveness of these activities has been confirmed by Graham and Perin (2007b). They found that sentence combining instruction was beneficial for low-performing students as well as students in general. Students may have learned skills to produce complex sentences by using connecting words, adding more adjectives and adverbs, and embedding adverbial/adjectival clauses, which led to a higher quality of writing.

Genre Awareness

Genre-based approaches are advocated by educators who are concerned about how to help students deal with academic tasks to gain social power (Cope & Kalantzis, 1993; Delpit, 1998). Commonly suggested approaches entail a focus on the mastery of academic genres such as reports, explanations, summaries, and argumentative essays. However, little empirical research has been conducted on the outcome of genre-based writing instruction. The above reviewed meta-analysis studies (Graham & Perin, 2007b; Hillocks, 1984) do not include genre-based writing research.

Upon closer examination of these studies, some methods with potential for teaching genre awareness can be found. These instructional methods include the use of models, the design of inquiry activities, and writing for content-area learning. First, presenting models in writing class is one of the classic approaches, but its effect still holds in current writing classrooms. Commonly, in the study of models students are presented with sample texts to discuss the effective elements of such texts with a goal to have them emulate those elements in their own compositions. Another method, the use of inquiry activities, involves students collecting data, hypothesizing, and testing those hypotheses. Compositions written through inquiry activities enable students to think about words, phrases, and sentences to describe their predictions, analyses, or arguments. A last but still important method is writing for content-area learning, the purpose of which is content-area mastery through the practice of writing. This rather new approach, reviewed only in the more recent study (Graham & Perin, 2007b), has been employed in 26 studies of writing. Most of these studies reported positive effects.

Integration of Skills

In classroom, many teachers employ Flower and Hayes' research (1977, 1980, 2006) on the writing process. However, this research does not make clear the pedagogical strategies that might best enable students to cultivate at these three processes. Studies of teachers' practices recommend that skills instruction needs to be combined with process writing (Cutler & Graham, 2008; Graham, Harris, Fink-Chorzempa, & MacArthur, 2003; Graham & Perin, 2007b). Writing skills (e.g., spelling, sentence generation/combining, proper use of text structures) taught alone are inadequate unless applied to real tasks that are completed in the process cycles of planning, translating, and reviewing. For example, the explicit teaching of grammar out of context is associated with having a negative effect on student writers (Graham & Perin, 2007b; Hillocks, 1984), and therefore has been shunned in practice. On the other hand, process writing with a lack of emphasis on language structures may inadequately prepare students to meet the challenges of writing (Scarcella, 2003). This inattention to explicit grammar instruction may result in a large number of students taking remedial English courses in college, regardless of their grades in high school English or their language learner status. The integration of skills and process writing supports what Hillocks (1984) had already recognized decades ago. That is, writing tasks necessitating skills students should learn with external assistance were more successful than tasks only requiring students' existing abilities, such as free writing. This implies that well-incorporated skills instruction with process writing may fit into the zone of proximal development (Vygotsky, 1978), stimulating the further development of writing skills. However, teaching the recognition and use of language structures as part of a process writing curriculum is difficult, especially given how these structures are often obscured within texts. A new text format, supported by technology-based tools, may allow for this more integrated pedagogical approach to teaching both explicit language structures as part of the writing process.

VISUAL-SYNTACTIC TEXT FORMATTING IN LITERACY CLASSROOM

Despite current research on effective strategies for teaching language structures to support writing, the way texts are presented on the page poses a challenge. Although organized in paragraphs to reflect ideas, syntactic structures are not salient. For example, two sentences with the same surface structure may have very different deep structures, or meanings. For example, the sentence, "The boy tickled the girl with the feather," may mean that the boy used the feather to tickle the girl or that the boy tickled the girl who was holding a feather. Even unambiguous sentences can be difficult to parse, particularly if they are long and include embedded clauses. Because of the difficulty in seeing the syntactic structure of sentences, young

writers may find it particularly challenging to learn more complex grammar and language structures.

We now turn our attention to a kind of technology that may make natural text structures more salient, that is, visual-syntactic text formatting. To convert traditional linear text format into this specific format as shown in Figure 1, computer-based parsing engines apply algorithms that analyze each sentence using both visual and linguistic criteria and determine optimal positions for segment breaks and indentation patterns (Walker, Schloss, Fletcher, Vogel, & Walker, 2005). As a result of automatic parsing processing, VSTF creates unique cascading patterns that reflect syntactic hierarchies. This text format is expected to support readers' ability to skim texts,

Figure 1. Text converted into visual-syntactic text formatting. Syntactic structures in the linear text on the top are complicated, as shown in the figure in the middle, where some clauses are nested within larger ones. In order to represent such complex structures, several millions of computer calculations are performed for each sentence in the text. As a result, the text on the bottom depicts how phrases and clauses are hierarchically related, rather than simply grouping words into a series of phrases.

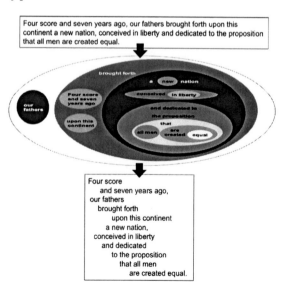

process word meanings, and better understand the text. Syntactic scaffolding is accomplished by segmenting the text along meaningful phrase units (Fodor & Bever, 1965; Jarvella, 1971). Reading these meaning segments may lessen working memory overload that often requires readers to go back to previously read words (Garrod, 1992). The resulting freed cognitive resources can then be devoted to making sense of texts. Studies on the cognitive process have demonstrated that meaningful unit-based segmentation of information has beneficial effects on learning, either by reducing repeated attention-switching between old and new information (Barrouillet & Camos, 2007) or by reducing the cognitive load by taking advantage of the psychological reality of linguistic phrases (Schwan, Garsoffky, & Hesse, 2000; Wouters, Paas, & van Merriënboer, 2008). VSTF with explicit segmentation along syntactic phrase boundaries, may help reduce readers' cognitive loads, resulting in more focus on the other cognitive processes of reading, so that readers can retain and consolidate multiple phrases in their mind (Walker et al. 2005).

The effects of this distinctive presentation have been examined in terms of reading comprehension, speed, retention, and proficiency (Walker et al., 2007; Walker & Vogel, 2005). In one study, 48 college students read three passages in standard block format and three in VSTF on computer screens (Walker et al., 2005). Participants answered comprehension questions with 40 percent greater accuracy for the passages read in VSTF than those read in block format. Further, participants read the passages 20 percent faster with the VSTF presentation. Thus, VSTF led to gains in both reading efficiency and comprehension for college students.

The effects of VSTF were also investigated among high school students for their reading retention in content courses (Walker et al., 2007, Walker & Vogel, 2005). For example, 10th grade students who read their history texts in VSTF showed greater improvement in their ten unit exams and final exam throughout the school year compared to their control peers. Overall, the effect size of the difference in exams in the second half of the year (.55) was larger than the effect size of the differences in the first half (.38). In these studies, the positive impact on reading proficiency is evidenced by the results of state standardized tests, the Measure of Academic Progress Test by the Northwest Educational Association (NWEA). A total of 384 sixth through eighth graders and 184 ninth and tenth graders took reading comprehension tests of the NWEA, of which passages are all formatted in block text. The analysis of changes between the NWEA at the beginning of the school year and the NWEA at the end of the school year showed that VSTF readers made greater improvements than did their counterparts in the block format condition.

Of greater relevance to this chapter, the unique presentation feature of VSTF and its fast and easy conversion of texts pose affordance as a writing instructional tool. In contrast to the traditional assumption that reading and writing are separate cognitive operations (Tompkins, 1997), reading and writing are postulated to share common underlying knowledge or processes (Fitzgerald & Shanahan, 2000; Tierney & Shanahan, 1991). In particular, Fitzgerald and Shanahan (2000) suggest four basic types of knowledge—metaknowledge, domain knowledge about substance and content, knowledge about universal text attributes, and procedural knowledge and skill to negotiate reading and writing. The latter two types of knowledge are pertinent to the knowledge of language structures—syntax and genre—that we address in this chapter. Text attributes include the rules for constructing sentences or larger chunks of text, while procedural knowledge refers to knowing how to generate knowledge in a given area, which is required for genre awareness. Drawing on this theoretical contention, VSTF, which facilitates students' understanding of language structures, is hypothesized to help teach and learn how to write sentences, paragraphs, and longer units of text.

Its fast conversion of texts makes VSTF potentially useful for the revision process. Students can review their written texts in VSTF, which makes their structures evident in order for writers to improve their writing by correcting mistakes in their drafts. This process can be expedited due to features of VSTF that may lessen working memory overload, a problem which may cause lower text quality and shorter sentence length as well as reduced writing fluency (Ransdell, Levy, & Kellogg, 2002). Even if earlier drafts contain a number of unfinished, run-on, or overly-simplistic sentences, such inferior sentences become obvious with VSTF. In fact, working memory plays an important role when writing skills progress to develop through three main stages in Bereiter and Scardamalia's (1987) model—knowledge telling, knowledge transforming and knowledge crafting. In the first stage, when writers generate texts to say what they want to say, they are expected to develop text representation, such as sentence generation and handwriting. Stable development of text representation is mainly limited by working memory capacity. Furthermore, a lack of basic skills to generate texts prevents writers from easily entering the next stages, because attention may not be given to planning and reviewing ideas, while text representation consumes most of writers' working memory (Kellogg, 2006).

Our two projects, one an experimental study in California and the other an action research project in Colorado, shed further light on this topic. For the first study, pre-converted digital textbooks were used, with which readers easily navigated to the section they were seeking. For the second study, software called ClipRead was used, which is available from Live Ink (www.liveink.com), the company that developed VSTF. With this tool, teachers and students can copy and paste any digital text into the program for quick conversion to VSTF, and then read through it.

An Experimental Study in California

Despite great effect sizes reported in the aforementioned studies with VSTF, these studies include weaknesses regarding their research designs, such as a less well-defined target population, risk of selection bias, effects of the treatment manipulation, or carry-over effects. These limitations may be mitigated by a large randomized study such as the one the first three authors carried out. The purpose of this study is to investigate the effects of reading texts in VSTF on sixth grade students' literacy development (Park, Warschauer, Farkas, & Collins, 2012). In particular, we were interested in which components of literacy are most affected by VSTF reading.

In this study, with 569 sixth graders in two southern California school districts, the treatment students ($n = 347$) received instruction in English language arts (ELA) and social studies with the VSTF program for one school year, while the students in the control group ($n = 222$) read the same texts in traditional format. The treatment students were exposed to individual (or pair work) VSTF reading for 30 to 120 minutes weekly for ELA and for 30 to 100 minutes biweekly for social studies. The control students read their regular texts in block format for approximately the same amount of time. Changes in students' performance over a school year were measured by comparing their achievements on the two classroom tests in each subject (one in fall and one in spring). Students also took the English portion of the California Standards Tests (CST) for two consecutive years, one before and one after the treatment. The English test in the CST contains five subtests: word analysis, reading comprehension, literary response, writing strategies, and written conventions.

Although there were inconclusive results on school-based unit tests, multiple regression analyses confirmed that students in the VSTF classrooms showed greater gains in ELA writing achievement. Students in the treatment group had CST ELA scores .22 standard deviations higher than those in the control group. More specifically, these students outperformed their control group peers in the subtest of word analysis by .38 standard deviations, writing strategies by .19 standard deviations, and written conventions by .18 standard deviations. However, these students showed no significant improvement on the reading comprehension and literary response subtests. These differences may reflect the syntactic scaffolding students had received throughout the year. For example, the word analysis subtest requires test takers to use word, sentence, and context clues to interpret words with novel or multiple meanings. The written conventions subtest requires students to use both simple and complex sentence structures to express complete thoughts. Writing strategies requires students to choose the form of writing that best suits the intended purpose, develop the topic with supporting details using precise vocabulary and coherent organizational patterns, and revise texts to improve the organization and consistency of ideas. In contrast, the two subtests that did not differentiate between VSTF and control students, reading comprehension and literary response, require a command of English beyond structural features, such as expository critiques of assertions or inferences in texts and narrative analysis or literary criticism. Thus, the effects of reading grade-level texts using VSTF were targeted to skills tapping the structural features of English.

An Action Research Project in Colorado

Despite noticeably improved performance on the writing portions of CST in our first study, VSTF was not directly used as a writing aid. Although to date the integration of VSTF into writing instruction has not yet been investigated using controlled randomized trials, our fifth author, Charles Vogel, conducted an action research project, aiming to explore possible ways of using VSTF as a writing scaffold in his social studies class.

Drawing on his successful reading intervention study with VSTF (Vogel, 2002), Vogel has encouraged a number of ELA or content area teachers in a Colorado school district to use VSTF as a reading scaffold in their fourth to 12th grade classes. These teachers' common practice was exemplified by including a reading section that engaged students in cultivating cognitive skills, cooperative learning, and fluency practice. VSTF also served both high-performing students who wanted to read above-grade-level texts and low-performing students who needed remedial reading intervention. Seeing the positive impact of VSTF on reading improvement across school subjects over the last decade, Vogel decided to conduct action research, taking advantage of VSTF to assist his students to write in his class. His students were asked to write an essay in response to what they read in their social studies class. He took notes on pedagogical strategies he used, which he continually adjusted to better suit his students' needs.

He described how in a typical writing session, his writing class format extended from his reading activities; the transition to writing with VSTF was smooth. All of the learning materials were provided in VSTF, making it possible to present grammatical rules of English via projector during class. Authentic examples from texts, ranging from simple to complex forms, were visually displayed. Especially at this stage of writing instruction, students were required to pay attention to linguistically accurate use of language, such as subject-verb agreement, verb conjugation, passive/active voice, parts of speech, and compound sentences. While dealing with grammatical rules, the teacher encouraged students to make more complex sentences by introducing how to combine sentences. VSTF was also used to highlight the visual architecture of texts, giving students a template to follow in all the controlled modeling exercises demanded from them (Figure 2). In their own composition, students then modeled their

Figure 2. Text examples for teaching language structures. The text to the left is an example of a narrative (excerpt from Charlotte's Web by E. B. White, 1952). The text to the right is an example of an expository text (excerpt from "Bacon's Philosophy, and Macaulay's Criticism of it" by B. B. Minor & J. D. Wells, 2007 in The Southern Literary Messenger 1834-1864 [Vol. 29 p. 181]). Vogel used the first example to explain subordination with the conjunctive adverb when, and the second example to show parallel structures emphasizing basic contrasts.

Figure 3. Writing samples in VSTF written by a tenth grade student before and after revision. The text to the left is her first draft and the one to the right is her last draft. Both texts are truncated in the middle due to space limitation. The last draft was originally twice as long as the first draft. Vogel and students discussed how to improve the first draft, which had sentence fragments, punctuation errors, and lacked transitions and sentence diversity. After this discussion, the draft was rewritten with changes in word choice and overall organization, which resulted in the last draft.

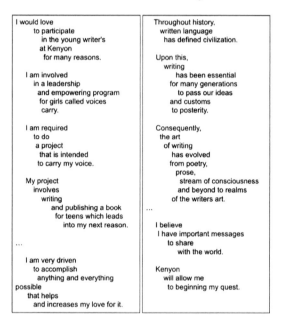

```
Next morning                    The aim
   when the first light            of the Baconianphilosophy
   came into the sky               was to provide man
   and the sparrows                   with what he requires
      stirred in the trees,            while he continues
   when the cows                         to be man.
      rattled their chains       The aim
         and the rooster crowed     of Platonic philosophy
   and the early automobiles        was to raise us
      went whispering                  far above vulgar wants.
         along the road,         The aim
WILBER AWOKE                        of Baconianphilosophy
   AND LOOKED FOR CHARLOTTE.        was to supply
                                       our vulgar wants.
                                The former aim was noble;
                                   but the latter
                                      was attainable.
```

writing on these examples. The teacher then had students input their own writing into ClipRead to present drafts in VSTF. Afterwards, the teachers and students together examined whether drafts that reflected students' thoughts were disorganized or not. Such reviewing sessions were done as a whole class activity or pair work. Students' writing with many problems, which were clearly highlighted through the VSTF conversion, were rewritten and resubmitted (for a student's writing samples, see Figure 3). Reading students' written pieces in VSTF, the teacher was able to better assess the needs of students, especially in terms of language structures, and tailor his feedback accordingly (see Figure 3).

Although no comparative outcome data were collected from his project, the author reported extensive benefits of using VSTF in writing activity (Vogel, 2011). Use of VSTF seems to benefit both students and the teacher. Not only did students obtain a better sense of language structures, according to Vogel, but they also learned to review and improve their own writing. For instance, through the discussions prompted by VSTF, Vogel suggested that students were able to rephrase their ideas, move phrases to their correct positions, add transitions, and witness how their drafts evolved from a rough, disorganized draft and into a well-organized final composition. Likewise, the teacher was assisted by VSTF in his history class, simultaneously addressing the issues of language acquisition and content instruction. While teaching content knowledge and using authentic texts, Vogel found that he was able to teach language structures, encourage students' literacy activities, provide appropriate feedback, and assess students' written products.

Integrating writing instruction is typically very challenging for content teachers, even though they are acutely aware of the language and reading challenges faced by their students (Newman, Samimy, & Romstedt, 2010). Though further research is needed, Vogel's project suggests that VSTF may enable content teachers to better integrate these types of writing activities into their curriculum.

GENERAL DISCUSSION

Taken together, our studies point to indirect and direct benefits of using VSTF for student writing development, and further suggest a possible way to help with writing assessment. In our California study, students saw indirect benefits. VSTF was used in the context of improving reading comprehension and made syntactic structures salient, leading to improved writing achievement. Even though this achievement, confined to written conventions and writing strategies, does not include the skills to write extended pieces, this indirect benefit contributing to improving writing skills may evidence the shared knowledge between reading and writing, namely syntactic knowledge.

In our project in Colorado, the effect on student writing appeared to be more direct. VSTF was used in writing instruction in two particularly interesting ways. First, students learned how to generate more sophisticated sentences and texts. For instance, by juxtaposing two model texts of two different genres, or two sample texts with/without transition words in VSTF, it seemed that students were able to get clearers ideas about structures than they would have in linear text format. Second, VSTF use often prompted students to review their drafts. Revision is an important but sometimes ignored part of the writing process. Using students' already

written texts as a springboard for generating ideas appears to be especially effective in the second half of the writing process (Van den Bergh et al., 2009). In enabling students to see their compositions in a different way, VSTF might encourage students to revisit their texts. Another study found that even students with high revision skills often fail to apply such skills, while postponing the rereading, evaluating, and revising activities (van der Hoeven, 1997). Because a writer who has little aptitude in one of the three writing sub-processes can compensate for it with another sub-process skill (Whitaker, Berninger, Johnston, & Swanson, 1994), taking full advantage of the revision process can increase writing quality even in the case of poorly planned pieces.

Additionally, our project suggests VSTF possibly assists writing assessment. Issues regarding writing assessment have historically focused on the use of a clear scoring rubric in order to obtain inter- or intra-rater reliability. Reliability is presumably reached by rigorous training, but such training sessions are often criticized for their focus on reliability at the expense of validity (Elder, Knoch, Barkhuizen, & von Randow, 2005; Hamp-Lyons, 2007; Huot, 1990; Moss, 1994; Weigle, 1994). In other words, students' valuable responses might be less appreciated when too much emphasis is placed on agreement between raters about the surface features of student writing. Assessing texts in VSTF with syntactic structures salient may leave more opportunities for raters to concentrate more on the content of texts rather than structures.

THE FUTURE: RESEARCHERS AND TEACHERS

Although writing instruction better reflects research than it did decades ago, current classroom writing is too often characterized by completing exercises or copying from the board rather than original student writing (Applebee & Langer,

2011). Therefore, students have few chances to describe their thoughts or knowledge through writing activities. Our findings suggest that the use of VSTF can increase the quality and quantity of writing done at school. The instructional strategies suggested in our studies can be employed across curricula, including in content areas. More time for writing in content areas makes it possible to learn how to connect the breadth and depth of knowledge students learn in reading to their composition. Through writing instruction in content area classes, students can have more chances to use cognitive and linguistic knowledge at the right moment. More frequent revisiting of drafts, supported by VSTF, helps students internalize the writing processes, thereby facilitating the development of student autonomy, or self-regulation, in the writing process. By presenting language structures and prompting the development of skills in context, VSTF can enhance writing instruction and student writing.

The flexibility of VSTF creates additional research possibilities. First, using the same technology across a variety of writing processes may show which processes are affected by instruction and how these processes are related to the quality of the resulting texts. Although the cognitive processes of writing and expert writers' characteristics have been revealed by Flower and Hayes' research (1977, 1980, 2006), their famous research method, think-aloud protocols, has not provided all the information we need for a clear understanding of novice writers' development. This is because the think-aloud method requires participants to verbalize their cognitive activities, which is not always possible or may be somewhat biased (Kellogg, 2001). In contrast, converting students' drafts into VSTF across the writing process can provide a series of written records showing the developmental changes of students. When such written texts are examined in relation to the instructional histories that students experience, researchers will be able to describe what are the learned features of language structures. Second, more empirical

studies are called for in order to obtain more detailed descriptions of instructional conditions under which learning may be transferrable. Our studies imply that structural knowledge can be transferred from reading to writing, but could not demonstrate this phenomenon empirically. Third, those who have limited working memory capacity might benefit from utilizing VSTF during this revision process to improve their writing quality. Future research that methodologically includes a working memory assessment can verify this hypothesis. Fourth, VSTF for assessment can be easily examined if VSTF is given to raters even without being used as an instructional tool. If future studies confirm the usefulness of VSTF as an assessment aid, the tool may help make writing instruction more accessible in schools, alleviating teachers' burden to evaluate and give feedback to large classes.

More interestingly, both instruction and research can be designed specifically for language minority learners. VSTF is hypothesized to benefit these students who hear and/or speak a language other than English at home. A number of research studies demonstrate that language minority learners have comparable growth trajectories to their English-only counterparts in decoding and phonological awareness skills, which are basic linguistic skills that need to be in place for reading. However, these language learners tend not to close the gap in higher-order linguistic skills, such as reading comprehension and writing (Chiappe, Glaeser, &Ferko, 2007; Geva, Yaghoub-Zadeh, & Schuster, 2000; Lesaux, Lipka, & Siegel, 2006; NCES, 2012d). In this sense, breaking sentences down into meaningful units, as VSTF does, could be appropriate scaffolding for this group of students. By enabling these students to recognize rules and characteristics in the English language and notice differences in English texts across genres more easily, VSTF helps increase writing development. This will be especially beneficial to those who have sufficient English language skills to graduate out of English language development classes (or English-as-a-second-language classes) but lack the knowledge in academic language and genre necessary to succeed in mainstream classrooms. It is also necessary to empirically explore whether VSTF use is favorable or unfavorable for these language minority students.

As discussed above, VSTF contains a palette of applications of potential value for writing instruction and research. Continued research may confirm the effectiveness of VSTF in enhancing students' learning and performance. Furthermore, research with VSTF, through more fine-grained analysis of intervention, is expected to produce more elaborated theoretical accounts of the conditions under which students learn writing skills and expand their knowledge.

REFERENCES

Applebee, A. N., & Langer, J. A. (2011). A snapshot of writing instruction in middle schools and high schools. *English Journal*, *100*(6), 14–27.

Barrouillet, P., & Camos, V. (2007). The time-based resource sharing model of working memory. In Osaka, N., Logie, R. H., & D'Esposito, M. (Eds.), *The cognitive neuroscience of working memory* (pp. 59–80). Oxford, UK: Oxford University Press. doi:10.1093/acprof:oso/9780198570394.003.0004.

Bereiter, C., & Scardamalia, M. (1987). *The psychology of written composition*. Hillsdale, NJ: Lawrence Erlbaum Associates, Inc..

Chiappe, P., Glaeser, B., & Ferko, D. (2007). Speech perception, vocabulary, and the development of reading skills in English among Korean-and English-speaking children. *Journal of Educational Psychology*, *99*(1), 154–166. doi:10.1037/0022-0663.99.1.154.

Common Core State Standards Initiative. (2010). Common core state standards for English language arts & literacy in history/social studies, science, and technical subjects. Washington, DC: National Governors Association Center for Best Practices and the Council of Chief State School Officers. Retrieved from www.corestandards.org/assets/CCSSI_ELA%20Standards.pdf

Cope, B., & Kalantzis, M. (1993). *The powers of literacy: A genre approach to teaching writing*. Pittsburg, PA: University of Pittsburgh Press.

Cutler, L., & Graham, S. (2008). Primary grade writing instruction: A national survey. *Journal of Educational Psychology*, *100*, 907–919. doi:10.1037/a0012656.

Daiute, C. (1986). Physical and cognitive factors in revising: Insights from studies with computers. *Research in the Teaching of English*, *20*, 141–159.

Delpit, L. D. (1998). The silenced dialogue: Power and pedagogy in educaitng other people's children. *Harvard Educational Review*, *58*(3), 280–298.

Elder, C., Knoch, U., Barkhuizen, G., & von Randow, J. (2005). Individual feedback to enhance rater training: Does it work? *Language Assessment Quarterly*, *2*, 175–196. doi:10.1207/s15434311laq0203_1.

Fitzgerald, J., & Shanahan, T. (2000). Reading and writing relations and their development. *Educational Psychologist*, *31*(1), 37–41.

Flower, L., & Hayes, J. R. (1977). Problem-solving strategies and the writing process. *College English*, *39*, 449–461. doi:10.2307/375768.

Flower, L., & Hayes, J. R. (1980). The dynamics of composing: Making plans and juggling constraints. In Gregg, L. W., & Steinberg, E. R. (Eds.), *Cognitive processes in writing* (pp. 31–50). Hillsdale, NJ: Erlbaum.

Flower, L., & Hayes, J. R. (2006). A cognitive process theory of writing. In Villanueva, V. (Ed.), *Cross-talk in composition theory: A reader* (2nd ed., pp. 273–297). Urbana, IL: NCTE.

Fodor, J. A., & Bever, T. G. (1965). The psychological reality of linguistic segments. *Journal of Verbal Learning and Verbal Behavior, 4,* 414–420. doi:10.1016/S0022-5371(65)80081-0.

Garrod, S. (1992, April). Reconciling the psychological with the linguistic in accounts of text comprehension. Paper presented at the NORD-TEXT Symposium. Espoo, Finland.

Geva, E., Yaghoub-Zadeh, Z., & Schuster, B. (2000). Understanding individual differences in word recognition skills of ESL children. *Annals of Dyslexia, 50*(1), 121–154. doi:10.1007/s11881-000-0020-8 PMID:20563783.

Graham, S., Harris, K. R., Fink-Chorzempa, B., & MacArthur, C. (2003). Primary grade teachers' instructional adaptations for struggling writers: A national survey. *Journal of Educational Psychology, 95,* 279–292. doi:10.1037/0022-0663.95.2.279.

Graham, S., & Perin, D. (2007a). What we know, what we still need to know: Teaching adolescents to write. *Scientific Studies of Reading, 11*(4), 37–41. doi:10.1080/10888430701530664.

Graham, S., & Perin, D. (2007b). *Writing next: Effective strategies to improve writing of adolescents in middle and high schools.* New York, NY: Carnegie Corporation.

Grejda, G. F., & Hannafin, M. J. (1992). Effects of word-processing on 6th graders' holistic writing and revisions. *The Journal of Educational Research, 85,* 144–149. doi:10.1080/00220671.1992.9944430.

Hamp-Lyons, L. (2007). Worrying about rating. *Assessing Writing, 12,* 1–9. doi:10.1016/j.asw.2007.05.002.

Hillocks, G. (1984). What works in teaching composition: A meta-analysis of experimental treatment studies. *American Journal of Education, 93*(1), 133–170. doi:10.1086/443789.

Huot, B. (1990). The literature of direct writing assessment: Major concerns and prevailing trends. *Review of Educational Research, 60,* 237–263. doi:10.3102/00346543060002237.

Jarvella, R. J. (1971). Syntactic processing of connected speech. *Journal of Verbal Learning and Verbal Behavior, 10,* 409–416. doi:10.1016/S0022-5371(71)80040-3.

Kellogg, R. (2001). Competition for working memory among writing processes. *The American Journal of Psychology, 114,* 175–191. doi:10.2307/1423513 PMID:11430147.

Kellogg, R. T. (2006). Professional writing expertise. In Ericsson, K. A., Charness, N., Feltovich, P. J., & Hoffman, R. R. (Eds.), *The Cambridge handbook of expertise and expert performance* (pp. 389–402). New York, NY: Cambridge University Press. doi:10.1017/CBO9780511816796.022.

Lesaux, N. K., Lipka, O., & Siegel, L. S. (2006). Investigating cognitive and linguistic abilities that influence the reading comprehension skills of children from diverse linguistic backgrounds. *Reading and Writing, 19*(1), 99–131. doi:10.1007/s11145-005-4713-6.

Moss, P. (1994). Can there be validity without reliability? *Educational Research, 23,* 5–12.

National Center for Education Statistics. (2012a). *The nation's report card: Mathematics 2011 (NCES 2012–458).* Washington, DC: Institute of Education Sciences, U.S. Department of Education.

National Center for Education Statistics. (2012b). *The nation's report card: Reading 2011 (NCES 2012–457).* Washington, DC: Institute of Education Sciences, U.S. Department of Education.

National Center for Education Statistics. (2012c). *The nation's report card: Science 2011 (NCES 2012–465).* Washington, DC: Institute of Education Sciences, U.S. Department of Education.

National Center for Education Statistics. (2012d). *The nation's report card: Writing 2011 (NCES 2012–470).* Washington, DC: Institute of Education Sciences, U.S. Department of Education.

Newman, K., Samimy, K., & Romstedt, K. (2010). Developing a training program for secondary teachers of English language learners in Ohio. *Theory into Practice, 49*(2), 152–161. doi:10.1080/00405841003641535.

Park, Y., Warschauer, M., Farkas, G., & Collins, P. (2012). The effects of visual-syntactic text formatting on adolescents' academic development. Manuscript submitted for publication.

Ransdell, S., Levy, C. M., & Kellogg, R. T. (2002). The structure of writing processes as revealed by secondray task demands. L1—Educational Studies in Language and Literature, 2(2), 141-163.

Rijlaarsdam, G., Van den Bergh, H., Couzijn, M., Janssen, T., Braaksma, M., & Tillema, M. et al. (2012). Writing. In Anderman, E., Winne, P. H., Alexander, P. A., & Corno, L. (Eds.), *Handbook of educational psychology* (pp. 189–227). New York, NY: Routledge.

Roberts, K. L. (2012). The linguistic demands of the common core state standards for reading and writing informational text in the primary grades. *Seminars in Speech and Language, 33*(2), 146–159. doi:10.1055/s-0032-1310314 PMID:22538710.

Scarcella, R. (2003). Accelerating academic English: A focus on English language learners. Oakland, CA: Regents of the University of California.

Schwan, S., Garsoffky, B., & Hesse, F. (2000). Do film cuts facilitate the perceptual and cognitive organization of activity sequences? *Memory & Cognition, 28,* 214–223. doi:10.3758/BF03213801 PMID:10790977.

Tierney, R. J., & Shanahan, T. (1991). Research on the reading-writing relationship--Interactions, transactions, and outcomes. In Barr, R., Kamil, M., Mosenthal, P., & Pearson, P. D. (Eds.), *Handbook of reading research* (pp. 246–280). New York, NY: Longman.

Tompkins, G. E. (1997). *Literacy for the 21st century: A balanced approach.* Upper Saddle River, NJ: Prentice Hall.

Van den Bergh, H., Rijlaarsdam, G., Janssen, T., Braaksma, M., Weijen, D., & Tillema, M. (2009). Process execution of writing and reading: Considering text quality, learner and task characteristics. Quality Research in Literacy and Science Education, 399-425.

van der Hoeven, J. (1997). *Children's composing: A study into the relationships between writing processes, text quality, and cognitive and linguistic skills (Vol. 12).* Atlanta, GA: Rodopi.

Vogel, C. (2011, February). CSAP and ACT bootcamp: Using the Liveink reading format. Paper presented at the Colorado Council International Reading Council Annual Conference. Denver, CO.

Vogel, C. A. (2002). A program evaluation of the live ink format. (Unpublished dissertation). University of Denver College of Education, Denver, CO.

Vygotsky, L. S. (1978). *Mind and society: The development of higher psychological processes.* Cambridge, MA: Harvard University Press.

Walker, R., Gordon, A. S., Schloss, P., Fletcher, C. R., Vogel, C., & Walker, S. (2007). Visual-syntactic text formatting: Theoretical basis and empirical evidence for impact on human reading. Paper presented at the IEEE Professional Communication Conference. Seattle, WA.

Walker, R., & Vogel, C. (2005, June). Live ink: Brain-based text formatting raises standardized test scores. Paper presented at the National Educational Computing Conference. Philadelphia, PA.

Walker, S., Schloss, P., Fletcher, C. R., Vogel, C. A., & Walker, R. (2005). Visual-syntactic text formatting: A new method to enhance online reading. *Reading Online*, 8(6).

Weigle, S. (1994). Effects of training on raters of ESL compositions. *Language Testing*, *11*, 197–223. doi:10.1177/026553229401100206.

Whitaker, D., Berninger, V., Johnston, J., & Swanson, H. L. (1994). Intraindividual differences in levels of language in intermediate grade writers: Implications for the translating process. *Learning and Individual Differences*, *6*, 107–130. doi:10.1016/1041-6080(94)90016-7.

Wouters, P., Paas, F., & van Merriënboer, J. J. G. (2008). How to optimize learning from animated models: A review of guidelines based on cognitive load. *Review of Educational Research*, *78*, 645–675. doi:10.3102/0034654308320320.

KEY TERMS AND DEFINITIONS

Common Core State Standards: A U.S. education initiative that seeks to align diverse state curricula by following the principles of standards-based education reform.

Genre Awareness: A metacognitive understanding of genres that students encounter in multiple disciplines, which helps students view a text in terms of its rhetorical and social purpose.

Knowledge Transforming: Transforming ideas retrieved from memory with the effort to resolve a conflict between the ideas and the rhetorical goal, which may result in the generation of new ideas and a deeper understanding of the subject.

Language Structures: Rules or principles that predict how sounds, sound sequences, words, sentences, and texts are made and how these units convey meaning.

Process Writing: An approach to writing that emphasizes working through various stages of the process—planning, transcribing, and reviewing.

Sentence Combining: Activities that encourage students to weld simple sentences into more diverse sentence types through explicit instruction, such as cutting out needless repetition and adding conjunctions.

Visual-Syntactic Text Formatting: Live Ink TechnologyTM that transforms traditional block text into cascading patterns helping readers identify syntactic structures.

Working Memory: The brain system that temporarily stores information necessary for tasks such as learning, comprehending, and reasoning.

Chapter 3
Using Digital Portfolios to Enhance Students' Capacity for Communication about Learning

Brian Kissel
University of North Carolina – Charlotte, USA

S. Michael Putman
University of North Carolina – Charlotte, USA

Katie Stover
Furman University, USA

ABSTRACT

There is a clear consensus that students need to be proficient in the use of digital technologies to help them become knowledgeable participants in an era of global information sharing (International Reading Association, 2009). Acknowledging this, the current study was situated in the belief that writers, when engaged in online composition and the creation of digital portfolios, engage in processes that differ from traditional pencil-paper types of writing. A qualitative approach was utilized to examine student writing samples and reflections over a two-year timeframe as the students transitioned from traditional writing portfolios to those created and maintained digitally on a wiki. The results demonstrated that digital portfolios provide a platform for students to communicate, express their ideas, share their understandings, and collaboratively construct meaning with an authentic audience. Correspondingly, it also demonstrates the necessity of adjusting teaching practices to accommodate for conditions that arise from the unique opportunities presented by the digital environment.

INTRODUCTION

In the 21st century classroom, technology-infused texts are primary within the practices of today's writers as they engage with ever-emerging tools to write in communicative, collaborative, and exploratory ways (Taylor, 2012). Students live in a world that is focused upon social interaction and new digital tools for communication have emerged, "changing ways of producing, distributing, exchanging and receiving texts" (Lankshear & Knobel, 2003, p. 16). Authorship now reaches wider domains and increases the potential for partnership and creativity as students have the opportunity to write for a variety of purposes and

DOI: 10.4018/978-1-4666-4341-3.ch003

interact with an authentic audience (Merchant, 2005). In the world of instant information, planning, revision, and editing are often replaced with a quick draft and an even quicker push of the publish button. Writers have the capacity to post comments and publish instantly for an entire virtual world to read. In essence, the tools of writing have changed. The audience has widened. The result is a new generation of writers who have redefined what it means to be literate (Hansen & Kissel, 2010).

It is within this context that we acknowledge the need to know more about how young students use technology as writers; to understand how writing is a tool they use to communicate and collaborate. We must also know practical ways teachers can bring technology into their classrooms so students have opportunities to engage in communicative and collaborative acts as writers. This chapter seeks to address this need as we examine how fourth grade students used technology in their classrooms as a mode of communication and collaboration while moving from paper-based portfolios to digital portfolios, thus allowing a third-space for peers to digitally communicate with one another about their learning.

THEORETICAL FRAMEWORK

Sociocultural Theory

Sociocultural theory (Bakhtin, 1981; Scribner & Cole, 1981; Vygotsky, 1978) addresses the learner as an individual as well as part of a context of learning and interaction with others. Risko et al. (2008) describe sociocultural theory as "not simply what happens in the brain of an individual but what happens to the individual in relation to a social context and the multiple forms of interactions with others" (p. 253). Within this perspective, individual meaning (knowledge) is developed within socially-situated contexts through semiotic mechanisms, including language, writing, and other symbol systems (Vygotsky, 1978).

While sociocultural theorists (see Vygotsky, 1978, Bakhtin, 1981) acknowledge the various mechanisms present within social interactions, language is viewed as a primary tool for communication and representation, and, as a result, learning. It enables thought processes, but also serves the dual purpose of facilitating social contact and mediating human behavior (Vygotsky, 1978). For Bakhtin (1981), language represented the mediator within discourse that was culturally and contextually influenced. He theorized, "The word in language is half someone else's. It becomes 'one's own' only when the speaker populates it with his own intention, his own accent, when he appropriates the word, adapting it to his own semantic and expressive intention" (Bakhtin, 1981, p. 293). He articulated the concept of dialogism to describe individuals' motives for the content of their interactions within specific contexts (Bakhtin, 1981). This was exemplified through dialogue affected by the speaker's recognition of the respondent's meaning as well as socially-constructed conventions, such as turn-taking.

Considering the premise that interaction and communication facilitate the development of "ideas, language, values, and dispositions" (Vasquez, 2006, p. 36), meaning is therefore negotiated through social interactions and is reliant on social constructs. Within a classroom, the social nature of learning is exhibited within literacy practices involving co-constructed meaning through shared ideas and social identities of the teacher and the students. Construction of thinking and knowing through social interaction demonstrates the value of shared understanding through collaboration with others. Interactions allow participants to develop and grow as "each participant makes significant contributions to the emergent understanding of all members" (Palincsar, Brown, & Campione, 1993, p. 43). Social construction of meaning in this format compliments Vygotsky's (1978) belief that the groups are central in helping learners construct knowledge.

Social interaction also influences the role of the teacher within sociocultural theory as she assumes the role of an "enabler" who helps the learner construct understandings (Vygotsky, 1986). Through her interactions or dialogue with students, the teacher facilitates the development of capabilities beyond a learner's current level of independent performance. Vygotsky (1978) articulated this process as achieving maximum impact when it occurred within the zone of proximal development (ZPD), or "the distance between the actual developmental level as determined by independent problem solving and the level of potential development as determined through problem solving under adult guidance or in collaboration with more capable peers" (p. 86). Within this process, dialogue or social interaction is used to guide learning. As proficiency increases, the teacher's dialogue gradually becomes less directive and more facilitative, dependent upon the resulting feedback and needs of the student.

For Vygotsky (1978), all aspects of learning and development were social. However, the social context shifted within the process of development of the learner. Learning began between people as an interpersonal process and progressed to an internal orientation, also referred to as intrapersonal. Vygotsky (1986) described this transformation as internalization, and associated it with higher level mental functioning. The primary function of this internal dialogue, referred to as inner speech, was to direct activities such as remembering and reasoning (Vygotsky, 1986). Bruner (1962) described inner speech as "the internalization of external dialogue that brings the powerful tool of language to bear on the stream of thought" (p. vii). The emerging processes of inner speech evolve as a result of constant, incremental changes that result from external and internal factors; the mind, therefore, is in a constant state of change. Thus, for Vygotsky (1978), language not only represented an instrument for developing thought, but was concurrently advanced through thought.

Sociocultural Theory and Writing

Sociocultural theory has particular applicability within the context of a classroom setting where literacy practices are co-constructed through shared ideas and social identities of the teacher and the students (Street, 1984). In this setting, all members are involved in the collective construction of meaning through interactions centered on content from readings or written works that allow learners to share ideas and understandings. Fish (1980) referred to these groups of learners as interpretive communities. Construction of thinking and knowing through social interaction demonstrates the value of shared understanding through collaboration with others. It is within this environment, and through the teacher's ability to adjust and adapt the environment, i.e. context, that Vygotsky (1978) further emphasized the necessity of authentic purposes for literacy, i.e. writing and reading. In his view, writing should be natural and aligned with the learner's environment. Vygotsky wrote that learners should approach "writing as a natural moment in her development, and not as training from without…in the same way as they learn to speak, they should be able to learn to … write" (1978, pp. 118). Thus, there is a focus on discourse that facilitates development from socially mediated activities within a community of practice to internalized competencies.

Several researchers have posited the importance of creating a community of learners within a shared space for interaction (see Gee, 2008; Vasudevan, Schultz, & Bateman, 2010). Having such shared spaces as well as a medium for text production provides an authentic audience for their written work. In other words, the writers have a purpose for their text creation. As a result, according to Graham and Harris (2007), students were more likely plan their writing, and, subsequently, to analyze, edit, and clarify writing. In essence, they were more likely to reflect upon their writing within the process.

Reflection is an important component if the learner is to internalize the processes addressed within the discourse or develop the behaviors associated with internalization (Vygotsky, 1986). First, it offers the opportunity to for students to establish goals and to monitor their progress towards achieving writing specific goals (Bransford, Brown, & Cocking, 2000). As teachers teach and reinforce reflective practices within writing, developing the contextual support within students' ZPD, the students will be more likely to demonstrate them, eventually incorporating the process into their everyday practices within writing (Griffin, 2003). The challenge, however, may lie in creating authentic contexts to practice reflection as well as specifically teaching the skills associated with it as children are unlikely to develop these skills without guidance (Bransford, et al., 2000).

Writing Instruction and Portfolios

One method that has been used by teachers to both provide an authentic context for writing and to promote reflective practices is the writing portfolio. Writing portfolios represent a collection of artifacts that are presented to fulfill a specific purpose. For example, they can be used to demonstrate in-process learning/growth over time (Abrami & Barrett, 2005; Barrett, 2007) or to showcase multiple, finished exemplars to demonstrate proficiency in specific skills (Denton, 2012). The inherent advantage of the use of writing portfolios is the flexibility in both form and function to fulfill the specified purpose.

Zubizarreta (2004) described a model for portfolios that emphasized the interaction of three elements: reflection, evidence, and collaboration. According to his research, learning can be accomplished using portfolios when two of the three components are activated; yet, a combination of all three elements facilitates opportunities for greater engagement and, potentially, enhanced learning. However, research on these outcomes has proven challenging, notably due to the variability

in process and context (Barrett, 2007). This is especially true of K-12 research as the majority of the investigations into portfolio use have come from higher education and adult education (Barrett, 2007).

The research that has been conducted, however, has shown that portfolios can serve an important role as a tool to support active reflection by students. These reflections on the pieces of evidence can include such information as the rationale for the selection of a piece of evidence, a personal evaluation of the work, and key information learned from the portfolio (Abrami & Barrett, 2005; Klenowski, Askew, & Carnell, 2006; Loughran & Corrigan, 1995; Smith & Tillema, 2003). In essence, portfolios allow students to become active participants in their learning as they describe what, how, and why they have learned as well as what challenges occurred within the process (Zubizarreta, 2004).

With the emergence of digital tools, educators have the capability of moving the traditional writing portfolio into an electronic format. According to Abrami and Barrett (2005), an electronic portfolio is "a digital container capable of storing visual and auditory content including text, images, video and sound…designed to support a variety of pedagogical processes and assessment purposes" (p. 2). Digital portfolios can serve many of the same purposes as the traditional portfolio (Niguidula, 2005). However, they can also "help students develop the self-awareness required to set their own learning goals, express their own views of their strengths, weaknesses, and achievements…[and] be shared with peers, parents, and others who are part of students' extended network" (United States Department of Education, 2010, p.12).

Digital portfolios appear to have several benefits unique to the environment. They can:

- Facilitate the use of different formats, including writing that integrates text, hyptertext, and multimedia elements (Abrami & Barrett, 2005; Heath, 2005; Wade, Abrami, & Sclater, 2005).

- Help students develop and model new technology skills (Abrami & Barrett, 2005; Wall, Higgins, Miller, & Packard, 2006).
- Distribute writing to a much broader, more authentic audience (Wade et al., 2005).

The capacity for sharing means the ability to exchange ideas and give/receive feedback is enhanced (Abrami & Barrett, 2005), potentially creating a community of practice centered upon the portfolios. Consequently, the elements associated with sociocultural theories are manifest in practices as feedback and discourse allows students to acknowledge contributions from others as well as take on responsibility for the each others' growth (e.g., Bakhtin, 1981; Vygotsky, 1978).

Perhaps the most significant shortcoming associated with digital portfolios in K-12 contexts is a general lack of research in this area. As technologies continue to emerge, there still exists a great need for additional knowledge about processes students use to compose and publish texts in online environments. Investigating the use of digital portfolios as a means to support children's writing development offers an opportunity to expand on what we currently know and may provide important implications for how technology can further influence our ideas about writing and instruction in the classroom.

The following research was undertaken to continue to refine and expand our knowledge in this area.

METHODOLOGY

For this study, we asked the following question: What happens throughout the digital portfolio process of fourth and fifth grade students? To answer this question, we employed an interpretivistic, ethnographic approach to study the culture of one classroom of students during a two year stretch as they looped from fourth grade to fifth grade with the same teacher (Erickson, 1986). This approach

is intended to acknowledge the multiple truths that existed in the culture of the classroom. We developed themes by reading and rereading the collected corpus of field notes, transcripts of conversations, and interviews. We then compared them with the written documents and digital portfolios created by the students. To describe their digital portfolio processes, thick descriptions of the classroom acts were employed to explain how participants engaged in this process (Geertz, 1973). The goal of the description was to make clear the events that occurred in the classroom. Descriptions of the classroom events were collected as field notes and then systematically studied to acknowledge emerging patterns and themes.

Site and Population Selection

The chosen classroom was a fourth/fifth grade classroom in a Southeastern town in the United States. The school was a publicly funded charter school. The school has maintained its charter status for over 11 years and is considered one of the most successful charter schools in the state.

The Classroom Teacher

Diana, a 42-year-old woman of European American descent, has been an elementary teacher for over 10 years. She is also a former vice principal. After several years in an administrative position, Diana missed teaching in the classroom. When the opportunity arose for her to teach within the school, she decided to enter the classroom.

Students in Diana's class participated in an hour of daily writing through a Writer's Workshop based on Fletcher and Portalupi's (2000) model for writing instruction. Each day, children gathered for a mini-lesson based on their writing needs, then engaged in writing of self-selected topics. In their fifth grade year, students published four major products for a wide audience: 1) a multigenre book based on their experiences at a three-day field trip to a coastal island within the state, 2) poetry they performed for a poetry slam at a local coffee house, 3) an opera in which the students composed the music and lyrics, created the sets, and performed in front of the school, and 4) a social action research project in which students used writing to enact change for a cause that was important to them. Many of these published pieces became selections of their digital portfolios.

The Fourth/Fifth Grade Students

This study, conducted over two years, examined the portfolio process of one classroom of 24 students as they moved from fourth to fifth grade. Combined, there were 12 boys and 12 girls. The majority of the students were of European-American descent (n=20). Two students were African American and two others were of Latino(a) descent. All names included within this article are pseudonyms to protect the identity of the participants examined in this study.

Data Sources and Procedures

This study is situated within an interpretivistic paradigm (Erickson, 1986) and uses a case study design (Dyson & Genishi, 2005; Merriam, 1998). Over the course of 18 months (9 months in year 1, 9 months in year 2), data were collected on children's writing processes and practices. Observations of the class, interviews with the children and teacher, and written documents of the children were primary sources of data. During Year 1, the researcher collected data in the classroom for the entire school year, once a week, for 2–3 hr each visit. In total, 37 visits to the classroom were made, which totaled approximately 82 hours. During Year 2, data were collected during the entire school year for approximately 2 hours for each visit. Thirty-eight visits were made for a total of 76 hours. During each of these visits, the primary researcher observed and wrote field notes about the children as they wrote. The children's conversations were captured using audio record-

ings. At the end of each day, the primary researcher elaborated on his field notes and wrote an analytic memo describing the themes that emerged from the data (Miles & Huberman, 1994). These field notes were filed with the transcribed interactions and scanned copies of the children's writing.

Data Analysis

Students' portfolio processes were analyzed using Jane Hansen's (1998) self-evaluation process as noted in her book *When Learners Evaluate*. In her work with various students across all grade levels, Hansen noticed an emerging self-evaluation process conducted by the students. This process involved a self-evaluative loop in which students collected, selected, reflected, projected, and affected, using artifacts from their reading and writing.

The primary researcher noticed a similar process within the fourth/fifth grade classroom with one notable change when students projected their digital portfolios: students enacted affection through connection. The commenting feature within the digital portfolios allowed students to offer responses to their peers in the forms of comments, questions, compliments, and personal connections.

The primary researcher used an interpretivist paradigm to scour the corpus of data to analyze how students enacted a self-evaluation process using their digital portfolios (Erickson, 1986). Interpretation of these data came from the researcher's understanding of the group interactions that occurred as he was embedded in the classroom for extensive periods of time. A constant comparative analysis (Glaser & Strauss, 1967) was used as the primary researcher read the transcripts and compared them with the documents collected from the students. Based on these careful readings, the researcher attempted to capture the essence of the children's compositions and his interpretations of those compositions (Dilthey, 1911/1977).

A recursive analytic process was employed to analyze the data (Miles & Huberman, 1994). From the corpus of data, the field notes, transcripts, and writing documents were reduced into one- to two-page analytic memos that summarized emerging themes. Through this reduction technique, patterns emerged.

To answer the research question, the researcher poured through the analytic memos, student transcripts, and writing documents to find instances where students engaged in their self-evaluative digital portfolio process. Using the analytic memos and data displays, themes were made about the students' digital portfolio process that led to the conclusions in this study. Based upon these thematic categories the following findings emerged.

RESULTS

Students in this classroom created a digital writing portfolio. The portfolio assignment was established by the teacher in conjunction with the students to answer the question, *What have you learned as a writer in our class this year?* The teacher asked students to pour through their writings (published pieces, drafts, plans, revisions, edits, notes, etc.) to show what they have learned throughout the year. They were asked to pick 4-6 pieces to submit to their portfolio. This section unpacks the digital portfolio process that unfolded in Diana's classroom through three themes. In Theme One, we explain the collection and selection phase of the students' portfolio process. We highlight the many places students searched to collect pieces of writing for their portfolios, and then examine their selection criteria for the pieces they chose to place on their digital portfolio wiki. Next, in Theme Two, we examine the students' reflection phase of the portfolio process. We reveal their purposes for the chosen pieces by examining several reflections written on their digital portfolio wiki page. Finally, in Theme Three, we show how students used their digital portfolio wikis to

project, affect, and connect. These three phases of the process became more important when students switched from a paper-based portfolio system to a digital portfolio system.

Theme 1: Portfolio Processes – Collect and Select

During this first phase of their portfolio self-assessment, *collection and selection*, students gathered all their writing materials from three primary sources: daybooks, in-progress folders, and published work. Diana made clear that the students could think of their portfolios in multiple ways; that is, students were not limited to collect and select items for their portfolio that reflected finished work or even their best work. The portfolios had to show their thinking and progression as writers over time.

Choosing and selecting artifacts proved to be a complex task for the students. First, students needed to find artifacts that revealed themselves as learners. That required careful collection of their materials and thoughtful consideration of their choices. Next, they had to make decisions. They asked themselves, "Of all the writings before me, what shows something important that I've learned?" This question required thoughtful inquiry and insight. Finally, they needed to consider audience. That is, not only did they have to consider their own learning, they had to justify this learning to others—to somehow reveal themselves through their writings, possibly teach others something about what they know, and persuade an audience that they learned something as a writer in Diana's class.

Collecting Artifacts

The artifacts students collected came from three sources: students' daybooks, published writing pieces, and folders of work deemed "in progress." The *daybooks* (see Murray, 1968), contained daily life experiences of the writers as well as observational notes, quotes, snippets of writing, plans, quick drafts, handouts given out in class, newspaper clippings, drawings, outlines, titles, to name a few. In Diana's classroom the daybook served as the container where students began their writing. When Diana gathered students, they brought their daybooks to the carpet. Oftentimes, they took notes in them, glued in instructional handouts from the teacher, or instantly applied a lesson to a draft of their writing. For example, one day, when Diana instructed the students on quotation marks, the students opened their daybooks to a draft and instantly applied the editing lesson on a piece of their writing.

The daybooks were an important source for the students' portfolio entries. Of the 95 pieces of writing uploaded onto the students' digital wiki page, 56 of the pieces came from their daybooks. This represented the largest majority of student selections. Another important source for the students' portfolio entries came from students' published work. This came from four major writing projects, which were previously described, that Diana conducted in the classroom. Of the 95 pieces of writing uploaded onto their digital wiki pages, 37 pieces came from one of these four published projects. Less influential were students' in-progress folders. Only two students selected a piece from that resource.

Selecting Artifacts

Student selected artifacts that represented a diverse range of genres (Table 1). The primary genre was poetry, with almost every child selecting poetry for at least one portfolio entry. Other selections included informational texts, memoirs, and persuasive texts. Students were given opportunities to study these genres in depth and received instructional support as they navigated through the various genres. Other selections ranged from student-generated quizzes to comics to lessons conducted by the teacher.

Table 1. Genres of portfolio selections

Genre	Number of Representational Portfolio Pieces
Poem	35
Informational Text	18
Memoir	16
Persuasive Texts	9
Lessons from the Teacher	5
Realistic Fiction	3
Comic/Graphic Novel	2
Informational How-To	1
Opera Lyrics	1
Other Content Areas (Math)	1
Total	95

When asked why he selected his portfolio pieces one student, Seymore, commented, "I just wanted to show everyone all the things I did as a writer. I did a lot of different stuff." For Seymore, the digital portfolio gave him an opportunity to show his diversity as a writer—to allow the reader to see his divergent thinking and his ability to adapt to changing writing terrains.

Another student, Audriana, was asked the same question and replied, "I'm really proud of my writing and I was excited to show everything I've learned as a writer. I think I'm getting better at it every day. This portfolio shows that." Audriana's portfolio selections allowed her to display her learning and to show her progression over time.

When other children were asked the same question, the answers varied from student to student. Some wanted to display published pieces because they represented, "my best work." Others showed comics they composed because they "showed that I'm funny and I can make others laugh." Still others made selections based on what they could teach peers. Serafina commented, "I just want my friends to learn something from me." With the digital portfolios, as opposed to the paper-based portfolios they created the year before, audience seemed to drive portfolio selection decisions.

Their work would become more public than ever; as such, they constructed their digital portfolios with a clear audience in mind.

Theme 2: Portfolio Processes – Reflect

After students gathered to collect and select their portfolio pieces, Diana taught a lesson about reflection—the next phase of the portfolio process. Diana urged students that it was not enough for writers to just pick written pieces and upload them to a wiki page. They had to reflect on why they picked their particular pieces. They used agency to explain their decisions while informing their audience.

An analysis of the reflective statements written by the students revealed multiple purposes for selecting particular pieces. Several students selected pieces because they revealed their knowledge of a particular genre. Christopher (Figure 1) chose a published poem to upload to his wiki page. In his reflection, Christopher noted the power of poetry as something that allows the writer and reader to have "an almost spiritual connection with the soul."

Students, through reflections, were able to provide commentaries about the genres they wrote within and the important reasons why writers might select specific genres to convey their thoughts.

Other students chose pieces for their portfolios because their self-selected topics reveal something about them as people. For example, Jeremy uploads a selection about his trip to New York City (Figure 2). He writes, "I picked this piece because it shows what I did during my summer of N.Y and I think its [sic] cool that I went to N.Y." When portfolios go public, and a classroom of peers will read the writer's work, students may want to make revelations about themselves so their peers may learn more about them.

A common reason for portfolio selection choices was the writer's desire to show a writing skill they learned and how they applied that skill within their writing. Emma (Figure 3) chooses a non-fiction draft from her daybook. In her reflection, she describes her revision of this piece. A skill she has learned as a writer is to revise while it is fresh on her mind. This is a tip peer writers might benefit from when reading through Emma's portfolio.

Figure 1. Christopher's reflection on his choice of poetry

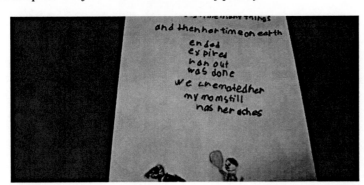

Portfolio Piece #4

The piece I picked is a poem my mom and I wrote together. It is a poem that describes the events of Julia "Butterfly" Hill's Life.

The reason I picked this piece is that I wrote it with my mom and that I used a lot of my writing skills working on it.

I have learned as a writer that I love to write poetry more than anything else. To me, it has an almost spiritual connection with the soul. It goes extremely deep.

I can use this piece of writing to teach others how powerful poetry really is, and, how sometimes it can change someone's feelings in a heart beat.

Figure 2. Jeremy's reflection reveals a life experience

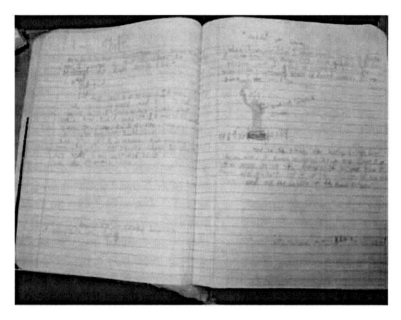

I picked "Empire state"
I picked this piece because it shows what i did during my summer at N.Y and i think its cool that i went to N.Y
I learned that i am a very deceptive writer and i can take things from my life and put it on paper
i think i can teach other people how to take something simple and make a whole story.
you just need to be wide eyed
i also would have not picked non-fiction writing any day but i still love to write it.

Figure 3. Emma's reflection on a writing skill

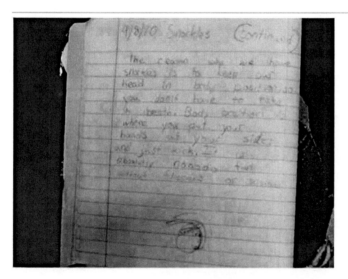

This is a non-fiction piece I wrote on my swimming equipment.
I chose this piece because it shows how I revise my pieces.
It has some bullet points where I've added onto the piece to make it better.
I revised right after I wrote it so I wouldn't forget what was on my mind.
I learned that if I really focus I can write more than one page.
I can use this piece to show others to write about their interests to excite others.

When writers reflect on their portfolio selections, they justify their portfolio decisions. They describe their selections, reveal their reasoning for choosing these selections, and offer thoughts about what other writers might learn from their writing. When students wrote paper-based portfolios in fourth grade, the only audience was the teacher. In fifth grade, audience expanded and so did their reflections. Students now began to consider their peers when they wrote their reflections. They began to use their digital portfolios to inform peer writers who would read their work on this wiki and offer comments—the focus of the third theme.

Theme 3: Portfolio Processes – Project and Connect

First, students collected and selected portfolio pieces. Next, they reflected on their choices. The first three endeavors were individualistic ones that revealed the inner thinking of the writer. The next phases of the process—projection and connection—moved the writer away from their individual thinking and encouraged the writers to consider the broader audience who might read their work. When portfolio writers project, they find a way to display their writing for readers. When they connect, they make notations about what they learned from others through the comment feature of their digital wikis.

Because this was the first time Diana asked students to make comments on peer digital portfolio pages, she did not anticipate the types of responses students would make. During her initial analysis of the students' comments, she grew distressed by the types of comments students made. She noticed that students were using text-like language and offered perfunctory comments like, 'What's up?' or 'How's it going?' Several students wrote song lyrics or funny comments unrelated to the writing. This prompted Diana to teach a lesson about appropriate comments—an important part of the *projection* and *connection* processes of the writer.

Project

As fourth graders, students constructed portfolios using three-pronged folders and inserts. They photocopied pieces of writing and added them to their folder. When completed, they turned them into Diana. She read them, asked students questions pertaining to the portfolio, and used them to initiate discussion for parent conferences. The folders were then sent home with the student. Portfolios were constructed within a paper-based space and the paper-based projection of the portfolios limited the number of people who viewed it (Figure 4).

The digital portfolios added a new dimension for the writer. In fifth grade, the projection of the portfolios entered a digital space. Whereas in fourth grade 2-3 other people viewed the paper-based portfolio, in fifth grade, with the introduction of a digital media, at least 25 people would view the writer's work, adding nuance and complexity to writers' decisions (Figure 5).

When interviewed about the shift from paper-based portfolios to digital portfolios, students offered differing opinions:

Alley noted, "I liked the digital one better. More people saw my writing. And I liked making comments on my friend's writings."

Chaz added, "I liked digital better. I love computers. I'm kind of like a computer whiz. Any time we can use computers in the classroom, I feel much happier."

Figure 4. Photo of paper-based portfolio

Figure 5. Photo of written-reflection vs. digital reflection

Hand-written reflection in 4ᵗʰ Grade

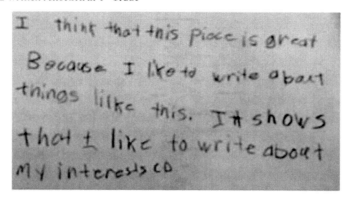

Digitally-written reflection in 5ᵗʰ Grade

Portfolio Piece #4

The piece I picked is a poem my mom and I wrote together. It is a poem that describes the events of Julia "Butterfly" Hill's Life.

The reason I picked this piece is that I wrote it with my mom and that I used a lot of my writing skills working on it.

I have learned as a writer that I love to write poetry more than anything else. To me, it has an almost spiritual connection with the soul. It goes extremely deep.

I can use this piece of writing to teach others how powerful poetry really is, and, how sometimes it can change someone's feelings in a heart beat.

Other students disagreed, preferring the paper-based portfolio model better.

Cindy explained, "I thought it was hard. I'm not good on computers. I thought it was hard to add things to it. I really needed someone to help me. Once someone showed me, I felt better about it."

Samantha concurred, "I thought the digital portfolio was harder. It was just easier to put paper in a sleeve and just put it in the folder. Here I had to take pictures, figure out how to upload them, and type reflections. I'm not a good typer. I thought it was hard."

The projection portion of the students' writing process changed from fourth grade to fifth grade. In fourth grade, students projected their portfolios using folders. Limited audiences saw their work. In fifth grade, portfolios were projected digitally. For some students, this was a welcome change. They wanted to use newer technology and they like the expanded audiences. Other students felt anxious using the digital space. The digital medium was unexplored territory and it required adjustments. They now had to do unfamiliar things as writers—and they had to adjust to the new writing terrain.

Connect

The connection component of the portfolio process represented the biggest change for the writers as they shifted from a paper-based system in fourth grade to a digital-based system in fifth grade. When their work became digital, and their pages became public, students were able to go onto their peers' wikis and make connections through comments.

Through the commenting feature, students offered suggestions to their peers, asked questions, gave compliments, and made personal connections. In this regard, the *connection* portion of the process presented students with the greatest shift in their portfolio experience.

The following snippet from Chaz's portfolio page shows the types of comments students made on the wiki pages of their peers (Figure 6). Students make several comments including: 1) compliments (e.g. "very, very well done, bravo!"), 2) specific feedback about a writing skill (e.g. "I like your description."), 3) suggestions (e.g. "You might want to tell more about what you learned as a writer."), 4) interest in topic (e.g. "The mud pit of doom sounds interesting and funny."), 5) evaluative statements (e.g. "This reflection shows that you are smart.")

Chaz's portfolio wiki page is representative of the portfolio pages of his peers. These varied peer comments affected the writers. The writers realized that an audience read their work. It made them consider future pieces of writing they would include on their portfolio.

Emma explains, "I didn't really think about who was going to read this at first. Now I do. I want my friends to learn from me. And, I guess I want to learn something from them." Digital portfolios offer a portal for connection. The comments from peers become part of the portfolio process—something that never happened when Diana's portfolios were paper-based. Digital portfolios added new dimensions to the writer's self-evaluation process.

IMPLICATIONS

As the digital world continues to evolve, there is a continuing need to expand our knowledge about how students use technology as writers to create, communicate, and collaborate. In the self-evaluative loop that framed this research on digital portfolios, writers found voice in their own writ-

Figure 6. Peer comments on a portfolio page

very, very well done. bravo!
P.S., very descriptive.

Awesome!!! I like your description.
you might want to tell more about what you learned as a writer.

PS I didn't know the mud pit was doom.

The mud pit of doom sounds discusting and funny. This reflection shows that you are smart.

I love the description

ing and offered their voices to other writers. The digital space made this important work possible.

The digital portfolio wiki offered a space where students could create individual pages for specific documents, linking their reflections as well as peers' comments directly to the individual portfolio selections. The latter facets were critical within this environment as, unlike traditional portfolios where students rarely have opportunities to communicate with wider audiences (Merchant, 2005), the digital environment allowed writers to publish information to a larger and more public audience, obtain feedback, and collaborate with others regardless of time and context. This socially-situated process engaged the class within a participatory approach to learning that has been associated with improved understandings of the learning process and outcomes for students (see Davidson & Goldberg, 2009; Gee, 2008). Meaning was negotiated through social interactions and involved co-constructed meaning through shared ideas. This construction of thinking and knowing through social interaction demonstrated the value of shared understanding through collaboration with others. This has implications for classroom teachers. Digital portfolios provide a space for students to create, collaborate, and communicate with peers that goes beyond the classroom walls. Children no longer are restricted by time and place. It is possible for creation, collaboration, and communication to occur in multiple places during various times.

Previous research (see Graham and Harris, 2007) has shown that when students are presented with opportunities to engage in writing for authentic purposes, e.g. interaction and collaboration, there is an increased likelihood that they will engage in reflection. Within this research, when the shift was made from the use of traditional portfolios to digital portfolios, the presence of an authentic audience also shifted the process of reflection from an internal, individualized one to a more externally-focused, metacognitive one. Students had to think about their work within the

selection and projection process as they were engaged with writing for a specified, authentic goal (Bransford, et al., 2000). The audience became a specific focal point within the selection process, as identified by the reflections associated with selections. Prior to the implementation of the digital portfolios, reflection was limited beyond noting the selection of individual pieces as representing students "best work", e.g. more skill-driven. The reflections also revealed students utilized the opportunity to reach wider audience as a mechanism to teach other students about themselves as well as the writing process itself.

Several implications for continued research relative to student outcomes associated with the digital environment are noted. With the expanded student awareness of audience, it is important to examine correlations between level of participation and growth/writing outcomes, e.g. quality of writing (see Corden, 2007). For example, as students continue to write for authentic audiences, how does the information they have about the audience influence their writing and, relatedly, how does the feedback received from the audience help them refine their writing? Similarly, examinations of students' perceptions of themselves as writers as well as their motivation to write will inform us how implementation of authentic writing experiences in a digital environment impacts affective constructs.

This research also reinforced that there is still much to learn about methods for teachers to use digital writing to support communication and collaboration (see Zammit & Downes, 2002). Notably, flexibility represented an important facet within the process. In several instances, Diana had to teach new skills that were not applicable within traditional writing portfolios. For example, the students' ability to offer suggestions, ask questions, and make connections was initially limited. The students were engaging in social practices, yet in a non-constructive manner. As a result, Diana had to specifically teach the students how to critically examine writing to facilitate connections between their own understandings and knowledge and to, subsequently, write effective comments. This reinforces previous research that teachers wishing to implement portfolios within this context must direct attention towards the development of skills considering the audience for the writing (Holliway & McCutchen, 2004). In this regard, we suggest additional research specifically focusing on the teacher and the teaching processes used to develop skills for participation as well as reflection to help enhance the related benefits of the digital environment and authentic audience.

It was revealed that not all students may feel (or be) proficient with the technology used for the portfolios, including typing skills. Teachers will need to direct attention toward technology skills to ensure students possess or can be taught necessary skills to create and collect their digital pieces as well as comment on others' work. With the proliferation of tools on the Internet that allow users to upload and create content, it is important research is directed towards the most effective methods in helping students develop these proficiencies (see National Governors Association Center for Best Practices and Council of Chief State School Officers, 2010) to ensure they can participate in a global society and increasingly interconnected network.

CONCLUSION

The meaning and description of what it means to be literate has certainly evolved due to the rapidly changing nature of the technology used both within and outside of our educational contexts. Regardless, we must still consider how to provide students with "the space and support to communicate critically, aesthetically, lovingly, and agentively" (Hull, 2003, p. 230). Digital portfolios may represent one mechanism that provides the space, while simultaneously preparing our students in the ever-evolving skills necessary to write and communicate in the 21st Century.

REFERENCES

Abrami, P. C., & Barrett, H. C. (2005). Directions for research and development on electronic portfolio. *Canadian Journal of Learning and Technology, 31*(3). Retrieved from http://cjlt.csj.ualberta.ca/index.php/cjlt/article/view/92/86.

Bakhtin, M. M. (1981). *The dialogic imagination: Four essays*. Austin, TX: University of Texas.

Barrett, H. C. (2007). Researching electronic portfolios and learner engagement: The REFLECT initiative. *Journal of Adolescent & Adult Literacy, 50*, 436–449. doi:10.1598/JAAL.50.6.2.

Bransford, J., Brown, A., & Cocking, R. (2000). *How people learn: Brain, mind, experience, and school*. Washington, DC: National Academy Press.

Bruner, J. (1962). Introduction to L. S. Vygotsky. In Hanfmann, E., & Vakar, G. (Trans. Eds.) *Thought and language* (pp. v–x). Cambridge, MA: MIT Press.

Corden, R. (2007). Developing reading and writing connections: The impact of explicit instruction of literary devices on the quality of children's narrative writing. *Journal of Research in Childhood Education, 21*(3), 269–289. doi:10.1080/02568540709594594.

Davidson, C. N., & Goldberg, D. T. (2009). *The future of learning institutions in a digital age*. Cambridge, MA: MIT Press.

Denton, D. (2012). Improving the quality of evidence-based writing entries in electronic portfolios. *International Journal of ePortfolio, 2*, 187-197. Retrieved from http://www.theijep.com/pdf/IJEP76.pdf

Dilthey, W. (1977). *Descriptive psychology and historical understanding* (Zaner, R. M., & Heiges, K. L., Trans.). The Hague, The Netherlands: Nijhoff. (Original work published 1911).

Dyson, A., & Genishi, C. (2005). *On the case: Approaches to language and literacy research.* New York, NY: Teachers College Press.

Erickson, F. (1986). Qualitative methods in research on teaching. In Wittrock, M. (Ed.), *Handbook of research on teaching* (3rd ed., pp. 119–161). New York, NY: Macmillan.

Fish, S. (1980). *Is there a text in this class?* Cambridge, MA: Harvard University Press.

Fletcher, R., & Portalupi, J. (2000). *Writing workshop: The essential guide.* Portsmouth, NH: Heinemann.

Gee, J. P. (2008). *Social linguistics and literacies: Ideology in discourses* (3rd ed.). New York: Taylor and Francis.

Geertz, C. (1973). *The interpretation of cultures.* New York, NY: Basic Books.

Glaser, B., & Strauss, A. (1967). *The discovery of grounded theory: Strategies for qualitative research.* Chicago, IL: Aldine.

Graham, S., & Harris, K. R. (2007). Best practices in teaching planning. In MacArthur, C. A., Graham, S., & Fitzgerald, J. (Eds.), *Best practices in writing instruction* (pp. 119–140). New York: Guilford.

Griffin, M. (2003). Using critical incidents to promote and assess reflective thinking in preservice teachers. *Reflective Practice, 4,* 207–220. doi:10.1080/14623940308274.

Hansen, J. (1998). *When learners evaluate.* Portsmouth, NH: Heinemann.

Hansen, J., & Kissel, B. (2010). K-12 students as writers: Research to practice. D. Lapp & D. Fisher (Eds.), The handbook of research on teaching the English language arts (3rd ed.), (pp. 271-277). New York: Routledge.

Heath, M. (2005). Are you ready to go digital? The pros and cons of electronic portfolio development. *Library Media Connection, 23,* 66–70.

Holliway, D. R., & McCutchen, D. (2004). Audience perspective in young writers' composing and revising. In Allal, L., Chanquoy, L., & Largy, P. (Eds.), *Revision: Cognitive and instructional processes* (pp. 87–101). Norwell, MA: Kluwer. doi:10.1007/978-94-007-1048-1_6.

Hull, G. A., & Nelson, M. (2005). Locating the semiotic power of multimodality. *Written Communication, 22*(2), 224–261. doi:10.1177/0741088304274170.

International Reading Association. (2009). *New literacies and 21st century technologies: A position statement of the international reading association.* Newark, DE: International Reading Association.

Klenowski, V., Askew, S., & Carnell, E. (2006). Portfolios for learning, assessment and professional development in higher education. *Assessment & Evaluation in Higher Education, 31,* 267–286. doi:10.1080/02602930500352816.

Lankshear, C., & Knobel, M. (2003). *New literacies: Changing knowledge and classroom learning.* Buckingham, UK: Open University Press.

Loughran, J., & Corrigan, D. (1995). Teaching portfolios: A strategy for developing learning and teaching in pre-service education. *Teaching and Teacher Education, 11,* 565–577. doi:10.1016/0742-051X(95)00012-9.

Merchant, G. (2005). Electronic involvement: Identify performance in children's informal digital writing. *Discourse: Studies in the Cultural Politics of Education, 26,* 301–314. doi:10.1080/01596300500199940.

Merriam, S. (1998). *Qualitative research and case study applications in education.* San Francisco, CA: Jossey-Bass.

Miles, M., & Huberman, A. (1994). *Qualitative data analysis: An expanded sourcebook.* Thousand Oaks, CA: Sage.

Murray, D. (1968). *A writer teaches writing: A practical method of teaching composition.* Boston: Houghton Mifflin.

National Governors Association Center for Best Practices & Council of State School Officers. (2010). *Common core state standards for English language arts & literacy in history/ social studies, science, and technical subjects.* Washington, DC: Authors. Retrieved January 13, 2013, from http://corestandards.org/assets/CCSSI_ELA%20 Standards.pdf

Niguidula, D. (2005). Documenting learning with digital portfolios. *Educational Leadership, 63,* 44–47.

Palincsar, A. S., Brown, A. L., & Campione, J. C. (1993). First-grade dialogues for knowledge acquisition and use. In Forman, E. A., Minick, N., & Stone, C. A. (Eds.), *Contexts for learning: Sociocultural dynamics in children's development* (pp. 43–57). New York, NY: Oxford University Press.

Risko, V. J., Roller, C. M., Cummins, C., Bean, R. M., Block, C. C., & Anders, P. L. et al. (2008). A critical analysis of research on reading teacher education. *Reading Research Quarterly, 43,* 252–288. doi:10.1598/RRQ.43.3.3.

Scribner, S., & Cole, M. (1981). *The psychology of literacy.* Cambridge, MA: Harvard University Press.

Smith, K., & Tillema, H. (2003). Clarifying different types of portfolio use. *Assessment & Evaluation in Higher Education, 28,* 625–648. doi:10.1080/0260293032000130252.

Street, B. (1984). *Literacy in theory and practice.* Cambridge, UK: Cambridge University Press.

Taylor, D. B. (2012). Multiliteracies: Moving from theory to practice in teacher education. In A. B. Polly, Mims, & K. Persichitte (Eds.), *Creating Technology-Rich Teacher Education Programs: Key Issues* (pp. 266-287). Hershey, PA: IGI Global.

United States Department of Education. (2010). *Transforming American education: Learning powered by technology.* Washington, DC: US Department of Education. Retrieved from http://www.ed.gov/sites/default/files/netp2010.pdf

Vasquez, O. A. (2006). Cross-national explorations of sociocultural research on learning. *Review of Research in Education, 30,* 33–64. doi:10.3102/0091732X030001033.

Vasudevan, L., Schultz, K., & Bateman, J. (2010). Rethinking composing in a digital age: Authoring literate identities through multimodal storytelling. *Written Communication, 27,* 442–468. doi:10.1177/0741088310378217.

Vygotsky, L. S. (1978). *Mind in society.* Cambridge, MA: Harvard University Press.

Vygotsky, L. S. (1986). *Thought and language.* Cambridge, MA: MIT Press.

Wade, A., Abrami, P. C., & Sclater, J. (2005). An electronic portfolio to support learning. *Canadian Journal of Learning and Technology, 31*(3). Retrieved from http://cjlt.csj.ualberta.ca/index.php/cjlt/article/view/94/88.

Wall, K., Higgins, S., Miller, J., & Packard, N. (2006). Developing digital portfolios: Investigating how digital portfolios can facilitate pupil talk about learning. *Technology, Pedagogy and Education, 15,* 261–273. doi:10.1080/14759390600923535.

Zammit, K., & Downes, T. (2002). New learning environments and the multiliterate individual: A framework for educators. *Australian Journal of Language and Literacy, 25*(2), 24–36.

Zubizarreta, J. (2004). *The learning portfolio: Reflective practice for improving student learning.* San Francisco, CA: Jossey-Bass.

Chapter 4
Preparing Young Writers for Invoking and Addressing Today's Interactive Digital Audiences

Ewa McGrail
Georgia State University, USA

J. Patrick McGrail
Jacksonville State University, USA

ABSTRACT

Twenty-first century technologies, in particular the Internet and Web 2.0 applications, have transformed the practice of writing and exposed it to interactivity. One interactive method that has received a lot of critical attention is blogging. The authors sought to understand more fully whom young bloggers both invoked in their blogging (their idealized, intentional audience) and whom they addressed (whom they actually blogged to, following interactive posts). They studied the complete, yearlong blog histories of fifteen fifth-graders, with an eye toward understanding how these students constructed audiences and modified them, according to feedback they received from teachers as well as peers and adults from around the world. The authors found that these students, who had rarely or never blogged before, were much more likely to respond to distant teachers, pre-service teachers, and graduate students than to their own classroom teachers or peers from their immediate classroom. The bloggers invoked/addressed their audiences differently too, depending on the roles that they had created for their audiences and themselves. The authors explore how and why this came to be the case with young writers.

INTRODUCTION

Twenty-first century technologies, in particular the Internet and Web 2.0 applications, have transformed the practice of writing (Andrews & Smith, 2011). Where once the concept of a writer's "audience," in distinction from that of a speaker's, was described as "at best, an abstraction, a theory, or a metaphor" (Magnifico, 2010), the advent of social networking has now provided many Internet writers - or bloggers, as they are more often known in these media – immediate feedback from a variety of responders. These

DOI: 10.4018/978-1-4666-4341-3.ch004

responders form a potentially international, and very "real" audience (Jenkins, 2006).

The construct of an audience, whether real or imagined, has suffused the large literature about teaching writing for a substantial period of time (Barbeiro, 2010; Graves, 1975; Kos & Maslowski, 2001; Lapp, Shea, & Wolsey, 2010/2011; Long, 1980; Ong, 1979). When Ede and Lunsford (1984) first grappled, more than a quarter century ago, with the dual questions of whether an actual audience existed for an individual writer, and, if it did, whether it should influence that writer's output, they took the position that then-current models for and against such a construct were inadequate to describe the process of actual writing. At that time, Mitchell and Taylor (1979) had observed that some scholars were urging teachers to instill in students a desire to privilege their own messages' sincerity and integrity, while others were advising them to be hyperaware of their audience and its particular needs (Hairston, 1978). Pfister and Petrik (1980) were exhorting students to "construct in their imagination an audience that is as nearly a replica as is possible of those many readers who actually exist in the world of reality" (p. 214). Despite this, prior to the late 1990s, however skillful one might be in such an exercise, "[f]or a writer, the audience [was] not *there* in the sense that the speaker's audience, whether a single person or a large group, is present" (Ede & Lunsford, 1984, p. 161, italics theirs). Ong (1979) explained this challenge from the student writer perspective in this way:

The problem is not simply what to say but also whom to say to. Say? The student is not talking. He is writing. No one is listening. There is no feedback. Where does he [student writer] find his 'audience'? He has to make his readers up, fictionalize them (p. 11).

That was then. Now we possess the technologies and predilection to textually communicate with and potentially witness and counter-respond to a few, some, or many others from around the world who comment upon our work (Andrews & Smith, 2011). Within this context, "writers and readers can become active listeners and conversation partners for each other" (Magnifico, 2010, p.168).

What is different about composing for such an audience, compared to writing using traditional technologies such as pen and paper? And what are the implications for writing with a digital audience in mind for audience awareness development and the teaching of it to young writers? This chapter attempts to explore these questions, by drawing insight from a year-long research project with fifth-grade bloggers. During the project, these young writers engaged in written conversations with a truly worldwide digital audience about what they were learning in and beyond their classrooms. The blogging community they joined was interactive and diverse; it consisted of audiences from different age groups, cultures, nations, continents and geographical locations.

Defining Blogging

Blogging has been defined and conceptualized in several different ways. For example, some scholars see blogging as "a personal knowledge artifact" (O'Donnell, 2006, p.7), which reveals the writer's emerging knowledge that is documented in writing and reflections posted on a blog. Others see blogging as a hybrid of conversations with the self and with others (Efimova & de Moor, 2005)—a practice and authorship that "combine two oppositional principles: monologue and dialogue" (Wrede, 2003, para. 1 Weblogs and Discourse).

Blogging has also been characterized as public and private spaces for individual reflection and social interaction (Davies & Merchant, 2007; Deng & Yuen, 2011). Self-expression and self-reflection support the individual in "expressing one's thoughts and emotions, as well as recording one's experiences" (self-expression) and deriving meaning from them (self- reflection) (Deng

& Yuen, 2011). Social interaction and reflective dialogue, on the other hand, are used "for the purpose of enhancing social presence" and joining "the cognitive presence within a learning community" (p. 443). Viewed from this perspective, blogging can provide young writers with the opportunity to develop "effective writing processes and strategies that enable them to use writing for an array of personal and social processes" (Chapman, 2006, p. 20).

Blogging can be both synchronous and asynchronous. Internet messaging (IM) which is less common today, and texting are examples of synchronous blogging. In synchronous blogging, responses mimic, in time elapsed, the amount of time that a spoken reply might take in a face to face interaction. When blogging is asynchronous, the writer and reader do not communicate at the same time. Rather, they write or access others' writing at their own schedule. More recently, newer technology permits the embedding of audio, video, or graphical material in and with blogs, and in this way can amplify the tools the writer has available for meaning-making and communication with others (Andrews & Smith, 2011; Davis, 2005) Such a development has greatly enhanced – and been enhanced by – "microblogging" practices such as Twitter.

In the past half-decade, blogs and blogging have begun appearing with greater frequency on such "megasites" as Facebook and Instagram. Blogging and writing on social networking sites such as these have also been described as a social practice (Rowsell, 2009). The writers in these spaces have been observed to develop and adopt certain conventions and behaviors, which go beyond writing conventions and include social norms or "practices, habits of mind, and texts" that have then become second nature to the users of these spaces (Rowsell, 2009, p. 97). These social networking sites are now available to anyone with Internet access anywhere in the world, and because they are also extremely well-known, these spaces provide access to a wider and more diverse audi-

ence (Jenkins, 2006). These technical affordances and the social practices that they engender also enable new relationships with readers both known and unknown, in both familiar and unfamiliar contexts (Wrede, 2003). As such, these spaces boast the potential to both extend and transform the writing and communication practices of their users (Andrews & Smith, 2011; Rowsell, 2009). Therefore, in order to address the complexity of these changes in teaching writing, we need to know more about practices such as blogging and the reader/writer nexus that evolves in this new writing context.

Writing and Blogging

There is a growing body of scholarship on blogging as a subset in the scholarly field of writing. Studies have examined blogging as intervention (Lamonica, 2010; Wong & Hew, 2010) genre (Efimova & de Moor, 2005; O'Donnell, 2006) and as social practice (McGrail & Davis, 2011; Penrod, 2007). For example, Lamonica (2010) explored the blogging writing program for fourth-grade students and noted that what she termed an "intervention" had had a positive impact on children's motivation and engagement, as well as on their writing skills. The study reported an increase in vocabulary and language use; for example, "the sentences invited expressive reading and were strong and varied" (p. 35). The researchers attributed this growth to both the opportunity for the students to "take ownership over what they write and what they want to write about" (p. 28) and the ability to engage with an audience beyond the classroom. However, the study did not elaborate on the nature of engagement with the audience.

McGrail and Davis (2011) examined fifth-graders' writing in a blogging/writing program, one that focused on reflective, persuasive, and narrative pieces, for audiences both within and beyond the classroom. The initial analysis from this study examined student writing and the writing process, paying attention to the following aspects of writing: attitude, content, voice, connections and relationships, thinking, and craft. The researchers found that student bloggers do become aware of and connect to the audience. They also observed these bloggers develop as active and empowered members of a blog community. The researchers associated this positive outcome with the commenters' and teachers' focus on idea development in responding to student writing, rather than focusing merely on writing conventions and language issues.

Wong and Hew (2010) analyzed interviews, writing, and observations of fifth-grade Asian students in a Singapore classroom, noting the influence of blogging on narrative writing development. The intervention the researchers examined consisted of specific questions about the story development such as what the story was about, followed with the when, where, who, and other questions. While the bloggers in this study appreciated blogging, and especially the feedback they received on their writing, they were disappointed with the limited peer response and the teacher's focus on the language issues rather than ideas in their writing.

In Glogowski (2008), blogging was used with eight-grade students in support of developing an online class community. Within this context, Glogowski examined "the notion of dialogic critique - peer discussions and critiques of written texts - and its impact on the quality of student writing, sense of ownership, confidence, and engagement in learning" (p. 11). Similarly to the findings from Lamonica (2010) and McGrail and Davis (2011), this study reported student gains in engagement and an increased investment in learning and writing. The study also noted the positive impact of dialogic critique on student writing and made a call for the teacher to "extend the classroom discourse beyond traditional academic texts, abandon the evaluative and authoritarian voice, and enter the community as a reader and a co-contributor"(p. 12).

Other studies have looked at the influence of blogging and related practices on the development of motivation and agency or identity formation among blog writers (Farmer, 2004; Swanson & Legutko, 2008). For example, using a pretest-posttest design, Swanson and Legutko (2008) examined the effect of the Book Blog writing intervention on 3rd grade-student levels of motivation and engagement. The intervention allowed these students to interact with peers about their responses to book reading while the traditional paper reading response cohort did not have this option. The study reported an increase in motivation for all students who had blogged with their peers and teachers about their reading on a wiki site. Similarly, in a case study of ESL students' use of instant messaging for academic writing development (Jin & Zhu, 2010), the use of instant messaging was found to have influenced "the formation and shift of students' motives within and across the computer-mediated peer response tasks" (p. 284). Such an influence could be construed as of either a positive or negative nature, based on the degree of motive competitiveness for each participant during peer response interactions mediated by instant messaging. This means that the readers' and audience's prior experiences with either technology or a writing task may have shaped their motives for participating in online communication.

Collectively, all these studies underscore the importance of audience in an online interactive environment and call for extending it beyond the classroom teacher and peers. Such a finding has implications for classroom pedagogy. If this is true, what should pedagogy for blogging look like?

Blogging Pedagogy

There are many guides for using traditional blogs in the classroom (Boiling, Castek, Zawilinski, Barton, & Nierlich, 2008; Gelbwasser, 2011; Johnson, 2010; Parisi & Crosby, 2012; Penrod, 2007; Zawilinski, 2009) and for "microblogging," as in Tweeting or instant messaging (Greenhow & Gleason, 2012). These guides offer practical advice on how to establish, manage, and maintain a classroom blog, how to sustain a community, and how to deal with Internet safety and privacy issues. Some describe ways to integrate blogging into literature discussion or a reading and writing workshop. For example, Johnson (2010) explained how to use blogs for engaging writers with young adult literature book authors. Others discussed blogging in creative writing such as digital poetry (Curwood, 20011) and digital story (Davis, 2005) or in general for self- expression and publishing (Fiedler, 2003; Downes, 2004).

Empirical research on teacher pedagogy for blogging is scarce. For example, Luehmann and MacBride's (2009) study investigated, through content analysis and teacher interviews, how high school science and mathematics teachers used blogs in support of content area instruction. The researchers categorized the teacher blog uses into six different classroom blogging practices: (a) sharing resources; (b) responding to teacher prompts; (c) recording lessons' highlights; (c) posting learning challenges; (e) reflecting on what was learned; and (f) engaging in on-line conversations (para. Conclusion). They also noted that even though all these uses reflected student-centered learning, student voice and participation levels in online conversations varied greatly in the classrooms of these teachers. While one teacher opened the class blog to a wider audience and allowed students to initiate posts and take ownership of their learning, the second teacher assumed more of a "take charge" attitude, initiating blog posts and directing the flow and the content of the conversations among the participants. The researchers concluded that the ways these teachers' blogs were structured and the affordances the teachers chose (e.g., opening or not opening the blog to the public and adding chat rooms for further dialogue) reflected distinct philosophical and practical realizations of student-centered peda-

gogy, as well as different ways to adapt blogging to fit in within these frames of reference.

McGrail and Davis (2013) examined blogging pedagogy in a somewhat different manner. Specifically, they applied the Technological Pedagogical Content Knowledge (TPACK) framework (Koehler & Mishra, 2008) to explore the teacher pedagogy and student experiences of blogging in a fifth-grade classroom. The TPACK framework explores the interplay of three sources of knowledge: Content (CK), Pedagogy (PK), and Technology (TK) in the development of pedagogy for technology integration in educational contexts. The researchers found that the teacher in this study understood and applied the framework in her class successfully. This was reflected in pedagogically integrating blogging technology into her writing instruction and capitalizing on this technology's affordances to extend the audience beyond the classroom. For this to happen, the teacher had to move away from a teacher-centered writing instruction style to a more participatory pedagogy. This shift, the researchers noted, "called for the blogging teacher to act both as an insider – fulfilling the traditional roles of a teacher in a classroom- as well as an outsider – a member of the larger blogging beyond the classroom community" (p. 279). It also required from the teacher to "rethink teacher, student, and commenter roles in the learning/teaching process" (p. 285).

Will exposure to such a participatory pedagogy in the blogging environment also make student writers rethink their understanding of audience? Will it also help them reevaluate the teacher as an audience as well? This work is an attempt to explore these questions.

Audience Awareness, Young Writers, and Blogging

In general, young writers tend to have a weak understanding of the concept of audience (Barbeiro, 2010). As a result, in their writing they tend to "simply and briefly report an experience without regard for the reader, the readers' perspectives, or the need for engagement" (Lapp, Shea, & Wolsey, 2010/2011, p. 33). New and growing research shows, however, that good writers are aware of and know their audience well (Kellog, 2008). Knowledge of the reader allows skilled writers to envision and assign to the reader particular characteristics and to identify and address their needs during writing (Barbeiro, 2010; Holliway, 2004). Audience awareness encourages, too, dialogic writing, with a hypothetical (imagined) or a real reader (Frank, 1992). It is not necessary for young writers to obtain encyclopedic knowledge of the demographic or psychographic makeup of their audience; what is required is for them to set the stage before they permit the actors of their stories to walk upon it. They must provide needed context.

Young writers tend to be self-centered in their writing (Blau, 1983), and struggle with this imagining, or invoking of the reader (Kos & Maslowski, 2001). They "must be taught to move beyond themselves as they learn to consider the dimensions of the audience for whom they write" (Lapp, Shea, Wolsey, 2010/2011, p.33). Blau (1983) used the term "decentering" (p.300) for the process of moving young writers beyond themselves, and described it as the writer's ability to evaluate critically and modify their writing with the readers in mind.

Blogging's most attractive feature may be that it offers opportunities for young writers to interact with an audience beyond the classroom (Boiling, Castek, Zawilinski, Barton, & Nierlich, 2008). Because such writing is on its face intended to be shared with others, blog writing also relies on response from the audience. As Penrod (2005) notes, "Without a response, there is no communication. If there is no communication happening, then there is no understanding as to whether one's words make meaning or fall silent" (p.2). The audience in blogging is therefore potentially an active agent, often functioning "as complex conversational partner; a listener with whom the speaker is attempting to communicate "(Magnifico, 2010, p.168). Writers in these spaces thus have the opportunity to "speak with, ask questions, and be influenced by audience of readers" (Magnifico, 2010, p.168) and readers too have the opportunity to direct questions and comments to writers. Within this context, "writers and readers can become active listeners and conversation partners for each other" (Magnifico, 2010, p.168). What are the implications of such an audience on student audience awareness and writing development?

One of the few research studies in this area is Lapp, Shea, and Wolsey's (2010/2011) case study of second grade student bloggers. Through content analysis of student blogs as well as interviews and pre/during/post-blogging surveys with students, the study investigated students' growth of awareness of their audience through their participation in blogging. The researchers observed growth in student audience awareness and also "a concern for what the audience thinks" (p. 41). The findings from this study suggest several questions: How are young writers negotiating the vast and different audiences in the cyberspace? Do they know for whom they write? For whom do they intend to write? As Magnifico (2010) argues, revisiting these questions in "new media-infused learning environments" (p. 167) such as blogging is necessary. This work responds to this call as it explores further young writers' emerging understanding of the audience in the blogging milieu. It describes audience awareness development, paying attention to the following questions:

1. Whom are young bloggers *invoking* in their writing?
2. Whom are young bloggers *addressing* in their writing?

THEORETICAL FRAMEWORK

In a note in Ede and Lunsford's (1984) article, they explore various terms that mirror the dichotomy between "invoking" and "addressing" an audience. They provide "identified/envisaged," "real/fictional," and "analyzed/created" (p. 156) as suggestive of the same concept in invoked/addressed. The addressed audience for them "refers to those actual or real-life people who read a discourse" while an invoked audience refers to an audience "called up or imagined by the writer" (1984, p. 156).

When Lunsford and Ede (2009) revisited some of the precepts addressed in their influential 1984 article (Ede & Lunsford, 1984), technology had changed the framework under which questions of "audience" and "authorship" would apply. Now, in a very present way, audiences could and would respond to the posts of bloggers, whereas in the earlier period, both the concept and reality of an audience could only make itself felt to a student writer in a more gradual and ephemeral manner. They note that "new literacies are...expanding the possibilities of agency, while at the same time challenging older notions of both authorship and audience" (2009, p. 43). Nevertheless, for Lunsford and Ede, important questions remained for young writers about the size, composition and nature of an audience, however transformed it may have become. They revisit several questions:

- In a world of participatory media – of Facebook, MySpace, Wikipedia, Twitter and Del.icio.us – what relevance does the term *audience* hold?
- How can we best understand the relationships between text, author, medium, context, and audience today? How can we usefully describe the dynamic of this relationship?
- To what extent do the invoked and addressed audiences that we describe in our 1984 essay need to be revised and expanded? What other terms, metaphors or images might prove productive? What difference might answers to these questions make to twenty-first-century teachers and students? (2009, p. 43).

Because we remain primarily interested in how the above questions manifest themselves in school settings, among fledgling writers, our own study is poised to address these questions through the lens of young writers, who are at times only dimly aware of an outside audience (Barbeiro, 2010), even as they seek to make meaning for others in blogs by choosing words and phrases that seem to them to best express their emotions and states of mind.

In their earlier work, the principal difficulty expressed in invoking an audience was that a writer alone could not "know" his audience in the way that a public speaker could (Ede & Lunsford, 1984). Presumably, the speaker could, through the instant response of applause, silence, boos, cheers and other audiovisual cues, know, in a very direct way, whether he or she has "reached" his audience, and made her meaning felt. At the same time, blogging has reduced for writers the temporal distance between the act of publication and the act of response (Penrod, 2007). Now it is possible within seconds or minutes to know whether those reading a post approve or disapprove of it, or feel compelled to respond to it in one way or another. The speaker and the writer have moved closer together in their embrace of audience.

Applying the concepts of *audience addressed* and *audience invoked* (Ede & Lunsford, 1984; Lunsford & Ede, 2009) to writing in blogging environments, this chapter examines the ways in which fifth-grade bloggers interacted with a quickly responding audience, and the manner by which such an accelerated level of response shaped their understandings of *addressed* and *invoked* audiences.

METHODOLOGY

The Participants and the Context

The fifteen fifth-grade student writers who wrote on the blog consisted of ten girls and five boys - nine Caucasian, five Hispanic, and one African-

American. Two students were in the gifted program and one was in the special education program, but we did not methodologically differentiate these students from the rest. All students were new to blogging, but many were familiar with word processing and searching the Internet. The student participants reflected the school student population's ethnic and socioeconomic backgrounds, with 81% considered economically disadvantaged in this Title 1 School in a southern state of the United States.

The research site was selected because a member of the research team had worked with teachers on blogging projects in the same school in previous years. The teacher whose classroom is discussed in the current study had also expressed an interest in blogging. The program described here is a response to this teacher's interest in blogging.

Since the focus of the blog writing program was providing students with opportunities to interact with the audience beyond the classroom, the researchers recruited commenters for the research project from among retired teachers and graduate students in their courses. Additional commenters who emerged from the larger blogging community came from several different countries and continents (Canada, Scotland, New Zealand, Australia and the US).

Student Blogging

Blogging was embedded into a language arts block period once a week for four hours over a period of one year in a computer lab. The writing curriculum was guided by classroom teachers, who suggested assignments for the students that could be completed by the act of blogging. There was a self-descriptive assignment, where students chose sentences that described them; there was a persuasion assignment, where students needed to write convincingly about a subject about which they had a conviction. Generally, however, the young bloggers were free to expostulate and respond to the many commenters that responded to their posts, and who came from many walks of life, and parts of the world.

In addition, students were introduced to blogging as technology and as a social practice (McGrail & Davis, 2011) through the exploration of a Webquest that reviewed aspects of blog writing such as questioning, thinking, writing, collaborating, reflecting, commenting, linking, and proofreading. They also reviewed an ABCs-type *"Blook on Blogging."* The *Blook* book was an unpublished online book created by a group of previous elementary student bloggers who used creative idioms and appealing drawings in story format to describe what blogging meant to them. Both the Webquest and the *Blook* provided the necessary background knowledge the student bloggers needed before they began to apply their own understandings about blogging in their own writing. Teachers also discussed safety guidelines on a class wiki and established a class blog to model blog writing to students. The areas the class blog modeled for students included: how to develop and sustain dialogue in posts and comments, how to ask and answer questions, and how to develop a unique voice. Student blog writers also learned how to write on the blog in respectful and responsible ways with the larger audiences. Some of the blog posts that served this goal included topics such as understanding the nature and conventions of public writing; giving credit to others' words; and respecting others and their viewpoints. The class blog also served as a catalyst for conversations about learning and new topics for future conversations and learning.

The teacher and student individual blogs were created with Typepad software because this software was available through the university connection to the research site. Additional interactive Web-based components such as podcasts, Skype, Gizmo, and Google Maps applications were used during blogging sessions to facilitate communication with commenters and readers, locally and globally.

Data Collection and Analysis

The data analyzed in this work included young writers' posts and their readers' comments, for a total of 659 single-spaced pages of blog scripts. Using a qualitative content analysis method (Creswell, 2007), we began with developing a coding sheet that included audience types (domains) and their descriptors (See Table 1). Ede and Lunsford's (1984) and Lunsford and Ede's (2009) concepts of *audience invoked* and *audience addressed* provided both the theoretical and analytical framework for defining and describing the audience typology reported in this work. The data were next analyzed in two steps.

In Step 1, which asks what audience is invoked, we qualitatively coded the data (i.e. the student blogs) using our initial coding sheet. Throughout the data analysis process, adjustments were made to the coding sheet, as informed by our ongoing individual and collective data analysis. Detailed analytical memos were written and were used to identify the themes that emerged from the data. The memos helped to member check (Creswell,

2007) our analysis. Excerpts from the memos were also used to provide elaboration on the key findings reported here.

In Step 2, utilizing descriptive statistics methodology (Bogdan & Biklen, 2006) several sorting and organizational tasks were completed on the raw data of the student blogs. This is because the blogging output of the students may be roughly classified as falling into one of two groups: pure self-expression not directed at anyone, and commentary that responded to what someone had written. In order to make this bifurcation meaningful, we determined where and when the students' posts initially addressed specific people or groups of people. In certain instances, this was self-evident, as when a student addressed other bloggers by name. In others, it was more difficult to determine, because students would refrain from, or neglect to name addressees. In these latter cases, both coders had to agree on the identity of the addressee of the blog. Notably, all of the blogs featured a mix of addressing specific people, specific groups, and pure self-expression directed to no one in particular.

It was also important for us to attempt to determine to whom a student blogger was responding when a comment, or body of comments, was made to one of their posts from one or more outside per-

Table 1. Audience typology

Audience	Descriptors
You Generic	No one in particular
You Specific	Anyone with specific qualities
We	Audience that includes the I and You
Classmate	Student who is in the same grade and classroom
Peer (Wide Audience)	Student who is close in age but is not in the same classroom
Teacher (Wide Audience)	Someone who is a teacher but is not a classroom teacher in the project
Teacher	A teacher who teaches the class in the project
Graduate Student (Wide Audience)	An adult who is not a peer or close in age and who is in graduate school
Harley (dog)	The dog who has a blog that is maintained by a retired teacher
Other	Anyone in the larger community who comments on student blogs

sons. This is because such a determination gives us valuable clues as to how a blogger addresses his or her actual audience, following a burst of commentary from a wide swath of interested people. These different responders were grouped according to the following scheme: *Classmates, Peers from a Wider Audience, Classroom Teachers, Teachers from a Wider Audience, Graduate Students*, and *Others* (see Table 2). *Classmates* included students blogging with them in that class. *Peers from a Wider Audience* were grade-school and middle school students from around the country (and the world) who were also engaged in blogging. *Classroom Teachers* were just that; the teachers that directly and personally instructed the students, and monitored their blogs. *Teachers from a Wider Audience* were teachers from classrooms

around the US and the world. *Graduate Students* were pre-service teachers and doctoral students at a large urban southern US university. The group *Others* consisted of persons from anywhere who contacted the students for their own reasons and commented, either on sundry affairs or on the students' blogs in particular.

One of the challenges in organizing the data was compensating for the fact that the overall amount of blogging done by each student differed greatly. Some students were prolix, and others were more reticent about communicating. Still others hovered around the average level of output. We decided to measure the output of each blogger by the number of pages that person output, rather than the quantity of words, sentences or phrases. This was partly because a blog post can

Table 2. Audience addressed

Pseudonym	# of pgs	AI	C	P(WA)	T (WA)	T	GS	Other	Total
Johnny	73	YG	0	4.1	23.3	6.8	9.6	16.4	60.2
Emmy	42	YS; YG; We	4.8	14.3	14.3	9.5	21.4	9.5	73.8
Victoria	66	YG	6.1	7.6	31.8	6.7	12.1	21.2	85.5
Michael	57	YS	0	1.8	54.4	7	8.8	19.2	91.2
Rosalinda	34	YG	2.9	0	50	5.9	17.6	17.6	94
Mia	54	We	16.7	14.8	35.2	13	7.4	11.1	98.2
Leslie	13	YG; YS	23.1	0	23.1	7.7	23.1	30.8	107.8
TK	25	YS	4	0	40	12	28	24	108
Eddie	75	YG; We	0	26.6	46.6	6.6	26.6	2.7	109.1
Dulce Maria	21	YG; We	9.5	19	52.4	9.5	19	0	109.4
Anni	32	YG; We	12.5	6.3	43.8	25	18.8	3.1	109.5
MV	38	YS	21	7.9	42.1	13.2	23.7	5.3	113.2
Lindsey	40	YG	5	15	25	12.5	35	27.5	120
Tina	41	YG; We	22	14.6	58.5	4.9	29.3	12.2	141.5
Mary	41	We	9.8	12.2	75.6	17.1	19.6	17.1	151.4
Total			137.4	144.2	616.1	157.4	300	217.7	1572.8

Note: Addressed Audience: YG- You Generic; YS- You Specific; C- Classmate; P (WA) - Peer (Wide Audience);T(WA); Teacher (Wide Audience); GS- Graduate Student

The numbers in the cells are standardized values representing the number of times each of the bloggers in our study responded unambiguously to persons in the differing categories, proportionate to the total amount of blogging the student did. Thus, higher numbers represent more frequent addressing of persons in a given category corrected for the total amount of blogging.

consist of many words or a single word, and in some cases, of a series of letters only (e.g. LOL, ROFL). Because it was crucial for us to determine the proportion of blogging that each student created that was mostly or solely a response to outside commentary, we had to create a metric that reflected proportionality. To determine the response rate of each of our bloggers to posts by others, we treated the total number of pages of each blog as a necessarily rough estimate of the size of a given student blogger's output. Therefore, because students varied widely in the total amount of blogging that they did, and hence the total number of pages, the number of responses to outside comments was proportionately adjusted according to the number of printed pages of blogs that each student blogger was responsible for. Each category of person that the student blogger was responding to (*Classmates, Classroom Teachers,* etc.) was given a score that represented the proportion of their response to that category, compared to their total blogging output. Thus for example, if one student had 50 pages of blogging material and 10 responses to persons in the Graduate Student category, this was given a ratio of 10/50 or 1/5, and treated the same as that from a student with 25 pages of blogging material and 5 responses to graduate students (5/25 or 1/5). Using these proportional scores, we rank-ordered the data to determine which responder groups, after accounting for each student's total, were the more frequent respondents of these students.

FINDINGS

Step 1: Whom Are Young Bloggers Invoking in Their Writing?

The audience that these fifth-graders invoked - or constructed without specific readers in mind - most often in their blog writing was the *You Generic* audience. For some writers, this type of audience was a very broad audience, such as "people in our

society," as Eddie wrote in his first post, or even the world at large. [Note: Quotations herein have been preserved with the idiosyncratic spelling produced by the participants.] Rosalinda spoke of such an audience in this reflection of hers on blogging: "I love blogging! Bloging is fun and entertaining. It's fun knowing about what is going on in other places of the world."

For others, the *You Generic* audience referred, simply, to no one in particular, rather than to an invoked world. This was certainly true for Johnny, who seemed to consider blogging to be a method for the release of his stream of consciousness and therefore addressed such self-expressive writing to all who could understand or relate to his thoughts. Johnny wrote with the *You Generic* audience in mind in the following post, which had no title attached to it:

1. Maybe if I butter up my mom she will give me that new I Phone.
2. If you say something too much People will think you are crying wolf.
3. Everyone in this world has gone Bananas.
4. Get out there and break a leg.
5. If you go out there alone you're a sitting duck.

Still other bloggers perceived the *You Generic* audience in more concrete terms. This understanding of such an audience was evident when student bloggers assigned some qualities to otherwise rather generic audiences. A good example of such audience invoking is Anni's introductory post:

Hi!!!!!!!!!!! My name is Anni and this is my first time that I blog. I think that this will be fun because I am already having a great time blogging. I think I am funny and nice. I hope you blog to me. Bye!!

In this post, the *Generic You* audience that Anni wished to address was narrowed down to the persons who, like her, like having fun and who would appreciate writing back to someone who is "funny and nice." TK, on the other hand, wrote to football lovers and fans, with a similar understanding of them as the audience in this post:

My Passion is Football because I am Athletic. I started liking football when i was about 5 or 6 years old. Every time when a football game comes on, right away i go and turn that TV on and i watch the football game...

It is important to note that the student bloggers in this study invoked the *You Generic* audience not only at the early stages of blogging, when they were beginning to write for an audience that they did not yet know, but throughout the history of their posts. They did this by asking questions of their invoked addressed audiences frequently. To illustrate, when Victoria learned that her fictional story of a girl transported to another world contained errors, a fact about which she felt "embaranced [*sic*]," she resolved to ask her invoked *Generic* audience, "Do you have another way I could catch my mistakes?" (p. 12). Lindsey also welcomed the give and take from the *You Generic* audience at different points of time: "If you have any questions on my blog you just write back to me and I will answer. I am alays [*sic*] here to type to you and any body that writes me."

The second type of audience these young writers invoked was the *We* audience. Typically, student bloggers invoked this audience type when they were asked to write persuasively for their blogs. Such writing was often on a topic about which they were passionate or cared deeply. Maria Dulce's post on saving the trees is a good example of the *We* style of audience summoned with this purpose in mind:

I believe we should stop cutting trees down in U.S. The more you cut trees down, the more hotter is going to be. Each year thousands of trees are cut down. We won't have any trouble if we stop doing that. Some animals live on trees or in trees like owls, birds, and other animals and they need

homes to live. A lot of animals are already dying because people are cutting trees down. Everybody might not see anymore animals like snakes and squirrels. So we don't want animals to extinct...

In this piece, Maria used the "we-you-everybody" language to indicate the specific audience she had in mind for her writing, and to encourage the members of this audience to join her in her cause. Mia, too, implored the *We* style audience for a different cause, which was her call to add P.E. (physical education) to the curriculum "everyday." Here is an excerpt from this call:

The first reason I believe we should have P.E. everyday is.... It will be a great exercise. Everyday a new exercise and activity could be done. Some news reporters say that people and mostly kids are getting fatter and they are overweight. So to stop that I think we should have P.E. every day. The second reason is by exercising everyday and making goals for ourselves. This will bring our grades up...

The least frequently invoked audience in the original posts of these bloggers was the *You Specific* audience. For example, Michael believed he possibly knew who might blog back to him. In his first post he wrote:

Hi, my name is Michael. I just entered the world of blogging and it is fun. I like posting comments on other blogs. I also like writing blogs online. My favorite subject in school is science. If you are new person like me I think you should read this. My friend is Mary.

Emmy too exhibited a *You Specific* audience that sometimes moved from a "You Generic" over to "We." This was particularly true when she concentrated on her accomplishments, as evident in this post about a legislative event, at which she represented her class and her school:

I am at the Georgia Depot and I am interviewing legislatures [sic] *and I have had wonderful answers especially Jimmy Pruett. We have given them the opportunity to answer and record questions. I have been able to get a caricature drawing done of me and the food is great (and free)....*

Step 2: Whom Are Young Bloggers Addressing in Their Writing?

Addressing was herein constructed to mean specific individuals to whom the bloggers would either greet or respond. The first observation of note that can easily be seen when examining Table 2 is the category with the overall least number of "hits," i.e. *Classmates*.[1] Evidently, almost all of the students regarded communicating with more distant groups as more important than with students sitting close by. For no blogger that we studied was the frequency of responses to the *Classmates* category greater than that for another group. However, it was not the only category ignored by some of the bloggers. Whereas Eddie, Johnny and Michael did not connect with anyone in the *Classmates* group, an equal number of students – Leslie, T.K., and Rosalinda – did not connect with anyone in the *Wider Peer Audience* group.

By comparison, the group that received the overall most hits was the *Teacher (Wider Audience)* group. The highest single score was received in this group, and overall scores were very robust here. As a group, they received over twice the number of aggregate responses (a score of 616.1) than the next most numerous group, *Graduate Students* (which had a score of 300). We do not have the data to completely answer why this occurred. Perhaps because these teachers were accomplished writers and bloggers, their facility with language, and ability to "draw out" shy students led them to be very popular with the student bloggers. Perhaps the fact that the students were aware that these experienced people would not be grading them was a factor. Notably, one of these *Teacher (Wider Audience)* group members, Lani, was responded to by literally every blogger, and

was singly responsible for a plurality of the comments from this category.

Another interesting finding was that students overall significantly varied in the proportion of their overall commentary to their responses to commenters. On the lower end, Johnny, despite 73 pages of blogging material, responded, on average, only 40% as often to the comments of any other bloggers as the high scorer in the group, Mary. Part of the reason for this was Mary's exceptionally high personal score for responding to *Teachers (Wide Audience)*, at over 75. This was more than three times Johnny's score of 23.3. It is reasonable to assume that Johnny and Mary each regarded the blogging experience as having very different purposes. Mary seems to have viewed the feedback from experienced teachers as being essential to her success as a blogger, whereas Johnny obviously found that this was less important for the blogging he wanted to do.

A more typical median score was that of Eddie, another profuse blogger who produced 75 pages of material. Unlike Johnny, he responded to everyone except to *Classmates*, and in perhaps the most balanced way. However, he, too, seems to have privileged the remarks of *Teachers (Wide Audience)*, since they receive his highest score as well (46.1).

When we reanalyzed the blogs to search for clues as to what might have motivated this privileging of certain groups over others, we noticed that comments made by other students (*Classmates*) were often ignored, dismissed, or treated superficially by these bloggers. An example of such a response to a classmate is Emmy's reply to Johnny's critique of her post on a favorite school subject:

Johnny: I wish you had talked more about what science projects you did In science class. And more about what you do In basketball do you go to games. Or Is It a fun thing you do at home? Jhonny I didn't talk about the science projects because I was just saying that I only liked them. I only said that I liked basketball. Emmy.

On the other hand, our second search also showed that the commentary by outside groups was privileged not only by the frequency with which the bloggers responded, but by the praise and gratitude shown by the students toward these more experienced people – teachers and graduate students. To illustrate, in this post, Anni thanked Lani, a teacher from the wider audience, for inspiring her as a writer and for helping her improve her own writing (note Anni named this teacher "the best writer" and used nine exclamation marks to communicate this high opinion of this teacher to her audience):

My best writer !!!!!!!!!

I really enjoy all of Lani's post .They really help me because when I have trouble with prepositions she helped me .This is one comment that she was helping me on " You said you were having difficulty with prepositions at school and you asked: "Do you have problems with some part of speech?" Can you tell me which words are prepositions in this paragraph or in the paragraph above this one?"Now I am better at prepositions. She also helps me with words that I don't know defonition of.

Thank You Lani

Maria Dulce, another blogger, included a graduate student in her "thank you" note to the teachers from the wider audience as well:

mY THANK YOU COMMENT (emphasis from the original quotation)

I'm thanking to everybody who comment me and I'm so glad people really did. The first person I'm thanking to is Lani you said alot of nice comments and I 'm glad you liked my story's. Did you know your were the first person to blog me? The next person was realy special to me and her name is Ms. Best. I think you tried your best in every thing

too and I 'm very glad your glad to be a Latino. I 'm Latino and I'm very happy about my culture too. Finlay is some one who tells the truth if she liked it or not. Chris I know you didn't understand my story is just I couldn't think what to write. I promise I will do a better story next time...

Another category that the students responded more often than *Classmates* was that of *Other*. Since people in the *Other* category seemed to be from other walks of life altogether, it was difficult for us to discern why the students enjoyed responding to them, other than that they appeared, in a few cases, to be people the students knew (i.e., family members or friends, such as "Uncle John," who wrote to Michael).

The most prolix blogger, Eddie, was also the blogger that most often responded to *Peers (Wide Audience)*, but other students did not give this group a high score. They thus were ranked second to last.

In third to last place was the classroom teacher (*Teacher*) category. Because this particular year-long session of blogging had some of the features of an "assignment," we believe that the comparative reluctance shown by these bloggers in addressing or responding to the classroom teacher may have been simply the maintenance of a respectful distance. We also observed that although classroom teachers offered comments on ideas in student writing, they tended to also give much attention to grammar, language or other issues in student writing. A response to Tina from this classroom teacher illustrates this kind of feedback:

Hi Tina,

I wish you had used spell check on this post because it is filled with so much good information. Always run spell check because it will pick up those errors. Also, remember to proof your work by reading it out loud.

You do such good thinking and contribute a lot to class. I think you are a good blogger! Reach for the stars! Mrs. C

As we can see, "Mrs.C" intertwines praise with a practical tip for a better result. Such advice is of course putatively helpful, but it also serves to reinforce that the blogging done by the students was performed in a school setting, and therefore possessed some of the features of "schoolwork."

How Do Young Bloggers Invoke/ Address their Audiences?

The bloggers in this study used different strategies to invoke or address their audiences, and these reflected their personalities as well as the roles they envisioned for themselves and for their audiences. For example, Victoria always named the persons to whom she responded, immediately before the post, unless she was writing an assignment that she was sharing with the blogosphere. She was respectful of teachers, as with her response to Mrs. A's criticism of a post: "You flatter me with your comments." She also seemed to mollify and curry favor with the graduate students and teachers, as when, in response to a comment from Chris, she said, "Thank you for telling me that I need to work on my puncuation [*sic*] skills. Since you told me that, I can tell you are a person who is helpfull. And a person who tells the truth. What do you do for a living?" These quotes indicate that Victoria appeared to view blogging as a challenging game to improve at, rather than as an opportunity to reveal herself. She wrote, "Ever since my first day of blogging I have been learning to write, read, use descriptive words, and to do better in my writing!"

The role that she created for her audiences was that of a supporter. She seemed to be interested in cultivating good public relations with her classmates, teachers and the other people she encountered on the blog, rather than using the blog to further compositional goals per se. To do this, she sometimes seemed to use her frequent questions as a kind of pleasant distraction, rather than to allow her blog posts to reveal things about her. Her classmate Eddie, who is also studied here, spoke about his interest in marine biology. In responding, Victoria replied, "You're a very smart guy so use your knowledge that way you can have a good future when you grow up. POP QUIZ! If you had $100,000,000,000 how would you spend it? See you in class."

Eddie, on the other hand, did not conceal how he felt about the subjects that he wrote about. When describing the untimely death of his dog, he resorted to all caps – "DEAD." In his otherwise lighthearted post on Jamaica, he delved into something he regarded as unfair – why he was denied an earlier visit to the island:

Last time I was going to go but my brother got bad grades and we couldn't go. This time i'm going by myself although my brother got bad grades. My parents finally saw that it wasnt fair to get held back for my brother's mistakes. can't wait for that ocean water to hit my body.

Eddie apparently assumed that respondents and readers would warm to the subjects that he recounted and he saw his audiences as friends and supporters. As a result, he did not hold back much. In the course of completing writing assignments on the blog, his vivid language both signaled his interests to a very general audience and attracted certain members of it. When responding to queries about those more general statements, he sincerely and comprehensively covered any subject that his respondents asked about. In doing this, he successfully made the distinction between statements made for a more general audience, and those made to specific individuals. Compare:

I always thougt that time square was the only square. I can't belive you guys go through the prosses of making maple syrup. It looks so cool. When we have fairs in our town we have a pie eating contest. The rules are to eat the pie but you cant use your hands. What other cind of festivals do you have in Ohio? [Eddie was writing this post to the new peers he met online]

And:

Well in science class Iv'e learned about the different parts of earth. The crust, mantle, and the core. The crust is the outermost layer of earth. The mantle is the middle layer of earth. The mantle is made of molten rock which shoots out of volcanoes. The last layer of earth is called the core. The core is actually made of many metals (mostly magnetic to be exact).It is made of iron, nickle, alloy,and some other unidentified metals.

Johnny did not "invoke" his actual audience much at all and therefore created no real role for them; they reacted by often assuming the teacher role, as when they asked him to proofread his work. However, in certain posts, Johnny would heartfully express his joy and concern over important personal issues. A good example is this post in response to his teacher having a child:

Guess what just came in our teacher just had a baby that is not somthing you hear evry day in blogging it was just so exiting our teacher had a baby boy named Eli I am so happy for her I wonder if he will come to blog for us and be in her class I just cant wait it is just so exititing [sic] blogging will never be the same because she wont be back for six weeks but it doesnt matter I may be sad but I also happy mostly happy I mean my teacher is having a baby i just cant believe it can you please everybody pray he will be a strong and be able to do any thing he wants to when he puts his mind to it.

His blending of disparate sentences and thoughts and the lack of proper punctuation and spelling made decoding this piece difficult, but one can see true affect and concern for another here. Therefore, while Johnny was primarily self-expressing through his blog, he was not unconcerned with the welfare of others.

Alternatively, Mia appeared to view blogging as a social opportunity, and as a result, preferred to focus much of her writing about likes and dislikes. Her incuriosity about the likes and desires of others, and the somewhat brusque quality of her posts meant that she tended to treat everyone similarly. When *Peer(Wider Audiences)* member Kara wrote:

Mia,

You remind me so much of myself. My favorite colors are pink and green and consider myself to be sassy and sweet also! I enjoyed reading your poem and I look forward to reading more of your writing. Is this your first blog? If so, how is your experience with it so far?

Mia wrote:

Kira [sic],I feel proud of myself because I made you feel the same you again. Most of the people that I know don't like the color pink, so happy right now. I can be sweet some times, But I always feel sassy. I consider this as my first bloging.My experince so far is preety good my teachers tell me that I use fantastic word in my bloging and I really admire what my teachers say about me.

Tina too assumed that her audience would be interested in her personal stories. She therefore channeled them into the Friend category. In one touching story, she described briefly the history of her dog ownership:

I enjoyed getting to see Harley your dog I used to have a dog just like him but he died last year. When he was little I was a baby and when I cried he came running to me to check on me. He was always the first thing I always saw when I came home from school. He also slept with me in my bed at night when I went to bed. He was a good dog and last year on his leg it hurt him and his bone was showing so my grama took him to the vet and they said he would die that night. All I have of him now is a picture.

Tina used this story for developing new social relationships with her audiences—her new friends; and she found it rewarding to be able to talk to them about her dog.

Mary, yet another blogger, took pains to communicate with others on a cheerful and evenhanded level. She was polite, responsive and grateful for constructive criticism. Because Mary allowed the comments of others to influence her blogs, the audience she invoked, while of course dissimilar in some ways from the actual audience, approached it in others. She named the people whose comments she addressed, and amended her own work in response to this. For instance, she wrote:

Chris, when you commented on my first 'The Disappointment Turned Great!' you discouraged me. Now I understand you just wanted it to be longer and have fewer exclamation marks. It touched my heart that you took a long time to go through and comment kindly.

Later on, in that blog entry she wrote to her commenters, "Keep commenting truly from the heart." This shows that Mary also attempted to engage the emotions of her audience when she wrote. She evidently intuited that the processes she used to clarify her own thoughts on the page would likely make her blog entries more intelligible to others. Therefore, she was sometimes "discouraged" when others did not enjoy her entries, and became "encouraged" again when what they said appeared to help those entries. Thus, she saw her audience as both supporters and critics.

Other student bloggers' ways of invoking and addressing their audiences fell under one of the types of response illustrated above.

DISCUSSION AND IMPLICATIONS FOR PRACTICE

Based on the number of pages of the total blog-script (659 single-spaced pages), it is obvious that the blogging experiment yielded important fruit in stretching the writing muscles for the blogging students who participated. Since the text corpus also consisted heavily of exchanges among student bloggers and their readers and commenters, it was evident to us that the audience in this study indeed became an interactive and participatory audience, and did in fact affect the intentions and modify the blogs of the students. Put differently, "Blogs create audiences, but audiences also create blogs" (Liu & LaRose, 2008, p. 7). Baker, Rozendal, and Whitenack's (2000) work, along with that of Jenkins (2006), has noted that interactive technologies such as blogging invite such roles from the audiences that use these communication tools. Our study has shown that our young writers embraced this kind of audience and the participatory interaction that it offered to them. It is through interaction with such an interactive audience that these young writers were able to sharpen their audience awareness, a concept, as we note above, that is often an abstract and difficult one for young writers (Barbeiro, 2010; Carvalho, 2002; Kos & Maslowski, 2001). For these student bloggers, however, the audience often became real and authentic people whom they chose to both invoke and address in their writing, and whose questions and needs they often recounted in their responses to them. The *You Generic/Specific* and *We* audiences that they invoked in their writing indicated that they indeed were in conversation with their participatory audiences.

The ways in which they invoked and addressed their audiences were different nevertheless. Sometimes, the bloggers saw their readers as friends and supporters; at other times, they saw in them teachers and critics. Others still did not see the need to hear from the audience at all and thus did not assign their readers any particular roles. Interestingly, some of these roles reflect the conception of blogging as a space for self-expression (Fiedler, 2003; Downes, 2004) and some reveal the perception of blogging as a space for social interaction (Davies & Merchant, 2007; Deng & Yuen, 2011). What these bloggers struggled with, however, was finding an effective way to combine what Werde (2003) described as two oppositional principles of authorship - monologue and dialogue – that is, how to carry conversations in the blogging space with the self and with others (Efimova & de Moor, 2005). As a result, some blog posts read like a stream of consciousness and the authors of these posts appear to "invite the audience's gaze," rather than a dialogue with it (Scheidt, 2006 as cited in Liu & LaRose, 2008, p. 6). Other posts were somewhat limited, in terms of interactivity and sustainable levels of dialogue and multiplex relationships. That is, the bloggers who composed the latter posts conversed with their readers about numerous topics and the issues these topics raised for them, and did so even frequently, rather than explore deeper but fewer areas of interest with more readers and commenters. This was partly because of what these bloggers were asked to do in different writing prompts. It may have also been partly because these young writers chose to not return to certain topics and conversations even when they were invited to write freely on self-selected topics.

There are several implications for practice from these findings. First, young writers need opportunities to interact with real audiences for an extended period of time, to help them develop a concept of the interactive and participatory audience. Everyone – the student bloggers, the classroom teacher, and the researchers – were surprised and delighted when interested persons, definitely not part of the ostensible blogging project, offered interesting opinions and viewpoints that came from many nations. The rich communication that this engendered was *sui generis*, and had its own kind of reward. We believe that the students were immeasurably served by it. It led the bloggers to ponder and respond to states of mind and states

of life that had thereunto been foreign to them. They became aware of, and sought to serve, an external, and very real audience. Skillful writers rely on such audience awareness as they imagine and address the needs of their readers in their writing (Barbeiro, 2010; Holliway, 2004). Writing in class with a teacher or peers as the only audience, as has been the experience for so many students in our classrooms (Gilbert & Graham, 2010), will not suffice in today's digital milieu. It is true that teachers can provide essential help in the actual structuration of their students' posts; grammar, spelling and narrative order are important ways that a classroom teacher can contribute. We do not anticipate that this will change in the future. However, responding only to a teacher or to students in the immediate vicinity is necessarily a limiting act.

Second, the fact that blogging as a genre often brings together two oppositional principles of authorship, monologue and dialogue (Werde, 2003), is a new writing experience for young writers. That is why young bloggers will need teachers to scaffold the ways in which they can learn to negotiate these seemingly competing writerly agendas and writing spaces. That is, young people must be taught to maintain a balance between that writing done for the self and that which is done for others. This balance is the essence of the blogosphere. Liu and LaRose (2008) observe that such negotiation requires from blog authors the ability to "maintain two delicate balances: the balance between satisfying different types of audiences, and the balance between satisfying themselves and their audiences" (p. 7). Helping students with satisfying their audiences will require particular attention from writing instructors, since we know that young writers have a hard time with not being self-centered in their own writing (Blau, 1983).

Third, moving young writers beyond themselves in their blog writing will also require teaching them about the needs of a variety of audience types that they may encounter in the blogosphere. Such an audience, as was the case in this study, is

71

sure to be heterogeneous (Liu & LaRose, 2008). It will consist of the known and unknown (Lenhart, 2005), the expected and unexpected (Li, 2005), the invoked and the addressed (Ede & Lunsford, 1984), and will be both approving and critical at times. Exposure to such diverse audiences will expand the facility blog writers will possess in both invoking and addressing these group types as they write.

Young writers in our study were very strategic with the choices that they made about the audiences that they invoked, and in particular about the audiences they addressed. With the exception of the few who responded to nearly all commenters, the majority of the young writers responded very selectively to their audiences, choosing the readers to whom they wished to write back. Being strategic about composing for an audience is an important skill for writers to possess (Dean, 2006). Young writers should be provided with opportunities to exercise such choices with the writing they produce for authentic audiences. Our young writers, however, seemed to be invoking outside group teachers and readers more often than their classroom teachers and classmates. Perhaps these bloggers felt constrained by, or uncomfortable in interacting with the classroom teacher as an audience. Perhaps they associated their teacher's reader role to be primarily that of an assessor or judge of their writing, even though the classroom teachers in this study assumed commenter and respondent roles as well. Ede and Lunsford (1984) note that the teacher-as-reader role in the classroom has already been "established and formalized in a series of related academic conventions" (p. 163). These roles have also been validated through the giving of grades, as well as the teacher power to render other important decisions about these young writers' futures, such as being promoted to the next grade level. Given these facts, it is perhaps understandable why these bloggers chose to address distant teachers who acted only as sympathetic and experienced writers. The emotional safety that these teachers from the wider audience could provide to these young writers may have allowed them to take risks with their writing.

There is some research that teachers as authority figures may command respect, but not camaraderie per se (Pace, 2007). It is possible, therefore, that there is a trade-off of free expression in student blogging in a classroom setting, under the watchful eye of the teacher, for the bonus of a more organized and fruitful experience. Young writers may otherwise lack the discipline to continue blogging in a focused way on their own without such supervision.

As did the classroom teachers in this study, all digital writing teachers play an important role in not only getting blogs started, but more importantly in scaffolding young writers into the "practices, habits of mind, and texts" (Rowsell, 2009, p. 97) of blogging. Accordingly, the students in our study were urged to explore their creativity in a way that demanded more of them as writers than merely conversing in a written way with their peers and other readers. The classroom teachers assigned poetry, fiction and non-fiction as blogging assignments that were then loosed to be commented upon by the world at large. This at times breathtakingly broad opportunity for review, from an abundance of peers and mentor figures, must be viewed in a positive light. We believe that the directed, organized and longitudinal nature of the blogging we analyzed, especially because it was not sporadic and scattershot, led to significant gains in expressive power and the inculcation of the needs of the external audience in the work of many of the bloggers whose posts we analyzed. Because of this, teachers may consider focusing on a small number of genre-specific assignments in a single blogging project and aim at more in-depth and sustained conversations on fewer topics that young writers can discuss with their readers over a longer period of time.

Another preference that our bloggers evinced was that of preferring an adult commenter or reader over a peer, irrespective of whether that peer was a fellow student from their immediate class, or a student from another classroom somewhere else in the world. Perhaps these bloggers felt that they required a writing mentor who could act not only as a "more knowledgeable other" to use Vygotsky's (1978, p. 128) term that describes a mentor in the apprenticeship learning model, but one who could also provide a different point of view than those from their peer age group.

IMPLICATIONS FOR RESEARCH

In this study, the largest audience that the students addressed was the teacher, if we broadly define this to include graduate students and pre-service teachers. However, the response of the student bloggers to their immediate classroom teacher was meager. Could the experience of the classroom teacher as an ever-present respondent and commenter have limited these young writers' abilities to invent other types of readers/audiences and the roles they wished for them in their writing? Secondly, would they have invoked or addressed their audiences differently if the readers and commenters on their blogs were made up solely of peers from a wider audience? These questions are difficult to answer with the data at hand, and further research should be implemented to help answer them.

Since blogging affords the merging of self-expressive writing and writing for social interaction (Davies & Merchant, 2007; Deng & Yuen, 2011), and this was an area of challenge to our student bloggers, we need to know more about the ways in which writers invoke and address their audiences within such spaces. For instance, how do they negotiate the tensions and conflicts when these two distinct authorship experiences meet? Equally, it is important to examine the ways in which these contact zone (Pratt, 1991) authorial experiences inform or augment each other. How does this benefit both the writer and the reader? Blogging permitted these young writers to draw ever nearer to both intended and unintended audiences. How they might best serve these audiences in an authentic way, through cogent and effective

writing, is the question that further research should, as an intended audience, address.

REFERENCES

Andrews, R., & Smith, A. (2011). *Developing writers: Teaching and learning in the digital age.* New York: Open University Press.

Baker, E., Rozendal, M., & Whitenack, J. (2000). Audience awareness in a technology-rich elementary classroom. *Journal of Literacy Research, 32*(3), 395–419. doi:10.1080/10862960009548086.

Barbeiro, L. F. (2010). What happens when I write? Pupils' writing about writing. *Reading and Writing, 24*(7), 813–834. doi:10.1007/s11145-010-9226-2.

Blau, S. (1983). Invisible writing: Investigating cognitive processes in composition. *College Composition and Communication, 34*(3), 297–312. doi:10.2307/358261.

Bogdan, R., & Biklen, S. (2006). *Qualitative research for education: An introduction to theory and methods* (5th ed.). Boston: Allyn & Bacon.

Boling, E., Castek, J., Zawilinski, L., Barton, K., & Nierlich, T. (2008). Collaborative literacy: Blogs and internet projects. *The Reading Teacher, 61,* 504–506. doi:10.1598/RT.61.6.10.

Carvalho, J. (2002). Developing audience awareness in writing. *Journal of Research in Reading, 25*(3), 271–282. doi:10.1111/1467-9817.00175.

Chapman, M. (2006). Research in writing, preschool through elementary, 1983-2003. *L1 Educational Studies in Language and Literature, 6*(2), 7-27.

Creswell, J. W. (2007). *Research design: Qualitative, quantitative, and mixed methods approaches* (3rd ed.). Thousand Oaks, CA: Sage.

Curwood, J. H. (2011). iPoetry: Creating space for new literacies in the English curriculum. *Journal of Adolescent & Adult Literacy, 55*(2), 110–120. doi:10.1002/JAAL.00014.

Davies, J., & Merchant, G. (2007). Looking from the inside out: Academic blogging as new literacy. In Lankshear, C., & Knobel, M. (Eds.), *A new literacies sampler* (pp. 167–197). New York: Peter Lang.

Davis, A. (2005). Co-authoring identity: Digital storytelling in an urban middle school. *Technology Humanities Education Narrative, 1*. Retrieved from http://thenjournal.org/feature/61/

Dean, D. (2006). *Strategic writing: The writing process and beyond in the secondary English classroom.* Urbana, IL: NCTE.

Deng, L., & Yuen, A. (2011). Towards a framework for educational affordances of blogs. *Computers & Education, 56*(2), 441–451. doi:10.1016/j.compedu.2010.09.005.

Downes, S. (2004). Educational blogging. *EDUCAUSE Review, 39*(5), 14–21. Retrieved from http://www.educause.edu/pub/er/erm04/erm0450.asp.

Ede, L., & Lunsford, A. (1984). Audience addressed/audience invoked: The role of audience in composition theory and pedagogy. *College Composition and Communication, 35*(2), 155–171. doi:10.2307/358093.

Efimova, L., & de Moor, A. (2005). Beyond personal webpublishing: An exploratory study of conversational blogging practices. In *Proceedings of the Hawaii International Conference on System Sciences* (HICSS-38). Manoa, Australia: IEEE Computer Society Press. Retrieved from http://blog.mathemagenic.com/2004/09/15.html#a1353

Farmer, J. (2004). Communication dynamics: Discussion boards, weblogs and the development of communities of inquiry in online learning environments. In R. Atkinson, C. McBeath, D. Jonas-Dwyer, & R. Phillips (Eds.), *Beyond the comfort zone: Proceedings of the 21st ASCILITE Conference* (pp. 274-283). Perth, Australia: Australasian Society for Computers in Learning in Tertiary Education.

Fiedler, S. (2003). Personal webpublishing as a reflective conversational tool for selforganized learning. In Burg, T. D. (Ed.), *BlogTalks* (pp. 190–216). Vienna, Austria: Academic Press.

Frank, L. A. (1992). Writing to be read: Young writers' ability to demonstrate audience awareness when evaluated by their readers. *Research in the Teaching of English, 26*(3), 277–298.

Gelbwasser, M. (2011). Running a classroom blog. *Instructor, 120*(4), 76–77.

Gilbert, J., & Graham, S. (2010). Teaching writing to elementary students in grades 4-6: A national survey. *The Elementary School Journal, 110*(4), 494–518. doi:10.1086/651193.

Glogowski, K. (2008). *Tracing the emergence of a blogging/writing community: Critical transformations in a grade eight classroom.* (Doctoral dissertation). Retrieved from ProQuest Dissertations and Theses database (Order No. 978-0-494-44706-2).

Graves, D. H. (1975). An examination of the writing process of seven year old children. *Research in the Teaching of English, 9*, 227–242.

Greenhow, C., & Gleason, B. (2012). Twitteracy: Tweeting as a new literacy practice. *The Educational Forum, 76*(4), 464–478. doi:10.1080/00131725.2012.709032.

Hairston, M. (1978). *A contemporary rhetoric* (2nd ed.). Boston, MA: Houghton Miffin.

Holliway, D. R. (2004). Through the eyes of my reader: A strategy for improving audience perspective in children's descriptive writing. *Journal of Research in Childhood Education, 18*(4), 334–349. doi:10.1080/02568540409595045.

Jenkins, H. (2006). *Fans, bloggers, and gamers: Media consumers in a digital age.* New York: New York University Press.

Jin, L., & Zhu, W. (2010). Dynamic motives in ESL computer-mediated peer response. *Computers and Composition, 27*(4), 284–303. doi:10.1016/j.compcom.2010.09.001.

Johnson, D. (2010). Teaching with authors' blogs: Connections, collaborations, creativity. *Journal of Adolescent & Adult Literacy, 54*(3), 172–180. doi:10.1598/JAAL.54.3.2.

Kellogg, R. T. (2008). Training writing skills: A cognitive developmental perspective. *Journal of Writing Research, 1*(1), 1–26.

Koehler, M. J., & Mishra, P. (2008). Introducing TPACK. In AACTE Committee on Innovation & Technology (Eds.), Handbook of technological pedagogical content knowledge for educators (pp. 3–29). New York: Routledge.

Kos, R., & Maslowski, C. (2001). Second graders perceptions of what is important in writing. *The Elementary School Journal, 101*(5), 567–578. doi:10.1086/499688.

Lamonica, C. (2010). *What are the benefits of blogging in the elementary classroom?* (Master's thesis). Retrieved from http://reflectivepractitioner.pbworks.com/f/Lamonica+Capstone+Paper.pdf

Lapp, D., Shea, A., & Wolsey, T. D. (2010/2011). Blogging and audience awareness. *Journal of Education, 191*(1), 33–44.

Lenhart, A. (2005). *Unstable texts: An ethnographic look at how bloggers and their audience negotiate self-presentation, authenticity, and norm formation.* (Unpublished master's thesis). Georgetown University, Washington, DC.

Li, D. (2005). *Why do you blog: A uses and gratification inquiry into bloggers' motivations.* (Unpublished master's thesis). Marquette University, Milwaukee, WI.

Liu, X., & LaRose, R. (2008). The impact of perceived audiences on blogging. Paper presented the meeting of the National Communication Association. San Diego, CA.

Long, R. C. (1980). Writer-audience relationships: Analysis or invention? *College Composition and Communication, 31*, 221–226. doi:10.2307/356377.

Luehmann, A., & MacBride, R. (2009). Classroom blogging in the service of student-centered pedagogy: Two high school teachers use of blogs. *Technology Humanities Education Narrative, 6*. Retrieved from http://thenjournal.org/feature/175/

Lunsford, A., & Ede, L. (2009). Among the audience: On audience in an age of new literacies. In Weiser, M. E., Fehler, B. M., & González, A. M. (Eds.), *Engaging audience: Writing in an age of new literacies* (pp. 42–73). Urbana, IL: NCTE.

Magnifico, A. (2010). Writing for whom? Cognition, motivation, and a writer's audience. *Educational Psychologist, 45*(3), 167–184. doi:10.1080/00461520.2010.493470.

McGrail, E., & Davis, A. (2011). The influence of classroom blogging on elementary student writing. *Journal of Research in Childhood Education, 25*(4), 415-437. Doi: http://dx.doi.org/10.1080/02568543.2011.605205

McGrail, E., & Davis, A. (2013). Blogversing with fifth graders: The intersection of blogging, conversations, and writing. In Young, C. A., & Kajder, S. (Eds.), *Research in English language arts and technology* (pp. 265–290). Charlotte, NC: Information Age Publishing.

Mitchell, R., & Taylor, M. (1979). The integrating perspective: An audience-response model for writing. *College English, 41*(3), 247–271. doi:10.2307/376441.

O'Donnell, M. (2005). *Blogging as pedagogic practice: Artefact and ecology*. Paper presented at the Blog Talk Downunder Conference. Sydney, Australia. Retrieved from http://incsub.org/blogtalk/?page_id=66

Ong, W. J. (1979). The writer's audience is always a fiction. *PMLA, 90*(1), 9–21. doi:10.2307/461344.

Pace, J. L. (2007). Understanding authority in classrooms: A review of theory, ideology, and research. *Review of Educational Research, 77*(1), 4–27. doi:10.3102/003465430298489.

Parisi, L., & Crosby, B. (2012). *Making connections with blogging: Authentic learning for today's classrooms*. Eugene, OR: Society for Integration of Technology in Education.

Penrod, D. (2005). *Composition in convergence: The impact of new media on writing assessment*. Mahwah, NJ: Lawrence Erlbaum.

Penrod, D. (2007). *Using blogs to enhance literacy: The next 21st-century learning*. Lanham, MD: Rowman & Littlefield Education Publishers.

Pfister, F.R. & Petrik. (1980). A heuristic model for creating a writer's audience. *College Composition and Communication, 31*, 213–220. doi:10.2307/356376.

Pratt, M. L. (1991). Arts of the contact zone. *Profession, 91*, 33–40.

Rowsell, J. (2009). My life on Facebook: Assessing the art of online social networking. In Burke, A., & Hammett, R. F. (Eds.), *Assessing new literacies: Perspectives from the classroom* (pp. 95–112). New York, NY: Peter Lang Publishing.

Scheidt, L. (2006). Adolescent diary weblogs and the unseen audience. In Buckingham, D., & Rebekah, W. (Eds.), *Digital generations: Children, young people and new media*. London: Lawrence Erlbaum.

Swanson, K., & Legutko, R. (2008). The effect of book blogging on the motivation of 3rd-grade students. *Online Submission*, 1-8.

Vygotsky, L. S. (1978). *Mind in society: The development of higher psychological processes*. Cambridge, MA: Harvard University Press.

Wong, R. M., & Hew, K. F. (2010). The impact of blogging and scaffolding on primary school pupils' narrative writing: A case study. *International Journal of Web-Based Learning and Teaching Technologies, 5*(2), 1–17. doi:10.4018/jwltt.2010040101.

Wrede, O. (2003, May). *Weblogs and discourse: Weblogs as a transformational technology for higher education and academic research*. Paper presented at the Blogtalk Conference. Vienna, Austria. Retrieved from http://wrede.interfacedesign.org/articles/Weblogs-and-discourse

Zawilinski, L. (2009). Hot blogging: A framework for blogging to promote higher order thinking. *The Reading Teacher, 62*(8), 650–661. doi:10.1598/RT.62.8.3.

Chapter 5
Composing Online:
Integrating Blogging into a Contemplative Classroom

Kendra N. Bryant
Florida A&M University, USA

ABSTRACT

"The Internet is the most appealing and expressive technology that humanity has ever encountered; the point for teachers is not to push that round peg into our square hole, but to make the Internet a productive technology for what people inherently want to do, make sense with each other."-Fred Kemp

This chapter invites writing instructors to consider integrating blogging practices as a writing exercise that both supports the 21ˢᵗ Century Google-aged learner and the contemplative writing classroom. The author suggests that blogging mirrors traditional personal voice writing and, if supported by a mindful practice such as freewriting, can assist students in bringing all of their faculties into the classroom, thus providing a more holistic and meaningful learning experience.

INTRODUCTION

Five years ago, I did not know anything about blogging, nor did I belong to any online social network. So when I was required to use WordPress, Twitter, and Facebook while in my doctoral program, I felt like a fish out of water. I did not own a laptop or smartphone, and I did not feel I was as technologically adept as my white peers. As the only African American in my program, I felt much like the African American students that Samantha Blackmon (2007) acknowledges do not have equal material and intellectual access to computers in comparison to their more affluent white counterparts. Needless to say, I kind of hated the Rhetoric and Technology course I was required to take, and my dis-ease exhibited itself in the shoddy work I produced. I did not want to engage in Twitter discussions, create a classroom community through Facebook, or blog my responses to classroom readings. I wanted pen and paper. And I wanted to be in an embodied classroom, where, according to Janet Emig (2001), "learning takes place within authentic communities of inquiry with physical others" (p. 273).

I eventually got over my disdain for composing with technologies, perhaps simply because I could not get around it. When I began teaching Professional Writing, the textbook I adopted heavily supported online communities for professional

DOI: 10.4018/978-1-4666-4341-3.ch005

networking, Websites for professional portfolios, and wikis for collaborative work. I could not ignore the responsibility I had as a classroom composition teacher to meet my Google Generation students where they were and to equip them with the necessary tools to be meaningful contributors to their technologically empowered communities. I needed to get with the program—literally—and effectively integrate technologies into my writing curriculum so that I could help writing students make meaning of themselves and others with the communication technologies with which they were familiar. And of course, as any good teacher does, I had to first familiarize myself with these technologies, particularly with blogging.

I have been using WordPress in my writing classrooms for four years now, and my appreciation of it increases with each new group of students. This essay explores my most recent endeavor with integrating WordPress into a contemplative reading and writing space I created for Florida A&M University's (FAMU) Improving Writing students.

THEORETICAL FRAMEWORK

Understanding Freewriting as a Contemplative Practice

As defined by the *Oxford Education Dictionary*, contemplation is "the action of beholding or looking at with attention and thought; the action of thinking about a thing continuously; attentive consideration, study." It is an exercise in deep concentration, which, in a contemplative classroom, can be honed by using the first ten minutes of class time to engage students in mindful breathing wherein they sit quietly and focus on their breath. According to Amy Saltzman, founder of the Association for Mindfulness in Education, "Mindfulness practices help students focus and pay attention. A few minutes of mindfulness practice can improve the learning environment" (*mindfuleducation.org*, 2013). By focusing on

the breath, students are being trained to let go of the "monkey mind" that mindful practitioners (Jon Kabat-Zinn, Arthur Zajonc, and Thich Nhat Hanh) claim contribute to feelings of inferiority, loneliness, confusion, and fragmentation. And so, a contemplative *writing* pedagogy is an approach to writing instruction that infuses traditional writing practice with the experience of present awareness. Peter Elbow's freewriting exercise, when done mindfully, can garner such present awareness. His freewriting practice is akin to a meditative writing practice because it encourages writers to write without stopping for an allotted time—usually ten minutes—thus mirroring mindful breathing practice.

Like breathing meditation, where students are trained to acknowledge their thoughts and to let go of them by refocusing their attention to their breaths (Kabat-Zinn, 1990; mindfuleducation.org, 2013), freewriting allows students to let go of their thoughts (including inhibitions, inferiorities, confusions about writing, reading, or even the day's events) through non-stop writing. According to Elbow, once writers are able to give up control of their writing—particularly regarding English pragmatics, conventions, and standards—their writing skills will increase, for they will be uninhibited by the insecurities that result in "bad writing" (1981, p. 5). And so, the practice of nonstop writing and letting go is a practice in mindfulness.

Mindfully freewriting becomes a contemplative writing practice in two ways: 1). It anchors students' attention to the day's lesson, thus allowing them to be more deeply engaged; and 2). It records students' ideas, allowing them to notice their thoughts so that they can identify and interrupt patterns that keep them stuck in old habits that do not serve their whole person—mind, body, and soul. Other examples of classroom mindfulness practice include paying attention to sounds in the classroom, feeling the stomach rise and fall with each breath, and engaging in mindful looking by way of eye trick images. When students are able to focus their attention and fall into still, quite spaces, they make room for creativity and new ways of thinking and being (Kabat-Zinn, 1991; Hanh 1991; *mindfulness.org*, 2013). This practice in mindfulness enables them to interrupt patterns that keep them stuck in dis-eased behaviors such as hatred, loneliness, and confusion, so that transformation is made possible—which is one of the goals of contemplative practice: to enter into the still, quiet place of one's personhood wherein lies patience, love, peace, and understanding of self and others. With this goal in mind, contemplative classroom practices are essential to the well-being of students living in this Digital-Reality TV-WorldStarHipHop[1] Age.

Understanding the Relationship between Freewriting and Blogging

Because freewriting is a traditional writing practice with which most composition teachers are familiar (Tobin, 2001, p. 8), it serves as a point of reference for understanding how blogging is an appropriate activity for the 21st century contemplative writing classroom. A blog—in the context of my discussion—is simply an online journal, similar to the commonplace books that Renaissance students were required to keep (and similar to modern day writing portfolios). In commonplace books, Renaissance students collected significant passages and quotes, notes from their readings, and other important phrases (Miller & Shepherd, 2009, p. 1464)—all of which expanded their thoughts, developed their intellect, and nourished their spirits. A blog, then, is like a 21st century commonplace book, for it is a place where students can collect significant videos, graphics, text, and images, so they, too, can focus their attention and develop their personhood.

What's more, the act of blogging is journaling (Stefanone & Jang, 2008). Since St. Augustine wrote himself into a peace of mind with his *Confessions* (398 AD), composition theorists, particularly advocates of the 1960s Process Movement, (Elbow,

1973; Moffett, 1982; Gallehr, 1994) support journaling and personal narrative writing as exercises in both personal development and agency. Such "expressivist" writing was important in helping students, especially struggling writers, to find their voices in the academy, as well as to assist students in making meaning for themselves during times of increased political rhetoric and civil unrest (Clark, 2003, p. 1-29; Reynolds et al., 2004, p. 7-8). Undoubtedly, then, during this current age of war, environmental pollution, publicized hatred, and continued racism, human beings have turned to blogging for the solace and affirmation that personal journals and diaries once provided. "The blogger is her own audience, her own public, her own beneficiary," says Miller and Shepherd (2009, p. 1461). Since writing has drastically shifted as a result of computer technologies, blogging is apropos to current space-time—especially if writing instructors aim at meeting students where they are and enabling them to understand themselves and the world around them on their own terms.

Integrating Technology into a Contemplative Classroom Space

The idea of integrating a computer technology practice into a contemplative reading and writing space seems daunting. Many scholars (Kabat-Zinn, 1990; Pearsall, 1998; Siegel, 2007) support contemplative pedagogies as a remedy to the fatigue, fragmentation, weariness, and attention deficits that technology use seems to induce in most learners. Integrating technology into the contemplative reading and writing space appears counterproductive to the goal of a contemplative pedagogy—to nourish innate qualities via silent, calm spaces. Popular debates regarding technology's "programming" support these contemplative educators' notions.

According to Carr (2008), Goldstein (2009), Mowe (2010), and Richtel (2010), too much technology use can actually deter the brain from processing lengthy texts, prohibit it from solidifying experiences, and keep it from cultivating new ideas. In his 2008 "Is Google Making Us Stupid?" Nicholas Carr argues that the Internet shapes people's thought processes: "[W]hat the Net seems to be doing is chipping away my capacity for concentration and contemplation. My mind now expects to take in information the way the Net distributes it: in a swiftly moving stream of particles" (p. 2). Carr believes he is becoming the technology he uses, and therefore, is no longer "a scuba diver in the sea of words," but is a guy on a jet ski, zipping along the surface (p. 2). His experiences, which reflect the experiences of most avid Internet users, suggest that technology use may actually conflict with a contemplative reading and writing classroom.

Similarly, Douglas Rushkoff in *Program or Be Programmed* (2010) claims computers and networks "not only copy our intellectual processes. . . but they also discourage. . . our higher order cognition, contemplation, innovation, and meaning making" (p. 23). He also argues that social networking communities, with which most students are active members, are places of decentralization (p. 41). If social networking communities contribute to the fragmentation that I propose demands a contemplative pedagogy, why would I even consider integrating WordPress—an online social networking community—into the contemplative reading and writing classroom? As members of a busied society that is already so injured by wars, sickened with disease, fragmented by hate, lonely from detachments—and now, experiencing disconnection with each other because of its strong connection to technology— a learning environment devoid of computerized technologies would appear to be the first step in cultivating a contemplative classroom; it would, at least, be the easiest step.

However, while Rushkoff claims that users should "program or be programmed," and Carr questions if "Google is making us stupid," they both acknowledge that human beings can become efficient and productive as a result of technology use, that innovative computer technologies have allowed people to read and write more now than they did in the 1970s or 1980s, and that "[t]here is a place for humanity . . . in the new cybernetic order" (Rushkoff, 2010, p. 18). I believe one of those places for writing students is in classroom blogging, particularly if supported by a contemplative freewriting practice.

Considering Blogging as an Exercise in Attention Focusing

A blog is an online writing space that—with the ability to insert links, post videos and images, compose texts, and receive comments—is a possible place for increased focus and attention, as well as creativity. In a Digital Age wherein students have tossed leather journals, paper collages, and processed film for Facebook, Instagram, and Tumblr—blogging seems to be a communications technology that is conducive to this generation of student writers. As Carr notes, this computer generation of people are engaged in a different kind of reading, "and behind it lies a different kind of thinking—perhaps even a new sense of the self" (2008, p. 2). He claims that hyperlinks, blinking ads, and other digital trinkets, cause readers to glance at these distractions while trying to read (or skim) an Internet source (p. 5). "The result is to scatter our attention and diffuse our concentration," he says, and because our brains are malleable, "we inevitably begin to take on the qualities of those technologies"—which do not include contemplation (pp. 4-5).

But, WordPress—as a content management system (similar to traditional writing portfolios) that allows users to essentially create a Website and write a blog enhanced by video clips, images, and links—could possibly invite students' scattered brains into a space that encourages a focused attention.

In "Concentration and Contemplation: A Lesson in Learning to Learn" (2007), Robert Altobello claims that college-level learning unfolds in three stages including "acquiring and understanding intellectually challenging information"; "developing a critically reflective posture in relation to the information"; and "integrat[ing] the student's creative thought processes with the learning developed in the first two stages" (p. 355). He claims that the third stage of learning "characterizes a mature upper-division level of discourse" that illustrates a student's ability to deeply understand, critically reflect, thoroughly research, and creatively engage with material, that they eventually begin to own (p. 355). Altobello then makes a clear distinction between concentration and contemplation, noting that concentration is "the focusing of attention," while contemplation is "the engaging of one's focused attention" (p. 357). He concludes, "Students need to develop models of learning that immerse them in the material they are studying" and that the intellectual tools that teachers provide students to deepen their "immersion" be an energy that reflects student interest (p. 357). Integrating WordPress into the contemplative writing classroom, then, is a familiar and popular computer technology that has the potential to assist students in engaging Altobello's three levels of higher learning. In addition, Altobello's ideas regarding the significance of contemplative practices to hone students' attention are deeply rooted in Peter Elbow, who in *Writing without Teachers* (1973), likens the writing process to cooking.

Altobello's first level regarding intellectual acquisition can be achieved by way of traditional freewriting practice wherein students practice concentration by pouring all of their attention into a particular writing topic. After their freewriting period, students can then engage Altobello's second stage—reflection—by silently reading over their freewritten page(s), as well as collaboratively discussing their ideas with other classmates. Finally, students can achieve Altobello's third stage of learning by way of a blogging activity that requires students to totally immerse themselves into that particular topic by integrating links, videos, and graphics into their final compositions. In a way,

blogging gives students the tools and the space to engage in a *mestiza rhetoric*—which, according to Gloria Anzaldúa, is a "rich mixture of genres" that allows a writer to find her voice in the multiplicity of artistic voices (Lunsford, 2004, p. 35). By integrating technology, particularly blogging practices, into the contemplative reading and writing classroom, teachers can assist the jet ski writer in learning how to scuba dive so she can be a more holistic student who doesn't fragment her mind through technology use, but is able to focus and deepen her mind with it.

METHODOLOGY AND PEDAGOGY

Purpose

FAMU's Improving Writing course requires me to cover four basic units: business writing, contemporary issues, film, and grammar and mechanics. I am not required to integrate technology in the writing classroom—a fact that would have relieved me five years ago, but alarms me now. As an African American professor who has graduated from a Predominantly White Institution (PWI), I experienced how crucial writing with communications technologies is to one's academic and professional endeavors. As a matter of fact, during my first year teaching freshman composition at a PWI, one of my black male students dropped out of school because he said he could not keep up with the technological requirements of the university; he was a transfer student from a historically black university.

According to Snipes, Ellis, and Thomas (2004), "The African American community is far behind the white community in terms of computer and Internet usage, and the digital divide is large between white and African American college students" (p. 383)—which would explain why that student I encountered grappled with the technological requirements of the University. However, according to Zickhur & Smith's *2012*

Pew Internet and American Life Project Report, while "differences in [I]nternet access still exist among different demographic groups," those differences are not reflected in African Americans' use or access (*pewinternet.org*, 2013). According to their report "Digital Differences," African Americans are trailing closely behind White Americans in their Internet use; 71% of African Americas use the Internet, while 80% of White Americans use it. But, more African Americans than White Americans own smartphones and use their smartphones to access the Internet. Table 1 offers more evidence of the changes in the Digital Divide.

While the gap between Internet access and use has drastically shifted between African Americans and White Americans—much of which is a result of how growing technologies allow one to access the Internet—the fact remains that African Americans are still far behind White Americans in their ability to use current technologies to improve their writing, to compose a professional online persona, and to make meaning of themselves and others. And so, the changes in the Digital Divide do not determine African Americans' ability to use computer technologies in their writing classrooms. While African Americans outnumber White Americans in their access to and use of the Internet via their smartphones (*pewinterent.org*, 2013), many of them are solely *consumers* of technology whose ownership has more to do with "swag" than it does academic growth

and development. Therefore, failing to teach African American students how to write, utilize, and make meaning of themselves and others with current technologies can potentially push some of them further toward the margins; for many do not know how to use computer technologies to write themselves into existence—let alone into an academic and professional space, or a space for social change. Due to this threat of marginalization, at FAMU I began using WordPress to equip my students with marketable skills, all while accomplishing the four basic units of the Improving Writing course, so that they could write themselves into a digital writing environment that Blackmon claims excludes African Americans.

In addition to integrating communications technologies into a predominantly black writing classroom whose students needed instruction in technology use, I wanted to create a contemplative classroom space for my Improving Writing students because at the time of this study FAMU was cloaked in negative energy: FAMU made (and remained in) national news regarding a hazing incident that resulted in the death of a " Marching 100" band member; the University was also placed on a year-long accreditation probation, and it was ranked four on the FBI's "The 25 Most Dangerous College Campuses"—although later reports confirmed faulty methodology in the FBI's rankings (Adams, 2012). Considering the stress employed on FAMU and its students—3,000 of which are also on academic probation—I figured

Table 1. Digital divide

Online Activities	Search	Email	Buy Products	Use Social Networks	Bank Online
Race/Ethnicity					
White, Non-Hispanic	93%	92%	73%	63%	62%
Black, Non-Hispanic	91%	88%	74%	70%	67%
Hispanic (English and Spanish-Speaking)	87%	86%	59%	67%	52%
(Statistics taken from *Pew Internet and American Life Project Report* at *pewinterent.org*, 2013)					

I could help students to nourish their spirits and to ground their attention to classroom matters by providing them with a contemplative classroom space complete with mindfulness activities and contemplative reading and writing assignments. Since blogging is similar to journaling, blogging, when supported by freewriting, allowed me to integrate technology into the writing classroom while maintaining the integrity of a contemplative classroom space.

Participants and Setting

Students participating in this study were undergraduates at FAMU. With the exception of one female Hispanic teenager, 49 students who participated are African American. Forty-one students were between 20 and 29 years old; eight students were under 20; and one student was between 40-54 years old. Many of the students are products of low-income housing and are first generation college students. In addition, many of them have experienced homelessness, gun violence, sexual abuse, teenage pregnancy, learning disabilities, and divorce. (Student experiences were exposed after the curriculum was developed.) Each student enrolled in Improving Writing 2300 because the course met their requirements for graduation; none of them were English majors. Instead, students' course of study included Criminal Justice, Business, or Social Work.

The study took place at the predominantly and historically black Florida A&M University, which was founded in 1887 to meet the needs of the underrepresented and underprivileged. It is the only historically black university in the eleven member State University System and currently services circa 13,000 students—99% of which receive financial aid. In 2012, *Forbes Magazine* named FAMU one of "America's Top Colleges" as well as one of America's "Best Research Colleges." In 1997 *Time Magazine-Princeton* selected FAMU as the "1997-1998 College of the Year."

Classroom Survey

Because a digital divide does exist between black and white students regarding computer access and familiarity, (Blackmon, 2007; Snipes, Ellis, & Thomas, 2006) I did not assume that neither my African American students nor Florida A&M University had the same level of computer access like the students I taught at the University of South Florida (USF). So, before introducing students to a technologically-integrated writing curriculum, I used Acrobat's Adobe *FormCentral* to survey their computer access and use, as well as to gather demographic information and to get a feel of their writing habits and beliefs (See Figures 1-4).

Out of 49 African Americans and one Hispanic student surveyed, each of them had computer access at either home or work, school or the public library. In addition, each student accessed the Web via smartphone and/or computer and belonged to a social network; four of them already had a WordPress account. However, with the exception of those four students, none were familiar with WordPress, nor were any engaged in regular blogging. Once I understood that each student did have out of school access to computers and the Internet, I proceeded with my curriculum.

Required Resources

I adopted two textbooks for my Improved Writing course at FAMU: Bovée and Thill's 4th edition of *Business Essentials* (2009) and *Power to the Pen: Finding Agency through Argument* (2010), a textbook anthology that a former colleague and I edited for the First Year Composition program at USF. I also recommended Purdue University's Online Writing Lab (OWL). These three references allowed me to introduce students to business writing, blogging, responding to film and contemporary issues, as well as practicing standard American grammar, punctuation, and

Figure 1. Student demographics. This figure provides demographical information on the students who participated in blogging activities.

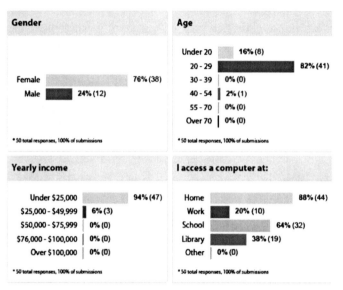

Figure 2. Student technology use. This figure provides information on how student technology use.

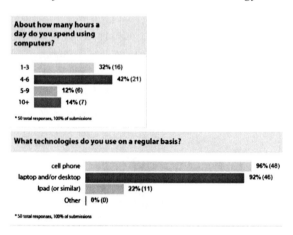

Figure 3. Student online communities. This figure details the online communities to which student participants belong.

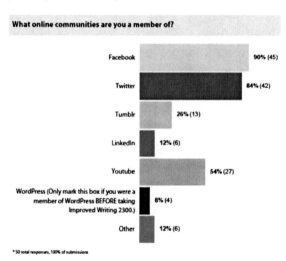

capitalization—the four required units for the Improving Writing course.

Resource requirements, along with summaries of the course description, its objectives, method of instruction, policies, grading criteria, and tentative weekly schedule were made available through the syllabus. The class syllabus also included a brief note that mentioned my contemplative approach

to teaching. Both O'Reilley (1998) and Schiller (1999) contend that including a paragraph or so about a contemplative approach to teaching encourages students who are not usually asked to bring their heart matters into the classroom to remain receptive and patient.

Figure 4. Student writing habits. This figure provides some insight on student writing habits and preferences.

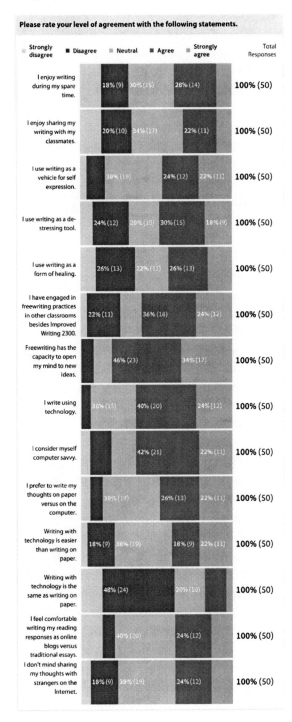

Creating a Contemplative Classroom Space

For the first class assignment, students were required to type and email as a Word attachment an essay responding to the question: "What Is Your Purpose?" As is the case for most English teachers, I used this essay in order to gauge students' writing skills, their personalities, as well as their computer abilities. This essay was not graded, but heavily commented on—specifically with personal comments that allowed me to forge a connection with each student. Building relationships with students by engaging their interests through teacher comments, as well as knowing each student by his or her name, are the first steps in creating a mindful classroom space (Schoeberlein & Sheth, 2009). I also placed students in accountability groups.

With an enrollment of 50 students—25 students in each class—there were five groups of five students. While I have experienced student resentment with group work in the past, these particular groups were not required to complete a group assignment for grading. Instead, they were required to read and discuss each other's responses (freewritten and blogged), engage in peer review, help one another understand challenging readings, as well as offer and submit work for absent classmates. Essentially, students collaboratively practiced mindful listening, reading, and speaking, while also practicing empathy, patience, and loving-kindness with one another. According to Schoeberlein & Sheth, "Academic performance improves when students feel safe and connected" (p. 71). Once students became more familiar with each other and with me, we were able to freely engage one another as a community of learners.

Moreover, our mindful classroom space was enhanced by a clean environment, equipped with spacious student desks, a teacher computer and projector, a wall of windows, as well as dimming lights. I usually held class with the lights dimmed allowing natural light to illuminate our classroom space. It provided a more relaxed and calming atmosphere, which a contemplative classroom requires.

(Initially) Building WordPress Accounts

Aside from the initial essay that students wrote, students did not engage in other class readings and assignments until they created a WordPress account. As is my method for all classes I teach, I gave students relatively brief instructions for the account; I wanted to see where students were in regards to their ability to follow directions and complete tasks. And so, via email, I sent students a memo directing them to go online and build a WordPress account using their first and last name as their address. Their account required three pages entitled "About Me," "My Resume," and "My Personal Philosophy." Students were also required to personalize their accounts by choosing a theme that illustrated their personalities, uploading a professional picture of them for their "About Me" page, and replacing WordPress's default tagline with a quote that best represents their philosophies. They were also required to write and post an autobiographical sketch to their "About Me" pages; the other two pages were to be completed at a later date. I also provided students the link to my own WordPress portfolio as an example of the work they would be producing throughout the semester, along with a chapter reading from Bovée and Thill about blogging. Finally, I suggested that they meticulously read through the WordPress site, and Google or contact WordPress Tech Support for any questions and/or problems they could potentially face. Students had two weeks to build their accounts and to send the link to their Wordpress addresses to me via email. From their submissions, I determined what skills I needed to help students develop and practice. Once accounts were created, with my personal WordPress account

projected for the class to follow, I dedicated an entire class period to answering student questions and concerns regarding WordPress. I also showed them how to link pages, insert video and graphics, as well as save Word documents as PDFs.

Building Professional Portfolios with WordPress

With chapter readings from Bovée and Thill, along with my instruction and suggestions from Purdue OWL, students were directed to write the resume, application letter, and personal statement. Each assignment was peer and teacher reviewed; students' business documents were also used to assess and practice class issues with grammar, punctuation, and capitalization. Once in final draft form, students were required to add their resumes and personal statements to their WordPress pages. (Because application letters are usually written for a specific company or person, application letters were not uploaded to student WordPress sites. I did not want to "narrow" students' online portfolios.) Students had the option of either uploading their full documents or linking them as Word or PDF documents to their pages.

Freewriting about Contemporary Readings and Blogging Responses

A contemplative classroom doesn't necessarily require "contemplative" readings. However, assigning readings that provoke emotion assist students in connecting with the author and/or character(s) and evaluating their own personhood, thus allowing them to more readily engage in contemplative reading practice (Suhor, 2002). With emotive readings in mind, I required students to read essays such as Parkers' "What Is Poverty?" (1971), the introduction to Alice Walker's *We Are the Ones We Have Been Waiting For* (2006), Langston Hughes' "Salvation" (1940), Audre Lorde's "Poetry is Not A Luxury" (1977), and even a poem about my own molestation, "For Me, For

My Mother, and For Those Who Keep Secrets" (2004). Students received the readings as PDFs prior to class meetings so they could be prepared to discuss them during class time. Students also received lecture and chapter readings on how to critically and actively read. Also, as a contemplative reading practice, I advised students to mark words, lines, or small passages that particularly connected with them—an exercise similar to the monastic reading practice called *lectio divina* that assists readers in making meaning of a text (Lichtmann, 2005).

At the start of each class meeting, after grounding students into the classroom community by calling each student by his or her name and literally asking each student how he or she was, I engaged students in a 10-minute freewrite about the assigned reading. For instance, after assigning Walker's *We Are the Ones*, students were required to freewrite about the text. No rules. No guidelines. No professor commentary. Just write for ten minutes about the reading. After the ten minutes expired, students were then directed to get into their accountability groups and discuss both the reading and their freewrite responses. I allotted 15-20 minutes for collaboration, at the end of which, one spokesperson from each group summarized their group members' ideas for the entire class. This activity further engaged students in mindful listening practice. Group summaries led to whole class discussions about the reading and eventually evolved into students' sharing their joys and sorrows, prejudices, insecurities, and confusions. For homework, students were directed to reread Walker's text and to post a blog (inclusive of links, videos, and images if they choose) in response to the reading. They were reminded to contemplate their freewrites, group collaboration, and class discussion. They were also required to comment on each of their group members' postings, in an attempt to build an online community and engage their classmates as authors.

DATA COLLECTION

Student blog responses were not graded, but students were required to submit a hard copy of their posts to me so that I could comment on them and give them a completion credit. While I followed each of their blogs online, I did not want to provide teacher-like comments in their public blogging spaces. As a member of their blogging community, when I left comments on student posts, I was not a teacher, but another blogger. However, in the classroom space, I wrote comments on their hand-submitted posts that were intended to improve their basic writing, comprehension, and critical thinking skills. And so, for the 14-week semester, about 10 of which were actually devoted to blogging practices, I collected student blogs and traditionally assessed them for English pragmatics, student participation, comprehension, and thought processing.

In addition to collecting, reading, and comparing student blogs throughout the semester, I also gave students weekly four-five question quizzes that served as informal evaluations (for my own research) regarding their reading and blogging practices as well as determined their homework participation; quizzes also encouraged on-time attendance. Quiz questions included inquiries such as:

- When you went home to blog about Walker's *We Are the Ones*, was your blog an extension of your freewrite or did you choose a specific part of your freewrite to expand on? Explain.
- Do you think if our class was held in a computer lab, blogging about the readings would feel different? Explain.
- Do you think had you sat in front of a computer freewriting versus writing with pen and paper that you would have produced the same thoughts? The same number of pages? Why or why not?

I also collected data by way of observation and class discussion. While students worked in their accountability groups, I walked around the classroom listening to (and sometimes engaging in) their conversations. I paid close attention to how students interacted with one another, for one of my class objectives was to forge classroom community and to improve student empathy. During our class discussions, I usually asked one student from each group to share their group's responses with the whole class. Group "leaders" could share responses from blogs, in-class freewrites, or that day's group discussion. These group reports usually led to healthy debates about religion and spirit, forgiveness, and writing practices, and often served as spaces for testimony—both of which further enabled me to gauge the effects of integrating blogging practices into a contemplative classroom space.

At the semester's end, students were required to write a final blog to be posted under their Personal Philosophy tab on their WordPress pages. This final blogging exercise challenged students to think about themselves as both writers and human beings. Students were required to use class readings, discussions, freewrites, and blogs to support the personal philosophies they were declaring in their final narratives. Although this assignment served as students' final writing project, it served as an assessment regarding the possibility of blogging as a practice that improves student writing, as well as attends to and develops students' personhood.

Moreover, during the last week of classes, students were asked to respond (in-class) to an informal, anonymous ten question questionnaire that asked them about their feelings and future plans regarding blogging.

RESULTS AND DISCUSSION

- Contemplative classroom reading and writing assignments supported by mindful practices nurtured and opened student minds and hearts.

On the last day of classes, my Improving Writing students gave me their hearts; their offerings were quite unexpected. I was giving my end-of-the-semester spiel, and at its close, I opened the floor for any questions regarding final grades and the like. The one Hispanic student in the class raised her hand first, and as soon as I thought she was going to ask me when I'd have their final papers graded, she told me, instead, how much she appreciated the class. The classroom readings validated her, she said. And when she flew to New York to interview for a job there, she was able to use her classroom experiences to answer the question: *How would you use technology to improve writing?* "I wouldn't have been able to answer that question had I not been in your class," she said. "I am really glad you taught us about blogging."

Then another student (who termed me "tree hugger") raised his hand, and he confessed that before taking this class he had not enjoyed reading, but now he wants to read all of the time. Then he turned around to his classmates and thanked them for allowing him to share his ideas with them. That student was misplaced by, but survived, Hurricane Katrina. During our reading of Audre Lorde's "Poetry Is Not A Luxury," he read an original poem aloud to his classmates about having to swim through New Orleans' muddy waters in order to retrieve food for his family. His reading to the class was his first time sharing his poetry with an audience.

Then another hand shot up—from a student who was newly mothered and married. She shared with me her experienced childhood sexual abuse after the class read and discussed "For Me, for My Mother, and for Those Who Keep Secrets." "Initially," she said, "I was offended by all of the comments you'd write on my papers because they made me feel like I wasn't a good writer. But your feedback helped me to improve my writing, and so, I really appreciate you for taking the time to read my work." The students laughed and echoed her sentiments, one claiming that she used to talk back at her papers after taking them home for revision.

And another student—who went home for Thanksgiving that semester to find that her mother could not afford to pay the water and electric bill, thus forcing her to relive the poverty that attending FAMU was relieving her from—claimed that she learned more in this class than she had in any of the English classes she had taken at FAMU thus far. In her Thanksgiving blog, she shared her misfortunes with her classmates, but she also acknowledged her mother's efforts and claimed her appreciation for simply being with her mother.

When class ended, students hugged me and shook my hand, and those who didn't share with the class, extended their gratitude to me privately. With the exception of high school classrooms, I had not experienced such expressions of gratitude in the postsecondary environment. And so, one thing I know for sure is that creating a contemplative classroom space complete with contemplative reading and writing assignments invites empathy, understanding, forgiveness, gratitude, community, and love into the classroom. A contemplative classroom makes possible a meaningful learning experience for both students and teachers.

- Blogging did not free students from the writing demands and expectations that often contribute to student inferiority and "voicelessness," but actually contributed to student censorship.

Considering that many students seem to both waive their privacy rights and rights to standard American English while engaged in particular social networks such as Twitter, Facebook, and Instagram, I found students' concerns regarding posting their reader responses to a public site quite contradictory to their current online behaviors. However, for many students, blogging with Word-Press felt like an academic exercise; it felt quite scholarly, for blogging required students to claim a writer's hat. So, students paid careful attention to writing conventions because they didn't want to appear "stupid" to their vast public audience.

Although their desire to "sound smart" improved their proofreading, editing, and revising abilities, it also got in the way of their writing as authentically as they did in their classroom freewrites. Some of their blogs actually sounded like the "Engfish" Macrorie discusses in his *Telling Writing* (1970), and therefore, the blogs initially sounded . . . well, they absolutely bored me. I could not sense my students' genius, for they concealed their personhood with an institutional voice they thought I wanted to hear (or could understand).

In Figure 5 are a few student responses to the question: "Was blogging about the in-class poem, 'For Me, for My Mother, and for Those Who Keep Secrets,' different than freewriting about it in class?" They illustrate students' angst regarding blogging.

I thought I could remedy students' "Engfish," as well as their angst by encouraging them to integrate their personal stories into their responses and to type their first thoughts, which, according to Natalie Goldberg (2005), "have tremendous energy" and "are unencumbered by ego" (p. 9). I advised students to stop editing while typing and to stop thinking about the length of the page and anything else that clouded their free thinking and silenced their voices—which were vibrant and beautiful and black. I even suggested that they meditate for five to ten minutes before blogging and made space for some meditation practice in class, because according to mindfulness practitioners, meditating before class starts improves student focus and relieves their anxiety (Ball, 2011; Chawkin 2012; Mack, 2010; Suttie, 2009).

- Blogging convinced students to control and/or edit their emotions.

Once students familiarized themselves with blogging, they also became more conscious of their audience, which increased student awareness and fear regarding the exposure of their writing skills and personal information to a wider Internet audience. Many students confessed that they would

Figure 5. Student responses to blogging. The student responses provided here detail students' feelings about blogging responses versus freewriting them.

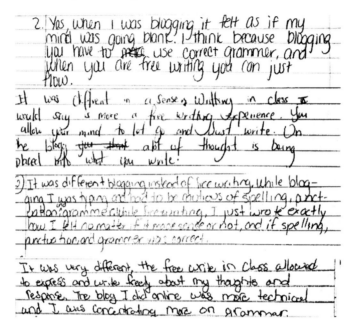

never publicly submit their freewrites and would not even give them to me because they were so emotionally charged. While students appreciated freewriting as a mindfuless practice that assisted them in contemplating a topic for blogging, they adamantly assured me that they would not publish such vulnerable writing in a public space; that kind of writing was too personal, they said. So, they took their freewritten essays and revised them into blogs that sounded more "academic," which based on their traditional American schooling, meant devoid of spirit and heart.

Sample ("Academic") Blog Responses to Naomi Klein's "No Logo"

Student Sample #1

This is a piece on company branding. It explains how huge companies went through phases of "branding". Where the focus was not on the products they produced but the image of the company to the consumers. These companies invested billions of dollars in this form of marketing with no real promise of it being wisely invested. The story shifts at certain points in history usually when one major company is struck by a misfortune. This has shown to change the direction of all the major companies listed in the story.

Student Sample #2

The article "No Logos" by Naomi Klein is about the history of brands and its impact on our modern world. This article describes its function and it evolution from promoting new inventions to the expansion of the company ego from advertisement and popularity. The article explain that after the depression there was a need for businesses to manufacture and produce their own products. However, as time progressed companies found it more efficient to manufacture overseas. This not only helped the companies save money on employment but, put their focus and money on the marketing aspect of business.

From student submissions and in-class discussions, I realized that students did not need help in freewriting or blogging, but in negotiating between the space between academic and personal writing. Students needed practice in developing an academic voice that reflected their personhood—a voice that reflected both their brains and their hearts. So, I eventually did away with the contemplative readings—which required some critical thinking skills—because students claimed that the readings contributed to their angst about academic writing. And so, I replaced readings with contemplative writing topics such as, "If you could describe your current disposition with a song, what song would you sing?" and "Describe your God." Blogging became easier for students, as did commenting on their peers' blogs; students had more to say about their personal experiences than they did about the readings, which encouraged their desire to maintain their blogs and to read their classmates' submissions.

Sample ("Non-Academic") Blog Responses to "Describe Your God"

Student Sample #1

I believe that you don't know God with without first knowing yourself, or at least taking steps to finding yourself. As you get to know yourself you find purpose, and through finding your purpose you live your life in a way that is conducive to fulfilling that purpose. I do not believe that heaven and hell exists in they way the bible teaches it, but that each individual creates his or her own heaven and hell on earth. An individual's inability to self reflect makes it hard for that person to spiritually grow. Through learning myself I found God, I journal everyday and that helps me record my progress or any setbacks.

Student Sample #2

I believe in God, his son Jesus Christ, and the Holy Spirit. As a child growing up I was forced to go to church and sit through very long services. All I really remember from my childhood being in church was that I could not chew gum, go to sleep in the front row, and I had to be in the Easter plays every year. There was no foundation being laid in who I was supposed to be praising and what all of it meant. I did not get a true meaning of who God was until I married my husband.

The task of helping students to find and retain their voice in academic settings still remains my challenge as a writing instructor. Clearly, integrating computer technologies into the writing classroom does not necessarily make students better, confident, or even more contemplative writers; and the publicity that technology garners definitely deters students from publishing "expressivist" writing.

- Blogging assisted students in forging online community that further enhanced their in-class community, as well as developed their empathy for one another.

Although students were already required to work in accountability groups throughout the semester, the act of blogging in a public space allowed students to forge relationship with students who were not in their groups. In other words, students were able to acquaint themselves with each of their classmates by engaging in their classmates' blogs. In the sample below, for instance, in her blog, Student #1 claims that she is not talented enough to write poetry. Student #2, though she does not name her target audience, responds to Student #1's declaration:

Student Sample #1

Every time I hear someone recite a poem I feel the power and emotion resonate through their poem. Poetry gives you the courage and power to do things because it allows you to explore yourself, and to also free yourself from whatever hurt or pain you are feeling. I honestly love reading and hearing poetry because it is so liberating. I just wish that I had the talent to write healing poetry so that I can tap into my inner self.

Student Sample #2

Many of my peers feel that they are not "deep enough" to write a poem, but little do they know that they create poetry every time they wake up just being themselves. They just haven't written it on a page yet.

In addition to building relationships by communicating with their peers directly through their blog posts, WordPress's commenting feature also encouraged student relationships.

Sample Student Comments to Student Blog Post on "Describe Your God"

Sample Student Comment #1

I don't exactly agree with you because I believe in a totally different God, but I respect your opinion. Everyone is entitled to their own beliefs. I do agree on the part where you stated "My God does not judge or hate" because my God doesn't either. God is known as Love but he is also known as a ruler of all the Earth. I cannot bash you or feel a certain way about you because we do not believe

in the same God. All I can say is God will show himself in due time.

Sample Student Comment #2

I enjoyed reading your response and really respect your opinion. My cousins feel the same way you do currently because my uncle forced religion down their throats and always preached about the way they should live rather than letting them be who they are. You are human and are entitled to your beliefs about any situation. You had several strong points I love that your "God is love" and "It does not judge or hate". The way you feel about God does not by any means hinder the view I have of you as a person because everyone's God is different and to each its own.

- Blogging required students to shift from a teacher-focused audience to a public audience, therefore encouraging student writers to actually speak to their readers. Student blog titles were also more creative than titles that usually accompany traditional writing assignments.

All too often, students write essays and the like for their English teacher because as the reader, commenter, and grader, the teacher, by default, becomes the students' sole audience. While composition instructors do well to urge students to "'consider your audience,'" says Irene Clark (2003), conceptualizing a fictional audience is challenging for writing students. From my teaching experience, students' obsession with grades deters them from writing to an audience outside of their teacher because that fictional audience is not grading their assignments. But blogging—because it is a publicized practice—enables students to consider various audiences; their teacher becomes an audience, their classmates, and possible Internet surfers. And if students linked their blogging sites to their other social networks, then their family and friends become possible audience members as well. As a result of students' awareness of audience, students' writing became more engaging, for students talked directly to their readers by way of pronoun reference, inquiry, and side notes. Students also played with fonts, as evidenced in the sample below:

Sample Student Blog Post to Parker's "What Is Poverty?"

*We ought to be ashamed of ourselves. Some people feel like they can't spare a few dollars to a homeless person begging for help. Some folks spit at the feet of those who can't help themselves. Some don't even consider the repercussions that will affect thousands of people if Medicare or social security is cut or 'vouched'. Some people do all of these things, but a lot of people do not even look back and consider assisting others. If everyone stopped and tried to support others this world would be a much better place. But sadly, we are all too busy thinking only of ourselves. We can't stop focusing on our needs and wants even though there are some who really need help. If we all got together and helped each other out no one would have to suffer. This is the type of world we should **need** to be striving for.*

Sample Student Blog Post to "Describe Your Current Disposition through Song"

Once I realized my potential I had to do better for myself and the future that I want. In "On and On" by Erykah Badu she sings If we were made in his image then call us by our names... We all have the ability to get in tune with ourselves to mold our own reality, but first one must realize their

power. I make sure to journal to free my mind, eat better (currently 4 months meat-free) to maintain my health, and do things that make me happy.

Awareness of audience also inspired more interesting student blog titles. Of the majority of student papers I receive—whether they are argumentative essays or personal narratives—students' titles usually lack creativity, personality, and clarity. However, because blogs are so public, students paid more attention to their titles, for they understood the title's role in inviting (or enticing) readers toward their posts. (See Table 2 for sample student blog titles)

- Blogging encouraged students to synthesize information and to apply their own knowledge to writing tasks.

Most students enter the classroom as if they are empty vessels to be filled, and so, they sit there, stale faced, waiting—and often wanting—teachers to pour knowledge into their heads. As often as Paulo Freire (1968), bell hooks (1994), and other liberatory education aficionados have argued against this "banking" concept of education, many students welcome the opportunity to be told what to think, how to think, when to think, and how

Table 2. Sample student blog titles

Blogging Topic	Student Titles
"What song describes your current disposition?" Note: Student titles are not actual song titles, but are variations or lines taken from their song choices.	Keep Your Head Up and Eyes Open "It's okay not to be okay" "Knowing my condition is the reason I must change…"
"Describe Your God."	I am not a Whack Job Atheist My God Alpha and Omega Supernova
"Write A Response to 'For Me, For My Mother, and For those Who Keep Secrets.'"	Breaking the Silence No Tolerance
"Write a Response to Naomi Klein's 'No Logos.'"	Logos Oh No Dear Cheerios

to express their thoughts—not because they are actually empty vessels to be filled or even believe they have nothing to contribute. However, many students' obsession with grades causes them to become machines, if you will. And they believe (and some of their classroom experiences support their notion) that regurgitating their teachers' lectures and philosophies will warrant them a passing grade.

This way of being in the classroom is often evident in traditional student essays wherein the novice writer fails to include any of his or her prior knowledge to the writing task. Since many students misbelieve that they don't know how to integrate their personal voices into their academic voices, students tend to ignore their personhood—including their experiences—and adopt an "Engfish" that purports to mimic good, academic writing. But blogging, perhaps because it is a type of journaling, enables students to freely write. Subconsciously, then, freewriting students are able to recall prior experiences, as well as summarize and synthesize information, thus increasing the interest, depth, and clarity of their writing assignments (Elbow, 1973). In addition, since the act of blogging carries an academic aura, students subconsciously, and successfully, teeter between their academic and personal voices, as evidenced in the student sample below:

Sample Student Blog Response to "Describe Your God"

I treat people how I want to be treated and learn how to trust my instincts. I try my best to not place judgement on others because I have my own skeletons and I understand that whatever energy I give out to this world I get back. Ralph Waldo Emerson and Henry David Thoreau wrote two of my favorite essays, "Nature" by Emerson and "Walden" by Thoreau. Both of these writes understood that it is necessary for man to understand and acknowledge their place on earth through solitude. Emerson

wrote "Standing on the bare ground, — my head bathed by the blithe air, and uplifted into infinite space, — all mean egotism vanishes. I become a transparent eye-ball; I am nothing; I see all; the currents of the Universal Being circulate through me; I am part or particle of God."

Integrating blogging practices into a contemplative classroom space did not make students more contemplative writers, per se. However, it did make students more mindful of their audience, their classmates, and their writerly selves. While English teachers usually direct students to mind their audience, their classmates, and their writer's voice, the act of blogging itself invoked students' awareness—which more or less placed the writing student in the teacherless classroom (Elbow, 1973). But, while teaching students how to blog afforded them the opportunity to use technology to improve their writing, integrating computer technologies into a contemplative reading and writing classroom actually contributed to the bulk of responsibilities I already had as a classroom teacher.

Certainly, blogs have garnered much popularity throughout the nation, but blogging on a social network like WordPress was just as, if not more challenging than, teaching students traditional journaling practice. As research already claims, the nature of the Internet has altered the way people read and write (Carr, 2008; Rushkoff, 2010). Reading has become an exercise in skimming pages, thus contributing to shallow writing; not to mention, most students, especially non-English majors, hate writing. Therefore, a social communications network like WordPress that requires bloggers to do much more than tweet or update their status was initially laborious for most of my Google-aged students who resembled Carr's jet skiers. Not only did they have to learn how to use this communications technology, but they also had to 1). read essays, one of which was at least 12 pages long; 2). freewrite their initial responses in class; 3). blog their contemplated responses—

which had to be at least one page each; 4). and if they so desired, revise their blogs.

Although students were required to blog outside of the classroom, many of them needed hands-on instruction for such tasks as uploading images, inserting links, adding videos, and manipulating their accounts. Watching me demonstrate WordPress use on a projected screen was not enough instruction for many students, and we did not hold class in a computer lab. So, until I was able to reserve the library's computer lab (FAMU's English Department doesn't have one of its own), I dedicated class time for WordPress instruction, stayed after class to assist students with their accounts, and even tried my best to instruct them via email. Surely, those who integrate any computer technology into their classroom space will probably have an easier, less time-consuming experience than I did, should their classroom be equipped with student computers. Likewise, students' classroom computer use will allow students to immediately blog responses to readings and writing prompts, which may then encourage teachers to do away with traditional freewriting—depending on the teacher's objectives, of course.

Nevertheless, during our one computer lab day, students spent the entire period on desktop computers updating, revising, tweaking, and understanding WordPress. I began that particular class reviewing the requirements for the WordPress account and showing students how to upload, link, and attach documents and media. Then I spent the remainder of the class time assisting students individually. But, at the end of that class, I no longer had to instruct students on WordPress use. In fact, a few of them closed the period through an informal presentation of their WordPress sites to the entire class. Not only had they grasped how to use important features of the program that allowed navigating the technology easier, but students felt skilled enough to teach their peers how to further develop their own WordPress sites. My students were no longer consumers of technology, but were

becoming users who could make the technology work for their personal growth.

At the start of the semester, however, I had not planned to have to dedicate so much of my time and energy into teaching students how to navigate WordPress. As members of the Google-aged generation, I grossly assumed that students could—or at least wanted to—independently work through computer technologies. And I had not realized then that my black students were "smartphone swaggers" versus computer users. But, because I was creating a contemplative classroom space and students had engaged in some meditation practice, both I and my students approached computer technologies more patiently and openly.

By the semester's end, students were deeply reading, openly collaborating, passionately freewriting, and thoughtfully blogging; they were significantly improving their writing, as they were practicing skills that assisted them in what Yagelski (2009) phrases, "writing themselves into being." And ultimately, that is my goal as a writing instructor: to help students uncover their brilliance and to teach them how to use their inherent knowingness to write their own stories. In an email one of my students sent me mid-semester, he said: "I have been patient with WordPress and every time I get on the site, I learn something new. Thanks for introducing WordPress to us! I can honestly say that thanks to your class I am becoming a better writer. I notice major improvements."

IMPLICATIONS

Despite the challenges and busyness that English teachers with little to no technology training encounter when teaching students how to use technologies, integrating a computer technology into the traditional classroom is fundamental to students' growth and development—specifically because the 21st Century is so technologically engrossed. Blogging allows students to practice basic computer skills, to build personal Websites, to find their online voices, to participate in and become members of online communities, and to create an online persona that contributes to their marketability.

As a practice in composition, blogging assists students in understanding audience, negotiating between their academic and personal voice, synthesizing and integrating prior knowledge, and peer reviewing each other's work. In addition, when supported by mindful freewriting practice, blogging invites students to contemplate their feelings and ideas; and as a content management system, the blog archives students' submissions making possible re-envisioning. In other words, as long as students have a WordPress account, they can read their thoughts over and over again—and perhaps identify fixed ideas and judgments that disrupt their peace of mind and/or contribute to their false notions of self and preconceived ideas of others. Blogging also awakens and encourages student creativity, as well as focused attention, as it allows students to enhance their posts with links, videos, and images. Furthermore, because WordPress is a public space, blogging fosters classroom relationship and empathy, as well as student agency, for students can more readily (and courageously) participate in class discussions by way of reading and commenting on each other's blogs.

CONCLUSION

During the last week of class, a male student informed me that he shared his blogging experiences with his mother, who is a middle school teacher. "I told her we are like real life Freedom Writers up in here," he said. His mother was so inspired by his classroom experiences and his enthusiasm that she employed WordPress in her own middle school class. Certainly, WordPress is a space that beckons the Freedom Writer in all students, for blogging invites students to holistically and truth-

fully engage in and explore their relationship with self and other beings.

As perhaps one of America's favorite pastimes, blogging has evolved from being a computer technology specific to USENET newsgroups who hosted discussions and publications to being a mainstream platform for breaking political news and pop-culture happenings (*wikipedia.org*, 2012). Such humble beginnings grew to 181 million blogs in 2011; three of them—Blogger, WordPress, and Tumblr—claimed top ten social networking spots, with viewership of 80 million (*nielsen.com*). Clearly, the advent of social technologies such as Twitter, Tumblr, Facebook, Wikipedia, and the like have catapulted the notion that Elbow suggested 40 years ago in his groundbreaking *Writing without Teachers* (1973). He claimed that students are inherently writers, thus charging compositionists to reconsider their purposes in the classroom as well as how they teach writing. And while composition theorists like David Bartholomae (1995) challenged Elbow's notions, claiming students need teachers to teach them how to write, today's computer technologies have forged a digital divide that now requires teachers to question, "What is 'writing'? Where is writing? [and] What does writing *do*?" [author's emphasis] (Eyman, 2011, p. 329).

While freewriting and "expressivist" writing are practices in mindfulness that support a contemplative reading and writing class, blogging is an appropriate and meaningful writing activity for a contemplative classroom made up of 21st century Google-aged learners. Freewriting before blogging allows students to release and contemplate their ideas, while blogging impels students to contemplate their writerly selves, their emotions and ideas, as well as their audience; and with WordPress users ability to insert links, images, and graphics, blogging invites students' focused attention.

And so, blogging practice—which for many students translates into "making my 'freewrites' public"—conjures students' awareness of audience. Such awareness helps students to be more mindful writers, as they are forced to reconsider their ideas, their voices, their writing approaches, their word choices, and the like. Such awareness also inspires student creativity—much of which has been doused by high school assessments. Hopefully student awareness of themselves as writers and composers will also make them more aware of their higher selves and their relationship to the rest of the world. On the contrary, however, student awareness of audience can potentially invite self-inflicted censorship. But even *that*—students' decision to censor and/or edit themselves—is self-liberating, for students take ownership of their writing and their personhood; they choose how much of their selves they want to offer the world.

Our students are supernovas, and teachers have to simply provide them the space to shine. "To teach is to create a space, [which] describes experiences of everyday life," says Parker Palmer (1983, pp. 69-70). Since technology is a staple in our society, teaching students how to use it to improve their writing and to compose their online personas make possible more centered, intuitive human beings who can more efficiently and effectively contribute to the technological world in which they live. For blogging practices supported by freewriting invite both right and left brain thinking—an integration of the heart and mind that allows students to be creative and logical, academic and organic; it invites the whole learner into the classroom for a more meaningful learning experience. And the blog, as a content management system (or online writing portfolio), allows students to interrogate their own ideas as well as develop a personal/professional Website that contributes to their marketability and efficacy in a Web-driven society.

REFERENCES

Adams, R. (2012). Revised list drops FSU, FAMU from 25 most dangerous campuses. *WCTV.TV*. Retrieved from http://www.wctv.tv

Altobello, R. (2007). Concentration and contemplation: A lesson in learning to learn. *Journal of Transformative Education*, 5(4), 354–371. doi:10.1177/1541344607312549.

St. Augustine. (398). *Confessions*.

Ball, J. (2011). How meditation can give our kids an academic edge. *Huffpost Living*. Retrieved from www.huffingtonpost.com

Bartholomae, D. (1995). Writing with teachers: A conversation with Peter Elbow. *College Composition and Communication*, 46(1), 62–71. doi:10.2307/358870.

Blackmon, S. (2007). (Cyber)conspiracy theories? African-American students in the computerized writing environment. In P. Takayoshi & P. Sullivan's (Eds.), Labor, writing technologies, and the shaping of composition in the academy: New directions in computers and composition (pp. 153-166). New York: Hampton Press.

Bovée, C., & Thill, J. (2009). *Business essentials* (4th ed.). Hoboken, NJ: Prentice Hall.

Bryant, K. (2004). *For me, for my mother, and for those who keep secrets. As I roc the mic* (pp. 43–46). Indianapolis, IN: Xlibris Corporation.

Bryant, K., & McKee, J. (Eds.). (2010). *Power to the pen: Finding agency through argument.* Boston: Bedford/St. Martin's.

Carr, N. (2008). Is Google making us stupid? What the Internet is doing to our brains. *The Atlantic*. Retrieved from http://www.theatlantic.com

Chawkin, K. (2012). *Meditation in the classroom: An antidote to stress.* Retrieved from http://www.nestressfreeschool.org

Clark, I. (2003). Process. In I. Clark's (Ed.), Concepts in composition: Theories and practice in the teaching of writing (pp. 1-29). Hoboken, NJ: Lawrence Erlbaum Associates.

Elbow, P. (1973). *Writing without teachers*. New York: Oxford University Press.

Elbow, P. (1981). *Writing with power: Techniques for mastering the writing process*. New York: Oxford University Press.

Emig, J. (2001). Embodied learning. *English Education, 33*(4), 271–280.

Eyman, D. et al. (2011). Computers and composition 20/20: A conversation piece, or what some very smart people have to say about the future. *Computers and Composition, 28*, 327–346. doi:10.1016/j.compcom.2011.09.004.

Freire, P. (1970). *Pedagogy of the oppressed*. New York: Continuum.

Gallehr, D. (1994). Wait and the writing will come: Meditation and the composing process. In Brand, A., & Grave, R. (Eds.), *Presence of mind: Writing and the domain beyond the cognitive* (pp. 21–30). Portsmouth, NH: Boynton/Cook.

Goldberg, N. (2005). *Writing down the bones: Freeing the writer within*. Boston: Shambhala.

Goldstein, E. (2009). Is it time to unplug? Technology and overconnection. *Psych Central*. Retrieved from http://blogs.psychcentral.com/mindfulness

Hanh, T. (1991). *Peace is every step: The path of mindfulness in everyday life*. New York: Bantam Books. hooks, b. (1994). *Teaching to transgress: Education as the practice of freedom*. New York: Routledge.

Hughes, L. (1940). Salvation. In Fine Clouse, B. (Ed.), *Patterns for a purpose: A rhetorical reader* (pp. 203–204). Boston: McGraw.

Kabat-Zinn, J. (1991). *Full catastrophe living: Using the wisdom of your body and mind to face stress, pain, and illness*. New York: Dell Publishing.

Lichtmann, M. (2005). *The teacher's way: Teaching and the contemplative life*. New York: Paulist Press.

Lorde, A. (1977). Poetry is not a luxury. In *Essays and speeches by Audre Lorde* (pp. 36–39). Thousand Oaks, CA: Crossing Press.

Lunsford, A. (2004). Toward a mestiza rhetoric: Gloria Anzaldúa on composition and postcoloniality. In A. Lunsford & L. Ouzgane's (Eds.), Crossing borderlands: Composition and postcoloniality studies (pp. 33-66). Pittsburgh, PA: University of Pittsburgh Press.

Mack, M. (2012). Meditation in schools. *Wildmind Buddhist Meditation*. Retrieved from http://www.wildmind.org/

Macrorie, K. (1970). *Telling writing*. Rochelle Park, NJ: Hayden.

Miller, C., & Shepherd, D. (2009). Blogging as social action: A genre analysis of the weblog. In Miller, S. (Ed.), *The Norton book of composition studies* (pp. 1450–1473). New York: W.W. Norton & Company, Inc..

Moffett, J. (1982). Writing, inner speech, and meditation. *College English, 44*(3), 231–246. doi:10.2307/377011.

Nielsen. (2011). *State of the media: U.S. digital consumer report, Q3-Q4 2011*. Retrieved from http://www.nielsen.com/us/en/insights/reports-downloads/2012/us-digital-consumer-report.html

O'Reilley, M. (1998). *Radical presence: Teaching as a contemplative practice*. Boynton/Cook Publishers.

Palmer, P. (1983). *To know as we are known: Education as a spiritual journey.* New York: HarperOne.

Parker, J. (1971). What is poverty? In Fine Clouse, B. (Ed.), *Patterns for a purpose: A rhetorical reader* (pp. 546–549). Boston: McGraw.

Pearsall, P. (1998). *The heart's code: Tapping the wisdom and the power of our heart energy.* New York: Broadway Books.

Reynolds, N., Bizzell, P., & Herzberg, B. (Eds.). (2004). *The Bedford bibliography for teaching of writing* (6th ed.). Boston: Bedford/St. Martin's.

Ritchel, M. (2010). Digital devices deprive brain of needed downtime. *New York Times.* Retrieved from http://www.newyorktimes.com

Rushkoff, D. (2010). *Program or be programmed: Ten commands for a digital age.* Berkeley, CA: Soft Skull Press.

Saltzman, A. (2013). *Association for mindfulness in education.* Retrieved from www.mindfuleducation.org

Schiller, S. (1999). Spirituality in pedagogy: A field of possibilities. *JAEPL, 5,* 57–68.

Schoeberlein, D., & Sheth, S. (2009). *Mindful teaching and teaching mindfulness: A guide for anyone who teaches anything.* Boston: Wisdom Publications.

Siegel, D. (2007). *The mindful brain: Reflection and attunement in the cultivation of well-being.* New York: W.W. Norton.

Snipes, V., Ellis, W., & Thomas, J. (2006). Are HBCUs up to speed technologically? One case study. *Journal of Black Studies, 36,* 382–395. doi:10.1177/0021934705278782.

Stefanone, M., & Jang, C. (2008). Writing for friends and family: The interpersonal nature of blogs. *Journal of Computer-Mediated Communication, 13,* 123–140. doi:10.1111/j.1083-6101.2007.00389.x.

Suhor, C. (2002). Contemplative reading—The experience, the idea, the applications. *English Journal, 91*(4), 28–32. doi:10.2307/822453.

Suttie, J. (2009). Mindfulness and meditation in schools for stress management. *Greater Good Magazine.* Retrieved from http://greatergood.berkeley.edu/

Tobin, L. (2001). Process pedagogy. In Tate, G., Rupiper, A., & Schick, K. (Eds.), *A guide to composition pedagogies* (pp. 1–18). New York: Oxford UP.

Walker, A. (2006). Introduction. In *We are the ones we have been waiting for: Inner light in a time of darkness.* New York: The New Press.

Wikipedia. (n.d.). *Blogging.* Retrieved November 30, 2012, from http://www.wikipedia.org

Yagelski, R. P. (2009). A thousand writers writing: Seeking change through the radical practice of writing as a way of being. *English Education, 42*(1), 6–28.

Zickhur, K., & Smith, A. (2012). Digital differences. *Pew Internet and American Life Project.* Retrieved from http://www.pewInternet.org

ENDNOTES

[1]   WorldStarHipHop is a Website notorious for publicizing violence. Similar to YouTube, it allows people to upload and share video online. However, WorldStarHipHop users usually showcase disruptive, violent, hateful, and dehumanizing behaviors to either embarrass and denigrate others or popularize self.

Chapter 6
The Disappearing Trace and the Abstraction of Inscription in Digital Writing

Anne Mangen
Oslo and Akershus University College, Norway

ABSTRACT

Due to increasing digitization, more and more of our writing is done by tapping on keyboards rather than by putting pen to paper. As handwriting is increasingly marginalized both inside and outside of schools, and children learn to write by typing "ready-mades" on different kinds of keyboards rather than by shaping each letter from scratch, we ought to acknowledge the physical and sensorimotor aspect of writing, in addition to the more typically studied cognitive and linguistic aspects. The shaping of letters and words in handwriting involve distinct kinesthetic processes that differ markedly from the kinesthesia involved in tapping keys on a keyboard. The ways in which we use our fingers and hands play an important role in perceptual and cognitive processing; hence, the shift from handwriting to typewriting might entail far-reaching cognitive as well as educational implications. This chapter reflects on some largely neglected aspects of the ongoing shift from handwriting to typewriting, focusing in particular on potential cognitive and phenomenological implications of the increasing abstraction of inscription entailed in typing on a keyboard, and the intangibility of the resulting text on screen compared to that produced by handwriting with pen on a material substrate such as paper.

INTRODUCTION: TOOLS AND TECHNOLOGIES – BODIES AND BRAINS

What is writing? It may seem uninformative, or perhaps redundant, to begin an article on the impact of digitization on writing with a question of such general nature. After all, we intuitively know what writing is; and if we do not, the steadily growing research literature on writing can inform us that it is a complex process involving the coordination of a number of cognitive or mental tasks (see, e.g., Alamargot & Chanquoy, 2001). However, as I will attempt to show in the following, the current digitization should make us pause to reflect on some fundamental and yet largely ignored dimensions of the physical nature of the writing process itself. More precisely, we might want to reconsider common notions of writing as primarily if not exclusively a cognitive process involving,

DOI: 10.4018/978-1-4666-4341-3.ch006

according to the most commonly referred model in cognitively oriented writing research (Flower & Hayes, 1981), planning (i.e., developing the writing plan and setting goals), translating (i.e., converting the plan into text), and reviewing (i.e., text reading and editing). The digitization of writing entails radical transformations of the very act of writing at a sensorimotor, physical level, and the (potentially far-reaching) implications of such transformations are far from properly understood. Hence, narrowing in on the physical, sensorimotor dimensions of the act of writing by hand and by different kinds of keyboards, combined with an awareness of the mediating role of the tools and technologies employed during the different writing processes, might uncover aspects in need of greater theoretical, empirical, and pedagogical consideration in a time when writing by hand is increasingly marginalized by a host of digital technologies.

Writing has always relied on the use of technologies and media that provide means of materializing mental content into visible symbols and representations. From the use of clay tablets and animal skins via the medieval manuscript and the ancient papyrus roll, to the printing press and the current digitization, writers have always had to handle some writing implements and use these in dexterous ways to generate inscriptions, traces or representations on some medium, substrate or display. Crucial to the present context is that both implements and substrates have certain affordances[2] which will impact the writing process, in subtle and more obvious ways. Whether considered a challenging intellectual skill, a deeply satisfying creative process, or a means of communication, writing therefore by definition involves and depends on the human body, the human mind/brain, and some tool by means of which we write, and a substrate or display (medium) on which the writing appears.

Today, thanks to the ubiquity of digital technologies, we arguably write more than ever. However, the ways in which we write are notice-ably different from earlier times. In particular, the physical aspect of the writing process is different: the ways in which we use our fingers and hands differ profoundly when tapping keys on a keyboard compared with writing and shaping each letter by hand. As our writing tools and technologies change, the particular affordances of the tools make themselves more readily apparent, and we may begin to glimpse the more profound implications of such a shift:

Changing the technologies of writing has profound implications, at least in part, because different technologies are *materially configured in profoundly different ways*. That is, different writing technologies set up radically different spatial, tactile, visual, and even temporal relations between the writer's material body and his or her material text. [...] Hence, the body [...] is the mechanism by which the mediation of the mental and the material occurs. (Haas, 1996, p. 5; italics mine)

When writing with digital technologies, for instance, less precise and less discriminating manual movements are required than when handwriting with pen on paper (Mangen & Velay, in press). In many respects, digitization contributes to making the relationship between the embodied, sensorimotor input (i.e., the physical process of writing) and the perceptible output (i.e., the visible "trace" of the writing process; the product) generated by the technology, more abstract and detached. Needless to say, such increasing abstraction might have far-reaching implications, educationally and practically as well as phenomenologically and biophysiologically.

Nevertheless, it is not easy to find empirical studies actually comparing handwriting and typewriting with respect to different aspects or outcomes. The scarcity of studies stands in stark contrast to countless prophesies and questions about the increasing marginalization of handwriting in schools: will we need to know how to write by hand in a future which is increasingly digital? Is anything important being lost if we lose the ability to write by hand? Will it matter to our children's current well-being, or their academic achievements later in life, if they are taught the alphabet on a keyboard rather than by putting pen to paper?

The digitization of writing can also be reasonably expected to have an impact on a different area of writing, namely, the creative writing of professional authors of different literary genres. The research literature is steadily growing also in this domain; however, I will briefly touch upon just a few questions pertaining in particular to the aspects of digitization having to do with the ergonomics of the writing process and the affordances of the implements and substrates involved.

In what follows I will attempt to address some of the phenomenological, psychological, pedagogical and, albeit to a lesser extent, creative/expressive implications of the digitization of writing. However partial, such an endeavor necessarily warrants venturing into a number of theoretical paradigms and a variety of empirical research in different disciplines. I contend that the nature of the topic in question requires an extensively cross-disciplinary approach, combining perspectives from philosophy of technology and phenomenology of human-technology relations with psychology, physiology, (cognitive & experimental) neuroscience and theories of human cultural and biological evolution. In particular, I will focus on the differences in tangibility between the virtual, conditionally existing trace of the digital text and the fixed and sensorially salient trace of the handwritten inscription. Explicitly stated, when we write something by hand on some physical substrate, we have immediate tactile access to the product of our writing – the text – in a way that we do not when writing on a keyboard. During typewriting, in other words, the product of our writing – the text – appears and evolves at a location, i.e., the screen, which is separated from the activity of our fingers, i.e., the keyboard. Moreover, the text written by hand on a piece of paper (for instance) has a fixed visual appearance which is physically contiguous with

the medium, i.e., the paper. A digitally produced text, by contrast, has no such physical contiguity with its medium, i.e., the computer (or any other digital device).

A combination of research findings from fine-grained, analytic, experimental approaches with holistic, top-down, philosophical (phenomenological) approaches might shed some light on commonly neglected aspects and dimensions of the transition from writing by hand by putting pen(cil) to paper, to digitized writing by tapping keys on virtual and mechanical keyboards. Furthermore, such an approach might pave the way for a more epistemologically comprehensive, cross-disciplinary, and conceptually unifying approach to studying relations between handwriting and typewriting. By accommodating approaches and perspectives originating from fundamental aspects of, firstly, the materialities of the tools and devices employed in writing, and, secondly, the sensorimotor contingencies[3] of such materialities on equally fundamental aspects of the writer's psycho-physiological dispositions, such an approach might be a way to attenuate further theoretical-methodological dispersal and disciplinary fragmentation. Promising recent signs of cross-disciplinary consolidation and theoretical-methodological advancement[4] notwithstanding, the field of writing research continues to be marred by epistemological schisms and lack of communication between involved disciplines: the field of graphonomics (the scientific study of handwriting [and other graphic skills]) is largely populated by neurologists and (cognitive) neuroscientists, whereas a majority of empirical studies of (hand)writing outside of the graphonomics field is carried out in psychology departments, often as collaborative projects between (educational/cognitive) psychologists and (psycho)linguists. Most importantly (and regrettably), it seems reasonable to say that too little knowledge resulting from either of these two dominant writing research domains finds its way to the field of pedagogy, whether theoretically, practically, or with respect to policy making.

IT IS ALL IN THE HAND(S): MATERIALITIES, AFFORDANCES, AND SENSORIMOTOR CONTINGENCIES INVOLVED IN HANDWRITING AND TYPEWRITING

Adept tool use is a prerequisite for any writer. At a fundamental level, writing requires the employment of appropriate tools – writing implements – in appropriate ways for some communicative, artistic, or aesthetic purpose. Obviously, any use of tools crucially depends on and involves human hand-eye-brain relationships. The pivotal role of the hand in human evolution is widely acknowledged, and scientists such as Frank Wilson (1998), John Napier (1993) and Raymond Tallis (2003) have all written informed treatises about the fundamental role and position of our dexterous hands and fingers in cultural as well as biological evolution.

Nevertheless, the importance of the hand remains largely ignored in much of the research on writing and, to an even larger extent, literacy, in social sciences and humanities. This lack of attention might at least in part explain the relative lack of studies addressing issues having to do with the changing haptics in the digitization of writing (haptics is defined as a combination of the sensation of touch [e.g., tactility] with the active movement involved in exploration of our surroundings by the use of our fingers). When writing is defined and studied as primarily visual, cognitive processes or as sociocultural practices, questions concerning the haptic and tactile aspects of the writing process remain largely unaddressed (see also Mangen & Velay, 2010).

Handwriting and typewriting differ in a number of ways, some of which may appear immediately obvious, whereas others are more subtle and perhaps, for that reason, particularly important since they tend to be downplayed or even ignored. The hand- and finger-movements we perform "ex nihilo" (Mangen & Velay, in press) when writing by hand differ from the movements we perform when writing on a keyboard. By corollary, hand-eye coordination and hand-eye-brain connections necessarily differ in the two writing modalities. Empirical and theoretical research within the emergent, cross-disciplinary paradigm of embodied cognition (see, e.g., Calvo & Gomila, 2008; Shapiro, 2010; Varela, Thompson, & Rosch, 1991) has established that the fundamental role and function of the human brain is action and movement (Glenberg, Jaworski, Rischal, & Levin, 2007), and not thinking and cognitive information processing, as one might be tempted to believe. Seen in this light, the changing movements required by and involved in writing by hand vs. writing by keyboard warrant extra consideration, on evolutionary and cultural as well as educational and phenomenological grounds. This alone would be a strong argument in favor of an increased awareness of research findings from the biological and natural sciences in applied (writing) pedagogies at both beginning and advanced levels (Glenberg, 2008). Moreover, it points to a need to scrutinize the potential impact of digitization of writing at more fine-grained, (neuro)psychological/-physiological and bodily-oriented level than is common, in particular among pedagogically oriented writing researchers.

Handwriting involves shaping each letter or sign, consisting of more or less elaborate patterns of strokes, lines, dots and circles with intrinsic directionality and a system of interrelationships which, to be learned, requires long periods of repetitive practice and sensorimotor as well as cognitive commitment. Typewriting, no doubt, also requires practice. However, the practice involved in learning to type consists in building an elaborate mental map of the distribution of letters and signs on a keyboard, and then positioning the hands and fingers accurately in order to hit the correct key for each letter. In handwriting, the task of the beginning writer is to learn the draw the shape of a figure from scratch, and to reach a level of perfection and standardization so that each idiosyncratic, personal variant of the letter resembles, to an acceptable degree, the correct one. In typewriting, by contrast, the learning and acquisition of the skill of typing entails reaching a speed level and a familiarity with the location of letter-keys on the keyboard so that all ten fingers are equally adept at finding and performing their role in the manual "tap-dance" of touch typing.

From this rather coarse description we can infer that there are radically different skills and processes involved in the two writing modalities, from low-level neurophysiological and –psychological processes and how these relate to perceptual and cognitive processes, to the experiential, phenomenological, felt sense of the writing processes themselves. At a fundamental level, handwriting is a process requiring the integration of visual, proprioceptive (haptic/kinesthetic), and tactile information (Fogassi & Gallese, 2004). Hence, the acquisition of handwriting skills involves a perceptual component (learning the visual shape of each letter) and a graphomotor component (learning the trajectory producing the letter's shape, a process involving the appropriate movements with the writing implement in order to create the character) (van Galen, 1991). In typing, obviously, there is no such graphomotor component involved, as the typing of each letter entails locating it as a ready-made on a keyboard.

Other differences between the two modalities manifest themselves at different levels and in other phases of the writing process. For instance, handwriting involves only one hand and might very well be one of the most lateralized of bodily processes, in that very few people master it equally well with both hands. In contrast, typewriting most commonly involves (more or less, depending on skill and expertise) both hands and, ideally, all ten fingers. However, it is worth mentioning that, while the execution process of handwriting, i.e., the process of shaping the letters and words and putting them down on paper, is by essence unimanual, the non-writing hand is not left idle in the process. As shown by Yves Guiard (1987), when writing on a piece of paper, the non-writing hand plays a complementary, though largely covert, role by continuously repositioning the paper in anticipation of pen movement. The nondominant hand "frames" the movement of the dominant hand and "sets and confines the spatial context in which the 'skilled' movement will take place" – whether this movement is dart throwing or embroidery (Guiard, 1987, p. 492; see also Mangen & Velay, 2010).

Beyond crucial questions addressing how, to what extent and under which conditions changes in hand-eye coordination might impact neural substrates of writing, these changes also have implications due to the fact that whenever we write, by necessity, we also, at the same time, read. Recent technological developments have made it possible to conduct fine-grained observations of the writer's "reading during writing", by combining online measures of the sensorimotor input process of either handwriting or typewriting, with online measures of visual behavior using eye tracking methodology. Programs and applications such as Eye and Pen (Alamargot, Chesnet, Dansac, & Ros, 2006), ScriptLog (Strömqvist, Holmqvist, Johansson, Karlsson, & Wengelin, 2006) and InputLog (Leijten & Van Waes, 2006) allow researchers to study in depth reading during writing, and to investigate how the coordination and integration of the processes of writing and reading shed light on distinctive online and offline characteristics of writing.

During handwriting, our visual attention is commonly restricted to the point where the pen hits the paper during the execution (Mangen & Velay, 2010). In this respect, handwriting takes place in a very limited space – literally, at the endpoint of the pen or pencil, where ink or graphite flow out of the core of the writing implement, leaving continuously evolving, visible traces on the substrate of, e.g., paper. The attention of the writer is concentrated onto this particular point both spatially and temporally, enabling a close and intimate spatiotemporal contiguity between the motor space and the space of visual attention. Seen in an evolutionary perspective, such contiguity is what our species, homo faber (the tool-making man) has, literally speaking, grown up with: "Traditionally, hand, eye, and tool converged in one place: when the hand worked on a material, the eye followed it continuously, or the hand held a paper, while the eye read." (McCullough, 1996, p. 35) Moreover, such a flow-like process, where visual attention is constrained, directed, and strongly unified with the sensorimotor input, resulting in an immediately tangible and tactilely sensed output, is likely a large part of the explanation why the distinctly felt experience of writing something by hand is often said to generate an experience having meditative qualities. Conscious attention and skilled sensorimotor action are closely related, enabling a meditative quality wherein "participation depends on both lower, automatic-level, preceptor-motor actions, as well as the highest understandings of focus and intent." (McCullough, 1996, pp. 141-142) The potential educational and pedagogical benefits inherent in the attentional nature of such meditative qualities are easily found: The ability to focus and to sustain concentrated focus on a task over a period of time remains a building block in learning, and the experience of flow and absorption in a task is commonly considered a major facilitator to this effect (see, e.g., Csikszentmihalyi, 1990).

In contrast, when typing on a keyboard (and, in particular, with a keyboard which is mechanically and physically detached from the screen display), the process of writing is clearly divided into two distinct spaces: the motor space (the keyboard) and the visual space (the screen) (Mangen & Velay, 2010). Depending on the writer's skill and whether or not she is an expert touch typist, the keyboard writer's attention is oscillating between these two spatiotemporally distinct spaces. This division, and the resulting oscillation, is however considerably reduced with tablet technologies where the virtual keyboard appears as part of the screen and where the distance between the two spaces is minimal, compared to that of conventional computer and laptop keyboards. It remains to be established empirically whether and to what extent such spatial closeness might attenuate potential negative effects of divided attention and oscillation between motor space and visual space during writing. Another factor likely to affect the tablet and touch screen typing process is the diminished haptic and tactile feedback from a touch keyboard, compared with a conventional computer keyboard. Some preliminary (though still largely anecdotal) evidence for this potential effect lies in the fact that typing on a touch keyboard tends to result in a larger number of typos, something which is also most likely due to the much smaller size of the screen-based touch keyboards compared with conventional computer keyboards.

THE DISAPPEARING TRACE IN DIGITAL WRITING

As evidenced by historians and neuroscientists alike (Classen, 2012; Hatwell, Streri, & Gentaz, 2003; Wilson, 1998), the sense of touch is of fundamental importance to humans, culturally as well as psychologically: "From an ontogenetic [i.e., the origin and development of an organism from embryo to adult] perspective, touch is the most important form of communication of the human baby. And from a phylogenetic [i.e., the evolutionary history of a kind of organism] perspective, touch is older." (Chandler, 1995, p. 165) This runs counter to a common human tendency to consider sight the superior source of learning and exploration. Besides proprioception (our sense of balance), the sense of touch is actually the most fundamental of human sensory modalities. Hence, the tactile and haptic aspects of handwriting and typewriting merit some closer inspection, not least because one of the fundamental differences between the two modalities is the ways in the resulting "trace" of digital writing, i.e., the digital/electronic text, is intangible and, hence, "un-touchable".

Evidence for the evolutionary importance of the sense of touch for human beings is easily found in the scientific literature. Tallis (2003), for instance, points to how the neural support for tactile as well as manipulative activity is reflected

> not only in the extraordinary density and sensitivity of nerve endings, but also in the enlargement of the spinal cord in the neck and, more strikingly in the disproportionate representation of the fingers (and in particular the thumb) in the sensory part of the cerebral cortex. The homunculus represented on the sensory (and indeed the motor) cortex, indicating which parts of the cortex are dedicated to servicing which part of the body, has grossly – indeed grotesquely – swollen fingers. (p. 29)

In this respect, it makes a key difference between writing by hand on paper and typewriting on a keyboard that our primary relation with digital technologies can safely be said to be visual rather than tactile. Admittedly, particularly through recent developments of force feedback and other haptic or tactile digital implementations, touch technologies and tangible computing[5] have made some headway. Nevertheless, digital interfaces are still primarily visually mediated. According to professor of architecture and information design Malcolm McCullough, this explains why the most common complaint about computers is not overload, but deprivation (1996, p. 130): we tend to not like the computer for artistic/creative processes and creations because we are not allowed to touch our work.

Due to its digital nature, texts produced via either mechanical or virtual keyboard or a digital stylus, and displayed on some kind of screen, are by definition intangible. Unless printed out and, hence, no less digital, the digitally implemented and displayed product of digitized writing differ in fundamental ways from the product of something written on a material substrate.[6] The sensorimotor contingencies and ergonomic affordances of a material substrate such as paper, entail that defining features such as texture and graininess might differentially influence the speed and smoothness of the writing process, depending on the material qualities of the writing implement (e.g., a pencil or quill) as well as the substrate (e.g., cardboard or rice paper).

When writing with a pen or pencil on a sheet of paper, the material solidity of paper provides a degree of "resistance" (friction) which can in different ways and to different degrees influence both temporal and spatial aspects of the writing process. The very fact that handwriting on paper in this way to different degrees slows down the writing process has been shown to be a matter of importance for some creative writers (see, e.g., Chandler, 1995), claiming that they prefer to write their first drafts by hand because they need the resistance of the paper and the concomitant slowness of the handwriting to ensure that their thoughts are allowed adequate time to develop. The slowness intrinsic to the material substrate of paper, combined with the sensorimotor contingencies of the flow of handwriting, ensures enough time to think before putting thoughts to paper, as the Norwegian author Thorvald Steen explained in a radio interview.[7] Despite the fact that he suffers from a muscular disorder which undeniably makes the process of writing long stretches of text by hand even more cumbersome, Steen continues to insist on writing his novels by hand, on average wearing out 25 ballpoint pens and 4 pencils per novel. When asked why he wouldn't write on a keyboard, he replied that the computer keyboard doesn't allow him enough time to think before writing and that the quality of his thoughts and, hence, the quality of his novels, depends in crucial ways on the slowing-down of the process that handwriting enforces. In short, handwriting with pencils and ballpoint pens on paper ensures that he doesn't get "too talkative", as he expressed it.

SOME POTENTIAL EDUCATIONAL IMPLICATIONS OF REPLACING HANDWRITING WITH TYPEWRITING

Replacing handwriting by typing during learning to write might have an impact on the cerebral representation of letters and thus on letter memorization (Velay & Longcamp, 2012). In two behavioral studies, Longcamp et al. investigated the differences between handwriting and typing, one in children (Longcamp, Zerbato-Poudou, & Velay, 2005) and one in adults (Longcamp, Boucard, Gilhodes, & Velay, 2006). Both studies demonstrated that letters or characters learned through handwriting were subsequently better memorized and recognized than letters or characters that participants had learned to write by typing. In a subsequent study (Longcamp et al., 2008), fMRI data showed that processing the orientation of handwritten and typed characters did not rely on the same brain areas. Greater activity related to the sensorimotor process involved in handwriting was observed in several brain regions known to be involved in the execution, imagery, and observation of actions (e.g., Broca's area). These findings indicate that the physical movements of the process of writing during handwriting may contribute to memorizing the shape and/or orientation of characters. Preliminary findings from another study replicating the behavioral studies of Longcamp et al. indicate that the effect of writing modality (handwriting or typewriting) is not necessarily restricted to memorizing at the level of single letters or characters. In a within-subjects design Mangen et al. (submitted) compared participants' free recall and recognition of words written down by the use of pen and paper, a touch keyboard on an iPad, and a conventional laptop keyboard. Preliminary findings show that, on the subsequent tests of free recall, participants remembered more of the words they had written down with pen on paper.

These findings largely concur with the findings from a study by Smoker et al. (2009), which used a between-subjects design to compare the effects of writing modality (handwriting vs typewriting on a computer keyboard) on subsequent memory for words. Results from their study showed that memory on the recall task approached significance in favor of the handwritten words, $F(1, 59) = 3.34$, $p = .065$; and the effect of writing modality was significant in the recognition task, $F(1, 59) = 4.63$, $p = .036$, indicating that participants in the handwriting condition performed significantly better than participants in the typewriting condition on the word recognition measure. Smoker et al. (2009) conclude that the results support the hypothesis that due to additional kinesthetic information provided by handwriting, subjects tend to remember words better when they have written them by hand than when they have written them by keyboard. However, caution should be taken with respect to their findings, considering that the sample size (N = 61) of their study is fairly small for a between-subjects design. Moreover, the authors did not administer any screening or pretests to ensure group homogeneity. For these reasons, similar findings would be considered more robust in a within-subjects design allowing greater experimental control.

Other studies, however, have not found an advantage to writing by hand rather than by keyboard (Cunningham & Stanovich, 1990; Vaughn, Schumm, & Gordon, 1992). Considering the scarcity of experimental studies specifically targeting this issue, it is far too early to conclude on this topic. However, the fact that existing research has provided some fairly robust indications that there might be some perceptuo-cognitive advantages intrinsic to handwriting warrants consideration and should be granted far more attention from pedagogically oriented research on writing and literacy than is currently the case. The ongoing digitization of writing entails an abstraction and disembodiment of the physical act of writing. The educational implications of such abstraction and disembodiment are still largely unexplored, and we need much more empirical research on the differences between the two processes of writing and how they may strengthen and preserve as well as attenuate and potentially hinder crucial aspects of writing development at different levels of instruction. Fundamentally, the mere fact that digital technologies frequently entails increased abstraction and disembodiment merits greater awareness in a time when research evidence from psychology and neuroscience increasingly indicates the importance of bodily, sensorimotor processes for cognition and learning.

In his philosophy of education, Alfred North Whitehead (1929) underscores the crucial role of the body, and in particular the hands, for learning and cognitive development. Establishing as an educational axiom that any teacher "will come to grief as soon as you forget that your pupils have bodies", Whitehead claims that

The connections between intellectual activity and the body though diffused in every bodily feeling, are focused in the eyes, the ears, the voice, and the hands. There is a coordination of senses and thought, and also a reciprocal influence between brain activity and material creative activity. In this reaction the hands are peculiarly important. It is a moot point whether the human hand created the human brain, or the brain created the hand. Certainly, the connection is intimate and reciprocal. (1929, p. 50)

Obviously, we will need to learn our children to write with keyboards and any other writing implement that future technologies might bring about. However, we need to balance a fascination for new technologies with a sharpened awareness of what is entailed in the "old" modes of writing, with pen and pencil on a piece of paper or cardboard. A richer and more nuanced comprehension of what is involved in handwriting, and how it works, might make us realize the full complexity of the skill and, hence, what we might want to make an extra effort to preserve. After all, handwriting, says Daniel Chandler, "may be important in ways that we are not altogether aware." (1995, p. 159)

CONCLUDING REFLECTIONS ON HANDWRITING AND THE FUTURE OF WRITING RESEARCH

Reciprocal and symbiotic rather than effectual and unidirectional, the affinities between tools, technologies, media and human creativity, communication and cognition evolve in a multifaceted manner, impacting each other small-scale and large-scale, with both short-term and long-term effects (Mangen & Velay, in press). The ways in which we read, write, talk, and think, are closely connected with and shaped by the affordances of these tools, technologies and media. In other words, the tools and technologies with and on which we write affect, in complex and profound ways, our modes of thinking. This points to the need to frame and phrase our questions about the future of handwriting differently and at different levels than is typically the case, in a time of remarkably successful and increasingly sophisticated digital interfaces which are able to transcode and algorithmically reconfigure even the idiosyncrasies of our handwritten signature (Piper, 2012). Pertaining as they do to what it means to be human, questions concerning whether or not we need handwriting in the future are too important for them to be discussed merely or primarily in pragmatic, communicational, technological, or even educational terms.

As outlined in some depth above, the human hand plays a vital role in human evolutionary as well as cultural development. The connections between the hand and the brain are as intimate as they are intricate: "the skill of the hand lies in the brain and it is here that dexterity and adroitness (or clumsiness) originate. The hand is a mirror of the brain; therefore there can be no such combination as dexterous hands and clumsy brains." (Napier, 1993, p. 25) The hand, says Wilson, is "the real-life focal point – the lever or the launching pad – of a successful and genuinely fulfilling life [...]" (Wilson, 1998, p. 14). As I hope to have shown, the human hand is at fundamental levels involved in human learning, thinking, creativity, expression, and communication. In a time of increasing digitization and concomitant abstraction, this might make us pause to reflect on some of Wilson's questions: "What is there in our theories of education that respects the biologic principles governing cognitive processing in the brain and behavioral change in the individual? [...] Could anything we have learned about the hand be used to improve the teaching of children?" (1998, pp. 277-278)

There is, moreover, always a cost/benefit ratio to any technological change where existing tools and technologies are complemented or replaced by innovations. For this reason, Nickerson advocates, "we should be alert to the fact that when the technology makes specific skills obsolete in practical situations, it undoubtedly decreases the likelihood that those skills will be acquired and retained. That may be acceptable in the case of some skills and not in that of others." (2005, p. 24) In a time where the shift to digital means of production and creative expression is in full swing, McCullough urges us to "carefully consider potential losses and gains [...]. Does further abstraction necessitate further decline of human skill, particularly of the hand?" (1996, p. 28)

As experimental research in graphonomics and different strands of neuroscience continues to provide empirical support to (more or less widespread and reported) phenomenological experiences of the changing nature of the act of writing, the field of writing research has a way to go in terms of adequately accommodating such theoretically and methodologically different approaches. In a special issue on writing development in the *Journal of Research in Reading*, the editors remark that, of all the papers submitted to the special issue, "most were located firmly in either linguistics or psychology, and none drew on multiple perspectives. The time is clearly ripe for research in writing to take a new turn, affording the complex act of writing theoretical and empirical

scrutiny which acknowledges multi-paradigmatic insights" (Myhill & Fisher, 2010, p. 3).

The title of the special issue in question is "Writing development: cognitive, sociocultural, linguistic perspectives." Cross-disciplinary as this may seem; as long as writing (and reading) research remains built on and dominated by this tripartite theoretical-methodological framework (i.e., cognitive, sociocultural, linguistic), fundamental questions concerning the impact of digitization on writing will remain inadequately addressed. Perspectives combining theoretical paradigms from cognitive psychology with analytical procedures and insights from linguistics certainly contribute to our knowledge of writing; however, understanding in more depth how the new technologies of writing impact the processes and experiences, in constructive and less constructive ways, short-term and long-term, requires in my view that we expand our horizon beyond a definition of writing as a primarily visual, cognitive, and linguistic process. The act of writing involves our bodies and entails sensorimotor interaction with and employment of tools and technologies whose affordances will have a significant impact on the process as well as the product of writing. Hence, the social turn (Pearson, 2009) so evident in research on reading and literacy overall needs, in my view, to be supplemented by a "bodily" (physical and/or psychobiological) turn "inward", towards fine-grained, (neuro)psychological and physiological processes taking place at an individual level of embodied engagement with different material implements and substrates (see also Mangen & Schilhab, 2012).

I would, therefore, like to conclude by suggesting a kind of interdisciplinary writing research which is different in kind and degree from the ones commonly pursued. Inspired by the emerging and rapidly growing field of educational neuroscience, I suggest *transdisciplinarity* (Samuels, 2009) as a promising and plausible alternative to the more familiar inter- and multidisciplinary approaches. Transdisciplinarity entails integrating disciplines at the level of particular issues (e.g., the impact of the digitization of the writing tool/implement and the substrate of the text, for the multisensory, embodied processes during writing). The type of knowledge pursued in a truly transdisciplinary approach is not the sum of individual knowledge shared by the experts involved (which would characterize multidisciplinarity), nor the knowledge that is created at the intersection of already established disciplines (i.e., interdisciplinarity). In contrast, transdisciplinarity is characterized by a common issue or research question to which all researchers and disciplines involved apply their particular expertise, perspectives and understanding, and where the common goal is to reach a holistic understanding of the issue. (Samuels, 2009) This, obviously, is challenging. However, considering what's at stake for the future of writing and writing research, it is, arguably, worth a try. I'll end by paraphrasing Rose et al. (2009) who emphasize the importance of pursuing true interdisciplinarity in the emerging field of educational neuroscience: to realize the full potential of writing research as a transdisciplinary science, scholars must be willing to "go where their questions take them, not simply where their past disciplinary training left them" (Rose, Daley, & Rose, 2011, p. 160).

REFERENCES

Alamargot, D., & Chanquoy, L. (2001). General introduction: A definition of writing and a presentation of the main models. In Alamargot & Chanquoy (Eds.), Through the models of writing: With commentaries by Ronald T. Kellogg & John R. Hayes (pp. 1-29). Amsterdam: Kluwer Academic Publishers.

Alamargot, D., Chesnet, D., Dansac, C., & Ros, C. (2006). Eye and pen: A new device for studying reading during writing. *Behavior Research Methods*, 38(2), 287–299. doi:10.3758/BF03192780 PMID:16956105.

Amadieu, F., Tricot, A., & Mariné, C. (2009). Prior knowledge in learning from a non-linear electronic document: Disorientation and coherence of the reading sequences. *Computers in Human Behavior*, 25(2), 381–388. doi:10.1016/j.chb.2008.12.017.

Calvo, P., & Gomila, A. (Eds.). (2008). *Handbook of cognitive science: An embodied approach.* Amsterdam: Elsevier.

Chandler, D. (1995). *The act of writing: A media theory approach.* (Doctoral dissertation). University of Wales, Wales, UK. Retrieved from http://www.aber.ac.uk/media/Documents/act/act.html

Classen, C. (2012). *The deepest sense: A cultural history of touch.* Urbana, IL: University of Illinois Press.

Csikszentmihalyi, M. (1990). *Flow: The psychology of optimal experience.* New York: Harper & Row.

Cunningham, A. E., & Stanovich, K. E. (1990). Early spelling acquisition: Writing beats the computer. *Journal of Educational Psychology*, 82, 159–162. doi:10.1037/0022-0663.82.1.159.

Flower, L., & Hayes, J. R. (1981). A cognitive process theory of writing. *College Composition and Communication*, 32(4), 365–387. doi:10.2307/356600.

Fogassi, L., & Gallese, V. (2004). Action as a binding key to multisensory integration. In Calvert, G. A., Spence, C., & Stein, B. E. (Eds.), *The handbook of multisensory processes* (pp. 425–441). Cambridge, MA: MIT Press.

Gibson, J. J. (1979). *The ecological approach to visual perception.* Boston: Houghton Mifflin.

Glenberg, A. M. (2008). Embodiment for education. In Calvo, P., & Gomila, A. (Eds.), *Handbook of cognitive science: An embodied approach* (pp. 355–372). Amsterdam: Elsevier. doi:10.1016/B978-0-08-046616-3.00018-9.

Glenberg, A. M., Jaworski, B., Rischal, M., & Levin, J. (2007). What brains are for: Action, meaning, and reading comprehension. In McNamara, D. S. (Ed.), *Reading comprehension strategies: Theories, interventions, and technologies* (pp. 221–240). New York: Lawrence Erlbaum Ass.

Guiard, Y. (1987). Asymmetric division of labor in human skilled bimanual action: The kinematic chain as a model. *Journal of Motor Behavior, 19*, 486–517. PMID:15136274.

Haas, C. (1996). *Writing technology: Studies on the materiality of literacy.* Mahwah, NJ: L. Erlbaum Associates.

Hatwell, Y., Streri, A., & Gentaz, E. (Eds.). (2003). *Touching for knowing.* Amsterdam: John Benjamins.

Leijten, M., & Van Waes, L. (2006). Inputlog: New perspectives on the logging of on-line writing. In Sullivan, K. P. H., & Lindgren, E. (Eds.), *Computer keystroke logging and writing: Methods and applications* (pp. 73–94). Amsterdam: Elsevier.

Longcamp, M., Boucard, C., Gilhodes, J.-C., Anton, J.-L., Roth, M., Nazarian, B., & Velay, J.-L. (2008). Learning through hand- or typewriting influences visual recognition of new graphic shapes: Behavioral and functional imaging evidence. *Journal of Cognitive Neuroscience, 20*(5), 802–815. doi:10.1162/jocn.2008.20504 PMID:18201124.

Longcamp, M., Boucard, C., Gilhodes, J.-C., & Velay, J.-L. (2006). Remembering the orientation of newly learned characters depends on the associated writing knowledge: A comparison between handwriting and typing. *Human Movement Science, 25*(4-5), 646–656. doi:10.1016/j.humov.2006.07.007 PMID:17011660.

Longcamp, M., Zerbato-Poudou, M.-T., & Velay, J.-L. (2005). The influence of writing practice on letter recognition in preschool children: A comparison between handwriting and typing. *Acta Psychologica, 119*(1), 67–79. doi:10.1016/j.actpsy.2004.10.019 PMID:15823243.

Mangen, A., Anda, L. G., Oxborough, G. H. O., & Brønnick, K. (submitted). *Handwriting versus typewriting: Effect of writing modality on word recall and recognition.* Submitted to Memory &Cognition.

Mangen, A., & Schilhab, T. S. S. (2012). An embodied view of reading: Theoretical considerations, empirical findings, and educational implications. In S. Matre & A. Skaftun (Eds.), Skriv! Les! (pp. 285-300). Trondheim, Norway: Akademika forlag.

Mangen, A., & Velay, J.-L. (2010). Digitizing literacy: Reflections on the haptics of writing. In Zadeh, M. H. (Ed.), *Advances in Haptics* (pp. 385–402). Vienna, Austria: IN-TECH Web. doi:10.5772/8710.

Mangen, A., & Velay, J.-L. (2013). Cognitive implications of digital media. In Ryan, M.-L., Emerson, L., & Robertson, B. (Eds.), *The Johns Hopkins guide to new media and digital textuality.* Baltimore, MD: Johns Hopkins University Press.

McCullough, M. (1996). *Abstracting craft: The practiced digital hand.* Cambridge, MA: MIT Press.

Myhill, D., & Fisher, R. (2010). Editorial: Writing development: Cognitive, sociocultural, linguistic perspectives. *Journal of Research in Reading, 33*(1), 1–3. doi:10.1111/j.1467-9817.2009.01428.x.

Napier, J. (1993). *Hands.* Princeton, NJ: Princeton University Press.

Nickerson, R. S. (2005). Technology and cognition amplification. In Sternberg, R. J., & Preiss, D. (Eds.), *Intelligence and technology: The impact of tools on the nature and development of human abilities* (pp. 3–27). Mahwah, NJ: Lawrence Erlbaum Ass.

Noë, A. (2004). *Action in perception.* Cambridge, MA: MIT Press.

O'Regan, J. K., & Noë, A. (2001). A sensorimotor account of vision and visual consciousness. *The Behavioral and Brain Sciences*, *24*(5), 939–973. doi:10.1017/S0140525X01000115 PMID:12239892.

Pearson, P. D. (2009). The roots of reading comprehension instruction. In Israel, S. E., & Duffy, G. G. (Eds.), *Handbook of research on reading comprehension* (pp. 3–31). New York: Routledge.

Piper, A. (2012). *Book was there: Reading in electronic times.* Chicago: University of Chicago Press. doi:10.7208/chicago/9780226922898.001.0001.

Rose, L. T., Daley, S. G., & Rose, D. H. (2011). Let the questions be your guide: MBE as interdisciplinary science. *Mind, Brain, and Education*, *5*(4), 153–162. doi:10.1111/j.1751-228X.2011.01123.x.

Samuels, B. M. (2009). Can the differences between education and neuroscience be overcome by mind, brain, and education? *Mind, Brain, and Education*, *3*(1), 45–55. doi:10.1111/j.1751-228X.2008.01052.x.

Shapiro, L. A. (2010). *Embodied cognition.* New York: Routledge.

Smoker, T. J., Murphy, C. E., & Rockwell, A. K. (2009). *Comparing memory for handwriting versus typing.* Paper presented at the Human Factors and Ergonomics Society Annual Meeting. New York, NY.

Strömqvist, S., Holmqvist, K., Johansson, V., Karlsson, H., & Wengelin, Å. (2006). What keystroke logging can reveal about writing. In Sullivan, K. P. H., & Lindgren, E. (Eds.), *Computer keystroke logging and writing: Methods and applications.* Amsterdam: Elsevier.

Tallis, R. (2003). *The hand: A philosophical inquiry into human being.* Edinburgh, UK: Edinburgh University Press.

van Galen, G. P. (1991). Handwriting: Issues for a psychomotor theory. *Human Movement Science*, *10*, 165–191. doi:10.1016/0167-9457(91)90003-G.

Varela, F. J., Thompson, E., & Rosch, E. (1991). *The embodied mind: Cognitive science and human experience.* Cambridge, MA: MIT Press.

Vaughn, S., Schumm, J. S., & Gordon, J. (1992). Early spelling acquisition: Does writing really beat the computer? *Learning Disability Quarterly*, *15*, 223–228. doi:10.2307/1510245.

Velay, J.-L., & Longcamp, M. (2012). Handwriting versus typewriting: Behavioural and cerebral consequences in letter recognition. In M. Torrance, D. Alamargot, M. Castelló, F. Ganier, O. Kruse, A. Mangen, L. Tolchinsky, & L. van Waes (Eds.), Learning to write effectively: Current trends in European research (pp. 371-373). Emerald Group Publishing Limited.

Whitehead, A. N. (1929). *The aims of education and other essays.* New York: Macmillan.

Wilson, F. R. (1998). *The hand: How its use shapes the brain, language, and human culture.* New York: Pantheon Books.

Wolf, M. J. P. (2000). *Abstracting reality: Art, communication, and cognition in the digital age.* Lanham, MD: University Press of America.

ENDNOTES

1. "Verba volant, scripta manent" is a Latin proverb (whose origin is in dispute), with the literal translation: "spoken words fly away, written words remain."

2. Coined by J.J. Gibson (1979), the concept of "affordances" denotes an intrinsic quality or feature of an object in the human environment, which allows an individual to perform certain actions while inhibiting others. Besides being determined by features of the object, an affordance also depends on the abilities for action pertaining to different organisms. What affords certain actions for certain organism does not necessarily afford the same actions for other organisms – for instance, a tree affords climbing for a monkey, but not for an elephant.

3. According to the sensorimotor contingency theory proposed by O'Regan & Noë (Noë, 2004; O'Regan & Noë, 2001), each sensory modality—audio, vision, touch, smell, taste, haptics, kinesthetics—is a mode of exploration of the world that is mediated by knowledge of sensorimotor contingencies, i.e. practical and embodied knowledge of sets of structured laws pertaining to the sensory changes brought about by one's movement and/or manipulation of objects. For instance, visual experience depends on one's knowledge of the sensory effects of our eye-contingent operations – for example, the fact that closing our eyes will yield no visual input. In contrast, closing our eyes will not bring about significant changes in auditory perception. Our practical knowledge of the laws governing these contingencies is built up by our lifelong experience from exploring the physical environment.

4. Initiatives and communities such as the EARLI (European Association of Research in Learning and Instruction) SIG Writing group, and the EU-funded COST Action ERN-LWE (European Research Network – Learning to Write Effectively) have served to consolidate and effectuate important cross-disciplinary research on writing.

5. See for instance the Tangible Media Group at MIT, whose vision is to replace the GUI (graphical user interface) with TUI (tangible user interface): http://tangible.media.mit.edu/

6. Strictly speaking, "digital" can only refer to data represented or stored in digital form; as output, in whatever form (e.g., computer graphics, digital text), the representations are analog. In order for us to be able to read it, a digitally produced text must "re-enter the domain of the physical world, and in doing so there is an inevitable shift back to analog form. This is similar to the idea that no one has ever seen a perfect circle, a circle is only perfect when it exists as a mathematical entity; once it is drawn up or printed out, imperfections in physical media, albeit small ones, render it imperfect" (Wolf, 2000, preface).

7. In "Ekko," NRK (Norwegian public broadcast), October 26, 2012.

Chapter 7
Error or Strength?
Competencies Developed in Adolescent Digitalk

Kristen Hawley Turner
Fordham University, USA

ABSTRACT

A study by the Pew Internet and American Life Project has indicated that teens are writing more than ever and that much of this writing is done in digital spaces. However, digitalk, the informal language used, often breaks from Standard English, and adults are concerned about the effects of digitalk on literacy skills in general. This chapter reports research that focuses on what language teens use in their digitalk and why they make the choices they do. With analysis of digital writing from 81 adolescents, researchers identified 18 conventions of digitalk. In a second phase of research, teens were surveyed and interviewed about their linguistic choices. Findings indicate that adolescents attend to audience, and they consider personal voice in their digital writing. Teens develop these competencies in a community of writers – outside of school.

INTRODUCTION

we hangin later?

i gotta meet my moms after skoooool today. tom?

yeah, fo sho

fo sho...we can meet behind the yard

k. see u then

HOLLA

Is this text conversation between two adolescents riddled with errors? Does the following exchange evidence "lax punctuation and grammar" (Lenhart, Arafeh, Smith, & Macgill, 2008, p. 3)?

Heyyy ! how you getting home tomorrow?

Hey um I think my mom will pick me up I guess

Oh alrighttt ... do you think she could give me a ride home? My mom's working, and I don't wanna be the loser senior on the bus. HAHA

haha prob I didn't even ask if she could bring me lol

DOI: 10.4018/978-1-4666-4341-3.ch007

ohhhhhh haha okayyy... . . let's go out to lunch for your birthday!

Hey I wish I could but I have soo much to do! Lol

Ughh okay well we must do something!

okk ok well I gotta ttyl:)

Byeeee!

A study by the Pew Internet and American Life Project (Lenhart et al., 2008) indicated that teens are writing more than ever and that much of this writing is done in digital spaces. The conversations above represent examples of that writing. Noticeably, the writers of these texts do not adhere to standard conventions and instead adopt language that is popularly known as "textspeak." The Pew report noted that this nonstandard language troubles "a considerable number of educators and children's advocates" who "are concerned that the quality of writing by young Americans is being degraded by their electronic communication, with its carefree spelling, lax punctuation and grammar, and its acronym shortcuts" (Lenhart et al., 2008, p. 3). This view, that the language is "carefree" and "lax," has also been seen in popular media, where titles like "The Gr8 Deb8 of Teen Txting: Text Messaging Ruining the English Language?" (Howard, 2012) have revealed an inherent prejudice against digital language.

What is interesting about the headline of Howard (2012) is that it captures a commonly held perception that teens regularly substitute numbers for sounds (e.g., Gr8). Surprisingly, this practice is rarely used by adolescents (Turner, 2011). In fact, adults hold many misconceptions about the digital language that teens use on a daily basis. As evidenced by the conversations cited above, adolescents easily communicate with each other via texting, instant messaging, and social networking. The language that they use blends formal and nonstandard English to serve a purpose for

a community of writers. This digitalk (Turner, 2010, 2011) allows adolescents to participate in a digital community even as it helps them to identify themselves among their peers (Turner, in press).

A careful examination of the digital messages that begin this chapter reveals that they were composed by four individuals. Reading down each column uncovers a distinct voice. For instance, the first teen wrote somewhat abruptly in short lines while his friend extended "skoooool" and used ellipses for flow. In the second conversation, the first writer repeated letters, as in "heyyy" and "ohhhhhh," but her friend did not adopt this convention. Each person created a noticeable style, a practice reflective of expert writers. Far from being lax, the adolescents used language purposefully, and their manipulations may reflect strengths of digital writers. A growing body of research has suggested that use of digitalk supports the development of literacy skills (Kemp & Bushnell, 2011; Plester, Wood, & Bell, 2008; Plester, Wood, & Joshi, 2009; Powell & Dixon, 2011; Wood, Jackson, Hart, Plester, & Wilde, 2001). This chapter will add to that literature by articulating competencies developed by adolescents who participate in a community of digital writers.

THEORETICAL FRAMEWORK

Studies that support a negative relationship between digitalk and grammar skills (e.g., Singel & Sundar, 2012) often isolate language from context. In contrast, the present study evolved from a sociocultural frame (cf. New Literacy theories (Barton, 1994, 2001; Gee, 1996, 2000; Street 1995, 1999)) that has viewed literacy as contextually based.

Gee (2008) recognized that language cannot be divided from "its social context" (p. 2). He distinguished between "big D Discourses," which "include much more than language" (p. 2), and lowercase discourses, which refer to issues of language alone. Understanding that language use varies according to context and that individuals shift registers depending upon the people and places that surround them, Gee (2000) explained that "the very form of language is always an important part of Discourses" (p. 204). However, Discourses also include "ways of behaving, interacting, valuing, thinking, believing, speaking, and often reading and writing" that contribute to "socially situated identities" (Gee, 2008, p. 3).

The examination of Discourses is inherently tied to social participation, and in the digital age, social groups form in virtual spaces. These virtual communities are saturated with tools of Information and Communication Technology (ICT) that enable efficient, written messages. Within digital communities, individuals have embraced ICTs to communicate, developing a language system that combines elements of Standard Written English (SWE) with abbreviations, fragmented sentences, "initialisms" (Jacobs, 2008, p. 204), emoticons, and other manipulations of conventional SWE. This digital language has evolved with the development of new technologies.

Whereas once teenagers communicated by telephone, with the introduction of computer chat programs, "talk" transformed. Conversations began to take place via writing, albeit in real time. Though the technology afforded new lines of communication, it also enabled the possibilities of overlapping utterances. Therefore, to more efficiently communicate ideas, shortcuts that involved fewer keystrokes became standard practice among many users (Crystal, 2001). As Gee (2008) might have argued, this evolving digital language represented both a discourse (language) and a Discourse (literacy) practice.

From their introduction instant messaging programs held great appeal to teenagers who wanted to connect with their friends outside of school. Further advancements in technology led to text messaging on mobile phones and communication via social networks, and adolescents similarly embraced these tools and the language that allowed for efficient communication with them. A

historical chronicling of what is commonly termed "textspeak" reveals that Crystal (2001) originally labeled the nonstandard, digital language as "net-speak." As both text*speak* and net*speak* suggest, teens have adapted their language when they "talk" to their friends, yet neither of these terms captures the true nature of the language. Writing in many digital venues blends elements of written discourse with those of spoken word (Baron, 2008; Gee & Hayes, 2011). However, patterns of language cross technological boundaries. They are neither net-based nor texting-based.

Therefore, the language that adolescents use in their virtual communities might better be called digitalk (Turner, 2010, 2011). The term captures the nature of the writing, which in most cases replaces verbal communication, and it encompasses the wide variety of digital technologies that allow for this exchange. Becoming an adept user of digitalk requires practice and knowledge of both the discourse and Discourse systems of a community. Digital Discourses allow for creativity on the parts of individuals, and teens have welcomed the freedom to experiment, which in turn has helped shape language within their communities of practice (Wenger, 1998). The present study has attempted to understand both the nature of the language, the discourse, and the underlying Discourse practices that influence teens' linguistic choices in their digital writing.

METHODOLOGY

The data for this study were collected and analyzed in a two-phase method by a multiple-member research team. First, researchers examined digital writing samples that were self-selected and submitted by 81 teenagers (ages 13 – 18) from a large geographic area that included a large city in the Northeast and several suburban communities surrounding it. Though researchers asked adolescents to provide examples from a variety of media (i.e., texts, instant messages (chats), emails, blog posts, social network posts, and other digital language), the participants submitted only texts, instant messages, and social network posts. The lack of data in other domains helped the research team to define digitalk as writing in these three media, where teens regularly "talk" to each other, and it influenced the decision to look for conventions across media rather than within one type of writing as other research has done. (See, for example, Baron, 2008; Cherny, 1999; Crystal, 2001; Crystal, 2008; Haas, Takayoshi, Carr, Hudson, & Pollock, 2011.)

After determining the features of language employed across media, researchers selected eight participants to interview about their language choices. Using the students' own writing, in a form of stimulated-recall (Dipardo, 1994), researchers probed the reasons why the teens used particular conventions. These interviews informed the creation of a "user-choice" survey that was completed by 75 teens. In addition, researchers conducted additional interviews with some of these new participants to explore fully the second research question.

Detailed description of the methodological decisions made in this study has been published elsewhere (Turner, Abrams, Katíc, & Donovan, in press). This chapter highlights the process of data collection and analysis, which may guide both researchers and teachers in future study of language practices. Table 1 presents an overview of the two-phase method described here.

Phase 1: What Do They Do?

To explore the question "What are the conventions of digitalk?" researchers asked teenagers to submit samples of their digital writing that did not conform to SWE. Teens were encouraged to share examples of their language that they considered typical of their digital writing but that also might not be "proper English." Each sample that was submitted was filed according to the media where

Table 1. Summary of data collection and analysis

Phase	Data Collection	Analysis
Phase 1	Writing samples collected from 81 adolescents	Coded for linguistic features and developed list of conventions
Phase 2	Interviewed 8 of the same participants to discuss language choices in their submitted samples	Developed broad themes that guided development of User-Choice survey
	Created and piloted User-Choice Survey with the same 8 students	
	Administered User-Choice Survey to the original 81 participants	Low response rate
	Recruited additional participants to complete survey	Counted frequencies and coded qualitative responses for 75 surveys
	Interviewed 16 of the new participants to discuss language choices	Coded interviews focusing on purposes of language use
	Conducted 3 classroom workshops that included 60 new participants (not included in survey results)	Coded transcripts focusing on purposes of language use

it was produced: (1) text message, (2) instant message, or (3) social networking post.

After this organization of the data, researchers coded the samples according to the five features of written language identified by Crystal (2001). The team looked for data manipulations in the following categories: (1) graphic (design, symbols, emoticons), (2) orthographic (spelling, punctuation, capitalization, emphasis), (3) grammatical (sentence structure, word order), (4) lexical (vocabulary, word changes), (5) discourse (structure, organization, coherence). Through an iterative process, independent coders inductively developed sub-codes in each area and then worked collaboratively to refine the code list, using the work of Crystal (2008) as a guide. The final list included 46 codes. (See Appendix for complete code list.) Inter-coder reliability was over 95%.

While Ling and Baron (2007) identified differences in patterns of language between texting and instant messaging, in contrast, the present study looked for features across media in an attempt to highlight both d/Discourse practices. Because texts, IMs, and social network posts dominated the data that was self-selected by teens, researchers concluded that manipulations to SWE occurred most often in these media and that commonalities among the media may help in understanding the community of writers as a whole. Therefore, the team charted the number of occurrences of each feature within each media. Also interested in the number of individuals who used each feature of language, researchers also charted the features according to participant.

Lewis (1969) suggested that conventional behavior within a culture develops when members of a particular community may reasonably expect others in that community to understand and accept their behaviors. For this analysis, researchers determined that features of language used by a majority of teens in the sample represented conventions; if most of the adolescents used the language features, they clearly expected others to accept and understand them. This analysis was conducted for the entire teen community (81 participants) and for sub-communities grouped geographically as "urban" (within city limits) and "suburban" (beyond city limits). The hope was to find conventions that crossed geographic boundaries and to discern any unique characteristics of the smaller communities.

Phase 2: Why Do They Do It?

Once the team understood *what* this population of teenagers was doing in their digital writing, researchers turned to the second question, "Why do teenagers make the language choices they do when they write texts, instant messages, and social network posts?" This phase of data collection and analysis cycled back to the first phase as data collected in phase one served to focus the work in phase two.

To begin the exploration of the question, interviewers used a form of stimulated-recall methodology (Dipardo, 1994), showing individual participants the writing samples they had submitted and asking them to discuss their language choices within those samples. Though the interviews were designed in the spirit of the work of Dipardo (1994), the present study did not attempt to capture the teens' thinking in the moment of composition. Rather, interviewers used the students' writing to prompt conversation about the language conventions present and why she or he used them. Three members of the research team independently reviewed the transcripts of these interviews, noting broad themes that identified several possible reasons why teens used the language features that had been uncovered in the analysis of their writing. At the research team meeting to discuss these individual reviews of the transcripts, questions about the role of technology in user choice arose. In order to ascertain the impact of the specific tools on language choices, the team decided to administer a user-choice survey that asked specific questions about autocorrect technologies.

The qualitative survey focused dually on the role of technology and other purposes (e.g., personal voice, community membership) that researchers had identified in the focal interviews. It consisted of two major sections. The first part asked closed questions (yes or no) that focused on technology; the second section asked participants to translate two samples of digitalk, to indicate whether they had used similar conventions in their own writing, and to provide insight into the purposes of using such conventions. (See Appendix for survey questions.) After being piloted with the focal students who had been interviewed, the survey was distributed to a larger group of adolescents.

In conjunction with collecting this survey data, researchers invited 16 teenagers to participate in a paired or group interview to discuss the conventions, the survey, and their own digital writing. The lead researcher also recorded three separate workshops, where she facilitated a high school class and engaged students in discussion of these topics. The 60 students who consented to participation in the study from these classes were not included in the survey data reported here; however, their verbal contributions were coded in conjunction with the interviews. Through a collaborative process, researchers independently coded data, discussed their interpretations, and developed a coding scheme. Ultimately, transcripts of these interviews and lessons were coded to highlight the purposes of the teen writers. Broadly, these codes focused on the major purposes of (1) efficiency, (2) community membership (including audience), and (3) individual identity (including personal voice).

FINDINGS

Conventions of Digitalk

Understanding that digitalk represents a discourse practice, and therefore a register of a particular Discourse, this study hoped to identify patterns of language that crossed technological media. The first phase focused on *what*, that is which features of language adolescents had conventionalized in their digital communities, and *how* the writers manipulated SWE. Overwhelmingly, teens in the sample manipulated SWE at the orthographic level (72% of coding frequency). Grammatical (12%), lexical (12%), and graphic (4%) codes surfaced in the analysis, but changes in spelling, punctuation, and capitalization dominated the data and the list of non-standard conventions of digitalk. This finding was not surprising in light of public views of "texting language," including media headlines that often play with orthographic features when mimicking the register. (See, for example, Ferenstein, 2012). What is interesting,

however, is that acronym shortcuts, which fall into the category of lexical changes, and "lax" grammar, both of which were cited by adults in the Pew Study (Lenhart, et. al, 2008) as problematic in teens' texting, were less apparent in the data than popular opinion might presume.

Table 2 presents a list of conventions adopted by the writers who participated in this study. To be considered a convention, more than 50% of the participants used it, and it was used across all three media of texting, instant messaging and social networking. First noticeable in this table is the blend of standard and nonstandard conventions adopted by this teen community. Of the 18 features of language identified as conventions, five adhere to SWE. These include (1) complete sentence, (2) question mark used, (3) standard capitalization, (4) end period used, and (5) apostrophe used. In fact, nearly every individual in the sample used complete sentences in digitalk. Thus, the notion that digitalk breaks completely from SWE was not supported by the data.

Despite the fact that 97% of the teens used complete sentences, fragments and run-ons were also frequently found in the data. These constructions, which might be viewed as errors by prescriptive grammarians, are not surprising in light of the seminal research by Shaughnessy (1977) that showed that student writers often used these constructions, and furthermore, conversations in oral language often consist of fragmented thoughts. Since digitalk blends oral and written language, it is predictable that adolescents use these conventions with frequency. Participants indicated that digital writing represented first-draft writing. They did not proofread, and they did not revise. Feedback from the receiver/reader indicated whether a message was understood, and as long as understanding occurred, sentence structure was irrelevant.

An interesting point to make about the list of conventions lies in the seemingly contradictory usages. For example, teens accepted as practice both conventional and non-conventional capitalization.

Table 2. Percentage of participants using conventions of digitalk

Convention	Percentage of Participants	Breaks from SWE	Category
Complete Sentence	97%	N	Grammatical
End Period Not Used	96%	Y	Orthographic
Non-standard Capitalization	94%	Y	Orthographic
Acronym	76%	Y	Lexical
Question Mark Used	74%	N	Orthographic
Standard Capitalization	72%	N	Orthographic
Abbreviation (Cut off End)	71%	Y	Lexical
Logograms (Letters for Sounds)	68%	Y	Lexical
Apostrophe Not Used	65%	Y	Orthographic
Fragment	65%	Y	Grammatical
Lowercase i	63%	Y	Orthographic
Run-On	63%	Y	Grammatical
Compound Words	62%	Y	Lexical
Multiple Consonants	60%	Y	Orthographic
End Period Used	59%	N	Orthographic
Ellipses	54%	Y	Orthographic
Apostrophe Used	54%	N	Orthographic
Multiple Vowels	50%	Y	Orthographic

Similarly, the teens were nearly as likely to use an apostrophe as they were not to use an apostrophe. In early days of digitalk, the nonstandard uses made sense; to be efficient and to minimize keystrokes, users abandoned capital letters and apostrophes. With the advent of autocorrect technology, these purposeful errors have been dramatically reduced. Many of the teens reported that they allowed their phones and computers to "fix" their writing. When the technology did not interfere and meaning was not threatened, however, they chose efficiency over correctness. Some, however, specifically chose to deactivate autocorrect features or to use lowercase letters, particularly lowercase i. For many of the survey respondents, this choice related to appearance, or as one participant said, using the lowercase i "looked cooler."

Another interesting contradiction in the data occurred in the use of end punctuation. Nearly every teen in the sample chose not to use end periods in their writing. On the other hand, over half of these same teens did use periods at times. Most often these periods separated thoughts within a line, as in the message provided at the beginning of this chapter: "i gotta meet my moms after skoooool today. tom?" However, periods at the end of a message, as one student said, were "not really necessary." The break in the message caused by hitting *send* served the purpose of the end punctuation. In addition, some of the participants suggested that using a period helped in creating a tone. As Lenny, a sophomore from a suburban school, stated, "If you're making like a serious point, you put a period at the end. You know, like if you want to be taken seriously." In this case, using the period contributed to the writer's voice. Similarly, question marks, which

Table 3. Unique conventions of digitalk and percentage of users by geographic area

Urban Conventions	Users	Unique	Suburban Conventions	Users	Unique
Complete Sentence	100%		Complete Sentence	94%	
End Period Not Used	97%		End Period Not Used	94%	
Non-standard Capitalization	95%		Non-standard Capitalization	94%	
Logograms (Letters for Sounds)	86%	x	Acronym	81%	
Phonetic Spelling	84%	x	Run-On	74%	
Question Mark Used	81%		Lowercase i	71%	
Abbreviation (Cut off End)	81%		Apostrophe Not Used	68%	
Standard Capitalization	76%		Standard Capitalization	68%	
Acronym	73%		Question Mark Used	65%	
Compound Words	70%		Multiple Consonants	65%	
Slang	70%	x	Apostrophe Used	65%	x
Fragment	68%		Fragment	61%	
Apostrophe Not Used	62%		Abbreviation (Cut off End)	58%	
End Period Used	62%		Logogram (Noises for Actions)	58%	x
Ellipses	62%	x	End Period Used	55%	
Lowercase i	57%		Multiple Vowels	55%	x
Multiple Consonants	57%		Compound Words	52%	
Run-On	54%				
Abbreviation (missing vowel)	54%	x			
Capital I	51%	x			

were used by 74% of the participants, captured inflection that reflected oral language.

In fact, capturing "voice" was important to the teens, and this purpose for using language could be seen when the data were disaggregated by geographic area. Table 3 suggests that urban teens conventionalized three features of language that relate to sound. Logograms (Crystal, 2008) that substitute letters for sounds (e. g., "r" for are, "c" for see, as in "cya") focus directly on the way a word sounds. In addition, phonetic spellings (e.g. "skool," "dat") and slang (e.g., "mad good," "homie") capture oral language in an authentic way. These features helped to create a distinct voice of the urban data, a style the teens purposefully chose to accept into their community. Similarly, suburban teens conventionalized logograms that identified noises made through or with actions (e. g., haha, eek). These slight differences in the

conventions of the community may indicate that the groups attempted to achieve the same goal (i.e., capturing voice) in unique ways.

The list of conventions of the communities of writers in this study reflect the assertions of Baron (2008) and Gee and Hayes (2011), who noted that digital language is a blend of spoken and written discourses. As teens "talk" to each other using written words, they compose using standard conventions that enable a systematic language, yet they manipulate features in order to communicate efficiently and to capture their voices. These acts reflect the choices that expert writers make. Digitalk, then, allows adolescents to develop competencies as writers.

Competencies Developed in Digitalk

Audience

Nystrand (1986) suggested that writers do not compose in isolation from their eventual readers. Instead, writing is a collaborative act: under a contract of reciprocity, each individual "presupposes—indeed counts on—the sense-making capabilities of the other" (p. ix). Teen writers immersed in a world of digitalk do not disregard rules of reciprocity. On the contrary, they strive as a community to adopt conventions that will be understood by its members. In part because of their unspoken understanding of reciprocity, adolescents who write in digital communities develop a keen sense of audience.

This competence became clear as participants in the present study discussed the intended receivers of their messages. For example, Charlie and Andie, two juniors in a suburban school, explained that their choice of language depended upon "the person you're talking to." The following conversation began with a discussion of multiple vowels, specifically the use of more than one "y" in the word "heyyyy."

Andie: That means he likes someone or the closer you are with them.

Interviewer: The more Ys you put?

Charlie: Yeah like if you like someone, usually the more Ys you put, the more excited you are to talk to them kind of thing.

Interviewer: Yeah I kind of see, wait, you mean "like," like meaning boy and girl like or meaning like -

Andie: Usually it's more like, yeah, it's like if you want to go out with someone, but it can be like a best friend or something like that.

Interviewer: So somebody that you don't know very well you would -

Charlie: You just put hey.

Andie: Like if you're -

Charlie: Or even hi.

Interviewer: Oh hi, instead of hey?

Andie: Yeah. A lot of people write like a lot of I's if you're excited to talk to someone.

Interviewer: Oh really?

Charlie: I've never heard of the I's but I just know -

Andie: I do that. I know if I'm texting like one of my really good guy friends.

Interviewer: So it's different if you're texting a girl or a guy?

Andie: Yeah.... It depends on your relationship with that person. If they're just a friend, usually it doesn't matter but if it's someone you like - I know like I have friends and sometimes I stress over, should I put two Ys or three Ys?

Charlie: So it depends on the person you're talking to. For example, I have friends who are very nit-picky with grammar. So if I put "hey" or like if I don't capitalize my I's or anything, they go OCD [obsessive].

Andie: It depends who's on the other side of the message.

Andie and Charlie indicated that they considered their relationship with the intended receiver, the audience, as they chose language conventions. They made specific choices for close friends, for acquaintances, for romantic interests, and for friends whose "grammar has to have everything right." As Andie suggested, "It depends. It really depends on who's on the other side of the phone."

Interestingly, both Andie and Charlie acknowledged that a few of their teen friends expected standard grammar in their digital communications. Though this was not a common theme in the data, and in fact, most of the teens felt that they were not judged by their friends for their language choices, many of the participants did suggest that they wrote more formally for some receivers. For their grammar-conscious friends, Andie said she will "capitalize everything," and Charlie affirmed he will "put the periods in." However, most of the adolescents in the study indicated that they saved formal language for adults. As another participant,

Doug, noted, "You can't write your mom like that because she'll be, like, 'what?' She wouldn't understand what you're writing."

Reciprocity played a key role in the teens' decisions to write more formally with the adults in their lives. According to their explanations, adults would not understand digitalk. Friends Lebron and Ray explained:

Lebron: Only with my grandmother, that's when I text proper. She really doesn't understand the abbreviations so -

Ray: Yeah, I only speak to my friends like that.

Interviewer: But you would never just type the word? You would always use the symbol?

Ray: I mean only with my friends do I use these symbols. My mom or my grandmother when texting, they don't understand all the symbols we use. Cause we already know what it's about, you know?

Interviewer: So what wouldn't your mom or grandmother understand about this particular conversation [that you wrote]?

Ray: Basically nothing.

Lebron: If I said "whaddup" to my grandmother, she knows what it means, but she'll, she'll look at me like "why you writing me like that?"

These ideas—that adults would not understand digitalk nor would they accept it—permeated the data. One student even defined the age of understanding as "under 30," a line that many of the teens seemed to have drawn between "old" and young. This attention to reciprocity, or the knowledge that the receiver must be able to understand the message, demonstrates a developing knowledge of audience, a key element of the process of expert writers (Flower & Hayes, 1981).

Voice: A teen from an urban school, Sherry, made it clear that language "depends on the situation and the audience I'm speaking to." This understanding of the connection between audience and language represents one competency that teens develop through their communities rooted in digitalk. They also cultivate a sense of voice, or "the medium employed by the writer to create his or her presence in the text" (Yancey, 1994, p. x). Voice is closely linked to personal style; it is what allows a reader to distinguish easily between the writing of F. Scott Fitzgerald and his contemporary Ernest Hemingway. The linguistic styles of these two authors were distinct, and as such, readers familiar with their individual voices recognize their work. For writers, "voice is a powerful tool" (Frank & Wall, 1996, p. 6), but according to Frank & Wall (1996), it is also "hard to identify" (p. 6) and "most writers struggle to unearth voice" (p. 6). Digitalk, however, allows youth on a daily basis to experiment in language, to identify themselves, and to begin to "unearth" their voices.

For example, Tabitha, a freshman in a large city school, explained that using multiple letters was a way for teens to "express themselves." Her classmate, Nash, suggested that replacing letters with numbers (e.g., '3' replacing 'e') made the writing "unique." These ideas indicated that language helped the teen writers to identify themselves, and as John, a junior in a suburban district, said, "There's some things that you do because you, like, want it to be you." Charlie, also a junior in a suburban school, connected digitalk explicitly to voice: "It's kind of weird. But I can actually hear their voices sometimes. Like the way that they're writing is the way that they're speaking."

John and his friend Emily talked extensively about how they "sound" when they write in digitalk. They attempted to capture an authentic voice, and they recognized the voices of their peers. As Emily remarked, "Like I can tell sometimes if it's not that person texting you from that number." As the two dissected a sample text conversation, they discussed Emily's style.

Interviewer: Well what does [Emily] do that makes it known that you know it's her?

John: Like, like she does like extensive things sometimes. Like, she does do faces, like it's all random for her, and she'll do, like, sometimes you will do extended letters like, 'soooo...whatsss up?'

Emily: I don't do the S's.

John: You'll do like 'soooo' or something like that. I don't know, but, like, yeah I can tell when Emily – like, Emily likes to be proper in her writing, but she likes to be, like, funny or, like, easy about it. Like she would write - like what would she write? {looking at text conversation} Like she would write like this part {pointing}; she would never write like that {pointing to another section}.

Interviewer: I didn't see the first part. It's like the 'i got pizzaa'?

John: She'd write like Lily's part. She would never write like Michael.

Emily: I wouldn't write like this. What are you talking about?

John: Like -

Emily: 'Ima', 'pizzaa' - that's just weird.

John: No, you wouldn't write like that. Like short things like 'soooo' you would write extensive. Like, like simple words.

Emily: OK. Her dot-dot-dots - I would do that.

John: She'd do that.

From Emily's emphatic, "I wouldn't write like this," to John's affirmation that Emily would use ellipses similar to those in the sample conversation, it was clear from this exchange that both teens recognized the power of language to identify a writer.

Ray and Lebron shared a similar sentiment in their interview. When asked how a friend would know that it was Ray who was writing, the young man replied, "They know how I talk.... Just like the way I write... just that alone they already know it's me." Lebron concurred, offering a specific linguistic "signature" for his friend.

Lebron: Like how I would know it was Ray is he doesn't write S's; he writes 5's.

Ray: Yeah.

Interviewer: And only Ray does that?

Lebron: Yeah, basically.

Ray: Yep, that's how they know that it's me.

Interviewer: And why do you do 5's and not S's?

Ray: I don't know. Just to have, just to have me there.

Interviewer: So -

Ray: It makes people know it's me.

Though they do not label it as such, Ray, Lebron, John, and Emily all suggested that digitalk allows them to identify themselves, a process that helps in developing their writer's voice. In part this voice is literal, linked to how an individual sounds when he or she speaks. A group of middle school girls made this connection.

Ashley: But about the s and z thing, the transformation. Sometimes I say that to sound crazy or funny or something. Like "pizzazzz" "I'm going to go eat some pizzazzz"

Patti: "Pizzazzz" it's catchy.

Interviewer: Yeah, you said it with, like, all this attitude in your voice.

Ashley: Yeah, attitude. When they write, like I said this before, their attitude, how they feel. Like sometimes if you write schools with the "s," it's nothing. But "schoolz" with a z, that's like more catchy.

Jayla: Cool -

Ashley: Cool, catchy.

Jayla: And they like pay attention. Not like pay attention to you more, but like, well, I can't explain it.

Interviewer: They notice you?

Jayla: Yeah, they get you.

This conversation shifted from Ashley's point that language can capture "sound" to Jayla's revelation that manipulation of language can help the receiver "get you." In essence, these girls revealed that digitalk – with its freedom to experiment and manipulate – helped them to capture their voices in their writing. Like many of the teens in the study, these girls were developing competence in understanding voice through their digital communities.

IMPLICATIONS

Thurlow (2006) investigated the media's portrayal of computer-mediated discourse (CMD) and found that digital language has been viewed negatively. However, he asserted:

What is less certain is the degree of accuracy and the specificity of detail offered in media representations of computer-mediated discourse. For this reason, if no other, future research should pay greater attention to the linguistic and orthographic dimensions of CMD and undertake more situated analyses of CMD practice. (p. 690)

The present study has added to the growing body of research that answers Thurlow's call. To date, however, these studies have focused on adult users, and they have been limited to articulating *what*, or descriptions of language features that are used in various digital venues. The methodology employed in the present study adds to both the questions about and the analysis of digital language by situating digitalk as part of community practice. As such, the focus has been as much about the purposes of the writers within a community as it is about the linguistic features themselves. The two-phase method allowed for a deeper understanding of the Discourse practices of the teens.

In articulating the features of language used by adolescents in their digitalk, the present study found that teens manipulate language primarily at the orthographic level and that they both adhere to and break from SWE. These findings push against popular conceptions of "texting language," suggesting that adults may make inaccurate as-

sumptions about the *what* and the *why* of digitalk. These false beliefs have led to stereotypes of laziness (Lenhart, et. al, 2008), which were echoed by some of the teens in the sample. Focusing on digitalk as *wrong* cultivates language prejudice, and this prejudice may conceal any competencies that do exist in the non-standard practice. This conversation is not new (e.g., Delpit & Dowdy 2002/2008); however, the present study suggests that it be expanded to include digital language.

Language practices are complex, and adolescents must navigate multiple d/Discourses – both in and out of school. There is no question that digitalk is different from academic English. However, the difference does not make it deficient. Rarely do adults commend teens on their experimentation with language, on their creativity, or on their ability to navigate social norms in a community of practice. Rarely are teens proud of their competencies in their out-of-school communities. In fact, the Pew study indicated that 60% of teens do not see their digital writing as "*real*" writing" (Lenhart et al. 2008, p. 4). Their views may be shaped by the fact that they use the term "talk" to refer to their interactions with their friends online. However, their dismissal of texting, IM, and social networking, all of which takes place using written words, might also be a product of the societal bias against the informal language, or digitalk, they use in these spaces.

When given the opportunity to talk about their digitalk, teens articulated clear purposes for the manipulation of SWE. These purposes related to audience and voice, and the participants demonstrated attention to reciprocity (Nystrand, 1986). In other words, they used language that they believed would capture their individual persona and that their recipients would understand. This finding alone has implications for the teaching of writing. If educators can help teenagers to recognize digitalk as a legitimate use of language within a specific community, and if teen writers can articulate the purposes behind their language choices in that community, they may be able to consciously apply their knowledge of audience and voice, which they have developed in their digital communities, to writing that they do in school.

To achieve this goal, a shift in thinking must occur. Rather than seeing *error* in students' digitalk, teachers and researchers must focus on *strength*. To this end, first, adults must recognize that many mainstream perceptions of digitalk are not accurate. The analysis of writing from the adolescents in this study indicated that some popular notions (e.g., using numbers to replace sounds, as in "b4") may be outdated. Secondly, those outside the digital, teen community must view this group as writers who use language for communicative purposes.

Without fear of a red pen, by using digitalk adolescents are developing their awareness of audience and their understanding of voice in an authentic space. Because most teens write in their digital communities every day, they have the opportunity to practice and receive immediate feedback from their peers in this process. Students of the digital era enter writing classrooms with this experience, and educators have the potential to engage these competencies in an academic venue by fostering metalinguistic awareness and helping teens to make purposeful linguistic choices in all contexts. This work begins with asking students about their out-of-school writing and the language that they use, rather than simply telling them that they *should* be using SWE in academic tasks. Though this study documented the work completed by researchers that examined the writing of a diverse group of students, the method could be replicated by classroom teachers. The data revealed that language choices are, indeed, influenced by communities of practice. Instruction in language, then, could begin by understanding the community in the classroom – and the communities of those writers outside of school.

The present study has complicated the way researchers and teachers might view digital language and suggests that rather than focusing on (in)correctness, adults consider the competencies that teen writers demonstrate in their out-of-school communities. The suggestions for practice outlined above embody questions for future research to explore. For example, "How might teens transfer their knowledge of audience and voice, gained in their digital communities, to academic tasks?" This question of transfer lies at the heart of the instructional implications presented here, and researchers should work closely with teachers in designing and evaluating instruction to reveal the potential of bringing the out-of-school literacies to academic writing.

Future research might also look more closely at digitalk and its role in developing teens' understanding of writing. The present study revealed that adolescents develop a sense of audience and personal voice through their digitalk; however, neither the questions nor the method uncovered the process of doing so. How does an individual develop a sense of self in his or her digital writing? How does this sense of self evolve? Exploring these questions may have further implications for writing instruction, and attention to these issues will place value on the Discourse practices of adolescents.

Adolescence is a period of identity development (Erikson, 1968); this development occurs alongside of, and perhaps through, digital communication, and digitalk may very well represent changes in self and negotiation of individual identity within a community of practice. The link between literacy and identity has been drawn by others (e.g., Moje & Luke, 2009); new media allows for writing in new ways, namely by introducing authentic contexts and audiences for writing on a daily basis. It is important to explore these new contexts, as well as the effects they have on teens' writing. Because the community of teen writers is in constant flux, with members growing and evolving, the language will also change.

The research community should continue to attend to these linguistic movements, validating or challenging popular assumptions about what is happening, and it should also allow adolescents to voice their perspectives of the writing that they do in authentic contexts.

CONCLUSION

Is the following conversation riddled with errors?:

- we hangin later?
- i gotta meet my moms after skoooool today. tom?
- yeah, fo sho
- fo sho...we can meet behind the yard
- k. see u then
- HOLLA

Perhaps not. Perhaps this exchange with its phonetic spellings, its abbreviations, and its non-standard punctuation and capitalization embodies the voices of two writers. Perhaps these writers chose particular conventions in order to belong to a community, to communicate a message efficiently, and to express their individual identities. Finally, perhaps both the research and teaching communities can learn from these teens, valuing the competencies that they develop in an authentic way. These competencies in digitalk reflect the strengths of these digital writers.

REFERENCES

Baron, N. S. (2008). *Always on: Language in an online and mobile world*. New York, NY: Oxford University Press.

Barton, D. (1994). *Literacy: An introduction to the ecology of written language*. Oxford, UK: Blackwell.

Barton, D. (2001). Literacy in everyday contexts. In Snow, C., & Verhoeven, L. (Eds.), *Literacy and motivation* (pp. 23–37). Mahwah, NJ: Lawrence Erlbaum Associates.

Cherny, L. (1999). *Conversation and community: Chat in a virtual world*. Stanford, CA: CSLI Publications.

Crystal, D. (2001). *Language and the internet*. New York, NY: Cambridge University Press. doi:10.1017/CBO97811391647771.

Crystal, D. (2008). *Txtng: The gr8 db8*. New York, NY: Oxford University Press.

Delpit, L., & Dowdy, J. K. (Eds.). (2002/2008). *The skin that we speak*. New York: New Press.

Dipardo, A. (1996). Stimulated recall in research writing: An antidote to I don't know, it was fine. In Smagorinsky, P. (Ed.), *Speaking about writing: Reflections on research methodology* (pp. 163–181). Thousand Oaks, CA: Sage Publications.

Erikson, E. (1968). *Identity: Youth and crisis*. New York: Norton.

Ferenstein, G. (2012, Aug. 1). Study: Texting iz destroying student grammar. *Tech Crunch*. Retrieved from http://techcrunch.com/2012/08/01/study-texting-iz-destroying-student-grammar/

Flower, L., & Hayes, J. (1981). A cognitive process theory of writing. *College Composition and Communication*, *32*, 365–387. doi:10.2307/356600.

Frank, T., & Wall, D. (1996). *Finding your writer's voice: A guide to creative fiction*. New York: St. Martin's Griffin.

Gee, J. (1996). *Social linguistics and literacies: Ideology in Discourses* (2nd ed.). London: Taylor & Francis.

Gee, J. P. (2000). Discourse and sociocultural studies in reading. In Kamil, M. L., Mosenthal, P. B., Pearson, P. D., & Barr, R. (Eds.), *Handbook of Reading Research* (*Vol. 3*, pp. 195–207). Mahwah, NJ: Lawrence Erlbaum.

Gee, J. P. (2008). *Social linguistics and literacies: Ideology in discourse* (3rd ed.). New York, NY: Routledge.

Gee, J. P., & Hayes, E. R. (2011). *Language and learning in the digital age*. New York, NY: Routledge.

Haas, C., Takayoshi, P., Carr, B., Hudson, K., & Pollock, R. (2011). Young people's everyday literacies: The language features of instant messaging. *Research in the Teaching of English*, *45*, 378–404.

Howard, C. (2012, February 14). The Gr8 Deb8 of teen Txting: Text messaging ruining the English language? *World Now*. Retrieved from http://www.khq.com/story/16937099/the-gr8-deb8-of-teen-txting-text-messaging-ruining-the-english-language

Jacobs, G. E. (2008). We learn what we do: Developing a repertoire of writing practices in an instant messaging world. *Journal of Adolescent & Adult Literacy*, *52*(3), 203–211. doi:10.1598/JAAL.52.3.3.

Kemp, N., & Bushnell, C. (2011). Children's text messaging: Abbreviations, input methods and links with literacy. *Journal of Computer Assisted Learning*, *27*, 18–27. doi:10.1111/j.1365-2729.2010.00400.x.

Lenhart, A., Arafeh, S., Smith, A., & Macgill, A. R. (2008). *Writing, technology and teens*. Retrieved from http://www.pewInternet.org/PPF/r/247/report_display.asp

Lewis, D. (1969). *Convention: A philosophical study*. Cambridge, MA: Harvard University Press.

Ling, R., & Baron, N. S. (2007). Messaging and IM: Linguistic comparison of American college data. *Journal of Language and Social Psychology*, *26*(3), 291–298. doi:10.1177/0261927X06303480.

Moje, E. B., & Luke, A. (2009). Literacy and identity: Examining the metaphors in history and contemporary research. *Reading Research Quarterly*, *44*(4), 415–437. dx.doi.org/10.1598/RRQ.44.4.7 doi:10.1598/RRQ.44.4.7.

Nystrand, M. (1986). *The structure of written communication: Studies in reciprocity between readers and writers*. Orlando, FL: Academic Press.

Plester, B., Wood, C., & Bell, V. (2008). Txt msg n school literacy: Does texting and knowledge of text abbreviations adversely affect children's literacy attainment. *Literacy*, *42*, 137–144. doi:10.1111/j.1741-4369.2008.00489.x.

Plester, B., Wood, C., & Joshi, P. (2009). Exploring the relationship between children's knowledge of text message abbreviations and school literacy outcomes. *The British Journal of Developmental Psychology*, *27*, 145–161. doi:10.1348/026151008X320507 PMID:19972666.

Powell, D., & Dixon, M. (2011). Does SMS text messaging help or harm adults' knowledge of standard spelling? *Journal of Computer Assisted Learning*, *27*, 58–66. doi:10.1111/j.1365-2729.2010.00403.x.

Shaughnessy, M. P. (1977). *Errors and expectations: A guide for the teacher of basic writing*. Oxford, UK: Oxford University Press.

Singel, D., & Sundar, S. S. (2012). Texting, techspeak, and tweens: The relationship between text messaging and English grammar skills. *New Media & Society*, *14*, 1304–1320. doi:10.1177/1461444812442927.

Street, B. V. (1995). *Social literacies: Critical approaches to literacy in development, ethnography, and education*. New York: Longman.

Street, B. V. (1999). Literacy and social change: The significance of social context in the development of literacy programmes. In Wagner, D. A. (Ed.), *Future of literacy in a changing world* (pp. 55–72). Cresskill, NJ: Hampton Press.

Thurlow, C. (2006). From statistical panic to moral panic: The metadiscursive construction and popular exaggeration of new media language in the print media. *Journal of Computer-Mediated Communication, 11*, 667–701. doi:10.1111/j.1083-6101.2006.00031.x.

Turner, K. H. (2010). Digitalk: A new literacy for a digital generation. *Phi Delta Kappan, 92*(1), 41–46.

Turner, K. H. (2011). Digitalk: Community, convention, and self-expression. In Rowsell, J., & Abrams, S. A. (Eds.), *Rethinking Identity and Literacy Education in the 21ˢᵗ Century* (pp. 263–282). New York: Teachers College Record Yearbook.

Turner, K. H. (2013). The challenge of acceptance: Digitalk and language as conformity and resistance. In Spielhagen & Schwarz (Eds.), Adolescence in the 21st Century: Constants and Challenge. Information Age.

Turner, K. H., Abrams, S., Katic, E., & Donovan, M. J. (2013). Digitalk: The what and the why of adolescent digital language. *Journal of Literacy Research*.

Wenger, E. C. (1998). *Communities of practice: Learning, meaning and identity*. New York, NY: Cambridge University Press.

Wood, C., Jackson, E., Hart, L., Plester, B., & Wilde, L. (2011). The effect of text messaging on 9- and 10-year-old children's reading, spelling, and phonological processing skills. *Journal of Computer Assisted Learning, 27*, 28–36. doi:10.1111/j.1365-2729.2010.00398.x.

Yancey, K. B. (2004). Definition, intersection, and difference – Mapping the landscape of voice. In Yancey, K. B. (Ed.), *Voices on voice: Perspectives, definitions, inquiry (vii – xxiv)*. Urbana, IL: National Council of Teachers of English.

APPENDIX

Code List for Phase I

- Abbreviation (change word)
- Abbreviation (cut off end)
- Abbreviation (missing consonant)
- Abbreviation (missing vowel)
- Acronym
- All Caps
- Apostrophe Not Used
- Apostrophe Used
- Capital I
- Complete Sentence
- Compound Words
- Double negative
- Ellipses
- End Period Not Used
- End Period Used
- Exclamation point used
- Expressions
- Fragment
- Inconsistency
- Line Break
- Logograms (#s as sounds)
- Logograms (letters for sounds)
- Logograms (noises for actions)
- Logograms (symbols)
- Lowercase i
- Missing Word
- Multiple Consonants
- Multiple Punctuation
- Multiple Vowels
- Non-Standard Capitalization
- Non-Standard Punctuation
- Nonsense Typing
- Numbers written
- Omitted Preposition
- Omitted Subject
- Omitted Verb
- Phonetic Spelling
- Pictograms
- Question Mark Not Used

- Question Mark Used
- Run-On
- S-V Agreement
- Slang
- Spanish used
- Standard Capitalization
- Standard punctuation used
- Thoughts Run-On
- Typo

User-Choice Survey Part I Questions

- Do you use a phone that automatically capitalizes "I" for you?
- Do you use a computer that shows you that you have not capitalized "i"?
- Do you ever use a lowercase "i" on purpose?
- If yes, why do you do this?
- Do you use a phone that automatically capitalizes the beginning of a new sentence for you?
- Do you use a computer that shows you that you have not capitalized the beginning of a new sentence?
- Do you ever choose not to capitalize the beginning of a new sentence?
- If yes, why do you do this?
- Do you use a phone that capitalizes proper nouns for you (like New York City or Michael)?
- Do you use a computer that shows you that you have not capitalized proper nouns (like New York City or Michael)?
- Do you ever choose not to capitalize proper nouns?
- If yes, why do you do this?
- Do you ever choose not to put a period at the end of your sentences?
- If yes, why do you do this?
- Do you use a phone that wants to expand a word for you (like "prob" turned into "probably")?
- Do you ever choose to let the phone insert the expanded word?
- Do you use a phone that shows you when you spelled a word wrong?
- Do you use a computer that shows you when you spelled a word wrong?
- Do you ever choose to let the phone autocorrect your spelling?
- Do you ever choose to let the computer autocorrect your spelling?
- Do you have a phone plan that limits how many text messages you can send?
- Do you have a phone plan that limits how long your outgoing text messages can be?
- Do you use abbreviations when you text because of the phone plan you have?
- Do you know what types of phones your friends have?
- Do you adjust your texting to fit your friends' phones?
- Do you use language differently depending on whether you text, IM, or write social network posts? If yes, why do you do this?

- **Instant Messaging:** Is there anything else you want to tell us about the way you use language in instant messaging (IM)?
- **Text Messaging:** Is there anything else you want to tell us about the way you use language in text messages?
- **Social Networking:** Is there anything else you want to tell us about the way you use language in social networking?

User-Choice Survey Part II Questions

Translate this message into Standard English:

"sameee...so wat did u get on the chem test"

Translation: Why do you think the author used the following? (See Table 4.) Write your reason in the box and check whether you have ever done something similar, have seen it but never done it yourself, or have never seen it.

Translate this message into Standard English:

Table 4.

	Why do you think the author used this?	Done it	Have seen it	Have never seen it
sameee (rather than same)				
...				
wat (rather than what)				
u (rather than you)				
chem (rather than chemistry)				

"ahh that sucksss. im gonna have to make it up =/"

Translation: Why do you think the author used the following? (See Table 5.) Write your reason in the box and check whether you have ever done something similar, have seen it but never done it yourself, or have never seen it.

Table 5.

	Why do you think the author used this?	Done it	Have seen it	Have never seen it
sucksss (rather than sucks)				
im (rather than I'm)				
gonna (rather than going to)				
=/				

Section 2
New Tools for Revision and Feedback

How can writing instructors provide feedback that nurtures and develops students' growth as writers? How do educators teach students to effectively respond to others' writing during peer-review opportunities in the classroom? Issues surrounding how to provide effective feedback and engage students in the revision and feedback process have been long-standing research questions in the field of writing. Teachers often encourage students to engage in collaboration and self-reflection through peer review opportunities; however, peer review is often difficult for students. Too often students aren't taught how to provide feedback, they have concerns about alienating peers, or feel they lack the knowledge to give feedback. Even teachers find that providing writers with specific feedback can be challenging. New online environments and tools have prompted researchers to examine platforms that teachers and students might use to respond to writing during instruction. The chapters in this section explore specific digital tools and online platforms for revision and feedback.

The first two chapters focus on middle school students' engagement and learning about the peer-feedback process in online writing environments. Hunt-Barron and Colwell examine how seventh grade students participated in peer-feedback using a Ning, a social network environment. During this 13-week study, students wrote, requested feedback from their peers, provided feedback, and responded to the feedback provided. This study found students learned how to provide feedback to others and were able to incorporate revisions in their writing. McCarthey, Magnifico, Woodard, and Kline provide a case study of one middle school student, Tom, to specifically analyze the affordances of using Scholar, an online writing tool for revision. Using Scholar provided Tom opportunities to consider his audience, increased his motivation for writing, and scaffolded his learning of writing and responding to other's writing. Lack of access to technology at home, as well as focus a scripted reading program used in the classroom, created constraints for Tom as a writer.

The last chapter in this section analyzes the research on digital feedback at the college level. Hopton examines how digital feedback allows professors to effectively give students' feedback on their writing and manage writing assessments. Digital tools are featured that can provide both formative and summative feedback. Hopton argues that more research is needed to examine the effectiveness of these tools.

This section is guided by the idea that feedback from peers and teachers is essential for the writing process and that digital tools provide support during this task.

Chapter 8
Illuminating Change:
Technology, Feedback, and Revision in Writing

Sarah Hunt-Barron
Converse College, USA

Jamie Colwell
Old Dominion University, USA

ABSTRACT

Using the method of a formative experiment, this investigation examines how the use of peer revision and collaboration in an online environment, specifically a social network, could be implemented in a middle school classroom to increase revision over multiple drafts and improve the quality of student expository writing. Thirty-six students in two sections of a seventh-grade English language arts class participated in the study. Quantitative and qualitative data were collected prior to, during, and after the intervention to establish baseline data, as well as determine progress toward the pedagogical goal. Analyses reveal improvement in the amount of student revision and quality of student writing, as well as improved peer feedback using an online community for peer revision and collaboration. The enhancing and inhibiting effects of technology in this intervention is examined, as well as the unanticipated effects of the intervention.

INTRODUCTION

As digital technologies have changed, so has writing. Web 2.0 tools are in common use and, as part of an increasingly participatory culture, we are all creators of media for public consumption (Jenkins, Clinton, Purushotma, Robison, & Weigel, 2009; Yancey, 2009). According to research by the Pew Internet and American Life Project, 95% of teens are now online with 70% of teens taking the

time to go online daily (Lenhart, Madden, Smith, Purcell, Zickuhr, & Rainie, 2011). Teens are active users of social networking sites, with 80% of teens actively engaged in some kind of online social media (Lenhart, Madden, Smith, Purcell, Zickuhr, & Rainie). Therefore, most teenagers aged twelve to seventeen are using some form of electronic personal communication, from sending email to text messaging to posting comments on social networks. Many online spaces foster collaboration and interaction with others through writing, yet, for students, the literacy of their

DOI: 10.4018/978-1-4666-4341-3.ch008

everyday lives, or out-of-school literacy, and the literacy valued in schools is not always apparent (Rhodes & Robnolt, 2009; Tyner, 1998). Further, teachers may not view students' out-of-school literacy skills, specifically the writing skills students engage in outside of school, as sufficiently rigorous (Williams, 2005).

Thus, critical questions concerning writing instruction in adolescent education remain. For example, how can educators effectively engage students in writing? How can teachers help students develop as readers and writers and prepare them with skills necessary in the 21st century and relevant to their out-of-school lives? These questions were considered as we designed this study. Studying online and digital technologies is one relevant method to address 21st century skills. Also, the writing workshop model is inherently collaborative, and activity focused on peer revision holds promise to improve students' critical writing skills. Capitalizing on collaborative online environments during peer revision may be a promising method to engage students in writing. Our study, which was conducted as a formative experiment, considered an intervention, which used a collaborative online writing environment to support peer revision in a middle-school classroom. This chapter describes our methods, the intervention and its implementation, and our findings to discuss the effectiveness of the intervention in the setting in which our study was conducted. First, we consider the relative literature and theory.

THEORETICAL FRAMEWORK

Learning to write is a process deeply entwined in the social and emotional growth of learners (Bomer & Laman, 2004). It is situated and authentically embedded within activity, context and culture (Lave & Wenger, 1991), grounding much of the research on writing in socio-cultural theories of learning (Vygotsky, 1978) and situated cognition (Lave & Wenger, 1991).

Vygotsky's (1978) socio-cultural theory asserts that learning depends upon people's interactions with one another; learning is a social act and culture provides the tools that help learners develop understandings of the world around them. A cultural historical theoretical view of learning is sometimes used to capture the complexities of classroom environments (Guiterrez & Stone, 2000). This theoretical perspective embraces the notion that learning is a transactional process (Dewey & Bentley, 1949) mediated by cultural tools, including spoken and written language, as people participate in routine activities in communities of practice (Dyson, 2000; Gutierrez & Stone, 2000; Lave & Wenger, 1991).

Communities of Practice (COPs) are knowledge communities in which people invest their time and energy in a joint enterprise, developing a shared repertoire (Henderson & Bradley, 2008). Gee (2005) describes Lave and Wenger's (1991) community of practice as one in which learners "…pick up practices through joint action with more advanced peers, and advance their abilities to engage and work with others in carrying out such practices" (p. 77). Learners draw on their own Discourses (i.e. home, community, academic) and as members participate in the community, a new, shared Discourse emerges (Gee, 2005).

PEDAGOGICAL FRAMEWORK

This study particularly focused on peer revision in the writing process in an online setting. Teaching students how to successfully respond to peers' text, as well as to read and understand critiques of their own work, and provides adolescents with the skills they will need to move forward, both in academic environments and in the larger world. Revision gives students the opportunity to not only re-examine their own ideas, but also examine and internalize elements of effective writing in a variety of contexts (Bruffee, 1985). Although peer revision is an important component of the writing process, many classroom teachers spend little time on peer revision (National Writing Project, 2003), and adolescents struggle with the peer revision process.

For instance, students reported they were not always honest in their appraisal of one another's work, for fear of alienating peers (Styslinger, 1998; Styslinger, 2008). Also, differences in perceived writing ability, as well as group members who are reticent to speak, or group members who may overwhelm their peers, are also issues that have emerged in peer revision groups (Sommers, 1993). Peer status, gender, and race may also affect the feedback students receive from one another and whether that feedback is valued (Christianakis, 2010). In addition, it may take years for even high school students to develop necessary skills to become helpful peer reviewers (Simmons, 2003), and both teachers and students may become disenchanted and abandon the process (Lawrence & Sommers, 1996; Styslinger, 1998).

Yet, online writing environments and tools may hold potential in addressing these concerns. Online writing environments may alleviate adolescents' concerns regarding offering of constructive criticism or suggestions to peers; developing a Discourse (Gee, 2005) with peers online may allow students to try on new identities, offering potential avenues for honest feedback. Existing research suggests features such as tracking changes may be an effective technique for revision in classrooms (Carmichael & Alden, 2006). Further, peer response through digital communications may lead to more revision by writers (Tuzi, 2004) as well as more thoughtful feedback by reviewers (Crank, 2002).

However, the literature on peer revision in online settings is limited in K-12 education research, specifically in middle-school classrooms. The majority of studies of peer revision are situated in the context of freshman composition courses (Brammer & Rees, 2007; Carmichael and Alden, 2006; Crank, 2002; Eades, 2002; Strasma, 2009; Tomlinson, 2009), and a few studies examine revision in high school classrooms (Karegianes,

Pascarella, & Pflaum, 1980; Moran & Greenburg, 2008; Simmons, 2003; Styslinger 1998; Styslinger, 2008). This leaves middle-school teachers few resources to turn to when looking for effective ways to implement or enhance peer revision. In addition, few resources are available addressing the use of digital technology to enhance writing and peer revision. Research focusing on efforts to effectively integrate peer revision into the middle-school classroom using online resources and platforms is needed to address gaps in theory and pedagogy.

This study used a formative experiment to explore the use of online environments as new spaces for peer revision in a middle school classroom and to address current barriers to the integration of peer revision in classrooms. Specifically, our investigation examined how peer revision and collaboration in an online environment could be implemented in a seventh-grade classroom to increase revision of writing over multiple drafts and improve the quality of student expository writing.

METHODOLOGY

Formative experiments are one of several approaches to research referred to collectively with overarching terms such as design-based research or design experiments (Barab & Squire, 2004; Brown, 1992; Design-Based Research Collective, 2003; Hoadley, 2004; van den Akker, Gravemeijer, McKenney, & Nieveen, 2007). In a formative experiment, the investigator sets a pedagogical goal, instead of a research question, and selects an intervention that shows promise to achieve the goal or alternately designs an intervention that may help achieve the goal. The pedagogical goal for this formative experiment was:

Increase the amount of revision that occurs over multiple drafts of students' writing and improve the quality of student expository writing through online peer revision and collaboration in a middle school English language arts classroom.

In education, formative experiments are often seen as a means to bridge the gap between theory and practice (Reinking & Bradley, 2008) and to refine and develop pedagogical theories in authentic contexts (Bradley & Reinking, 2011). In a formative experiment, instructional difficulties, obstacles, and even failures are viewed as useful data that can inform instruction and help build pedagogical understanding. Nevertheless, the aim of formative experiments are not to offer prescriptive solutions to pedagogical needs; rather, the goal is to identify relevant factors, including obstacles, that inform how instruction can be carried out more effectively.

Participants and Context

Participants were 36 students in two sections of a required English language arts class at Wilson Middle School (pseudonym), one of several middle schools in a large Southeastern school district in the United States. Wilson consistently failed to make Annual Yearly Progress, as outlined by No Child Left Behind, and was following a mandated restructuring plan at the time of the study. Approximately 93% of students at the school received free or reduced meals. Student participants reflected the diversity of the school, with 14 students self-identified as African-Americans, 12 as Hispanic, and 10 as Caucasian. Of the 36 participants, 13 were female and 23 were male. A total of 11 participants were English language learners and 2 received special education services. No participants were identified as gifted and talented. Participants in this study had among the lowest writing scores in the state on the writing test given at the end of sixth grade, with just over 60% not meeting the required standard for basic proficiency.

Although this site was considered challenging for this investigation, it was selected because it was likely to be a supportive environment for this type of writing instruction and intervention, with one-to-one laptops, on-site technical support, an instructional coach who was formerly an English language arts specialist, and several teachers who completed coursework in both writing workshop and using technology in the classroom through a local university.

Ms. Piper, the teacher, had six years of teaching experience, all at Wilson. At the time of the study, Ms. Piper had completed a master's degree and also achieved National Board Certification. She was well versed in writing workshop, having completed coursework focused on writing, and was also a teacher-consultant with the local site of the National Writing Project. We recruited her to participate in the study because of her expressed commitment to writing in her classroom and openness to using technology in her classroom.

The Classroom Environment

Prior to the implementation of the intervention, we collected observational data to better understand the environment of the school and specifically to observe Ms. Piper's classes. The intent of these observations was to create a thick description of the classroom setting (Patton, 2002), a critical phase in conducting a formative experiment (Reinking & Bradley, 2008). The students' classroom and learning routines were well established when we gathered these data mid-year. Initial observations of this classroom revealed that students used laptops each day, for both reading and writing. Students were accustomed to composing on the computer, as well as saving their work to common spaces. Their school routines were established and structured. Students spent 60 minutes each day in their English language arts class, and had an additional 30 minutes daily devoted to sustained silent reading. They also had 30 additional minutes of English language arts each week with their teacher as part of an advisory/ tutorial program. The teacher allowed students to come in to work both before and after school if they needed extra time or assistance.

THE INTERVENTION

The intervention phase of the study lasted 13 weeks. For the purposes of this study, online peer revision and collaboration were defined as having the following components: (a) an online space for students to post work and provide feedback; (b) the ability for students to track changes made to their work; (c) the ability for a student to request feedback from peers in writing at any stage of their writing; and (d) the ability for students to respond to feedback from their peers. These components were essential to the intervention and were not subject to modification during the intervention.

Selecting the Online Space

Appeal is an important aspect of any intervention in a formative experiment (Reinking & Bradley, 2008). We selected a Ning (www.ning.com) as the platform for our online interactions. Nings might be best described as closed, social networks, with many features similar to Facebook that appeal to adolescents, such as built-in email, the ability to friend users, status updates, the ability to upload pictures to and maintain a user profile, and the ability to give gifts. Users can also upload documents, videos, and pictures. These features seemed likely to support four key elements to developing successful online communities: remuneration, influence, belonging, and significance (Howard, 2010). For our study, only those invited could see the Ning site, contact one another, and share documents, which made the school and teacher feel it was a safe option for instruction in school.

Function was another important consideration. Downloading and uploading documents was straightforward: the user clicked on a button and a dialogue box appeared with simple instructions. Students were able to compose in Microsoft Word and upload documents to the Ning. The Ning also allowed users to include messages about the uploaded documents; students could include specific requests for feedback or assistance with each file uploaded. More importantly, the Ning did not convert uploaded documents to another format. This feature was critical, as students could use the revision toolbar within Word to track changes and use the comment feature to make suggestions.

Implementing the Intervention

Students participated in peer revision in class at least once each week, both as a reader and a writer, responding to drafts at a variety of points in the writing process. This practice was based on both writing theory and research which suggest students should be given time to write and receive feedback throughout the writing process (Atwell, 1988; Calkins, 1986; Fletcher & Portaluppi, 2001). Meta-analyses also suggest the importance of peer assistance during the writing process for K-12 students (Graham & Perin, 2007a; Graham, McKeown, Kiuhara, & Harris, 2012). The intervention was implemented in two stages, based on research on successful peer revision in classrooms (Crank, 2002; Karegianes, Pascarella, & Pflaum, 1980; Moran & Greenburg, 2008; Simmons, 2003; Strasma, 2009), which suggested students needed face-to-face practice with peer revision before moving into the online model.

The first stage of the intervention, which lasted one week, included direct instruction on responding to peer writing, with practice responding in face-to-face groups. We chose to teach the students a technique (TAG – Tell, Ask, Give) to frame their responses to one another's writing with Ms. Piper modeling feedback during a mini-lesson using TAG to provide a scaffold for peer revision.

Stage two, which lasted 12 weeks, included the implementation of digital technologies in the writing process, including the use of tracked changes and comment features in Microsoft Word, students posting work to an online forum, and student response through the online forum. Ms. Piper modeled feedback on the Ning using the TAG structure previously taught, offering each student some feedback on the first piece they posted. Students then posted and offered feedback to one another through the online forum.

Ongoing instruction in responding to peer writing took place throughout the intervention, as suggested by research on peer revision (Moran & Greenburg, 2008; Simmons, 2003). This instruction was provided through mini-lessons and modeling, based on progress toward the goal. Throughout the intervention, we assumed the role of participant observers (Patton, 2002). The first author was present in the classroom observing students during the two days per week they were focused on writing. Ms. Piper taught mini-lessons and led the instruction and the first author took detailed field notes, often moving around the room to observe what students were doing. This approach created an environment where students treated the first author as an assistant teacher and another classroom resource for student questions. Students sometimes asked the first author to read something they had written and give her opinion or offer help with surface features (spelling, etc.), but students turned to Ms. Piper for instruction and clarification on the assignments at hand.

DATA COLLECTION AND ANALYSIS

The first author was the lead researcher in this study and was primarily responsible for designing and implementing the intervention and data collection. The second author served as a literacy resource and provided insight into data analysis and findings. Our study used a mixed-methods approach (Creswell, 2003). Qualitative data was systematically collected and analyzed to measure progress toward the pedagogical goal and identify factors that enhanced or inhibited the intervention. These data included participant observations, field notes, classroom artifacts such as student work samples, and all electronic communications between participants on the Ning. Scored writing samples provided quantitative data to measure writing progress. Student writing samples composed over a period of time with peer feedback

were collected for all students the month prior to the intervention, at week 7 of the intervention, and again at the conclusion of the intervention.

We selected 9 focal students, 4 from the smaller below-grade level class section and 5 from the on-grade level class section, for close analysis during the intervention, a common practice in formative experiment research (Reinking & Bradley, 2008). Selected students represented the range of students in the classrooms: students with positive and negative attitudes toward writing (as reported on a writing dispositions survey, see Piazza & Siebert, 2008), and students who enjoyed school as well as those who were disengaged, based on field notes and teacher input. Focal students were also representative of the school's gender and race demographics.

Using previous formative experiments as models, weekly analyses of field notes, student-writing samples, classroom artifacts, and electronic communications informed the progress of the intervention and were used to make justifiable modifications to the intervention based on data analysis. In addition to these on-going modifications, data helped to determine the degree to which the environment was transformed by the intervention, using retrospective analysis (Gravemeijer & Cobb, 2006), which is a holistic analysis conducted after all data have been collected.

All quantitative data was examined using a pre-post model, with baseline data gathered before the intervention and again at the end of the intervention. Trained scorers, using the National Writing Project's Analytic Writing Continuum, scored writing samples independently, and on a scale of 1-6, based on content, structure, stance, sentence fluency, diction, and conventions. Each piece also received a holistic score, which scorers assigned independently of the individual attribute scores. All samples were scored twice and inter-rater reliability, defined as having identical scores or scores within one single point of one another, was 95%. Using paired t-tests, we analyzed scores before and after the intervention.

Beginning at the outset of the intervention phase and continuing through retrospective analyses, qualitative data was analyzed using sequential data analysis (Miles & Huberman, 1994) using a process of open coding, allowing emergent themes and patterns to develop (Miles & Huberman, 1994). We also looked for disconfirming evidence during the following observation for each theme identified to assess whether these were representative (Miles & Huberman, 1994) and trustworthy (Lincoln & Guba, 1985).

To achieve triangulation (Creswell, 2003), a criterion for rigor in formative experiments (Reinking & Bradley, 2008), we considered and compared observational and interview data with student writing, electronic communications, and student think-alouds codes and themes. Member checks (Creswell, 2003) were also conducted with Ms. Piper throughout the intervention and data analysis process. After retrospective analysis, a final member check with Ms. Piper was conducted to confirm the validity of the identified themes.

RESULTS

Here, we examine the results of our formative experiment in terms of progress toward its goal and how technology enhanced and inhibited this intervention.

Improvement in Students' Expository Writing and Amount of Revision

Data suggested progress toward the pedagogical goal of both increasing the amount of revision and improving the quality of student writing. We analyzed the pre- and post-intervention writing samples (n=30) using a paired samples t-test. The results of the scored writing samples are found in Table 1 and indicate statistically significant differences (alpha = .05) between the pre- and post-writing samples overall, as determined by the holistic score, as well as across the six measured attributes: content, structure, stance, sentence fluency, diction, and conventions.

When examined as individuals, twenty-eight out of 30 students showed overall growth between the pre-writing sample and the post-writing sample, represented by the holistic score. Two students received the same holistic score pre- and post-intervention.

Qualitative data also consistently pointed toward progress in writing achievement and revision and will be discussed in the following subsections with representative data excerpts.

Enhanced Definitions of Revision

Both mid-intervention interviews with focal students and field notes suggest students developed

Table 1. Pre- and post-intervention means for student writing samples

Attribute	Pre-Mean (SD) (n=30)	Post-Mean (SD) (n=30)	Gain (SD) (n=30)
Holistic	2.65 (.95)	3.98 (.71)	1.33 (.87)
Content	2.68 (1.03)	4.12 (.91)	1.43 (.94)
Structure	2.45 (.83)	3.90 (.74)	1.450 (.96)
Stance	2.55 (.87)	4.23 (.73)	1.683 (.97)
Sentence Fluency	2.50 (.89)	3.87 (.71)	1.367 (.94)
Diction	2.58 (.98)	3.80 (.65)	1.217 (.97)
Conventions	2.55 (1.03)	3.73 (.68)	1.183 (.95)
p-value ≤.001 for all mean differences			

more complex and nuanced definitions of what it meant to revise their work as the intervention progressed. For example, in her pre-intervention interview, Dee described revision as, "To look over and see what mistakes you made or something." In our mid-intervention interview, Dee explained revision by stating, "To make sure the spelling's right and all that and make sure it makes sense and make sure you are not boring and you still have their attention or something." Dee continued to expand her definition of revision, explaining in her final interview that revision meant, "To check spelling and see if it makes sense. If it confuses you or something, you might want to change it or something. Add more information or take information out or rearrange it." Dee's progress was representative of other participants, and over time, student definitions of revision expanded.

Evidence of Revision

Data also provided evidence of increased revision in student writing. Field notes from observations of the classroom a month prior to the intervention indicated little revision. When students were engaged in revisiting their work, they focused primarily on editing.

One student, Javon, asked me to read his piece of so far. He had very little written and he wanted help correcting his spelling. I made the comment that he might consider focusing on the content of his piece first and he said, "What's content?" (field notes, 12/7).

As the intervention progressed, more evidence of revision became apparent in both classrooms. Field notes describe students in both classes working through multiple drafts and adding information, as well as giving one another feedback. A typical entry follows:

Juan has been working with the track changes on, adding new information from his notes and this is the first time I've seen that. With track changes

on, I saw more revision than I had seen in all their writing to date (2/15).

Teacher interviews also indicated revision increased during the intervention. Ms. Piper revealed some of the revision she was seeing in the classroom in her mid-intervention interview.

I see them having conversations about if a piece sounds right or finding more information to put into it. Devante said to me today, "I read this and I think I missed that." He noticed that it didn't make sense and said, "I'm going to go change it." He wasn't doing that before.

Student posts on the Ning, using the track changes feature in Microsoft Word, revealed that students were posting and revising throughout the writing process. Students wrote multiple drafts and revised them using feedback from peers throughout the intervention. Kimberly, a student reading below grade level prior to the intervention, provides an example of this revision and feedback process. Figure 1 is Kimberly's first draft of a "This I Believe" essay. Figure 2 is the feedback offered to her by another student, also considered to be reading below grade level. Figure 3 is Kimberly's final draft.

Role of Technology

Technological factors that enhanced the intervention included perceptions of playfulness and visibility of progress. However, qualitative data suggested a lack of support and an emphasis on delivery of instruction also played a role in the intervention, perhaps inhibiting progress toward the goal of increased student revision and improvement in the quality of writing.

Figure 1. Kimberly's first draft

Coupons, dollar tree, and goodwill

I believe in using coupons, going to goodwill and the dollar tree. My mom had taught me how to use coupons and going to the dollar tree and goodwill. Every time I go to goodwill. I always can find stuff for a dollar and it save me and my mom some money. A lot of my friends don't go to goodwill but I do, and at the dollar tree everything there is a dollar. So I can get all the stuff I need for only a dollar. We go other places to my mom are always to tell me to use coupons and go to the Clarence. I had got this make but it had cost more then I had but my mom had a coupon so then I can afford it. My mom says you have to save money because of price these days. When I am older and I have to pay bills I will be especially be using coupon and going to goodwill and dollar tree. My mom tells me she might not have food stamps and a lot of money but she has coupons and she can go to the dollar tree and goodwill.

Figure 2. Kimberly's draft, with suggestions from Roman

Coupons, dollar tree, and goodwill

I believe in using coupons, going to goodwill and dollar tree. My mom had taught me how to use coupons and going to the dollar tree and goodwill. I always i find stuff for a dollar and it save me and my mom some money. A lot of my friends don't go to goodwill but I do, and the dollar tree everything there is a dollar. So I can get what I need for only a dollar. We go other places to my mom are always to tell me to use coupons and go to the clearance. I had got this make but it had cost more then I had but my mom had a coupon so then I can afford it. My mom says you have to save money because of price these days. When I am older and I have to pay bills I will be especially be using coupon and going to goodwill and dollar tree. My mom tells me she might not have food stamps and a lot of money but she has coupons and she can go to the dollar tree and goodwill.

Why is it important to save money?
Do you have to work hard for your money? Is that important?

Technological Factors that Enhanced the Intervention

Perceptions of Playfulness

Qualitative data suggested that technology, specifically the Ning, offered students an online space with more appeal than the spaces they typically explored and occupied during school hours. Without exception, the focal students interviewed described their feelings about the Ning in positive terms. When asked what they liked about using the Ning, the majority of students made some reference to Facebook, such as "[I like] how you can send like a friend request like Facebook" and "It's fun, it's like Facebook."

The perception that this was a space where students could be more playful while at school was reflected in students' use of texting language in their electronic communications with one another on the Ning. Throughout the school day, students were asked to use Standard American English in their communication with both teachers and one another. For the Ning, students developed and recorded writing rules in class and in both sections students specifically sanctioned the use of texting language. The student recording the rules in the below-grade-level section chose to use the informality of text to make his point: "Yu cn use txt language 4 cmts." Data suggested all students followed this rule. Abbreviations common to texting are evident in their informal

Figure 3. Kimberly's final draft

Coupons, Dollar Tree, and Goodwill

I believe in using coupons, going to Goodwill and the Dollar Tree. My mom had taught me how to use coupons and going to the dollar tree and goodwill. Every time I go to Goodwill. I always can find stuff for a dollar and it save me and my mom some money. A lot of my friends don't go to goodwill but I do, and at the Dollar Tree everything there is a dollar. So I can get all the stuff I need for only a dollar.

We go other places to my mom are always to tell me to use coupons and go to the Clearance. I had got this make but it had cost more then I had but my mom had a coupon so then I can afford it. My mom says you have to save money because of price these days. When I am older and I have to pay bills I will be especially be using coupon and going to Goodwill and Dollar Tree.

My mom tells me she might not have food stamps and a lot of money but she has coupons and she can go to the Dollar Tree and Goodwill. I am not ashamed of going there and using coupons, it's the exact thing as the named brand stuff it just have a different name to it. We don't have to sacrifice - we just know how to save money. Some people might be ashamed using coupons and going to the dollar tree and the goodwill but I am not. Also and the cheap brands there is some stuff I like better. Its like food it tastes the same. Some people might think there to good for the Dollar Tree, Goodwill and using coupons but I don't care what other people think I like using coupons and going to Goodwill and also Dollar Tree.

communications with one another on the Ning, but were largely absent from their more formal writing assignments. Students also blended Standard American English with their own vernacular, including Spanish for bilingual students, in their comments to one another.

The playful tone of the Ning was also reflected in students' choices of monikers for themselves in the online space and the pictures they chose as icons. Students chose pseudonyms such as Tankhead, fallen_dark_$;angel, ~gummyboo~, starburst, and Wakko. Pictures students used to represent themselves ranged from religious figures to celebrities to cartoon characters. Other students chose to use pictures they had taken of themselves with cell phones.

Field notes and electronic communications also suggested students used the Ning as a way to communicate with one another, as well as for academic purposes. Ms. Piper recognized this use of the Ning for non-academic purposes as well and discussed it during her mid-intervention interview.

I know that they're sometimes not totally on task on there but I feel like in order to have the community that has to happen at some point like you have to feel like you're in the community, you know? So I haven't felt like that's been a big distraction probably just a good thing that they leave each other little gifts and stuff.

Although the online space afforded opportunities for students to be off-task, we felt it was important to maintain the social aspect of the community. Howard's (2010) concept of remuneration informed this decision; we wanted to provide students with a satisfying and engaging experience.

Visibility

The visibility of both student revisions, through the track changes feature on Microsoft Word, as well as through comments to one another using both the comment feature in Word and the Ning, made the work of both composition and revision visible to not only the teacher, but also to the students themselves. Data suggested that the visibility of work was an important factor in student revision.

Ms. Piper noted that she was seeing more revision when students started using the track changes feature in Microsoft Word. She noted in her mid-intervention interview, "Track changes I think was awesome. The fact that it's posted on the Ning and somebody's going to read it and reading other people's suggestions I think helped a lot." The visibility of track changes came up again in our post-interview. "Tracking the changes I think was so motivating and helped them to see the ways their writing changed."

Students also expressed appreciation for the visibility technology afforded them. Brad, a student who struggled as a writer throughout the intervention, noted after participating in the think-aloud protocol, "Now that I can see how people have helped me, I can help other people in that way... when they help me like, like I have you, then it helps me help other people." Other students also talked about the value of being able to see comments. Troy, a more willing writer, found it helpful to be able to go back and revisit comments when revising his writing. "Because like if I get a comment off the Ning that's like something that like I can remember to do, because it's on there, but if you're doing it face to face like you can forget to do it sometimes" (Post-intervention interview, 4/28). Troy also recognized that he learned from other students' feedback by commenting, "Somebody writes me with feedback, that's something else I can tell somebody else, because their writing could be similar."

In sum, technology enabled students to make their thinking visible to one another and encour-

aged students to make changes to their writing, resulting in more revision. It also offered students models for peer feedback, which students found helpful during the peer revision process.

Technological Factors that Inhibited the Intervention

Lack of Support

Although the school had a one-to-one laptop initiative, the laptops were four years old and needed repairs for issues like keys falling off the keyboard. When laptops were sent out for repair, it could be weeks or months before they were returned. At the start of the intervention, Ms. Piper had 22 functional laptops in her room available to students. By the end of April, there were 15 functional laptops in Ms. Piper's room. Toward the end of the intervention, Ms. Piper was sending students to other spaces to work on their writing. Because Ms. Piper approached writing using a workshop model, this detracted from instruction. Ms. Piper's ability to scaffold and target instruction to improve student writing was inhibited by this development.

Emphasis on Delivery of Instruction

Data also suggest that technology was typically used in the school for delivery of instruction, rather than to enhance instruction. Administrative support for using the laptops was focused on test taking. Due to budget constraints, benchmark tests in the school were delivered to students via laptops. Rather than printing copies of quizzes and tests, all quizzes and tests at the school were delivered online. Teachers were encouraged to closely monitor student use of the laptops. During the intervention, the administration asked Ms. Piper to rearrange her classroom so she could see every computer screen from the rear of the classroom. This vision of a teacher as a monitor and computers as a way to deliver instruction inhibited the intervention, as Ms. Piper had to alter her classroom instruction to some degree to satisfy the requirements set forth by school administrators.

DISCUSSION

Formative experiments consider practical as well as theoretical aspects of classroom research (Reinking & Bradley, 2008). Thus, in this section we discuss our findings by first presenting an unanticipated effect of the intervention on the classroom environment, which is an important component in conducting formative experiments (Reinking & Bradley, 2008) and then drawing connections to the literature base.

Unanticipated Effect of the Intervention

According to Reinking and Bradley (2008), formative experiments will likely have effects the researcher may not have anticipated at the start of the intervention. Analysis of data revealed one major unanticipated effect that was outside the original scope of the intervention: the possibility of accelerated learning by students in how to give effective peer feedback.

Although the intervention was intended to increase revision in student writing and assist students in giving one another meaningful feedback, we did not expect students to become expert in giving peer feedback over the course of the intervention. For example, Simmons (2003) suggested it might take years for students to become effective responders for one another.

Data suggested, however, that making feedback visible through the track changes feature and the Ning may have accelerated students learning process. During the think-aloud protocol, students independently focused their comments and suggestions on content and structure when offering suggestions on a cold piece of text. This

focus differed from the start of the intervention, when students own definitions of revision were limited to "fixing mistakes" which they defined as errors in grammar and punctuation. During post-intervention interviews, focal students reported learning how to become better peer reviewers. For example, Brad noted, "I learned how to actually give helpful suggestions rather than just criticizing people's writing...It helped me actually, since I know how to actually revise people's work now, it helped me learn how to revise mine better than I did." Ms. Piper also noticed a difference in her students' comments.

I think they gave each other really excellent feedback. It was a lot easier than I thought it would be. I thought they would not know what to say. I think they learned to enjoy it and to really think like a writer. I think by revising the other person's, they really learned how to look back at their own, too.

Ms. Piper reported that students seemed to have learned to offer one another effective feedback with little scaffolding or instruction on the part of the teacher.

One thing that really surprises me about the Ning is we don't have to say look for this or look for that and to scaffold their revising, like a lot teachers think you have to do. You know, give them a revision sheet to follow. They just needed that structure of somewhere to put their work.

Thus, students became more adept at offering feedback than the existing studies suggested may be expected.

Theoretical Implications and Considerations

In this investigation, an online community was established as a vehicle for students to offer one another peer feedback to increase the amount of revision in middle school students' writing over multiple drafts and improve the quality of their writing. The results of this study are significant for several reasons: the results support findings from college classrooms that asynchronous feedback may be an effective tool in peer revision (Crank, 2002; Honeycutt, 2001; Strasma, 2009) and the use of computers in K-12 environments may support improvement in the quality of student writing (Goldberg, Russell, & Cook, 2003; Moore & Karabenick, 1992). The results also offer support for the use of online spaces as potential academic communities of practice (Britsch, 2005; Clarke, 2009; Gunawardena, Hermans, Sanchez, Richmond, Bohley, & Tuttle, 2009). These findings, though not generalizable, may contribute to local theory and support the use of comparable interventions in middle-school settings similar to the one in this study (Firestone, 1993).

Admittedly, however, the context of this study may have fostered success. Despite the fact the school selected served many at-risk students with many students struggling to achieve grade level standards, Ms. Piper's openness to the idea of using technology in her classroom and commitment to writing may have counteracted these factors. Existing research suggests time to write (Cutler & Graham, 2008; Graham & Perin, 2007b; National Commission on Writing, 2003) and the ability to collaborate with peers (Coker & Lewis, 2008; Gere, 1987; Gere & Abbott, 1985; Graham & Perin, 2007b; Langer, 1999, 2000) are effective instructional tools in the teaching of writing. Ms. Piper's willingness to structure and organize her physical environment and instructional time to facilitate collaboration and revision among students was critical to the success of this intervention. Ms. Piper's awareness of student's need for social interaction likely helped maintain the feeling that the Ning was a space that allowed for play, as well as for the academic work of the classroom, which kept students engaged. Replication of this study across multiple environments is essential to better understand how the results may differ across contexts.

FINAL THOUGHTS AND CONCLUSION

The present investigation, although promising, is a very small part of a much larger picture. How do we help students develop habits of mind that encourage them to revisit and revise their work to improve writing in our schools? And, how do we encourage teachers, who are less enthusiastic about technology integration, to utilize online resources to improve writing and revision in schools? This formative experiment reveals one instructional strategy that may be promising to address both of those questions. Overall, we concluded that building an online academic community supports students as writers and fosters an environment and space where students feel comfortable engaging in revision and are encouraged to become editors. This study provides support for the implementation of similar online writing models in middle-school English classrooms. We believe, however, the present investigation should be replicated in a variety of contexts to add to pedagogical theory, provide useful models, and inform instructional practice in K-12 settings.

REFERENCES

Atwell, N. (1998). *In the middle: New understandings about writing, reading, and learning.* Portsmouth, NH: Boynton/ Cook.

Barab, S., & Squire, K. (2004). Design-based research: Putting a stake in the ground. *Journal of the Learning Sciences, 13*, 1–14. doi:10.1207/s15327809jls1301_1.

Bomer, R., & Laman, T. (2004). Positioning in a primary writing workshop: Joint action in the discursive production of writing subjects. *Research in the Teaching of English, 38*(4), 420–466.

Bradley, B. A., & Reinking, D. (2011). Revisiting the connection between research and practice using design research and formative experiments. In Duke, N., & Mallette, M. (Eds.), *Literacy research methodologies* (2nd ed., pp. 188–212). New York: Guilford Press.

Brammer, C., & Rees, M. (2007). Peer review from the students' perspective: Invaluable of invalid? *Composition Studies*, *35*(2), 71–85.

Britsch, S. (2005). But what did they learn? Clearing third spaces in virtual dialogues with children. *Journal of Early Childhood Literacy*, *5*(2), 99–130. doi:10.1177/1468798405054581.

Brown, A. L. (1992). Design experiments: Theoretical and methodological challenges in creating complex programs in classroom settings. *Journal of the Learning Sciences*, *2*(2), 141–178. doi:10.1207/s15327809jls0202_2.

Bruffee, K. A. (1985). *A short course in writing: Practical rhetoric for teaching composition through collaborative learning* (3rd ed.). Boston: Little.

Calkins, L. (1986). *The art of teaching writing*. Portsmouth, NH: Heinemann.

Carmichael, S., & Alden, P. (2006). The advantages of using electronic processes for commenting on and exchanging the written work of students with learning disabilities and/or AD/HD. *Composition Studies*, *34*(2), 43–57.

Christianakis, M. (2010). I don't need your help! Peer status, race, and gender during peer writing interactions. *Journal of Literacy Research*, *42*(4), 418–458. doi:10.1080/1086296X.2010.525202.

Clarke, M. (2009). The discursive construction of interpersonal relations in an online community of practice. *Journal of Pragmatics*, *41*(11), 2333–2344. doi:10.1016/j.pragma.2009.04.001.

Coker, D., & Lewis, W. E. (2008). Beyond writing next: A discussion of writing research and instructional uncertainty. *Harvard Educational Review*, *78*(1), 231–250.

Crank, V. (2002). Asynchronous electronic peer response in a hybrid basic writing classroom. *Teaching English in the Two-Year College*, *30*(2), 146–155.

Creswell, J. (2003). *Research design: Qualitative, quantitative, and mixed-methods approaches* (2nd ed.). Thousand Oaks, CA: Sage.

Cutler, L., & Graham, S. (2008). Primary grade writing instruction: A national survey. *Journal of Educational Psychology*, *100*(4), 907–919. doi:10.1037/a0012656.

Design-Based Research Collective. (2003). Design-based research: An emerging paradigm for educational inquiry. *Educational Researcher*, *32*(1), 5–8. doi:10.3102/0013189X032001005.

Eades, C. (2002). A working model of pedagogical triangulation: A holistic approach to peer-revision workshops. *Teaching English in the Two-Year College*, *30*(1), 60–67.

Firestone, W. A. (1993). Alternative arguments for generalizing from data as applied to qualitative research. *Educational Researcher*, *22*(4), 16–23. doi:10.3102/0013189X022004016.

Fletcher, R., & Portaluppi, J. (2001). *Writing workshop: The essential guide*. Portsmouth, NH: Heinemann.

Gee, J. P. (2005). Meaning making, communities of practice, and analytical toolkits. *Journal of Sociolinguistics*, *9*(4), 590–594. doi:10.1111/j.1360-6441.2005.00308.x.

Gere, A., & Abbott, R. D. (1985). Talking about writing: The language of writing groups. *Research in the Teaching of English*, *19*(4), 362–385.

Gere, A. R. (1987). *Writing groups: History, theory, and implications.* Carbondale, IL: Southern Illinois University Press.

Goldberg, A., Russell, M., & Cook, A. (2003). The effect of computers on student writing: A metaanalysis of studies from 1992 to 2002. *Journal of Technology, Learning, and Assessment, 2*(1). Retrieved December 20, 2012 from http://www.jtla.org

Graham, S., McKeown, D., Kiuhara, S., & Harris, K. R. (2012). A meta-analysis of writing instruction for students in the elementary grades. *Journal of Educational Psychology, 104*(4), 879–896. doi:10.1037/a0029185.

Graham, S., & Perin, D. (2007a). A meta-analysis of writing instruction for adolescent students. *Journal of Educational Psychology, 99*(3), 445–476. doi:10.1037/0022-0663.99.3.445.

Graham, S., & Perin, D. (2007b). *Writing next: Effective strategies to improve writing of adolescents in middle and high school.* Washington, DC: Alliance for Excellent Education.

Gravemeijer, K., & Cobb, P. (2006). Design research from a learning design perspective. In J. van den akker, K. Gravemeijer, S. McKenney, & N. Nieveen (Eds.), Educational design research (pp. 17-51). New York: Routledge.

Gunawardena, C. N., Hermans, M. B., Sanchez, D., Richmond, C., Bohley, M., & Tuttle, R. (2009). A theoretical framework for building online communities of practice with social networking tools. *Educational Media International, 46*(1), 3–16. doi:10.1080/09523980802588626.

Hoadley, C. M. (2004). Methodological alignment in design-based research. *Educational Psychologist, 39*, 203–212. doi:10.1207/s15326985ep3904_2.

Honeycutt, L. (2001). Comparing e-mail and synchronous conferencing in online peer response. *Written Communication, 18*(1), 26–60. doi:10.1177/0741088301018001002.

Howard, T. W. (2010). *Design to thrive: Creating social networks and online communities that last.* Burlington, MA: Morgan Kauffman.

Jenkins, H., Clinton, K., Purushotma, R., Robison, A. J., & Weigel, M. (2009). *Confronting the challenges of participatory culture: Media education for the 21st century.* Retrieved April 5, 2012 from http://digitallearning.macfound.org/site/c.enJLKQNlFiG/b.2029291/k.97E5/Occasional_Papers.htm

Karegianes, M., Pascarella, E., & Pflaum, S. (1980). The effects of peer editing on the writing proficiency of low-achieving tenth grade students. *The Journal of Educational Research, 73*(4), 203–207.

Langer, J. A., & National Research Center on English Learning and Achievement. (1999). *Beating the odds: Teaching middle and high school students to read and write well.* Retrieved May 6, 2012 from http://www.albany.edu/cela/reports.html#L

Langer, J. A., & National Research Center on English Learning and Achievement. (2000). *Guidelines for teaching middle and high school students to read and write well: Six features of effective instruction.* Retrieved May 6, 2012 from http://www.albany.edu/cela/reports.html#L

Lave, J., & Wenger, E. (1991). *Situated learning: Legitimate peripheral participation.* Cambridge, UK: Cambridge University Press. doi:10.1017/CBO9780511815355.

Lawrence, S., & Sommers, E. (1996). From the park bench to the (writing) workshop table: Encouraging collaboration among inexperienced writers. *Teaching English in the Two-Year College, 23*(2), 101–110.

Lenhart, A., Arafeh, S., Smith, A., & Macgill, A. R. (2008). Writing, technology and teens [Electronic version]. *Pew Internet & American Life Project*. Retrieved November 5, 2012, from http://www.pewInternet.org/Reports/2008/Writing-Technology-and-Teens.aspx?r=1

Lenhart, A., Madden, M., Smith, A., Purcell, K., Zickuhr, K., & Rainie, L. (2011). Teens, kindness and cruelty on social network sites: How American teens navigate the new world of digital citizenship. [Electronic version]. *Pew Internet & American Life Project*. Retrieved February 5, 2013 from http://www.pewInternet.org/Reports/2011/Teens-and-social-media.aspx

Lincoln, Y. S., & Guba, E. G. (1985). *Naturalistic inquiry*. Beverly Hills, CA: Sage.

Miles, M., & Huberman, A. (1994). *Qualitative data analysis*. Thousand Oaks, CA: Sage.

Moore, M., & Karabenick, S. (1992). The effects of computer communications on the reading and writing performance of fifth-grade students. *Computers in Human Behavior*, *8*(1), 27–38. doi:10.1016/0747-5632(92)90017-9.

Moran, P. P., & Greenberg, B. (2008). Peer revision: Helping students to develop a meta-editor. *Ohio Journal of English Language Arts*, *48*(1), 33–39.

National Commission on Writing. (2003). *The neglected R: The need for a writing revolution*. Retrieved January 2, 2011 from http://www.hostcollegeboard.com/advocacy/writing/publications.html

Patton, M. Q. (2002). *Qualitative research and evaluation methods* (3rd ed.). Thousand Oaks, CA: Sage.

Piazza, C. L., & Siebert, C. F. (2008). Development and validation of a writing disposition scale for elementary and middle school students. *The Journal of Educational Research*, *101*(5), 275–285. doi:10.3200/JOER.101.5.275-286.

Reinking, D., & Bradley, B. A. (2008). *Formative and design experiments: Approaches to language and literacy research*. New York: Teachers College Press.

Rhodes, J. A., & Robnolt, V. J. (2009). Digital literacies in the classroom. In Christenbury, L., Bomar, R., & Smagorinsky, P. (Eds.), *Handbook of Adolescent Literacy Research* (pp. 153–169). New York: Guilford Press.

Simmons, J. (2003). Responders are taught, not born. *Journal of Adolescent & Adult Literacy*, *46*(8), 684–693.

Sommers, E. (1993). *Student-centered, not teacher-abandoned: Peer response groups that work*. Retrieved from ERIC database.

Strasma, K. (2009). Spotlighting: Peer-response in digitally supported first-year writing courses. *Teaching English in the Two-Year College*, *37*(2), 153–160.

Styslinger, M. E. (1998). Some milk, a song, and a set of keys: Students respond to peer revision. *Teaching & Change*, *5*(2), 116–138.

Styslinger, M. E. (2008). Gendered performances during peer revision. *Literacy Research and Instruction*, *47*(3), 211–228. doi:10.1080/19388070802062815.

Tomlinson, E. (2009). Gender and peer response. *Teaching English in the Two-Year College*, *37*(2), 139–152.

Tuzi, F. (2004). The impact of e-feedback on the revisions of L2 writers in an academic writing course. *Computers and Composition: An International Journal for Teachers of Writing, 21*(2), 217–235. doi:10.1016/j.compcom.2004.02.003.

Tyner, K. (1998). *Literacy in the digital world: Teaching and learning in the age of information.* Mahweh, NJ: Erlbaum.

van den Akker, J., Gravemeijer, K., McKenney, S., & Nieveen, N. (2007). Introducing educational design research. In van den Akker, J., Gravemeijer, K., McKenney, S., & Nieveen, N. (Eds.), *Educational design research* (pp. 3–7). New York: Routledge.

Vygotsky, L. S. (1978). *Mind and society: The development of higher psychological processes.* Cambridge, MA: Harvard University Press.

Williams, B. T. (2005). Leading double lives: Literacy and technology in and out of school. *Journal of Adolescent & Adult Literacy, 48*(8), 702–706. doi:10.1598/JAAL.48.8.7.

Yancey, K. B. (2009). *Writing in the 21st century: A report from the national council of teachers of English.* Urbana, IL: NCTE.

Chapter 9
Situating Technology–Facilitated Feedback and Revision:
The Case of Tom

Sarah J. McCarthey
University of Illinois – Urbana-Champaign, USA

Alecia Marie Magnifico
University of Illinois – Urbana-Champaign, USA

Rebecca Woodard
University of Illinois – Chicago, USA

Sonia Kline
University of Illinois – Urbana-Champaign, USA

ABSTRACT

In this chapter, the authors present a case study of one writer, Tom, to uncover how his writing was mediated by school-level and individual factors. The online writing environment had three major affordances for Tom in this 8th grade classroom: the online writing environment increased Tom's access to peer response, motivated him write to a higher standard for an audience, and both scaffolded and increased his response repertoire. However, the larger policy context in which Tom's writing was embedded placed constraints on the classroom and school. Other constraints included Tom's lack of access to a computer at home, the teacher's highly structured task, and the online tool's assignment of random reviewers that forced Tom to continually write to a new audience of peers who lacked the previous context. In light of the situated nature of Tom's writing and responses in this classroom, the authors make recommendations for policy, research, and instruction.

DOI: 10.4018/978-1-4666-4341-3.ch009

INTRODUCTION

Writers learn by writing, but they also learn by externalizing their thinking as they commit words to paper or screen and by participating in larger institutions like classrooms and schools. By responding to iterative drafts, peers and teachers can help writers to identify which ideas are clear and which require additional explanation. Writers can then revise in response to these comments to produce more coherent texts. Interactions that surround the writing, reviewing, and revising of texts can produce a more collaborative environment. Designing an online environment that organizes revision and supports interaction, particularly among peers, lies at the center of our work. In this chapter, we trace one student using *Scholar*, a Web-based writing tool, through a six-week narrative project that involved writing, peer review, annotation, and revision.

Simply analyzing online artifacts of these activities, however, only shows one aspect of students' and teachers' experiences of the writing process. Equally important are teachers' pedagogies, and how their instructional design is enmeshed in such factors as school and federal policies. Teachers design writing curricula and assessment in response to their students' needs, but also in response to accountability and curricular mandates. In the classroom that we discuss in this chapter, the teacher, Ellen Anderson, implemented *Scholar* to enhance her students' experiences with writing but encountered challenges that limited their access to technology.

We examine the affordances and constraints of *Scholar* to support writing, peer review, annotation, and revision within classroom and school contexts. We also look at peer response as a mechanism of formative assessment that distributes feedback throughout the classroom, recasting the teacher in the role of guide (rather than sole assessor) and the students as active audience members. While online writing environments have the potential to enable a shift from the traditional classroom to a more collaborative one, Tom's case demonstrates the complex, situated nature of this transformation and how it is enacted.

In this chapter, we review relevant literature on technology policy and computer-mediated instruction as it relates to writing, peer response, and revision. We then present a case study of one writer, Tom, to uncover how his writing was mediated by school-level and individual factors such as his ambitious ideas for his story, the structure of Ellen's assignment and rubric, and his access to *Scholar* in and out of school. These influences supported and constrained Tom's writing in divergent ways. In light of the situated nature of his writing and responses in this classroom, we make recommendations for policy, research, and instruction.

LITERATURE REVIEW

Our inquiry into the use of *Scholar*, a technology-enabled classroom-writing tool, is informed by a situated view of teachers' instruction and students' learning. Such activity occurs within broad layers of context including federal, local, and school policy.

Scholar intervenes in educational systems at the level of classrooms, as an instruction-focused tool that aims to help teachers transform their classrooms into places where students write primarily to communicate about real problems and purposes -- rather than to write summaries and answer questions (e.g. Applebee & Langer, 2009; Nystrand, Gamoran, Kachur, & Prendergast, 1997). As Kalantzis and Cope (2012) put it, classrooms are currently oriented "vertically," with teachers serving as students' assessors and sole audience members, but they might be transformed to include more "horizontal, student-to-student" (p. 162) discourse. To this end, they offer seven design principles that are central to *Scholar*. We focus on three of these principles here: The first of these elements is *ubiquitous learning*, which means that students and teachers may work on their writing anywhere and anytime they have access to an Internet-enabled device (Cope, Kalantzis, McCarthey, Vojak, & Kline, 2011). In addition, *Scholar's formative assessment* tools enable teachers to design writing projects that develop with the help of classmates' feedback and leverage *collaborative intelligence* as students use this feedback to make subsequent revisions.

While there is a substantial body of research on literacy instruction that employs such collaborative peer response and peer review practices, few studies have contextualized such classroom practices within higher-level elements of instruction and teacher's pedagogical decision-making. To contextualize the case of Tom, we first examine literature on educational technology policy, peer response, and computer-mediated peer response. Then we turn to prior research on *Scholar* to show how this writing environment functions in classroom writing instruction.

Technology Policy

The context of educational policy shapes district and school approaches to instruction, which in turn play into teachers' classroom structures. For instance, the No Child Left Behind (NCLB) policies that implement standardized measures of accountability cascade into typical classroom foci on reading rather than writing (Yancey, 2009), particularly for students from marginalized populations (McCarthey, 2008). Educational technology policies, too, provide grants to support states as they seek to improve students' achievement through the use of technology (Enhancing Education Through Technology Act, 2001), and call for "revolutionary transformation" in the ways that states use technology to enhance students' learning experiences (Office of Educational Technology, 2010, p. v). In current responses to such mandates, schools have largely invested in technologies to manage accountability scores (Halverson & Shapiro, 2012), although research on

how teachers use high-level student performance data is unclear at best (Spillane, 2012). *Scholar*, on the other hand, is a technological tool designed for teachers and learners. Typically selected by teachers to enable collaborative work on writing assignments, *Scholar* reorganizes classroom work and offers teachers data on what students are writing, how they respond to each others' work, and how they revise in response to reviews.

Peer Response

Literature on classroom writing suggests that implementing peer response practices allows classrooms to shift from teacher-directed spaces to interactive spaces where students read and assess each other's writing. Black and Wiliam (1998, 2009) point out generally that this type of formative response encourages incremental learning, while Graham and Perin (2007) note that process-writing approaches (which commonly include peer review) have a small but significant positive effect on writing performance. In an early study of language use across secondary classrooms, Gere and Abbott (1985) reported that the highest proportion of talk focused on the content of writing, showing that students can and do respond to one another in meaningful ways. Freedman's (1992) study of ninth-grade peer response supports this finding, showing that peers working in writing groups remained on task, collaborated to accomplish their work, and discussed writing elements like format, mechanics, and content. Students become more effective responders as they gain peer review expertise, however. In three years of working with college-bound students, Simmons (2003) found that experienced students focused their comments on readers' needs and writers' strategies, whereas less experienced reviewers focused more on editing. This study also cautions teachers to offer alternatives to global "cheerleading" comments (e.g. "great paper"). Students offer such responses frequently, but they do not aid in classmates' revisions.

Computer-Mediated Peer Response

As new media environments have become more classroom-accessible, many researchers have compared Computer-Mediated Communication (CMC) with face-to-face peer response. Studies have taken place with college students in composition (Ellis, 2011; Hewett, 2000; Mabrito, 1991) and English as a Second/Foreign Language courses (Jones, Garralda, & Lock, 2006; Matsumura & Hann, 2004; Sullivan & Pratt, 1996). Mabrito's (1991) work compares electronic mail with face-to-face peer response and shows that students devoted more attention to revisions in the email condition than face-to-face. Similar studies have found that peer groups engaged in face-to-face commenting focus on broader matters such as global idea development and the writing tasks themselves, while CMC groups focus more clearly on their peers' texts (Hewett, 2000; Honeycutt, 2001). In general, such findings follow Honeycutt's (2001) conclusions, suggesting that students using CMC environments may offer more extended, specific comments, while students offering face-to-face feedback often speak more globally. In a recent study comparing on-paper and online blog feedback, Ellis (2011) extends these findings to show that the medium of feedback matters, as well: Students working with blogs offered more extended comments, suggestions for revision, affirmation, and attention to relationship-building. Students who physically marked up each others' papers focused on word-level details, commenting on surface features such as punctuation and grammar.

Peer Response and Revision

The goal of much instruction that employs peer response and student review—whether face-to-face or online—is to expose students to readers' feedback in order to motivate reflection on and revision of their writing. Nevertheless, most studies in this area report little global, meaning-changing revision, and much proofreading or word-level revision (Beason, 1993; Cho & MacArthur, 2010; Flower, Hayes, Carey, Schriver, & Stratman, 1986). Researchers have noted that students find high-level, abstract revision processes cognitively and procedurally challenging (Hayes & Chenoweth, 2006; McCutchen, 2000), which may explain these findings. Nelson and Schunn (2009) found that writers tend to avoid revising when they do not understand readers' feedback; when reviewers identify specific problems and give concrete solutions, writers revise more consistently. All of these studies point towards the necessity of both sufficient time for peer response and teachers' instruction about what constitutes helpful comments.

Peer Response and Revision in Scholar

Our own analyses of classrooms using *Scholar* confirm and extend findings in all of these areas. Across classrooms in different schools and with different demographic characteristics (Kline, Letofsky, & Woodard, in press; Magnifico, Kline, Woodard, Letofsky, Carlin-Menter, & McCarthey, 2013), peer reviews most often inform writers about the content of their work rather than directing changes or eliciting additional information. Students frequently use affirming language and only rarely criticize each other in demeaning ways. Contrary to teachers' fears that peers will drift off-task or bully one another, these studies confirm findings that peer responders focus on content (Freedman, 1992; Gere & Abbott, 1985). Particularly less-experienced students, however, act as "cheerleaders" rather than as constructive critics (Simmons, 2003), and such a focus on information and affirmation is associated with few revisions. At the same time, when multiple peers highlighted the same problems and made specific suggestions, many writers made efforts to address these ideas (Magnifico et al., 2013).

Accompanying analyses demonstrate that teachers' assignments and rubrics—their initiating texts (Prior, 2004)—presented in *Scholar* direct students' responses and revisions. Teachers' texts draw student attention to particular language features or essay structures, and students' reviews respond in kind. This finding is consistent with Goldin and Ashley (2012) as well as our earlier study of three *Scholar* classrooms, both of which show that prompts and rubrics influence students' peer reviews (Magnifico, et al., under review). As Goldin and Ashley (2012) put it, "rubrics affect the experience of students and instructors; they are not neutral" (p. 232). Similarly, classroom and school contexts are not neutral, and students and teachers are enmeshed in these environments as they write and respond to each others' work.

Using these college-level studies of peer review and our own earlier analyses of *Scholar* as a backdrop, we sought to investigate how an 8th grade student wrote within his online and face-to-face blended writing environment.

METHODS

We use a case study design (Stake, 1995) to focus on the textual revisions and responses of one student, Tom (all names of schools, teachers, and students are pseudonyms), within a larger classroom context. We first analyze Tom's writing and response to examine his composition and revision with particular attention to the ways in which initiating texts influence his writing. Using interviews with Tom and his teacher, as well as broader classroom context, we further situate this writing work within Tom's classroom and school system to examine *Scholar's* place within a broader educational ecosystem.

Participants and Setting

Tom was a student in Ellen Anderson's eighth grade class at Reed Junior High, a school in which the team piloted its first version of *Scholar*.

The Online Writing Environment: Scholar

The online writing environment, *Scholar*, is currently in its fourth year of development. We, the authors, all serve as educational researchers partnering with software developers to inform the design of *Scholar*. This means that we partner with teachers, observe closely as they implement *Scholar* in the classrooms, analyze data, and make recommendations to the software team about design challenges, particularly those that relate to writing pedagogy.

At the time of this data collection cycle, *Scholar* consisted of two major components: (a) Creator, a word processor where a student composes writing and multimedia; and (b) Publisher, a class database where teachers design and manage projects with forms of peer review. Within Creator, students compose multiple versions of texts as well as review and annotate peers' texts. Once student drafts are submitted, students complete peer reviews. Teachers can set up peer review groups randomly or intentionally, and have options for anonymity. With the review tool, they use a teacher-created rubric to numerically evaluate and comment on various facets of their peers' texts. With the annotation tool, reviewers highlight areas of the text and prompt changes such as "add" or "change." The annotation tool was a new addition to the program at the time this data was collected, so was of particular interest to the research team. Once peer reviews and annotations are completed and submitted, students receive these responses and annotations, and use them to guide revision. *Scholar* collects and stores data including draft versions, proofreading annotations, and rubric-based peer reviews.

Reed Junior High

Reed is a diverse school in a small urban community about 25 miles from a major university; 81% of Reed's students are from low-income homes (State Report Card, 2011). At the time of this study, the school had been on the State's "Academic Watch" list as a result of failing to make Adequate Yearly Progress (AYP) in accordance with No Child Left Behind (2001). As a result, Reed lost several teachers and the school had to reorganize. This reorganization placed teachers into teams and mandated a scripted, reading-focused curriculum for below-grade-level classes. Ellen was assigned two on-or-above-grade level language arts classes and one below-grade level class. In these on-or-above-grade level courses, she chose to use *Scholar*.

The Teacher: Ellen Anderson

Ellen Anderson was in her second year trialing *Scholar* in her eighth-grade English Language Arts classroom. She was selected for this study because she self-identified as a confident user of computer technologies and because she expressed a strong interest in engaging students in peer response as part of the writing process. Before using *Scholar*, Ellen had provided some opportunities for face-to-face peer response in the classroom. She was enthusiastic about using *Scholar* because she felt it made peer response much easier to organize. She also believed that *Scholar* would help her to promote writing as a process, which she considered very important.

The Focal Student: Tom

Tom is a white male who was in his second quarter of eighth grade when he completed the narrative writing assignment detailed in this case. He identified himself as a confident user of computer technologies and expressed interest in using *Scholar* for writing. Tom wanted to become a writer, he said, "I would love to be a writer but I am not quite there yet, which is why we are trying *Scholar*." He described himself as "spontaneous, imaginative, and overall probably creative," and his writing as "an escape."

Tom was selected as a focal student because Ellen believed he would benefit greatly from peer review. She described him as a strong writer who had difficulty recognizing the need to improve his work when she gave him feedback. Ellen hoped that a peer audience who read and reviewed his writing would encourage Tom to revise. From our standpoint as researchers, Tom's case was information-rich because he wrote extensively and provided his opinion willingly in interviews. He was motivated to both try the online environment and receive peer feedback, contributing to a potentially "best case" for benefitting from *Scholar*.

The Assignment: A Narrative Writing Project

Previous to her use of *Scholar*, Ellen allotted 80 minutes for language arts, but most of the time was devoted to reading. Writing assignments focused on short answers, not extended writing projects. Once she decided to use *Scholar* for writing, she devoted significantly more time to writing for the narrative project.

Ellen asked her students to write narrative stories successively over the course of six weeks; she expected that they would finish their work in the allotted classroom time rather than completing tasks at home. Before using *Scholar*, students were to complete a variety of pre-writing tasks, including developing ideas about the character and plot. Then students drafted each story section—the introduction, then the rising action, climax, falling action, and resolution—in order. After each story section was drafted, it went out for peer review. Once the reviews were in, students submitted a second draft of this section. When they had reached the end of the story, students put all of the sections together into a full narrative to be peer reviewed again. Ellen set up the assignment with these specific sections to promote accountability and peer review. She wanted her students to see that writing requires multiple revisions and that they could sustain work on a longer text over time. Breaking the narrative into smaller sections helped peer reviewers stay focused and allowed Ellen to monitor students' writing and reviews. At the same time, students often started reading and reviewing their peers' stories in the middle of the narrative rather than at the beginning.

The rubrics Ellen created for students' peer reviews featured three criteria within each section: plot (e.g., introduction, rising action, climax, falling action, resolution), descriptive writing, and effort/creativity. All criteria used a rating scale of 0-3. These criteria reflected Ellen's goals, including descriptive writing, "8th grade vocabulary" (e.g. "microscopic" instead of "small"), and creativity. She told students she wanted them to create "original work, not a remake of a movie they had seen." These initiating texts—the assignment and rubric, primarily—created the context for Tom to write his story, review others' texts, and revise his own.

Data Collection

One of the authors (Kline) had worked with Ellen for two years; in this study, she observed Tom's class 3-4 times weekly during the narrative writing project, and took fieldnotes. After providing a brief overview of how to use *Scholar*, she took on the role of a participant-observer who also provided technical support when needed. She formally interviewed Tom three times, and Ellen twice, and audio-taped and transcribed these interviews. In addition, she had many informal conversations with students and teacher. She also collected artifacts from the classroom and from *Scholar,* including the assignment and rubric; all of Tom's texts, reviews, and annotations; and peers' responses to Tom's texts.

Data Analysis

First, we recursively reread interview data and classroom fieldnotes (Corbin & Strauss, 2008). We analyzed Tom's interviews to understand his work as a writer/revisor and a reviewer/annotator.

Classroom observation data were used to provide information about the broader classroom and school contexts. The analysis of Tom's interviews, then, focus on three aspects: his views of himself as a writer, his attitudes toward and understanding of peer review, and his perceptions of working in the online writing environment.

Next, we analyzed Tom's responses and revisions using the linguistic analysis technique reported in a larger study of three classrooms (Kline, Letofsky, & Woodard, in press). We developed a coding scheme with categories informed by Gere and Abbott (1985) and Sinclair and Coulthard (1978). Each review comment was divided into idea units, and each unit was coded according to its linguistic function (Chafe, 1980): whether it *informed* the author about their writing, *directed* the author to make a change, or *elicited* information from the author. Additionally, we coded each review comment to note its focus of attention, problem identification, specific revision strategy, and affective function.

For the bidirectional artifact analysis (Halverson & Magnifico, in press; Magnifico & Halverson, 2012), we traced Tom's writing over the course of the assignment and connected his revision and rewriting to classroom observations and interview comments. To do so, we examined all of Tom's work in both "backwards" (i.e. how later drafts reflect earlier ideas and writing) and "forwards" (i.e. how early drafts and feedback direct revision) directions. All revisions were coded by type (e.g. addition, reorganization, correction of English conventions) and traced to peer feedback and/or contextualized with observations, interview comments, and classroom initiating texts where possible.

Finally, we identified themes about the affordances and constraints of *Scholar*, particularly related to peer response and revision. We arrived at the themes by looking across the interview, artifacts, and observational data to understand how the online environment and the classroom and school contexts influenced Tom's texts and reviews. We subsequently identified three affordances—Tom's increased access to peer response, heightened motivation to write, and broadening classroom language use. We also found four constraints—the teacher's highly structured writing assignment, the random assignment of reviewers in each phase, classroom time constraints, and lack of ongoing access to computers and Internet.

FINDINGS

To understand Tom's responses and revisions in *Scholar*, we discuss Tom as a writer, a reviewer and annotator, and as a member of Ellen Anderson's classroom. Tom's work is situated within broader classroom and school contexts, which create both opportunities for and barriers to *Scholar* use. We outline these affordances and constraints and argue that implementation of online tools such as *Scholar* must take into consideration the complex factors of teachers' assignments, school policies and curriculum, as well as broader issues such as access to computers and the Internet.

The Case of Tom

Tom as Writer and Reviser

Although Tom did not engage in extensive revision, he was highly engaged in writing his narrative and appreciated his peer feedback. He saw value in the writing assignment, believing that it gave him an opportunity to go beyond "typical" school assignments. Tom thought Ellen assigned it "to challenge us, to explore the possibilities, to see how far we can go to make a good story without relying on ourselves." His understanding of what was required went beyond the technical elements; as he understood it, the point of the assignment was to, "be creative, be genuine, and think it through... This can't be a generic story."

Tom's plan for his story, "Let It Rain," was ambitious and included several plot developments and an organizational structure that moved from present time to the past through flashbacks. This plot featured a main character who dreamed a whole series of terrible events while in a coma, and he knew that this story would be complicated to write and revise. Yet, *Scholar's* record of his work in Table 1 shows Tom only created a revision for one section of his story—the Rising Action.

Tom valued the peer feedback he received on each section. He liked that the annotation tool helped point out grammatical mistakes and things that "would not be part of spellcheck." He also thought that most of his reviews were "accurate." Using Ellen's criteria, readers liked his creativity, but suggested that he work on his vocabulary and use more colorful language. He found that the reviewers brought to his attention that "the sections need to be stories within themselves," and that his sections were "choppy." While he liked the draft feedback, he did not tend to use it to make revisions.

From his full, final draft, which features hundreds of words of new content that were not present in his initially-drafted sections, it appears that Tom consistently spent the writing time that Ellen envisioned for refinement of each section on lengthening and adding detail to his original ideas. Such an orientation to writing and revision—where revision largely means adding content rather than copy-editing, reorganizing, or engaging in other

Table 1. Tom's drafts and reviews

Story Section	Drafts	Reviews	Annotations
Introduction	1st draft	(none)	1 annotation
Rising Action	1st & 2nd drafts	2 reviews	2 annotations
Climax	1st draft	2 reviews	7 annotations
Falling Action	(none)	(none)	(none)
Resolution	1st draft	2 reviews	1 annotation
Full Story	1st draft	2 reviews	4 annotations
Synopsis/ Book Flap	1st draft	2 reviews	(none)

forms of substantial reworking— also explains Tom's general lack of revision. As shown in Table 1, he received reviews and annotations from his classmates, many of which directed him to make changes or suggested possible editing moves, but did not often act on these suggestions.

In the section of the story where two drafts do exist, the Rising Action, both of Tom's reviewers suggest that he remove a large, ambiguous space (e.g., Reviewer 1 noted in an annotation that "... if you were trying to creat [sic] a silence you use periods to create a silent moment"), and ask for more descriptive language (e.g. Reviewer 2 pointed out that Tom "didn't describe anything"). In draft 2, Tom removes the lengthy space and adds a capital letter to the beginning of a name, thus completing minor revisions. Most of his work, however, goes into adding 350 words of content that describes his main character's meeting with his friends. This new content is replete with descriptive language:

I trekked my way across the sandy desert trying to avoid cacti and various pointy "yucatan" plants. When I arrived at what looked like a rock solid column, I approached it and saw the piles of rocks that guarded the entrance. "I didn't know that Zacharius set up a security mechanism." I walked over to the string and pulled it with the lightest force. The rocks instantly lit fire and burned rapidly (from Rising Action, version 3).

Such a focus on description suggests that Tom likely took his reviewers' advice to heart. It also suggests that the students were attuned to Ellen's review criteria for "descriptive writing." At the same time, Tom's ambitious plan seems to have trumped his desire to revise according to his reviews. Tom had many story details to write in order to fulfill his plan, and as such, it seems that there was little time for rethinking and rewriting.

In the final, full story draft, Tom's revision process remained consistent with this pattern. While he reorganized a substantial part of his content, moving two paragraphs of the original "rising action" into the final draft's "introduction" section, most of his revision involved substantial additions to the story. Tom added descriptive content to the introduction, as well as a transition to clarify a scene change in the rising action. He added a full new "climax" section that explains how his main character's best friend falls to his death in a Colorado canyon. The section where this death occurs, initially labeled "resolution" in earlier drafts, was moved to the end of the climax. Finally, Tom added 5 short sentences in which the remaining characters try to save their friend's life. While this is not a "resolution"—especially considering Tom's original plan for his story—he did reach a stopping place for this part of the narrative.

Tom did not finish his final story during the allotted class time. He noted that while an author's work is "never done," and that there are always "afterthoughts," he felt "guilty" about not completing this story. He felt that he had let readers down since he had included so much plot in his synopsis, yet never delivered a satisfactory resolution. Despite his disappointment in not completing the narrative, Tom believed that his story "conveyed emotion through words," and to some degree met his goal of making it "movie-like." His greatest challenges, he found, were tying the characters and plot together, especially given the separate sections of the story prompted by the teacher's outline. He wished he had made "smoother entrances into the sections." However, compared to his previous stories, he felt that "Let It Rain" was deeper because it "expressed humanity" and he was able to elicit "sadness and sympathy" for the character.

Primarily, Tom did not finish his story because he ran out of time. There was "so much to write up" that he found it "overwhelming" and felt a "sense of awe" in trying to write so much. He also noted that his lack of home Internet access limited his ability to finish. If he could have accessed *Scholar* at home, he would have been writing "24 hours a day." From Tom's texts and interviews, it becomes clear that he was invested in writing to an audience. Although he did not engage in much actual revision, he continued to value the process of writing and reviewing and found that *Scholar* facilitated this process.

Tom as Reviewer and Annotator

In addition to writing and revising his own story, Tom participated as a reviewer and annotator of his classmates' work, and he used the review and annotation tools in different ways. Table 2 provides the numeric results of the linguistic analysis of the reviews Tom received (Reviews & Annotations for Tom's Writing), an analysis of the reviews (Tom's Reviews for Other Writers), and annotations (Tom's Annotations for Other Writers) he provided for his peers.

Tom provided feedback to five students during the narrative project. His review strategies tended to inform (70.2%) rather than direct (27.7%) or elicit (2.1%). His informing strategy can be seen in his response to Vivian's character description, "I love how every word you say is detailed when it comes to talking about your character's characteristics. I love how I can just imagine the character's face and body structure because of how you describe them." He also directs her to make some changes when he wrote, "you could be better when it comes to creating a more. . . miscellaneous, fun, and energetic settings and scenarios."

Tom usually responded to the content of classmates' stories (46.8%) in his reviews. Tom's focus on the elements of a successful story is apparent in his reviews of Ruth's story, "Decisions, Decisions. Who shall live?" Tom wrote, "I like your falling action. It seems as though the action is over as falling action should be." Tom, however, did point out some grammatical issues as well. In his response to Ray's story, "The missing Mona Lisa: Narrative." Tom wrote, "Work on your grammar! Most of these are run on sentences."

Tom identified problems in classmates' writing (48.9%) about half of the time. When he gave an explicit strategy for changing the text, it tended to be to add to the story as in this comment to Ray, "Oh, and add more descriptive words." Tom frequently provided explicit affirming responses (44.6%) such as in his response to his peer, Cory's "Goodbye Pride: Climax" narrative. Tom wrote, "I love how this story has a "Lion king" feel to it! It's really rambunctious and fast-paced, as well as being insanely descriptive and creative."

While Tom followed a typical pattern of mostly informing while using the review tool, he used more directing language in the annotation tool. Such in-text citation tools allowed Tom and other students to use a greater variety of language than response to teacher-created rubrics alone. He was much more likely to give a change strategy in his annotations (100%) than his reviews (10%), and he provided a greater variety of change strategies than in his reviews. However, his dominant change strategy in both annotations and reviews was to recommend additions such as "Finish the climax!! (please)." He tended to provide more specific comments without pronounced affect in the annotation tool, as evidenced by his comment, "Leave out 'like." In the review tool, Tom was more likely to offer affirmations such as "You really do know what your [sic] doing though!!"

Tom was sensitive to how peers might react to his comments. He was especially attuned to not affecting the writer's confidence as well as the need for considering Ellen's rubric criteria, such as descriptive language and 8th grade vocabulary. He noted that "you don't want to tear somebody's confidence out" with negative reviews, and that it is important to describe a scene clearly so that the reader can picture the details, "...almost like going to the theater and watching Harry Potter, you've got to have a lot of description and you know, color words, eighth grade vocabulary, things of that nature."

On the one hand, the review and annotation tools assisted him in giving feedback on his own

Table 2. Tom's reviews and annotations

	Reviews & Annotations for Tom's Writing	Tom's Reviews for Other Writers	Tom's Annotations for Other Writers	Total
Total # Idea Units	**65 idea units = 100%**	**47 idea units = 100%**	**9 idea units = 100%**	**121 idea units = 100%**
Linguistic Function				
Inform	37 (56.9%)	33 (70.2%)	0 (0%)	**70 (57.9%)**
Direct	26 (40%)	13 (27.7%)	9 (100%)	**48 (39.6%)**
Elicit	2 (3.1%)	1 (2.1%)	0 (0%)	**3 (2.5%)**
Focus of Attention				
Content	22 (33.8%)	22 (46.8%)	1 (11.1%)	**45 (37.2%)**
Conventions	8 (12.3%)	2 (4.3%)	3 (33.3%)	**13 (10.7%)**
Assignment Guidelines & Formatting	7 (10.8%)	0 (0%)	0 (0%)	**7 (5.8%)**
Sentence Fluency & Word Choice	19 (29.2%)	7 (14.9%)	5 (55.6%)	**31 (25.6%)**
General	5 (7.7%)	10 (2.1%)	0 (0%)	**15 (12.4%)**
Other	2 (3.1%)	5 (10.6%)	0 (0%)	**7 (5.8%)**
Unclear	2 (3.1%)	1 (2.1%)	0 (0%)	**3 (2.5%)**
Identifying a Problem				
No	26 (40%)	24 (51.1%)	0 (0%)	**50 (41.3%)**
Yes- Explicit	21 (32.3%)	12 (25.5%)	0 (0%)	**33 (27.3%)**
Yes- Implicit	18 (27.7%)	11 (23.4%)	9 (100%)	**38 (31.4%)**
Give Explicit Strategies				
No	40 (61.5%)	32 (78.7%)	0 (0%)	**72 (59.5%)**
Yes	21 (32.3%)	10 (21.3%)	9 (100%)	**40 (33.1%)**
Add	10 (15.4%)	7 (14.9%)	2 (22.2%)	**19 (15.7%)**
Elaborate	0 (0%)	1 (2.1%)	0 (0%)	**1 (0.8%)**
Correct	8 (12.3%)	1 (2.1%)	4 (44.4%)	**13 (10.7%)**
Delete	0 (0%)	0 (0%)	2 (22.2%)	**2 (1.7%)**
Reorganize	0 (0%)	0 (0%)	0 (0%)	**0 (0%)**
Substitute	2 (3.1%)	0 (0%)	0 (0%)	**2 (1.7%)**
Reread	1 (1.5%)	0 (0%)	1 (11.1%)	**2 (1.7%)**
Other	0 (0%)	1 (2.1%)	0 (0%)	**1 (0.8%)**
Unclear	4 (6.2%)	5 (10.6%)	0 (0%)	**9 (7.4%)**
Pronounced Affective Function				
No	39 (60%)	22 (46.8%)	9 (100%)	**70 (57.9%)**
Affirm-Explicit	18 (27.7%)	21 (44.6%)	0 (0%)	**39 (32.2%)**
Affirm- Implicit	6 (9.2%)	2 (4.3%)	0 (0%)	**8 (6.6%)**
Demean- Explicit	0 (0%)	1 (2.1%)	0 (0%)	**1 (0.8%)**
Demean- Implicit	2 (3.1%)	1 (2.1%)	0 (0%)	**3 (2.5%)**

time, and concentrating on the text rather than the writer. He could also give specific feedback related to teacher criteria through the review tool, and point to specific aspects of the writing with the annotation tool. However, he did not provide much clarification or elaboration in the review tool, rarely asked questions to encourage dialogue, and used a limited variety of language types in his responses. This indicates some of the challenges with written peer feedback: It takes enormous amounts of time to learn how to provide meaningful feedback, whether reviews are conveyed in face-to-face or online environments (Beach & Friedrich, 2006).

Tom as a Student in Ellen's Classroom

Tom's texts and his reviews of peers' texts were also embedded within Ellen's pedagogical choices and *Scholar*'s design. His story aligned to her rubric's review criteria (i.e., plot elements, descriptive writing, effort/creativity), and her assignment's narrative categories (i.e. introduction, rising action, climax, falling action, and resolution/denouement). His initial and revised texts showed a focus on descriptive writing, and his tendency to continually add text demonstrated his effort. Students' responses to his texts, as well as Tom's reviews and annotations of peers' work, aligned with Ellen's review criteria as well. This finding indicates that the teacher's initiating texts and her rubrics had a major impact on both Tom's texts and his response to others' writing, and is consistent with our analyses of 10 classrooms demonstrating the influence of teachers' initiating texts on students' responses and revisions (Woodard, Magnifico, & McCarthey, 2013).

However, Ellen's decisions about structuring the assignment into small segments, such as rising action, seemed to have a somewhat deleterious effect on Tom's revision. He was in continual conflict between meeting Ellen's and his peers' expectations of revising the existing content, and his own goal of writing a lengthy, complex story

within the allotted classroom time. Likewise, his reviews and annotations of his peers' texts showed that he was somewhat constrained by Ellen's review criteria as he focused many of his comments on description. While Ellen believed she was facilitating students' revision processes and monitoring students' completion by breaking the assignment into plot features, the constant need to review others' work within each feature appeared to undermine Tom's ability to revise or complete the project. The criterion of descriptive writing with the expectation to use "8th grade vocabulary" may have resulted in an overwhelming sense of adding details for their own sake as opposed to moving the plot forward. By combining effort with creativity into one criterion, Tom seemed to conflate creating something unique ("not unlike a movie") with the amount of time spent on the task. His focus on description came to overshadow almost all other criteria, and effort was not discussed at all.

Ellen also believed that the random assignment of peers to review parts of the story would result in gaining more viewpoints about each aspect. However, the result was that the same student never had the opportunity to read a narrative from its inception to its completion. Peers attended to the three criteria only within a given section, but did not respond to the text in its entirety nor see how the plot developed. Although Tom recognized that he needed to summarize or make smoother transitions for the reader, the overall effect of the writing process appeared fragmented, resulting in Tom's frustration of not meeting his own goals.

AFFORDANCES OF CONSTRAINTS OF AN ONLINE WRITING ENVIRONMENT

The case of Tom highlights both the affordances and constraints of an online writing and review system, *Scholar*, used in a middle school setting. The case also exemplifies how school-based online writing practices are always situated within teacher's pedagogical choices, classroom norms, school settings, and larger policy contexts. While *Scholar* provided opportunities for Tom to engage in beneficial writing and peer review practices, the tool also had some shortcomings, particularly in that it did not encourage Ellen to radically transform her pedagogy. Contextual factors such as mandates related to standards, as well as a lack of technology access for all students, provided additional challenges.

Affordances

The online writing environment seemed to have three major affordances for Tom in this 8th grade classroom. First, the online writing environment increased Tom's access to peer response. Prior to implementing *Scholar*, Ellen had not used much peer review in the classroom. Working with this technology contributed to her valuing peer response more, and incorporating it into the writing process. Because she felt that *Scholar* provided access to peer response and made the writing process more visible, Ellen felt empowered to implement peer response. The result was that Tom had more opportunities to interact with his peers about writing and received more types of feedback—both rubric-based and annotations—than he did before the implementation of the online writing system.

These opportunities to interact with peers connected to the second affordance of *Scholar* for Tom—his motivation to write more and to a higher standard for an audience. For example, when asked about peer review using *Scholar* he said, "I think it is helpful. It lets you explore what's going to work for you and your audience because when it comes down to it writing isn't for yourself, it's for the people; it gives them something to look forward to and to explore and entertain themselves with." He saw the value of doing peer review, "So you need - like - somebody to bounce ideas off - . . .That's why you should explore with a partner

or peer review. They open up so many doors for you." His reviews by peers became a first step for writing to a larger audience; he found that peers using the online system could "notify not only what you need working on but (what) the public is going to like."

The online writing tool had another affordance for Tom: The wide variety of response tools scaffolded and increased his response repertoire. As an author, he found that the review criteria could help make his writing better by providing a way to organize his writing. He was able to understand and use the distinct functions of the review tool and the annotation tool, saying:

I like the annotation especially because it is just like little things that you might have missed that you yourself were unable to fix. . . "check" only checks spelling and not the order of the words, and how it sounds from somebody else's perspective. I think that is where annotations come in-- to really fix you up. They buffer your story and make it much better.

He took advantage of the annotation tool, using it differently than the rubric-referenced review tool in the responses he gave to his peers as well. These tools were more explicitly separate than students interacting in a face-to-face setting where they often focus on spelling and grammatical errors rather than larger issues of plot or character development (Ellis, 2011).

While the three affordances reflected the goals of the design of the *Scholar* environment, its implementation in Ellen's classroom shared some of the same problems as described in the literature on face-to-face writing response and revision processes, and also exposed some of the constraints with this stage of *Scholar*'s use. In addition, Tom's case highlights some of the problems with implementing online environments in schools with limited computer access and within current policy contexts.

Constraints

The constraints on Tom's writing included aspects of the assignment and the larger school and social contexts, as well as some specific limitations of *Scholar*. First, the larger policy context in which Tom's writing was embedded placed additional constraints on the classroom and school. Because the school had been on the State's "Academic Watch" list for not making Adequate Yearly Progress (AYP) the school focused primarily on reading, and adopted a scripted reading curriculum. These policy issues constrained most of the Reed teachers from engaging students in much writing, and made it difficult for Ellen to focus on writing throughout the year. Like teachers in low-income schools in McCarthey's (2008) study, who were limited in the writing opportunities they offered to students, school and policy factors tended to constrain Ellen's ability to provide continual access to the innovative writing environment.

Second, Tom lacked access to a computer at home. He had noted that he would have been writing "24 hours a day" if he had Internet access at home. Because many students, like Tom, did not have access to home computers, the school policy on homework mandated that only pencil and paper homework could be assigned. Thus, the *Scholar* project had to be completed during school time. School computer time was also limited since teachers had to sign up for the computer lab in advance, and Ellen became concerned that she was monopolizing the lab. Access was further limited due to the slowness of the wireless connectivity-- when the teacher and students logged on to see the texts and reviews, they often had to wait several minutes for their texts to appear.

Third, the online tool assigned random reviewers for each section of the narrative (e.g., rising action, plot, etc); therefore, peers did not have the full story to read and respond to throughout the cycle of the writing. This constrained Tom's writ-ing process because he was constantly writing to a new audience who lacked the previous context and details that were particularly salient to his lengthy narrative. He also was unable to establish a relationship with a group of peers as he revised.

Finally, Ellen set up a linear and highly-structured one draft-one review-one revision cycle. Her task of breaking the narrative assignment into parts such as introduction, rising action, climax, etc, with a review in each, did not allow Tom enough time to complete his story, give meaningful feedback, and revise his work in a timely manner. The need to complete reviews during school time also had a negative effect on Tom. For example, he provided lengthy oral comments when interviewed outside the classrooms about what a student should revise, but his online review comments tended to be brief.

Tom's brief response comments can be explained by two constraints: the tool and Ellen's timelines. *Scholar* was set up for students to simultaneously review each others' texts only after 80% of the students submitted their assignment to the online environment. Because the system precluded individual students from completing their texts and then requesting reviews as needed, Ellen gave frequent ultimatums for students to complete reviews in 10 minutes to keep students on a timeline toward completion. The effect was that many students tended to rush into giving generic feedback while students who read more carefully tended to run out of time and reduced their standards in responding.

Factors such as limited access to the Internet and the policy contexts, including the pressure to increase achievement on reading tests and the scripted curriculum imposed on teachers for below-grade level classes, shaped the classroom context and Ellen and Tom's use of *Scholar*. The affordances and the constraints of online writing environments, then, must be viewed within these broad contexts.

IMPLICATIONS

Implications from this case study of Tom's online peer response and review in *Scholar* can be extended more broadly to writing in technology. We begin with policy implications, then move to research and pedagogical implications.

Policy

Access to technology and curricular mandates related to national standards and assessments all came into play in Tom's work in *Scholar*. First, Tom only had access to online writing technology because of Ellen's commitment to peer interaction and writing. Most of the other teachers who started using *Scholar* at the same time as Ellen stopped using it because of the school's concern with making AYP on state reading tests, and their resulting mandated curriculum policies. Even Ellen did not use *Scholar* with her below grade-level class because of the skill-based mandated reading curriculum they used. In fact, that class did much less writing in general than Tom's class. However, Tom's access to *Scholar* was limited because he did not have a computer at home, and could not use the program on a handheld device. The implications of high-stakes testing, curricular mandates that privilege reading over writing, and student access to technology are also essential issues in discussions of writing with technology.

Research

Methodologically, we found that *Scholar* had great potential to support a process-oriented view of student writing within the Web-based system. The system, which was designed to encourage multiple versions of texts that are continually reviewed by peers, is consistent with a process orientation to writing (Calkins, 1998; Graves, 1990; Murray, 1979), and it appears that Ellen adhered to the process view as she designed her narrative assignment. When studying online writing environments,

researchers need to examine the kinds of pedagogy they best support. Because *Scholar* collects and stores data including multiple drafts, annotations, and rubric-based peer reviews, students (like Tom), teachers (like Ellen), and researchers all have access to a wealth of data. However, the artifacts alone only tell part of the story; to really understand students' writing in online spaces, researchers must trace into classroom interactions and pedagogy, and outwards to policy and access issues. Such efforts reflect Prior's (2004) focus on contextualizing students' literacy practices across initiating texts, learning situations, and conversations, as well as the bidirectional artifact analysis employed in this study to understand revision (Magnifico & Halverson, 2012).

Instructional

Online writing environments like *Scholar* can certainly motivate students like Tom, and help teachers implement more peer response and writing process pedagogy. However, as in offline classrooms, teachers must design writing projects to align with student goals and to create flexible writing process possibilities. Specifically, when teachers use online writing environments to facilitate text-based annotation they allow students to use directing language and encourage specific revision strategies. Teachers and students also gain greater access to data that can be used for formative assessment and peer review.

However, school, teacher, and student goals for writing are often misaligned. Ellen's goals misaligned with Tom's at various points throughout the project, and ultimately resulted in fairly surface-level revisions (e.g., the addition of new content or descriptive language, rather than reorganization or cutting). It is worth exploring ways for teachers to develop initiating texts (assignments and rubrics) that also account for students' goals (e.g., rubric co-construction). Similarly, the ways teachers design the writing process impacts student response and revision.

Teachers and writing environments, like *Scholar*, need to address the needs for a more flexible writing process, and on-going writing partners and groups over time. Ellen's highly structured writing process, use of different anonymous peer reviewers for various sections of drafts, and assumptions about access hindered Tom's revision process. While *Scholar's* design at the time of this study certainly contributed to Ellen's pedagogical decisions, we believe that many of these constraints may hold true in other online writing environments.

For example, teachers' pedagogies might take advantage of annotation tools that allow students to comment freely on various aspects of writing. While much writing assessment focuses on teacher-driven rubrics, annotation encourages students to use a wider variety of language and to make personal choices about response to their classmates' writing. More research is needed to understand how teachers might better design formative assessment to scaffold a variety of student feedback and encourage more directing and eliciting language.

Online environments provide rich formative assessment data that teachers and students can use to improve writing and instruction. These data afforded Ellen with a rich picture of each student's writing that allowed her to monitor each student's drafts and reviews, and to consider how to improve the project for future use. That said, Ellen increasingly took on the role of monitor (rather than facilitator or guide), to move the students through the writing process at her planned pace. Tom also had access to the multiple versions of his story that could allow him to see the revisions he made over time; however, the system itself could not provide him with the time and access he needed to complete his project and reflect on his texts.

CONCLUSION

As we close this chapter, we reflect on the principles of assessment that drive our work on *Scholar* (Cope et al., 2011) and pose questions about the potential of similar online writing environments. An underlying principle of *Scholar* is that online writing is ubiquitous. As we saw in Ellen's classroom where she had to reserve the computer lab in advance, and in Tom's case where he lacked Internet access at home, Web-based writing can only occur when all classrooms and all students truly have access anywhere and anytime. While formative assessment and collaborative intelligence continue to be worthwhile goals that can be enhanced by online writing environments such as *Scholar*, it is still the teacher's pedagogical design and initiating texts (projects and rubrics), as well as the relationships among teachers and students, that will advance teaching and learning in writing. The classroom, school, and larger policy contexts will continue to influence teaching and learning regardless of the technology used. However, well-designed tools that promote writing and reflection can still play a major role in helping to shape students' thinking about writing. Further refinement of these tools to take advantage of teachers' and students' experiences as well as continued research on their uses in classrooms can move writing instruction forward.

ACKNOWLEDGMENT

This work was supported by grants from the Institute of Education Sciences: "Assessing Complex Performance: A Postdoctoral Training Program Researching Students Writing and Assessment in Digital Workspaces," U.S. Department of Education (Common Ground Publishing LLC) "U-learn. net, Phases 1 and 2," and "The Assess-As-You-Go Writing Assistant: A Student Work Environment That Brings Together Formative and Summative Assessment" (Bill Cope, PI).

REFERENCES

Applebee, A., & Langer, J. (2009). What is happening in the teaching of writing? *English Journal*, *98*(5), 18–28.

Beach, R., & Friedrich, T. (2006). Response to writing. In MacArthur, C. A., Graham, S., & Fitzgerald, J. (Eds.), *Handbook of writing research* (pp. 222–234). New York, NY: Guilford Publications.

Beason, L. (1993). Feedback and revision in writing across the curriculum classes. *Research in the Teaching of English*, *27*, 395–422.

Black, P., & Wiliam, D. (1998). Assessment and classroom learning. *Assessment in Education*, *5*(1), 7–74. doi:10.1080/0969595980050102.

Black, P., & Wiliam, D. (2009). Developing the theory of formative assessment. *Educational Assessment, Evaluation and Accountability*, *21*(1), 5–31. doi:10.1007/s11092-008-9068-5.

Calkins, L. M. C. (1986). *The art of teaching writing*. Portsmouth, NH: Heinemann.

Chafe, W. L. (1980). The deployment of consciousness in the production of a narrative. In Chafe, W. L. (Ed.), *The pear stories: Cognitive, cultural, and linguistic aspects of narrative production*. Norwood, NY: Ablex Publishing Corporation.

Cho, K., & MacArthur, C. (2010). Student revision with peer and expert reviewing. *Learning and Instruction*, *20*, 328–338. doi:10.1016/j. learninstruc.2009.08.006.

Cho, K., & Schunn, C. D. (2007). Scaffolding writing and rewriting in the discipline. *Computers & Education*, *48*, 409–426. doi:10.1016/j. compedu.2005.02.004.

Cho, K., Schunn, C. D., & Charney, D. (2006). Commenting on writing: Typology and perceived helpfulness of comments from novice peer reviewers and subject matter experts. *Written Communication*, *23*, 260–294. doi:10.1177/0741088306289261.

Cope, B., Kalantzis, M., McCarthey, S., Vojak, C., & Kline, S. (2011). Technology-mediated writing assessments: Principles and processes. *Computers and Composition*, *28*, 29–96. doi:10.1016/j. compcom.2011.04.007.

Corbin, J. M., & Strauss, A. L. (2008). *Basics of qualitative research: Techniques and procedures for developing grounded theory*. Thousand Oaks, CA: Sage.

Ellis, M. J. (2011). Peer feedback on writing: Is on-line actually better than on-paper? *Journal of Academic Language & Learning*, *5*(1), 88–99.

Enhancing Education Through Technology Act. (2001). Retrieved from http://www2.ed.gov/ policy/elsec/leg/esea02/pg34.html

Flower, L., & Hayes, J. R. (1980). The cognition of discovery: Defining a rhetorical problem. *College Composition and Communication*, *31*(1), 21–23. doi:10.2307/356630.

Flower, L., Hayes, J. R., Carey, L., Schriver, K., & Stratman, J. (1986). Detection, diagnosis, and the strategies of revision. *College Composition and Communication*, *37*(1), 16–55. doi:10.2307/357381.

Freedman, S. W. (1992). Outside-in and inside-out: Peer response groups in two ninth-grade classes. *Research in the Teaching of English*, *26*, 71–107.

Gere, A. R., & Abbott, R. D. (1985). Talking about writing: The language of writing groups. *Research in the Teaching of English, 19*, 362–385.

Goldin, I. M., & Ashley, K. D. (2012). Eliciting formative assessment in peer review. *Journal of Writing Research, 4*(2), 203–237.

Goldin, I. M., Ashley, K. D., & Schunn, C. D. (2012). Redesigning educational peer review interactions using computer tools: An introduction. *Journal of Writing Research, 4*(2), 111–119.

Graham, S., & Perin, D. (2007). A meta-analysis of writing instruction for adolescent students. *Journal of Educational Psychology, 99*, 445–476. doi:10.1037/0022-0663.99.3.445.

Halverson, R., & Shapiro, R. B. (2012). *Technologies for education and technologies for learners: How information technologies are (and should be) changing schools* (WCER Working Paper No. 2012-6). Madison, WI: Wisconsin Center for Education Research, University of Wisconsin-Madison.

Hayes, J. R., & Chenoweth, N. A. (2006). Is working memory involved in the transcribing and editing of texts? *Written Communication, 23*(2), 135–149. doi:10.1177/0741088306286283.

Hewett, B. L. (2000). Characteristics of interactive oral and computer-mediated peer group talk and its influence on revision. *Computers and Composition, 17*, 265–288. doi:10.1016/S8755-4615(00)00035-9.

Honeycutt, L. (2001). Comparing e-mail and synchronous conferencing in online peer response. *Written Communication, 18*, 26. doi:10.1177/0741088301018001002.

Jones, R. H., Garralda, A., Li, D., & Lock, G. (2006). Interactional dynamics in on-line and face-to-face peer-tutoring sessions for second language writers. *Journal of Second Language Writing, 15*, 1–23. doi:10.1016/j.jslw.2005.12.001.

Kalantzis, M., & Cope, W. (2012). *Literacies.* New York: Cambridge University Press. doi:10.1017/CBO9781139196581.

Kline, S., Letofsky, K., & Woodard, R. L. (2013). Democratizing classroom discourse: The challenge for online writing environments. *E-Learning and Digital Media, 10*(4).

Mabrito, M. (1991). Electronic mail as a vehicle for peer response. *Written Communication, 8*, 509–532. doi:10.1177/0741088391008004004.

Magnifico, A. M., Kline, S., Woodard, R. L., Letofsky, K., Carlin-Menter, S., McCarthey, S., & Cope, B. (2013). *A formative investigation of peer response and revisions in an online writing environment.*

Matsumura, S., & Hann, G. (2004). Computer anxiety and students' preferred feedback methods in EFL writing. *Modern Language Journal, 88*, 403–415. doi:10.1111/j.0026-7902.2004.00237.x.

McCarthey, S. (2008). The impact of no child left behind on teachers' writing instruction. *Written Communication, 25*, 462–505. doi:10.1177/0741088308322554.

McCutchen, D. (2000). Knowledge, processing, and working memory: Implications for a theory of writing. *Instructional Science, 37*, 375–401.

Nystrand, M., Gamoran, A., Kachur, R., & Prendergast, C. (Eds.). (1997). *Opening dialogue: Understanding the dynamics of language and learning in the English classroom.* New York, NY: Teachers College Press.

Office of Educational Technology. (2010). *Transforming American education: Learning powered by technology: National educational technology plan 2010.* Washington, DC: US Department of Education.

Prior, P. (2004). Tracing processes: How texts come into being. In Bazerman & Prior (Eds.), What writing does and how it does it: An introduction to analyzing texts and textual practices (pp. 167-200). Mahwah, NJ: Lawrence Erlbaum Associates.

Simmons, J. (2003). Responders are taught, not born. *Journal of Adolescent & Adult Literacy, 46*, 684–693.

Sinclair, J., & Coulthard, M. (1975). *Towards an analysis of discourse*. Oxford, UK: Oxford University Press.

Spillane, J. P. (2012). Data in practice: Conceptualizing data-based decision-making phenomena. *American Journal of Education, 118*(2), 113–141. doi:10.1086/663283.

Stake, R. E. (1995). *The art of case study research*. Thousand Oaks, CA: Sage.

Sullivan, N., & Pratt, E. (1996). A comparative study of two ESL writing environments: A computer-assisted classroom and a traditional oral classroom. *System, 24*, 491–501. doi:10.1016/S0346-251X(96)00044-9.

Woodard, R. L., Magnifico, A. M., & McCarthey S. J. (2013). Supporting teacher metacognition about formative assessment in online writing environments. *E-Learning and Digital Media, 10*(4).

Yancey, K. B. (2009). *Writing in the 21st century: A report from the national council of teachers of English*. Urbana, IL: NCTE. Retrieved from http://www.ncte.org/library/NCTEFiles/Press/Yancey_final.pdf

Chapter 10
Rebooting Revision:
Leveraging Technology to Deliver Formative and Summative Feedback

Sarah-Beth Hopton
University of South Florida, USA

ABSTRACT

In the past decade, digital feedback tools to review and revise student writing have proliferated. Scholarship in rhetoric, composition, and professional writing has yet to consider how digital feedback systems might offer a promising alternative to traditional and arguably broken feedback practices. This chapter offers a review of the latest scholarship on the digital feedback and revision practices of students and professors, and demonstrates the use of a heuristic customized to college writing applications and programs, which can help professors review and assess new digital tools used to manage an electronic feedback and assessment protocol.

1. INTRODUCTION

One central frustration for English professors is the time it takes to offer quality feedback on the writing assignments of their students. This frustration is often coupled with questions about whether, and to what extent, students act on the formative feedback offered by their professors. Technology can ease these frustrations and make the work of offering quality feedback on writing assignments more effective and efficient while simultaneously offering professors a view into the revision practices of their students. Or, at least, this is what the advocates of digital feedback technology promise. Limited studies have measured the effectiveness of various digital feedback

technologies like Camtasia and Google Docs, but these studies need to be replicated to confirm their claims that digital feedback technologies are preferable to analog practices. Further compounding the issue is the difficulty in selecting appropriate software to manage feedback protocols. Untrained in usability principles, and lacking relevant heuristics, many English professors are overwhelmed by the sheer volume of technology options for feedback delivery. As a way of alleviating some of this frustration, in this chapter, I review some innovative practices using technology as a way of delivering formative and summative assessments. I then turn to a discussion of the revision practices of students as a way of helping professors to see how assessment can enhance the revision practices of their students. And, before I end, I offer an overview of areas in the field of digital

DOI: 10.4018/978-1-4666-4341-3.ch010

feedback technology that require further study. My final analysis concerns the heuristics of choosing between delivery technologies. In short, I attempt to offer aid to English professors by proposing a good model for selecting between software to deliver formative and summative feedback.

2. DEFINING THE DIGITAL FEEDBACK PROTOCOL

Advancements in technology and the rise of the "app"—short for an application built to optimally function on digital devices—affords English professors an array of tools to call upon to assess the writings of their students. However, today, writing is much different from what it was when many of our professors were in college. Now, most college papers are written on a computer, not paper; essays are now turned in via e-mail, not attached by paperclips and plopped down on a desk at the beginning of class; peer reviews are managed using collaborative digital technology like MyReviewers, not in small groups; and conversations between professors and students are increasingly conducted via voice-over-Internet-protocols like SKYPE, not the old twentieth century mode of the telephone. Moreover, because technology is affordable and easily accessible to most, devices like Apples's iPad have changed how we access textbooks and how English departments across this nation are experimenting with knowledge transfer and adaptive learning technology. Indeed, even the very *idea* of what constitutes text has changed. Concerning textbooks specifically, in the past textbooks were bound objects of static information complimented by two-dimensional images, but today's digital textbooks are haptically responsive, multi-modal, and to an increasing degree customizable. Professors can use technology, when soundly selected and cleverly employed, to better assess the writing abilities of, and promote

good revision practices among, their students. But what *is* a digital feedback protocol? And how do English professors manage such protocols amid a constantly shifting backdrop of new technologies?

Innovations in digital technology are much too rapid and dynamic to expect professors who are not technologically savvy to maintain fluency across multiple tools and applications. Nevertheless, formative feedback (commentary) is generally regarded as a significant factor in motivating learning and improving knowledge and skill acquisition (Epstein et al., 2002; Moreno, 2004). Formative feedback helps students identify their strengths and weaknesses and target areas of writing that need improvement. Formative feedback also helps professors monitor, and in some cases, customize content to improve student learning. Summative feedback, on the other hand, evaluates student learning; it evaluates learning relevant to a particular point in time, usually with a grade. Formative feedback can be considered the endnote an instructor writes on a student's essay that offers global suggestions for revision. Such suggestions might include issues with organization, sources, or argumentation. Formative feedback can also include "local" suggestions for revision such as suggestions for improving style, grammar, and punctuation. By contrast, summative assessments are generally thought of as grades, though summative assessments can be used formatively when students or faculty use them to guide their efforts in subsequent writing activities. Both formative and summative assessments are used to develop student writing, but formative feedback is particularly important to professors who subscribe to writing process pedagogy (Emig, 1971; Perl, 1979; Flower & Hayes, 1971). Stated simply, then, digital feedback and revision protocols establish procedures for offering formative and summative feedback on student writing assignments using a digital device, software program, an application, or combination of such tools.

3. DIGITAL FEEDBACK PRACTICES IN THE COLLEGE WRITING CLASSROOM

Writing professors lament over the time it takes to offer quality formative feedback on the writings of their students. Those who work with undergraduate writers are particularly motivated to find and adopt technology that enables them to be more efficient and effective in their feedback practices. The advocates of digital feedback technology promise to meet this need, and offer the added benefit of allowing professors a view of the revision practices of their students. But English professors' willingness to integrate digital feedback technology into their writing classrooms has been tried by the gap between what the advocates of digital technology promise and what they have been able to deliver up to this point. Hawisher, LeBlanc, Moran and Selfe (1996) have observed that the early work in the field of computers and writing tended to focus on the possibility that computers could be programmed to "read" and assess student writing, and thereby do for composition professors what the "calculator ha[s] done for mathematics" professors (p. 31). Unfortunately, however, digital tools like word processing programs, which can automate certain writing and revision functions, have a much more difficult task because writing mechanics, tone, and style are not easily reducible to algorithmic-friendly parts in the way that addition and subtraction equations are.

Nevertheless, when word processors were first available as teaching tools, writing professors viewed programs like Microsoft Word as a godsend, but eventually such programs were found to be of limited value in reducing the amount of time professors spent on assessments. Spelling and grammar checkers cannot, for example, distinguish between homonyms, detect words outside the program's internal dictionary, or easily recognize colloquialisms. Automatic feedback programs might offer the English professor a point of departure from which to begin editing for grammar and style, but even advanced programs like ETS's E-Rater, which automatically generates formative feedback on issues of style, grammar, and punctuation, requires an instructor to verify the computer-generated suggestions are indeed accurate, making the feedback process hardly automatic.

Although technology has not fully lived up to its promises, digital writing tools are ubiquitous in the college writing classroom because they alleviate several specific complaints about giving and receiving formative feedback. A study conducted by Comer and Hammer demonstrates that when instructors use digital technology to offer feedback on assignments, students report improvements in legibility, efficiency, clarity and ease of revision (Comer & Hammer, 2008). Instructors say that features like Word's "Track Changes"—and editing command inside Word that keeps track of changes made to a document—are efficient, thereby allowing them to offer more extensive feedback. Advanced program users further maximize productivity by automating common comments using macros, embedding links to outside resources, and utilizing version control to manage multiple drafts of student work. Digital feedback is considered more dialogic too, as drafts of papers can be e-mailed and sensitive critiques delivered in a medium conducive to private conversations. Physically, digital files take up less space, can be manipulated easily, and reduce wasting paper. And with the advent of cloud computing—the process of using remote servers to host and process information—student writing assignments and instructor comments are always accessible, safely stored, and easily distributable among groups for collective peer review.

So, while easily composing, revising, editing, and storing student writing assignments digitally are advantages, can we accurately say that new video capture programs like Camtasia or audio tools further improve the efficiency and effectiveness of professors offering feedback?

There is no universally agreed upon "average time" spent assessing student assignments. The depth of feedback given, the delivery mechanism used—even the time of day—affects how long it takes a professor to assess the writings of his/her students. Anecdotal evidence suggests that writing professors spend between fifteen and twenty minutes assessing an essay of average length (four pages). In 2007, Russell Stannard of the University of Westminster conducted a case study that looked at an innovative way of providing feedback on student work in an English Language Teaching course: screen capture. Stannard's case study found that students not only did students prefer video feedback to traditional forms of feedback, he also claimed offering video feedback reduced grading time down to a matter of minutes. That said, he noted that his commentary was disorganized and Stanndard was not commenting and editing four-page compositions. At the 2006 Conference on College Composition and Communication, Scott Warnock presented results from a small class study that compared three modes of feedback given to his students in class across three essay assignments: a) written feedback via a rubric, b) face-to-face conference(s), and c) video feedback via Camtasia. For the first essay, he offered written feedback via the Waypoint rubric program. For the second essay he conferenced. For the third essay, he gave feedback with Camtasia. Warnock concluded that video feedback took the least amount of time. By his own calculation, he could complete four essays per hour with margin comments, five per hour using the rubric, and six per hour using A/V captures.

Warnock calculated that he could do four essays per hour if he wrote margin comments, five per hour if he used Waypoint, and six per hour using A/V captures. Further, Warnock confirmed Stannard's findings that students prefer this form of feedback to written comments alone, noting that thirty-five percent of students favored conferences and twenty-seven percent favored A/V feedback; fifteen percent favored written comments and twenty-three percent had no preference (Fred Siegel, 2006). These results however, have not been verified through comparative experimental studies across wider samples of students, and they assume a certain level of programmatic experience, which, frankly, many professors do not have. If Warnock's findings are replicable, then screen capture software could be shown to effectively doubles instructor's feedback output, but again, his findings do not account for technology gone awry, learning time, or different instructor practices and experiences.

Camtasia Studio is an application used to create videos to comment on the assignments of students. While it is not particularly complicated, using it does not necessarily improve the speed with which a professor assesses student work. Users can specify the exact screen area to "capture" and record while simultaneously recording audio from a standard input source. Users can also apply built-in tools like highlighters, text boxes to markup, or add comments on screen in real time. Once the software is activated, all screen movements are recorded into a raw video file, which then can be edited and uploaded on a hosted platform. Screen capture tools are most commonly used to deliver feedback on student writing by calling the student's essay onto the screen and recording what amounts to a think-aloud feedback protocol. In my own experiments with Camtasia, I found that it significantly increased the time it took me to deliver video feedback because of the time it took to render the video upon export, load it to the server, manage glitches that resulted in poor audio quality, and e-mail the student, among other things. So, it is unclear how Warnock calculated the final grading time. In other words, one might ask: Did his per-essay time include time spent rendering, editing, uploading videos and notifying students? Or, did his finding of four-five minutes per essay only measure the time it took plan, prepare and record instructor commentary?

In part, the preference for audio and video feedback goes beyond improving efficiency to improving the effectiveness of the commentary itself. Audio and video recordings approximate the student writing conference, which is often considered the ideal environment in which to review student writing because writers learn the most when they share and reflect. In other words, shared writing is usually improved writing (Graham & McArthur 2007). Like the conference, audio commentary on student work is contextual and social, enabling professors to leverage tone and body language (Still, 2006). Like earlier studies, Still's study found that students prefer voice comments to written comments alone, and a combination of voice and written feedback is ideal (Still, 2006). Still's study suggests that the efficacy of feedback is greatly improved by the medium in which it is delivered. Professors who use A/V technology to deliver feedback tend to cover more issues, but if these issues were all highlighted on paper using, say, Microsoft Word's Track Changes, the paper would look butchered from a student's point of view. Even worse, marked up papers tend to overwhelm students and thereby make them less like to make revisions. Supplementing in-text comments with audio comments, however, decreases the tendency for students to feel overwhelmed. It might be a false perception, but in this case, just the perception of personalization seems to positively affect learning outcomes (Ice et al., 2007; Merry & Orsmond, 2008). More practically, tone is much easier to produce in an audio file than it is in print. "I can tell what I need to do just by listening," said one 23-year old female student from Still's 2006 study (Still 2006, p. 466). Such clarity is often missing in the written comments professors make in the margins of student essays, comments that frequently use shorthand or editors' marks, or do not thoroughly explain the proposed revision using language with which students are familiar.

Of course, the ideal writing feedback and assessment protocol then would use a single tool to compose, revise, analyze and customize feedback on assignments and it would integrate into standard learning management systems for grade and note keeping. This tool would incorporate multi-modal components, and it would include features that highlight the social nature and importance of writing as a process. Such a tool does not yet exist, but companies like Adapt Courseware, which create adaptive learning environments and texts, are working towards this end. TurnitIn, originally only used as a plagiarism detection software program, has also incorporated many such features, as it tries to accommodate the needs of writing professors. Such a tool or platform would offer an invaluable window into students' composing and revision processes, and it would increase the quality, efficiency, and consistency of instructor feedback. Indeed, these two goals guide many researchers. In fact, a team at the University of South Florida are using them as guides as they analyze more than 30,000 instructor comments generated in the endnotes of student papers housed in the MyReviewers database (Moxley). MyReviewers is a peer review program designed by Professor Joe Moxley. The endnote data was aggregated this year, and Moxley and his team hope to offer analysis that illuminates how and to what degree students act on formative feedback. For now, MyReviewers is a closed, proprietary system, but a similar open peer review system, Eli, is offered through the University of Michigan. Eli offers instructors the use of real-time data about the status and progress of a review. This allows professors to intervene in the writing process, store peer-to-peer feedback, and access drafts of their students' papers. This offers a more complete picture of how students use formative feedback during the revision process. Commercial options that illuminate how students incorporate formative feedback also exist. For example, many instructors have had great success using Google Docs and Google Drive to customize feedback, mimic real-time peer-review workshops, build online writing portfolios, and track the revision histories of their students.

Tools that show whether and how students are following formative commentary provide an important step in determining how much and what kind of feedback will be most effective. While few instructors argue against assessment as a tool for developing what Biggs (1999) calls "deep learning," instructors sometimes worry that their time spent offering feedback is wasted, especially if that time includes the time spent learning a new digital tool by which the feedback is distributed. It is beneficial to professors to have access to tools that compare drafts, like Google Docs, because comparative drafts allow professors to see if and how students make revisions based on their commentary. Over time, professors would be able to refine their feedback practices based on the metadata digital tools collected and stored. This is important because students need practice at making meaning through the very language of assessment. By studying instructors' digital commentary practices, the language they use to assess student writing, and how students execute revisions, we might create a more effective series of common comments that are easier for students to understand (Creme & Lea, 1997) and that significantly improve student writing.

Regardless of the medium through which it is delivered, the most helpful formative feedback has certain key elements: it is multidimensional, non-evaluative, supportive, timely, specific, credible, infrequent, and genuine (Brophy, 1981; Schwartz & White, 2000). Indeed, in 1998, Black and William conducted a meta-analysis of 250 studies of formative assessment and concluded that students learn better with rapid, systematic feedback focused on the quality of their work. A later study by Higgins and Hartley (2002) captured students' accounts of their experiences and understanding of assessment and feedback. Interviewing 19 students across two subjects and two institutions, Higgins and Hartley found students perceive feedback negatively if it isn't helpful, if it is too impersonal, too general, too vague, or too difficult to read. Digital feedback tools that allow

instructors to monitor student revision practices and adjust the level, tone, and depth of commentary will likely have the greatest impact on improving student writing. Good formative feedback, especially when delivered digitally, is iterative, and it is hard work. But feedback is deeply important to students and effective formative feedback clearly improves student-writing outcomes (Nelson & Schunn 2009)

In 2000, Hyland showed that students feel feedback improves their chances of getting a higher grade, but the grade itself is not what matters most. In this study, Hyland showed that students valued formative feedback because it stressed weaknesses and strengths, which helped them identify which writing behaviors to repeat and which to modify. The Higgins and Hartley study (2002) confirmed what other studies showed about global versus local feedback suggestions: global matters more. The feedback that focused on argumentation and critical analysis was most important to student writers (Higgins & Hartley 2002, p. 60). A digital tool that allows instructors to upload audio, video and insert in-text comments might improve the effectiveness of commentary for reasons already explained: instructors can provide extensive global comments without overwhelming students, while focusing on local comments in-text, and monitoring and adapting further feedback based on revision patterns.

4. AREAS FOR FUTURE STUDY AND DEVELOPMENT

One of the difficulties in offering a chapter on new media tools used to manage feedback protocols is the lack of experimental research measuring the efficacy of such technologies. It is particularly important to quantify the efficiencies and effectiveness of digital feedback technology because it is easy to rely on lore or conventional wisdom without empirical substantiation to drive the development of a feedback protocol, to assume that available tools will, by their very technological nature, make one more productive. It is important to study productivity tools as they relate to the writing classroom specifically because some of the most commonly used tools were not designed expressly for the writing classroom or for feedback management, and their adoption may waste time or perpetuate poor feedback and revision practices. Developing applications is becoming easier and cheaper, and it is not outside the realm of possibilities that an English professor interested in creating an application to manage his/her feedback protocol could do so. This makes it all the more important to articulate what the ideal tool for feedback would look like. More studies that replicate and extend the work of Stannard, Warnock, Brick & Holmes would help English studies arrive at an answer to the question of whether or not technology reduces grading time and fatigue while improving efficiency and effectiveness.

The Higgins-Hartley study demonstrated the need for English professors to refine their understanding of how students use feedback. Fortunately, adaptive technology and the availability of tools used to analyze big data make studying what instructors say and how students use the feedback possible. Nevertheless, adaptive technology is so new there are scant studies yet published about its applications or effectiveness. More importantly, however, there is a glaring gap in the research when it comes to measuring the effects of assessment language, or when it comes to measuring whether or not students actually understand the language instructors use to comment on their writing assignments. This is particularly important because of something I mentioned earlier, namely, overly marked papers that are difficult to understand overwhelm students and make them less likely to make revisions. Even more, such a study might provide answers to why so many students never revise their papers. Is it because they are overwhelmed by and don't understand the commentary of their professors? Is it because they are simply not interested in do-

ing so? Is it because the technology used to offer feedback is difficult, cumbersome, unwieldy? Or, is it for some other reason? Either way, in order to arrive at accurate answers to these questions we need to conduct further studies.

Measuring the reactions and solutions of students to formative feedback delivered digitally is also an area where more research is needed. One reason why such research is needed is so that we learn more about the thinking and writing processes of students, (Flowers & Hayes, 1994). Comment functions inside programs like TurnitIn—called QuickMarks—may one day soon include the ability to link to outside media and resources. The click-through rate of such links can be tracked, and, depending on the program and level of surveillance, instructors might see which students took the time to follow the link to recommended resources and how long they spent on the outside Website. Though time spent on an outside resource is not a measure of learning in itself, this kind of metadata is important for professors who want to eliminate reasons why a student isn't improving his/her writing. Checking reports that compile this kind of information is one way to determine if students are using the resources professors take the time to source and direct them to. Such detailed information could help professors customize learning exchanges. Such technological capability will undoubtedly inform teaching and learning practices in the writing classroom and during the peer review process, but research is needed to explain if these tools are available, how they are being used, and why, and under what conditions, student revision practices are changed.

There is little replicable, experimental data available specific to the use of video feedback in the writing classroom. Some of the more exciting areas of research in video feedback and assessment were conducted by Degenhardt (2006) and Samuels (2006). Degenhardt and Samuels's work uses video to capture offline and online screen activities without hindering the natural writing or reading processes of the user. This is important because it is another window into the writing and revision practices of students. Insights gleaned from student revision practices can also shape feedback practices among professors and so this research could have significant application to think-aloud protocols for both students and professors (Silva 14).

More importantly a quantitative study of digital feedback practices among writing faculty is needed. Some publishers, for example, found studying the effectiveness of their latest interactive e-textbooks nearly impossible because professors would not use all the tools' features (Weider, 2011) Such a study might give us insight into why English faculty are often resistant to using new digital tools and what features are most important to faculty using technology in the writing classroom, specifically as it concerns formative feedback. Of course, this is valuable data because resistance to technological adoption might be a usability issue or a usefulness challenge, both of which can be solved.

Computer-adaptive testing and responsive learning environments will also provide rich areas for future research (Chang 2004; Chang & van der Linden 2003, Zhang 2007). Adaptive formative and summative feedback systems will one day offer pre-writing diagnostics to test student understanding, identify areas of strength and weakness in drafts, and customize the writing process to individual students. Surveys given after writing assignments will identify degrees of progress in acquiring understanding and such environments will support social networks for the development of test items, feedback libraries, and peer review banks (Cope et. al, 2009 a, b).

5. USING A HEURISTIC TO SELECT DIGITAL TOOLS TO MANAGE A FEEDBACK PROTOCOL

The number of new applications, programs, plug-ins, and platforms available to assess the writings of students is dizzying. Given such diversity, one might ask: How does a professor choose which technology or combination of tools will be most effective for his/her purposes? Some institutions have in-house technology departments wherein most of the staff members are technology experts, not subject matter experts, and so their recommendations may not offer the level of specificity an English professor wants for a formative feedback tool. Most English faculty who are interested in using digital technology to manage a feedback protocol must experiment on their own in order to find the combination of tools that facilitates delivery of the most effective and efficient feedback on student writing. But even the most adventurous and willing professors need a guide.

By invoking standard usability protocols developed by experts like Jakob Nielsen, English professors can be guided through the process of selecting technology based on the heuristics of usefulness and usability. Of course, usefulness is an assessment of the value that the user experienced after using the technology. It measures whether the intended audience found the program or application meaningful and valuable. Usability, by contrast, is a property of the object under review. It measures whether the operations, displays, and content of the technology are easy to understand, access, learn, and navigate. Of course, these terms are not mutually inclusive. That is, an application might be easily usable but not useful for completing work tasks (Mirel 2004, p. 33). Conversely, an application can be useful for completing tasks but not easily useable. And, of course, ideally an application is be both useable and useful. As part of their toolkit, usability experts can consider conducting various tests of usability—cognitive walkthroughs, expert reviews, and heuristic evaluations (Neilsen, 1993; Holingsed & Novick 2007).

Nevertheless, here, I am concerned only with heuristic evaluations. Heuristic evaluations apply some form of severity rankings to judge whether or not a feature is a) included b) problematic and c) the degree to which the problem exists. Below is a standard severity ranking, but, since I am not conducting true usability testing I will modify the severity ranking to reflect if a desired feature is included and the extent to which its purpose is fulfilled.

Severity rankings typically look like this:

Level 5: Catastrophic error causing total loss of data.
Level 4: Severe problem causing possible loss of data.
Level 3: A moderate problem causing wasted time but no permanent loss of data.
Level 2: A minor but irritating problem.
Level 1: A minimal error (Wilson & Coyne, 2001).

(I have customized Wilson and Coyne's severity ranking system, but note that I have inverted the scale. An assignment of "3" means the tool has full functionality and the feature works with minimal flaws. Thus, a score of "3" is the best possible score, denoting the feature is both useable and useful. The higher the score the better the product or tool for delivering formative feedback on student writing.)

(1-3 with 1 being no functionality; 2 some functionality; 3 full functionality)

Level 3: Application supports this function and its benefit to the fullest extent.

Level 2: Application supports this function but there are problems.
Level 1: Application does not support this function.

A heuristic is an experience-based technique used to solve problems. Though the term is borrowed from technical communications and Web design, professors of writing will be familiar with it and its application in describing the writing process from Flowers' seminal work (1981). The heuristic below is intended to make the review and adoption of formative and summative assessment tools used in a feedback protocol easier. The following heuristic was adapted from a combination of sources. Many of the characteristics for each function and explanation were borrowed and extended from Nielsen's ten characteristics for user interface design.

The features in the heuristic were designed based on current writing pedagogy that sees writing as a recursive, social act, improved by summative and formative feedback delivered across technological mediums by both peers and instructors. There is no single digital tool that provides every feature listed, but by developing a heuristic based on an ideal specifically designed for writing situations and measuring the ideal against the features found in existing tools, English faculty may have an easier time of managing a digital feedback and revision protocol.

The heuristic is broken into four parts: the function, explanation, severity ranking, and notes. In the notes section, I have included an example that demonstrates the heuristic's real-world application. I reviewed TurnitIn, an internationally used plagiarism detection program. This program's severity score totaled 61 out of a possible 75. The severity label however, is misleading. That doesn't mean the program was severely deficient, but instead, that the program was found to have a high number of features with minimal problems deemed both useful and useable in a feedback protocol. And so, the higher the score using this method, the better the product in delivering formative and summative feedback in the writing classroom. Users will notice the features are not weighted. This heuristic is simply a guide; its features can be reorganized and weighted so the results will more or less reflect what the user feels is the most important aspect of a feedback program (see Figure 1 and Figure 2).

6. CONCLUSION

Here, I have offered a glimpse of the future through a straw, having reviewed what promises only to be a tiny spot on the horizon of digital and networked landscapes used to assess student writing. Digital tools will not solve all of the issues surrounding the efficiency and effectiveness of writing feedback, but new software programs and apps clearly provide needed opportunities to improve the delivery of formative and summative feedback. Using a heuristic to measure the applicability of a new tool to deliver feedback ultimately improves the field's disposition to technology adoption generally because it privileges the needs of writing professors not application developers. Furthermore, using a heuristic to test the usefulness and usability of feedback tools potentially saves time and the frustration of figuring out too late that the chosen tool used isn't very useful. Perhaps the heuristic can also ultimately serve as a template by which to build the ideal feedback and

Figure 1. Proposed heuristic for measuring the suitability and effectiveness of digital tools in managing a digital feedback and revision protocol

Function	Explanation	Severity Ranking	Example/Notes (Based on TurnitIn)
System Status Update	The system provides appropriate, timely feedback regarding system upgrades, updates, and problems.	3	Yes. Updates and comments are logged under the "What's New" tab; there is also a Twitter feed. I can sign up for e-mail updates as well. My support ticket was responded to in 24 hrs. There is also a system status update page.
Discourse Simulation	The system and its features emulate the language of the discourse communities it serves, making information appear natural and logical.	2	Somewhat. The auto-generated QuickMark (QMs) comments are inconsistent in their level of helpfulness/detail and their tone. There are POV shifts and the categories under which the QMs are managed do not always correspond to the classroom.
User Control	Emergency exits for each function are clearly marked. Users can leave an unwanted state without needing to exit through a series of extended back doors or dialogues. Common undo and redo functions are supported.	2	Somewhat. While there are exits they are not always clearly marked. It's difficult to tell how to get back to the main screen once inside an open assignment.
Consistency	The system uses consistent logic, meaning words, situations, and actions mean and do the same thing across multiple exchanges.	3	Yes. Most of the situations and actions function the same way across multiple exchanges. Roll-overs, external links, drop-down menus and drag and drop features abide the same logic.
Pattern Recognition	Objects, actions and options are visible and stable, minimizing the user's need to remember instructions. Complicated tasks are easily accessed via adaptive instructions and tool tips, or quick-launch tutorials.	3	Yes, once the system logic is learned, the system is stable and loading papers for feedback is fairly intuitive. One note of frustration: the open/due/post date settings are clunky. Most pages or actions have tool tips (in the form of a ? mark in top right hand corner) and most pages have guiding instructions on how to use the page.
Aesthetic	The structure of the site leverages a *minimal* aesthetic, deleting extraneous links, images, or features. Every unit of information works to improve the logic of the page and facilitate ease of use.	3	Yes, the aesthetic is minimal and well designed, utilizing white space and cascading menus to hide/reveal information. The header uses common tabs and actions seem to work in the interface as they do in other online environments.
Help and Documentation	Error messages are plainly stated with links to further documentation or suggested, adaptive solutions. Documentation is searchable, relevant and succinct.	3	Yes, the help center is complete, featuring documentation, video training, live walk throughs, ticket creation, support services and system status updates.
Open & Non-Commercial	The architecture is open and allows developers to create extension, applications, or functions that utilize core functionality, add new features, fix bugs, or crowdsource innovative upgrades. While the platform/program may not be free, it is freely accessible.	1	No, this is a proprietary system. Access is dependent upon university subscription. All bugs and fixes are internally regulated.
Accessible	The program/platform is compatible with assistive technologies like screen readers and speech synthesizers.	1	Somewhat. Some assistive technologies do not work well. Screen readers like JAWS work when non-standard settings are selected, but are hard to follow and navigate. Student with additional needs would have to submit their work online in advance or work with disability services.
Browser Independent	Users can access and use all major program/system functions with minimal disruption across multiple browsers.	2	Mostly. The system works well with Firefox 15+, Chrome 23+, Safari 5+, Internet Explorer 8 or 9. Browsers must be set to allow all cookies; Javascript must be enabled.

Figure 2. Continued from previous figure: proposed heuristic for measuring the suitability and effectiveness of digital tools in managing a digital feedback and revision protocol

No Additional Software	There are limited barriers to use. Components, add-ons, upgrades, widgets, and plug-ins are encouraged for greater range and functionality, but users do not have to purchase and install additional software for the core program/platform to work at full capacity.	2	Somewhat. The program can be used in open source LMSs like Moodle using a free plug-in but the system access is behind a paywall.
Textual & Graphic Annotations	The program supports rich annotation features. Users can add textual annotations to student's content (in-line) as well as to web pages that may be referenced within a student essay, offering further context to the original content. There are both public and private annotation options available. Graphic and audio annotations are supported. Annotations, like other feedback forms are social and can be tagged, shared, aggregated and printed.	1	Not really. Though the GradeMark feature allows users to add comments and create QMs, annotation features are clunky and do not link outside the interface. The instructor has to copy/paste the URL into the comment and the links aren't live. The instructor's view has a "social" component in the BETA version of the Activity Stream. None of the comments can be tagged but they are aggregated, shared and can be printed via PDF.
Linking & Sharing	The platform/program allows students to reference and anchor material from outside sources. This information aggregates into a printable report, providing taxonomic value and a window into student revision processes.	1	Not really. The student view generates a printable report. One of the more frustrating features is that the ETS eGrader is only activated once an instructor opens it for review unless using the Peer Mark Feature.
Reports	Users can collate and print metadata into structured reports, allowing the user to create their own learning materials for future reference and allowing instructors to shift learning goals based on student behaviors.	2	Somewhat. There is some metadata included in the Activity Stream and on certain reports, particularly the plagiarism report. The Student Engagement feature shows you if students have opened and viewed the GradeMark feedback on their papers.
Storage	Documents are stored and accessible by users at no additional cost. Users control the accessibility level of documents.	3	Yes.
Searching	All content is searchable.	3	Yes. Content on the web site is searchable. Content inside student essays is not.
Analytics	The program/platform offers robust analytics including reading/feedback/revision times, links visited, and relevant patterns of information access.	1	Not really. Though there are some analytics built into the latest version, the usefulness of the kinds of information collected is limited.
Adaptive	The platform/program supports adaptive technology and integrates adaptive functions where possible, specifically during the writing and feedback process.	1	Not really. The most adaptive technology is the eRater system and only an instructor can activate this system.
Plagiarism Detection Capability	Plagiarism detection software is built into the platform. If not offered as part of the suite, the platform/program is compatible with the major plagiarism detection software programs.	3	Yes. TurnitIn was built primarily as a plagiarism detection tool.
Free Trial Availability	The program/platform is available for a free trial, if purchase is required. The trail is substantive and open.	3	Sometimes. TurnitIn does not seem to support individual trials but will support institutional trials. Even so, these trials costs upwards of $5,000.
Individual & Group User Cost	There is an individual and group user cost offered, which accommodates users with and without institutional support.	1	No. There does not seem to be an option for individual license purchase. Institutional support is critical.
Multimodal Capabilities	The program/platform facilitates the use of multimodal feedback, including audio, video or screen capture capabilities.	2	Somewhat. Audio files of 3 minutes or less are supported. Video is not supported.
Collaboration	The program/platform incorporates opportunities for students to collaborate synchronously and a-synchronously. Options might include a stream of real-time status updates; like buttons, video chat and graphic annotation on student work.	2	Somewhat. Students can prewrite using an online discussion board but that is the limit of collaboration. This collaboration is also asynchronous. Status updates are for instructors only.
Conferencing	Users can synchronously conference by video. Chat, polling, virtual break-out rooms, group video relay, and screen capture with graphic annotation are part of the conferencing component.	1	No. There are currently no video features supported. Conferences are not supported though one could use a third-party vendor to screen capture the use of the product.
Multi-Modal Feedback	Automated and custom feedback at the point of error is supported. The mode of delivery is multiple, including audio, video and graphic. Anchors directing students to additional resources are supported.	2	Not really. Though some of the QMs are supported by additional information that links out to an internal information base, anchors directing students to web-based resources are not supported.
Rubric	Rubrics are supported, customizable, and tied to automatic grade calculation tables. A grade book is integrated into the platform/program or exports/imports easily into market dominate institutional learning management systems.	3	Yes. Rubric scorecards can be used to evaluate student work based on defined criteria and custom scales. The rubric scores are created by the administrator/instructor and shared among the class. Three types are supported: standard, custom, and qualitative.
Genres/Forms Promoted	Automated feedback is genre/form specific. Examples and tutorials are customized to the writing form. Tutorials are contained within the system/platform and follow established platform logic.	1	No. The automatic feedback offered through features like eRater does not focus on genres. There are tutorials for both students/instructors but they are not linked to the platform; they must be accessed by visiting the Help tab on the web site.
Process-Focused	Peer and instructor feedback workflows highlight the process of writing. Students have multiple opportunities to revise and resubmit and all revision metadata is collected, tracked, compiled and delivered providing a means to demonstrate student progress and points of further writing study.	2	Somewhat. The entire TurnitIn cycle of Originality Check/GradeMark/PeerMark was designed to mimic the iterative process of writing. Students can move through Originality Check and PeerMark several times before submitting a draft for evaluation with GradeMark but they do not have the benefit of GradeMark, which automatically checks grammar/style in Originality Check/PeerMark environment.
Customized Student Learning	The program/platform is "smart." It tracks, compiles, and reports student learning habits. Such smart reports offer students a customized learning plan that includes links to additional resources and recommendations for further writing study and development.	1	No. Customized learning plans are currently not supported.
Ease of use	The program/platform is stable and easy to use. Updates and new versions do not significantly alter the navigation or user logic. Administrators maintain system reliability and integrity and offer adequate, personal support and accessible documentation.	3	Yes. Though the UK version seems to have several issues as late as 2011, the US version (2012) seems to be fairly stable and easy to use. Based on user experience most issues seem to be focused around major LMS integrations or upgrades.

revision application. Technology may not provide the panacea for which early practitioners of computers and writing had hoped, but this is the price we pay for valuing writing not reduced to mere formulas, because, regardless of the technology that delivers commentary and feedback, the act of writing and assessing writing will always be a profoundly human endeavor.

REFERENCES

Biggs, J. B., & Tang, C. (2011). *Teaching for quality learning at university*. Maidenhead, UK: McGraw-Hill Education.

Brick, B., & Holmes, J. (2008). Using screen capture software for student feedback: Towards a methodology. In *Proceedings of the IADIS International Conference on Cognition & Exploratory Learning In Digital Age*, (p. 339). IADIS.

Brophy, J. (1981). Teacher praise: A functional analysis. *Review of Educational Research*, (1): 5. doi:10.3102/00346543051001005.

Chang, H.-H. (2004). Understanding computerized adaptive testing: From Robbins-Monro to Lord and beyond. In Kaplan, D. (Ed.), *The SAGE handbook of quantitative methodology for the social sciences* (pp. 117–133). London: Sage Publications. doi:10.4135/9781412986311.n7.

Chang, M.-W., Ratinov, L., & Roth, D. (2007). Guiding semi-supervision with constraint driven learning. In *Proceedings of the Annual Meeting of the Association of Computational Linguistics*, (pp. 280-287). Retrieved from http://acl.ldc.upenn.edu/P/P07/P07-1036.pdf

Comer, D. K., & Hammer, B. (2008). *Surveying the efficacy of digital response: Pedagogical imperatives, faculty approaches, and student feedback*. Academic Press.

Cope, B., & Alantzis, M. (2009b). Ubiquitous learning: An agenda for educational transformation. In Cope, B., & Kalantzis, M. (Eds.), *Ubiquitous learning*. Champaign, IL: University of Illinois Press.

Cope, B., & Kalantzis, M. (2000). *Multiliteracies: literacy learning and the design of social futures*. London: Routledge.

Cope, B., & Kalantzis, M. (2009a). Multiliteracies: New literacies, new learning. *Pedagogies: An International Journal*, 4, 164–195.

Cope, B., Kalantzis, M., & Magee, L. (2011). *Towards a semantic web: Connecting knowledge in academic research*. Cambridge, UK: Woodhead Publishing. doi:10.1533/9781780631745.

Creme, P., & Lea, M. (2007). *Writing at university*. Maidenhead, UK: McGraw-Hill Education.

Cynthia, L. S. (n.d). Three voices on literacy, technology, and humanistic perspective. *Computers and Composition*, (pp. 12309-310). doi:10.1016/S8755-4615(05)80069-6

Degenhardt, M. (2006). Camtasia and catmovie: Two digital tools for observing, documenting and analyzing writing processes of university students. In Van Waes Luuk, L. Mariëlle, & M. Neuwirth (Eds.), Writing and digital media: Studies in writing (pp. 180–186). Amsterdam: Elsevier.

Epstein, M. L., Lazarus, A. D., Calvano, T. B., Matthews, K. A., Hendel, R. A., Epstein, B. B., & Brosvic, G. M. (2002). Immediate feedback assessment technique promotes learning and corrects inaccurate first responses. *The Psychological Record*, 52(2), 187.

Flower, L. (1994). *The construction of negotiated meaning: a social cognitive theory of writing*. Carbondale, IL: Southern Illinois University Press.

Flower, L. S., & Hayes, J. R. (1984). Images, plans, and prose: The representation of meaning in writing. *Written Communication, 1*, 120–160. doi:10.1177/0741088384001001006.

Gail, E. H. (n.d). Research update: Writing and word processing. *Computers and Composition,* 57-27. doi:10.1016/8755-4615(88)80002-1

Graham, S., Fitzgerald, J., & MacArthur, C. A. (2007). *Best practices in writing instruction.* New York: Guilford Press.

Gruber, S., Sweany, M. F., & Hawisher, G. E. (1996). *Computers and the teaching of writing in American higher education, 1979-1994: A history.* Norwood, NJ: Ablex Pub..

Hawisher, G. E. (1986). Studies in word processing. *Computers and Composition, 4*(4), 6–31. doi:10.1016/S8755-4615(86)80003-2.

Hawisher, G. E. (1989). Computers and writing: where's the research? *English Journal,* 7889–7891.

Higgins, R., Hartley, P., & Skelton, A. (2002). The conscientious consumer: Reconsidering the role of assessment feedback in student learning. *Studies in Higher Education, 27*(1), 53. doi:10.1080/03075070120099368.

Hyland, F. (2000). ESL writers and feedback: giving more autonomy to students. *Language Teaching Research, 4*(1), 33–54.

Ice, P., Curtis, R., Phillips, P., & Wells, J. (2007). Using asynchronous audio feedback to enhance teaching presence and students' sense of community. *Journal of Asynchronous Learning Networks, 11*(2), 3–25.

LeBlanc, P. (1988). How to get the words just right: A reappraisal of word processing and revision. *Computers and Composition, 5*(3), 29–42.

LeBlanc, P. (1992). Letter from the guest editor. *Computers and Composition, 10*(1), 3–7. doi:10.1016/S8755-4615(06)80012-5.

Mary Lourdes, S. (n.d). Camtasia in the classroom: Student attitudes and preferences for video commentary or microsoft word comments during the revision process. *Computers and Composition,* 291-22. doi:10.1016/j.compcom.2011.12.001

Mayer, R. E. (2009). *Multi-media learning* (2nd ed.). New York: Cambridge University Press. doi:10.1017/CBO9780511811678.

Merry, S., & Orsmond, P. (2008). *Students' attitudes to and usage of academic feedback provided via audio files.* Retrieved from http://www.bioscience.heacademy.ac.uk/journal/vol11/beej-11-3.aspx

Mirel, B., & Wright, Z. (2009). Heuristic evaluations of bioinformatics tools: A development case. In *Proceedings of the 13th International Conference on Human Computer Interaction (HCII-09) (LNCS),* (vol. 5610, pp. 329-338). Berlin: Springer.

Moreno, R. (2004). Decreasing cognitive load for novice students: effects of explanatory versus corrective feedback in discovery-based multimedia. *Instructional Science: An International Journal of Learning and Cognition, 32*(1-2), 99–113.

Moxley, J. (2012). *My reviewers.* Tampa, FL: University of South Florida.

Nelson, M. M., & Schunn, C. D. (2009). The nature of feedback: how different types of peer feedback affect writing performance. *Instructional Science: An International Journal of the Learning Sciences, 37*(4), 375–401. doi:10.1007/s11251-008-9053-x.

Nielsen, J. (1992). Finding usability problems through heuristic evaluation. In *Proceedings ACM CHI'92 Conference* (pp. 373-380). ACM.

Nielsen, J. (1994a). Enhancing the explanatory power of usability heuristics. In *Proceedings of ACM CHI'94 Conference* (pp. 152-158). ACM.

Nielsen, J. (1994b). Heuristic evaluation. In Nielsen & Mack (Eds.), Usability Inspection Methods. New York: John Wiley & Sons.

Nielsen, J., & Molich, R. (1990). Heuristic evaluation of user interfaces. In *Proceedings of the ACM CHI'90 Conference* (pp. 249-256). ACM.

Samuels, L. (2006). *The effectiveness of web conferencing technology in student-teacher conferencing in the writing classroom: A study of first-year student writers*. (Unpublished master's thesis). North Carolina State University, Raleigh, NC.

Schwartz, F., & White, K. (2000). Making sense of it all: Giving and getting online course feedback. In White, K. W., & Weight, B. H. (Eds.), *The online teaching guide: A handbook of attitudes, strategies, and techniques for the virtual classroom* (pp. 57–72). Boston: Allyn and Bacon.

Selfe, C.L., & Wahlstrom, B.J. (1979). *Beyond bandaids and bactine: Computer-assisted instruction and revision*. (ERIC Reproduction Service Document N. 232182).

Selfe, C. L., & Wahlstrom, B. J. (1983). The benevolent beast: Computer-assisted instruction for the teacher of writing. *Writing Instructor*, *2*(4), 192–193.

Siegel, F., & Warnock, S. (2006). Using video capture software for asynchronous A/V writing feedback. *CCCC 2006 Review*. Retrieved from http://wac.colostate.edu/atd/reviews/cccc2006/c24.cfm

Stannard, R. (2007). Using screen capture software in student feedback. *The Higher Education Academy*. Retrieved from http://www.english.heacademy.ac.uk/explore/publications/cas-estudies/technology/camtasia.php

Stannard, R. (2008). Screen capture software for feedback in language education. In *Proceedings of the Second International Wireless Ready Symposium*. Retrieved from http://wirelessready.nucba.ac.jp/Stannard.pdf

Still, B. (2006). Talking to students embedded voice commenting as a tool for critiquing student writing. *Journal of Business and Technical Communication*, *20*(4), 460–475. doi:10.1177/1050651906290270.

van der Linden, W. J., & Twente Univ. (2000). *Optimal stratification of item pools in a stratified computerized adaptive testing*. Research Report. Twente, The Netherlands: Twente University.

Wieder, B. (2011). *Publishers struggle to get professors to use latest e-textbook features*. Retrieved from http://chronicle.com.ezproxy.lib.usf.edu/blogs/wiredcampus/publishers-struggle-to-get-professors-to-use-latest-e-textbook-features/29683

Wilson, C., & Coyne, K. (2001). Tracking usability issues: To bug or not to bug? *Interaction*, *8*, 15–19. doi:10.1145/369825.369828.

Zhang, J. (2007). Conditional covariance theory and detection for polytomous items. *Psychometrika*, *72*, 69–91. doi:10.1007/s11336-004-1257-7.

Section 3
Online Spaces for Writing

There are many conversations about how young people spend a significant amount of time writing in online spaces, but what does it mean to write "online" or in a "digital environment"? What affordances do these new spaces provide writers? How do teachers use online spaces for writing instruction? The chapters in this section examine online spaces for writing and how writers use these spaces both in and out of the classroom. These chapters specifically examine how young adults writing in these online spaces have more opportunities for collaboration and engagement in a writerly community.

Lammers, Magnifico, and Curwood begin this section by examining two online spaces, FanFiction. net and Scholar. Using case studies of two young adults, the authors explored the affordances and constraints of these two spaces. The authors noted the young adults' engagement in the spaces differed as FanFiction.com was an out-of-school space and Scholar was used for classroom instruction. Both spaces, however, allowed the writers to view writing as a collaborative endeavor, and the writers became more aware of their audience.

Dwyer and Larson explored online literature circles that took place between sixth-grade students from Ireland and the United States. The students in both countries read e-books on digital reading device, wrote digital thinkmarks, and composed on message boards during literature circle discussions. Students' engagement in digital reading and writing provided opportunities for community-building and peer collaboration surrounding situated responses to literature.

The final chapter in this section examines the program Making Connections, an epistolary community created through email exchanges between bilingual Latino middle school students and first-generation Latino university students. Over 10-weeks the middle school and university students exchanged emails about their lives, experiences and shared interests. The research found technology and writing allowed the middle school and university students to engaged in collaborative partnerships.

This section offers readers an opportunity to consider new online spaces for writing and writing instruction. The chapters in this section highlight the specific affordances and constraints of writing in online spaces.

Chapter 11
Exploring Tools, Places, and Ways of Being:
Audience Matters for Developing Writers

Jayne C. Lammers
University of Rochester, USA

Alecia Marie Magnifico
University of Illinois – Urbana-Champaign, USA

Jen Scott Curwood
University of Sydney, Australia

ABSTRACT

This chapter explores how writers respond to interactions with readers and audience members in two technology-mediated writing contexts: a Hunger Games fan's use of FanFiction.net and a classroom using Scholar to write original narrative texts. The authors look across the two spaces to analyze similarities in how the technology is used to foster interaction with readers and develop writers' craft through these interactions. In particular, they analyze how writing functions in each space as a tool, a place, and a way of being. By considering the affordances of these two contexts, the authors argue that technology is changing how we write and learn to write, in and out-of-school, by connecting writers with an audience that can significantly shape their goals, skills, and processes.

INTRODUCTION

Young people spend increasing amounts of time writing in technology-mediated spaces (Lenhart, Arafeh, Smith, & Macgill, 2008), and educational researchers continue to call for studies to theorize these practices (Alvermann, 2008; Moje, 2009). As English teacher educators and literacy researchers, we are also interested in exploring connections

between young people's writing practices in in-school and out-of-school contexts. This chapter draws on our research within technology-mediated writing spaces to consider: How is technology changing how we write? How is technology changing how we learn to write, both in and out of schools? Comparing case studies of *Hunger Games*-related writing on FanFiction.net and *Scholar*, a classroom Web-based technology for writing and peer review, we argue that these spaces leverage technology in ways that afford different

DOI: 10.4018/978-1-4666-4341-3.ch011

practices and encourage developing writers to attend to audience in new ways. As we continue to investigate ways technology is changing how we write, we find it helpful to return to existing metaphors used to make sense of the Internet (Markham, 2003) and of literacy (Steinkuehler, Black, & Clinton, 2005). Drawing on case studies of two adolescent writers, we conceptualize technology-mediated writing as a tool, a place, and a way of being.

As tools, both *FanFiction.net* (FFN) and *Scholar* connect writers with an audience and they become repositories for writing. Within each space, the technology provides other tools, such as drag-and-drop functionality and Author Notes that encourage writers to engage in particular practices. Thus, these technology-mediated writing context can exemplify the tool metaphors of conduit, extension, prosthesis, and container that Markham (2003) describes. However, we remain mindful not to perpetuate an oversimplification of what happens in these writing spaces by focusing only on the tools that these technologies provide: "By absenting context, individuals, and meaning from the conceptual framework, one derives a framework for Internet technologies which unproblematically transfer knowledge from one person or place to another. As long as there is access, there will be knowledge" (p. 6). Similarly, Steinkuehler et al. (2005) reinforce this notion that an understanding of the tool must be contextualized within each space. In other words, reviews and feedback are tools that shape writing each of these contexts, but writers employ such tools differently in each context.

As places, these technology-mediated writing spaces are "sociocultural places in which meaningful human interactions occur" (Markham, 2003, p. 6). Thus, our research attends to how the culture of each context is created as we examine the interactions between writers and audience that are afforded by FFN and *Scholar*. Our focus on exchanges between participants "does not only require a sense of architecture, but also requires a sense of presence with others" (p. 8). Yet, in defining them as places, we recognize the "fuzzy boundaries" (Steinkuehler et al., 2005, p. 98) of FFN and *Scholar*, noting that not all of the interactions with audience and all of the writing may happen solely within the technology-mediated writing space.

Finally, as ways of being, FFN and *Scholar* establish patterns and practices that fundamentally shift what it means to be a writer in these spaces. As each of the case studies will illustrate, these technology-mediated writing spaces encourage participation that is self-directed, multi-faceted, and dynamic (Lammers, Curwood, & Magnifico, 2012). Markham (2003) notes that the way of being metaphor encourages us to see that "the self's relation to Internet technologies is much closer and one can begin to see a collapse of the distinctions that separate technology, everyday life, self, and others" (p. 9). Similarly, Steinkuehler et al. (2005) posit that technology-mediated writing spaces, when conceived of as ways of being, might collapse these distinctions as they bring the dynamics of face-to-face communication into these spaces. As fans and teachers alike incorporate these technology-mediated writing spaces into their fandom and curriculum, practices begin to change and online/offline dichotomies are blurred, if not broken down altogether.

With these metaphors in mind, we turn to articulating the theories of affinity spaces and audience that frame our research. We continue by describing FFN and *Scholar*, introducing our focal participants, and explaining the data collection and analysis procedures used for this chapter. Then, we present findings related to how each technology-mediated writing space exemplifies the tool, place, and way of being metaphors, focusing on interactions between writers and their audience. In doing so, we begin with the FFN case to demonstrate how voluntary participation in an online affinity space connects adolescents with a worldwide audience that shapes writers' processes and practices in particular ways. We then continue with the *Scholar* case to present an in-school instantiation of technology-mediated writing, examining how adolescents interact with an audience made up of their classmates who provide peer reviews, in line with the constraints of school and mandated participation in the space. In the final section, we discuss comparisons and unique affordances of each space, with an eye toward what this analysis contributes to the field's understanding of technology's potential to shift the relationships between writers and audiences.

THEORIZING AFFINITY SPACES AND AUDIENCE

Important to our inquiry into how technology affords new audience-writer relationships in both FFN and *Scholar* is an explanation of how we conceptualize affinity spaces and how we understand the role of audience within these spaces.

Affinity Spaces

We frame our understanding of these two technology-mediated writing contexts by drawing on the concept of *affinity spaces*. According to Gee (2004), these physical, virtual, and blended spaces facilitate informal learning where "newbies and masters and everyone else" interact around a "common endeavor" (p. 85). Affinity spaces spread across multiple sites, and can include in-person meeting spaces as well as online Websites and social networking tools, each serving as a *portal*, or entry point, to the space. Fan-based affinity spaces develop practices in which much of the interaction between participants involves sharing and reviewing transformative works, such as fan fiction stories, poems, videos, art, or other content related to the fandom. In our previous work (Lammers, et al., 2012), we updated Gee's concept to further define nine key features of contemporary affinity spaces:

1. A common endeavor is primary.
2. Participation is self-directed, multi-faceted, and dynamic.
3. Portals are often multimodal.
4. Affinity spaces provide a passionate, public audience for content.
5. Socializing plays an important role in affinity space participation.
6. Leadership roles vary within and among portals.
7. Knowledge is distributed across the entire affinity space.
8. Many portals place a high value on cataloguing and documenting content and practices.
9. Affinity spaces encompass a variety of media-specific and social networking portals.

Key to our understanding of affinity spaces is that they encourage participants to self-direct their interest-driven participation in the space. Affinity spaces make multiple paths of participation available and thus legitimate multiple roles within the space. Though affinity spaces support myriad passions, as literacy researchers, we are particularly interested in how they can encourage writing. Consequently, this chapter highlights how these spaces offer developing writers passionate and knowledgeable audience members who read and respond to their transformative works.

Audience

Historically, research suggests that writers think about their audience in abstract ways, imagining a fictional reader and then writing with that person's imagined interests in mind (Gibson, 1950; Ong, 1975; Porter, 1996). Cognitive process studies suggest that many expert writers construct purposes, genres, and audiences to guide their writing even when these constraints are unclear (Berkenkotter, 1981; McCutchen, 2000), while others use themselves as a model audience (e.g. Elbow, 1987). Such findings have led to writing curricula in which students plan their work via pre-writing techniques (e.g. Pressley, 2005) and read classmates' writing in small-group workshops (e.g. Atwell, 1998). Since traditional schooling and publishing often create relationships in which writers write for an audience, but rarely receive feedback directly from readers (other than evaluators like teachers or editors), several designs have sought to help students find "authentic" readers for their work. For instance, Cohen and Reil (1989) and Freedman (1992) matched students with penpals, while Purcell-Gates, Duke, and Martineau (2007) and Shaffer (2006) have created situations in which students work with and present their writing to community organizations. In all of these studies, results show that students write more successfully for real readers.

Research exploring online writers' conceptualization of audience also frames this chapter. Out of school, writers and readers of new media are no longer trapped in the one-sided relationships that are typical to schools and print media. Instead, they can become active readers, writers, and conversation partners (Magnifico, 2010). As Lunsford and Ede (2009) suggest, online writers must still consider an audience, but they now can stand "among the audience" (p. 42). Audience interactions can help writers to not only understand how their work fits into an affinity space's understandings and Discourses (Gee, 2008), but to internally reflect on their work, set new goals for themselves, and provide motivation to reconcile their ideas with their readers' reactions (Magnifico, 2010). These considerations of audience become important in the analysis of *The Hunger Games* fan fiction practices presented in this chapter.

Finally, our chapter also considers the Discourse of school, where recent movements towards accountability have led to mandated curricula, standardized assessments, and a focus on content knowledge evaluation. These tendencies lead teachers to focus on reading (Yancey, 2009), conventions and correcting errors (Dyson, 2006), as well as content-driven writings (Applebee & Langer, 2009). Thus, classrooms have maintained

an evaluation-centered "vertical" (Kalantzis & Cope, 2012), "knowledge telling" (Bereiter & Scardamalia, 1987) orientation to writing, with the teacher as the primary audience. However, as will become visible in this analysis, incorporating a technology-mediated writing space, such as *Scholar*, into schools has the potential to connect writers with an audience beyond the teacher.

METHODOLOGY

We worked in the framework of descriptive case analysis (Yin, 2003), drawing case studies from a focal participant in each technology-mediated writing context. Both cases highlighted here were part of larger studies that focused on the interaction of literacy practices and technology-mediated spaces. The adolescents discussed in this chapter, Alexa and Darrell, joined their respective spaces as middle school students. Alexa was a fan of *The Hunger Games* and quickly became an avid writer on FanFiction.net during her out-of-school time; Darrell was a seventh grade student who tapped into his affinity for the *Heroes of Olympus* series to complete a school writing assignment using *Scholar*. Thus, their similar ages and fan fiction writing practices make them comparable cases. However, since these two writers had different writing skills and different ways of navigating their respective writing spaces, they present an interesting contrast. Each research context, focal participant, and the specific data collection and analysis methods employed are explained in more detail below.

Research Contexts

FanFiction.net

Since its founding in 1998, FanFiction.net (FFN) has become the most popular fan fiction Website, with over two million users and stories in more than 30 languages. FFN offers nine main categories, including Anime/Magna, Books, Cartoons, Games, Comics, Movies, Plays/Musicals, Television Shows, and Miscellaneous. Once fans register for an account, they can create a profile, share their stories, review others' stories, list their favorite stories and authors, communicate via private messages, and participate in the forums. In effect, FFN blurs "any clear-cut distinction between media producer and media spectator" (Jenkins, 1992, p. 247) and provides fans with a supportive space to share their transformative works. *The Hunger Games* is a prime example of this phenomenon; by 2013, fans had written 29,753 *Hunger Games*-inspired stories and shared them on FFN. Curwood's ethnographic study of *The Hunger Games* affinity space has examined how fans use literature and popular culture as a springboard for their fan fiction stories, artworks, videos, songs, and role-playing games (Curwood, 2013a; Curwood, 2013b; Curwood, Magnifico, & Lammers, 2013). As a specific portal into *The Hunger Games* affinity space, FFN offers insight into how writers engage in this space.

In the first case study, we consider Alexa (all names are pseudonyms). At 13, she stumbled onto the world of fan fiction through an Internet search. Four years on, Alexa is an avid writer on FFN. In addition to the dozens of stories she has written, inspired by young adult literature and television shows, she also regularly reviews and offers feedback on others' writing. Alexa's online work extends to DeviantART and Tumblr, where she creates her own art and shares art that others have created based on her stories. Offline, Alexa lives in the eastern United States, is an accomplished student, and a member of her high school's Honor Society. In an interview, she shared her love for *The Crucible, The Adventures of Huckleberry Finn, Great Expectations*, and her all-time favorite, *To Kill a Mockingbird*. She then added, "Surprisingly, I do not like to read. I am not a big reader at all unless I have to read something for school. As for writing, I love it - depending on what the subject is that I am writing about."

Unlike most of her writing in school, FFN allows Alexa to draw on popular culture, engage in collaborative writing, and develop her characters and plots over a sustained period. Alexa's stories are inspired by young adult literature and television shows, including *The Hunger Games, Harry Potter, Twilight, Glee, Fringe*, and *Bones*. As a writer, Alexa has found that fan fiction offers her unlimited choices in her creative writing, including the opportunity to explore new plot lines and characters' perspectives. Moreover, FFN offers her a readily available audience for her creative work. To date, Alexa's stories total over 300,000 words and have 2,900 reviews. This chapter will focus on one of Alexa's recent *Hunger Games* stories. Since Alexa's work is posted within the public domain, details of her fan fiction story are omitted in order to retain her anonymity.

Scholar

Scholar (http://learning.cgscholar.com/) is an online, Web-browser-based workspace for writing and peer review in its fourth year of development. Currently, this tool is largely used in classrooms, but free accounts are available and individuals may use its tools and participate in professional networks. One of the authors, Alecia Magnifico, is a member of an educational research team that is partnered with *Scholar's* software development team. In this capacity, she has worked with interested teachers, observed as they implement these tools in their classrooms, analyzed data, and made design recommendations for further development. The team has studied *Scholar* throughout its development; another chapter in this volume (McCarthey, Magnifico, Woodard, & Kline, 2013), takes up the question of how students' peer review work is situated not only in *Scholar,* but within classrooms, schools, and public educational policies.

At the time of this data collection cycle, *Scholar* consisted of three major applications: Publisher, Creator, and Community. To set up *Scholar* assignments, teachers use the Publisher application to enter their assignment criteria, rubrics for formative assessment, and decisions about peer review (which can include one or more peers who are anonymous or named). Then, students use the Creator application to work on their writing from home or school, save versions, check their work, write and receive peer reviews, make annotation comments, and revise in response to this feedback. Students and teachers may also interact with fellow classmates in the Community space. Similar to Edmodo and Facebook, Community allows students and teachers to send messages, share links, and post resources, sample papers, and status updates (although in this case, the teacher elected to only allow students to send messages rather than to post resources).

In the second case study, we consider Darrell, a student in Natalie Barrett's language arts class, and his narrative writing in *Scholar*. Ms. Barrett teaches at a middle school located in a small urban community near a large university in the midwestern United States, and her 7th grade class is composed of 17 students from diverse backgrounds. Darrell is an enthusiastic member of this 7th grade and was selected for this case because, while he described himself as "not a great student" and his story as a "plain story," he became very engaged in this narrative writing assignment. He loves the author Rick Riordan, whom he describes as "a beast," particularly the *Heroes of Olympus* series and its final installment, *Mark of Athena*. Darrell is impulsive, often jumping between the desks as he walks into class or bouncing off his classmates, and Ms. Barrett frequently chides him for talking out of turn. At the same time, Darrell enjoys his reading and writing. He read *Mark of Athena* during silent reading time for the duration of the narrative project and described particularly enjoying using Riordan's universe as an inspiration for his writing, working "off of" the demigod theme and "put[ting] them [the book's ideas] into connection with [his] own experiences."

Ms. Barrett envisioned the narrative project described in this paper as the closing writing project for the first quarter of the year, when the students were studying narrative works in class. She described it to her students as the first of a series of written pieces in various genres that they would write for a class magazine over the course of the school year. Students began to think through their narrative stories before classroom observation began, journaling and pre-writing in their class notebooks, as well as completing plot and character worksheets. While students were familiar with planning and drafting writing, receiving feedback from Mrs. Barrett, and revising in light of these comments, *Scholar* provided their first chance to write reviews for each other and to write and revise in an online environment. This chapter will focus on Darrell's pre-writing and writing stages during one short story.

Data Collection

In each context, data collection involved systematic observation, interviews, and artifacts. Given the online nature of FFN and the in-person nature of middle school classrooms, however, these data were gathered in rather different ways. As part of Curwood's ongoing research into *The Hunger Games* affinity space, she has investigated multiple online portals and interviewed over thirty young adults from the United States, United Kingdom, Canada, and Australia. In order to understand the culture of this online affinity space, Curwood conducted systematic observation of Alexa's participation on FFN, DeviantART, and Tumblr. In addition to multiple interviews over Skype and email with Alexa, she collected artifacts, including Alexa's FFN profile, fan fiction stories, Author Notes, reviews, and private messages as well as her DeviantART artwork. As a participant-observer in the affinity space, Curwood's data collection includes four years of Alexa's current and historical transformative works and online posts.

Magnifico completed most of her data collection in person by observing in Ms. Barrett's class during seven days of the students' narrative writing project. Her observations began on the last day of pre-writing, which the students completed in their classroom, and continued in the school's computer lab as the class began to use *Scholar*. In this setting, she acted as a participant-observer, introducing *Scholar* to the students, providing technical support, and speaking informally with the students and teacher as they wrote. On each of these days, she jotted quick field notes during the class and wrote these observations up into more detailed memos immediately afterwards. On the final day of observation, students split their time in class between finishing their story writing and beginning a subsequent book project. Students who completed their stories (including Darrell) took part in 30-minute focus groups in which they reflected on their experiences with *Scholar*. These interviews were recorded and transcribed. Finally, all of the students' online writing artifacts—initiating texts, drafts, review comments, and annotations— were captured by *Scholar* and downloaded for analysis.

Data Analysis

We used a thematic analysis framework (Boyatzis, 1998; Saldaña, 2009) to perform several repeated rounds of qualitative coding, gradually consolidating and refining the participants' discussions of their writing practices into several broad patterns that illustrated the tool, place, and way of being metaphors. In our analysis, we considered how young people describe their writing processes, their real and imagined audience, and how online and school-based affinity spaces supported the development of their written work. We also examined participants' writing, feedback from their readers, and subsequent revisions in order to understand how their audience actively shaped their writing process.

In addition, because *Scholar* captures drafts and peer response comments, it provides researchers with fine-grained access to students' writing and their interactions with peer reviewers—their audience members—over time. To understand Darrell's writing throughout the assignment, Magnifico employed bidirectional artifact analysis (Magnifico & Halverson, 2012) to trace Darrell's writing "backwards" (i.e. to show how later drafts reflect earlier ideas and writing) and "forwards" (i.e. to show how early drafts and feedback direct revision). This technique contextualizes Darrell's writing, reviews, and revisions, noting the textual changes he made and connecting this work with observations that capture the classroom's activity, review comments that he received, and interview transcripts that discuss his perceptions of his ongoing work. All of Darrell's reviews, annotations, and revisions were coded by type and traced to peer feedback or observations where possible.

In considering how these two technology-mediated writing contexts function as tools, places, and ways of being, we read back and forth between our data from each case and Markham's (2003) framework. The findings we present below represent our interpretation of how the metaphors map onto each case.

FANFICTION.NET AND SCHOLAR AS TOOLS, PLACES, AND WAYS OF BEING

In order to gain insight into how audience shapes writers' processes and practices within various technology-mediated writing contexts, we offer case studies of two developing writers. Examining both FanFiction.net and *Scholar*, this section considers how writing and writing contexts function as tools, places, and ways of being. We begin with the FFN case, one in which writers voluntarily participate in a fan-based affinity space. We then move to the *Scholar* case, which represents mandated participation in an adapted affinity space implemented in a classroom setting. This organization allows us to explore a developing writer's interactions with audience "in the wild" (Hutchins, 1995), and then move to consider a more constrained case. To further reinforce the impact context has on writers' interactions with audience, and vice versa, we present our analysis of each case by first discussing the metaphor of place, then tool and way of being.

FanFiction.net

Online Writing Community as a Place

For Alexa, her development as a writer has been profoundly shaped by her participation in primarily online "socio-cultural places in which meaningful human interactions occur" (Markham, 2003, p. 6). These places extend beyond FFN to include other portals within the affinity space, including DeviantART and Tumblr. These three portals allow Alexa to engage with multiple transformative works, modes, and semiotic resources. Moreover, they also provide access to diverse audiences. For instance, Alexa uses DeviantART as a way to share the drawings, paintings, comics, and cover art that she and other fans have created for her FFN story. One of her DeviantART followers became an avid FFN reader as a result, adding that, "If fan fiction is always like this, I will definitely be reading more!" Similarly, Alexa connects with her audience via Tumblr. Recently, one reader shared that she had been patiently waiting for the next chapter and begged Alexa to write it soon. In posting her reader's comment and her reply, Alexa alerted her Tumblr followers about the next installment in her story.

Alexa sees her online writing as qualitatively different from her writing in school. She says, "Mostly my English teacher gives us questions and we discuss the author's purpose or describe what different sorts of symbolism are present throughout the stories." In school, Alexa reads classic works of literature and analyzes how au-

thors use literary devices. But outside of school, Alexa draws inspiration from popular culture, creates compelling plot lines, and deftly applies literary devices in her own transformative works. For instance, Alexa begins one chapter with an ominous tone:

At first I lie to myself that what happened was nothing more than a dream. That it was, in fact, a mere nightmare. That when I open my eyes and the darkness fades, I will be back within my room in the Capitol. But as consciousness envelopes me, I know that it is not the case.

Rather than simply being a consumer, Alexa's writing community encourages her to be a producer and an innovator. In school, she often has a limited audience; namely, her teacher. But online, Alexa has a wide audience who interacts with her by providing reviews and formative feedback, thereby motivating her to continue writing.

Alexa's writing community offers her a global audience, including eager reviewers and beta readers. Not only does FFN allow for asynchronous communication between writers and their audience, it also gives writers ample time to develop their craft. When Alexa first joined FFN, she wrote a number of stories about *Bones* and *Twilight*. Over the past four years, she began to explore new genres, characters, and themes. Today, Alexa is a dedicated writer. She shares, "I write fan fiction like nobody's business. I love it so much." Her interests and ideas—not external deadlines or high-stakes assessments—drive her writing. Moreover, Alexa's writing community includes fuzzy boundaries (Steinkuehler et al., 2005) and multiple portals. By posting her transformative works on FFN, DeviantART, and Tumblr, she shares her work in the public domain. As a place, Alexa's writing community is defined by the meaningful interactions she has in these multiple spaces and the keen sense of presence with her audience.

Author Notes as a Tool

As a writer, Alexa has been able to spend the past four years developing her craft as part of an online affinity space. In her profiles on FFN, DeviantART, and Tumblr, Alexa identifies herself as a writer, first and foremost. She uses all three portals as a way to interact with her audience. For instance, she includes links to her Tumblr on her FFN stories and she shares her own and others' fan art for her stories on DeviantART, thus these links become conduits (Markham, 2003) connecting Alexa's writing across the multiple portals. One of the primary tools that Alexa uses to interact with her audience is through her Author Notes, which Black (2008) has noted as a core feature of the fan fiction genre. Over the past ten months, Alexa has been writing a story about an unlikely romance between two *Hunger Games* characters. At 112,373 words long, each of the story's 30 chapters includes Author Notes at the beginning and end.

Author Notes serve multiple purposes for Alexa: they allow her to respond to readers' previous chapter reviews, anticipate readers' reactions to the current chapter, express appreciation to certain reviewers, and address any possible issues with her writing, such as proofreading issues or writer's block. As a tool, Author Notes connect Alexa with her audience. At the beginning of this particular story, her chapters generally included disclaimers ("I'm doing my best to keep them in character") and requests ("Please review, favorite, and author alert! It keeps me motivated"). Alexa uses Author Notes as a way to address her choices as a writer; for instance, she may have drawn attention to the chapter's suspenseful ending or explained why she depicted characters in certain ways. At other times, Alexa's Author Notes double as an apology for her perceived shortcoming as a writer and promises to proofread her chapter soon.

As her following has grown, Alexa's Author Notes have become more detailed and specifically respond to reviews. In general, reviewers offer Alexa positive feedback, including compliments on her characterization ("Your portrayal of the characters is outstanding!") and plot development ("I'm in love with the relationship between [the two main characters]. So thank you, for actually taking it slow. Their progress is gradual, and such a joy to read") as well as her attention to the original work, *The Hunger Games* ("Your story is really well-written and I love how you managed to stick to the canon in so many details"). Some reviewers request specific topics for Alexa to explore in future chapters; consequently, her Author Notes explain why she did (or did not) take incorporate readers' suggestions. As they bridge physical and virtual spaces and create a means for answering back to reviewers, Author Notes can be seen as a tool FFN writers like Alexa use in order to engage in a dialogue with their audience.

Writing as a Way of Being

Alexa has engaged in the online affinity space associated with *The Hunger Games* as a reader, a writer, a reviewer, and an artist. Alexa's identity as a writer shapes the way she sees herself and the world around her, and her participation on FFN has been integral to her development. This way of being is validated by others as Alexa is recognized within the affinity space as an accomplished writer. In one interview, she said, "I think I'm a rather well-known author on FFN. I'll go onto other sites and I'll have people say, 'Oh hey! You're the one who wrote [story title]. I love that story!' And I'll be like, 'Really?! Thank you!'" Alexa's acquisition of her ways of being as a writer did not happen overnight. Rather, through actively participating in FFN, Alexa developed her ability to craft believable characters and compelling storylines. Moreover, her development of a writerly Discourse was facilitated by her interaction with hundreds of reviewers as well as a few specific beta readers.

Mid-way through her story, a reviewer named Hope pointed out the value of beta readers who serve as peer reviewers, "I am so excited for the upcoming chapters. Me. Want. Have you ever thought about getting a beta?... Once they proof-read [your story], they send it back and it's ready for posting! I would actually love to beta for you, if you wanted a beta." Alexa quickly took Hope up on her offer and they have since forged a close relationship, without making distinctions between friendship and collaboration. Before Alexa posts her chapters online, she always sends them to Hope for review.

In one exchange, Hope's feedback to Alexa focused on her writing style and punctuation:

8th paragraph: Combine the first two sentences and make it "I chew on the inside of my cheek at the truth of his words." Take off the of at the end of the fourth sentence to make it "... I am unsure." Fifth sentence try to change it to something more like "Just like I am kept in the dark as to what's going on, shadows grow between him and me." (beautiful comparison, btw)

13th paragraph: Take off the question mark at the last sentence.

14th paragraph: Take out the comma after "I ask" and put a period in its place.

15th paragraph: Place a comma instead of a period after "Can't" and lowercase "he." Take out the apostrophe on the word "yours." Yours is already possessive. It doesn't need an apostrophe.

16th paragraph: Instead of chopping up her urges into separate sentences, make them one. "The urge to cry, to slap, to release my emotions somehow, builds until I feel I may burst."

Great job so far! Loving the tension between [the two characters]!

While reviews are publicly posted, beta readers share their comments through FFN's private message system. As a writer, this allows Alexa to have an initial audience of one who edits her story and offers constructive criticism. Recently, Alexa

and Hope established a joint account where they write alternating chapters based on two characters in *The Hunger Games* trilogy, collapsing distinctions between the two as writers. This collaborative project illustrates how participating in FFN encourages Alexa to see writing as something other than a solitary way of being, thus shaping her identity, her practices, and her relationships with others within the writing community.

Scholar

Classrooms as Writing Places

While *Scholar* aims to support classrooms as writing communities in which students help each other by formatively reviewing each others' drafts—similar to interactions in online affinity spaces—the socio-cultural contexts of classrooms construct writing places quite differently. Perhaps the key difference between most classrooms and most affinity spaces is the nature of participation itself. In online writing communities and affinity spaces, participation is often voluntary and "horizontal" (i.e. many writers comment freely on each others' work, see Kalantzis & Cope, 2012). Few operate under the premise that members must participate, and fewer still dictate the steps and terms of participation. In classrooms, however, students are required to complete certain assignments and they must complete them in certain ways.

While working on Ms. Barrett's narrative project, Darrell and his classmates were free to choose school-appropriate story topics, and many students started several narratives as they worked through their initial journaling and pre-writing worksheets. At the same time, *Scholar* and their teacher dictated their writing process. *Scholar's* architecture guided writers through the specific steps of drafting a story: submitting first drafts, reviewing and annotating each others' work, and revising with that feedback in mind. Failing to complete these activities on time would lead to a lower grade, a significant penalty since this narrative represented the class's first substantial writing project grade for the year.

Introducing *Scholar* to the classroom created a hybrid environment that had more-directive features of the classroom (e.g. rubric-centered reviews) and more-open features of a writing affinity space (e.g. sending messages to classmates in Community). Ms. Barrett remained a central presence in the classroom in many ways: she set assignments, created assessment guidelines, and circulated through the computer lab to answer questions and help students manage their writing. Review and annotation interactions in *Scholar* opened up the typical discourse among students, however, allowing Darrell and his classmates to meaningfully interact with each others' work by reading, providing help, and sharing ideas in ways that would be impossible if Ms. Barrett was their sole reader. For instance, Darrell described the reviews becoming "a circle of help" because the reviews that he received "g[ave] [me] a starting point on what to look out for in someone else's story." *Scholar's* online writing place broadened students' audience, allowing them to communicate ideas with their reviews and put writing lessons into practice, while Ms. Barrett opened up the classroom to students' narrative expression by assigning an open-ended story.

Scholar as a Writing Tool

Darrell was one of the few students who reported writing at home and thus *Scholar* became a tool for expanding the classroom and allowing interactions with his parents as readers. Most significantly, he experienced some data loss in the first draft of his story, *The Life of Jason Grace: the life of a demigod* [sic], when the computer that he was using in the lab classroom disconnected from the network. He was understandably upset at the time, but the next morning, Darrell bounded into class and reported that he had used *Scholar* to re-draft his story and asked his parents for a read-through: "Guess what! I got home last night, and I rewrote my story, and my parents helped me, and now it's way longer

and better. And I was scared it'd erase, so I saved like seven times!" Darrell's work logs in *Scholar* back up this description of his actions. Between draft 4 (saved after school) and draft 7 (saved in class the next day), Darrell re-drafted his story and copyedited his work. In the first paragraph of his story alone, Darrell made 17 large and small edits, including 14 corrections to conventions (e.g. correcting spelling) and three reorganizations (e.g. reorganizing run-on sentences into smaller sentences). The two remaining paragraphs share similar errors and corrections. While draft 4 includes many misspellings, capitalization errors, and run-on sentences, draft 7 transforms his sentences into more conventional English. This editing work confirms Darrell's report of working on his story and asking his parents for proofreading help, and it demonstrates how *Scholar* was a tool that connected him to his writing from home.

In this way, the "anywhere, anyplace" capability of *Scholar* aided Darrell. When an online tool can expand the classroom beyond its traditional place within the school walls, new opportunities and interactions become possible for students. Not only did Darrell ask his parents to become his readers, he used their ideas in the very document that he would eventually turn in for peer review and teacher evaluation. *Scholar* organizes work and provides access to audiences and readers (in this case, Darrell's parents) that might and offer help in multiple ways and at multiple times.

Reviewing as a Way of Being

Following his significant self-revision, the class began work on peer reviewing each other's stories. As a reviewer, Darrell provided feedback on three classmates' stories, mostly making informative (e.g. "i know the charecter know and how i can relate to her"[1]) and praising comments (e.g. "great thought good storie strong conflicts of charecters") in his reviews. Additionally, he annotated two of these stories extensively to correct various small errors. For example, he commented "5.4??????????????" on one classmate's phrase

"5.4 brothers." On another classmate's story, he noted spacing errors, "Iasked – space it." Darrell worked carefully on reading, annotating, and reviewing until day 6 of the project, the day before Ms. Barrett had planned for the students to finish and submit the final drafts of their stories.

Between his last two drafts—draft 7 and draft 9—Darrell did not revise significantly, possibly as a result of the time he spent reviewing others' work rather than revising his own. At the same time, he changed small details. For instance, Darrell added setting details such as the "small town of Norrisvile," included his character's name, and reorganized to provide information about his main character's motivations to run away. All of these revisions responded directly to review comments from his classmates, suggesting that Darrell began to see responding to reviews as a part of the writing process—something that writers do. Comments about setting, in fact, were key features of his reviews, since he received three suggestions about his (lack of) setting. For example, his classmate Kea writes "I didn't really get a really good idea of the setting as i was reading. I think that you should [add] the setting a little bit in between some words so i can imagine the setting."

These comments made it clear that missing setting information has consequences—Darrell's readers were not sure where his story happened. Similarly, his classmate Isaac explained his confusion with the beginning of the story, noting that the audience does not yet know Jason is a demigod. Facts and backstories must be explained to make the story make sense. Darrell appreciated the feedback that he got and the review process in general:

I really liked the fact that we were able to share stories with other people because we were able to get some input from other people... most of them were good comments but they were also very helpful.

What is interesting, however, is that he and several classmates reported wide-ranging conse-

quences as a result of their reading and reviewing. While students largely focused on this mutual help, they also reported thinking more metacognitively about editing and writing as a result of their reading. In the focus group, Darrell pointed out that his classmates' reviews helped him consider writing and reviewing as reciprocal, connected processes as he was reading their narratives:

When you see how this person's reviewing your story that also gives you a starting point on what to look out for in someone else's story... When they reviewed on my story, it gave me a starting point of what to think of while I read theirs.

Reading, in other words, feeds back into writing and reviewing, collapsing distinctions between the tasks of becoming a writer.

Students learned about each other by reading each other's writing, too, "like, where this person is coming from." Darrell noted, for instance, that he learned that a classmate "probably has a very wide span of imagination" by reading his humorous story about a baby penguin who travels to Jamaica. Whereas the students complained at first about having to review each others' stories—it was, after all, a whole extra step beyond their usual writing classwork—many found themselves excited to not only help each other, but to share personal insights that had, up until the reviews, been inaccessible.

FINAL THOUGHTS

Having presented data from the two case studies of developing writers, each working within a different technology-mediated writing context, we now turn our attention to discussing comparisons between and unique affordances of each space. Specifically, we consider how this analysis contributes to the field's understanding of technology's potential to shift the relationships between writers and audiences. In each context, we see that writers are encouraged to engage with and respond to feedback from their audience. Alexa had the assistance of a beta reader, who provided editorial suggestions for unpublished drafts, and readers who posted reviews on published chapters. She used the practice of including Author Notes as a tool for responding to audience feedback. Darrell received feedback from his parents and through peer reviews in the Creator tool in *Scholar*, and responded by making changes to his drafts. Additionally, for both Alexa and Darrell, writing took on a new way of being within these technology-mediated spaces. For Alexa, the FFN practice of having beta readers allowed her to see writing not as a solitary activity, but as a collaborative way of being. *Scholar* fostered the importance of review and revision as parts of the writing process, and allowed Darrell the opportunity to see writing as a way of getting to know his classmates in a different light.

The analysis also reveals important differences between these spaces. Though *Scholar* begins to create classroom writing spaces by providing tools that foster writerly practices of annotating, seeking feedback, and revising, that this technology-mediated writing context remains influenced by the Discourse of school cannot be ignored. *Scholar* shifts classrooms towards greater participation and collaboration by allowing students to serve as each other's readers, and its review elements are similar to those experienced by Alexa in FFN. At the same time, Ms. Barrett dictated Darrell's writing assignment and assessment, and chose to curb students' posting of information in *Scholar's* Community application. While these limitations make sense given school norms and parent expectations, as a result, the *Scholar*-mediated writing place remains necessarily hybrid, not as truly horizontal or interest-driven as FFN. We also see how the context affects each writer's development of a way of being. Alexa was able to take on the identity of a writer in *The Hunger Games* affinity space because FFN gave her the freedom to pursue the plots and characters in which she was most interested whenever she wanted to write. The mandated, time-limited, rubric-driven nature of

classroom writing, on the other hand, necessarily hindered Darrell's ability to adopt a writerly way of being, even though Ms. Barrett did allow her students free choice in several areas including narrative topic and form. Therefore, while technologies allow students to realize that they, too, sit "among the audience" (Lunsford & Ede, 2009), *Scholar* also remains committed to school.

Assessment was another important difference between these spaces. Ms. Barrett assessed Darrell's writing as a portion of his English grade, whereas Alexa's writing was assessed by reader reviews. The teacher's control of the writing context stands in stark contrast to the open, communicative writing observed in online affinity spaces. While adherence to genres, forms, and language conventions is a key skill for writers in both of these settings—and we observe both Alexa and Darrell attending to their own and others' writing in these ways—writing takes on different significance in spaces where creation for passionate online audiences is the central activity (Curwood, et al., 2013; Magnifico & Halverson, 2012). Alexa writes for enjoyment and to express her fandom of *The Hunger Games*. Darrell, though he similarly takes inspiration from popular culture in writing his demigod narrative, is writing to complete a school assignment.

We see potential for the design of affinity spaces to filter into school-based reading and writing, however. The Common Core State Standards conceptualize multi-genre writing, multimedia creation, ongoing collaboration, and peer review as valuable skills (NGA Center & CCSSO, 2010). However, the extent to which the assessments that follow from these standards enact these values remains to be seen. Educational technologies such as *Scholar* bring online content creation and peer review to classrooms, aiming to shift discourse patterns from a teacher-centered "vertical" to a more peer-to-peer "horizontal" framework (Kalantzis & Cope, 2012), much like Alexa's experience of working with reviewers and beta readers in FFN. Additionally, the technology affords students the opportunity to work beyond school walls, allowing

Darrell's parents to provide formative feedback on his draft as he worked from home. In this way, Darrell's work in *Scholar* supports Warschauer's (2006) findings that when students had daily access to Internet-connected laptops, they demonstrated increased levels of composition, revision, and publication, and they received greater feedback on their writing.

Finally, this analysis demonstrates how metaphors shape our perceptions, providing us different ways to think about writing. In contrast to thinking about writing as evaluation or writing as private self-reflection, these cases illustrate that writing can be public and collaborative, encouraging formative feedback from readers in the audience. Thus, these technology-mediated writing spaces afford different kinds of practices and create new writing cultures. By making the implicit writing relationship between author and audience more explicit, these spaces shift the culture of writing. While this may be more evident in online affinity spaces (see also Lammers, 2013), with the inclusion of *Scholar* in classrooms, we see the potential for a similar cultural shift in schools, too. This analysis begins to consider how *learning* to write is changing, and the next steps should include further research into how technology-mediated writing contexts can be used to *teach* writing in new ways.

ACKNOWLEDGMENT

The work on *Scholar* in this chapter was supported by grants from the Institute of Education Sciences: "Assessing Complex Performance: A Postdoctoral Training Program Researching Students Writing and Assessment in Digital Workspaces," U.S. Department of Education (Common Ground Publishing LLC) "U-learn.net, Phases 1 and 2," and "The Assess-As-You-Go Writing Assistant: A Student Work Environment That Brings Together Formative and Summative Assessment" (Bill Cope, PI).

REFERENCES

Alvermann, D. E. (2008). Why bother theorizing adolescents' online literacies for classroom practice and research? *Journal of Adolescent & Adult Literacy*, *52*(1), 8–19. doi:10.1598/JAAL.52.1.2.

Applebee, A. N., & Langer, J. A. (2009). EJ extra: What is happening in the teaching of writing? *English Journal*, *98*(5), 18–28.

Atwell, N. (1998). *In the middle: New understandings about writing, reading, and learning*. Portsmouth, NH: Boynton/Cook.

Bereiter, C., & Scardamalia, M. (1987). *The psychology of written composition*. Hillsdale, NJ: Lawrence Erlbaum Associates.

Berkenkotter, C. (1981). Understanding a writer's awareness of audience. *College Composition and Communication*, *32*(4), 388–391. doi:10.2307/356601.

Black, R. (2008). *Adolescents and online fan fiction*. New York: Peter Lang.

Boyatzis, R. E. (1998). *Transforming qualitative information: Thematic analysis and code development*. Thousand Oaks, CA: Sage Publications.

Cohen, M., & Riel, M. (1989). The effect of distal audiences on students' writing. *American Educational Research Journal*, *26*, 143–159. doi:10.3102/00028312026002143.

Curwood, J. S. (2013a). *The Hunger Games*: Literature, literacy, and online affinity spaces. *Language Arts*, *90*(6), 417-427.

Curwood, J. S. (2013b). Fan fiction, remix culture, and *The Potter Games*. In Frankel, V. E. (Ed.), *Teaching with Harry Potter* (pp. 81–92). Jefferson, NC: McFarland.

Curwood, J. S., Magnifico, A. M., & Lammers, J. C. (2013). Writing in the wild: Writers' motivation in fan-based affinity spaces. *Journal of Adolescent & Adult Literacy*, *56*(8), 677-685. doi:10.1002/JAAL.192.

Dyson, A. H. (2006). On saying it right (write), Fix-its in the foundations of learning to write. *Research in the Teaching of English, 41*(1), 8–42.

Elbow, P. (1987). Closing my eyes as I speak: An argument for ignoring audience. *College English, 49*(1), 50–69. doi:10.2307/377789.

Freedman, S. W. (1992). Outside-in and inside-out: Peer response groups in two ninth-grade classes. *Research in the Teaching of English, 26*(1), 71–107.

Gee, J. P. (2004). *Situated language and learning: A critique of traditional schooling*. New York: Routledge.

Gee, J. P. (2008). *Social linguistics and literacies: Ideology in discourses* (3rd ed.). New York: Routledge.

Gibson, W. (1950). Authors, speakers, readers, and mock readers. *College English, 11*(5), 265–269. doi:10.2307/585994.

Hutchins, E. (1995). *Cognition in the wild*. Cambridge, MA: MIT University Press.

Jenkins, H. (1992). *Textual poachers: Television, fans, and participatory culture*. New York: Routledge.

Kalantzis, M., & Cope, W. (2012). *Literacies*. New York: Cambridge University Press. doi:10.1017/CBO9781139196581.

Lammers, J. C. (2013). Fan girls as teachers: Examining pedagogic discourse in an online fan site. *Learning, Media and Technology*. doi:10.1080/17439884.2013.764895 PMID:23459677.

Lammers, J. C., Curwood, J. S., & Magnifico, A. M. (2012). Toward an affinity space methodology: Considerations for literacy research. *English Teaching: Practice and Critique, 11*(2), 44–58.

Lenhart, A., Arafeh, S., Smith, A., & Macgill, A. (2008). Writing, technology, and teens. *Pew Internet and the American Life Project*. Retrieved from http://www.pewInternet.org

Lunsford, A. A., & Ede, L. (2009). Among the audience: On audience in an age of new literacies. In Weiser, M. E., Fehler, B. M., & Gonzales, A. M. (Eds.), *Engaging audience: Writing in an age of new literacies* (pp. 42–69). Urbana, IL: NCTE.

Magnifico, A. M. (2010). Writing for whom: Cognition, motivation, and a writer's audience. *Educational Psychologist, 45*(3), 167–184. doi: 10.1080/00461520.2010.493470.

Magnifico, A. M., & Halverson, E. R. (2012). Bidirectional artifact analysis: A method for analyzing creative processes. In J. van Aalst, K. Thompson, M.J. Jacobson, & P. Reimann (Eds.), *The future of learning: Proceedings of the 10th International Conference of the Learning Sciences*, (Vol. 2, pp. 276-280). Sydney, Australia: International Society of the Learning Sciences.

Markham, A. N. (2003). *Images of internet: Tool, place, way of being*. Paper presented at the Fourth Annual Conference of the Association of Internet Researchers. Toronto, Canada.

McCarthey, S. J., Magnifico, A. M., Woodard, R. L., & Kline, S. (2013). Situating technology-facilitated feedback and revision: The case of Tom. In Pytash, K., & Ferdig, R. (Eds.), *Exploring technology for writing and writing Instruction*. Hershey, PA: IGI Global.

McCutchen, D. (2000). Knowledge, processing, and working memory: Implications for a theory of writing. *Educational Psychologist, 35*(1), 13–23. doi:10.1207/S15326985EP3501_3.

Moje, E. B. (2009). Standpoints: A call for new research on new and multi-literacies. *Research in the Teaching of English, 43*(4), 348–362.

National Governors Association Center for Best Practices (NGA Center) & Council of Chief State School Officers. (CCSSO). (2010). *Common core state standards*. Washington, DC: National Governors Association Center for Best Practices, Council of Chief State School Officers.

Ong, W. (1975). The writer's audience is always a fiThe w. *Publications of the Modern Language Association of America, 90*(1), 9–21.

Porter, J. E. (1996). Audience. In Enos, T. (Ed.), *Encyclopedia of rhetoric and composition: Communication from ancient times to the information age* (p. 43). New York: Routledge.

Pressley, M. (2005). *Reading instruction that works: The case for balanced teaching* (3rd ed.). New York, NY: Guilford.

Purcell-Gates, V., Duke, N. K., & Martineau, J. A. (2007). Learning to read and write genre-specific text: Roles of authentic experience and explicit teaching. *Reading Research Quarterly, 42*(1), 8–45. doi:10.1598/RRQ.42.1.1.

Saldaña, J. (2009). *The coding manual for qualitative researchers*. Thousand Oaks, CA: Sage.

Shaffer, D. W. (2006). *How computer games help children learn*. New York, NY: Palgrave Macmillan. doi:10.1057/9780230601994.

Steinkuehler, C., Black, R., & Clinton, K. (2005). Researching literacy as tool, place, and way of being. *Reading Research Quarterly, 40*(1), 7–12.

Warschauer, M. (2006). *Laptops and literacy: Learning in the wireless classroom*. New York: Teachers College Press.

Yancey, K. B. (2009). *Writing in the 21st century: A report from the national council of teachers of English*. Urbana, IL: NCTE.

Yin, R. K. (2003). *Case study research: Design and methods* (3rd ed.). Thousand Oaks, CA: Sage Publications.

KEY TERMS AND DEFINITIONS

Affinity Space: Physical, virtual, or blended sites of informal learning where interested participants gather for a common endeavor (see Lammers, Curwood, & Magnifico, 2012).

Beta Reader: Proofreader and/or copyeditor within a fan fiction space (see Black, 2008).

Communicative Writing: Writing intended as an interaction with readers, rather than for the purpose of self-reflection or evaluation.

Discourse: A socially-situated way of being in the world that encompasses not only language, but also behavior, interactions, values, and beliefs, to construct an identity as a certain kind of person that is recognized by others within a particular group (see Gee, 2008).

Fan Fiction: Fictional texts created by fans, derived from their fandom of a particular media such as a television show, movie, book, anime or manga series, or videogame, often to engage with or extend particular characters or storylines (see Black, 2008; Jenkins, 1992).

Peer Review: A process of evaluating work, in this case writing, that is conducted by one's peers.

Portal: An entry point into an affinity space (i.e. an online discussion board, a face-to-face gathering, a social networking site) that generates content related to the common endeavor.

Transformative Work: A creation that takes an existing text/media and turns it into something new, such as fan fiction, art, music, or videos (see http://transformativeworks.org/).

ENDNOTES

[1]   All quotations that refer to reviews are reproduced exactly as Darrell and his classmates wrote their reviews on each other's work.

Chapter 12
The Writer in the Reader:
Building Communities of Response in Digital Environments

Bernadette Dwyer
St. Patrick's, College, Dublin City University, Ireland

Lotta Larson
Kansas State University, USA

ABSTRACT

Digital reading environments are redefining the relationship between reader, text, activity, and sociocultural context. This chapter explores the nature of engagement, collaboration, and reader/writer response, as sixth-grade students from Ireland and the United States read and responded to electronic books within the context of an online global literature circle. In response to the readings, students composed digital thinkmarks, which served as springboards for subsequent written asynchronous message board discussions. Findings from this qualitative case study suggest that peer collaboration in an online literature discussion forum enabled the construction of social identity, community building, and a sociocultural situated response and engendered immersion in, involvement with, and interpretation of texts.

INTRODUCTION

Digital texts and digital interactions permeate our daily lives (Coiro, Knobel, Lankshear, & Leu, 2008), while digital reading environments are redefining the relationship between reader, text, activity, and sociocultural context (McEneaney, 2006; Rand Reading Study Group, (RRSG), 2002; Reinking, Labbo, & McKenna, 2000). The International Reading Association (IRA) (2009) emphasized the importance of integrating Information and Communication Technologies (ICTs)

into current literacy programs. An important step towards such integration involves redefining the notion of what constitutes text, as teachers seek alternative text sources including digital texts and electronic books (Booth, 2006; Kucer, 2005). Digital texts in electronic book formats offer the possibility of "scaffolded digital reading" environments (Dalton & Proctor, 2008, p. 303), which are flexible, supportive and responsive to the needs of students, through embedded multimodal supports, such as text-to-speech functionality, built-in dictionaries, and customizable font size (Hall, Strangman & Meyer, 2003). Furthermore, digital texts afford readers the role of writers, as they annotate or highlight passages or words

DOI: 10.4018/978-1-4666-4341-3.ch012

within the text and author digital thinkmarks, or notes, to capture and archive fleeting responses and thoughts as they read.

In a traditional literacy classroom, students read print texts, respond to reading in written response journals (whose only audience may well be the classroom teacher), and exchange ideas in traditional face-to-face literature discussions. In such instances, knowledge is mostly transmitted, not conducted (Carico, Logan, & Labbo, 2004). However, in the new literacies classroom, students assume diverse responsibilities as consumers and producers of information and effective learning is increasingly dependent on social and collaborative learning strategies which can potentially reach far beyond their classroom walls (Dwyer, 2013; Larson, 2009; Leu, Kinzer, Coiro & Cammack, 2004; Malloy, Castek & Leu, 2010; Wolsey & Grisham, 2012). The National Council for the Teachers of English (NCTE) (2013) urges teachers to use technologies to intentionally build cross cultural connections and collaborative relationships within a global community. In this way, students can redefine the boundaries of the classroom (Beach, 2012) to move beyond local context and culture to build "cosmopolitan dispositions and habits of mind" (Hull & Stornaiulo, 2010, p. 89). In this chapter, we will describe how students from Ireland and the United States read e-books on digital reading devices (Amazon Kindles) and participated in ICT-based literature circle discussions where they authored responses to text on an asynchronous message board. These experiences allowed them to interact with and respond to the texts in new and innovative ways.

THEORETICAL PERSPECTIVES

The study was underpinned by a range of diverse theoretical perspectives to allow for the consideration of "multiple perspectives from a constellation of theories and methodologies" (Harrison, 2008, p. 1292). These viewpoints included (a) new literacies perspectives, (b) sociocultural perspectives, and (c) reader response theories. Each of the theoretical perspectives, explored in the sections which follow, affords us a lens to view the complexity of literacy in the 21st century from cognitive, cultural, social and affective dimensions.

New Literacies

At present there is no single, unifying, theoretical perspective in the research literature to explain the evolving and deictic (Leu, 2000) nature of literacy in the 21st century (Reinking, 1998; Rideout, Foehr & Rideout, 2010). Perspectives include 'Multiliteracies' (Cope & Kalantzis, 2000; The New London Group, 2000) drawing on the multimodal nature of digital literacies within a global communication network in a flattened world (Friedman, 2005). 'New Literacies Studies' (Gee, 2003; Kress, 2003; Lankshear & Knobel, 2003; Pahl & Rowsell, 2005; Street, 1998) situate digital literacies within sociocultural perspectives, viewing literacy in terms of semiotic contexts, new discourses, social purposes, events and practices. Rooted in socio-constructivist and cognitive theories, 'New Literacies' perspectives (Leu, Kinzer, Cammack & Coiro, 2004) recognize that "social contexts have always shaped the form and function of literate practices, and been shaped by them in return" (Leu, Kinzer, Coiro, Castek & Henry (2013, p. 1151). Therefore, new literacies are constantly evolving, requiring new skills, strategies and dispositions to fully exploit the potential of digital literacies to enhance literacy, communication and learning. The juxtaposition of these multiple perspectives challenges educators to transform reading and writing instruction in response to emerging technologies and new possibilities for communication and collaboration across the world (IRA, 2009).

Sociocultural Perspectives

Sociocultural perspectives view literacy practices and learning as social activities where personal knowledge is co-constructed (Bruner, 1986; Vygotsky, 1978) through peer collaboration and the social construction of meaning. Knowledge is created within a social activity and evolves through negotiation. When students collaborate in constructing meaning from text, they have what Kucan and Beck (1997) referred to as "multiple resources at the reading construction site" (p. 289). Therefore, as students interact in social settings, they acquire both knowledge and the processes by which knowledge is constructed (Putney, Green, Dixon, Durán & Yeager, 2000). Knowledge is not merely "the sum of individuals' knowledge" but is rather "distributed among participants as the nature of their participation shifts" (Gutiér-rez & Stone, 2000, p. 160). In co-constructing meaning, group members may participate in collaborative communities to develop literacy practices and construct identity (Alvermann et al., 2012), develop a participatory culture (Jenkins, 2006), or an affinity space (Gee, 2004). In this way they can develop response and agency while examining their own knowledge and beliefs with those of others (Alvermann, 2009; Azmitia, 1988; Barron, 2000; Daiute & Dalton, 1993). Recent research (Castek, 2008; Dwyer, 2010) suggests that peer collaboration is an important component for developing new literacies in inquiry-based learning activities on the Internet as students co-construct effective online skills and strategies in collaborative learning environments. Talking about books in literature circles, book clubs, or other forms of oral response, fosters a desire to share personal connections and conversational reactions to literature within a community of readers and writers (Daniels, 2002; Raphael, Florio-Ruane, George, Hasty, & Highfield, 2004). With greater access to technology, online discussions are becoming increasingly common as a means to encourage learner engagement and literature discussions. Classroom studies posit that online literature discussions may foster literacy skills, strengthen communication, and build community (Carico, Logan, & Labbo, 2004; Evans & Po, 2007; Grisham & Wolsey, 2006, Larson, 2009; Maples, 2010; McWilliams, Hickey, Hines, Conner & Bishop, 2011).

Reader Response

Louise Rosenblatt's (1938, 1978) transactional reader response theory suggests an active, constructive experience in which readers create "meaning *with*, not from, the text" (Galda, 2010, p. 3, italics in original). In this transaction, the voices of the reader and author are blended, resulting in opportunities to create meaning by applying, reorganizing, or extending personal experiences and encounters with texts. In other words, meaning does not reside *in* the text or *in* the reader, but rather occurs during the transaction between the reader and the text (Rosenblatt, 2005). By challenging the notion of one true meaning of text, reader-response theory allowed for a range of student-constructed responses and interpretations of texts, recognizing each reader's unique perspectives as well as the social and cultural contexts in which the reading takes place. Consequently, this belief replaces the teacher's role of single authority of literary knowledge to one of literacy facilitator, creating room for increased student interpretation and collaboration (Karolides, 2000; Larson, 2009; Park, 2012).

Since the zenith of reader response research in the 1990s, educators have adjusted their focus to reflect continuing educational changes, including technological advances and increasingly diverse classrooms, while remaining devoted to honored reader response research traditions and perspectives (Hancock, 2008). Hence, many literacy educators advocate for moving beyond students' personal responses to more "critical and culturally responsive versions of reader-response pedagogies" in which students conceptualize reading as critical and collective practice (Park, 2012, p. 191). In addition to traditional literacies of paper and pencil, the increased use of digital literacies challenges educators to consider students' reactions to digital texts and the potential uses of ICTs to discuss and respond to readings. Technology can clearly provide a new vision and dimension for reader/writer response research and classroom practice. In this chapter, we will discuss how sixth-grade students from Ireland and the United States reached across a global community in time, space, culture, and context to share and expand personal perspectives in response to literature.

FRAMING THE STUDY: PARTICIPANTS AND SETTING

Two groups of sixth-grade students; one in Dublin, Ireland (Katie, Hanna, Jane, Colm, Niall, and Paul) and one in Kansas, USA (Judith, Elizabeth, Grace, John, Duane, and Ben); read and responded to e-books. To protect privacy, all students were assigned a pseudonym which they used throughout the study. Using purposive sampling (Patton, 2002), all participants were identified as strong readers and effective communicators by their classroom teachers; however, none of them had previous experience with literature circles or other forms of literature discussion groups. In an online pre-reading survey, students were asked about their perceptions of themselves as readers. Responses indicated that these students were motivated and engaged readers who read a range of literary genres including fiction and informational texts. Their perceptions of reading ranged from the functional aspects to aesthetic dimensions of reading. For example, Elizabeth, a student from Kansas commented, "I am a good reader I have been in reading enrichment for two years in a row. I also have never gotten lower than a 90 percent on a state assessment." Jane, a student from Dublin noted, "I LOVE reading! It's my favourite pastime! I would definitely call myself a bookworm! I like

reading Juvenile Fiction or just Fiction. I am a good reader because I know your language improves by reading and you learn more words and I have." Each student was given a digital reading device (Amazon Kindle) loaded with e-book versions of two young adult novels: *The Miraculous Journey of Edward Tulane* by Kate DiCamillo (2006) portrays the account of Edward Tulane, a haughty porcelain rabbit who loves only himself until he is separated from Abilene, the little girl who loves and adores him, and encounters new places, new adventures and many new owners until he finds the true meaning of friendship and love; in John Boyne's (2006) *The Boy in the Striped Pajamas*, Bruno, the son of a Nazi officer befriends a boy in striped pajamas who lives behind a wire fence of a large camp. While considerably different in content, both titles elicited heartfelt responses from the students. None of the students had any prior experience with either book.

Over a six-week period, students read pre-assigned chapters in the e-book and recorded digital thinkmarks and highlights on the digital reading device. Then each group met twice weekly in a face-to-face literature circle at their respective school. At these meetings, students shared their responses to and interpretations of the text. They also formulated questions and discussion prompt threads which they posted on an online, asynchronous message board. The message board functioned as the host of a larger global literature circle in which all students collaborated and engaged in discussion. The authentic voices of the students (including occasional errors in spelling and conventions) will be quoted throughout this chapter to bring their literature discussions to life. However, due to publication restrictions, it is not possible to truly capture the way the students created identity through the use of color, font size, font type, and highlighting features on the asynchronous message board. As an illustrative example, Figure 1 presents a visual representation of the message board.

Figure 1. Illustrative example of asynchronous message board discussion

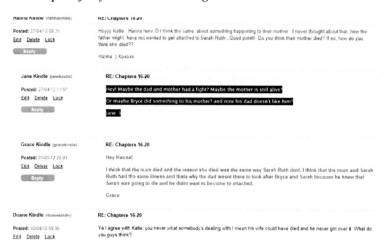

While reading, participants physically interacted with the texts by using e-book tools. For example, they adjusted text size, listened to the story through text-to-speech features, highlighted key passages, accessed the built-in dictionaries, and searched for key words or phrases within the book. In response to the readings, the students also annotated the text with notes or digital thinkmarks. These digital thinkmarks offered insights into the students' meaning-making processes and served as conduits to ongoing response writing and literature circle discussions (Larson, 2010; 2012).

METHODOLOGY

A qualitative case-study methodology was chosen to provide an expressive, narrative description within a natural setting (Creswell, 2003). Case studies are generally categorized as exploratory, descriptive, or explanatory depending on the nature of the research problem and questions (Yin, 2009); this study was exploratory in nature as the researchers aimed to investigate what happens when Irish and American students, in different social and cultural contexts, interact and collaborate in an online global literature circle while reading

and responding to e-books. The strength of case study research is in providing a rich description of complex phenomena, often derived from a qualitative research approach, focused on participants' experiences within the case (Creswell, 2003; Stake, 1995). Data sources included online discussion board transcripts, digital voice recordings of face-to-face group discussions, students' digital annotations in e-books, interviews with participants, pre- and post-reading surveys, and researchers' field notes.

Data sources were triangulated and coded, drawing on inductive methods of analysis, such as the constant comparative methodology (Glaser & Strauss, 1967), deductive methods of analysis (drawing on theoretical frameworks used within the study) and abductive methods (abstracting the best explanation for understanding one's study results) (Johnson & Onwuegbuzie, 2004) to discover patterns within the data until themes emerged (Bogdan & Biklen, 2003; Miles & Huberman, 1994). The coding process was carried out independently by the two researchers; one situated in Ireland, the other in the United States. Each researcher read all message board posts, segmenting them into descriptive units and finally classifying each unit through inferential and interpretive coding (Miles & Huberman, 1994) as belonging to certain indicator categories, such as reader/writer-response categories (immersion, involvement, and interpretation) or building community categories (including constructing identity, affinity or participatory culture). Initial coder-consensus (Kozlowski & Hattrup, 1992; Olsen, 2011) was calculated at 90% agreement, based on a sample of 20% of the total posts (n= 422). Subsequently, the researchers negotiated the disparate posts in a series of Skype video calls until reaching 100% coder consensus.

FINDINGS

Findings which emerged from meticulous examination of the data suggested that peer collaboration in an online literature discussion forum encouraged (a) a sociocultural situated response through the construction of a community identity and an affinity space, and (b) deepened reader/writer response to the literature. These findings are discussed below.

Constructing a Community Identity and an Affinity Space: Writing with Divided Attention

The students met in face-to-face literature circles and discussed the digital thinkmarks and highlighted passages they had created within the e-book texts. Then they participated in threaded discussions on an asynchronous message board. Analysis of the message board threads suggested that the students were writing with divided attention, i.e. they were authoring response to the literature while concurrently constructing a community culture, identity and affinity space.

Initially, the students drew attention to the affordances and supports provided by the digital reading devices ("we really like the vocabulary in these chapters. We used our Kindle dictionary to look up words"). They also created individual identity through the use of style signatures and

emoticons ("From Katie! xx:):)"), font theme and size, use of color, and highlighting features to proclaim who they were ("Heyyyy its Judith!!").

However, a prompt posted by the students in Dublin, with questions about the initial chapters in *The Miraculous Journey of Edward Tulane*, expressed concern about a spate of recent tornadoes in Kansas ("Hello!, how is it over there? We heard about the horrible tornado"). Students in Kansas, such as Duane, responded with similar concern for the Dublin students who lived in a coastal region beside the Irish Sea, "Oh ya thanks for our consern [concern] about the tornados. Starting now I'll watch the news for tsunamis or floods in your area." In the following example John, a student from Kansas, responds to the concern about the tornadoes, creates a sense of context, while simultaneously constructing a response to the text.

Hey, this is John and just like Abiline in the book, we have a town in Kansas and it is called Abiline also. Yes, there were 127 tornadoes that touched down and we are all ok. Thanks for thinking of us and we hope you enjoy the book, too. Well, a big change for Edward was when he felt his first emotion, being afraid. We really look forward to blogging with you.-John

Following this series of posts, students began to create threads which almost seamlessly shifted between response to text and creating a community culture. The students (a) engaged with one another, "I Think we all really need to pay attention to Pellegrina..... She is really mysterious and we should keep an eye on her"; (b) affirmed one another ("John you brought that to my attention, so thanks and good point"); (c) valued opinions ("We thought of these questions because we wanted to know what you thought"), and (d) contested ("I don't think every book has to have a happy ending to be a good book") in creating a community of readers and writers. The topics explored by the students in creating a community identity, affinity space, culture and social connection (Jenkins,

2006) included issues related to education, culture, religion and personal topics. For example, topics related to education involved the length of the school day and year and the subjects the students were studying. The students also commented on cultural aspects, such as Christian names which were common in both countries and the languages spoken by the students.

Paul interpreted the journey undertaken by Edward Tulane in religious terms when he annotated the e-book with the following digital thinkmark, "it reminds me of Jesus didn't eat or drink for forty days and nights. ...he looks like Jesus on the cross when he was crucified. I think that is very sad and mean:(." When Paul later posted a comment related to this religious interpretation of the story ("Edward's story is a bit like the story of Jesus-40 days and 40 nights in a rubbish dump-and being on the cross as a scarecrow and rising from the dead"), it resonated with many of the students. For example, John's response suggested a valuing affirmation and ease of response as a member of a community:

"I think that Edward is becoming more lifelike. He was afraid and then he kind of felt love. I like how you pointed out the Jesus thing with the 40 days and nights. I think that Abiline maybe would care for Edward and would take better care for him. I loved the saying that the fishing lady said, "What I say is, theres a use for everything, and everything has its use, thats what i say."

The students also related the texts to their own personal lives where they could be seen constructing identities as individuals who would be acknowledged and recognized by others in the community as "just like us" (Gee, 2008, p.3). The characters, Bruno and Gretel, in *The Boy in the Striped Pajamas*, were similar in age to the participating students and their relationship was according to Niall a "typical sibling relationship." He explained, "[I] love proving my siblings wrong but to be honest I'd be absolutely lost without

them." The sibling relationship between the characters in *The Boy in the Striped Pajamas* elicited a number of digital thinkmarks in the e-books with comments related to the students' own lives. In response to the post, "we could make connections with the books from our lives because Bruno and Gretel sometimes fight but sometimes get on well," there were a considerable number of posts and replies (n=13) on the asynchronous message board. For example, a reply from Colm suggested the volatility of relationships between children in families but also their powerlessness and inability to control the future. He noted:

I have a younger brother who is ten and we sometimes get along and sometimes we don't. But it was the same like how Bruno moved from fancy and great to a small and awful house. I used to live in Australia and we had a nice house and a pool and pretty much everything but when we moved to Ireland I got stuck in this little house with no pool or anything and I had to leave all my friends as well <:(

Concurrently to building a community affinity space and culture, students' written responses to the literature transformed over the six-week study. Reader/writer response to literature in e-book format through peer collaboration is discussed in the following sections.

Peer Collaboration in an Online Literature Discussion Forum Deepened Reader/Writer Response to Literature

Adapting Hancock's (1993) categories of literature response as a springboard for coding, analysis of the message board transcripts suggested that reader/writer response included immersion in, involvement with, and interpretation of texts (see Table 1 for definitions of these categories).

Analysis of the message board transcripts are presented in Table 2. *The Miraculous Journey of*

Table 1. Reader/writer response: Immersion in, involvement with, and interpretation of texts as defined in the present study

Reader/writer response	As defined in the present study (adapted from Hancock, 1993)
Immersion in texts	Readers make sense of emerging plot and character by (a) moving beyond summary to reflect personal understanding; (b) gaining insights into feelings, thoughts, and motives for behaviors of characters; (c) predicting events; and (d) expressing confusion or puzzlement through questions.
Involvement with texts	Readers become personally involved with the character and/or plot by (a) identifying with the characters; (b) judging or acknowledging the plot or characters' actions, values, and growth.
Interpretation of texts	Readers engage with the text at a higher level by (a) making intertextual connections, text-to-life connections, or text-to-media connections; (b) evaluating literary elements or the author's craft; and (c) changing the outcome or authoring parts of the text.

Edward Tulane consisted of 27 chapters. *The Boy in the Striped Pajamas* was a shorter text consisting of 20 chapters. Table 2 presents the percentages of responses at key stages for both texts (beginning, middle and end). Due to time constraints (ending of the school year), the number of responses were fewer for *The Boy in the Striped Pajamas*. However, it is interesting to note that the average length of responses grew from 195 characters in *The Miraculous Journey of Edward Tulane* to 324 characters for *The Boy in the Striped Pajamas*.

Crafting Reader/Writer Response at an Immersion Level

Early posts of the asynchronous message boards strongly supported students' immersion in *The Miraculous Journey of Edward Tulane* as they attempted to make sense of the emerging plot and characters. As shown in Table 2, 70% of students' message board posts were at the immersion level as they discussed and responded to the first part of the book. These responses (a) reflected personal understanding of plot and character, moving beyond basic summary ("I think edward is like an antique to show how rich they are. I also think that pellagrina is a really important character because she knows that edward has a mind"); (b) reflected students' insights into characters' feelings, thoughts, and behavioral motives ("I think that Pellagrina was telling Edward the story because she has some connection to Edward that Abilene doesn't know or a relationship of sort"); (c) predicted events ("Abiliene's mom or dad might buy her another bunny") and; (d) expressed students' confusion through questions ("But does Edward have feelings?... That is what I wander [wonder]"). While immersion responses were often short in length, they did serve as a foundation for thoughtful response and community building. Members from both groups contemplated others' posts before submitting thoughtful replies to answer direct questions or offer personal opinions or ideas.

Immersion responses were also found in the digital thinkmarks crafted by the students within the e-books. For example, Duane consistently authored digital thinkmarks that supported his understanding ("so Abilene already has a kid"), predicting of events ("I think the chef will be arrested"), and confusion ("Can Edward drown i mean he doesnt have a nose and his mouth is glued shut"). When asked about his digital thinkmarks, Duane stated "I write things that help me remember what I'm reading."

Crafting Reader/Writer Response at an Involvement Level

As the plot evolved and students established a stronger community of readers and writers, they also became more involved in the story. As shown in Table 2, students' responses to *The Miraculous Journey of Edward Tulane* moved from the immersion level to the involvement level indicating students' ability to (a) identify with the characters or (b) judge or acknowledge the characters' actions, values, and growth (Hancock, 1993). For example, Elizabeth put herself in Edward's shoes as he longed for his home and original owner, "I would get so sick of being away from my family. I couldnt stand it." After reading about the abusive father of Bryce and Sarah Ruth, two young protagonists who cared for Edward, Elizabeth quickly judged the father's actions: "The father is ridiculous and very rude I cant believe he would treat his family like that. I wonder if they had child abuse services back then if they do he should be turned in immediately."

Clearly, the students were angry with the father, but they also tried to make sense of his actions.

Katie stated, "I think that Bryce's father shouldnt be judged too soon, We never know what happened in his past, I think maybe he didnt want to get too attached to Sarah Ruth because of something that maybe happened to her mother.:)" Ben agreed, " i think Bryce's dad didn't realize that he loved her [Sarah Ruth] untell she died some people don't love untell someone is lost." On the message board, responses at the involvement level often sparked longer threads, inviting multiple perspectives and strong opinions. At times, students' thinkmarks served as a springboard for subsequent message board posts. For example, before joining the passionate discussion concerning Bryce's abusive father, Elizabeth had already noted to herself, "Why does he [the father] slap Bryce to get out his frustration? there are better ways to deal with life." John's digital thinkmarks suggested that he kept upcoming message board conversations in mind as he composed questions for the other students, "the dad has no right yelling at bryce. why do you think he is yelling at him?" and "what do you think of the guy that said it's a sin for a rabbit to dance?" clearly prepared him for both written discourse and face-to-face discussion.

Table 2. Percentages of types of student reader/writer response at immersion, involvement, and interpretive levels for both e-books in the study

	The Miraculous Journey of Edward Tulane			The Boy in the Striped Pajamas		
	(9 threads; 310 responses; average length of responses equates to 195 characters)			(9 threads; 112 responses; average length of responses equates to 324 characters)		
Reader/writer response categories	Beginning (chs.1-5)	Middle (chs.11-15)	End chs.21-27)	Beginning (chs.1-5)	Middle (chs.11-15)	End (chs.16-20)
Immersion	70%	41%	9%	32.5%	1%	7%
Involvement	27%	59%	33%	35%	8%	14%
Interpretation	3%	0%	58%	32.5%	91%	79%

Crafting Reader/Writer Response at an Interpretative Level

Not surprisingly, the students engaged in very little interpretation of text (see Table 2) at the beginning of *The Miraculous Journey of Edward Tulane*. While the level of interpretation grew to 58% at the end of *The Miraculous Journey of Edward Tulane* the level of interpretation in *The Boy in the Striped Pajamas* increased as the students became more confident in expressing opinions and interpretations and critiquing the author's craft within a community of readers and writers.

The following sections explore aspects related to interpretative reader responses (as defined in Table 1) in relation to (a) making intertextual links and connections; (b) critiquing literary elements, including those related to author's craft; and (c) authoring the text or the writer in the reader.

Making Intertextual Links and Connections

The students authored threads and responses which suggested that they made intertextual links and connections to themselves, the media, and the world around them. In crafting responses they also created community and social connectedness and drew parallels between each other's lives at a personal level and in cultural, educational, religious and social contexts. The example below illustrates the initial post addressing chapters 1-5 in *The Boy in the Striped Pajamas,* in which students in Dublin made intertextual links between the characters of Edward and Bruno in the two e-books. Additionally, they made connections to themselves and their world knowledge at age twelve (they had studied the second world war) which they acknowledged is very different from that of Bruno, (a "vulnerable nine year old" who "didn't understand what heil hitler meant"). Interestingly, the students in Dublin engaged in subtle community building where they ascertained the prior knowledge of students in Kansas vis-à-vis this period in history ("did they know who the fury [führer] was? and what was outside the house?").

The book was very well written especially the ends of the chapters… it made us want to read on. This book is very different from Edward Tulane although we were making connections between the two because both Edward and Bruno had to move away from their homes. The story is told through the eyes of a nine year old boy, he is very vulnerable because he didn't understand what heil hitler meant. We could make connections with the book from our lives because Bruno and Gretel sometimes fight but sometimes get on well. We thought that his father treated him like an adult because he shakes his hand instead of giving him a hug and because his office was out of bounds with no exceptions. We've done projects and research on the history of the second world war so we know a lot about that time. Who do you think the Fury is? Do you know what's outside the house?

Critiquing Literary Elements, Including Those Related to Author's Craft

It was clear from the numbers of digital thinkmarks created and responses posted on the asynchronous message board that the students had a number of critical points to make regarding literary elements in the text. They critiqued the author's craft and technique with regard to the ending of *The Miraculous Journey of Edward Tulane*. Elizabeth stated:

The author left us hanging just a little …the story didn't seem done…They need a sequel because there is a lot of things we still need to figure out I wonder if it was like that doter sues [Doctor Seuss] book that he never finished before he died.

Jane commented on the author's use of flashbacks in *The Boy in the Striped Pajamas* noting:

it was strange how the author chose to write the book because most of the chapters were flashbacks, the Fury coming to dinner, the fight between grandmother and father at Christmas. I don't want to criticise the author but I don't think it was a good way to write a book"

In general, they approved of the literary decisions made by the authors ("The chapters were described really well and I think that the author put loads of thought into the chapters. I love the way they described Bryce's eyes. 'brown with flecks of gold shining in them." Finally, they often became emotionally involved in the stories ("oh my god!! It's Abilene and she never stopped loving Edward!! She wore his pocket watch around her neck!! This made me really happy!!...This was by far one of the best books I have ever read").

Authoring the Text or the Writer in the Reader

Analysis suggested that while the students made intertextual links and connections and commented on the author's craft, they were also identifying with the author and reading like a writer (Smith, 1988) to become what could be termed co-collaborators with the author in writing the text. For example, the students in Kansas commented on the author's use of a coda in the *The Miraculous Journey of Edward Tulane*:

At the end of the book, did you guys read the coda. We were curious what it meant so we looked it up. It means the end or the summary of a book and it comes from the Latin word tail. What genre would you consider this book? I think it's fantsy but i am not sure. I think it's fantasy because it is a rabitt that is halfway alive. I'm not sure, but i'm curious what you guys think.

Again, this elicited comments from the students on the inclusion of a coda. If John ever "made" a book he would definitely have a coda. Niall "really enjoyed the coda!!!:)." He observed, "I think that every book should have a coda. I liked how it was like the whole book on a page and a bit!!"

Further, in discussing big ideas from *The Miraculous Journey of Edward Tulane*, both Elizabeth and John agreed that the book needed a sequel because "there is a lot of things we still need to figure out." Grace would have been "really mad if Edward and Abilene had not been reunited. Hanna wanted to "jump inside the book" as she explained in a post:

Hello! It's Hanna here!! Overall, I really enjoyed the book!! It really showed me a true meaning of friendship and seperation [separation]. He was owned by so many people, but then got sperated [separated] from them. When he said he wasn't going to love anymore so he wouldn't get hurt, I just wanted to jump inside the book and tell him to never give up!! What do you think the meaning of the book is?? If I was the author, I wouldn't know whether to make Edward go back to Abilene. Yes, it is a good ending, but when Neal cracked his head, I probably would've made him go to heaven and stay with Sarah Ruth. If you were the author, who would you make Edward stay with?

As students co-constructed responses to text it was clear that engaging in a community of readers and writers allowed them to act on textual possibilities with others (Hancock, 2008). Interacting in a malleable digitized reading environment blurred the lines between reader and writer, enhanced reader engagement, and deepened reader/writer response.

DISCUSSION AND IMPLICATIONS

Reinking (2008) reasoned, "online reading and writing, even more than their printed forms can never be understood entirely as simply literacy events. Instead they instantiate literacy practices because they are more overtly and consistently social acts" (p. 1178). Evidence from the study presented in this chapter suggests that digital texts by their nature tend to cultivate interactivity with text and a blurring of lines between reader and writer. Students in the study made sense of text through multimodal dialogue to co-construct meaning while building a community of readers and writers. Literacy as a social practice contributed to the construction of social identities (Alvermann et al., 2012) as students constructed an affinity space (Gee, 2004) which promoted agency (Cope & Kalantzis, 2010) and equality among members of an online participatory culture (Jenkins, 2006).

Results from the study suggest that peer-to-peer collaboration enabled the development of both generative and reflective processes (Daiute & Dalton, 1993). Collaboration among peers facilitated multiple transactions with the text and the co-construction of response. Such collaboration expanded individual response as students reflected on, examined, contested and evaluated their ideas with those of others within the global literature circle. Crafting response on an asynchronous message board provided both an archive for the students where they could revisit and reflect on response and also a powerful thinking tool for the students. While working both collaboratively and individually in response to the literature, students established a community of inquiry in which their questions, prompts, and personal commentary elicited divergent responses inspired by diverse and multiple perspectives (Dwyer, 2010; Larson, 2009). The Internet has truly "collapsed time and space" (Fridell & Lovelace, 2008, p. 179). Virtual literature discussion circles promote active engagement (Huang, 2006), provide authentic audiences (Boling, Castek, Zawilinski, Barton & Nierlich, 2008), deepen engagement with texts (Bowers-Campbell, 2011) and promote a socially constructed and collaborative learning environment (Dwyer, 2010; Larson 2009). The study presents a vision onto new possibilities of grand conversations, across time, space and cultures, in global communities of readers and writers as students exchange responses to literature.

While Birkerts (1994) argued that the level of personal reflection and engagement is not maintained in a digital environment; others (Agosto, 2002; Kuiper & Volman, 2008) pointed to the largely minimalist and consumerist nature of

students' learning in such environments. When moving from page to screen it is important that what we value most in terms of reader/writer response survives the transition (Reinking, 2009). Evidence from this study suggests that digitized text enhanced rather than negated a reflective reader/writer response as the students engaged in close reading, personal interpretation, critical thinking, and deep response to text through immersion in, involvement with and interpretation of text within a community of readers and writers. Digitized text not only afforded an enhanced reading experience, through the presence of scaffolds and supports, but also provided a malleable reading environment where students could annotate the text through digital thinkmarks and highlights to capture fleeting thoughts and responses. The asynchronous message board also provided an archival space where students could thoughtfully, through written discourse, create dialogue and response (Grisham & Wolsey, 2006). Recently, Karchmer-Klein and Shinas (2012) addressed the potential fear of new literacies replacing or hindering traditional literacies; they suggested that teachers "must set aside those concerns and replace them with knowledge that, when taught well, new literacies can support and extend students' abilities to read and write for real purposes" (p. 293). The asynchronous format provided students equitable opportunities to share their thought and voice their opinion about the readings. In a traditional literature circle, some students - particularly those who are shy, linguistically diverse, or struggle as readers - may hesitate to share their thoughts in group settings (Larson, 2009). While all participants in the study were proficient readers and strong communicators, they too benefited from the extra thinking time provided by the asynchronous format to formulate and post responses. As e-books, along with opportunities to respond to literature through ICTs, become increasingly common in today's classrooms, it is crucial that researchers and educators alike consider the affordances of such technologies. However, existing research is rather limited, focusing on feasibility and efficacy in controlled contexts or small cases (Biancarosa & Griffiths, 2012). Undoubtedly, future research will benefit from larger, longitudinal studies, as well as research with specific focus on how English Language Learners, struggling readers, or students with special needs can benefit from using e-book features including built-in dictionaries, text-to-speech functions, and options for customizing a wide range of text features.

Furthermore, this study suggested a blurring of the lines between readers and writers, consumers and creators, and authors and audiences as students co-constructed response to text. The participants added digital thinkmarks to their books in support of their reading comprehension. Reflective of comprehension strategies commonly taught in classrooms, most digital thinkmarks started out at the immersion level with students making predictions, restating main ideas, and asking questions. Over time, the digital thinkmarks evolved into a deeper involvement with and interpretation of the text, often progressing into posts on the online message board conversations.

It is commonly known that students, when provided opportunities to discuss language in books, learn to notice what writers do; they come to understand that authors constantly make deliberate choices as they compose and they draw upon this knowledge in their own writing and their own evaluation of and appreciation for texts (Galda, 2010). As exemplified by Hanna who wished to "jump inside the book," the students in this study expressed a strong desire to manipulate the story outcome and offer suggestions to the author. Smith (1983) explained that true engagement takes place when readers read like a writer, anticipating what the author will say; the author becoming an unsuspecting partner in helping children respond to what they have read and express themselves in writing. Hence, teachers have the critical responsibility to offer relevant reading materials and provide opportunities for students to engage as writers. Today's technologies provide

further options for interacting with, responding to, and composing texts. As the students read the assigned literature on digital reading devices, they were able to add annotations and interact with the digital text in multiple ways. The online message board offered a forum for an authentic audience of peers. As students posted literature responses, they quickly became accustomed to frequent and collaborative peer feedback (Corrigan, 2010). This study supports Hancock's (2008) claim that "the exchange of reader response to literature between related groups of readers is no longer confined by distance or contexts" (p. 108). The aesthetic and cognitive domains of reader response to commonly read literature promise interactions and experiences through ICTs that share and expand personal perspectives on response to books.

Research in technology as a mode of reader/writer response is still in its infancy. Exploring how students of all reading capabilities and backgrounds respond to various forms of digital texts; utilize blogs, message boards, or social media to discuss or respond to literature; and access online resources to extend and enhance reading experiences are just a few research possibilities for the future. Even as the context of Rosenblatt's transactional theory is preserved, technology itself can offer fresh insights into the responses that occur through digital reading, writing, and communications about literature (Hancock, 2008).

As today's students encounter a plethora of new literacies in addition to the traditional literacies associated with paper, pencil, and print texts (IRA, 2009), it is important to keep clear literacy goals and outcomes in mind. Rather than something to be fitted into an already crowded literacy curriculum, technology should be conceptualized as affording tools that support teachers in empowering all students to become engaged and capable readers, writers, and communicators in a global society (Dwyer, 2012). As epitomized in this study, technology can support students' deep engagement with literature as they establish communities of readers and writers across time, space, and culture. In accommodating (Reinking, Labbo & Mc Kenna, 2000) technology tools, researchers and educators should shift the focus from the technology tools themselves towards the technological, pedagogical, content knowledge (Mishra & Koehler, 2006) necessary to construct a curriculum to enhance literacy development and deepen engagement with text; thereby enriching student learning.

REFERENCES

Agosto, D. E. (2002). Bounded rationality and satisficing in young people's web-based decision-making. *Journal of the American Society for Information Science and Technology*, *53*, 16–27. doi:10.1002/asi.10024.

Alvermann, D. E. (2009). Sociocultural construction of adolescent and young people's literacies. In Christenbury, L., Bomer, R., & Smagorinsky, P. (Eds.), *Handbook of adolescent literacy research* (pp. 14–28). New York: The Guildford Press.

Alvermann, D. E., Marshall, J. D., McLean, C. A., Huddleston, A. P., Joaquin, J., & Bishop, J. (2012). Adolescents' web-based literacies, identity construction, and skill development. *Literacy Research and Instruction*, *51*(3), 179–195. doi:10.1080/19388071.2010.523135.

Azmitia, M. (1988). Peer interaction and problem solving: When are two heads better than one? *Child Development*, *59*(1), 87–96. doi:10.2307/1130391.

Barron, B. (2000). Achieving coordination in collaborative problem-solving groups. *Journal of the Learning Sciences*, *9*(4), 403–426. doi:10.1207/S15327809JLS0904_2.

Beach, R. (2012). Digital literacies: Constructing digital learning commons in the literacy classroom. *Journal of Adolescent & Adult Literacy*, *55*(5), 448–451. doi:10.1002/JAAL.00054.

Biancarosa, G., & Griffiths, G. G. (2012). Technology tools to support reading in the digital age. *The Future of Children*, *22*(2), 139–160. doi:10.1353/foc.2012.0014 PMID:23057135.

Birkerts, S. (1994). *The Gutenberg elegies: The fate of reading in an electronic age*. Boston: Faber & Faber.

Bogdan, R., & Biklen, S. (1992). *Qualitative research for education: An introduction to theories and methods* (2nd ed.). Boston: Allyn and Bacon.

Boling, E., Castek, J., Zawilinski, L., Barton, K., & Nierlich, T. (2008). Collaborative literacy: Blogs and Internet projects. *The Reading Teacher*, *61*(6), 504–506. doi:10.1598/RT.61.6.10.

Booth, D. (2006). *Reading doesn't matter anymore: Shattering the myths of literacy*. Portland, ME: Stenhouse.

Bowers-Campbell, J. (2011). Take it out of class: Exploring virtual literature circles. *Journal of Adolescent & Adult Literacy*, *54*(8), 557–567. doi:10.1598/JAAL.54.8.1.

Boyne, J. (2006). *The boy in the striped pajamas*. London: David Fickling Books.

Bruner, J. (1986). *Actual minds, possible worlds*. Cambridge, MA: Harvard University Press.

Carico, K. M., Logan, D., & Labbo, L. D. (2004). A generation in cyberspace: Engaging readers through online discussions. *Language Arts*, *81*(4), 293–302.

Castek, J. (2008). *How do 4th and 5th grade students acquire the new literacies of online reading comprehension? Exploring the contexts that facilitate learning*. (Unpublished doctoral dissertation). University of Connecticut, New Haven, CT.

Coiro, J., Knobel, M., Lankshear, C., & Leu, D. J. (2008). Central issues in new literacies and new literacies research. In Coiro, J., Knobel, M., Lankshear, C., & Leu, D. J. (Eds.), *Handbook of research on new literacies* (pp. 1–21). Mahwah, NJ: Lawrence Erlbaum Associates.

Cope, B., & Kalantzis, M. (2000). *Multiliteracies*. London, UK: Routledge.

Cope, B., & Kalantzis, M. (2010). New media, new learning. In Cole, D. R., & Pulllen, D. L. (Eds.), *Multiliteracies in motion: Current theory and practice*. New York, NY: Routledge.

Corrigan, J. (2010). Improving writing with wiki discussion forums. *Principal Leadership, 11*(3), 44–47.

Creswell, J. (2003). *Research design: Qualitative, quantitative, and mixed methods approaches* (2nd ed.). New York: Sage Publications.

Daiute, C., & Dalton, B. (1993). Collaboration between children learning to write: Can novices be masters? *Cognition and Instruction, 10*(4), 281–333. doi:10.1207/s1532690xci1004_1.

Dalton, B., & Proctor, C. P. (2008). The changing landscape of text and comprehension in the age of the new literacies. In Coiro, J., Knobel, M., Lankshear, C., & Leu, D. J. (Eds.), *Handbook of research on new literacies* (pp. 297–324). Mahwah, NJ: Lawrence Erlbaum Associates.

Daniels, H. (2002). *Literature circles: Voice and choice in book clubs and reading groups* (2nd ed.). Portland, ME: Stenhouse.

DiCamillo, K. (2006). *The miraculous journey of Edward Tulane*. Somerville, MA: Candlewick Press.

Dwyer, B. (2010). *Scaffolding internet reading: A study of a disadvantaged school community in Ireland.* (Unpublished doctoral dissertation). University of Nottingham, Nottingham, UK.

Dwyer, B. (2012). *Reading today: Election statement for the international reading association board of directors*. Retrieved February 20, 2013 from http://www.reading.org/General/Publications/blog/BlogSinglePost/reading-today-online/2012/11/19/candidates-for-the-2013-ira-board-election

Dwyer, B. (2013). Developing online reading comprehension: Changes, challenges and consequences. In Hall, K., Cremin, T., Comber, B., & Moll, L. (Eds.), *International handbook of research in children's literacy, learning and culture*. London: Wiley-Blackwell. doi:10.1002/9781118323342.ch25.

Evans, E., & Po, J. (2006). A break in the transition: Examining students' responses to digital texts. *Computers and Composition, 24*, 56–73. doi:10.1016/j.compcom.2006.12.003.

Fridell, M., & Lovelace, T. (2008). Creating a digital world: Five steps to engage students in multicultural learning. *The International Journal of Learning, 15*(3), 179–183.

Friedman, T. L. (2005). *The world is flat: The globalised world in the twenty-first century*. London, UK: Penguin.

Galda, L. (2010). First thing first: Why good books and time to respond to them matter. *New England Reading Association Journal, 46*(1), 1–7.

Gee, J. P. (2003). *What video games have to teach us about learning and literacy*. New York: Palgrave MacMillan. doi:10.1145/950566.950595.

Gee, J. P. (2004). *Situated language and learning: A critique of traditional schooling*. London: Routledge.

Gee, J. P. (2008). *Social linguistics and literacies: Ideology in discourses* (3rd ed.). New York, NY: Routledge.

Glaser, B. G., & Strauss, A. L. (1967). *Discovery of grounded theory: Strategies for qualitative research*. Chicago: Aldine.

Grisham, D. L., & Wolsey, T. D. (2006). Recentering the middle school classroom as a vibrant learning community: Students, literacy, and technology intersect. *Journal of Adolescent & Adult Literacy, 49*(8), 648–660. doi:10.1598/JAAL.49.8.2.

Gutierrez, K., & Stone, L. D. (2000). Synchronic and diachronic dimensions of social practice: An emerging methodology for cultural-historical perspectives on literacy learning. In Lee, C. D., & Smagorinsky, P. (Eds.), *Vygotskian perspectives on literacy research: Constructing meaning through collaborative inquiry* (pp. 150–164). New York: Cambridge University Press.

Hall, T., Strangman, N., & Meyer, A. (2003). *Differentiated instruction and implications for UDL implementation*. Wakefield, MA: National Center on Accessing the General Curriculum. Retrieved August 7th 2012 from http://aim.cast. org/learn/historyarchive/backgroundpapers/differentiated_instruction_udl

Hancock, M. R. (1993). Exploring the making-making process though the content of literature response journals. *Research in the Teaching of English, 27*(4), 335–368.

Hancock, M. R. (2008). The status of reader response research: Sustaining the reader's voice in challenging times. In Lehr, S. (Ed.), *Shattering the looking glass: Challenge, risk, and controversy in children's literature* (pp. 97–116). Norwood, MA: Christopher-Gordon.

Harrison, C. (2008). Researching technology and literacy: Thirteen ways of looking at a blackboard. In Coiro, J., Knobel, M., Lankshear, C., & Leu, D. J. (Eds.), *Handbook of research on new literacies* (pp. 1283–1293). Mahwah, NJ: Lawrence Erlbaum Associates.

Huang, H.-J. (2006). Promoting multicultural awareness through electronic communication. *International Electronic Journal for Leadership in Learning, 10*(7).

Hull, G. A., & Stornaiuolo, A. (2010). Literate arts in a global world: Reframing social networking as cosmopolitan practice. *Journal of Adolescent & Adult Literacy, 54*(2), 85–97. doi:10.1598/JAAL.54.2.1.

International Reading Association (IRA). (2009). *New literacies and 21st century technologies: A position statement*. Newark, DE: IRA. Retrieved February, 1, 2010 from www.reading.org/General/AboutIRA/PositionStatements/21stCenturyLiteracies.aspx

Jenkins, H. (2006). *Confronting the challenges of participatory culture: Media education for the 21st century*. White paper for the Mac Arthur Foundation. Retrieved September, 1, 2011 from www.digitallearningmacfound.org

Johnson, R. B., & Onwuegbuzie, A. J. (2004). Mixed methods research: A research paradigm whose time has come. *Educational Researcher, 33*(7), 14–26. doi:10.3102/0013189X033007014.

Karchmer-Klein, R., & Shinas, V. H. (2012). Guiding principles for supporting new literacies in your classroom. *The Reading Teacher, 65*(5), 288–293. doi:10.1002/TRTR.01044.

Karolides, N. J. (Ed.). (2000). *Reader response in secondary and college classrooms*. Mahwah, NJ: Lawrence Erlbaum Associates.

Kozlowski, S., & Hattrup, K. (1992). A disagreement about within-group agreement: Disentangling issues of consistency vs consensus. *The Journal of Applied Psychology, 77*(2), 161–167. doi:10.1037/0021-9010.77.2.161.

Kress, G. (2003). *Literacy in the new media age*. London: Routledge. doi:10.4324/9780203164754.

Kucan, L., & Beck, I. L. (1997). Thinking aloud and reading comprehension research: Inquiry, instruction and social interaction. *Review of Educational Research, 67*(3), 271–279. doi:10.3102/00346543067003271.

Kucer, S. B. (2005). *Dimensions of literacy: A conceptual base for teaching reading and writing in school settings* (2nd ed.). Mahwah, NJ: Lawrence Erlbaum.

Kuiper, E., & Volman, M. (2008). The web as a source of information for K-12 education. In Coiro, J., Knobel, M., Lankshear, C., & Leu, D. J. (Eds.), *Handbook of research on new literacies* (pp. 267–296). Mahwah, NJ: Erlbaum.

Lankshear, C., & Knobel, M. (2003). *New literacies: Changing knowledge and classroom learning*. Philadelphia, PA: Open University Press.

Larson, L. C. (2009). Reader response meets new literacies: Empowering readers in online learning communities. *The Reading Teacher, 62*(8), 638–648. doi:10.1598/RT.62.8.2.

Larson, L. C. (2010). Digital readers: The next chapter in e-book reading and response. *The Reading Teacher, 64*(1), 15–22. doi:10.1598/RT.64.1.2.

Larson, L. C. (2012). It's time to turn the digital page: Preservice teachers explore e-book reading. *Journal of Adolescent & Adult Literacy, 56*(4), 280–290. doi:10.1002/JAAL.00141.

Leu, D. J. (2000). Literacy and technology: Deictic consequences for literacy education in an information age. In Kamil, M. L., Mosenthal, P. B., Pearson, P. D., & Barr, R. (Eds.), *Handbook of reading research* (pp. 743–770). New York: Erlbaum.

Leu, D. J., Kinzer, C. K., Coiro, J., & Cammack, D. (2004). Towards a theory of new literacies emerging from the internet and other information and communication technologies. In Ruddell, R. B., & Unrau, N. (Eds.), *Theoretical models and processes of reading* (5th ed., pp. 1570–1613). International Reading Association.

Leu, D. J., Kinzer, C. K., Coiro, J., Castek, J., & Henry, L. A. (2013). New literacies and the new literacies of online reading comprehension: A dual level theory. In Unrau, N., & Alvermann, D. (Eds.), *Theoretical models and processes of reading* (6th ed.). Newark, DE: International Reading Association. doi:10.1598/0710.42.

Malloy, J., Castek, J., & Leu, D. J. (2010). Silent reading and online reading comprehension. In Hiebert, E., & Reutzel, R. (Eds.), *Revisiting silent reading* (pp. 221–240). Newark, DE: International Reading Association.

Maples, J. (2010). The digital divide: One middle school teacher attempts to connect with his students in online literature discussions. *The Language and Literacy Spectrum, 20*, 25–39.

McEneaney, J. E. (2006). Agent-based literacy theory. *Reading Research Quarterly, 41*(3), 352–371. doi:10.1598/RRQ.41.3.3.

McWilliams, J., Hickey, D., Hines, M., Conner, J., & Bishop, S. (2011). Using collaborative writing tools for literary analysis: Twitter, fan fiction and the crucible in the secondary English classroom. *Journal of Media Literacy Education, 2*(3), 238–245.

Miles, M. B., & Huberman, A. M. (1994). *Qualitative data analysis: An expanded sourcebook* (2nd ed.). Thousand Oaks, CA: Sage.

Mishra, P., & Koehler, M. J. (2006). Technological pedagogical content knowledge: A new framework for teacher knowledge. *Teachers College Record, 108*(6), 1017–1054. doi:10.1111/j.1467-9620.2006.00684.x.

National Council for Teachers of English (NCTE). (2013). *Context for NCTE's 21ˢᵗ century framework*. Retrieved February, 22,2013 from http://www. ncte.org/positions/statements/21stcentframework

Olsen, N. S. (2011). Coding ATC incident data using HFACS: Inter-coder consensus. *Safety Science*, *49*, 1365–1370. doi:10.1016/j.ssci.2011.05.007.

Pahl, K., & Rowsell, J. (2005). *Literacy and education: Understanding the new literacy studies in the classroom*. London, UK: Paul Chapman Publishing.

Park, J. Y. (2012). Re-imaging reader-response in middle and secondary schools: Early adolescent girls' critical and communal reader responses to the young adult novel *Speak*. *Children's Literature in Education*, *43*, 191–212. doi:10.1007/s10583-012-9164-5.

Patton, M. Q. (2002). *Qualitative research and evaluation methods* (3rd ed.). Thousand Oaks, CA: Sage Publications.

Putney, L. A. G., Green, J., Dixon, C., Durán, C., & Yeager, B. (2000). Consequential progressions: Exploring collective-individual development in a bilingual classroom. In Lee, C. D., & Smagorinsky, P. (Eds.), *Vygotskian perspectives on literacy research: Constructing meaning through collaborative inquiry* (pp. 86–126). New York: Cambridge University Press.

RAND Reading Study Group (RRSG). (2002). *Reading for understanding: Toward a research and development program in reading comprehension*. Pittsburgh, PA: Office of Educational Research and Improvement.

Raphael, T. E., Florio-Ruane, S., George, M., Hasty, N. L., & Highfield, K. (2004). *Book club plus! A literacy framework for the primary grades*. Lawrence, MA: Small Planet Communications.

Reinking, D. (1998). Synthesizing technological transformations of literacy in a post-typographical world. In Reinking, D., McKenna, M. C., Labbo, L. D., & Kieffer, R. D. (Eds.), *Handbook of literacy and technology: Transformations in a post-typographic world* (pp. xi–xxx). Mahwah, NJ: Lawrence Erlbaum.

Reinking, D. (2008). Thoughts on the Lewis and Fabos article on instant messaging. In Coiro, J., Knobel, M., Lankshear, C., & Leu, D. J. (Eds.), *Handbook of research on new literacies* (pp. 1175–1187). Mahwah, NJ: Erlbaum.

Reinking, D. (2009). Valuing reading, writing, and books in a post-typographic world. In Nord, D., & Rubin, J. (Eds.), *The history of the book in American* (pp. 485–502). Cambridge, UK: American Antiquarian Society and Cambridge University Press.

Reinking, D., Labbo, L. D., & McKenna, M. C. (2000). From assimilation to accommodation: A developmental framework for integrating digital technologies into literacy research and instruction. *Journal of Research in Reading*, *23*(2), 110–122. doi:10.1111/1467-9817.00108.

Rideout, V. J., Foehr, U. G., & Roberts, D. F. (2010). *Generation M2: Media in the lives of 8- to 18-year olds*. Menlo. Park, CA: Henry J. Kaiser Family Foundation.

Rosenblatt, L. M. (1938). *Literature as exploration*. New York: Appleton-Century-Croft.

Rosenblatt, L. M. (1978). *The reader, the text, the poem: The transactional theory of the literary work*. Carbondale, IL: Southern Illinois University Press.

Rosenblatt, L. M. (1978). *The reader, the text, the poem: The transactional theory of the literary work*. Carbondale, IL: Southern Illinois University Press.

Rosenblatt, L. M. (2005). *Making meaning with texts: Selected essays*. Portsmouth, NH: Heinemann.

Smith, F. (1983). Reading like a writer. *Language Arts, 60*, 558–567.

Smith, F. (1988). *Joining the literacy club: Further essays into education*. Portsmouth, NH: Heinemann.

Stake, R. (1995). *The art of case study research*. London: Sage Publication.

Street, B. (1998). New literacies in theory and practice: What are the implications for language in education? *Linguistics and Education, 10*(1), 1–24. doi:10.1016/S0898-5898(99)80103-X.

The New London Group. (2000). A pedagogy of multiliteracies designing social futures. In Cope, B., & Kalantzis, M. (Eds.), *Multiliteracies: Literacy learning and the design of social futures* (pp. 9–37). London: Routledge.

Vygotsky, L. S. (1978). *Mind in society: The development of higher psychological processes*. Cambridge, MA: Harvard University Press.

Wolsey, T. D., & Grisham, D. L. (2012). *Transforming writing instruction in the digital age: Techniques for grades 5-12*. New York: The Guilford Press.

Yin, R. K. (2009). *Case study research: Design and methods* (4th ed.). Thousand Oaks, CA: Sage.

Chapter 13

"Write Me Back!"
Diasporic Identities and Digital Media: Creating New Spaces for Writing in School

Michelle A. Honeyford
University of Manitoba, Canada

ABSTRACT

This chapter addresses the disconnect between in- and out-of-school writing spaces. Drawing from a larger study of the writing of bilingual Latino immigrant youth in a middle school English language class, the author examines the epistolary community created through an exchange of emails with a group of first-generation Latino university students. The author draws on an ecologies of writing framework to explore writing and place-based identities and the notion of writing across digital and cultural communities in order to analyze the relational, locational, and collective work the students were engaged in. The chapter suggests implications for creating new spaces for writing in school, drawing on social and digital media to participate in imaginative and intellectual literacy work.

INTRODUCTION

One of the key distinctions between in-school and out-of-school writing is the role of an authentic audience. No matter how interesting the assignment or valid the purpose for writing it, if the teacher is the only audience, its power is limited. Aware of the critical role of audience, writing educators have long argued for the need to situate school writing in authentic contexts, positioning students as authors of petitions, newsletters, or editorials, as published poets, picture book authors, short story writers, and essayists (Atwell, 1998; Christensen, 2009; Bomer & Bomer, 2001). Such opportunities

also contribute to students' developing identities as writers—and as citizens, activists, and artists.

The disconnect between writing in and out of school seems to be growing only wider, particularly for young adolescents. With their increasing access to digital and social media, youth are writing more than ever (Lenhart, Arafeh, Smith & Macgill, 2008; NCTE, 2009). Though much of this writing is in abbreviated forms (e.g., texts, tweets, updates, comments, in-app or in-game messaging) and is produced in semiotic modes that look substantively different from standard forms of language, youths are increasingly engaged in written interactions with others. And, whether they are "hanging out," "geeking out," or "messing around" (Ito, Baumer, Bittani, boyd, Coy, Herr-Stephenson, et al., 2009), their writing reflects the kinds of everyday social

DOI: 10.4018/978-1-4666-4341-3.ch013

practices that Barton & Hamilton (1998) and others (Street, 1984; Gee, 1996) have argued are literacy: forms of writing (and reading) that are deeply embedded in sociocultural contexts, used for authentic purposes, and connected to their identities. In school, however, youths' opportunities to write are primarily individual, inauthentic, and assessment-oriented. For example, Ife (2012, p. 64-65) found that her middle school students believed that real writing only occupied spaces outside the classroom and that class assignments were merely opportunities to earn a grade. More importantly, they defined the dramatic contrast between writing in school (responding to literature, essay prompts, and answering questions at the end of a reading selection) versus writing at home (texting, updating social network sites, blogging, and maintaining personal poetry or rap books).

The contrast Ife's students experienced is of particular importance when we consider the school experiences of immigrant youth learning English as an additional language. The kinds of writing Ife's students practiced at home (e.g., texting, updating, blogging, writing poetry or rap) are deeply connected to their social and cultural identities, occur in spaces that are inclusive of transcultural and even global participants, and offer youths a sense of connection and belonging in communities that share their interests. For youth who are often marginalized by their linguistic and cultural differences in school, these kinds of spaces are potentially transformative. While recent research has pointed to the efficacy of such third spaces in afterschool media and literacy programs for young adolescents (Hull & Schultz, 2001; Kafai, Peppler, & Chapman, 2009), there are far fewer examples in school spaces, and fewer yet that focus on immigrant and bilingual youth. In their meta-analysis of research on writing, Juzwik et al. (2006) found that although research "on bilingual and multilingual writing is the second most active area of research,…little…is occurring at P-12 levels—crucial years for language acquisition, literacy development, and identity

formation. Especially scarce are studies…at the middle school level" (p. 467).

This chapter focuses on a study of the writing of bilingual Latino immigrant youth in a middle school English as a New Language class. Mediated by technology (email), the students in this class located an authentic audience for their writing in a group of first-generation Latino/a university students. In this chapter, I draw on a cultural ecologies model of writing to explore the written exchanges of one pair of students. A cultural ecologies approach understands how students' writing is situated in their local contexts, as well as the more global ecologies of which students are a part (Pahl, 2012). Through an analysis of their emails, I examine how the students' writing references their relationships to the environments around them but also affords them the opportunity to make connections with one another across those contexts. Based on the study, I argue that to be relevant in the 21st Century, school-based writing pedagogies need to acknowledge students' connectedness to the cultural ecologies in which they are located, but even more importantly, to engage them in meaningful writing across them. I suggest that this can be facilitated, at least in part, by creating digital communities that connect immigrant youth to others in order to recognize, draw on, and extend their personal and collective knowledge and experiences in potentially transformative ways.

THEORETICAL FRAMEWORK

The research discussed in this chapter is more broadly framed by sociocultural theories of literacy, research in New Literacy Studies (NLS), and youths' out-of-school practices with digital media and writing. Within this conceptual framework, literacy is understood as socially and culturally mediated sets of practices that people use in the contexts of their everyday lives to communicate with one another and participate in the world (Gee,

1999; Street, 1984; Barton, Hamilton, & Ivanic, 2000). There are then multiple literacies, and our ability to read and write effectively requires us to be able to understand and use the discourses privileged by specific groups within particular contexts (Gee, 1996; New London Group, 1996). Thus, reading and writing are viewed not as sets of autonomous skills to be acquired, but as ideological practices that are connected to our subjectivities and implicated in complex systems of power (Street, 1984; Lewis, Enciso & Moje, 2007; Blackburn & Clark, 2007; Janks, 2010). Research in digital media and writing has highlighted the practices by which youth, in particular, are actively engaging with digital media to connect with one another, access and produce knowledge, play and create, and participate in affinity spaces (Lenhart, Arafeh, Smith & Macgill, 2008; Ito, Baumer, Bittani, boyd, Coy, Herr-Stephenson, et al., 2009; Gee & Hayes, 2011). For this chapter, I draw more specifically on research and theory related to a cultural ecologies approach to writing, exploring the implications of such an approach for conceptualizing digitally mediated forms of writing; notions of space, place, and community; and cultural identity.

An Ecologies of Writing Framework

From an ecologies of writing perspective, writing is contextualized in the local spaces and places in which it occurs (Pahl, 2012), but writing also signals the connections of writers to the larger ecologies of which they are a part. For "just as students' cultures and contexts are not limited to the physical space and context of the classroom, their engagement with texts and writing extend to the diverse contexts and communities they inhabit outside of the classroom" (McLean, 2012, p. 231). The contribution of an ecologies of writing framework is an understanding of the simultaneity of experience of diasporic writers (Honeyford, 2013b), the recognition that transcultural writers may experience a social location that spans

multiple contexts and communities. As McLean (2012) theorizes, the writing of immigrant students bridges "*H/home*: the home (place of residence and local and virtual communities in which they participate), Home (cultural practices of native country and region) and host environments.... the concept of *H/home* bring[s] together [the] transnational social worlds and D/discourses... these young persons navigate" (p. 231).

As a model for writing, a cultural ecologies framework conceptualizes how writing connects social interactions with the local and global environments in which they occur (Kells, 2007). Writing instruction then, should seek to facilitate students' critical responses to the multiple semiotic systems they encounter in the environments that circulate through the spaces of their lives. In practice, a cultural ecology model "challenges writers to recognize that every rhetorical situation represents complex social configurations and interdependent relations" in order to make more visible the "interdependence and interrelationships integral to community development and survival" (Kells, 2007, p. 98, 97). Writing is thus understood as a complex social practice that writers engage in with others in authentic contexts, an activity that demands writers recognize specific semiotic systems and how they work, and use them appropriately. In any such contexts—digitally mediated or not—writers have the potential to use writing to affect the larger ecology around them; writing has transformative power as well as real ecological consequences.

Writing and Place-Based Identities

Within a writing ecologies framework, writing is recognized as a process and product that is both connected to specific contexts and able to navigate across them. Writers are located in place, but "place-identity can operate on a variety of socio-spatial scales, from the home, to the neighborhood and beyond to the nation" (Benwell & Stokoe, 2006, p. 212). The socio-spatial scales are further expanded in online environments, where place-identities may reference membership and activity in particular spaces, mark movement across digital spaces, or be effectively relegated to the background or even hidden in order to foreground other aspects of identity. The notion of boundaries is thus particularly salient, as "boundaries function as symbolic resources in identity construction" (Benwell & Stokoe, p. 212). Boundaries are often socially constructed, separating people, but also serving as "the mediators of contact between them" (Benwell & Stokoe, p. 212). Boundaries may also be collectively negotiated, in both digital and non-digital environments, as groups define who belongs and what it means to be a member.

The discursive construction of place-identities recognizes the role of writing, and literacy and language more generally, as modes through which the "everyday experiences of self-in-place form and mutate" (Dixon & Durrheim, 2000, p. 32). Further, "it is through language that places themselves are imaginatively constituted in ways that carry implications for 'who we are' (or 'who we claim to be')" (Dixon & Durrheim, 2000, p. 32). Through written (and often multimodal) interactions with others, new places and spaces may be created (literally or figuratively) and thus new ways of defining ourselves made possible. From their literacy practices, we can better understand how youth shape identities that are both defined by the boundaries around them and also "deterritorialized [in] online spaces that offer multiple points of social and cultural contact with individuals from diverse backgrounds" (Black, 2009, p. 398).

Writing Across Digital and Cultural Communities

It is important for this study to understand how an ecologies of writing framework conceptualizes the ways technology mediates writers' access to and interactions with others. Although physically situated in one local place/space, digital and social media make it possible for youth to navigate the larger ecologies in which they are a part. The "attention to broader contexts and dispersed locations across geographical sites necessitates new ways of understanding the spatial dimension of literacy" (Eva Lam & Warriner, 2012, p. 192).

In practice, a writing ecologies approach suggests that schools acknowledge the alternative discourse practices and funds of knowledge (González, Moll, & Amanti, 2005) or "learning incomes" (Guerra, 2008) of culturally diverse students. Building on Kells' (2007) cultural ecology model of writing, Guerra (2008) argues that rather than "writing across the curriculum," new models of writing instruction should emphasize "writing across communities," an ideological and pedagogical shift that positions students "as citizens of multiple spheres" (Kells, 2007, p. 97) or, as Haitian author Edwidge Danticat (2010) suggests, as diaspora "with their feet planted in both worlds" (p. 51).

Such a shift reflects more accurately the ways in which transnational youth use "oral, written, and visual practices with texts…to reach across time and space, to create and sustain social connections, and to facilitate participation in communities of learning" (Eva Lam & Warriner, 2012, p. 203). It also necessitates that educators recognize writing as "a dialogic process…fraught with the tensions of negotiating…not only the push and pull of public and private positioning but also of local-global, native and adopted cultures" (McLean, 2012, p. 232). Simultaneously, an ecological approach to writing would remind "us all of the extent to which communication cuts across the natural and human world in which we live, and especially of its tendency to migrate and to be carried by us from one physical, social, or cultural context to another" (Guerra, 2008, p. 298).

This is critical to realizing the full inclusion of immigrant youth in authentic authoring spaces, which are made all the more possible through digital and social media. Far too often, the transnational identities of immigrant youth "can affect [their] interaction in the world, and limit the kinds of places [they] can connect with" (Benwell & Stokoe, 2006, p. 214). As researchers focus more attention on how transnational youth "interact with literacy learning in educational settings, and how institutional structures of schooling position youths' transnational experiences and affect their literacy learning and educational opportunities" (Eva Lam & Warriner, 2012, p. 201), there is also a greater possibility for change.

METHODOLOGY

Context, Participants, and Researcher's Role

My six-month study of the literacy activities of a middle school English as a New Language (ENL) class in the U.S. Midwest included *Making Connections*, a collaborative partnership established with a university Latino student organization. I had initially selected the classroom for my research because of the teacher's commitment to creating spaces alongside the official curriculum for students to engage in authentic issues that drew on their linguistic and cultural repertoires of knowledge while they learned new ones. I had begun my research at the school several years earlier, when it received federal funds for a one-to-one laptop program. The ENL teacher, Beth[1], regularly integrated technology into the official curriculum and also into the "second" spaces of the classroom (Campano, 2007) as she supported students in creating multimodal products to share their work with the school and community (Honeyford, 2013a).

At the time of collecting data for this part of the study, I had been a researcher in the classroom for a couple months. Students knew me as someone affiliated with the university who had an interest in language, literacy, and immigrant youth. My role in the classroom was of participant-observer; I observed, took notes, and audio- and video-taped classroom activities, but I also regularly helped students with homework and interacted with them. Beth had readily agreed to "host" me as a researcher in her classroom, and in turn, I had honored her request to support her pedagogically in exploring ways to extend opportunities for reading and writing. This included the first novel study for the ENL class, *The House on Mango Street* (Cisneros, 1984); reading and writing poetry about immigration, culture, and identity; exploring the representation of immigrant and transcultural identities in public murals, art, and digital photography; and writing profile essays (Christensen, 2009). Beth and I met weekly to look at student work, reflect, and plan. It was in one of our weekly conversations that Beth related the story of an immigrant student in the school who, in his conversation with the assistant principal (upon being sent to the office by a teacher), questioned why he should "try" in school as he knew that his (undocumented) status would prevent him from ever attending college anyway. We began talking about ways to establish a stronger connection for immigrant youth with the university. The idea for *Making Connections* came from those conversations.

The six students in the Grade 7/8 Advanced ENL class had all been born in Mexico and spoke Spanish as their first language. They had been placed in the Advanced class because of their scores on the state's English proficiency exam and Beth's assessments of their progress the prior year. The goal of *Making Connections* was for the middle school students to "meet" a first-generation Latino/a university student who had also immigrated to the U.S. and learned English as an additional language. Through their correspondence, we hoped the middle school students would make connections with their writing partner, with the idea of attending a college or university, and with the possibility of realizing the futures they barely dared dream about.

Over a 10-week period, the middle school and university students exchanged a series of letters (4-5 each) via email. The middle school students composed their letters on the laptops in class, and then, to adhere to policy, saved them to a shared folder on the school's server where Beth retrieved and sent them via email. The university students emailed Beth directly; Beth then distributed the emails to her students in hard-copy. The study included the six students in the class as well as two of the six university students who participated in *Making Connections*[2]. To explore the connections between the students and, in their writing, to the ecologies around them, this chapter focuses on the emails exchanged between one pair of students, Gabriel, a popular 7th grade student, and Enrique, an advanced undergraduate student.

Data Analysis

In my initial analyses of the emails exchanged during *Making Connections*, I noted that though asynchronous, many of them—particularly the first two emails—strongly reflected the structure inherent in conversations. For instance, the students practiced turn-taking, providing stories, personal details, and answers to the questions posed by their partner. This prompted me to look at turn design: how turns were related to the social actions being conducted through the larger exchange (which I labeled "relational moves") and also how they indexed the identities students were evoking in relationship to those themes and one another ("membership categorization devices") (See Table 1). A method for analyzing identity "based in systematic analyses of social action in everyday settings" (Benwell & Stokoe, 2006, p. 67), membership categorization analysis (MCA) focuses on the ways in which the participants orient themselves in their interactions with others.

My observations were consistent with Stanley's (2004) research of epistolary communities as *dialogical*, *emergent*, and *perspectival*. As I found by tracing both the themes (topics of conversation) and relational moves, extended exchanges between the writers reflected the dialogical structural properties of "turn-taking and reciprocity" (Stanley, 2004, p. 202). In my analysis, I also found that although the university students had been provided with suggestions for their introductory letter, the emergent quality of epistolary communities ensured that by even the second and third exchanges, the letters were "not occasioned, structured, or their content filled by researcher-determined concerns. Instead, they [had] their own preoccupations and conventions and indeed their own epistolary ethics; and these aspects… change[d] according to particular correspondences and their development over time" (Stanley, 2004, p. 203).

The letters also characterized the perspectival nature of epistolary communities, as the dynamic structure and content of the letters reflected the writers' specific location and time: "Letters fascinatingly take on the perspective of the 'moment' as this develops within a letter or sequence of letters, and may utilize a particular 'voice' adopted by the writer or a particular 'tone' rhetorically employed" (Stanley, 2004, pp. 202-203). For instance, I noted how students' greetings and sign offs shifted over time, from formal salutations that signaled the letters as a school literacy activity to informal greetings that reflected their growing familiarity with one another, the more conversational tone of personal emails, and the movement of the activity into a liminal space between home and school.

However, an ecologies of writing perspective goes further, "focusing on the relationships between the data and the much larger world of which they are a part" (Pahl, 2012, p. 212). As Pahl suggests, this process "of untangling meaning" involves following "the 'Ariadne's threads' that [extend] outwards from texts to practices while acknowledging the material reality of the text" (p. 212). Thus, I decided to look more closely at the letters written by Gabriel and Enrique as a case study, exploring the threads woven between their letters and the larger ecologies connected to them.

Table 1. Relational moves

	References*	Sources**	Students				
			G	I	A	J	M
Providing personal details	29	17	8	8	2	7	4
Describing likes/dislikes	19	10	0	6	6	4	3
Expressing desire to meet	13	10	4	1	2	3	3
Asking questions	13	9	6	2	1	1	3
Invoking shared experiences	12	8	5	3	1	2	1
Telling stories	11	10	3	1	4	1	3
Sharing conflicts	8	6	0	2	4	1	1
Following up	8	7	2	1	2	1	2
Expressing desire to exchange more letters	8	8	3	1	0	3	1
Describing other	8	5	3	0	0	3	2
Sharing values	7	6	2	2	1	0	2
Answering questions	7	5	4	0	2	0	1
Sharing pictures	5	5	2	2	1	0	0
Expressing thanks	5	4	1	0	1	2	1
Describing everyday experiences	5	4	0	2	0	1	2
Extending friendship	4	3	0	0	0	1	3
Showing emotion	4	3	0	0	2	0	2
Acknowledging compliment	3	2	2	1	0	0	0
Empathizing	3	2	3	0	0	0	0
Sharing knowledge related to interests	3	2	2	0	0	1	0
Providing explanations	2	2	0	1	0	0	1
Describing personal qualities	1	1	0	0	0	1	0
Demonstrating solidarity	1	1	1	0	0	0	0
Recognizing accomplishments	1	1	1	0	0	0	0
Recognizing unique attributes/differences	1	1	1	0	0	0	0
Relating good wishes	1	1	1	0	0	0	0
Encouraging	1	1	0	0	0	1	0
Total			46	25	27	26	31
Range			19	14	13	16	17

*The distinct number of times that move was used.
**The distinct number of letters in which that move was made.

Case Study: Gabriel and Enrique

The nine emails exchanged between Gabriel and Enrique most clearly illustrated the dialogic and relational nature of this epistolary community.

Gabriel, a 7th grade boy, utilized a greater number and wider range of relational moves than any of his peers, including several that were unique (see the shaded "G" column and rows in Table 1). I looked to Gabriel and Enrique's exchanges to better understand the relationships between their letters and the ecologies around them. How did their interactions reference their relationships to the local and global environments in which they were situated? I also wanted to look more closely at how Gabriel and Enrique discursively constructed their cultural identities through their letters. How did they relate to one another? How did they define their individual and collective identities in relation to the places and systems around them? Finally, I was interested in exploring the epistemological implications around notions of writing across communities. What kinds of inquiries did Gabriel and Enrique make into their experiences? What kinds of knowing were privileged in that work? And what possibilities did they imagine in their writing that might suggest the transformative potential for authentic, digitally mediated writing communities in the classroom?

FINDINGS

Writing Relationally

Enrique's first letter reads like a *testimonio*, relating his traumatic experiences as a Mexican immigrant student in American schools and also his eventual success—the first in his family to earn a college degree.

My name is Enrique, I am [age], and I grew up in Mexico...I was born in a little village in [state], Mexico. I grew up in Mexico until I was 10 years old... My father was always in the United States working and I only got to see him for a few months during the winter. ...Getting enrolled in Middle school was one of my worst experiences. I was very traumatized by the sudden change. I was in culture shock just like the rest of my family...I did not speak English at all and that is what made it so hard. I did terrible academically because I could never pass any exams, I copied all of my homework assignments, and I was made fun off

[sic] by my classmates almost everyday...During middle school I did not even thought [sic] of going to college. I used to laugh every time the teacher asked, "What do you want to be when you grow up and go to college?" College seemed so far and a dream that was out of my reach (Enrique, Letter 1).

After receiving Enrique's letter, Gabriel, a social student who liked to talk and interact with others while he worked, made an unprecedented move: he took the letter and a laptop to an extra desk at the front of the room where he wouldn't be disturbed, and spent the rest of the period (more than 20 minutes) absorbed in writing.

Enrique,

Hey, I am Gabriel [last name]. I am a boy and I am [age]. I come from Mexico. I don't know where in Mexico. I came here when I was a little boy like 6 or 7. I really like it here, but my family and I are leaving in [date]. I don't want to go.

I read your letter that you sent us. I am sorry that happened to you. That happened to me too. Now I understand English a little more, but am still not that good. I am getting there. One day I hope to go to college like [yours] or [a rival]. It had to be really hard for you when you got here but someday maybe you and I can be better than the ones that made fun of you and me. (Gabriel, Letter 1)

Gabriel's letter follows the structural flow of Enrique's letter, echoing the identity categories he shares with Enrique: a native of Mexico, an immigrant, and a student. He expresses empathy and solidarity. Gabriel's letter demonstrates an attentive response to Enrique's narrative; he has listened closely to Enrique's story and responds by sharing bits of his own, following the pattern Enrique set.

Gabriel and Enrique's initial exchanges read much like an extended dialogue. In fact, when I asked Gabriel—as he sat, hunched over the laptop writing his second letter to Enrique—how he was deciding what to write about, he said he was following Enrique's letter and writing back to it. The form of these letters shows their thematically parallel constructions (see Table 2).

Their recursive conversations reveal the ways Gabriel and Enrique interact with one another as they reference their relationships to the local and global environments in which they are situated. Through their memberships and their relational moves, they discursively construct their cultural identities, building a basis for their own friendship and acknowledging the larger social networks they share and/or value (See Table 3).

This example (similar to many others related to friends, swimming, and other topics) reveals the emergent nature of Gabriel and Enrique's writing (Stanley, 2004) as they explore instances of what Erickson (1975) called "situational co-membership," a revelation between speakers (or writers, in this case) that they hold "some attribute of social identity" in common. Of course, *Making Connections* was consciously designed to recruit university students who would share membership in the larger cultural and linguistic groups with which the middle school students identified. Those significant sources of situational co-membership were anticipated and may have contributed to the instances of assumed understanding implicit in Gabriel's—and other students'—writing (as explored next). Nevertheless, a close look at Gabriel and Enrique's letters reveal their writing as relational: organized in structural patterns that attend to their emerging interests, made visible

Table 2. Thematic construction in second exchange of letters

Enrique, Letter 2	Gabriel, Letter 2
Greeting	Greeting
Friends & Family	Family & Friends
Soccer & Swimming	Soccer & Swimming
Gabriel's Careers	Careers
Enrique's career goals	Response to Enrique's goals
Questions regarding Gabriel's 1st letter	Answers to questions posed by Enrique
Closing	Closing
	Attached pictures

Table 3. Soccer dialogue

Writer, Letter #	Text Segment	Membership Categorization Devices	Relational Moves
Gabriel, Letter 1	I like to play soccer, basketball, swimming, and a little football (but not that much). I like soccer more than any other sport....Sometimes I go to the gym and play with my friends and they are good.	Soccer/sports player Friend	Expressing likes/dislikes Sharing details related to interests
Enrique, Letter 2	I have a small brother who just turned [age] in December. You guys are around the same age. My brother and other family members also enjoy soccer and basketball.	Family (brother)	Identifying commonality Talking about family
Gabriel, Letter 2	What's your brothers' name? My whole family likes soccer. I play it at the [community program]. It's where I play the most. My brother and I play for a team that goes and plays with other teams in [the state].	Family (brother) Soccer/sports player	Showing interest (Asking questions) Sharing details related to interests
Enrique, Letter 3	My brother's name is Manuel (pseudonym). My brother and my dad also like soccer. What is your favorite soccer team? What is the name of the team where you and your brother play?	Family (brother)	Identifying commonality Asking questions

in their shared identity memberships, and characterized by relational moves that demonstrate interested questioning and attentive listening practices.

Writing Locationally

The relational work being accomplished in Gabriel and Enrique's writing is also locational work. Throughout their letters, Gabriel and Enrique use a number of rhetorical devices to reference their common locational perspectives as immigrant youth. Their writing spans *H/home* as does the writing of the young women McLean (2012) studied, but it does so collectively, suggesting the shared boundaries of their immigrant experiences as well as shared ways of knowing, mediated by their common place-identities. As Enrique (Letter 2) states, "It sounds like you and I have a lot of things in common. We both came from Mexico at an early age and have struggle[d] through school."

Their shared place-perspectives are referenced, particularly by Gabriel, through spatial and proximal deixis (Benwell & Stokoe, 2006). In his first letter, for example, Gabriel writes, "I came *here* when I was a little boy like 6 or 7. I really like it *here*" (emphasis added). Gabriel continues the pattern in Letter 2, using *here* to set up an implicit contrast to Mexico, a comparison Gabriel may have felt he did not need to make explicit to Enrique due to their shared immigrant experience.

I want to be a pro soccer player but I have to work so hard for that and its cold here and I don't get to go play outside that much…Yeah it's hot sometimes here too and I go swimming. I like swimming and play soccer. (Gabriel, Letter 2, italics added for emphasis)

Likewise, in telling this story about visiting family out of state, Gabriel refers to a shared understanding of rural life in Mexico (and again, to the contrast in weather):

I have family from…[a U.S. state]. One time I went there it was really cold and there were cows and you know how like in Mexico to take cows like in a walk and to get water. Well, I did that but with a four wheeler. It was really fun but yea it was cold. I had to wear like 3 socks and like this big thing that covered my nose. (Gabriel, Letter 2)

In his response, Enrique expresses his surprise to discover they both have family living in the same U.S. state. He shares his similar experiences (and reactions to) the cold weather and takes up Gabriel's reference to Mexican rural life by talking about his experiences on his grandparents' farm:

I was really surprised that you too have a family member in [same state]. My sister and her family live [there]. Yeah, it's very cold up north. When I go to visit my sister, I also take two sweaters… My grandparents have a big farm in Mexico. They own cows, horses, goats, chickens, and much more. When I was little I helped my grandparents in looking after their goats. It was very entertaining. (Enrique, Letter 3)

Gabriel and Enrique's shared place-identities extend to other structures of their similar social locations: they explore their present and desired future socio-economic status (e.g., references to class, making money), their familial and generational locations (e.g., siblings, parents, and grandparents), and ideological locations (e.g., values related to working hard, going to university). Their relational connections are made stronger by their shared locational connections, and through their letters they locate themselves as members of a larger diasporic ecology. As Moya (2006) explains, "Insofar as identities reference our understanding of ourselves in relation to others, they provide their bearers with particular perspectives on a shared social world… ways of making sense of our experiences" (p. 97).

Writing Collectively

In these exchanges, Gabriel and Enrique maintain what could be characterized as a peer-to-peer-like orientation, or "footing" (Goffman, 1981; Erickson, 2004) to one another. Their sustained footing across these exchanges shows a "participation framework" through which they are writing reflexively, about what they know about themselves, and writing relationally, to know more about one another and their worlds.

What is interesting about their footing is what it reveals about the stances Enrique and Gabriel have taken in their writing. Although Enrique could have positioned himself as an "expert" or "mentor," he takes such a stance only when Gabriel asks about areas in which Enrique has more expertise or experience. He also acknowledges Gabriel's knowledge and experience, even though Gabriel is eight years younger. Gabriel and Enrique show an equitable interest in one another's lives, but they also expand their focus to the broader Latino immigrant community. In these exchanges, they often reference the future, writing to explore how their personal experiences in their respective positions/places offers a perspective from which they collectively consider the changes they wish to see.

Gabriel imagines a future in which cultural and linguistic differences are not cause for bullying. In his response to Enrique's narrative about his social and academic struggles in school, Gabriel empathizes, "It had to be really hard for you when you got here." He then suggests to Enrique that their experiences might help others know a different future: "[B]ut someday maybe you and I can be better than the ones that made fun of you and me." Through a story that Enrique might have intended to use to relate to Gabriel, Gabriel responds by positioning them both ("you and I") vis-à-vis "the ones that made fun of you and me." He realizes the potential for collective change, a move to end discrimination by a generation of immigrant youth who know what it is like to be discriminated against. In turn, when Gabriel

shares details about his family's plans to return to Mexico, Enrique empathizes, saying he, too, has family members who are undocumented, but that for change to come, "we all have to be united and work together."

In one shift in footing, Enrique responds to Gabriel's interest in attending university (to be an architect and a pro soccer player). Referencing his own experience as well as the collective experience of first-generational Latino university students, Enrique writes, "Yes, [Gabriel] we all have to work very hard to accomplish our goals, but it is all worth it at the end. I admire that even though you are young, you already have many plans and goals." Gabriel and Enrique's emails are personal, woven around their own lives and experiences, but they also index the greater social, cultural, institutional, economic, and political structures in which they live and write. Gabriel and Enrique are engaged in writing in an academic sense; they are "conveying meaning and communicating." They are also participating in writing "as a way of knowing" (McLean, 2012, p. 230), exploring through their relationship with one another more about their collective relationship with the world around them.

IMPLICATIONS AND CONCLUSION

Although *Making Connections* was facilitated by technology, it reflected more closely the temporality of letter writing than emailing or, of course, the almost instantaneous replies awarded by texting.[3] The immediacy of response was removed; Gabriel and Enrique's nine letters were exchanged over a period of 10 weeks. The space created by their correspondence, however, was immediate in its value to Gabriel, who made writing to Enrique a priority. It was also immediate in their regard for one another; when they finally met in person at the university, Gabriel and Enrique treated one another like brothers. This is not to underestimate the role of technology—email provided a cost- and time-effective way to facilitate *Making Connections* and both groups of students were very comfortable with email as a mode of correspondence. But it is important to recognize first the social and participatory practices of students in the space created by the program and, second, to consider the kinds of digital and social media that can help facilitate the creation of authentic writing communities in the classroom.

As Gabriel and Enrique's emails demonstrate, the program created a space for students to write about their day-to-day activities, explore their future dreams, and open up with one another about the realities of their current lives. Through their emails, the students created a space for learning about one another that effectively met them where they were; *Making Connections* became a community "based on using students' present reality as a foundation for further learning rather than doing away with or belittling what they know and who they are" (Nieto, 2010, p. 131). It was clear in their choices of topics and relational moves that the students had effectively established safe spaces to think out loud and take risks. Their emails were a kind of "sandbox" for experimenting, their writing a rehearsal for participating in larger conversations about their experiences, concerns, and desires.

Their email exchanges also point to how the students productively merged their out-of-school email practices (e.g., with friends and family) for in-school purposes, pointing to how youth flexibly adapt media to accomplish their goals. The exchanges between Gabriel and Enrique demonstrated their facility with digital literacy practices to relate to one another. When, for instance, Enrique asked Gabriel what he meant by swimming "freestyle," Gabriel attached an image he found on the Internet. In return, Enrique copied images of one of his favorite activities, fencing, and his laboratory work. They utilized the visual to enhance their texts and get to know one another, embedding digital images and occasionally incorporating "text speak" abbreviations and symbols to communicate their mood and intended tone.

The dialogical, emergent, and perspectival traits of this epistolary community (Stanley, 2004) also seem to have reflectd the convergence of in- and out-of-school literacy practices. Gabriel and Enrique created community by conscientiously attending to the content and structure in one another's letters; their responses showed they were carefully "listening" to one another and reciprocating in their efforts to make connections. And while at first their letters mapped the topics and ideas suggested by Beth, over time, new topics emerged in their writing as Gabriel and Enrique felt more comfortable sharing their day-to-day activities. As they got to know one another, the perspective of their emails also shifted; their letters looked less like in-school assignments and more like informal exchanges between friends (e.g., shorter sentences, fewer structured paragraphs, more emoticons and symbols, less contextual cues, more colloquial word choice). Their final emails seem to have found a "middle ground" perspective—more formal letters of thanks and appreciation acknowledging the end of *Making Connections* as a class project, while also warmly expressing their mutual respect for one another and their interest in continuing to write.

Through their digital correspondence, the students created new connections between these two communities. In his first letter, Enrique explained to Gabriel that when he was a middle school student, he could not imagine attending university. Through Enrique, Gabriel could explore what university was like. In his letters, he asked questions about the courses Enrique was taking, what he did in his free time, and what the Latino cultural center meant to him as a first-generation Latino student. Gabriel's physical experience of the university (during the class's visit) was prefaced by this extended virtual, vicarious experience facilitated through Enrique's writing. Gabriel was thus able to imagine the university as part of his larger ecology in a way that Enrique had never been able to do. In his final letter, Gabriel shared his impressions not just of the campus ("P.S. it was really BIG"), but also of the students: "When I was there I saw a lot of people. It seems really fun to be in college and at [this university]."

Through *Making Connections*, the students' academic identities extended to new spaces: Enrique's into the middle school ENL classroom (where his letters were read aloud and he was often invoked in conversation) and Gabriel's into a university campus where he could imagine himself as a student, playing soccer, hanging out at the center, and studying to be an architect. Their writing became a mediating tool, contributing to "a classroom community of difference" between the middle school and university "that makes use of all the spatial, cultural and linguistic resources of its participants" (Gutiérrez et al, 1999, p. 287). Gabriel and Enrique's letters point to the ways third space writing pedagogies can be mediated by digital and social media for the purposes of creating new critical communities of writers by expanding the modes, genres, and audiences for writing in school.

Making Connections also suggests that an important aspect of such communities is *confianza*: Gabriel and Enrique demonstrated care and trust in their interactions with one another, realizing in their common experiences a shared future that relies on their ability to move from their individual experience to collective knowledge building and action. Another component in such a critical and participatory writing pedagogy for immigrant youth is a stance that is both imaginative—authoring selves in relationship to other people, places, and futures (Holland, Lachicotte, Skinner, & Cain, 1998; Appadurai, 1996; Black, 2009) —and intellectual, acknowledging the role of collective experience as a source of knowledge and social change (Nieto, 2010).

Digital and social media afford powerful tools for this kind of transmediation, the movement of students' writing across communities. Taken up in school, through collaborative partnerships like *Making Connections*, a writing ecologies pedagogy acknowledges the fluid ways immigrant youth negotiate language and literacy across their daily contexts (Gee & Hayes, 2011; Pahl, 2012; Guerra, 2008). But such a pedagogical stance also repositions writing in school as personally and collectively relevant, recognizing the potential for students' writing not only to move across but also to transform the spaces and communities through which it circulates.

REFERENCES

Appadurai, A. (1996). *Modernity at large: Cultural dimensions of globalization*. Minneapolis, MN: University of Minnesota Press.

Atwell, N. (1998). *In the middle: New understandings about writing, reading, and learning* (2nd ed.). Portsmouth, NH: Boynton/Cook Publishers.

Barton, D., & Hamilton, M. (1998). *Local literacies: Reading and writing in one community*. London: Routledge. doi:10.4324/9780203448885.

Barton, D., Hamilton, M., & Ivanic, R. (Eds.). (2000). *Situated literacies: Reading and writing in context*. London: Routledge.

Beach, R., Campano, G., Edmiston, B., & Borgmann, M. (2010). Literacy tools in the classroom: Teaching through critical inquiry, grades 5-12. New York: Teachers College Press/National Writing Project.

Benwell, B., & Stokoe, E. (2006). *Discourse and identity*. Edinburgh, UK: Edinburgh University Press.

Black, R. (2009). Online fan fiction, global identities, and imagination. *Research in the Teaching of English*, *43*(4), 397–425.

Black, R. W. (2005). Online fanfiction: What technology and popular culture can teach us about writing and literacy instruction. *New Horizons for Learning Online Journal, 11*(2).

Blackburn, M., & Clark, C. (Eds.). (2007). *Literacy research for political action and social change.* New York: Peter Lang Publishing, Inc..

Bomer, R., & Bomer, K. (2001). *For a better world: Reading and writing for social action.* Portsmouth, NH: Heinemann.

Campano, G. (2007). *Immigrant students and literacy: Reading, writing, and remembering.* New York: Teachers College Press.

Christensen, L. (2009). *Teaching for joy and justice: Re-imagining the language arts classroom.* Milwaukee, WI: Rethinking Schools, Ltd..

Cisneros, S. (1984). *The house on mango street.* New York: Random House, Inc..

Danticat, E. (2010). *Create dangerously: The immigrant artist at work.* New York: Vintage Books.

Dixon, J., & Durrheim, K. (2000). Displacing place-identity: A discursive approach to locating self and other. *The British Journal of Social Psychology, 39*(1), 27–44. doi:10.1348/014466600164318 PMID:10774526.

Erikson, F. (1975). Gatekeeping and the melting pot: Interaction in counseling encounters. *Harvard Educational Review, 45,* 224–229.

Eva Lam, W. S., & Warriner, D. (2012). Transnationalism and literacy: Investigating the mobility of people, languages, texts, and practices in contexts of migration. *Reading Research Quarterly, 47*(2), 191–215.

Gee, J. (1996). *Social linguistics and literacies: Ideology in discourses* (2nd ed.). London: Taylor & Francis.

Gee, J., & Hayes, E. (2011). *Language and learning in the digital age.* New York: Routledge.

Gee, J. P. (1999). *An introduction to discourse analysis: Theory and method.* New York: Routledge.

Goffman, E. (1981). *Forms of talk.* Philadelphia: University of Pennsylvania Press.

González, N., Moll, L., & Amanti, C. (2005). *Funds of knowledge: Theorizing practices in households, communities, and classrooms.* Mahwah, NJ: Lawrence Erlbaum Associates.

Guerra, J. (2008). Writing for transcultural citizenship: A cultural ecology model. *Language Arts, 85*(4), 296–304.

Gutiérrez, K., Baquedano-López, P., & Tejeda, C. (1999). Rethinking diversity: Hybridity and hybrid language practices in the third space. Mind, Culture, and Activity, 6(4), 286-303.

Heath, S. B. (1983). *Ways with words: Language, life, and work in communities and classrooms.* New York: Cambridge University Press.

Herrington, A., Hodgson, K., & Moran, C. (Eds.). (2009). *Teaching the new writing: Technology, change, and assessment in the 21st-century classroom.* New York: Teachers College Press/National Writing Project.

Holland, D., Lachicotte, W., Skinner, D., & Cain, C. (1998). *Identity and agency in cultural worlds.* Cambridge, MA: Harvard University Press.

Honeyford, M. (2013a). Critical projects of Latino cultural citizenship: Literacy and immigrant activism. *Pedagogies: An International Journal, 8*(1), 60–76.

Honeyford, M. (2013b). The simultaneity of experience: Cultural identity, magical realism, and the artefactual in digital storytelling. *Literacy.* doi:10.1111/j.1741-4369.2012.00675.x.

Hull, G., & Schultz, K. (2001). Literacy and learning out of school: A review of theory and research. *Review of Educational Research, 71*(4), 575–611. doi:10.3102/00346543071004575.

Ife, F. (2012). Powerful writing: Promoting a political writing community of students. *English Journal, 101*(4), 64–69.

Ito, M., Baumer, S., & Bittani, M. boyd, d., Cody, R., Herr-Stephenson, B., et al. (2009). Hanging out, messing around, and geeking out: Kids living and learning with new media. Cambridge, MA: MIT Press/MacArthur Foundation.

Janks, H. (2010). *Literacy and power*. New York: Routledge.

Jenkins, H., Clinton, K., Purushotma, R., Robinson, A. J., & Weigel, M. (2009). *Confronting the challenges of participatory culture: Media education for the 21st century*. Chicago, IL: MacArthur Foundation.

Juzwik, M., Curcic, S., Wolbers, K., Moxley, K., Dimling, L., & Shankland, R. (2006). Writing into the 21st century: An overview of research on writing, 1999-2004. *Written Communication, 23*, 451–476. doi:10.1177/0741088306291619.

Kafai, Y., Peppler, K., & Chapman, R. (Eds.). (2009). *The computer clubhouse: Constructionism and creativity in youth communities*. New York: Teachers College Press.

Kells, M. (2007). Writing across communities: Deliberation and the discursive possibilities of WAC. *Reflections: The SoL Journal*, 87–108.

Kress, G. (2003). *Literacy in the new media age*. New York: Routledge. doi:10.4324/9780203164754.

Lenhart, A., Arafeh, S., Smith, A., & Macgill, A. (2008). *Writing, technology and teens*. Washington, DC: Pew Internet & American Life Project.

Lewis, C., Enciso, P., & Moje, E. (2007). *Reframing sociocultural research on literacy: Identity, agency, and power*. Mahwah, NJ: Lawrence Erlbaum Associates, Inc..

Lu, M. L. (1990). Writing as repositioning. *Journal of Education, 172*, 18–21.

Luke, A. (2008). *Introduction. Literacy and education: Understanding the new literacy studies in the classroom* (pp. x–xiv). Thousand Oaks, CA: Sage.

Mahiri, J. (Ed.). (2004). *What they don't learn in school: Literacy in the lives of urban youth*. New York: Peter Lang.

Maybin, J. (2000). The new literacy studies: Context, intertextuality and discourse. In Barton, D., Hamilton, M., & Ivanic, R. (Eds.), *Situated literacies: Reading and writing in context* (pp. 197–209). London: Routledge.

McLean, C. (2012). The author's I: Adolescents mediating selfhood through writing. *Pedagogies: An International Journal, 7*(3), 229–245.

Moya, P. M. L. (2006). What's identity got to do with it? Mobilizing identities in the multicultural classroom. In Alcoff, L. M., Hames-Garcia, M., Mohanty, S. P., & Moya, P. M. L. (Eds.), *Identity politics reconsidered* (pp. 96–117). New York: Palgrave Macmillan.

National Council of Teachers of English. (2009). *Writing between the lines and everywhere else*. Urbana, IL: NCTE.

New London Group. (1996). A pedagogy of multiliteracies: Designing social futures. *Harvard Educational Review, 66*(1), 60–92.

Nieto, S. (2010). *The light in their eyes: Creating multicultural learning communities*. New York: Teachers College Press.

Pahl, K. (2012). A reason to write: Exploring writing epistemologies in two contexts. *Pedagogies: An International Journal, 7*(3), 209–228.

Pahl, K., & Rowsell, J. (2008). *Literacy and education: Understanding the new literacy studies in the classroom*. Thousand Oaks, CA: Sage.

Stanley, L. (2004). The epistolarium: On theorizing letters and correspondences. *Auto/Biography, 12*, 201–235. doi:10.1191/0967550704ab014oa.

Street, B. (1984). *Literacy in theory and practice*. Cambridge, UK: Cambridge University Press.

Street, B. (2003). What's "new" in new literacy studies? Critical approaches to literacy in theory and practice. *Current Issues in Comparative Education, 5*(2).

ENDNOTES

[1]   All names are pseudonyms.

[2]   Though all the university students have been invited to participate, only two agreed. The researcher contributes this not to their unwillingness but in the difficulties in contacting them after the end of the semester/graduation.

[3]   It should be noted that none of the students had a cell or smart phone, but they regularly communicated via email to family in Mexico.

Section 4
Writing Instruction

Teachers' instructional practices must be guided by a strong conceptual framework that includes knowledge of writing and the pedagogical approaches effective for the teaching of writing. Technology has influenced our conceptions of what it means to write as students are now engaged in multimodal compositions and digital writing. What does this shift in writing mean for the pedagogical strategies used to teach writing? The chapters in this section explore how instruction is changing to meet the new demands of writing with technology. How should teachers teach writing with technology? The chapters in this section address these important questions.

This section begins with an investigation lead by Higgs, Miller, and Pearson examining four elementary and middle school teachers' expectations and experiences with incorporating of a tablet application to facilitate classroom discussions. The tablet application featured a collective reading platform and embedded discussion tools. Higgs, Miller, and Pearson's analysis of the teachers' instructional approaches led them to propose Classroom Digital Interaction (CDI), a pedagogical lens for both digital and face-to-face discussions.

The next two chapters highlight the connection between reading and writing, emphasizing that inquiry opportunities to analyze the reading of digital content can facilitate the learning of writing digital texts. Wolsey, Lapp, and Fisher review the literature to analyze how reading and writing are influenced by and interact in digital environments. They provide specific implications for how educators can use digital texts as exemplary sources for students' written work. O'Bryne presents the Online Content Construction (OCC), an instructional model, for teaching students to use digital texts and tools to construct or design online texts. The OCC model incorporates the theoretical underpinnings of cognitive apprenticeship and research on writing to detail an instructional approach that moves students through the process of deconstructing and designing online content.

The final chapter in this section was penned by Yim and Warschauer. The authors use a framework-based analysis of achievement, change, and power, to synthesize current research and provide pedagogical implications for technology use for non-native speakers of English. Their chapter examines technology's teaching effectiveness and transformative power. Yim and Warschauer propose that the power framework, which focuses on technology and writing practices, can improve second language learners' educational, social, and economic opportunities. Their examination provides implications for the educational benefits of using technology to teach writing to non-native speakers of English.

The chapters in this section represent how technological changes influence writing instruction.

Chapter 14
Classroom Digital Interaction:
High Expectations, Misleading Metaphors, and the Dominance of Netspeak

Jennifer Higgs
University of California – Berkeley, USA

Catherine Anne Miller
University of California – Berkeley, USA

P. David Pearson
University of California – Berkeley, USA

ABSTRACT

As Computer-Mediated Communication (CMC) is increasingly adopted for literacy instruction in K-12 classrooms, careful attention should be paid to its instructional benefits and challenges. In this chapter, the authors take a careful look at how the metaphors of social interaction guiding teacher translation of CMC into their lessons mask the full range of affordances and limitations of CMC. Using a linguistic lens, they analyze teacher interviews and student online discussion data to make a case that using Classroom Digital Interaction (CDI) as a pedagogical tool requires a close look at the aims of literacy instruction and the constraints and affordances of computer mediated discussion.

INTRODUCTION

It is well established that new communication technologies have had a profound impact on language use, particularly with regard to written communication (Herrington, Hodgson, & Moran, 2009; Yancey, 2009; Warschauer, 2007; Jewitt, 2005). Writing researchers and linguists have paid increasing attention to the ways in which synchronous and asynchronous computer-mediated communication (CMC) engender new forms of writing, writing in which the hybridization of spoken and written language is often strikingly divergent from the writing produced for academic or "official" purposes (Haas & Takayoshi, 2011; Goddard, 2011; Tagliamonte & Denis, 2008; Crystal, 2006; Ferrara et al., 1991; Biber & Finegan, 1997; Davis & Brewer, 1997; Eldred & Fortune, 1992). For literacy teachers and researchers seeking to capitalize on outside-school writing practices as a way of supporting in-school achievement (Mahiri, 2011; Reinhardt & Zander, 2011; Vie, 2008; Hull & Schultz, 2002), the use of CMC in the classroom is particularly intrigu-

DOI: 10.4018/978-1-4666-4341-3.ch014

ing, as it combines the generative interaction of discussion and writing (Dysthe, 1996; Nystrand et al., 1998) with students' everyday social practices in an increasingly digitized, multimodal communication landscape (Lankshear & Knobel, 2011; Carrington & Robinson, 2009; Coiro et al., 2008; Hull & Nelson, 2005).

There is considerable evidence, however, that teachers continue to struggle with using CMC in ways that maximize potential literacy learning, despite widespread access to and use of information and communication technologies designed for education (Beach, Hull, & O'Brien, 2011; Honan, 2009; Tearle, 2003; Cuban, Kirkpatrick, & Peck, 2001). Researchers have attributed teacher approaches to technology to a variety of contextual factors, including infrastructural obstacles, teachers' technological knowledge, and teachers' beliefs about the role of technology (e.g., Prestidge, 2012; Hutchison & Reinking, 2011; Starkey, 2010; Honan, 2009; Harris, Mishra, & Koehler, 2009; Stolle, 2008), but less attention has been paid to the ways in which the common metaphors for CMC (i.e., discussion, chatrooms, messaging, texting, collaborating) influence teachers' interpretations of how to implement communication technology for instruction. Metaphors, as Lakoff and Johnson (1980) have notably argued, structure our perceptions and shape our expectations. Thus, it is no surprise that metaphors for defining technology (e.g., e-book, tablet, email, chat) can be simultaneously helpful and dangerous, with descriptive language facilitating use of the "new" by evoking the "old", while also potentially ossifying our understandings of a particular technology and thereby clouding important conceptual differences (Eldred & Fortune, 1992). In other words, the metaphors we use to frame new communication tools both define use and obscure affordances of the technology. In light of the persuasive power of metaphoric interpretation, teachers' perceptions of CMC seem salient to the implementation of technology in classrooms, and particularly to the literacy classroom which remains organized largely around print-based paradigms of writing and reading (Beach et al., 2011).

This chapter examines metaphor as an influential factor contributing to rudimentary uses of communication technologies in the classroom, drawing on interviews and observations to illustrate how metaphors constrained teachers' uses of a collaborative tablet reading platform for composition and discussion. Specifically, we look at the ways in which teachers' metaphors led to a conflation of digitally mediated and Face-To-Face (FTF) discussion that ultimately undermined their original purposes for implementing the online platform's embedded discussion tool. Following our analysis, we propose a pedagogical lens we refer to as Classroom Digital Interaction (CDI), which we conceptualize as a tool for practitioners to use when evaluating the affordances of learning tools that travel the range of oral, written and digital registers. A CDI lens encourages educators to take into account the pedagogical purpose of discussion in the literacy classroom, whether face-to-face or digitally mediated, and how pedagogical purpose and practical affordances of a register interact in a complex manner to support students' learning.

CONTEXT AND PURPOSE

In the fall of 2012, we were contacted by an educational technology company to examine how teachers were using a tablet application the company had created. The application takes the form of a collective reading platform that incorporates social media tools to encourage multimodal discussion and collaborative meaning making "inside" the pages of a digital book. Users can create reader profiles, participate in multiple book discussion groups (school and non-school texts; all books accessible through Google Play are available for download), post questions to other readers and answer notes, link to Web content, and create/complete quizzes and assignments. Users' interactions across these discussion-oriented communication modes are "published" as they are posted and appear as digital marginalia in the e-book. From a New Literacies perspective, this kind of platform has the potential to engage students in multimodal communication forms that mirror the literacies in which they engage outside of school (e.g., Facebook comment threads), thus opening up the repertoire of traditionally school-sanctioned meaning-making spaces.

Due to the fact that the application's inaugural semester as an e-reader in classrooms was Fall 2012, there were no investigations that attended to teachers' perceptions of the application, the challenges and affordances associated with using the application for classroom instruction, and how teachers use this platform with their students. As such, our initial research questions focused on teachers' uses and perspectives: 1) Why are teachers using this application in their classes?; 2) How are teachers using this application to support literacy instruction?; and 3) What do teachers perceive as the challenges and benefits of using this tool?

LITERATURE REVIEW

There is a substantial body of research that suggests on the importance of face-to-face (FTF) classroom discussion. With the rise of communication technology and its adoption in the classroom, more attention has been paid to the use of digital tools to facilitate discussions among learners and expand interaction beyond traditionally bounded learning times and spaces. In an effort to clarify what we know to date about the affordances of conventional FTF interaction and those of discussion forms embedded in digital contexts, we offer here a brief review of empirical work examining FTF classroom discussion and computer-mediated asynchronous discussion in K-12 settings.

Affordances of FTF Classroom Discussion

As language and literacy scholars have long suggested, language use cannot be separated from learning (Halliday, 1980) and the way we talk matters in that learning process. The potential of peer-led talk has become of increasing interest to researchers as attention has shifted from discussions that replicate the teacher initiation, student response, and teacher evaluation (IRE) pattern of classroom interaction (Cazden, 2001, 1997, 1986) to focus more on teacher-facilitated, peer-led discussions (Almasi, 1995; Maloch, 2002). Peer-led classroom discourse, which Cazden describes as having the qualities of authentic, everyday discussions, offers learners more opportunities for response and control and can support sophisticated meaning making strategies and deeper understandings as learners interact (Gambrell, 1996; Gilles & Pierce, 2003; Britton, 1969/1990). Literacy scholars conducting research on text-based discussions invoke various theories to argue for the use of peer-led, collaborative dialogue as a means of promoting students' reading comprehension, including cognitive, sociocognitive, and sociocultural perspectives on learning and teaching (Tsai & Wilkinson, 2010).

From a cognitive perspective, empirical evidence supports the importance of discussion in improving students' reading comprehension and facilitating active engagement in making meaning from text (McKeown, Beck, & Blake, 2009; Wilkinson & Son, 2011; Wolf, Crosson, & Resnick, 2005). McKeown and colleagues (2009) found in a two-year quasi-experimental study with fifth grade students that collaborative discussion produced higher scores on standard comprehension measures (e.g., narrative recall), while Wolf, Crosson, and Resnick (2005) found in their quantitative analyses of classroom talk that students' demonstration of knowledge had positive, significant links to the level of rigor in the classroom lesson. From a sociocognitive perspective, literary discussion may offer a forum in which one's ideas about a text are challenged and changed by conflicting information revealed during social interaction. For example, in her study of 97 fourth-graders' sociocognitive conflicts in peer-led and teacher-led literary discussions, Almasi (1995) found that students in peer-led (decentralized) groups were able to recognize and resolve conflict more successfully than students in teacher-led (centralized) groups, resulting in internalization of cognitive processes associated with engaged reading. These sociocognitive conflicts (Bloome, 1985) can create "room to grow" for students as they confront diverse textual interpretations and worldviews. Sociocultural scholars have found that authentic discussion aids students' co-construction of knowledge and understandings of text as well as their internalization of the knowledge, skills, and dispositions needed to transfer to the reading of new texts (Nystrand, 2006; Wells, 2007). The tension and conflict between relative perspectives and competing voices in discussion about text helps shape discourse and students' comprehension (Bakhtin, 1953/1986; Nystrand, 2006). The learner must gain intersubjectivity, progressing from an egocentric understanding of a topic to a decentered understanding of a topic.

The potential of discussion in K-12 literacy classrooms has been well documented. A number of studies carried out in elementary and secondary classes have shown that students' reading comprehension improves with classroom interaction with their teachers and peers, including small-group (e.g., Soter et al., 2008) and whole-group discussions (e.g., Juzwik, Nystrand, Kelly, & Sherry, 2008; Juzwik & Sherry, 2007; Van den Branden, 2000). These findings support Nystrand's (1997) earlier research on open-ended, dialogic discourse in eighth- and ninth-grade ELA, which suggested that students regularly engaged in discussion (defined as "an open exchange of ideas among

students and/or between at least three participants and the teacher that lasted at least 30 seconds") recalled their readings better and understood them in more depth than students taught in more traditionally organized classes (e.g., lecture, recitation, seatwork). Applebee and colleagues (Applebee, Langer, Nystrand, & Gamoran, 2003) and Langer (2001) further established the positive correlation between ELA classes characterized by dialogic discussions and increases in high student achievement.

Asynchronous Computer-Mediated Communication

The research on FTF classroom discussion suggests that effective talk in classrooms is collaborative, resembling a give-and-take format as interlocutors explore ideas, improvise, confront notions conflicting with their own, and integrate new perspectives. With the abundance of available asynchronous online discussion platforms and the promise of flexible access to content at any time or place (Xie, DeBacker, & Ferguson, 2006), increased interest in locating Computer-Mediated Discussions (CMD) within the catalogue of tools for discourse-based learning is understandable.

The nature of online discussions in post-secondary learning contexts can change depending on the design of questions and the facilitation of discussion by the teacher (Garrison & Cleveland-Innes, 2005). A recent meta analysis from the Department of Education and Technology identified the pertinence of this difference between FTF discussion and asynchronous communication. However, of the major findings of this report was the lack of empirical studies on comparing K-12 students' achievement in FTF and online forums. (Means, Toyama, Murphy, Bakia, & Jones, 2010). In our review of the literature we found relatively few empirical studies to date that describe and explain the communication and learning affordances of CMD in K-12 classroom learning contexts, although some empirical work has been done on

K-12 virtual schools (e.g., Rice, 2006) as well as on CMD in the context of literacy methods courses and teacher education (e.g., Deoksoon, 2011; Mills & Chandra, 2011; Wake & Modla, 2012). Although the burgeoning nature of research on CMD in K-12 settings precludes conclusive generalizations about its effects on learning, we can outline some of the technical affordances that may contribute to the growing popularity of CMD in elementary and secondary schools.

As CMD is often asynchronous, it offers students opportunities for communication with peers at any time and from any distance. Asynchronous online discussion environments may be defined as "text-based human-to-human communication via computer networks that provide a platform for the participants to interact with one another to exchange ideas, insights and personal experiences" (Hew & Cheung, 2003, p. 249). Unlike synchronous discussion formats such as Instant Messaging, asynchronous online discussion does not take place in "real time" and therefore enables the extension of learning activities beyond traditional classroom time and space. CMD is also text-based, which requires students to express their thoughts and opinions in writing. Researchers have argued that computer mediated writing offers more time for participants to form and edit ideas and responses (Daiute, 2000; Dennen, 2005) and encourages the kind of reflection that promotes higher level thinking skills such as analysis, synthesis, and evaluation (Newman, Johnson, Webb, & Cochran, 1997). The text-based nature of CMD may be particularly appealing to teachers who hope to leverage increasingly interactive and collaborative technologies to transform socially-situated writing, reading, and critical thinking activities (Hungerford-Kresser, Wiggins, & Amaro-Jimenez, 2012; Dredger, Woods, Beach, & Sagstetter, 2010). Written versus oral communication may also facilitate practice with writing in an authentic interactive context. Studies in the past decade suggest that students participating in asynchronous online discussions may take more time articulating their ideas in comparison to students in FTF discussion groups (Wang & Woo, 2007) and may also engage in more complex and elaborated syntactic structures, particularly with regard to ESL students (Sotillo, 2000).

Another commonly referenced affordance of CMC in the classroom is the potential for increased equity among students (Flores, 1990; Selfe, 1990; Sutherland-Smith, 2002). Supporters of this perspective view the use of computer-mediated discussion as an opportunity to "empower students" and alter classroom dynamics by "modeling a more egalitarian mode of dialogue" among peers (Flores, 1990, p. 112). Although this notion of peer-led equity has been contested (e.g., Cook-Sather, 2002; Moje & Shepardson, 1998; Wade & Fauske, 2004), many teachers believe that computer-mediated discussions can improve learning for disenfranchised students by offering increased opportunities for participation in less conventional, less threatening, and more culturally open ways.

THEORETICAL FRAMEWORK

Informing our study are three strands of research that triangulate to form the basis for understanding the use of digital interaction spaces in the classroom. We draw upon Eldred and Fortune's (1992) perspectives on how the metaphoric interpretation of communication technologies define and constrain classroom application, which remain relevant to 21st century discussions of technology integration and tool use in school spaces. Extending Lakoff and Johnson's seminal work on metaphors (1980) to writing instruction and new communication technologies, Eldred and Fortune contend that although metaphors are integral to meaning making, we must "ensure our descriptive metaphors are working for us" (p. 60), for such language directs and often undermines how teachers conceive of and employ technology for literacy instruction. The danger of a literal interpretation of common technology metaphors in the classroom, they argue, is that such metaphors are invariably aligned with spoken language (e.g., chatting, conversation, discussion, collaboration), whereas research has suggested that digital interactions display more features of written discourse. Thus students are often required to acknowledge the demands of written discourse while engaging in interactions that share similarities with spoken and written language but are in actuality unique hybrids that defy stable classifications.

To illustrate this point, Eldred and Fortune build on previous work examining structural differences between written and spoken language (Biber & Finegan, 1997; Chafe & Tannen, 1987; Tannen, 1982; Ochs, 1979; Olson, 1977) to produce a language continuum (Figure 1) that incorporates communication technologies into the speech/writing continuum. According to the authors, this representation of spoken and written language lifts the veil of metaphor that often conceals a technology's full range of uses by focusing on online interactions that feature both spoken and written language without "belonging" to either category. Using email, for example, as "traditional mail, but faster" (Eldred & Fortune, 1992, p. 58) hides the range of asynchronous (archived, not "live") and synchronous (simultaneous, "live") communication possibilities currently available on Webmail servers. Webmail supports synchronous features such as videochat and instant messaging alongside its asynchronous features and can therefore be seen as moving fluidly along the continuum based on use; this movement counters static notions of email as a mere transmitter of electronically transcribed letters. The continuum below illustrates where Webmail might fall.

Another strand of research informing this study complements and extends Eldred and Fortune's perspectives by promoting a more linguistically informed examination of the specific differences between metaphoric online discussion and FTF discussion, and written discourse and digital interaction. Davis and Brewer (1997) found that classroom digital interaction complicated the metaphor of "classroom discussion" in particular and predictable ways. Features of electronic interaction that both emulated and differed from spoken or written language included: (a) time-boundedness [online interaction reads like conversation, but interaction is delayed by seconds, minutes or days]; (b) turn-taking is unlike conventional conversation [natural interruptions and overlaps are not possible; interaction draws on two time frames, that of the sender and that of the receiver, so "turns" may not reflect actual timing of responses]; (c) use of graphics [emoticons, capitalizing letters to convey emotion]. Unlike Eldred and Fortune, Davis and Brewer view online interaction as something beyond the confines of a "traditional" speech and writing language continuum (Figure 2). Significantly, online interaction does not include some essential elements of FTF interaction that make discussion useful in literacy/learning environments, including the gestural cues, interruptions and overlaps that occur in spoken language. This more expansive view of the digital speech/written language continuum provided Crystal (2001) with the foundation for his conception of Netspeak, a term Crystal coined to represent the new forms of communication arising across different uses of communication tools in different digital spaces.

Figure 1. Eldred and Fortunes (1992) speech to writing continuum

Written Prose	Email	Net Talk	Speech
Written Language			Oral Language

Figure 2. Crystal's live to online continuum

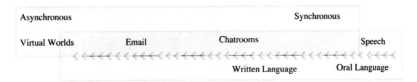

METHODS

The findings reported here are part of a larger study designed to understand teachers' perceptions and uses of a specific tablet application, a collective reading platform, as well as the potential affordances and constraints of using the tablet application during classroom instruction.

Participants

Four elementary and middle school public school teachers participated in this study: Karen, a 6th grade teacher with 24 years of teaching experience; Diana, a 4th grade teacher with 15 years of teaching experience; Jamie, an 8th grade teacher with 34 years of teaching experience; and Sally, a 7th grade teacher with 20 years of teaching experience. Sally and Jamie taught at the same mid-western middle school, while Diana and Karen taught in separate West Coast elementary schools. The company recommended these particular teachers because they were actively using the application with their students and seemed to be interested in sharing their experiences in the classroom. Karen, Jamie, Sally, and Diana self-identified as being very comfortable with classroom technology and receptive to experimenting with new pedagogical approaches. Additionally, all taught in classrooms

with 1:1 tablet programs; although only Diana's students were able to take the tablets home.

Study Design

Over the course of two months in the fall of 2012, we worked with the teachers as they began using the tablet application with their students. In order to compare teachers' expectations for and experiences with the application, we conducted interviews with each study participant, observed in person and remotely (using Skype), and engaged teachers in reflection after lessons. This cross-case approach enabled us to look at the variations and similarities across the teachers' perceptions and uses (reported and observed) of the tool. Adopting a cross-case design seems particularly helpful in exploring different uses of a new digital tool, as this methodology offers opportunities for analysis that can enhance generalizability and deepen understanding (Miles & Huberman, 1994, p. 173).

Data Sources

Qualitative methods were used to collect data over a two-month period in the form of teacher interviews, reflective post-lesson conversations with teachers, field notes of in-person and remote class observations, and screenshots of teachers' online participation in the application.

Interviews

We conducted, audio/video recorded, and transcribed four semi-structured interviews with Karen, Diana, Jamie, and Sally. The purpose of the semi-structured interviews was to learn more about teachers' previous experiences with classroom technology; their motives for using the technology with their students; their perceptions of the affordances and constraints of using the platform for literacy instruction; and their uses of the platform during a recent lesson. We also asked teachers to describe a recent lesson using the application that they deemed successful (using their own definition of success) so that we could better understand their conceptions of effective classroom implementation of the platform.

Field Notes from Classroom Observations

Due to our geographic distance from the teachers, we designed the study so that we would conduct observations in-person and remotely using Skype. As we observed, we wrote down chronologically ordered jottings of main events and ideas, which we developed into full field notes as soon as possible afterward. When we were present in the classroom, we walked around to see what students were working on, but we spent more time observing than participating.

Teacher Reflections

We asked teachers to reflect post-lesson on how the platform was used during the observed class in order to assess differences between teachers' perceived tool use and their actual tool use. Teacher reflections were audio recorded and transcribed for analysis.

Screenshots of Classroom Interactions

Teachers granted us access to their class e-books (we were approved as group members and were therefore able to view all student responses) so that we could follow the digitally mediated class interactions. Being "inside" the book provided us with a different observation perspective, as we could see how teachers actually posed questions and framed student interactions. We collected several screenshots illustrating teachers' online participation on the platform (e.g., teacher-facilitated prompts embedded in digital texts)

Data Analysis

We mixed inductive and deductive strategies as we coded transcribed data. From our research questions, we drew broad deductive codes for teachers' reasons for adopting the reading platform, how they implemented the platform in the classroom, and what they perceived as benefits and challenges of using the platform. The list of sub-codes developed for these deductive codes, however, were devised inductively as we scanned the data and looked for categories that emerged from the transcripts of the teacher interviews. Inductive approaches, as Miles and Huberman (1994) note, are intended to assist the researcher in developing an understanding of raw data through "data reduction," or summarization of themes and categories. This coding strategy led us to our focus on how the participating teachers were translating metaphors of communication technology into their instruction and the elements of Netspeak that appeared in their technology use that complicated their metaphors. Our four focal participants shared a great deal of information during our interviews, so a combined deductive/ inductive approach to analysis enabled us to keep focused on our research objectives while still allowing key sub-categories to emerge from a close reading of the transcripts. After creating this initial list of descriptive codes (level I), we identified pattern codes (Miles & Huberman, 1994) that represented emergent findings (level II). We next identified categories of either metaphor or Netspeak (level III), and last identified linguistic patterns that related to the continuums of speech and writing (level IV) after which we returned to the data and recoded for those themes.

Following data coding, we created a partially ordered meta-matrix (Miles & Huberman, 1994) to organize our cross-case analysis of the four teachers' motivations for using the app in their classes, uses of the tool (reported and observed), and perceptions of technology challenges and benefits, which enabled us to efficiently identify similarities, differences, and outliers in teachers' use. In order to ensure the accuracy of our findings, we triangulated data collection methods and moved iteratively between the matrix and data sources throughout analysis to check the validity of cross-case patterns.

FINDINGS

Analysis of teacher interviews suggested that although teachers unanimously reported being motivated to use the application in ways that would offer a wide variety of communication modes to their 21st century learners, their actual uses of the application were constrained by the type of literal interpretation of metaphor that Eldred and Fortune describe. These teachers' classroom practices, as we will show, were shaped by the language they adopted to define the technology, thus concealing certain limitations and affordances associated with online interaction. Specifically, we focus here on teachers' interpretations of the discussion features in the application, first discussing how literal interpretations of metaphors shaped teachers' uses of the application for literacy instruction, and then

describing differences between live discussion and online discussion that complicated the teachers' objectives for using CMD as a learning tool.

"Meeting" the 21st Century Learner

A theme running through the four teachers' reasons for adopting the application was a desire to accommodate the educational needs of what they all independently referred to as "the 21st century learner." Diana, Karen, Sally, and Jamie seemed to share a common vision of a "new" type of student who learns best with technology and in collaboration with peers, and they all employed variations of the phrase "meeting [the students] where they are" in describing their willingness to adopt the application in their classrooms. Their use of this phrase positioned the application as a metaphorical bridge that enabled teachers to journey across the chasm dividing familiar "old" ways of teaching and the "new" territory of digitally mediated, collaborative learning. Karen's reflection on changes in the educational landscape encapsulates the teachers' beliefs regarding the 21st century learner they set out to "meet":

… this is what they're used to, this is their world … if we're going to make an impact and get these guys ready for their future, we need to teach them skills that we just simply didn't need to have … So just meeting them where they are … no teacher can afford to teach the way they used to teach. (Interview, 10/17/2012)

Diana, Jamie, and Sally shared Karen's perspective that their students were accustomed to learning with "cutting edge technology" and that teachers had an obligation to "capture their interests" and prepare students with skills for a "different" world. The teachers reported that their decisions to integrate the application in their classrooms were based on its "cutting edge" nature and fostering of collaborative learning, a skill the teachers viewed as a necessity for success in school and the workplace. They perceived the application as a tool that would create opportunities for students to work together in creating textual meaning through student-led discussions, thus moving away from teacher-as-expert teaching models by positioning students as co-creators of knowledge "inside" a text. The application was therefore adopted to empower students as well as acknowledge their facility with technology.

Metaphoric Interpretations of the Application

One of the most common uses of the application reported by the teachers was the embedded online discussion feature, which acted as a chatroom space for participating readers. Due to the universal use of the discussion feature by the teachers in this study, as well as the significant role that discussion plays in the composition process (Dysthe, 1996; Nystrand, Gamoran, & Carbonaro, 1998), we have decided to highlight teachers' approaches to the discussion feature to illustrate their application of metaphor to classroom practice.

Diana, Karen, Sally, and Julie reported that online discussion was an important "cutting edge" tool for fostering students' understandings of texts. Although the teachers stated their belief that online discussion was different from FTF discussion, their lesson planning conflated digital and FTF discussion. All four teachers stated that their approaches to lesson plans featuring digitally mediated communication were identical to those they would create for FTF discussion, and this equation of digital and FTF communication was illustrated in how they structured discussion with the e-book. The teachers relied exclusively on formulating and posting questions in the class e-books ahead of instructional time, as they might formulate a list of questions for a class discussion. They would then direct students to read texts silently while utilizing the digital discussion space (accessed through the "discuss" button under each teacher-provided prompt) to "talk" with their classmates.

During class observation, we noticed that teachers would urge their students to "talk a lot" because they wanted to "see a lot of discussion happening." No additional instructions for students' digitally mediated discussion were provided by the teachers beyond these general guidelines, which suggested that teachers assumed that the contexts (the situation as the speaker finds it, prior to the moment of speaking) and participation structures (the rights and obligations of participants regarding who can say what and when) of FTF discourse and digital discourse were the same (Cazden, 1986; Green, 1983; Erickson & Schultz, 1977).

Teachers' articulations of their "ideal" uses of the application offer further evidence of this conflation of digital and FTF interaction. For example, Diana stated that her ideal use of the application would take the form of "students doing their own thing" while she would "[walk] around the room with [her] iPad and checking in on what they're doing, what their discussion is." This approach mirrors FTF strategies often used by teachers, such as the Think-Pair-Share activity (Lyman, 1987), during which students turn to talk to each other about an idea before a whole group discussion. The teacher during this activity does not direct student talk but rather monitors students' progress, as Diana envisions herself doing by "checking in on what they're doing" by looking at their activity on the tablet application.

Similarly, Sally saw the application as being useful in providing opportunities to "call out" or to address the entire class as one would do during a "live" classroom discussion (e.g., "Hey, what does this mean?"). To support her struggling readers, Sally often turned to discussion-based strategies to help students' meaning making processes. Guided reading, a verbal strategy used by teachers to help struggling students develop comprehension through discussion (Duke & Pearson, 2008), was one such strategy that she found particularly useful, and she reported that she was able to "translate" the kinds of guided reading discussions in "live" classrooms into the digital environment. She shared with us that she thought "guided reading inside the book is so huge, for those of us teaching reading strategies and reading skills … good reading in the book -- wow, that is powerful." For Sally, digital interactions offered all the affordances of FTF interactions. Guided reading strategies "inside the book" were believed to help foster students' "good reading habits" to the same extent that FTF guided reading might, which was another reason why Sally found the application "powerful." Reading discussions in the digital environment were thus seen as equivalent to FTF guided reading discussions.

Features of Netspeak that Complicate the Metaphor of "Discussion"

The literal adoption of the online discussion metaphor is evident in these teachers' applications of technology. Taking the metaphoric discussion capabilities of the platform literally, teachers simply replaced the FTF discussions that they planned with digital interactions, suggesting that they interpreted these as equivalent communication modes. Students were instructed to trade ideas, respond to embedded questions, take quizzes, and write responses to the reading without engaging in FTF conversation, all under the umbrella of "discussion." But as Crystal (2001) and Davis and Brewer (1997) have pointed out, computer mediated discussion—Netspeak-is something beyond speech and written language.

We know that the number of characteristics shared between online and live discussion is quite limited (Crystal, 2001; Davis & Brewer, 1997). In fact, online discussion is a different language altogether, requiring users to understand what can and cannot be accomplished within that medium in relation to the purpose for using it. Drawing upon what we know about the nature of language and the nature of writing online, researchers interested in the affordances of CMD have identified some of the fundamental differences

between FTF and CMD. One striking difference that sets CMD apart from spoken language is the characteristic time lag between a 'speaker' and a 'respondent' online. Crystal, using a linguistic lens to describe how this difference sets CMD apart from FTF communication, explains that time lag breaks our conversational expectations of question-and-response and thus introduces a host of potentially disruptive messages that can undermine effective communication in what he calls "lag wars." Crystal explains that unlike the conventional strategies we use when a silence occurs on a phone call, the silence of a lag between an online question waiting for response has more ambiguity and fewer solutions:

The linguistic strategies which underpin our conversational exchanges are much less reliable in chatgroups. Colin may never get a reaction to his reply to Jane because Jane may never have received it (for technical reasons), may not have noticed it (because there are so many other remarks coming in at the same time), may have been distracted by some other conversation (real or online), may not have been present at her terminal to see the message (for all kinds of reasons), or simply decided not to respond. Equally, she may have replied, and it is her message which has got delayed or lost. When responses are disrupted by delays, there is little anyone can do to sort such things out (p. 32).

This characteristic of Netspeak can appear in classroom CMD when school-wide networks run slowly or go off-line. Although the teachers were generally pleased with the platform as a tool that incorporated social media features to support classroom literary discussion, they did express some frustration with certain aspects of using the platform. These frustrations related generally to the technical aspects of using a digital tool that highlighted (to us, the researchers) the differences between CMD and FTF discussion. All four teachers noted the problem of keeping students engaged in learning when slow Internet connection speeds stalled the progression of a lesson. While they did not explicitly associate this connectivity problem with the platform, the fact that slow connections affected all classroom lessons is consistent with the characteristics of CMD that must be attended to when online discussion is used in a classroom context. Diana expressed a response typical among the four teachers regarding the technical challenges of using an online tool in the classroom: "The part that is just kind of been a thorn is our network is sometimes full-out streaming and sometimes there are pockets that it seems no matter what we do, it keeps loading, loading, loading."

Other teachers described what happened during lessons in which the students using the reading platform were not connected online at the same time. Karen said, "[One challenge is] the network problems, and that's frustrating [speaking as the inner voice of a student], 'How come the person sitting right next to me is not having a problem logging in and I'm having a problem logging in?'" Sally echoed a similar concern regarding student engagement when students were not reading and responding in sync with their peers: "Right, or I'm so far ahead and all of a sudden they're pushing buttons they shouldn't, and they're in a place they can't get out of, you know."

Research on interaction patterns in online spaces has found that without deliberate and active engagement from the instructor, CMD takes on characteristics of IRE (Initiation, Response, Evaluation) discourse patterns that do not support the pedagogical goals of authentic classroom discussion (Cazden, 2001, 1986; Hsieh & Tsai, 2012). Research in CDM for post-secondary students provides evidence that active and 'deep learning' supported by the affordances of authentic discussion can happen, but requires careful attention to instructional design (Bradley, Thom, Hayes, & Hay, 2008). In particular, the types of question posed and an active teacher presence online (Garrison & Cleveland-Innes, 2005) are associated with CMD that is interactive and re-flective in ways that provide some of the powerful learning benefits of FTF classroom discussion. As the research for these studies included samples much older than elementary school students, the transferability of the findings may be marginal. However, post-secondary research provides a potential reference point to consider the data we found in our elementary and middle school sample.

All of the teachers in our sample said that there was "no difference" between planning and giving lessons FTF or within the CMD platform. We use this evidence of teacher perception of CMD as a way to understand our data on the discourse characteristics of the CMD between teachers and students. Our initial finding was consistent with the research on standard CMD in instructional settings, as teachers and students interacted in a characteristic IRE pattern. In the discussion transcript below, we see an example of the best of intentions gone awry: The teacher posed an open question, one that clearly allowed students a wide berth for personal connections, yet as the CMD unfolded, it morphed into a teacher-initiated question with student response (I and R, no E) (see Figure 3).

The student responses shown here are representative of the kinds of interactions we saw as students used the platform and responded to teacher-posed prompts. Even though teachers expressed goals of facilitating outside-school communication modes for literary discussion, and supported those goals by embedding questions that were often both open-ended and personally relevant, they did not meet their objective. Instead of a dynamic peer-led exchange facilitated by a teacher prompt, students responded only to the teacher and did not engage in cross-discussion characteristic of authentic high-quality classroom discussion (Cazden, 1986). Students may have benefitted from the extra time and thought they could put into their responses, but if the intention of this prompt was to promote deeper thinking spurred by peer-led interaction, that goal was subverted by the nature of CMD.

Figure 3. Teacher prompt with student responses

Teacher Prompt:

> 1) Here Clay asks another question about decisions Hannah made. Why do you think Hannah goes with Courtney?
> 2) Connecting--tell a time when you made a decision to do something a friend wanted you to do when you knew you shouldn't.

Student Responses:

> She wanted to be popular.
> I went to this party and I really shouldn't of [sic] gone.

> 1) She wanted to be noticed more. And popular
> 2) I was at the mall and my friend said we should throw bouncy balls down the second floor and I said no.

> 1) I think Hannah goes to the [party] because she wants to be seen with Courtney because Courtney is popular and Hannah isn't
> 2) this one time this girl asked me to go to the gas station at 3 in the morning so I went I thought nothing of it but I didn't know she went there for smoking. BIG MISTAKE

> She wanted to be more noticeable so she went with Hannah
> Yes like every weekend

> Hannah want [sic] to be cool with Courtney

> 1 Hannah wants to be friends with Courtney.
> 2 I went to a party also.

> 1) she wants everyone to think she is cool
> 2) my friend told me to help me hack black ops 2 [video game] n u can get in trouble and they can ban u

> 1: She wanted to be popular
> 2: Me and Trey [were] getting out of a bus and this [one] lady and her mom flicked us and we flicked off them and said couple of things and she got out of her car and tried to get us and we ran

From what we know about CMD, this is not a surprising result, although teachers did not cite the lack of student cross-discussion as an instructional challenge in our interviews. The data in this case were significant for their absence; teachers' lack of acknowledgement of this student interactional pattern may indicate that teachers were not aware of the importance of peer-to-peer interaction for authentic discussion or of the natural interchange fueled by the mechanics of turn-taking absent from asynchronous online interaction. Our data show that teachers posed plausible questions for a FTF classroom discussion, but within the CMD they elicited responses characteristic of IRE. From what we have learned from post-secondary research on CMD, and to the extent that the research can transfer to K-12 school settings, teachers must be deliberate in the way they pose and monitor student responses if they wish to engage students in deep learning online. The relevance of turn taking has implications in setting expectations about student interaction in asynchronous online discussions (Garrison & Cleveland-Innes, 2005).

Fundamental characteristics of online discussion are the absences of prosody and kinesics, which are integral to FTF discussion. Prosody refers to the volume and intonation of speech that provides information beyond the mere words uttered. Kinesics refer to the physical cues used mostly unconsciously (e.g., facial expressions, hand gestures, body position) that provide information beyond what is shared in spoken language. Efforts to embed this information into CMD include the now ubiquitous use of emoticons and exaggerated spellings to convey emotions that result from a loss of self-control (see Goffman, 1981, on response cries). These features have evolved as a way to avoid the ambiguity of written text (Crystal, 2001; Goddard, 2011; Walther & D'Addario, 2001). However, a common complaint that surfaced during the teacher interviews concerned students' uses of casual and playful graphic features in their discussion responses that strove to create a closer approximation to FTF discussion with their peers. Diana cited "inappropriate" student uses of graphics as a challenge associated with classroom use of the application. She expected student-to-student digital interactions inside the book to reflect conventional academic writing. What she saw instead was the type of digital interaction characteristic of CMD:

...they were asked to post to response to other people's paragraphs, and then what was happening was we were getting, "Oh, that's so cool," or just emoticons across [the] post, so then it takes

to a step back, to teach ... proper academic posting, and then to go back into it ... doing it justice is using it to its capacity.

For Diana, the application was a tool for building students' academic discourse through "proper academic posting." This approach aligned with her literal interpretation of the discussion metaphor, as it left no space to acknowledge other forms of language that might emerge in the digital environment. Despite her interest in encouraging student discussion, she envisioned a specific way to "do [the application] justice" in the classroom, including "using it to its capacity" to support academic interactions that were not "cool" but formally sanctioned. Emoticons were perceived as non-academic and therefore as having no place in classroom digital interactions, despite the fact that emoticons strive to replace the prosody characteristic of FTF discussion (Crystal, 2001; Walther & D'Addario, 2001).

The excerpt below, taken from one of Sally's lessons on the novel *13 Reasons,* provides an example of student responses that challenged the metaphor of discussion as teachers attempted to foster "proper" and "academic" interactions within the application. The interaction among Sally's students, beginning with a teacher-posed question, reveals students playfully responding to a text-based question. In the novel, Alex, a high school student, has circulated a list ranking attractive girls at his school. One of the girls on the list, Hannah, reads it, starting a series of events that leads to her suicide. Sally posted a question about this list within the application and required students to respond.

- **T:** What is the list Hannah is talking about and who wrote it?
- **S1:** I think Justin
- **S2:** Justin wrote it
- **S3:** Justin...Maybe?
- **S4:** I think Justin wrote it (Bieber:))
- NVM. ALEX wrote it.

- **S3:** Lol ^^^
- **S3:** Just kidding...It was Alex..
- **S5:** Justin
- **S6:** Is going to be Justin
- **S7:** Jjjjuuussssttiin (hehe)
- **S8:** U fruity Namibia and Justin
- **S9:** JUSTIN HE TALKING BOUT JUSTIN AYE HOLLA @ ME

The question was designed to elicit a quick comprehension check by asking for factual information in the novel. In a FTF interaction, this discussion would allow students to quickly confirm or correct misunderstandings about the story. The students responded both to the question and to each other using graphics and response cries (Goddard, 2011; Goffman, 1981), including a:), LOL (laugh out loud) and ^^^ (indicating the writer pointing to the posting located above). These graphics are rich with the prosody substitutes characteristic of CMD. Ironically, while Sally and the other teachers viewed these sorts of interactions as examples of students "being silly" or "goofing off," these instances were the ones that offered the most authentic representations of the kinds of student interactions that teachers were trying to accommodate by using the online platform. These kinds of student responses were not "academic" in the manner hoped for by the teachers, but they did capture the peer-generated energy and interaction that teachers wished to leverage for text-related writing, reading, and discussion.

DISCUSSION

We know that live communication and online communication are different. We also know that in the classroom there are some differences in modes of communication that matter. Our data on the benefits and challenges of using digital interaction in the classroom illustrate some of the ways in which these differences matter. In this chapter, we have argued that teachers who do not understand the nature of digital interaction as something beyond the metaphoric online "discussion" are less likely to attain their pedagogical objectives when employing digital discourse tools in the classroom. The unique linguistic modes used in digital spaces rely on characteristics that morph digital interaction into a convergence of speech and writing characteristics, spilling into linguistic forms culturally and technically unique to digital interaction.

When FTF discussion becomes the primary metaphor for understanding and implementing online discussion, which was certainly a major force in shaping the expectations, plans, and instructional moves for the participating teachers in our study, it fails to do its work as a guiding framework. It is insufficiently clear, even potentially confusing, to student users, who are often encouraged by the teacher to "talk a lot" using social media features but are required to apply their writing skills in order to do so. Likewise, the FTF metaphor is insufficient and potentially confusing to teachers, who are encouraged by the metaphor to supplant FTF discussion with online discussion without considering the skills that their students will need to use, as well as how using those skills may or may not help achieve their ultimate teaching goals.

Rather than adopting rigid metaphors of discussion that preclude understanding the nuances of interactive written discourse (Ferrara et al., 1991), it is our belief that digital interaction in the classroom is "a new species of communication" with unique conditions of use (Crystal, 2001, p. 48; Eldred & Fortune, 1992; Davis & Brewer, 1997), conditions that depend upon communication purpose and the affordances of the digital media employed. Classroom discussion has purposes and conventions that reach beyond the kinds of informal discussions that might unfold in a coffee shop (for example), so the use of digital tools for learning in the classroom must reach beyond conceptions of the casual social networking and

"talk" that might unfold online between friends or in other informal communities.

What types of tools do literacy teachers need in order to utilize the affordances of CMD powerfully in classrooms? We believe teachers' goals and purposes for using digital interaction tools can be realized only when they understand the distinct affordances of those tools and are able to assess the differences between digital and face-to-face learning environments. To that end, we propose a pedagogical lens that we refer to as Classroom Digital Interaction (CDI), which we conceptualize as a tool that may help practitioners develop more nuanced evaluations of learning tools that encompass written, oral, and digital (Netspeak) registers. As this study suggests, teachers need to understand the limitations and affordances of digital media in order to apply them meaningfully as learning tools. Although current research on the application of CMD in learning contexts provides generative foundations for thinking about the nature of digital interaction, as well as valuable insight into the differences between live speech and writing and online speech and writing, less attention has been paid to the unique pedagogical purposes of discussion in a learning environment.

A CDI lens encourages educators to first take into account the pedagogical purpose of discussion in the literacy classroom, whether face-to-face or digitally mediated, and then consider how those purposes interact with the practical affordances of oral, written, and digital registers to support student learning. Unfortunately, examples of what this might look like in primary or secondary school settings did not arise in our study, and examples from the research literature are sparse. The vast majority of empirical work on online classroom learning has used samples from post-secondary contexts, focusing on the instructional design elements of collaboration and cognitive processing in asynchronous groups. For example, some studies on purely online instruction provide support for active student-teacher interaction. These studies make a strong case that meaningful learning takes place when student-teacher interaction is deliberate, active, and based on theories of collaborative learning (Hsieh & Tsai, 2012; Garrison & Cleveland-Innes, 2005; Schellens & Valcke, 2005). Even the type of questions posed in online discussion elicits qualitatively different answers (in quality and volume) from student respondents (Bradley et al.,; Markel, 2001; Wang & Woo, 2006). Also, tools or features prompting students to reflect on their learning can be instrumental in improving student outcomes (Means et al., 2010). This body of work acts as a useful springboard as we consider future directions for effective digital interaction in in K-12 contexts.

Research on digital reading platforms and their embedded discussion functions is still nascent, and our study revealed a number of areas for future examination. One important area on which to focus future K-12 studies is on how the design of technologies might support the pedagogical objectives of the Common Core Curriculum (National Governors Association, 2010). The Common Core will undoubtedly be delivered through multiple media and may serve as a pretext for elevating the use of CDI. Two possibilities exist. First, the Common Core emphasizes rich text-based discussion leading to summaries of text that will eventually inform writing from sources (i.e., those texts already summarized in the unit in which students are currently working). If students were required to share and to critique one another's summaries, they would end up with a rich source of ideas for their writing projects. Second, speaking and listening standards could be invoked to improve the quality of CDI. Standard 1 in the Speaking and Listening strand rubrics and guidelines emphasizes the integration of information in diverse media and formats (e.g., orally, visually) within and between digital spaces. If students were required to use computer simulations as the basis for oral discussion, for example, they would have a rich source of expert knowledge to draw upon when negotiating meaning with both peers and teachers.

Another area for further study is on the kind of professional development needed to help teachers develop a deep understanding of the affordances and limitations of varied digital interaction tools, and how those affordances and limitations augment or undermine their learning goals. Similarly, how might we help teachers develop their digital interactive platform literacy, so that they gain fluency in uses of digital interaction tools? Too often professional development focuses on the seductive quality of a specialized digital platform's novelty, but what this approach (which often manifests as discrete training workshops) does not accomplish is helping teachers figure out how they might apply what they learned in a workshop to their everyday teaching and learning goals. A workshop can create excitement around a new tool, but it is rare that one focuses on tool appropriation for effective, flexible, and sustained classroom use. We propose CDI as a theory of classroom-based tool appropriation that can help teachers truly meet the needs of the 21st century learner with purposeful and pedagogically appropriate implementation of digital discourse tools.

Future work might also build upon existing post-secondary research on best uses of discussion for online discussion to focus on CDI in K-12 settings. As we have noted elsewhere in this chapter, there are many more available examples of successful use of digital interaction at the post-secondary education level than at the primary or secondary levels. Mining that body of work for examples that might transfer to elementary, middle, and high schools strikes us as a worthy endeavor as we examine how we might help our struggling students evolve in their use of available registers.

REFERENCES

Almasi, J. F. (1995). The nature of fourth graders' sociocognitive conflicts in peer-led and teacher-led discussions of literature. *Reading Research Quarterly*, *30*(3), 314–351. doi:10.2307/747620.

Applebee, A. N., Langer, J. A., Nystrand, M., & Gamoran, A. (2003). Discussion-based approaches to developing understanding: Classroom instruction and student performance in middle and high school English. *American Educational Research Journal*, *40*(3), 685–730. doi:10.3102/00028312040003685.

Bakhtin, M. M. (1981). *The dialogic imagination. Four essays by M. M. Bakhtin. (M. Holquist* (Emerson, C., & Holquist, M. (Trans. Eds.)). Austin, TX: University of Texas Press.

Beach, R., Hull, G., & O'Brien, D. (2011). Transforming English language arts in a web 2.0 world. In D. Lapp & D. Fisher (Eds.), Handbook of research on teaching the English language arts (3rd Ed). IRA & NCTE.

Biber, D., & Finegan, E. (1997). Diachronic relations among speech-based and written registers in English. In Nevalainen, T., & Kahlas-Tarkka, L. (Eds.), *To explain the present: Studies in the changing English language in honour of Matti Rissanen* (pp. 253–276). Helsinki: Société Néophilologique.

Bloome, D. (1985). Reading as a social process. *Language Arts*, *62*(2), 134–142.

Bradley, M. E., Thom, L. R., Hayes, J., & Hay, C. (2008). Ask and you will receive: How question type influences quantity and quality of online discussions. *British Journal of Educational Technology*, *39*(5), 888–900. doi:10.1111/j.1467-8535.2007.00804.x.

Britton, J. (1969/1990). *Language, the learner, and the school* (4th ed.). Portsmouth, NH: Boynton-Cook.

Carrington, V., & Robinson, M. (2009). Introduction: Contentious technologies. In Carrington, V., & Robinson, M. (Eds.), *Digital literacies: Social learning and classroom practices* (pp. 1–9). London: Sage Publications.

Cazden, C. B. (1986). Classroom discourse. In Wittrock, M. C. (Ed.), *Handbook of research on teaching* (3rd ed., pp. 432–463). New York: Macmillan.

Cazden, C. B. (1997). Foreword. In Paratore, J. R., & McCormack, R. L. (Eds.), *Peer talk in the classroom: Learning from research* (p. v). Newark, DE: International Reading Association.

Cazden, C. B. (2001). *Discourse: The language of teaching and learning*. Portsmouth, NH: Heinemann.

Chafe, W., & Tannen, D. (1987). The relation between written and spoken language. *Annual Review of Anthropology*, 383–407. doi:10.1146/annurev.an.16.100187.002123.

Coiro, J., Knobel, M., Lankshear, C., & Leu, D. (2008). Central issues in new literacies and new literacies research. In Coiro, J., Knobel, M., Lankshear, C., & Leu, D. (Eds.), *Handbook of research on new literacies* (pp. 1–21). New York, NY: Taylor & Francis Group.

Cook-Sather, A. (2002). Authorizing students' perspectives: Toward trust, dialogue, and change in education. *Educational Researcher*, *31*(4), 3–14. doi:10.3102/0013189X031004003.

Crystal, D. (2001). *Language and the internet*. Cambridge, UK: Cambridge University Press. doi:10.1017/CBO9781139164771.

Cuban, L., Kirkpatrick, H., & Peck, C. (2001). High access and low use of technologies in high school classrooms: Explaining an apparent paradox. *American Educational Research Journal*, *38*(4), 813–834. doi:10.3102/00028312038004813.

Daiute, C. (2000). Writing and communication technologies. In Indrisano, R., & Squire, J. R. (Eds.), *Perspectives on writing: Research, theory, and practice* (pp. 251–276). Newark, DE: International Reading Association.

Davis, B. H., & Brewer, J. (1997). *Electronic discourse: Linguistic individuals in virtual space.* Albany, NY: State University of New York Press.

Dennes, V. P. (2005). From message posting to learning dialogues: Factors affecting learner participation in asynchronous discussion. *Distance Education, 26*(1), 127–148. doi:10.1080/01587910500081376.

Deoksoon, K. (2011). Incorporating podcasting and blogging into a core task for ESOL teacher candidates. *Computers & Education, 56*(1), 632–641.

Dredger, K., Woods, D., Beach, C., & Sagstetter, V. (2010). Engage me: Using new literacies to create third space classrooms that engage student writers. *Journal of Media Literacy Education, 2*(2), 85–101.

Duke, N. K., & Pearson, P. D. (2008). Effective practices for developing reading comprehension. *Journal of education, 189*(1), 107.

Dymoke, S., & Hughes, J. (2009). Using a poetry wiki: How can the medium support pre-service teachers of English in their professional learning about writing poetry and teaching poetry writing in a digital age? *English Teaching: Practice and Critique, 8*(3), 91–106.

Dysthe, O. (1996). The multivoiced classroom: Interactions of writing and classroom discourse. *Written Communication, 13*(3), 385–425. doi:10.1177/0741088396013003004.

Eldred, J. C., & Fortune, R. (1992). Exploring the implications of metaphors for computer networks and hypermedia. In Hawisher, G. E., & LeBlanc, P. (Eds.), *Re-imagining computers and composition: Teaching and research in the virtual age* (pp. 58–73). Portsmouth, NH: Boyton.

Erickson, F., & Schultz, J. (1977). When is a context? Some issues and methods in the analysis of social competence. *Quarterly Newsletter of the Institute for Comparative Human Development, 1*(2), 5–10.

Ferrara, K., Brunner, H., & Whittemore, G. (1991). Interactive written discourse as an emergent register. *Written Communication, 8*(1), 8–34. doi:10.1177/0741088391008001002.

Flores, M. (1990). Computer conferencing: Composing a feminist community of writers. In Handa, C. (Ed.), *Computers and community* (pp. 106–117). Portsmouth, NH: Boynton/Cook Heinemann.

Gambrell, L. B. (1996). What research reveals about discussion. In Gambrell, L. B., & Almasi, J. F. (Eds.), *Lively discussion! Fostering engaged reading* (pp. 25–38). Newark, DE: International Reading Association.

Garrison, D. R., & Cleveland-Innes, M. (2005). Facilitating cognitive presence in online learning: Interaction is not enough. *American Journal of Distance Education, 19*(3), 133–148. doi:10.1207/s15389286ajde1903_2.

Gilles, C., & Pierce, K. M. (2003). Making room for talk: Examining the historical implications of talk in learning. *English Education, 36*(1), 56–79.

Goddard, A. (2011). Type you soon! A stylistic approach to language use in a virtual learning environment. *Language and Literature, 20*, 184–200. doi:10.1177/0963947011413561.

Goffman, E. (1981). *Forms of talk*. Philadelphia: University of Pennsylvania Press.

Green, J. L. (1983). Research on teaching as a linguistic process: A state of the art. In Gordon, E. W. (Ed.), *Review of research in education.* Washington, DC: American Educational Research Association. doi:10.2307/1167138.

Groenke, S. L. (2007). Collaborative dialogue in a synchronous CMC environment? A look at one beginning English teacher's strategies. *Journal of Computing in Teacher Education, 24*(2), 41–47.

Haas, C., & Takayoshi, P. (2011). Young people's everyday literacies: The language features of instant messaging. *Research in the Teaching of English, 45*(4), 378–404.

Halliday, M. (1980). Three aspects of children's language development: Learning language, learning through language, learning about language? In Goodman, Y., Haussler, M., & Strickland, D. (Eds.), *Oral and written language development research: Impact on the schools I* (pp. 7–20). Urbana, IL: NCTE and IRA.

Harris, J., Mishra, P., & Koehler, M. (2009). Teachers' technological pedagogical content knowledge and learning activity types: Curriculum-based technology integration reframed. *Journal of Research on Technology in Education, 41*(4), 393–416.

Herrington, A., Hodgson, K., & Moran, C. (2009). *Teaching the new writing: Technology, change, and assessment in the 21st century classroom.* New York: Teachers College Press.

Hew, K. F., & Cheung, W. S. (2003). Evaluating the participation and quality of thinking of pre-service teachers in an asynchronous online discussion environment: Part 1. *International Journal of Instructional Media, 30*(3), 247–262.

Honan, E. (2009). Mapping discourses in teachers' talk about using digital texts in classrooms. *Discourse: Studies in the Cultural Politics of Education, 31*(2), 179–193. doi:10.1080/01596301003679701.

Hsieh, Y. H., & Tsai, C. C. (2012). The effect of moderator's facilitative strategies on online synchronous discussions. *Computers in Human Behavior, 28*(5), 1708–1716. doi:10.1016/j.chb.2012.04.010.

Hull, G., & Nelson, M. E. (2005). Locating the semiotic power of multimodality. *Written Communication, 22*, 224–261. doi:10.1177/0741088304274170.

Hull, G., & Schultz, K. (2002). *School's out: Bridging out-of-school literacies with classroom practice.* New York, NY: Teachers College Press.

Hungerford-Kresser, H., Wiggins, J., & Amaro-Jimenez, C. (2012). Learning from our mistakes: What matters when incorporating blogging in the content area literacy classroom. *Journal of Adolescent & Adult Literacy, 55*(4), 326–335. doi:10.1002/JAAL.00039.

Hutchison, A., & Reinking, D. (2011). Teachers' perceptions of integrating information and communication technologies into literacy instruction: A national survey in the U.S. *Reading Research Quarterly, 46*(4), 308–329.

Jewitt, C. (2005). Multimodality, reading, and writing for the 21st century. *Discourse: Studies in the cultural politics of education, 26*(3), 315-331.

Juzwik, M. M., Nystrand, M., Kelly, S., & Sherry, M. B. (2008). Oral narrative genres as dialogic resources for classroom literature study: A contextualized case study of conversational narrative discussion. *American Educational Research Journal, 45*(4), 1111–1154. doi:10.3102/0002831208321444.

Juzwik, M. M., & Sherry, M. B. (2007). Expressive language and the art of English teaching: Theorizing the relationship between literature and oral narrative. *English Education, 39*(3), 226–259.

Lakoff, G., & Johnson, M. (1980). *Metaphors we live by.* Chicago: University of Chicago Press.

Langer, J. (2001). Beating the odds: Teaching middle and high school students to read and write well. *American Educational Research Journal, 38*(4), 837–880. doi:10.3102/00028312038004837.

Lankshear, C., & Knobel, M. (2011). *The new literacies: Everyday practices and social learning.* Berkshire, UK: Open University Press.

Lyman, F. (1987). Think-pair-share: An expanding teaching technique. *MAA-CIE Cooperative News, 1*(1-2).

Mahiri, J. (2011). *Digital tools in urban schools: Mediating a remix of learning.* Ann Arbor, MI: University of Michigan Press. doi:10.3998/toi.10329379.0001.001.

Maloch, B. (2002). Scaffolding student talk: One teacher's role in literature discussion groups. *Reading Research and Instruction, 42,* 1–29.

Markel, S. L. (2001). Technology and education online discussion forums: It's in the response. *Online Journal of Distance Learning Administration, 4*(2).

McKeown, M., Beck, I., & Blake, R. G. (2009). Rethinking reading comprehension instruction: A comparison of instruction for strategies and content approaches. *Reading Research Quarterly, 44*(3), 218–253. doi:10.1598/RRQ.44.3.1.

Means, B., Toyama, Y., Murphy, R., Bakia, M., & Jones, K. (2010). *Evaluation of evidence-based practices in online learning: A meta-analysis and review of online learning studies. Technical Report.* Washington, DC: U.S. Department of Education.

Miles, M. B., & Huberman, A. M. (1994). *Qualitative data analysis: An expanded sourcebook* (2nd ed.). Thousand Oaks, CA: Sage.

Mills, K. A., & Chandra, V. (2011). Microblogging as a literacy practice for educational communities. *Journal of Adolescent & Adult Literacy, 55*(1), 35–45.

Moje, E. B., & Shepardson, D. P. (1998). Social interactions and children's changing understanding of electric circuits: Exploring unequal power relations in peer-led learning groups. In Guzzetti, B., & Hynd, C. (Eds.), *Perspectives on conceptual change: Multiple ways to understand knowing and learning in a complex world* (pp. 225–234). Mahwah, NJ: Erlbaum.

National Governors Association Center for Best Practices, Council of Chief State School Officers. (2010). *Common core state standards.* Washington, DC: National Governors Association Center for Best Practices, Council of Chief State School Officers.

Newman, D. R., Johnson, C., Webb, B., & Cochrane, C. (1997). Evaluating the quality of learning in computer supported cooperative learning. *Journal of the American Society for Information Science American Society for Information Science, 48,* 484–495. doi:10.1002/(SICI)1097-4571(199706)48:6<484::AID-ASI2>3.0.CO;2-Q.

Nystrand, M. (1997). *Opening dialogue: Understanding the dynamics of language and learning in the English classroom.* New York: Teachers College Press.

Nystrand, M. (2006). Classroom discourse and reading comprehension. *Research in the Teaching of English, 40,* 392–412.

Nystrand, M., Gamoran, A., & Carbonaro, W. (1998). *Toward an ecology of learning: The case of classroom discourse and its effects on writing in high school English and social studies.* Albany, NY: National Research Center on English Learning & Achievement.

Ochs, E. (1979). Planned and unplanned discourse. In Givón, T. (Ed.), *Syntax and semantics: Discourse and syntax* (pp. 51–80). New York: Academic.

Olson, D. (1977). From utterance to text: The bias of language in speech and writing. *Harvard Educational Review, 47*, 257–281.

Prestidge, S. (2012). The beliefs behind the teacher that influences their ICT practices. *Computers & Education, 58*(1), 449–458. doi:10.1016/j.compedu.2011.08.028.

Reinhardt, J., & Zander, V. (2011). Social networking in an intensive English program classroom: A language socialization perspective. *CALICO Journal, 28*(2), 326–344.

Rice, K. L. (2006). A comprehensive look at distance education in the K-12 context. *Journal of Research on Technology in Education, 38*(4), 425.

Schellens, T., & Valcke, M. (2005). Collaborative learning in asynchronous discussion groups: What about the impact on cognitive processing? *Computers in Human Behavior, 21*(6), 957–975. doi:10.1016/j.chb.2004.02.025.

Selfe, C. L. (1990). Technology in the English classroom: Computers through the lens of feminist theory. In Handa, C. (Ed.), *Computers and community* (pp. 118–139). Portsmouth, NH: Boynton/Cook Heinemann.

Soter, A. O., Wilkinson, I. A., Murphy, P. K., Rudge, L., Reninger, K., & Edwards, M. (2008). What the discourse tells us: Talk and indicators of high-level comprehension. *International Journal of Educational Research, 47*, 372–391. doi:10.1016/j.ijer.2009.01.001.

Sotillo, S. M. (2000). Discourse functions and syntactic complexity in synchronous and asynchronous communication. *Language Learning & Technology, 4*(1), 82–119.

Starkey, L. (2010). Teachers' pedagogical reasoning and action in the digital age. *Teachers and Teaching: Theory and Practice, 16*(2), 233–244. doi:10.1080/13540600903478433.

Stolle, E. (2008). Teachers, literacy, & technology: Tensions, complexities, conceptualizations & practice. In Y. Kim, V. Risko, D. Compton, D. Dickinson, M. Hundley, R. Jimenez, K. Leander, & D. Wells-Rowe (Eds.), *57th Yearbook of the National Reading Conference* (pp. 56–69). Oak Creek, WI: National Reading Conference.

Sutherland-Smith, W. (2002). Integrating online discussion in an Australian intensive English language course. *TESOL Journal, 11*(3), 31–35.

Tagliamonte, S. A., & Denis, D. (2008). Linguistic ruin? LOL! Instant messaging and teen language. *American Speech, 83*(1), 3–34. doi:10.1215/00031283-2008-001.

Tannen, D. (1982). *Spoken and written language: Exploring orality and literacy.* ABLEX Publishing Corporation.

Tearle, P. (2003). ICT implementation: What makes the difference? *British Journal of Educational Technology, 34*(5), 567–583. doi:10.1046/j.0007-1013.2003.00351.x.

Tsai, H. F., & Wilkinson, I. A. (2010). *Why should discussion affect reading comprehension? An analysis of theoretical frameworks.* Paper presented at the Annual Meeting of the American Educational Research Association. Denver, CO.

Van den Branden, K. (2000). Does negotiation of meaning promote reading comprehension? A study of multilingual primary school classes. *Reading Research Quarterly, 35*, 426–443. doi:10.1598/RRQ.35.3.6.

Vie, S. (2008). Digital divide 2.0: 'Generation M' and online social networking sites in the composition classroom. *Computers and Composition, 25*(1), 9–23. doi:10.1016/j.compcom.2007.09.004.

Wade, S. E., & Fauske, J. R. (2004). Dialogue online: Prospective teachers' discourse strategies in computer-mediate discussions. *Reading Research Quarterly*, *39*(2), 134–160. doi:10.1598/RRQ.39.2.1.

Wake, D. G., & Modla, V. B. (2012). Using wikis with teacher candidates: Promoting collaborative practice and contextual analysis. *Journal of Research on Technology in Education*, *44*(3), 243–265.

Walther, J. B., & D'Addario, K. P. (2001). The impacts of emoticons on message interpretation in computer-mediated communication. *Social Science Computer Review*, *19*(3), 324–347. doi:10.1177/089443930101900307.

Wang, Q., & Woo, H. L. (2006). Comparing asynchronous online discussions and face-to-face discussions in a classroom setting. *British Journal of Educational Technology*, *38*(2), 272–286. doi:10.1111/j.1467-8535.2006.00621.x.

Warschauer, M. (2007). Technology and writing. In Davison, C., & Cummins, J. (Eds.), *The international handbook of English language teaching* (pp. 907–912). Norwell, MA: Springer. doi:10.1007/978-0-387-46301-8_60.

Wells, G. (2007). Semiotic mediation, dialogue and the construction of knowledge. *Human Development*, *50*(5), 244–274. doi:10.1159/000106414.

Wilkenson, I. A. G., & Son, E. H. (2011). A dialogic turn in research on learning and teaching to comprehend. In Kamil, M. L., Pearson, P. D., Moje, E. B., & Afflerbach, P. P. (Eds.), *Handbook of Reading Research* (*Vol. 4*, pp. 359–387). New York: Routledge.

Wolf, M. K., Crosson, A. C., & Resnick, L. B. (2005). Classroom talk for rigorous reading comprehension instruction. *Reading Psychology*, *26*(1), 27–53. doi:10.1080/02702710490897518.

Xie, K., DeBacker, T. K., & Ferguson, C. (2006). Extending the traditional classroom through online discussion: The role of student motivation. *Journal of Educational Computing Research*, *34*(1), 67–89. doi:10.2190/7BAK-EGAH-3MH1-K7C6.

Yancey, K. B. (2009). 2008 NCTE presidential address: The impulse to compose and the age of composition. *Research in the Teaching of English*, *43*(3), 316–338.

Chapter 15
Digital Texts as Sources for Novice Writers

Thomas DeVere Wolsey
Walden University, USA

Diane Lapp
San Diego State University, USA

Douglas Fisher
San Diego State University, USA

ABSTRACT

In this chapter, the authors review literature describing how reading processes appear to work in online and other digital environments. In particular, the nature of reading, writing, and the academic utility of new literacies is explored and applied to the digital environments of secondary school students. Writing is described as an ill-defined domain and situated theoretically in classical discourse theories as well as cognitive-linguistic approaches that explain reading and writing interactions in digital environments. Specific considerations for using digital texts as sources for written work are explained, including the role of search engine optimization techniques on reading and how access to multiple varied sources changes what students can learn. Implications and suggestions for future research are provided.

INTRODUCTION

"What should I write about?" a common question. "Write about what you know," a common response. However, in writing, identifying what one knows is not clear-cut, and understanding how one comes to such identification is often far more complex than it first appears. Successful authors have long held that a key to writing something others deem worthwhile involves reading prodigiously (Langer & Flihan, 2000). Novice writers, who read digital content and reflect on the workings of the text as well as the content, may find insights gained from such scrutinization that support their writing improvement. There, however, is still much to learn about the nature of reading in digital environments and how doing so impacts one's writing.

It appears that readers approach reading digital texts, especially those found online, in ways that differ from printed texts. One significant difference that may change the dynamic relationship between reading and writing is that the Internet makes knowledge just a click away, thus, increasing the possibility of reading widely and abundantly. Digital texts are available on-demand and as

DOI: 10.4018/978-1-4666-4341-3.ch015

needed (cf., Stewart 1997). Availability of digital texts expands one's opportunities to explore varied points-of-view and perspectives. Access to many sources on the World Wide Web, as well as in other digital formats such as databases, provides a view of the world that is more expansive and inclusive than at any time in history (Friedman, 2000; Buchanan; 2002).

Reading and writing have always been technology-driven; one cannot write without a pencil, a keyboard, or a stylus. Similarly, one cannot read without a book, a scroll, or a screen. Technologies are tools, which are commonly thought of as computers, pencils, and the Internet; however, systems are also tools, though less tangible (Hughes, 2004). The systems of reading and writing are, thus, technologies, though one does not simply pick up a system as one would a tablet computer; nevertheless, the systems readers and writers rely upon weigh heavily on what one comprehends from reading and what one can compose. Succinctly, what a writer reads changes the nature of that writer's expertise; however, what is known about online reading (e.g. Coiro & Dobler, 2007) and its relationship to writing tasks still awaits further study. One purpose of the literature review found in this chapter is to expose areas in need of further examination (Hart, 1998). We explore the tools of reading digital texts, the limitations such texts impose on novice writers, and the possibilities for an expansive view of writing in digital environments.

EPISTEMOLOGY AND IDENTITY

Identity is a complex construction that is shaped as individuals navigate contexts of gender, race, class, and other cultural dimensions. Archer, Deweiit, Osborne, Dillon, Willis, and Wong (2010) working in the United Kingdom, reported their findings from focus group interviews drawn from schools representing a variety of contexts (e.g., urban, private religious, private elementary mainly

white). Though this work dealt with a wide array of identity constructions relative to science, these findings offer the seeds of two overarching and key concepts that are useful to the study of reading and writing relationships. They are 1) students can and will consult reading materials that support their interests, albeit outside of school, and 2) they can construct parts of their identities as to what it means to "do" science or be a scientist through what they read. As we shall see, writers seek to assert themselves as competent contributors in the world, and what they read, digitally and on paper, greatly informs their writing.

We can think of writing as an act of asserting oneself as a unique being in the world. Writers, particularly in academic settings, are not just demonstrating what they know; they are also defining themselves as cognitive beings in the world (e.g., Erikson, 1968; Yagelski, 2009) with something substantive to contribute. Even as students increasingly use digital tools, and their capacity to use them informs their identities, their ability to use them for academic writing purposes, such as reading to inform writing, may benefit from well-planned instruction.

Consistent with Erikson's characterization of identity formation, Meredith, Coyle, and Newman (2011) explored the relationships between motivation and recreational and academic reading, in both traditional and digital formats. They found that social sharing was an important predictor of reading frequency in both recreational and academic contexts (cf. Grisham & Wolsey, 2006).

The question that guides this chapter is the result of our inquiries into the nature of reading, writing, and the academic utility of new literacies. We wondered, "How do secondary students (e.g., middle and high school) read in digital environments to inform their writing? What we found leaves us with more questions than answers but also with a sense of direction.

Note: We have limited the scope of the present chapter to an examination of digital reading on writing tasks whether digital or more traditional in character. The nature of digital writing tasks will be examined in other chapters in this volume, and thus we do not explore them further here. Additionally, our examination of the literature on reading in digital environments does not include a discussion of technologies designed specifically for the purpose of teaching reading or improving reading comprehension online or offline because such a discussion is beyond the scope of the present chapter.

THEORETICAL FRAMEWORK

We draw on four traditions in our examination of the reading practices of high school students and how instruction may be improved if the unique challenges and advantages of digital tools are brought to bear on writing tasks. First, we provide an overview of cognitive flexibility theory (Spiro, 2004; Spiro, Coulson, Feltovich, & Anderson, 2004; Spiro, Feltovich, & Coulson, 1996) as it might be applied to writing and other composing tasks. Next, we consider the communication model approach (e.g., Kinneavy, 1971). We then turn to the shared knowledge and cognitive processes model of reading and writing relations (Fitzgerald & Shanahan, 2000), and finally employ the principles of Leu, Kinzer, Coiro, and Cammack (2004) toward understanding new literacies as a lens for considering the relationship between reading texts in a digital environment and writing tasks.

Writing as an Ill-Defined Domain

Cognitive flexibility theory (e.g., Spiro, Feltovich, & Coulson, 1996) has been applied to the medical field, computer-mediated environments, and reading (Spiro, 2004; Spiro, Coulson, Feltovich, & Anderson, 2004). We (Wolsey, 2010) have also asserted that it is useful in describing how novice writers approach composing tasks, and informing the types of written work students' produce, whether self-sponsored (cf., Emig, 1971)

or school-sponsored (cf., Hillocks, 1986). Cognitive flexibility theory proposes that some fields of endeavor are ill-defined; that is, they resist oversimplification, reduction, and disaggregation. Writing, treated as a complex endeavor, presents and encourages an expansive and flexible world view for novice writers learning to make a literate space in the world. Spiro and his colleagues (2004) call these endeavors approaches that avoid prescriptive views of complex concepts or single representations of products or processes.

Classical Origins and Communication Approach to Discourse

The tradition of reading to gain a view of an expansive world through writing may be found in Classical texts (e.g., Kinneavy, 1971). We can trace the outlines of this thinking forward to today as we consider new demands for high-quality written work (cf. Common Core State Standards [CCSS], 2010). One important way of knowing and understanding the world is to read about it. In the digital age, reading multiple texts about the world has never been more accessible.

Because traditional understanding of discourses implies a receptive aspect (e.g., listening, reading) and an expressive aspect (e.g., speaking, writing), a brief overview of the well-known communication triangle may provide insight as we consider the receptive or input aspects of reading online materials that eventually inform written discourse production. We rely on Kinneavy's representation of the model. For our purposes, this simplified representation will suffice; for a full explanation, see Kinneavy (1971). In this model, an encoder has a message to send while a decoder receives that message across the top of the inverted triangle (see Figure 1). At the nadir, we find the reality to which the encoder's message refers, and in the middle is the signal or carrier of the message. In our consideration of digital reading, the signal or media, as we shall see, is of

Figure 1. Communication triangle

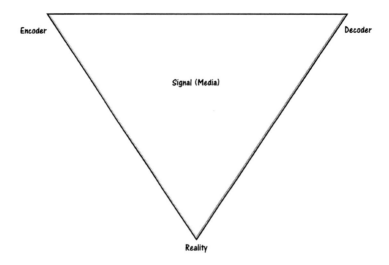

particular importance. Kinneavy further explains the purposes of discourse in terms of this triangle. Discourses overlap, of course, but the emphasis of a given discourse tends to emphasize one of the vertices more than the other (cf. Moffett, 1983). For example, referential-oriented discourses (e.g., informational and scientific discourse) tend to favor the vertex labeled "reality." Persuasive texts emphasize the vertex labeled "decoder" because the message is intended to have a direct effect on the recipient of the message. Expressive discourse, in this model, favors the encoder, and literary discourse favors the signal itself.

How Does Reading Improve Writing?

Writing is much more than the mirror image of reading, and composing places greater demands on working memory than reading tasks do (Berninger & Richards, 2002). Reading and writing are, simultaneously separable (that is, treated as separate domains with discrete differences in many respects) and interrelated (that is, they draw on shared knowledge of language between the domains and some common cognitive processes). The cognitive processes model of the reading-writing relationship (Fitzgerald & Sha-

nahan, 2000; Shanahan, 2006) asserts that some aspects of reading and writing share a "common substrata of abilities" (Shanahan, 2006, p. 174 ff). These substrata inform each other and provide a framework for "bootstrapping" competency in the counterpart. Fitzgerald and Shanahan theorize four substrata that inform development of reading-writing relationships from a cognitive perspective.

Reading and Writing Relationships and Development

A domain of content knowledge, or what the writing will be about, is cognitively available in both reading and writing processes. Readers draw on content knowledge to construct a mental representation of the text; writers similarly draw on this content knowledge, harking back to our opening paragraph that writers are often exhorted to write about what they know as they construct texts. Also, what one knows about the nature of written language, metaknowledge, can assist readers with insights into what a writer's purposes might have been in constructing the text. Similarly, the features of language, such as orthography, word recognition skills, and so on, inform both reading and writing processes and are often bidirectional (e.g., word recognition skills in reading are a predictor of spelling capacity). Finally, procedural knowledge related to access, use, and generation of information function as a common substratum between reading and writing processes. Though the reading and writing processes are correlated, they are not necessarily symmetrical (Shanahan, 2006).

Fitzgerald and Shanahan (2000) suggested that cognitive development, at least in proficient readers, proceeds in stages based on the work of Chall (1996). The fifth stage of this model focuses on proficient readers and writers at the high school level (approximately ages 14-18). Stage four, roughly descriptive of middle school (ages 9-13) focuses on syntactic structures, text structures, and creating and using word meaning and connected texts. Though the model described the development of proficient language users, it can also inform researchers and practitioners about the possible needs of readers and writers who struggle. In stage five of this framework, termed "multiple viewpoints," the progression of tasks focuses on larger blocks of text, multiple texts that tend to develop ability to choose and apply cognitive strategies when reading, facility with text structure, and working with ever more complex and connected texts. The ability to work with multiple texts and understand the point-of-view of others overlaps significantly with new literacies theories.

Framework for Considering New Literacies

Digital literacies, as Dodge, Husain, and Duke (2011) point out, are thought of as a set of functional skills needed to navigate the digital environment and they are conceptualized as social practices within digital environments. Leu et al. (2004) suggest central principles of new literacies that will eventually inform a theory of the new literacies perspective. New literacies encompass digital literacies, and these principles emphasize the social nature of new literacies as well as the functional or strategic knowledge necessary to work within the digital environment. More specifically, Leu et al. suggest that new literacies require attention to speed, and they are deictic, meaning that they are in a state of constant change, encompassing a multiplicity of tools and dispositions.

DIGITAL TEXTS AS SOURCES FOR NOVICE WRITERS

The four common cognitive substrata that reading and writing share are explored through a new literacies perspective in the following section. In each, we note possibilities and suggest possible routes for further inquiry into the nature of reading digital texts to inform effective writing and writing pedagogies.

Metaknowledge

Metaknowledge refers to a constellation of knowledge that readers and writers, in this case, hold and can employ in relation to their knowledge of purposes for literacy activities, motivation to engage in those activities, and the capacity for monitoring learning and composing processes. The substratum of metaknowledge may be the most thoroughly explored of the four processes common to both reading and writing. Regarding motivation, Archer et al. (2010) note that students wanted something that made their brains work. Problems that require deep thinking about problems that are complex and ill-defined (e.g., Spiro et al., 2004) tend to be motivating for students. Similarly, the pervasive nature of digital technologies and the novelty of new tools can be motivating, as well.

Domain Knowledge

Texts are always about something; they must attend to content in some substantive way if they are to serve communication purposes. What students write about is critically important, and how they develop an understanding of those topics has changed as digital texts are increasingly available.

Disciplinary literacy focuses on what is unique to the texts in a given field of study as well as the thinking in a given field of inquiry. The concept of disciplinary literacy or domain knowledge is not new and much is known about the characteristics of text in many disciplines (cf. Moje, 2007). In school, this notion is sometimes characterized as "thinking like a…" historian, mathematician, and so on. Using the domain of history as one illustrative example, Hynd (1999) suggested that historians think of documents as arguments, typically constructed from many other sources, rather than as discrete facts to be learned and points out the dichotomy between how historians work and how history is presented in textbooks (Estes, 2007). The approach to the study of history and the sources on which that study relies informs the literacies on which professionals in that field employ (e.g., Drake & Brown, 2003).

In the example of primary sources in the study of history, students now have access to a wide variety of texts via databases and Websites (e.g. http://catalog.loc.gov/, http://ipr.ues.gseis.ucla.edu/), some curated and some not. In earlier times, a set of primary sources, limited in number, were reproduced and given to students; in the second decade of the 21st century, students have access to a wide variety of primary sources and an increasing collection housed in multiple online locations. How students navigate these archives, identify appropriate resources for academic purposes, and interpret digitized materials is less well investigated. Our review of the literature shows this to be true in other disciplines, as well, even as the quantity of reliable sources is increasingly available.

Knowledge of Universal Text Attributes

Universal attributes of text include vocabulary and orthographic knowledge (e.g., Chomsky, 1970), knowledge of text structures, letter-sound correspondences, and syntax. Though educators sometimes decry the effect of emoticons (e.g., smileys) and abbreviated words and phrases found in texting environments, it appears that students do know the difference and can code-switch when expected to do so for academic purposes. A 2009 study (Plester, Wood, & Joshi) reported that there was no relationship between students' use of textisms and their capacity to use traditional spellings and language features.

Text structures in paper-based works have been documented thoroughly in the literature (e.g., Dymock, 2005). These include description and list structures, cause and effect, comparison and contrast, sequence structures. Often, such structures are identified using headings, organizational graphics, and introductory text that specifically indicate the structure of the text to follow. Instruction intended to improve comprehension through attention to text structures has permeated the literature for practitioners (e.g., Armbruster, Anderson, & Ostertag, 1989). English teachers frequently ask students to write in the style of a given author, sometimes as a parody (e.g., Bintz, 2012; Gardner, n.d.). By mimicking or riffing on the style of a mentor text, novice writers learn to attend to the syntactic features and word choices professional authors make. However, digital texts can differ substantively from paper-based texts. Reinking (1997) illustrated how non-linear text characterizes digital content; that is, the entry point is not always page one and the next section of text may not be page two. Digressions and alternate paths permit readers to move through text skipping some portions and deeply exploring others depending on their purposes and interests for reading (also see Protopsaltis, 2008). Texts transformed for the eReader format or written specifically for these venues (e.g. iPad, Kindle, Inkling) may introduce new complexities and suggest new frameworks for thinking about text, as well (e.g., Wilson, Zygouris-Coe, Carullo, & Fong, 2013).

Though there is a great deal of description of non-linear text, additional research about the way students navigate these types of texts and effective instructional approaches is needed if students are to use hypertext to their advantages in positioning themselves as authors who have something worthwhile to say as a result of their cognitive work with digital texts. Moreover, such texts allow linking to other texts (including multimodal texts), often created by others, that could change the nature of the discourse itself. Tseng (2010) found that the limitations of the online environment (e.g., limited ability to annotate texts, eyestrain, being distracted by other elements of the online environment) were problematic for English-as-a-foreign language students at university.

How readers approach text bears on their comprehension, as well. When readers go online to a search engine, their reading of the search result tends to skip wide swaths of text as they search for the content they need (Neilsen, 2012). Eye movements can be tracked, and during perusal of a search result, the places where the reader's gaze tends to be most concentrated resembles an 'F' shape. The reader takes in key terms most often on the left side of the screen and sweeps across other places forming the arms of the 'F.' As important, once readers do select a Web source to read, they tend to follow the same pattern during initial reading of the Webpage. Because reading on the screen is somewhat different than reading on paper, Web designers actually take advantage of this F-shaped pattern and write text using headings and key words that fall within the F-zone in an effort to gain the reader's attention. The challenge for teachers and the readers in their classes is deciding when to use this strategy and when to go beyond this approach and read a bit more thoroughly and perhaps slowly (cf. Newkirk, 2012).

Purcell, Rainie, Heaps, Buchanan, Friedrich, Jacklin…Zickuhr (2012) noted that teachers in a survey drawn from a sample of Advanced Placement instructors and the National Writing Project believe that digital search tools have a mostly positive effect on student reading; however, they also note that students are more easily distracted and expect that information will be relatively easy to locate. At the same time, the report points out that the teachers believe students are overwhelmed with the amount of information and are thus discouraged from employing the wide range of sources that might otherwise inform their research. Given the tendency of online readers to use the F-shaped pattern as they read voluminous Webpages and the possibility that high school readers might be inefficient and discouraged readers of online sources, further research into instructional routines and pedagogies that promote close reading of online materials may, at times, be appropriate. A working definition of close reading is in order: "Close reading is characterized by the use of evidence from the text to support analysis, conclusions, or views of texts" (Wolsey, Grisham, & Hiebert, 2012, p. 2). The Partnership for Assessment of Readiness for College and Careers (2012) explains close reading:

Close, analytic reading stresses engaging with a text of sufficient complexity directly and examining its meaning thoroughly and methodically, encouraging students to read and reread deliberately. Directing student attention on the text itself empowers students to understand the central ideas and key supporting details. (2012, section 3, para. 3).

In traditional close reading approaches, the teacher prereads the material, identifies challenges, and develops guiding or text-dependent questions that push the reader back to the text (e.g., Schleppegrell, Greer, & Taylor, 2008) to analyze all dimensions of the how the text works including language, form, rhetorical tropes, argument, and ideologies within texts (Brummett, 2010; Fisher, Frey & Lapp, 2012).

When students work online, the likelihood increases that students select texts that were not chosen by the teacher, and the teacher may not have vetted the texts in terms of reading challenges or appropriateness for the reading task, composing task, grade level, and so on. Nevertheless, in spite of all that is known about the construction of Webpages for search engine optimization, long-standing practices that rely upon close reading, and increased demands that students read texts closely, we found no empirical studies of how students read texts closely in digital environments in a large database of scholarly papers using the keywords "close reading."

Procedural Knowledge

Reading to write tasks include two dimensions (Lenski, 1998): social context (what the teacher's purposes and expectations are and the student's interpretation of those purposes and expectations). Such tasks also call for problem-solving proficiency in relation to finding appropriate sources, working within the structure of the task, and so forth. She points out that writing that draws upon reading sources selected during research, students draw far less on memory for content and rely on the sources they find and read. "Teachers believe that they assign research papers so students will engage in inquiry and learn about the topic under discussion. Students, on the other hand, think that research papers are a process of information gathering that shows their degree of competence about locating source material" (p. 291). This is congruent with Kinneavy's (1971) characterization of referential discourse.

Digital Texts

That students should be instructed in how to evaluate Websites they find and may choose to employ in support of their own compositions has enjoyed

some attention in the research literature (cf. Castek, Leu, Coiro, Gort, Henry, & Lima, 2007) and the literature intended to inform pedagogy (e.g., Schrock, 2001; Fisher, Lapp, & Wolsey, 2009). Students may attend to the attributes of sources (e.g., venue, date, title) to varying degrees and place more weight on some attributes over others (Braasch, Lawless, Goldman, Manning, Gomez, & MacLeod, 2009). In spite of instruction, online readers often do not apply principles successfully for evaluating sources even if they know they should do so (e.g., Leu, Zawilinski, Castek, Banerjee, Housand, Liu, & O'Neil, 2007).

In addition to considerations regarding the reliability of any given source is the match between that source and the writing task the student envisions. For example, an expressive essay may be useful as a source, but unless it is accompanied by referential (e.g., informative) text, a science teacher may balk. The level of difficulty represented by texts is also problematic for students conducting inquiry in a digital environment. Tools such as Twurdy.com may assist students to find texts that are suitable for the topic of the inquiry but also a challenging but appropriate fit for the reader's level of proficiency with text in general (cf. Miltsakaki & Troutt, 2007).

The type of resources students consult, whether they cite them or not, comprise a topic of ongoing debate and offer a potential for informative research. One example is the online encyclopedia as a source of information. Bélisle (2005) wonders about the format of encyclopedic content online, while others debate the social nature of Wikipedia and the nature of expertise (e.g. Giles, 2005; Waters, 2007).

Though there is an evidence base about the strategies students might employ in evaluating a Web source, there is very little empirical research describing the strategies students employ or the instructional routines teachers use to assist online readers in initially choosing an appropriate search venue. Though Google is arguably the most used search engine (e.g., Soames, 2012), other search engines employ algorithms that foreground different aspects of online research that may prove useful in different academic contexts. Moreover, search engines tend to be subject to Search Engine Optimization (SEO), a method Web designers use to make their Websites float to the top of a search query, sometimes regardless of the relevance to the original search string (cf. Cahill & Chalut, 2009). Virtually ignored in the empirical literature is how students make use of databases (e.g., InfoTrac Junior) and index services (e.g., WorldCat) that archive, index, and organize journal and magazine articles as well as other content that is not generally available on the World Wide Web.

Multiple Sources

It has been apparent for some time that students need to read, and read widely, in service of learning (cf. Hynd, 1999; Short & Harste, 1996). More specifically, they must be able to interpret, accurately characterize, and synthesize what they learn as a result of reading in composing processes, notably through written texts they create. Students tend to learn more efficiently when they read from multiple sources (Allington, 2002) in general because they make connections between texts, and between texts and their own experiences. Novice writers also tend to employ vocabulary in more precise ways (Wolsey, 2010) when they draw on multiple sources and across disciplines. More specifically, they learn to think critically within disciplines when they learn to use evidence found in reading (cf. Grim, Pace, & Shopkow, 2004; Schmoker, 2007) and in the world beyond representative texts to construct understandings which they can explain, describe, narrate, and explore through their own written work. Digital environments make possible access to a wide variety of texts, but not all such texts are suitable for specific academic purposes. Moreover, those texts found in digital environments call for new skills and understanding of the social nature of both reading and composing processes.

Written tasks in secondary schools demand that students develop proficiency with a wide variety of composing tasks, as well. Students must learn to write in expository, narrative, persuasive, and informative/referential modes while drawing on their own experiences and observations and the work they find through reading. Reading, increasingly, is done in digital environments (e.g., Ranie & Duggan, 2012). What students compose as a result of their reading of traditional and digital texts will increasingly demand the rigor of solid argumentation (Toulmin, 2003) and the capacity to put argumentation based on evidence and solid reasoning into practice (e.g., Graff & Birkenstein, 2007).

Additional Pedagogical Considerations

In this chapter, we have taken some pains to refer to secondary level students as novice writers (cf. Heller, 2010). We recognize that students are not miniature versions of adult or expert writers, and that they are developing their skills as writers who seek to understand the world through the discourses they read and those they create. Though we have drawn examples from the disciplines of history and science, these are intended to be illustrative while keeping some coherence to the chapter rather than comprehensive and inclusive of all disciplines. It would be possible to draw examples from mathematics, physical education, music, the plastic arts, and so on, as well. Overemphasis on general research processes can impede genuine inquiry (e.g., Lenski, 1998), and we believe this applies to novice writers who are looking for ways to be interested in the research they do in digital environments, as well. One important area relative to student composition and reading processes that we have not addressed is that of plagiarism and academic honesty (e.g. Ma, 2007). The topic is an important one that would encompass another entire chapter.

IMPLICATIONS AND FURTHER RESEARCH

While some empirical evidence exists connecting the interest young writers have for what they read and how that flows to what they are asked to write, especially relative to argumentation (Ariasi, Del Favero, & Ballarin, 2011), there is still much work to be done. Gil, Bråten, Vidal-Abarca, and Strømsø (2010) in their study of summarization tasks across multiple texts suggested they may be best scaffolded relative to argumentation tasks; that is, students who summarized were more likely to remember what they read while those who composed argumentation directly after reading were less likely to do so. Bråten and Strømsø (2010) found that law students were more capable of working with contradictory ideas when they believed that concepts were highly interrelated even when they seemed contradictory than those students who treated knowledge as a simple accumulation of facts (p. 638). Thus, the role of background or prior knowledge is foregrounded and more research seems indicated relative to how such knowledge is acquired from text and applied to further reading and writing opportunities where those opportunities are used in ways that facilitate understanding. This seems especially so in digital environments where the opportunities to engage with multiple and sometimes conflicting texts are possible in contrast to the era of the single source textbook. That prior knowledge must be then translated into accurate pedagogical models (e.g., Fisher & Frey, 2013) such that the nuances of digital reading and writing opportunities are leveraged and the nuances of the text are not lost.

In our research, we have found that students more robustly use tier II words (Beck, McKeown, & Kucan, 2002) or technical vocabulary (Coxhead, 2000) that is not specific to any one discipline but are also not common terms when their writing draws from sources across disciplines (e.g., literature, science, social studies) (Wolsey, 2010). While the Internet affords students the opportunity to access a variety of sources, these findings are not specific to online reading. However, we further investigated the nature of sources students drew upon (Wolsey, Lapp, & Fisher, 2012) in their composing processes. The interview and survey responses of tenth-grade teachers were compared with the interview and survey responses of their students. The written products of the students were used as a point of triangulation for all interview and survey data. We learned that while students were often aware of the sources that informed their writing, they often did not attribute those sources in their written work. Moreover, many of those sources were found online.

Students were reluctant to identify these sources, however, in their writing. For example, students reported using a popular search engine to learn more about a topic, but they did not explicitly refer to these sources even when their work required a referential stance. On the other hand, another tenth grader was able to explain the importance of supporting claims in written work with evidence and warrants. Indeed, she was able to do so in terms of the Toulmin model (2003). We speculate that at least one reason for their reluctance was because their teachers expected them to rely on the resources the teachers provided (e.g., textbooks, lectures). However, students also failed to attribute sources even when their sources were lectures provided by the teacher. It seems students can situate their own learning in terms of the sources on which they draw if they are taught to do so.

If students are expected to be conversant in the discourses of school and specific disciplines, they might reasonably be expected to be familiar with the written work that informs the discipline. Students may assume that the knowledge they encounter is to be taken for granted, a tautology as students might perceive it, and thus should not be attributed in their composing processes. The school itself may reinforce this notion by requiring students to rely on a limited set of texts (e.g., teacher lecture and one textbook in any given subject).

As students have increasing access to texts they find online, the problem for educators deepens. The purpose of this chapter has been to explore how reading in digital environments affects students' writing processes, and also to uncover areas for further research. What is known of traditional texts provides a context for inquiry into the nature of reading in digital environments to write; however, the media can and does change the message. Possible future research, suggested in this chapter, revolves around five areas.

First, how do students search for and choose digital resources to read that support their writing? Though some attention has been given to how students can evaluate individual search results, there is little in the literature that describes how students select the tools (such as various search engines and databases) they might employ to find materials to read. Second, how do students synthesize, apply, and create compositions that draw on digital texts? The strategies and skills students use in digital environments is also underexplored. Understanding when and if students select digital texts that match those found in the field of inquiry could prove fruitful. Third, how do students strategically read digital texts? How they determine whether to slow down and read closely or speed up by skimming may be an interesting area for additional research. Fourth, how might close reading in digital environments differ as opposed to close reading of paper-based texts? In what ways do online texts within the disciplines differ from paper-based texts (such as a journal or trade book)? Fifth, to what degree are students aware of the nature of the discourse (e.g., referential, persuasive, expressive) and how the discourse changes what they may learn from a given digital source? Finally, how do readers who struggle navigate and learn from digital texts? With all we know about reading in digital environments and what we know about connections between reading and writing processes and tasks, there remains much research and pedagogical work still to do.

REFERENCES

Allington, R. L. (2002). You can't learn much from books you can't read. *Educational Leadership*, *60*(3), 16–19.

Archer, L., Deweiit, J., Osborne, J., Dillon, J., Willis, B., & Wong, B. (2010). "Doing" science versus "being" a scientist: Examining 10/11-year-old schoolchildren's constructions of science through the lens of identity. *Science Education*, *94*, 617–639. doi:10.1002/sce.20399.

Armbruster, B. B., Anderson, T. H., & Ostertag, J. (1989). Teaching text structure to improve reading and writing. *The Reading Teacher*, *43*(2), 130–137.

Beck, I. L., McKeown, M. G., & Kucan, L. (2002). *Bringing words to life: Robust vocabulary instruction*. New York: Guilford Press.

Bélisle, C. (2005). Academic use of online encyclopedias. In P. Kommers & G. Richards (Eds.), *Proceedings of World Conference on Educational Multimedia, Hypermedia and Telecommunications 2005* (pp. 4548-4552). Chesapeake, VA: AACE. Retrieved from http://www.editlib.org/p/20794

Berninger, V. W., & Richards, T. L. (2002). *Brain literacy for educators and psychologists*. Boston, MA: Academic Press.

Bintz, W. P. (2012). Using parody to read and write original poetry. *English Journal*, *101*(5), 72–79.

Boscolo, P., Ariasi, N., Del Favero, L., & Ballarin, C. (2011). Interest in an expository text: How does it flow from reading to writing? *Learning and Instruction*, *21*, 467–480. doi:10.1016/j.learninstruc.2010.07.009.

Braasch, J. L. G., Lawless, K. A., Goldman, S. R., Manning, F. H., Gomez, K. W., & MacLeod, S. M. (2009). Evaluating search results: An empirical analysis of middle school students' use of source attributes to select useful sources. *Journal of Educational Computing Research, 41*(1), 63–82. doi:10.2190/EC.41.1.c.

Bråten, I., & Helge, I. S. (2010). When law students read multiple documents about global warming: Examining the role of topic-specific beliefs about the nature of knowledge and knowing. *Instructional Science, 38*(6), 635-657. doi: http://dx.doi.org/10.1007/s11251-008-9091-4

Brummett, B. (2010). *Techniques of close reading.* Thousand Oaks, CA: Sage.

Buchanan, M. (2002). *Nexus: Small worlds and the groundbreaking science of networks.* New York: W. W. Norton and Company.

Cahill, K., & Chalut, R. (2009). Optimal results: What libraries need to know about Google and search engine optimization. *The Reference Librarian, 50*(3), 234–247. doi:10.1080/02763870902961969.

Castek, J., Leu, D. J. Jr, Coiro, J., Gort, M., Henry, L. A., & Lima, C. (2007). Developing new literacies among multilingual learners in the elementary grades. In Parker, L. (Ed.), *Technology-mediated learning environments for young English learners: Connections In and out of school* (pp. 111–153). Mahwah, NJ: Lawrence Erlbaum Associates.

Chall, J. S. (1996). *Stages of reading development.* Fort Worth, TX: Harcourt Brace.

Chomsky, N. (1970). Reading, writing, and phonology. *Harvard Educational Review, 40*(2), 287–309.

Coiro, J., & Dobler, E. (2007). Exploring the online reading comprehension strategies used by sixth-grade skilled readers to search for and locate information on the internet. *Reading Research Quarterly, 42,* 214–257. doi:10.1598/RRQ.42.2.2.

Common Core State Standards Initiative. (2010). *Standard RL.9-10.3: Common core state standards for English language arts & literacy in history/social studies, science, and technical subjects.* Washington, DC: Council of Chief State School Officers and the National Governors Association. Retrieved from http://www.corestandards.org/the-standards/english-language-arts-standards/reading-literature-6-12/grade-9-10/

Coxhead, A. (2000). A new academic word list. *TESOL Quarterly, 34*(2), 213–238. doi:10.2307/3587951.

Dodge, A. M., Husain, N., & Duke, N. K. (2011). Connected kids? K-2 children's use and understanding of the internet. *Language Arts, 89*(2), 86–98.

Dymock, S. (2005). Teaching expository text structure awareness. *The Reading Teacher, 59,* 177–182. doi:10.1598/RT.59.2.7.

Emig, J. (1971). *The composing processes of twelfth graders.* Urbana, IL: National Council of Teachers of English.

Erikson, E. H. (1968). *Identity: Youth and crisis.* New York: W.W. Norton.

Estes, T. (2007). Constructing the syllabus: Devising a framework for helping students learn to think like historians. *The History Teacher, 40*(2), 183–201.

Fisher, D., & Frey, N. (2013). Reading and reasoning: Fostering comprehension across multiple texts. *Engaging the Adolescent Learner.* Retrieved from http://www.reading.org/Libraries/members-only/fisherfreyjan2013.pdf

Fisher, D., Frey, N., & Lapp, D. (2012). *Teaching students to read like detectives: Comprehending, analyzing, and discussing texts.* Bloomington, IN: Solution Tree Press.

Fitzgerald, J., & Shanahan, T. (2000). Reading and writing relations and their development. *Educational Psychologist, 35*(1), 39–50. doi:10.1207/S15326985EP3501_5.

Friedman, T. L. (2006). *The world is flat: A brief history of the twenty-first century.* New York: Farrar, Strauss, & Giroux.

Gardner, T. (n.d.). *Literary parodies: Exploring a writer's style through imitation.* Retrieved from http://www.readwritethink.org/classroom-resources/lesson-plans/literary-parodies-exploring-writer-839.html

Gil, L., Bråten, I., Vidal-Abarca, E., & Strømsø, H. I. (2010). Summary versus argument tasks when working with multiple documents: Which is better for whom? *Contemporary Educational Psychology, 35*(3), 157–173. doi:10.1016/j.cedpsych.2009.11.002.

Giles, J. (2005). Internet encyclopaedias go head to head. *Nature, 438*(7070), 900–901. doi:10.1038/438900a PMID:16355180.

Graff, G., & Birkenstein, C. (2007). *They say, I say: The moves that matter in persuasive writing.* New York: W.W. Norton.

Grim, V., Pace, D., & Shopkow, L. (2004). Learning to use evidence in the study of history. *New Directions for Teaching and Learning, 98,* 57–65. doi:10.1002/tl.147.

Grisham, D. L., & Wolsey, T. D. (2006). Recentering the middle school classroom as a vibrant learning community: Students, literacy and technology intersect. *Journal of Adolescent & Adult Literacy, 49,* 648–660. doi:10.1598/JAAL.49.8.2.

Hart, C. (1998). *Doing a literature review: Releasing the social science research imagination.* Thousand Oaks, CA: Sage.

Heller, R. (2010). In praise of amateurism: A friendly critique of Moje's "call for change" in secondary literacy. *Journal of Adolescent & Adult Literacy, 54*(4), 267–273. doi:10.1598/JAAL.54.4.4.

Hillocks, G. Jr. (1986). *Research on written composition: New directions for teaching.* Urbana, IL: NCTE.

Hongyan, M., Yong Lu, E., Turner, S., & Guofang, W. (2007). An empirical investigation of digital cheating and plagiarism among middle school students. *American Secondary Education, 35*(2), 69–82.

Hughes, T. P. (2004). *Human-built world: How to think about technology and culture.* Chicago: University of Chicago Press.

Hynd, C. R. (1999). Teaching students to think critically using multiple texts in history. *Journal of Adolescent & Adult Literacy, 42*(6), 428–436.

Kinneavy, J. L. (1971). *A theory of discourse: The aims of discourse.* New York, NY: W. W. Norton.

Langer, J., & Flihan, S. (2000). Writing and reading relationships: Constructive tasks. In Indrisano, R., & Squire, J. R. (Eds.), *Writing: Research/Theory/Practice.* Newark, DE: International Reading Association.

Lapp, D., Fisher, D., & Wolsey, T. D. (2009). *Literacy growth for every child: Differentiated small-group instruction K-6.* New York: Guilford Publishers.

Lenski, S. D. (1998). Strategic knowledge when reading in order to write. *Reading Psychology, 19*(3), 287–315. doi:10.1080/0270271980190303.

Leu, D. J., Kinzer, C. K., Coiro, J. L., & Cammack, D. W. (2004). Toward a theory of new literacies emerging from the internet and other information and communication technologies. In Ruddell, R. B., & Unrau, N. (Eds.), *Theoretical models and processes of reading* (5th ed., pp. 1580–1613). Newark, DE: International Reading Association.

Leu, D. J., Zawilinski, L., Castek, J., Benerjee, M., Housand, B., Liu, Y., & O'Neil, M. (2007). *What is new about the new literacies of online reading comprehension?* Retrieved from http://www.newliteracies.uconn.edu/pub_files/What_is_new_about_new_literacies_of_online_reading

Meredith, H., Coyle, V., & Newman, D. (2011). Digital media's role in adolescent recreational and academic reading. In M. Koehler & P. Mishra (Eds.), *Proceedings of Society for Information Technology & Teacher Education International Conference 2011* (pp. 3736-3741). Chesapeake, VA: AACE. Retrieved from http://www.editlib.org/p/36908

Miller, C., Purcell, K., & Rainie, L. (2012). Reading habits in different communities. *Pew Internet and American Life Project.* Retrieved from http://libraries.pewInternet.org/2012/12/20/reading-habits-in-different-communities/

Miltsakaki, E., & Troutt, A. (2007). Read-X: Automatic evaluation of reading difficulty of web text. In T. Bastiaens & S. Carliner (Eds.), *Proceedings of World Conference on E-Learning in Corporate, Government, Healthcare, and Higher Education 2007* (pp. 7280-7286). Chesapeake, VA: AACE. Retrieved from http://www.editlib.org/p/26932

Moffett, J. (1983). *Teaching the universe of discourse.* Portsmouth, NH: Heinemann.

Moje, E. B. (2007). Developing socially just subject-matter instruction: A review of the literature on disciplinary literacy teaching. *Review of Research in Education*, *31*, 1–44. doi:10.3102/0091732X07300046.

Neilsen, J. (2012). F-shaped pattern for reading web-content. *The Neilsen Norman Group.* Retrieved from http://www.nngroup.com/articles/f-shaped-pattern-reading-Web-content/

Newkirk, T. (2012). *The art of slow reading.* Portsmouth, NH: Heinemann.

Partnership for Assessment of Readiness for College and Careers (PARCC). (2012). Structure of the model content frameworks for ELA/literacy. *Achieve, Inc.* Retrieved from http://www.parcconline.org/mcf/english-language-artsliteracy/structure-model-content-frameworks-elaliteracy

Plester, B., Wood, C., & Joshi, P. (2009). Exploring the relationship between children's knowledge of text message abbreviations and school literacy outcomes. *The British Journal of Developmental Psychology*, *27*(1), 145–161. doi:10.1348/026151008X320507 PMID:19972666.

Protopsaltis, A. (2008). Reading strategies in hypertexts and factors influencing hyperlink selection. *Journal of Educational Multimedia and Hypermedia*, *17*(2), 191–213.

Purcell, K., Rainie, L., Heaps, A., Buchanan, J., Friedrich, L., Jacklin, A., et al. (2012). How teens do research in the digital world. *Pew Internet and American Life Project.* Retrieved from http://pewInternet.org/Reports/2012/Student-Research.aspx

Rainie, L., & Duggan, M. (2012). E-book reading jumps: Print book reading declines. *Pew Internet and American Life Project.* Retrieved from http://libraries.pewInternet.org/files/legacy-pdf/PIP_Reading%20and%20ebooks.pdf

Rand, A. (2010). Mediating at the student-Wikipedia intersection. *Journal of Library Administration*, *50*(7/8), 923–932. doi:10.1080/01930826.2010.488994.

Reinking, D. (1997). Me and my hypertext: A multiple digression analysis of technology and literacy (sic). *ReadingOnline.* Retrieved from http://www.readingonline.org/articles/art_index.asp?HREF=/articles/hypertext/index.html

Schleppegrell, M., Greer, S., & Taylor, S. (2008). Literacy in history: Language and meaning. *Australian Journal of Language and Literacy*, *31*(2), 174–187.

Schmoker, M. (2007). Reading, writing, and thinking for all. *Educational Leadership*, *64*(7), 63–66.

Shanahan, T. (2006). Relations among oral language, reading, and writing development. In MacArthur, C. A., Graham, S., & Fitzgerald, J. (Eds.), *Handbook of writing research* (pp. 171–183). New York, NY: Guilford Press.

Short, K. G., Harste, J. C., & Burke, C. (1996). *Creating classrooms for authors and inquirers* (2nd ed.). Portsmouth, NH: Heinemann.

Soames, C. (2012). Most popular search engines – UK, US and worldwide. *Smart Insights*. Retrieved from http://www.smartinsights.com/search-engine-optimisation-seo/multilingual-seo/search-engine-popularity-statistics/

Spiro, R. (2004). Principled pluralism for adaptive flexibility in teaching and learning to read. In Ruddell, R. B., & Unrau, N. (Eds.), *Theoretical models and processes of reading* (5th ed., pp. 654–659). Newark, DE: International Reading Association.

Spiro, R. C., Coulson, R. L., Feltovich, P. J., & Anderson, D. K. (2004). Cognitive flexibility theory: Advanced knowledge acquisition in ill-structured domains. In Ruddell, R. B., & Unrau, N. (Eds.), *Theoretical models and processes of reading* (5th ed., pp. 640–653). Newark, DE: International Reading Association.

Spiro, R. J., Feltovich, P. J., & Coulson, R. L. (1996). Two epistemic world-views: Prefigurative schemas and learning in complex domains. *Applied Cognitive Psychology*, *10*, 51–61. doi:10.1002/(SICI)1099-0720(199611)10:7<51::AID-ACP437>3.0.CO;2-F.

Stewart, T. (1997). *Intellectual capital: The new wealth of organizations*. New York: Doubleday.

Toulmin, S. (2003). *The uses of argument, updated edition*. New York: Cambridge University Press. doi:10.1017/CBO9780511840005.

Tseng, M. C. (2010). Subjective and objective evaluation of hypertext reading performance: In-depth analysis of contributing factors. *Journal of Educational Multimedia and Hypermedia*, *19*(2), 221–232. Retrieved from http://www.editlib.org/p/33201.

Waters, N. L. (2007). Why you can't cite Wikipedia in my class. *Communications of the ACM*, *50*(9), 15–17. doi:10.1145/1284621.1284635.

Wilson, N., Zygouris-Coe, V., Cardullo, V., & Fong, J. L. (2013). Pedagogical frameworks of e-reader technologies in education. In Keengwe, J. (Ed.), *Pedagogical applications and social effects of mobile technology integration* (pp. 1–24). Hershey, PA: IGI Global. doi:10.4018/978-1-4666-2985-1.ch001.

Wolsey, T. D. (2010). Complexity in student writing: The relationship between the task and vocabulary uptake. *Literacy Research and Instruction*, *49*(2), 194–208. doi:10.1080/19388070902947360.

Wolsey, T. D., Grisham, D. L., & Hiebert, E. H. (2012). What is text complexity? *Teacher Development Series*. Retrieved from http://textproject.org/tds

Wolsey, T. D., Lapp, D., & Fisher, D. (2012). Students' and teachers' perceptions: An inquiry into academic writing. *Journal of Adolescent & Adult Literacy*, *55*(8), 714–724. doi:10.1002/JAAL.00086.

Yagelski, R. P. (2009). A thousand writers writing: Seeking change through the radical practice of writing as a way of being. *English Education*, *42*(1), 6–28.

Chapter 16
Online Content Construction:
Empowering Students as Readers and Writers of Online Information

W. Ian O'Byrne
University of New Haven, USA

ABSTRACT

It is increasingly clear that this generation of adolescents is almost always connected to online information (Horrigan, 2010; Pew Research Center, 2010). Indeed, the Internet has quickly become this generation's defining technology for literacy, in part due to facilitating access to an unlimited amount of online information and media (Rideout, Foehr, & Roberts, 2010). Yet it is a paradox that history's first generation of "always connected" individuals (Pew Research Center, 2010) is not taught how to effectively and authentically use the digital texts and tools that permeate society. As society has incorporated dynamic and new media in everyday life, educators are required to expand traditional understandings of text and literacy that have replaced many of the ways that we communicate, create, and socialize (Sutherland-Smith, 2002; Alvermann, 2002). Put simply, there is a need to value and construct different kinds of texts, learning, and interactions within the classroom (Beach & Myers, 2001). To achieve this goal, this chapter presents a synthesis of theoretical perspectives and research into a new instructional model known as Online Content Construction (OCC). OCC is defined as the skills, strategies, and dispositions necessary as students construct, redesign, or reinvent online texts by actively encoding and decoding meaning through the use of digital texts and tools.

INTRODUCTION

A 21st century educational system must educate all students in the effective and authentic use of the digital texts and tools that permeate society. In the past, our educational system emphasized the use of traditional tools such as textbooks, chalkboards, overhead projectors, and composition books. Now, however, society has incorporated dynamic and

new media in everyday life. Educators are required to expand traditional understandings of text and literacy as technology-driven tools and systems have replaced many of the ways that we communicate, create, and socialize (Sutherland-Smith, 2002; Alvermann, 2002). More importantly, there is a need to value and construct different kinds of texts, learning, and interactions within the classroom (Beach & Myers, 2001). To achieve this goal, a synthesis of theoretical perspectives and research into a new instructional model known as

DOI: 10.4018/978-1-4666-4341-3.ch016

Online Content Construction (OCC) is necessary. OCC is defined as the skills, strategies and dispositions necessary as students construct, redesign, or reinvent online texts by actively encoding and decoding meaning through the use of digital texts and tools.

In this chapter, I will examine the changes that are occurring to expository or argumentative writing as a result of technology, and indicate the instructional model of OCC as one possible way to reflect these changes in instruction. I will then further define OCC and the theoretical perspectives used to this new work. These perspectives include research from multimodal design, new literacies, and cognitive apprenticeship. Following this examination of OCC, I will then detail the instructional model that was tested in two research studies that provides opportunities for students and teachers to construct online content in all disciplines. Finally, I will discuss implications of conducting work such as this in the traditional classroom.

WHAT IS ONLINE CONTENT CONSTRUCTION?

The writing process (Murray, 1972, 1999; Hairston, 1982) has been defined as including prewriting, drafting, revising, editing, and publishing. As the writing process moves from print to pixel many of these skills are employed as students construct online content. As student writing moves from page to screen the key difference between the traditional writing process and OCC is that teachers and students need to consider other elements that are particular to working with online informational text (e.g., semiotics, visual literacy, multimodal design). This framing of OCC moves the field of literacy research, and writing instruction further by providing opportunities to discuss and include this work in teaching and learning activities in the classroom, while remaining flexible as changes in technology warrant.

Authentically and effectively integrating the Internet and other communication technologies (ICTs) into the classroom is a social imperative given the ability to empower students in the reader/writer nature inherent in the online informational space. In computer science, read/write is defined as media that is capable of being displayed (read) and modified (write). In a literacy context, the reader/writer nature of online information could be viewed as a means to allow individuals to quickly and efficiently comprehend and construct online information. An easy way to understand this is the work associated with listening to, sharing, and revising audio files. Consider the use of records and LPs, and then cassette tapes, and finally now MP3 files and streaming online information. With records, it was very difficult to create, and remix music given these tools. Cassette tapes made it a little easier to create and share audio information, as long as the little plastic tab was not broken off. With MP3 and other audio file formats, it is very easy to create, remix, or mash-up and finally share audio content. This increasing ease in the creation, remixing, and sharing of audio information I believe extends to involve all forms of online, multimodal content. It is the duty of educators to empower their students in ways that they can have a voice and create content for the reader/writer Internet. There are two challenges associated with this. The first is a keen understanding of the literacies necessary (e.g., critical literacy, new literacy, multiliteracies) to thoughtfully comprehend and construct online content. The second aspect that needs to be understood by teachers and students is the acquisition of the knowledge, skills, and dispositions needed to skillfully encode and decode meaning online. For these two reasons OCC has been developed and tested for use in the classroom.

As students write and compose online content, the knowledge, skills, and dispositions change as a result of the affordances of the online space (Leu et al., 2005; Swenson, Young, McGrail, Rozema, & Whitin, 2006). This process grows more complex as students must consider the effect of multimodal content such as images, video and audio and the effect this has on their work product (Duncum, 2004; Sheppard, 2009). Students may consider visual aesthetics, elements of graphic design, and semiotic elements that may affect how the audience perceives their work (Serafini, 2011). Students may also consider aspects of critical literacy and sensitively prepare and present their thinking in their digital work product (Yelland, 1999). Work such as this is necessary given the increasing reliance of the Internet as a space for individuals to communicate, socialize, and learn (Shapiro, 2000; Oblinger, 2006). Online reading and writing has been described as a more social and interactive act than traditional communication because it focuses on both the process and the purpose of the participation of many, rather than the private act of an individual (Leu et al., 2009). The instructional model of OCC explores one method of preparing students to examine and employ the processes needed to critically read and write online information, both individually and collaboratively.

Numerous skills and strategies are needed in both the procedural and strategic use of digital texts and tools in writing. Given the deictic nature of literacy (Leu, 2000), viewing creation of content using ICT tools as belonging to only one skill set is problematic. Consider the multitude of tools and formats available to writers, or constructors of online information: (a) blogging, (b) wikis, (c) e-mail, (d) social networks, and (e) word processing. A broad spectrum of combined skills and tools is emerging in order to capture the aptitudes and attitudes necessary for students to construct online content. To that end, OCC was developed to define the abilities necessary to communicate the information assembled while searching, sifting, and synthesizing knowledge gained during the online inquiry process (Leu et al., 2004, 2008).

Knowledge, Skills, and Dispositions Involved as Students Construct Content

The goal of the OCC model is to provide teachers with pedagogical opportunities to move students from content consumers, to content curators, and finally constructors of online content. Content curation in this context refers to a meaning-making activity in which students collect, aggregate, and distill links of online information sources through the use of tools such as Pinterest. The knowledge, skills, and dispositions involved in this communication process are informed by previous research in writing instruction (Hayes & Flower, 1980, 1986; Collins & Gentner, 1980; Scardamalia, Bereiter, & Steinbach, 1984; Graves, 1994) and envisioned as a combination of skills students may employ as they construct online content. The five skills involved in OCC are planning, generating, organizing, composing, and revising. *Planning* is defined as a student creating internal and external representations of the content they intend to build and ensuring that it is logically appropriate for the task (Flower & Hayes, 1981). These representations may include paper sketches, graphic organizers, or original designs of future works planned. *Generating* is defined as the process in which a student creates or translates initial elements of the digital product based on their memory and organizers (Hayes & Flower, 1986; Collins & Gentner, 1980). These initial drafts and graphic organizers act as elements of the work completed to allow the student to begin reviewing and organizing materials. *Organizing* is defined as the process in which a student creates or manipulates the hierarchical or relational structure of their work product (Flower & Hayes, 1981). In this process, students maneuver content and categories of content to ensure they meet the goals of the inquiry and purpose of the content. Additionally, as students organize, they may attend to aesthetic decisions about the presentation and ordering of elements of the content (Carey, Flower, Hayes, Schriver, & Haas, 1989). *Composing* is defined as the process in which a student constructs the online content while weaving elements from the previous three phases into a cohesive composition that is representative of the goals of the inquiry process. *Revising* is defined as the process in which a student dedicates time to systematically review and examine with the intent of improving the overall work product (Hayes & Flower, 1980). The process of reviewing and revising may occur across all stages of the model, however this final step is one in which students consciously examine and evaluate constructed content before finishing the work process. Once again, many of these skills and strategies have been identified in traditional writing instruction, the key element that differentiates this from the online environment is the inclusion of the visual, digital, and multimodal design choices that must be made by students as they work.

Student Review of Work Process Embedded in the Instructional Model

Embedded within each one of these five skills is a recursive, metacognitive review process in which students retrospectively consider their ideas, evaluate this work in relation to task or purpose, and possibly share with others to obtain another perspective on their work. Much of this review process is informed by the complex pattern of goal setting, problem solving, and reflection known as "knowledge transformation" (Scardamalia & Bereiter, 1985). Embedded in OCC is an examination of the differences between "knowledge-telling" and "knowledge-transformation" strategies (Bereiter & Scardamalia, 1987). Knowledge-telling strategies were defined as the retrieval from long-term memory of ideas related to a rhetorical goal and their resultant transference into text (Bereiter

& Scardamalia, 1987). Knowledge-transformation strategies were defined as those ideas that were transformed in an effort to resolve a conflict between the original ideas and the intended rhetorical goal (Bereiter & Scardamalia, 1987). This review process has the potential to result in the generation of new knowledge and a deeper understanding of the student's content knowledge (Bereiter & Scardamalia, 1987; Collins, Brown, & Holum, 1991). This synthesis of discourse and content as students construct content has the potential to change incrementally as individual images, videos, and text are added, removed, or repositioned within a work product.

In terms of fully understanding the complexity of this metacognitive review process, it is also important to understand how the knowledge-telling and knowledge-transformation strategies espoused by Bereiter and Scardamalia have been revised. Galbraith (1998) identified "knowledge-constituting" as involving a "dialectic" between dispositional aspects of students as they attempted to make sense of their thinking as they constructed knowledge (Galbraith, 1996, 1998). This dialectic involves the student engaging in the processes detailed by Scardamalia and Bereiter (1987), but modifying it with each additional element of text that was constructed (Galbraith, 1996, 1998). This review process informs the work conducted in OCC by involving a cycle in which the students construct knowledge in the form of text and then consider if this idea is satisfactory or not (Galbraith, 1996, 1998). It is this metacognitive review process that assists instructors and students as they redesign, reinvent, or remix online texts.

Previous Work Similar to the Instructional Model

In many ways the OCC model is likened to the work on writing tasks that are ill-defined or ill-structured problems in which students do not have a ready-made procedure to produce and review content (Reitman, 1964; Simon, 1973). As opposed to traditional writing, OCC situates this cognitive process in a multimodal learning environment in which students operate as "designers" and try to "apply critiqued knowledge of the subject or topic synthesized from multimodal sources" during online inquiry (Kimber & Wyatt-Smith, 2006, p. 26). Fundamentally, OCC has students construct "representations of new knowledge" and communicate this knowledge to others with the intention of engaging their audience (Kimber & Wyatt-Smith, 2006, p. 26). Pedagogically, this multimodal design activity combines the "process and product" involved as students combine knowledge gained through online collaborative inquiry (New London Group, 2000).

Examples of this work have also been seen in the instructional design model known as "writing-to-learn" (Britton, 1970, 1972). Specifically, the "writing-to-learn" model can be used to engage students in writing activities using ICT tools. Students expressed learning through the use and creation of socially expressive digital media (Murray, 1999; Tewissen, Lingnau, Hoppe, Mannhaupt, & Nischk, 2001). In the "writing-to-learn" instructional model, students used computer-integrated classrooms to focus on individual learning and development of tools to enhance social and collaborative learning. As an instructional model, OCC expands upon this work by integrating a focus on new literacies and multimodal design research and practice.

Elements of this type of research have also been found in the work on Computer Supported Collaborative Learning (CSCL). CSCL focuses on elements included in the "writing-to-learn" research, but it also incorporates more writing of shorter pieces of text across various genres of online information and style (Romano, 2000). The goal of both of these research interests was to "restructure learning environments" (Flower & Hayes, 1994; Erkens, Kanselaar, Prangsma, & Jaspers, 2003) in an attempt to move student learning from knowledge transformation into knowledge constitution (Galbraith, 1999). A broader use of

these skills and learning environments has been applied to the work on Computer-Supported Intentional Learning Environments (CSILE) (Scardamalia & Bereiter, 1994). Similar to the work defined by OCC, CSILE builds on elements of cognitive apprenticeship and includes ICT use while students reflect on learning in the classroom.

It is important to note that OCC can occur concurrently and iteratively as students work individually or collaboratively in the online reading comprehension or online collaborative inquiry processes. As a result, students are asked to act as critical readers and writers of online information while applying knowledge learned from online and traditional information sources.

THEORETICAL PERSPECTIVES

The combination of the skills referred to as OCC integrates multiple lines of research from many fields (i.e., multiliteracies, new media, digital storytelling, digital literacy, gaming, and others). This integration of skills originates from content creation as defined by Livingstone (2004) in her theoretical definition of media literacy and the possibilities ICTs present in research and instructional practice. She maintained that to "identify, in textual terms, how the Internet mediates the representation of knowledge, the framing of entertainment, and the conduct of communication" the construct must be broad enough to allow for change in the future (p. 9). Thus, this reality dictates integration of these multiple lines of research within OCC.

Additionally, this model of content construction is made even more complex because of the evolution of ICT tools in conjunction with the expansion of various fields of multimodal design, visual literacy, and others (Doneman, 1997). As these technologies converge, some experts believe the tools associated with various Internet and communication technologies will merge as well (Fox, Anderson, & Rainie, 2005; Anderson & Rainie, 2008; Greenhow, Robelia, & Hughes,

2009). Thus, a broad spectrum of combined skills and tools has been emerging. This convergence affects the knowledge, skills, and dispositions teachers will need when empowering students as readers and writers of online information. To fully understand and implement these strategies, I used a multiple theoretical perspective approach (Labbo & Reinking, 1999) that integrated elements of multimodal design, new literacies, and cognitive apprenticeship. These three perspectives were reviewed to identify the instructional model of OCC and inform research in which students were encouraged to construct online content.

Multimodal Design

Multimodal design identifies the interchange between linguistic, visual, audio, gestural, spatial, and multimodal elements (New London Group, 2000; Kress & van Leeuwen, 2001; Jewitt, 2008). Information created using elements of multimodal design must consider the mode and media chosen by the student as a crucial concept in constructing meaning (Doneman, 1997). Research has found that "the ways in which something is represented shape both *what* is to be learned, that is, the curriculum content, and *how* it is to be learned" (Jewitt, 2008, p. 241). This section will define multimodal design as it informs the instructional opportunities informed by OCC. Additionally, this section will detail the use of multimodal design and multiliteracies as a means to empower students as they design applied knowledge.

Defining Multimodal Design

As an educational theory, multimodal design refers to the use of different "modes" to recontextualize a body of knowledge for a specific audience (Kress, 2003; Jewitt, 2008). The term "design" holds particular significance because it includes a sense of academic composition by students in which they skillfully construct the multimodal elements while considering the systematic and social conventions of the work they are constructing (Bezemer & Kress, 2008; Jewitt, Bezemer, Jones, & Kress, 2009). Conceptualized as a "domain of inquiry" (Kress, 2009, p. 54), multimodality encourages students to include elements of social semiotics (Kress & Van Leeuwen, 2001; Kress, 2010) to construct meaning through multiple representational, communicational, and situational resources. As opposed to traditional writing, when students construct online content they are asked to design multimodal representations of their work product, which convey not only the knowledge they learned during the work process, but also reflective of the conventions and critiques of the genre of the online information space they used in the design (Romano, 2000; Fletcher & Portalupi, 2001).

Designers of Applied Knowledge

As applied in OCC-based instruction, students are encouraged to operate as "designers" and try to "apply critiqued knowledge of the subject or topic synthesized from multimodal sources" (Kimber & Wyatt-Smith, 2006, p. 26). Students have the potential to construct "representations of new knowledge" and communicate this knowledge to others with the intention of engaging their audience (Kimber & Wyatt-Smith, 2006, p. 26). As a pedagogical tool, design combines the "process and product" (New London Group, 2000) and allows students to consider how literacy practices were used to understand and uncover truth (Street, 1984; Alvermann & Hagood, 2000).

The use of elements of multimodal design in OCC allows for the effective integration of student values, identity, power, and design in their work process and product. This allows instructors and students to dynamically construct identity in the classroom by examining the "ongoing design and redesign of identities across the social and cultural practices of meaning making" (Jewitt, 2008, p. 260). This instructional model situates instructors and students firmly within the various informational, technological, and sociological forces that impact society while providing learners with a tool to become "active participants" (Cope & Kalantzis, 2000). Based on elements of critical literacy, new literacies, and multiliteracies, this perspective is built on a pedagogical agenda of social change and empowerment of students as "active designers of social futures" (Cope & Kalantzis, 2000). Multiliteracies include critical literacy tenets of having students "reading the word and reading the world" (Friere & Macedo, 1987), while integrating the teaching of writing (Graves, 1994; Cope & Kalantzis, 2000) and ICTs. In effect, work such as this helps build aspects of critical engagement between students and text to promote social justice through process and product.

New Literacies

Student construction of online content is also informed by both the larger definition of New Literacies, as well as the more specific definition of new literacies, as it applies to online reading comprehension (Leu, O'Byrne, Zawilinski, McVerry, & Everett-Cacopardo, 2009). The larger definition of New Literacies broadly examines the changing nature of literacy and language as new technologies emerge and rapidly and repeatedly redefine what it means to be able to read, write, and communicate effectively (Leu et al., 2011). The more specific definition of new literacies as it applies to online reading comprehension examines the knowledge, skills, and dispositions students' use as they question, locate, evaluate, synthesize, and communicate online information (Leu et al., 2011). The work involved in OCC includes expository, persuasive, or argumentative texts formed by students while they are engaged in the online inquiry process.

Defining New Literacies

The nature of literacy is rapidly evolving as the Internet and other Information and Communication Technologies (ICTs) emerge (Coiro, Knobel,

Lankshear, & Leu, 2008). Developing the skills students needed to participate fully in a globalized community, the work defined by OCC is based on New Literacies theory. This perspective of the learning experience requires a continual examination of the knowledge, skills, and dispositions that impact students and instructors as they work together (Warschauer, 2000; Grimes & Warschauer, 2008). By encouraging students to construct online content as opposed to the traditional writing process, they are enabled to "communicate with one another using the codes and conventions of society" (Robinson & Robinson, 2003).

New literacies theory (Leu et al., 2009, 2011) works on two levels: uppercase (New Literacies) and lowercase (new literacies). Common findings and applications developed across the multiple perspectives of new literacies are then included in the broader concept of New Literacies.

The New Literacies of Online Reading Comprehension

The new literacies of online reading comprehension (Leu et al., 2009) frames the problem-based inquiry process that involves the new skills, strategies, dispositions, and social practices that take place when the Internet is used to solve problems and answer questions. At least five processing practices occur during online reading comprehension: (a) reading to identify important questions, (b) reading to locate information, (c) reading to evaluate information critically, (d) reading to synthesize information, and (e) reading and writing to communicate information. The skills, strategies, and dispositions that are distinctive to online reading comprehension, as well as others that are also important for offline reading comprehension, reside within these five areas. The previous research involving OCC used the online reading comprehension skills and inquiry process as a means to first have students work with online content before they constructed content (Author, 2009, 2012)

Cognitive Apprenticeship

Cognitive apprenticeship has been defined as an instructional theory in which a knowledgeable instructor imparts knowledge to apprentices in a structured, "scaffolded" process (Brown, Collins, & Duguid, 1989). Scaffolding is defined as a series of instructional supports provided for the student during the learning process which is tailored to the needs of learners to allow them to achieve their learning goals (Sawyer, 2006). There are usually four dimensions considered in cognitive apprenticeship (e.g., content, methods, sequence, sociology) when embedding learning in activity using a classroom's social and physical contexts (Brown, Collins, & Duguid, 1989; Collins, Brown, & Newman, 1989). These dimensions and the scaffolding associated with cognitive apprenticeship are important in instruction of OCC given the complex and deictic nature of online information.

Instructional practice informed by OCC includes the enculturation of students into authentic practices through activity and social interaction in an online environment (Hennessey, 1993) in an attempt to embed learning in activity (Brem, Russell, & Weems, 2001; Kiili, Laurinen, & Marttunen, 2008). This section defines cognitive apprenticeship as it has been used to frame OCC. Additionally, this section considers three ways in which cognitive apprenticeship impact the teaching and learning of OCC in the classroom: (a) by defining the sequencing of modeling, coaching, and fading of instruction; and (b) by outlining reflection on strategies used by students.

Defining Cognitive Apprenticeship

Embedded within a situated activity, cognitive apprenticeship describes conceptual knowledge as a set of tools (Brown, Collins, & Duguid, 1989), which can only be understood through their use. The student must understand this view of the world and accept the belief system of the culture in which the tools are used (Collins, Brown, & New-

man, 1989). During the online inquiry process, students have the opportunity to engage in several of its practices: (a) collectively solving problems, (b) displaying multiple roles, (c) confronting ineffective strategies and misconceptions, and (d) providing collaborative work skills (Brown, Collins, & Duguid, 1989).

Cognitive apprenticeship provides significant insight into learning and the way it is used to teach students the behaviors and belief systems that are important within social groups. Brown, Collins, and Duguid point out that students "pick up relevant jargon, imitate behavior, and gradually start to act in accordance with its norms" (1989, p. 34). This indoctrination into culture, including the accompanying tools and their value within society, not only raises the level of "participation" that students have within the social group, but also the value students place on the learning process (Herrington & Oliver, 2000; Hendricks, 2001). As a result, teaching and learning using elements of OCC affords opportunities for students to not only participate in global conversations, but also in some cases empower them for their future as literate individuals.

Fundamental in cognitive apprenticeship is a consideration and examination of learning experiences that are authentic and those that are not (inauthentic). Brown, Collins, and Duguid view authentic learning as activities that are "coherent, meaningful, and purposeful" while inauthentic learning activities are seen as "tasks" (1989). Put simply, having students comprehend and construct online content engages them in authentic learning activities that are defined as "ordinary practices of the culture" (Brown, Collins, & Duguid, 1989).

Modeling, Coaching, and Fading of Instruction

The instructional model used to enable OCC in the classroom contained phases of instruction guided by the modeling, coaching and fading steps cognitive apprenticeship theory detailed

(Collins, Brown, & Newman, 1989). These elements guided the comprehension-fostering and comprehension-monitoring strategies (Palincsar & Brown, 1984) students' employ as they learn how to be critical readers and writers of online information. Guided by the tenets of cognitive apprenticeship, this approach yields guidance on the skills and strategies instructors may use: (a) modeling, (b) coaching, (c) scaffolding, and (d) empowering students to acquire a role as a self-motivated learner (Scardamalia & Bereiter, 1985; Scardamalia, Bereiter, & Steinbach, 1984).

Reflection on Strategies Used

The second element of cognitive apprenticeship that influences teaching, learning, and assessment in the instruction of OCC includes the reflection strategies of students. Students should be encouraged to reflect on novice and expert perspectives in a problem-solving context to emulate aspects of an expert performance and make adjustments to improve their own performance (Collins & Brown, 1988; Collins, Brown, & Newman, 1989). The implicit goal of this process is to provide students with the knowledge and skills needed to move from a novice level to an expert level (Collins, 1991). This process of modeling, coaching, and then fading of instruction involves five important processes: (a) modeling an expert's performance; (b) understanding of the internal/external processes; (c) encouraging students to think and work like experts; (d) application of knowledge in different contexts; and (e) demonstrating how to cope with difficulties (Rogoff, 1990). Thus, while under the supervision and guidance of the instructor, this function of reflection can include "co-investigation" and/or abstracted replay by students (Scardamalia & Bereiter, 1983; Collins & Brown, 1988). In this context, abstracted replay is defined as a comparative metacognitive activity in which students reflected on strategies employed during the work process and how these related to those employed by an expert (Collins, Brown,

& Newman, 1989). In this process, students are encouraged to reflect on the critical decisions and thought processes used while constructing their work product. Through this reflection, they may be able to better understand the complexities of the strategies used while working individually and as a group. These reflective strategies labeled as "abstracted replay" refer to the students' "post-mortem" analyses in which they may analyze the knowledge, skills, and strategies employed during OCC and then compare them to those that would be utilized by an expert (Collins, Brown, & Newman, 1989). This reflective process enables students to consider their own working process and skills and the abilities they would need to advance to a higher skill level.

Cognitive apprenticeship theory (Brown, Collins, & Duguid, 1989; Collins, Brown, & Newman, 1989) suggests that by engaging students as "co-investigators" (Scardamalia & Bereiter, 1983) educators encourage them to reflect on strategies they have or may need. OCC utilizes elements of cognitive apprenticeship to engage students as "co-investigators" (Scardamalia & Bereiter, 1983) and guide student learning while reflecting on the process and product of their work. The sequencing of methods and reflective strategies used while students construct online content works in concert to expand knowledge of the ways in which students work to tell, transform, and re-constitute information learned in an online informational space.

INSTRUCTIONAL MODEL TO SUPPORT STUDENT CONSTRUCTION OF ONLINE CONTENT

The preceding sections of this chapter provided the rationale, definition, and theoretical framing that were used to define and instruct knowledge, skills, and dispositions necessary when having students construct online content. This section will detail the instructional model that has been developed for and proven effective in empowering students to construct online content (O'Byrne, 2009, 2012). The previous research studies (O'Byrne, 2009; 2012) represent two different quasi-experimental, mixed-method studies developed to investigate the use of the OCC model in improving the critical evaluation skills of adolescents required while reading online. These studies investigated the extent to which critical evaluation skills required during online reading comprehension could be improved in which the OCC model was used to empower adolescents as creators of online information. As appropriate, this section will include examples and screenshots from student work to detail the work and findings of the two studies that have tested the OCC model.

The first study (O'Byrne, 2009) was a pilot study conducted with forty seventh grade students from an economically challenged school district in the northeast United States. Although the findings from the pilot study helped identify the patterns and themes that exist as students evaluate and construct online content, more work was needed to develop an instrument to measure whether the OCC model was effective in building skills needed as students are involved in an inquiry-based task.

The most recent study (O'Byrne, 2012) includes a full examination of 197 seventh grade students from the same school used in the pilot study. Quantitative results from this study indicate that students' ability to recognize and construct surface level elements of online information can be improved using the OCC model (O'Byrne, 2012). Results also indicate that certain dispositions required for successful online reading comprehension by adolescents may be improved by having them synthesize discourse during the OCC model. Qualitative findings from the most recent study indicate that students working in groups effectively during the OCC model effectively demonstrated the knowledge, skills, and dispositions needed to recognize and construct elements needed to effectively critically evaluate online information

(O'Byrne, 2012). Results also indicate that student groups effectively supported each other during the work process by utilizing and sharing strategies and dispositions needed while constructing online content (e.g., critical stance, healthy skepticism, collaboration, flexibility).

The OCC model provides guidance on elements of cognitive apprenticeship, writing research and the use of ICTs as a tool to allow students to express learning and experience to themselves and others (Klein, 1999). The resultant instructional model provides students with an opportunity to express learning through the use and creation of socially expressive digital media (Tewissen, Lingnau, Hoppe, Mannhaupt, & Nischk, 2001). As a result, students use computer-integrated classrooms to focus on individual learning and develop skills to enhance social and collaborative learning. Ultimately, the goal of the OCC instructional model is an attempt to use digital texts and tools to restructure learning environments (Flower & Hayes, 1994; Erkens, Kanselaar, Prangsma, & Jaspers, 2003) and move student learning from knowledge transformation into knowledge constitution (Galbraith, 1999). The OCC instructional model relied on three phases in order to scaffold and support students as they work individually or collaboratively.

Phase 1 of the Instructional Model

The first phase of the instructional model involved elements of the online reading comprehension process and online collaborative inquiry process. In Phase 1, students reviewed examples of online information (Websites, blogs, video, photos) on the topic of inquiry or student research. In the research (O'Byrne, 2009, 2012) conducted that tested the OCC model, students were asked to review a series of Websites they normally would encounter during an online inquiry project. During this review process they were often provided hoax Websites to review in an attempt to assess students ability to effectively evaluate online information. An example of this type of information is the Website for "The Dog Island" (see Figure 1). A hoax Website is an online informational source which has been created for entertainment purposes, usually invoking the absurd, but maintained a "superficial appearance of scientific professionalism" (Brem, Russell, & Weems, 2001, p. 198). In the case of the Website for The Dog Island, the Website looks professional and contains cues that would lead a student to believe the information being presented. Students were encouraged to annotate these Websites and document the elements of Web design that they noticed (e.g., images, video, audio, text) and how this affected how they considered the information being presented.

During this phase of the model students reflect on what they have learned from this online information and the totality of information in relation to other sources on the same topic (see Figure 2). This process encourages students to review the information presented, determine the purpose, audience, and design aesthetics of this information. The questions and processes that guide the teacher and students online collaborative inquiry process can vary depending of the grade level, purpose, and student learning objectives.

In working with students to evaluate online information, students were encouraged to review

Figure 1. Screenshot of "The Dog Island" hoax website

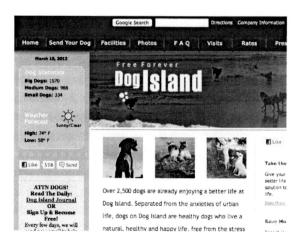

Figure 2. Example of a criteria chart completed during class review of online information

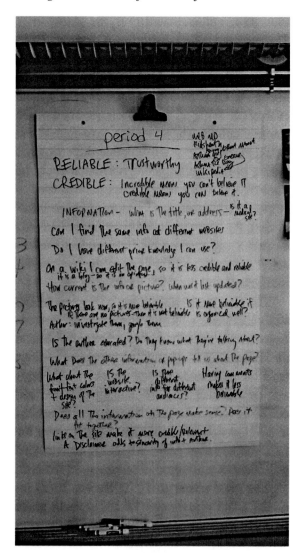

questions that identified the credibility and relevancy of a Website. How much have they learned from this Website? Why did the author publish this information? What did the author include, or leave out in the process? What textual and multimodal design choices did the author use to create this content? Classroom discussions focused on individual design elements and aesthetics of a Website in an attempt to understand how mood, tone, and meaning can be affected by the inclusion of text and images in a testimonial of a product (see Figure 3).

In Phase 1, students plan out the content they would like to construct using paper and graphic organizers to create detailed "mock-ups" of their work (see Figure 4). It is best to have them plan this out first with students on paper to assist them in identifying multimodal and textual elements they'll need to construct, and the design aesthetics that affect their work. These details and markers of online information should be collected and displayed in the class. This document can be used to guide students as they construct online content, it also can be used by the classroom teacher to develop rubrics for assessment of work produced by students. This integration of technology into writing in this planning stage requires teachers and students to work flexibly and think creatively about the construction process. Students need to be encouraged to have dialogue with the teacher and peers about the work process and how their planning and scaffolding tools inform the ultimate product. This work may be complex and

Figure 4. Example of student "mock-up" of webpage

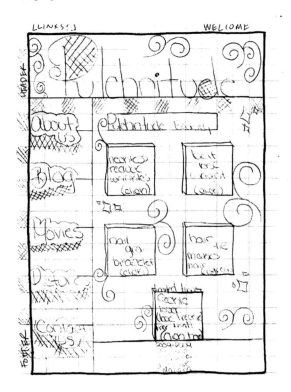

challenging as teachers and students may not fully envision the use tools and scope of the completed work product while planning.

Phase 2 of the Instructional Model

The second phase of the OCC model encourages students to use computers and ICT tools to construct the online content they have planned out on paper. Since the resultant content that students construct could take many forms (Websites, videos, photos, podcasts, blogs, wikis) the tools used in this process will vary. The important part is to have the students plan out their work ahead of time on paper. This allows them to return to the paper organizers if they have trouble during the process of constructing content.

During this phase of the OCC model, students work in groups in a one-to-one laptop environment using a variety of digital media editing software

Figure 3. Example of "testimonials" page from student constructed online content

(see Table 1). It should be noted that even though these tools were used successfully during the two studies, current work being conducted in OCC focuses on having teachers use free online tools to have students collaboratively construct content. Table 1 indicates the original tools used in OCC, but also the current tools being used online in a device agnostic policy. Device agnostic policy means that we provide multiple opportunities for teachers and students to work with whatever technological device is available. This may include a computer, tablet, or mobile device, but do not require a specific brand or operating system.

Please also keep in mind that some students may have experience with the varied ICT tools, while others might not have any background. To allay this concern, it is important to provide opportunities for students to work with the ICT tools and construct content throughout the school year without assessment, or grades associated with it. The major focus of assessment, at least during the initial times working in the OCC process should focus on the content, and knowledge transformation process, as opposed to quality or quantity of content produced.

During Phase 2, the classroom teacher is to work as a facilitator in the classroom and allow

students to work the majority of the time on the construction of online content. Teachers may start a classroom period with a "mini-lesson" (Atwell, 1998) to provide the entire class with instruction that is of importance to all members of the class. These mini-lessons may detail elements of ICT tool use, or excellent work by a student, or lessons learned while constructing content. The majority of instruction and scaffolding should be conducted while the teacher rotates through the groups as they work on their online content (see Figure 5).

Phase 3 of the Instructional Model

The third phase of the OCC instructional model begins as students are wrapping up their work building content on the computers. In this phase, the teacher provides students with real examples of online information that students can use to compare their work product to. Students are encouraged to review this exemplar material and review the work in relation to their own process and product completed to this point. The materials selected by the teacher are to be the same type (Website, video, image, text) as the work being constructed by the students. The work should also focus on the same theme that the student work product was focusing on. For example, a teacher would discuss and evaluate a Website for a beauty or hair care products with a group of students constructing a

Table 1. Online content construction tools used in previous studies

Tool Purpose	Tool Name	Revised Tool Name
Website Construction	iWeb	Google Sites, Mockingbird (Chrome extension)
Photo editing	Aviary (add-on for Firefox)	Pixlr Editor, Pixlr Express (Chrome extension)
Audio editing	Audible	Audible, Soundcloud
Video capture & editing	iMovie, Flip video cameras	WeVideo, mobile/tablet cameras/Webcams
Text editing	Microsoft Word, Evernote	Google Apps, Evernote

Figure 5. Teacher meeting with students during a "mini-lesson" to discuss group work

hoax Website about a new product line of "scratch and sniff" hair coloring products (see Figure 6).

Students are to review this exemplar material and identify elements of their own work process or product that they would like to change after their review (See Figure 7). This examination may identify that the author of the exemplar materials provided an "About Us" page, or included a title in their YouTube video. Students are then provided an appropriate amount of time to complete these revisions to their work before completing the work.

Following the completion of work process and submission of the product to the teacher, students should individually or collaboratively present their work to each other. This presentation can take the form of a showcase in which students rotate through the classroom and share their work with several other students and answer questions about their work and the resultant product. Much of the focus in this assessment process should be on the

Figure 7. Students revising work product following the review process

process involved in the construction of online content as documented by the reflections of students. Assessment of student work may also consist of a review of the work using the collaboratively constructed rubric that students have assembled for this project if this has been previously built. Classroom teachers should also meet with student groups to discuss the work process and product in the review and assessment of student work (see Figure 8). This step is necessary as assessment and evaluation of the process and product involved in OCC is challenging and may not be reflective of the work involved in the process. Additionally, classroom teachers may not feel confident or knowledgeable in understanding, valuing, and assessing elements of work that contain multimodal, visual, or semiotic elements of work. Conferences between students and the

Figure 6. Example of student constructed online content

Figure 8. Teacher meeting with students to assess design choices in student work product

teacher provide an opportunity to discuss the learning experience, and ways to possibly improve upon the process and ultimate product completed in future endeavors.

At the completion of the OCC instructional model, the work product of students was published online. These hoax Websites developed by students could now be shared with family, friends, and peers both in and out of the classroom. Student used this as an opportunity to showcase some of the new and exciting work they had completed in school. In this specific school the teachers and library media specialist used the project materials, and associated hoax Websites as a tool to teach strategies for evaluation of online information to staff and students. A listing of these initial hoax Websites created by students during the pilot study is available below.

Pulchritude

(http://newliteracies.uconn.edu/projects/hoax-sites/pulchritude/Site/Welcome.html): This Website was created by two students and the audience was identified by the students as "middle aged women". The purpose of the site was to sell jewelry that offered supposed health benefits to the individual that wore it.

Tikistar Island

(http://newliteracies.uconn.edu/projects/hoax-sites/tikistar/Site/Welcome.html): This Website was constructed by two students and the targeted audience was identified as "anyone that wanted to purchase an exotic animal". The purpose of the site was to sell exotic fish and pets from an island identified as Tikistar Island.

Toething

(http://newliteracies.uconn.edu/projects/hoax-sites/toething/Site/_welcome.html): This Website was constructed by three students and the targeted audience was any one that wanted to purchase their product. The purpose of the site was to market and sell toething, or "clothes for your toes."

DAT-a-Way

(http://newliteracies.uconn.edu/projects/hoax-sites/dat%20a%20way/Site/Welcome.htmh): This site was constructed by two students and the identified audience was described as "teenagers with acne problems". The purpose of the site was to market their product, an acne treatment formula that was made from the cleanest substance on the face of the earth, dog saliva.

Pillow3

(http://newliteracies.uconn.edu/projects/hoax-sites/Pillow3/Site/Home.html): This site was constructed by three students and the targeted audience was identified as "teenage boys". The purpose of the site was to market the newest installment of the Pillow game series, a videogame in which not only the game characters went to sleep, but many times the game players slept as well. The major advance of Pillow3 was that is was now a massive, multiplayer online game.

Fruitilicious

(http://newliteracies.uconn.edu/projects/hoax-sites/fruitiilicious/Site/VVellcome.html): This site was constructed by two students. The targeted audience was identified as "women of all ages." The purpose was to market a new hair color product that loosely was marketed as "scratch and sniff hair."

CLASSROOM DYNAMICS AND IMPLICATIONS

When students construct online content in the classroom, teachers are able to bring the knowledge, skills, and dispositions of these new and digital literacy practices into instruction. In this process of "doing" literacy, students construct online content and are empowered to not only understand, but also reframe "what counts as literacy" (Unsworth, 2001). Having students construct online content allows schools to more adequately represent the changes occurring to literacy as a result of technology while incorporating multiple forms and modes of text in the classroom (Alvermann, 2002; Gee, 2004; Leander, 2007).

Given the potential challenges that could occur while introducing these new literacies into instruction, classroom dynamics may need to change. The instructor must adopt a flexible disposition and an appreciation for the complexities, advantages, and limitations inherent in the online information space (Huffaker, 2004). Work such as detailed in this chapter engenders a degree of risk and trust amongst instructors and the students as they focus on productively accomplishing the necessary steps for comprehending and constructing online content (Alvermann, 2002; Livingstone, 2004). Implications of this work for pre-service and teacher preparation programs involve a need to have educators work with, and in some cases "play" with digital content. In this manner teachers are able to build some of the knowledge, skills, and dispositions necessary to authentically include online informational sources in instruction.

Researchers must constantly consider these changes to permit new concepts, processes, and approaches of information delivery to continue developing in society (Tyner, 1998; Sutherland-Smith, 2002). The OCC instructional model defined herein empowers instructors and students to work collaboratively together to define continually what it meant to be able to read, write, and communicate using online informational sources. Working within this context, instructors and students have to consider, and in some cases adapt, their roles to participate effectively in the learning experience (Luke 1994, 2000; Alvermann & Hagood, 2000; Mishra & Koehler, 2006). Re-

search needs to investigate the dynamics that exist between teacher and student, but also student and student as they work to construct online content in the classroom. Furthermore, research needs to be conducted to identify the opportunities and challenges that occur as students work individually and collaboratively in a learning environment such as the one detailed in this chapter.

Students also have an equal responsibility to undertake the discipline, responsibility, and flexibility required to work as an active participant in the ICT infused classroom (Greenhow, Robelia, & Hughes, 2009). Consequently, students need to reconsider the concept of "school" as they assume an active role in the learning process (Alvermann, 2002; Mishra & Koehler, 2006). In this instructional model, students are not only guided through online learning activities by the instructor, but in some cases they may take a leadership role in the development and application of learning (Ward, Peters, & Shelley, 2010). Students may have challenges in working with digital tools and content, or simply struggle with the changing dynamics of the classroom as detailed herein.

As these concepts evolve, educators must reflect on these changes and practices in our classrooms and also remain flexible to new developments. Bringing in the multiple perspectives and frameworks as identified in OCC allows educators and researchers to continue to examine these changes. The development of OCC as an instructional model is necessary as it allows educators to discuss this work in a classroom context in a language easy for practitioners to employ. This provides a common, approachable discourse in which educators and students can discuss this work and the work process and product that is included. In many ways this work expands upon work in traditional writing instruction to while identifying the complexity that occurs while including digital content in the construction process.

Literacy researchers are also provided an ample foothold in the changing landscape to allow for an informed examination and review of best practices associated with this work and the associated instructional model. The use of the dual-level new literacies theory allows OCC to be informed by, but also guide and further describe the complexity of New Literacies research. This instructional model allows for research including that previously described, but it also embeds elements of semiotics, visual literacies, and other elements of the contemporary social and technological backdrop. Cultivating the various theoretical boundaries and perspectives is an attempt to clarify the blurred distinctions that now exist between these "new and unsettled genres" (Romano, 2000; Jewitt, 2008). This compilation of research and perspectives integrated into the OCC model offer an opportunity to "build connections across discourses of specialized knowledges and everyday knowledges" (Jewitt, 2008; Zammit, 2011) that exist in our classrooms.

Of most importance in considering the inclusion of OCC in the classroom is the fact that it has the potential to empower students as "co-investigators" (Scardamalia & Bereiter, 1983) in the classroom. Students are empowered and encouraged to reflect on strategies they have or may need. This requires a potential shift in classroom power dynamics to provide opportunities for teachers and students to collaboratively reflect on the knowledge, skills, and dispositions needed to work with this content. The hope is that this structure of the instructional model provides fertile ground for teachers and students to exchange strategies and not be concerned that they do not know everything needed to conduct this work in the classroom. The goal would be on building the understanding and respect that they are working together to comprehend and construct content in an attempt to create their voice in the online informational space.

This consolidation of theory and research as detailed in OCC should be viewed as a starting point to identify possibilities for having students and teachers work on the process and product associated with construction of digital media. Instructional models such as this provide opportunities to empower students as they skillfully encode and decode meaning as a member of the reader/writer online informational space. Considering the increasing importance of online information, teaching effective ways to comprehend and construct online information to students is imperative to their future success as Internet users. As students increasingly use the Internet for social, academic and personal tasks, instruction in critical and thoughtful construction of online content will be essential.

REFERENCES

Alvermann, D. E. (2002). *Adolescents and literacies in a digital world*. New York: Peter Lang.

Alvermann, D. E., & Hagood, M. C. (2000). Fandom and critical media literacy. *Journal of Adolescent & Adult Literacy*, *43*, 436–446.

Anderson, J. Q., & Rainie, L. (2008). *The future of the internet III*. Washington, DC: Pew Internet and American Life Project. Retrieved December 15, 2010 from http://www.pewInternet.org/pdfs/PIP_FutureInternet3.pdf

Atwell, N. (1998). *In the middle: New understandings about writing, reading, and learning*. Portsmouth, NH: Boynton/Cook Publishers, Inc..

Beach, R., & Myers, J. (2001). *Inquiry-based English instruction: Engaging students in life and literature*. New York: Teachers College Press.

Bereiter, C., & Scardamalia, M. (1987). *The psychology of written composition*. Hoboken, NJ: L. Erlbaum Associates.

Bezemer, J., & Kress, G. (2008). Writing in multimodal texts: A social semiotic account of designs for learning. *Written Communication*, *25*(2), 166–195. doi:10.1177/0741088307313177.

Brem, S. K., Russell, J., & Weems, L. (2001). Science on the web: Student evaluations of scientific arguments. *Discourse Processes, 32*(2&3), 191–213. doi: doi:10.1080/0163853X.2001.9651598.

Britton, J. (1970). *Language and learning*. New York: Penguin.

Britton, J. (1972). *Writing to learn and learning to write*. Washington, DC: National Council of Teachers of English.

Brown, J., Collins, A., & Duguid, P. (1989). Situated cognition and the culture of learning. *Education Researcher, 18*(1), 32–42. doi:10.3102/0013189X018001032.

Carey, L., Flower, L., Hayes, J., Schriver, K., & Haas, C. (1989). *Differences in writers' initial task representations*. Pittsburgh, PA: Carnegie-Mellon University.

Coiro, J., Knobel, M., Lankshear, C., & Leu, D. (Eds.). (2008). *Handbook of research on new literacies*. Mahwah, NJ: Lawrence Erlbaum Associates.

Collins, A. (1991). Cognitive apprenticeship and instructional technology. In Idol, L., & Jones, B. F. (Eds.), *Educational values and cognitive instruction: Implication for reform* (pp. 121–138). Hillsdale, NJ: Lawrence Erlbaum Associates.

Collins, A., & Brown, J. S. (1988). The computer as a tool for learning through reflection. In Mandl, H., & Lesgold, A. (Eds.), *Learning issues for intelligent tutoring systems* (pp. 1–18). New York: Springer-Verlag. doi:10.1007/978-1-4684-6350-7_1.

Collins, A., Brown, J. S., & Holum, A. (1991). Cognitive apprenticeship: Making thinking visible. *American Educator, 15*(3), 6–11, 38–46.

Collins, A., Brown, J. S., & Newman, S. E. (1989). Cognitive apprenticeship: Teaching the craft of reading, writing, and mathematics. In Resnick, L. B. (Ed.), *Knowing, learning, and instruction: Essays in honor of Robert Glaser* (pp. 453–494). Hillsdale, NJ: Lawrence Erlbaum Associates.

Collins, A., & Gentner, D. (1980). A framework for a cognitive theory of writing. *Cognitive Processes in Writing*, 51-72.

Cope, B., & Kalantzis, M. (Eds.). (2000). *Multiliteracies*. London: Routledge.

Doneman, M. (1997). Multimediating. In Lankshear, C., Bigum, C., & Durant, C. (Eds.), *Digital Rhetorics: Literacies and technologies in education–current practices and future directions* (*Vol. 3*, pp. 131–148). Brisbane, Australia: QUT/DEETYA.

Duncum, P. (2004). Visual culture isn't just visual: Multiliteracy, multimodality and meaning. *Studies in Art Education*, 252–264.

Erkens, G., Kanselaar, G., Prangsma, M., & Jaspers, J. (2003). Computer support for collaborative and argumentative writing. In *Powerful learning environments: Unravelling basic components and dimensions* (pp. 159–177). Academic Press.

Fletcher, R., & Portalupi, J. (2001). *Writing workshop*. Portsmouth, NH: Heinemann.

Flower, L., & Hayes, J. R. (1981). A cognitive process theory of writing. *College Composition and Communication, 32*(4), 365–387. doi:10.2307/356600.

Fox, S., Anderson, J. Q., & Rainie, L. (2005). *The future of the internet*. Washington, DC: Pew Internet and American Life Project. Retrieved September 29, 2010, from http://www.pewInternet.org/pdfs/PIP_Future_of_Internet.pdf

Freire, P., & Macedo, D. (1987). *Literacy: Reading the word and the world*. Greenwood, CT: Praeger.

Galbraith, D. (1996). Self-monitoring, discovery through writing and individual differences in drafting strategy. In Rijlaarsdam, G., van den Bergh, H., & Couzijn, M. (Eds.), *Theories, Models and Methodology in Writing Research* (pp. 121–141). Amsterdam: Amsterdam University Press.

Galbraith, D. (1999). Writing as a knowledge-constituting process. *Knowing what to write: Conceptual processes in text production, 4*, 139-164.

Gee, J. P. (2004). *Situated language and learning: A critique of traditional schooling*. London: Routledge.

Graves, D. H. (1994). *A fresh look at writing*. Portsmouth, NH: Heinemann.

Greenhow, C., Robelia, B., & Hughes, J. (2009). Web 2.0 and classroom research: What path should we take now? *Educational Researcher, 38*(4), 246–259. doi:10.3102/0013189X09336671.

Grimes, D., & Warschauer, M. (2008). Learning with laptops: A multi-method case study. *Journal of Educational Computing Research, 38*(3), 305–332. doi:10.2190/EC.38.3.d.

Hairston, M. (1982). The winds of change: Thomas Kuhn and the revolution in the teaching of writing. *College Composition and Communication, 33*(1), 76–88. doi:10.2307/357846.

Hayes, J. R., & Flower, L. S. (1980). Identifying the organization of writing processes. *Cognitive Processes in Writing*, 3-30.

Hayes, J. R., & Flower, L. S. (1986). Writing research and the writer. *The American Psychologist, 41*(10), 1106. doi:10.1037/0003-066X.41.10.1106.

Hendricks, C. C. (2001). Teaching causal reasoning through cognitive apprenticeship: What are results from situated learning? *The Journal of Educational Research, 94*(5), 302–311. doi:10.1080/00220670109598766.

Hennessey, S. (1993). Situated cognition and cognitive apprenticeship: Implications for classroom learning. *Studies in Science Education, 22*, 1–41. doi:10.1080/03057269308560019.

Herrington, J., & Oliver, R. (2000). An instructional design framework for authentic learning environments. *Educational Technology Research and Development, 48*(3), 23–48. doi:10.1007/BF02319856.

Huffaker, D. (2005). The educated blogger: Using weblogs to promote literacy in the classroom. *AACE Journal, 13*(2), 91–98.

Jewitt, C. (2008). Multimodality and literacy in school classrooms. *Review of Research in Education, 32*(1), 241–267. doi:10.3102/0091732X07310586.

Jewitt, C., Bezemer, J., Jones, K., & Kress, G. (2009). Changing English? The impact of technology and policy on a school subject in the 21st century. *English Teaching: Practice and Critique, 8*(3), 8-20. Retrieved from http://education.waikato.ac.nz/research/files/etpc/files/2009v8n3art1.pdf

Kiili, C., Laurinen, L., & Marttunen, M. (2008). Students evaluating Internet sources: From versatile evaluators to uncritical readers. *Journal of Educational Computing Research, 39*(1), 75–95. doi:10.2190/EC.39.1.e.

Kimber, K., & Wyatt-Smith, C. (2006). Using and creating knowledge with new technologies: A case for students-as-designers. *Learning, Media and Technology, 31*(1), 19–34. doi:10.1080/17439880500515440.

Klein, P. D. (1999). Reopening inquiry into cognitive processes in writing-to-learn. *Educational Psychology Review, 11*, 203–270. doi:10.1023/A:1021913217147.

Kress, G. (2003). *Literacy in the new media age*. London: Routledge. doi:10.4324/9780203164754.

Kress, G., & van Leeuwen, T. (2001). *Multimodal discourse: The modes and media of contemporary communication*. London: Arnold.

Labbo, L., & Reinking, D. (1999). Negotiating the multiple realities of technology in literacy research and instruction. *Reading Research Quarterly, 34*(4), 478–492. doi:10.1598/RRQ.34.4.5.

Leander, K. M. (2007). You won't be needing your laptops today: Wired bodies in the wireless classroom. In Knobel, M., & Lankshear, C. (Eds.), *A new literacies sampler* (pp. 25–48). New York: Peter Lang.

Leu, D., Coiro, J., Castek, J., Hartman, D., Henry, L., & Reinking, D. (2008). Research on instruction and assessment in the new literacies of online reading comprehension. In Collins Block, C., & Parris, S. (Eds.), *Comprehension instruction: Research-based best practices* (pp. 321–346). New York: Guilford Press.

Leu, D. J. (2000). Literacy and technology: Deictic consequences for literacy education in an information age. In Kamil, M. L., Mosenthal, P., Barr, R., & Pearson, P. D. (Eds.), *Handbook of reading research* (*Vol. III*, pp. 743–770). Mahwah, NJ: Erlbaum.

Leu, D. J., Castek, J., Hartman, D., Coiro, J., Henry, L., Kulikowich, J., & Lyver, S. (2005). *Evaluating the development of scientific knowledge and new forms of reading comprehension during online learning*. Paper presented to the North Central Regional Educational Laboratory/Learning Point Associates.

Leu, D. J., Kinzer, C. K., Coiro, J., & Cammack, D. (2004). Toward a theory of new literacies emerging from the Internet and other information and communication technologies. In R.B. Ruddell & N. Unrau (Eds.), *Theoretical Models and Processes of Reading* (5th ed), (1568-1611). Newark, DE: International Reading Association. Retrieved October 15, 2008 from http://www.readingonline.org/newliteracies/lit_index.asp?HREF=/newliteracies/leu

Leu, D. J., McVerry, J. G., O'Byrne, W. I., Kiili, C., Zawilinski, L., & Everett-Cacopardo, H. et al. (2011). The new literacies of online reading comprehension: Expanding the literacy and learning curriculum. *Journal of Adolescent & Adult Literacy, 55*, 5–14.

Leu, D. J., O'Byrne, W. I., Zawilinski, L., McVerry, J. G., & Everett-Cacopardo, H. (2009). Expanding the new literacies conversation. *Educational Researcher, 38*(4), 264–269. doi:10.3102/0013189X09336676.

Livingstone, S. (2004). Media literacy and the challenge of new information and communication technologies. *Communication Review, 1*(7), 3–14. doi:10.1080/10714420490280152.

Luke, A. (1994). *The social construction of literacy in the classroom*. Melbourne, Australia: Macmillan.

Luke, A. (2000). Critical literacy in Australia: A matter of context and standpoint. *Journal of Adolescent & Adult Literacy, 43*(5), 448–461.

Mishra, P., & Koehler, M. J. (2006). Technological pedagogical content knowledge: A framework for teacher knowledge. *Teachers College Record, 108*(6), 1017–1054. doi:10.1111/j.1467-9620.2006.00684.x.

Murray, D. M. (1972). Teach writing as a process not product. *The Leaflet, 71*(3), 11–14.

Murray, D. M. (1999). *Write to learn*. New York: Harcourt Brace College Pub..

O'Byrne, W. I. (2009). *Facilitating critical thinking skills through content creation*. Paper presented at the 58th Annual National Reading Conference. Albuquerque, NM.

O'Byrne, W. I. (2012). *Facilitating critical evaluation skills through content creation: Empowering adolescents as readers and writers of online information*. (Unpublished doctoral dissertation). University of Connecticut, Storrs, CT.

Oblinger, D. (2006). *Learning spaces (Vol. 2)*. Washington, DC: Educause.

Palincsar, A. S., & Brown, A. L. (1984). Reciprocal teaching of comprehension-fostering and monitoring activities. *Cognition and Instruction, 1*(2), 117–175. doi:10.1207/s1532690xci0102_1.

Reitman, W. R. (1964). Heuristic decision procedures open constraints and the structure of ill-defined problems. In Shelly, M. W., & Bryan, G. L. (Eds.), *Human Judgments and Optimality*. New York: John Wiley & Sons, Inc..

Robinson, E., & Robinson, S. (2003). *What does it mean-discourse, text, culture: An introduction*. Sydney, Australia: McGraw-Hill.

Rogoff, B. (1990). *Apprenticeship in thinking: Cognitive development in social context*. New York, NY: Oxford University Press.

Romano, T. (2000). *Blending genre, altering style*. Portsmouth, NH: Boynton/Cook.

Sawyer, R. K. (2006). The Cambridge handbook of the learning sciences. New York: Cambridge.

Scardamalia, M., & Bereiter, C. (1983). Child as co-investigator: Helping children gain insight into their own mental processes. In Paris, S., Olson, G., & Stevenson, H. (Eds.), *Learning and motivation in the classroom* (pp. 83–107). Hillsdale, NJ: Lawrence Erlbaum Associates.

Scardamalia, M., & Bereiter, C. (1985). Fostering the development of self-regulation in children's knowledge processing. In Chipman, S. F., Segal, J. W., & Glaser, R. (Eds.), *Thinking and learning skills: Research and open questions* (pp. 563–577). Hillsdale, NJ: Lawrence Erlbaum Associates.

Scardamalia, M., & Bereiter, C. (1994). Computer support for knowledge-building communities. *Journal of the Learning Sciences, 3*(3), 265–283. doi:10.1207/s15327809jls0303_3.

Scardamalia, M., Bereiter, C., & Steinbach, R. (1984). Teachability of reflective processes in written composition. *Cognitive Science, 8*(2), 173–190. doi:10.1207/s15516709cog0802_4.

Serafini, F. (2011). Expanding perspectives for comprehending visual images in multimodal texts. *Journal of Adolescent & Adult Literacy, 54*(5), 342–350. doi:10.1598/JAAL.54.5.4.

Shapiro, A. L. (2000). *The control revolution how the internet is putting individuals in charge and changing the world we know*. PublicAffairs.

Sheppard, J. (2009). The rhetorical work of multimedia production practices: It's more than just technical skill. *Computers and Composition, 26*(2), 122–131. doi:10.1016/j.compcom.2009.02.004.

Simon, H. A. (1973). The structure of ill-structured problems. *Artificial Intelligence, 4*, 181–201. doi:10.1016/0004-3702(73)90011-8.

Street, B. (1984). *Literacy in theory and practice*. Cambridge, UK: Cambridge University Press.

Sutherland-Smith, W. (2002). Weaving the literacy web: Changes in reading from page to screen. *The Reading Teacher, 55*(7), 662–669.

Swenson, J., Young, C. A., McGrail, E., Rozema, R., & Whitin, P. (2006). Extending the conversation: New technologies, new literacies, and English education. *English Education, 38*(4), 351–369.

Tewissen, F., Lingnau, A., Hoppe, U., Mannhaupt, G., & Nischk, D. (2001). Collaborative writing in a computer-integrated classroom for early learning. In P. Dillenbourg, A. Eurelings, & K. Hakkarainen (Eds.), *Proceedings of the European Conference on Computer-Supported Collaborative Learning* (Euro- CSCL 2001), (pp. 593-600). Maastricht, The Netherlands: Euro-CSCL.

The New London Group. (1996). A pedagogy of multiliteracies: Designing social futures. *Harvard Educational Review, 66*(1), 60–92.

Tyner, K. (1998). *Literacy in a digital world: Teaching and learning in the age of information.* Mahwah, NJ: Erlbaum.

Unsworth, L. (2001). *Teaching multiliteracies across the curriculum: Changing contexts of text and image in classroom practice.* Buckingham, UK: Open University Press.

Ward, M., Peters, G., & Shelley, K. (2010). Student and faculty perceptions of the quality of online learning experiences. *International Review of Research in Open and Distance Learning, 11*(3), 57–77.

Warschauer, M. (2000). The changing global economy and the future of English teaching. *TESOL Quarterly, 34*(3), 511–535. doi:10.2307/3587741.

Yelland, N. (1999). Reconceptualising schooling with technology for the 21st century: Images and reflections. *Information Technology in Childhood Education Annual,* (1): 39–59.

Zammit, K. P. (2011). Connecting multiliteracies and engagement of students from low socio-economic backgrounds: Using Bernstein's pedagogic discourse as a bridge. *Language and Education, 25*(3), 203–220. doi:10.1080/09500782.2011.560945.

Chapter 17
Technology and Second Language Writing:
A Framework-Based Synthesis of Research

Soobin Yim
University of California – Irvine, USA

Mark Warschauer
University of California – Irvine, USA

ABSTRACT

This chapter aims to synthesize research on technology and second language writing through the lenses of three common and broad discourses surrounding literacy and technology: achievement, change, and power (modified from Warschauer & Ware, 2008). The authors discuss the meaning and relationship of each perspective to the field of technology and second language writing as well as provide an overview of recent research under each category. This framework-based analysis sheds new light on current research, offering researchers and teachers an opportunity to consider the weaknesses and strengths of each research focus as well as the gaps in the literature. Through examining the interwoven relationship between technology and second language writing under different perspectives, the authors ultimately aim to explore the ways we can maximize the educational benefits of technology use for non-native speakers of English.

INTRODUCTION

The ubiquitous presence of new technology has brought great changes in writing practices and instruction. Technology can have a powerful influence on students' writing; in turn, writing can maximize the potential benefits of digital media for education. One group of students who can benefit greatly from a strong connection between technology and writing is non-native English speakers. Since such students must increasingly demonstrate written communication skills in English as well as technology skills in order to participate and compete in a globalized economy, combining English and technology can provide students real-life purposes for writing and increase motivation and efficiency in learning. Furthermore, for tech-savvy students in countries such as Japan, Korea, or China, where access to broadband is widespread (Bleha, 2005; Kelly, Gray, & Minges, 2003; Reardon, 2005), English writing with technology can be both empowering

DOI: 10.4018/978-1-4666-4341-3.ch017

and synergizing; students can build their second language writing skills upon their already advanced technology skills.

Such synergistic relationships between technology and second language writing can also be explained in terms of a cultural modeling approach. In cultural modeling, students learn to consider their own cultural practices as valuable for learning classroom practices (Hull & Schultz, 2001). As technology-based activities such as online communication and Web searching become common cultural practices for students, second language learners find English not as a forced-to-learn core subject, but as a universal language in online spaces. In this context, English writing using technology becomes a more interest-driven, purposeful, and natural activity for second language learners.

The potential of technology to support second language writing has been illustrated in many studies over the past two decades. There has been fruitful research on diverse ways of incorporating technology in writing (e.g., Bruce, 2009), characteristics of second language writing with digital media (e.g., Schultz, 2000), and the challenges and benefits of technology use in second language writing (e.g., Bloch, 2007). Most recently, complex issues of culture, identity, and audience surrounding the use of technology and second language writing have also been explored (e.g., Lam, 2000; Black, 2009; Forte & Bruckman, 2010). In this era of fast-emerging research in technology and second language writing, scholars and practitioners may benefit from a review of research under a conceptual framework that facilitates interpretation of different perspectives and offers insight into how to maximize the benefits of technology use for non-native speakers of English.

In this chapter, we analyze research on technology and second language writing through the lenses of three common and broad discourses surrounding literacy and technology: *achievement*, *change*, and *power* (Warschauer & Ware, 2008). We begin the chapter by providing definitions of the three perspectives, whose emphases are

respectively on technology's teaching effectiveness, transformative power, and mission for socio-economic equality, and later discuss the meaning and relationship of each perspective to the field of technology and second language writing. Then we provide an overview of recent research on second language writing and technology under each category, drawing on both quantitative and qualitative research, as well as interventions and naturalistic studies of the field. This framework-based analysis will shed new light on current research, offering researchers and teachers an opportunity to consider the weaknesses and strengths of each research focus as well as the gaps in the literature. Through examining the interwoven relationship between technology and second language writing under different perspectives, we ultimately aim to explore the ways we can maximize educational benefits of technology use for non-native speakers of English.

FRAMEWORKS FOR TECHNOLOGY AND SECOND LANGUAGE WRITING

The relationship between technology and second language writing can be interpreted using broader discourses surrounding technology and literacy. Developing Warschauer and Ware's (2008) original framework that defined the three most common research themes in the field of technology and literacy, we put forward the achievement, change, and power frameworks, each with their own epistemological assumptions, set of practices, and evidence bases. In the *achievement* frame, the emphasis is typically on raising test scores on standardized measures of reading and writing, while in the *change* framework, the emphasis is on how literacy itself is transforming in radical ways because of revolutions in Information and Communications Technology (ICT). Lastly, the *power* framework focuses on relationships between technology access and use, and social and economic equality.

The three frameworks coexist and complement each other, but are distinguishable in their different orientations and goals. These frameworks can be thought of as corners of a triangle, as any educational or research perspective can fall on a continuum within a triangle rather than at one of its vertices (Warschauer & Ware, 2008). However, they differ in terms of how learner, literacy, and technology interact. The achievement framework emphasizes the impact of technology on the learner through literacy, while the change framework follows the social constructivist view of literacy, wherein students actively construct knowledge and understanding through interaction with technology. In the power framework, the focus is on how learners, or researchers and educators who support them, can deploy technology through literacy practices in order to improve educational, social, and economic opportunities. Rather than being a passive recipient, learners in this framework hold agency and creatively exploit technology to achieve desired ends.

The frameworks have both similarities and differences. Similar to the change framework, the power framework sees the flexible nature of literacies and values new literacy practices; however, it particularly focuses on how to use those practices to enhance social, economic, and educational power. The achievement and power frameworks are similar in that they view educational outcomes and test scores as important, but the power framework focuses on how to exploit students' use of technology in literacy practices in order to improve students' access to education, literacy, and academic gains. However, because such different foci can overlap, the frameworks should be viewed as a continuum of emphasis rather than as discrete categories.

In the subsequent sections, we discuss how the frameworks apply to the context of second language writing and what this implies for research and instructional practices. Below we provide the summary features of these three frameworks (see Table 1), followed by discussions on each framework and a research overview.

Table 1. Summary features of achievement, change, and power framework (modified from Warschauer & Ware, 2008)

Framework	Theoretical grounding	Research interests	Research tradition	Goal	Relevant field of inquiry	Target of critique
Achievement	Objectivism	Technology's impact on writing outcomes	Quantitative experiments, quasi-experiments, or correlational analysis	Raise writing test scores and improve student writing	Educational technology, educational administration, educational policy	Technology as a match for schools and learners
Change	Social constructionism	Relationship between home and school writing practices	Triangulation, mixed-methods, ethnography of communication, discourse analysis, phenomenology	Make school writing relevant by valuing new literacies	New literacy studies, cultural and media studies, games studies, computers and writing	Schools as conservative institutions
Power	Critical inquiry, social informatics	Access and use of technology-based writing for educational and social equity	Mixed-method approach, ethnographic approach, comparative case study	Empower writers through knowledge, access, and skill with socially relevant tools	Sociology, economics, development studies, critical pedagogy	Unequal power structures

Achievement Framework

The achievement framework addresses how technology can be incorporated in education, with outcomes measured through scores on standardized reading and writing tests (Warschaure & Ware, 2008). This framework focuses on literacy outcomes in the school context rather than literacy practices and interactions among learners outside school settings. In this framework, technology is simply seen as a new educational tool or learning system that replaces traditional overhead projectors or audiotape language labs (see Figure 1) to aid current literacy education. Its focus on measurable learning outcomes may overlap with the transmission-oriented pedagogy for computer-supported learning, the goal of which is to transmit information and skills articulated in the curriculum directly to students (Cummins, 2008).

In the field of second language writing, the main inquiry of this framework is how student writing can be supported, enhanced, or possibly limited with the integration of technology in school settings (Ware, Kern, & Warschauer, in press). With its focus on practical and measurable outcomes, research under this framework tends to follow an objectivist view, aiming to generalize the beneficial results of technology-enhanced writing interventions or teaching methods to English-as-a-Second-Language populations. Such research typically adopts quantitative methods including experimental, quasi-experimental, or correlational analysis. The most common topics explored include (a) technology as an instructional tool and (b) technology as a feedback tool, both of which will be discussed in detail later in the research review.

Change Framework

The advancement of technology and increasing bandwidth have transformed the way people read, write, communicate, and explore knowledge. Those revolutions, which can be compared with the diffusion of the printing press in 15th century (see Figure 2), have far-reaching effects on society. The change framework recognizes the interwoven relationship among technology, literacy, culture, and society, and views technology as embodiments of social and cultural relations (Warschauer & Ware, 2008). This framework also criticizes school systems for failing to recognize these radical reforms and subjecting students to outmoded and ineffective forms of education (Gee, 2004). Rather than focusing on the one-sided impact of technology on literacy and education within school settings, researchers adopting this framework turn their attention to out-of-school literacy practices that are not typically valued in schools (Hull & Schultz, 2002). Therefore, the goal of research is to make schooling relevant by valuing new literacies and exploring the relationship between home and school writing practices (Warschauer & Ware, 2008).

Figure 1. Central metaphors in achievement framework (Adopted from Warschauer & Ware, 2008)

Media in Education	Radio → Film → Television → Computer
Educational Technology	Blackboard → Overhead Projector → Software Programs → Internet
Learning System	Programmed Instructional Kits → Language Lab → Computer Lab

Figure 2. Central metaphors in change framework (Adopted from Warschauer & Ware, 2008)

Means of Communication	Language → Writing → Print → ICT
Carrier of Written Word	Papyrus → Codex → Book → Screen → Internet

In second language writing research under this framework, the focus of research shifts from static to interactive views of writing, from single authorship to multi-vocal texts, and from essay writing to multimodal textual production (Ware et al., in press). This framework views ICT as transforming second language writing by enabling the interactive nature of written communication (e.g., instant messaging, chat, and email), allowing new writing outlets through the production of multimedia and hypertexts, and bringing second language writers a limitless amount of information available from the Web (Warschauer, 1997; 1999).

The methodological approach of this framework includes, but is not limited to, ethnography of communication, which allows the researcher to explore the cultural environment that surrounds use of new technologies through interviews, journals, discourse analysis, and digital or video documentation (see, e.g., Lam, 2000). Participant self-report through written products or descriptive statistics from surveys are also common. Data analysis may involve triangulation across the aforementioned multiple types of data sources (Ware et al., in press). Researchers adopting this framework most commonly explore (a) changes in writing practices, and (b) changes in writer identity.

Power Framework

The power framework focuses on the associations of access and use of technology with social and economic equality. Figuratively, the revolutionary change that ICT brought to the entire society is to be compared to revolutions such as from the advance of steam power, electricity, or the printing press (see Figure 3). As with limited access

Figure 3. Central metaphors in power framework (Adopted from Warschauer & Ware, 2008)

Industrial Revolution	Steam Power → Electricity → ICT
Access Node	Phone Line → Internet
Literacy Node	Print Literacy → Electronic Literacies

to print literacy, the inability to access and use technology limits one's opportunities. The main goal of this framework is to empower youth through knowledge, access, and skill with socially relevant tools, and to investigate appropriate uses of technology to achieve desired ends (Warschauer & Ware, 2008).

In this framework, technology is seen as a tool to think with (e.g., for research, data analysis, knowledge production), rather than as a tutor (Warschauer, 2011). The power framework emphasizes multimodal pedagogies, by which students are positioned not as recipients of knowledge, but as active producers of knowledge drawing from blends of learning styles and practices (Luke 2003; Warschauer & Ware, 2008). With this emphasis, project-based learning, experiential learning, and collaborative critical inquiry are commonly employed, where students are encouraged to be active producers of knowledge rather than passive consumers. These practices are also in line with Cummins and Sayers' (1995) transformative pedagogy for computer-supported learning, which aims to enable students to gain insight into how knowledge intersects with power through technologies.

In second language writing, research adopting the power framework focuses on writing for the pursuit or production of knowledge rather than marginal activities such as text messaging or personal emails. Second language writing under this framework is seen as an instrument to enhance desired ends – increasing academic access and connecting to global society. Warschauer's (1999) case studies revealed that second language learners, especially those who are on the margin (e.g., immigrants in the United States or international students from developing countries), view the development of technology-based literacies as critical to their economic and social futures. This framework emphasizes the potential of technology to enhance the educational, social, and economic opportunities of those culturally and linguistically diverse students (Warschauer & Ware, 2008).

Under the power framework, students' second language writing is usually integrated as a part of a knowledge production process to increase access and equality through technology, rather than as a separate goal of instruction. Related research can greatly contribute to empowering language minority learners through knowledge, access, and skill with technology tools and might ultimately help alleviate the problems of educational and social inequity stemming from language barriers. Research exploring such potentials is rare but growing in the literature.

Two of the most representative methodological approaches under this framework are action research, where researchers implement changes to improve teaching and equality, and the comparative case study, where various methods ranging from highly ethnographic work to mixed-methods approaches are utilized (Warschauer & Ware, 2008). Through the use of multiple data sources, researchers can illuminate underlying power issues (Hagood, 2003). Salient topics of second language writing in this framework include (a) project-based learning and (b) language-as-an-asset approach.

RESEARCH OVERVIEW

Achievement Framework

Technology as an Instructional Tool

One of the major concerns in research under the achievement framework is whether or not technology enhances second language writing, which is measured by improved writing scores and outcomes. Research seeking to improve L2 students' writing ability through technology has reported the beneficial effects of teaching writing in a computer-supported context over teaching in a conventional classroom (Pennington, 2004; Lee & Swales, 2006). Most studies looked at the advantages of using a specific technological tool or program for writing. For example, Hegelheimer (2006) reported the positive effect of online grammar resources on ESL learners' writing skills, most markedly in reducing writing errors. Lee and Swales (2006) examined how an experimental corpus-based academic writing program may help ESL students to correct errors and revise their writing without the support of a native speaker.

A number of studies adopting the achievement framework took a closer look at how technology as an instructional tool affects second language writing. In a meta-analysis of 26 comparative studies, Goldberg, Russell, and Cook (2004) concluded that the writing process is more collaborative, iterative, and social in technology-based classrooms in comparison with traditional environments, students are more engaged and motivated in their writing, and they produce written work that is of greater length and higher quality. Findings from second language writing research echo these differences. Ferris and Hedgecock (2005) found that students in a computer lab setting have more one-on-one time between teacher and student. Chapelle (2003) noticed the benefits of instant feedback and easy access to online reference tools in technology-based second language writing.

Studies on how technology use affects the second language writing process have focused on issues of planning, revision, and peer collaboration. Pennington (2004) observed a recursive planning-drafting-revising process in a computer-assisted L2 writing class and suggested that this process emerged because the use of computers helped reduce students' stress and cognitive load, which are major challenges in L2 composition. Chuo (2007) evaluated the effects of Web-based language activities on second language writing, citing benefits such as the provision of rich, authentic, and current information, exposure to visual elements, enhanced flexibility of individual learning pace, reinforced learning of the subject matter, heightened motivation, and increased interest.

Technology as a Feedback Tool

Another important use of technology to support second language writing is as a feedback tool. As part of writing instruction, Automated Writing Evaluation (AWE) technology arose as a solution to support teachers and learners in solving practical difficulties surrounding feedback practices, such as time constraints and teacher workload. While feedback is a critical step in the writing process and crucial for revision, teachers' limited time and resources often lead to little revision in English Language Arts (ELA) classes (Breland, 1996, as cited in Grimes & Warschauer, 2010). In the last decade, AWE programs have been developed. These programs combine automated essay scoring software with a range of other tools for classroom use, such as model essays, scoring rubrics, graphic organizers, word banks, dictionaries, thesauri, and spelling, grammar, and usage checkers (Grimes & Warschauer, 2010). These features can benefit second language writers through scaffolding and by providing more practice opportunities, as well as equipping non-native English teachers with a tool to provide feedback to students.

Research exploring the value of AWE reported that these programs may facilitate more writing practice and increase students' motivation to write and revise (Elliot & Mikulas, 2004). In addition, AWE may help teachers to concentrate more on the content and organization of writing instead of mechanics (Grimes & Warschauer, 2010). There are also criticisms that AWE diminishes the role of teachers and distorts students' notions of good writing and the social interactions in writing (Cheville, 2004; Ericsson & Haswell, 2006). While studies indicate the potential of AWE for writing score improvement (Elliot & Mikulas, 2004), problems such as negative washback effects on writing or writing-to-the test practices raise concerns (Cheville, 2004). Most recent studies, however, stress that the success of AWE depends on how educators implement and integrate the tool with teaching and social writing process (Chen & Cheng, 2008; Grimes & Warschauer, 2010).

Change Framework

Changes in Writing Practices

Advances in technology have brought new genres, concepts of literacy, and pedagogical approaches to writing. One of the most salient topics in second language writing under the change framework deals with the transformation of writing practices outside school settings. Research investigating this topic focuses on different venues or types of writing, such as blogging, synchronous Computer-Mediated Communication (CMC), or wikis, with an aim of understanding how these new types of literacy modes in online spaces may shape second language writing and how writers interact with these new writing tools.

First, blogging, one of the most widely researched topics in second language writing and technology, may have a variety of positive effects on L2 learners. Researchers have found that blogging can help bridge the gap between English Language Learners' (ELLs') written and spoken communication skills (Chun, 1994); facilitate learners' idea exchanges and the ability to write for audiences outside the classroom (Sykes, Oskoz, & Thorne, 2008); and improve confidence in writing (Sykes, Oskoz, & Thorne, 2008), motivation, collaboration (Lee, 2011a), and English language development (Fellner & Apple, 2006; Zheng & Warschauer, 2012). While there is a concern that L2 learners' exposure to informal forms of the target language might have negative effects, such as fossilization of errors, Lee (2011b) found that blogging helps develop metalinguistic knowledge of lexical and morphosyntactical errors. Similarly, Bloch's (2007) case study of an immigrant L2 learner suggests that blogging can help develop academic writing skills in the target language.

Synchronous forms of CMC can also provide new opportunities for non-native speakers of English to improve their language and to collaborate with audiences. In terms of linguistic ability, Smith and Gorsuch (2004) found that CMC increases college ELLs' attention to form and usage of new vocabulary, through appropriate scaffolding of the target language. CMC was also found to enhance the writing process and improve student writing (Schultz, 2000) and facilitate the acquisition of certain linguistic structures (Salaberry, 2001). In addition, Abrams (2001) suggests that CMC fosters development of sociolinguistic and pragmatic competence among L2 learners through collaborations with an audience, which can be relevant to the potential of CMC to reduce anxiety and boost motivation for using the target language (Freiermuth, 2002).

Lastly, a good deal of research has discussed the potential of collaborative writing in wikis (Li, 2012). Wikis have been found to support communal knowledge formation and continual revision (Purdy, 2009). These tools can also facilitate interactive and collaborative writing processes (Lundin, 2008). Research unpacking the L2 learners' collaborative writing process in wikis has examined phases of group collective behavior (Kessler & Bikowski, 2010), revision processes (Mak & Coniam, 2008), and patterns of interaction (Li & Zhu, 2011). Kessler and Bikowski (2010) examined how English language learners (ELLs) co-constructed a class wiki and identified three main phases of group collaboration: build and destroy, full collaboration, and informal reflection. The three phases help our understanding of the nature of a communal knowledge production process. Mak and Coniam's (2008) study of students' joint creation of a school brochure using wikis revealed that students engage in four types of revision behaviors including adding, expanding, reorganizing of ideas and correcting errors. The authors emphasized the value of process-oriented writing and the ability to synthesize information in wikis, which mirror the challenges in real-life writing tasks. Li and Zhu (2010) analyzed patterns of interactions in small groups' collaborative problem solving activity in the wiki-mediated collaborative writing. By examining the wiki *discussion, page, and history*, the authors identified the distinct patterns in students' writing such as

authoritative vs. responsive pattern, and dominant vs. withdrawn pattern. They also found that these patterns relate to students' perceptions of their learning experiences on the wiki environment. Overall, the studies on L2 students' writing on new, but prevalent, technology tools reveal the power of technology in both shaping and improving their writing as well as enabling distinctively collaborative patterns of interactions.

Changes in Writers' Identities

Researchers investigating second language writers' identity construction have noted how multimedia creation can positively shape their identities. Gee (2004) pointed out that, because users of technologies take new social roles in online spaces, technology and literacy are intimately tied with expressions of individual and social identity. For second language learners, problems with limited language and writing often cause issues of identity development (Niiya, Warschauer, & Zheng, in press). The use of digital media for writing provides an effective way to help strengthen ESL writers' identities by creating comfortable writing contexts with multiple modes of expression and by providing authentic purposes and motivations for writing. Cummins (2008) also suggests that leveraging digital media as well as student sociocultural knowledge is essential for promoting the creation of identity texts in the classroom.

Important spaces that can also enable the identity development of second language learners are online communities such as fanfiction Websites. Online communities not only offer L2 learners rich opportunities for practicing their communication, sharing their writing, exchanging feedback, and collaborating with peers, but also a great sense of belonging and security. They also lessen the tensions and burdens of mastering L2 writing as part of classroom assignments (Niiya, Warschauer, & Zheng, in press). For example, Lam (2000) explored how a Chinese immigrant student reengaged with writing and developed a sense

305

of belonging and ownership through sharing his writing with online peers. Similarly, Black (2005; 2009) revealed the potential of fanfiction sites for empowering ELLs to contribute to community knowledge through posting, reviewing, and collaborating on stories. Black also illuminated how L2 learners incorporate digital media, including sounds, images, and movies, in creative writing. The use of multiple modalities can expand opportunities for ELLs to freely express themselves and strengthen their identities, overcoming the cultural and language barriers that otherwise potentially hamper their identity development.

Power Framework

Project-Based Learning

In the power framework, project-based learning aims to encourage students to engage in collaborative critical inquiry so that they can analyze their own lives and social problems. It also involves knowledge production, where students synthesize what they have learned from critical inquiry and ultimately share or publish their new knowledge. For second language learners, English writing is a critical component of such knowledge production and serves as a medium to deliver knowledge. In Project FRESA (Cummins, Brown, & Sayers, 2007), Spanish L2 students from farm-working families investigated their parents' work in the fields and published their results online using a variety of multimedia forms. They also engaged in authentic writing, such as emailing to the Governor of California and to students in agricultural communities of Paraguay and Chile. They used technology as a tool to generate new knowledge and engaged in collaborative critical inquiry into issues surrounding their lives (p.86). Teachers also integrated state content standards in geography, language arts, math, and science into the project, suggesting the compatibility of project-based learning with existing curriculum.

The successful integration of content-area literacy in project-based learning was also found in Ware and Warschauer's (2005) study. The authors investigated how autonomy in project-based learning empowered the elementary students, many of whom were non-native speakers of English. In the study, third and fourth graders designed educational math video games using multiple software programs and ultimately transformed the pedagogy from math drills and rote learning to collaborative knowledge sharing. Throughout the process, students conducted independent research, collaborated in groups, used both linguistic tools as well as multimodal (digital explanatory videos) means to create age-appropriate and engaging instructional materials (Warschauer & Ware, 2008). For second language learners, such autonomous activities offer opportunities to break down knowledge and redesign it according to their needs and level of content and linguistic proficiency. Authentic writing practices such as creating a storyboard for a game or using stories to explain mathematical concepts can be both engaging and effective for the L2 learners.

Language-as-an-Asset Approach

Second language research that focuses on how to empower students to achieve social and economic equality tends to adopt a language-as-an-asset approach (Ruiz, 1988). L2 learners' limited English language proficiency is often seen as a barrier to educational and social participation when approached from a deficit perspective. By contrast, an asset-based perspective builds on the home language of students and recognizes this as a fundamental strength, and aims to use this strength to maximize learners' potential as bilingual speakers.

Second language research adopting this approach recognizes the importance of nurturing positive L2 identity through technology-enhanced literacy activities in order to empower bilingual youth. Extending from the foundation of building positive identities, such research typically uses global networking activities, such as sister class projects, to broaden the opportunities for L2 learners to participate in global discourse and to engage in authentic English written communications. This research also focuses on creating an equal power relationship between the native and target language. Instead of forcing L2 learners to master the mainstream target language, such research aims to provide a setting for language exchange where both L1 and L2 learners learn each other's language.

One example that illustrates this approach is the DiaLogos Project (Kourtis-Kazoullis, 2002, as cited in Cummins et al., 2007). This project connected elementary school students in Canada and Greece through an Internet-based sister class. Over the course of two years, the Greek students learning English and the Canadian students learning Greek collaborated on writing projects where they used both languages to create a story. The authors reported students' improvement in writing abilities, engagement, motivation, and identity development as bilingual students.

Similarly, Chow and Cummins (2003) explored the value of *identity texts* in the Dual Language Showcase Project. The term *identity texts* describes the literacy practices and products where students invest their positive identities (Chow & Cummins, 2003), the creation of which in turn promotes cognitive engagement. In the Dual Language Showcase Project, first- and second-grade ELL students from a broad range of linguistic backgrounds initially created stories in English and then translated them into their home languages. They uploaded their dual-language texts as well as illustrations onto a Website to share with their relatives and friends in their home countries. This project shows how bilingual identity texts can help empower young learners to create, develop, and share their knowledge, as well as guide them to recognize the positive value of being bilingual.

Other effective ways to foster the language-as-an-asset approach through technology in-

clude gaming and simulation. The US-China Elanguage project has taken a gaming approach toward second language education. Designed as an adventure game, the software employs a multitude of technologies to help the students learn Chinese or English as a second language (Zhao & Lai, 2008). This game and the projects discussed above indicate the unique potential of technology in helping L2 students leverage their funds of knowledge (Greenberg, 1989) as well as their native language to produce and disseminate rich knowledge and globally connect with other learners, ultimately enhancing their educational, social, and economic opportunities.

DISCUSSION AND IMPLICATIONS

Careful examination of how the different approaches shape research under the three frameworks can ultimately help us identify the strengths and limitations of each approach, as well as the core issues educators should address in the research and practice of second language writing. Here we discuss the challenges and promises of each framework in L2 writing research, as well as their implications for issues such as writing assessment, teacher education, and pedagogy.

First, the strength of the achievement framework is that it seeks measurable evidence of L2 students' improvement in writing to better evaluate the effectiveness of technology use. However, the major challenge is that the benefits of using computers for writing may not appear on standardized tests (Warschauer & Ware, 2008; Warschauer, 2011). The framework also faces challenges of implementation and teacher education. Teachers reportedly decrease the amount of time they spend on computers in order to prepare students standardized tests—a necessary process when writing essays by hand (Russell & Abrams, 2004). Also, the effects of technology-based writing instruction can be compounded by instructors' prior experience and expertise with certain technologies or instructional contexts. Lastly, in terms of pedagogical goals, the achievement framework falls short of promoting broader 21st-century literacy skills because of its undue focus on test scores. It tends to reduce learning to test performance and can have a negative washback effect on classroom instruction (Warschauer & Ware, 2008). Since students are expected to learn what the curriculum dictates in a prescribed manner under this framework, technology often plays a minimal role (Cummins, 2008).

On the contrary, the change framework allows for a broad definition of learning and emphasizes the value of out-of-school literacies. It is critical for educators to explore ways to use such practices as an alternative learning opportunity for writing and academic achievement, ultimately incorporating them into their pedagogical goals. However, bridging students' engagement with academic literacy through out-of-school writing practices may pose challenges (Warschauer & Ware, 2008). It is also a daunting task to navigate the instability of genre in the 21st century. Since the concepts of new media literacy (New London Group, 1996) have blurred the definition of genre (Warschauer & Ware, 2008), how to evaluate and develop a model of writing based on these different genres is unclear. Additionally, researchers and educators should also consider how to minimize negative influence of out-of-school writing practices on L2 learners, such as a potential overemphasis on non-standard forms or informal styles of English.

Lastly, we see great potential in the power framework for its ability to promote 21st-century literacy skills through project-based, experiential learning, as well as through collaborative inquiry. As with transmission-oriented pedagogy, the power framework promotes greater gains in both content learning and second language learning (Cummins, 2008). It also acknowledges the importance of students' academic achievement and employs a variety of strategies to make project-based learning compatible with state standards and to assess – for example, through performance or portfolio evaluation – learning outcomes. However, as a social informatics approach informs, the benefits of technology use are possible only when we acknowledge the importance of interconnected relationships among people, organizations, and technology (Kling, 2000). In this sense, the success of project-based learning or critical inquiry approaches under the power framework may depend on how such methods are supported and implemented by researchers, policymakers, administrators, and most importantly, teachers.

Finally, while the power framework intends to promote bottom-up agency of learners through an amplification effect (Warschauer, 1999), technologies can also magnify pre-existing inequalities instead of closing the gap. Researchers have suggested that this gap stems from differential uses of technology leading to a second-level digital divide (Hargittai, 2002) or a pedagogical divide (Cummins, 2008). Additional research addresses the inequality of access to learning opportunities between inquiry-oriented pedagogy in high-SES schools and transmission approaches in low-SES schools (Warschauer, Knobel, & Stone, 2004; Warschauer, 2006). While research investigating this issue among L2 writers has not been conducted, the question of whether such disparities exist between L1 and L2 writers and how to narrow the gap would be worth investigating.

CONCLUSION

As we have seen, technology in second language writing can play different roles –as an educational tool in school contexts, as a force driving the transformation of writing practices, and as a gatekeeper for accessing knowledge and power – that provide complementary functions. Examining research on technology and second language writing under the three distinctive yet complementary conceptual frameworks can allow us to understand the broader context of research and to benefit from alternative viewpoints. The promises as well as challenges of each framework may help researchers and educators of second language writing to better support learners in both formal and informal settings, and may suggest how to create more optimal language learning environments for intended pedagogical goals. In our continued attempts to expand second language writers' engagement and academic achievement through use of digital media, we should be aware of both the potential positive as well as negative impacts of technology on L2 writers and avoid romanticism or technological determinism. Both researchers and educators interested in technology and second language writing will do well to exercise what Brown (1987) called "cautious, enlightened eclecticism" (p. 108); that is, choosing the combination of approaches that best matches their own belief system, context, and goals, and then continually making adjustments based on systematic evaluation of evidence.

ACKNOWLEDGMENT

We thank Melissa Niiya for her extensive and thoughtful feedback on an earlier version of this chapter.

REFERENCES

Abrams, Z. I. (2001). Computer-mediated communication and group journals: Expanding the repertoire of participant roles. *System*, *29*(4), 489–503. doi:10.1016/S0346-251X(01)00041-0.

Black, R. W. (2005). Access and affiliation: The literacy and composition practices of English-language learners in an online fanfiction community. *Journal of Adolescent & Adult Literacy*, *49*(2), 118–128. doi:10.1598/JAAL.49.2.4.

Black, R. W. (2009). Online fanfiction, global identities, and imagination. *Research in the Teaching of English*, *43*(4), 397–425.

Bleha, T. (2005). *Down to the wire*. Retrieved September 25, 2012, from http://www.foreignaffairs.org/20050501 faessay84311–p0/thomas-bleha/down-to-the-wire.htm

Bloch, J. (2007). Abdullah's blogging: A generation 1.5 student enters the blogosphere. *Language Learning & Technology*, *11*(2), 128–141.

Brown, H. D. (1987). *Principles of language learning and teaching*. New York: Longman.

Bruce, D. L. (2009). Writing with visual images: Examining the video composition processes of high school students. *Research in the Teaching of English*, *43*(4), 426–450.

Chapelle, C. A. (2003). *English language learning and technology: Lectures on applied linguistics in the age of information and communication technology*. Amsterdam: John Benjamins Pub..

Chen, C.-F. E., & Cheng, W.-Y. E. (2008). Beyond the design of automated writing evaluation: Pedagogical practices and perceived learning effectiveness In EFL writing classes. *Language Learning & Technology*, *12*(3), 94–112.

Cheville, J. (2004). Automated scoring technologies and the rising influence of error. *English Journal*, *93*(4), 47–52. doi:10.2307/4128980.

Chow, P., & Cummins, J. (2003). Valuing multilingual and multicultural approaches to learning. In *Multilingual education in practice: Using diversity as a resource* (pp. 32–61). Academic Press.

Chun, D. M. (1994). Using computer networking to facilitate the acquisition of interactive competence. *System*, *22*(1), 17–31. doi:10.1016/0346-251X(94)90037-X.

Chuo, T.-W. (2007). The effects of the WebQuest writing instruction program on EFL learners' writing performance, writing apprehension, and perception. *TESL-EJ*, *11*(3).

Cummins, J. (2008). Technology, literacy, and young second language learners: Designing educational futures. In Parker, L. L. (Ed.), *Technology-mediated learning environments for young English learners: Connections in and out of school* (pp. 61–98). New York: Lawrence Erlbaum Associates.

Cummins, J., Brown, K., & Sayers, D. (2007). *Literacy, technology, and diversity: Teaching for success in changing times*. Boston, MA: Allyn and Bacon.

Cummins, J., & Sayers, D. (1995). *Brave new schools: Challenging cultural illiteracy through global learning networks*. New York: St. Martin's Press.

Elliot, S. M., & Mikulas, C. (2004). *The impact of MY Access!TM use on student writing performance: A technology overview and four studies*. Paper presented at the Annual Meeting of the American Educational Research Association. San Diego, CA.

Ericsson, P. F., & Haswell, R. (Eds.). (2006). *Machine scoring of human essays: Truth and consequences*. Provo, UT: Utah State University Press.

Fellner, T., & Apple, M. (2006). Developing writing fluency and lexical complexity with blogs. *The JALT/CALL Journal, 2*(1), 15-26.

Ferris, D. R., & Hedgecock, J. C. (2005). *Teaching ESL composition: Purpose, process, and practice*. Mahwah, NJ: Erlbaum Associates, Inc..

Forte, A., & Bruckman, A. (2010). Writing, citing, and participatory media: Wikis as learning environments in the high school classroom. *International Journal of Learning and Media, 1*(4), 23–44. doi:10.1162/ijlm_a_00033.

Freiermuth, M. R. (2002). Internet chat: collaborating and learning via e-conversations. *TESOL Journal, 11*(3), 36–40.

Gee, J. P. (2004). *Situated language and learning: A critique of traditional schooling*. New York: Routledge.

Goldberg, A., Russell, M., & Cook, A. (2004). The effect of computers on student writing: A meta-analysis of studies from 1992 to 2002. *Journal of Technology, Learning, and assessment, 2*(1), 3–51.

Greenberg, J. B. (1989). *Funds of knowledge: Historical constitution, social distribution, and transmission*. Paper presented at the annual meeting of the Society for Applied Anthropology. Santa Fe, NM.

Grimes, D., & Warschauer, M. (2010). Utility in a fallible tool: A multi-site case study of automated writing evaluation. *Journal of Technology, Language, and Assessment, 8*(6), 1–43.

Hagood, M. (2003). New media and online literacies: No age left behind. *Reading Research Quarterly, 38*(3), 387–392.

Hargittai, E. (2002). Second-level digital divide: Differences in people's online skills. *First Monday, 7*(4). doi:10.5210/fm.v7i4.942.

Hegelheimer, V. (2006). Helping ESL writers through a multimodal, corpus-based, online grammar resource. *CALICO Journal, 24*(1), 5–32.

Hull, G., & Schultz, K. (2002). Connecting schools with out-of-school worlds: Insights from recent research on literacy in non-school settings. In Hull, G., & Schultz, K. (Eds.), *School's out! Bridging out-of-school literacies with classroom practice*. New York: Teachers College Press.

Kelly, T., Gray, V., & Minges, M. (2003). *Broadband Korea: Internet case study*. Geneva, Switzerland: International Telecommunications Union.

Kessler, G., & Bikowski, D. (2010). Developing collaborative autonomous learning abilities in computer mediated language learning: Attention to meaning among students in wiki space. *Computer Assisted Language Learning*, *23*(1), 41–58. doi:10.1080/09588220903467335.

Kling, R. (2000). Learning about information technologies and social change: The contribution of social informatics. *The Information Society*, *16*(3), 217–232. doi:10.1080/01972240050133661.

Lam, W. S. E. (2000). L2 literacy and the design of the self: A case study of a teenager writing on the internet. *TESOL Quarterly*, *34*, 457–482. doi:10.2307/3587739.

Lam, W. S. E. (2000). L2 literacy and the design of the self: A case study of a teenager writing on the internet. *TESOL Quarterly*, *34*(3), 457–482. doi:10.2307/3587739.

Lee, D., & Swales, J. (2006). A corpus-based EAP course for NNS doctoral students: Moving from available specialized corpora to self-compiled corpora. *English for Specific Purposes*, *25*, 56–75. doi:10.1016/j.esp.2005.02.010.

Lee, L. (2011a). Blogging: Promoting learner autonomy and intercultural competence through study abroad. *Language Learning & Technology*, *15*(3), 87–109.

Lee, L. (2011b). Focus on form through peer feedback in a Spanish-American telecollaborative exchange. *Language Awareness*, *20*(4), 343–357. doi:10.1080/09658416.2011.592589.

Li, M. (2012). Use of Wikis in second/foreign language classes: A literature review. *CALL-EJ*, *13*(1), 17–35.

Li, M., & Zhu, W. (2011). Patterns of computer-mediated interaction in small writing groups using wikis. *Computer Assisted Language Learning*. Retrieved Nov. 20, 2012, from http://www.tandfonline.com/doi/abs/10.1080/09588221.2011.631142

Luke, C. (2003). Pedagogy, connectivity, multimodality, and interdisciplinarity. *Reading Research Quarterly*, *38*(3), 297–314.

Lundin, R. W. (2008). Teaching with wikis: Toward a networked pedagogy. *Computers and Composition*, *25*, 432–448. doi:10.1016/j.compcom.2008.06.001.

Mak, B., & Coniam, D. (2008). Using wikis to enhance and develop writing skills among secondary school students in Hong Kong. *System*, *36*, 437–455. doi:10.1016/j.system.2008.02.004.

New London Group. (1996). A pedagogy of multiliteracies: Designing social futures. *Harvard Educational Review*, *66*(1), 60–92.

Niiya, M., Warschauer, M., & Zheng, B. (2013). Emerging literacies in digital media and L2 secondary writing. In de Oliveira, L. C., & Silva, T. (Eds.), *L2 writing in secondary classroom: Student experiences, academic issues, and teacher education*. New York: Routledge.

Pennington, M. (2004). Electronic media in second language writing: An overview of tools and research findings. In Fotos, S., & Browne, C. M. (Eds.), *New perspectives on CALL for second language classrooms* (pp. 69–92). Mahwah, NJ: Erlbaum Associates Inc..

Purdy, J. P. (2009). When the tenets of composition go public: A study of writing in wikipedia. *College Composition and Communication*, *61*(2), 351–373.

Reardon, M. (2005). *China to trump U.S. in broadband subscribers*. Retrieved Sep. 21, 2012, from http://news.zdnet.com/2100-6005_22-5695591.html

Ruiz, R. (1988). Orientations in language planning. In McKay, S. L., & Wong, S. C. (Eds.), *Language diversity: Problem or resource?* (pp. 3–25). New York: Newbury House.

Russell, M., & Abrams, L. (2004). Instructional effects of computers for writing: The effect of state testing programs. *Teachers College Record, 106*(6), 1332–1357. doi:10.1111/j.1467-9620.2004.00381.x.

Salaberry, M. R. (2001). The use of technology for second language learning and teaching: A retrospective. *Modern Language Journal, 85*(1), 39–56. doi:10.1111/0026-7902.00096.

Schultz, J. (2000). Computers and collaborative writing in the foreign language curriculum. In Warschauer, M., & Kern, R. (Eds.), *Network-based language teaching: Concepts and practice*. Cambridge, UK: Cambridge University Press. doi:10.1017/CBO9781139524735.008.

Smith, B., & Gorsuch, G. (2004). Synchronous computer mediated communication captured by usability lab technologies: New interpretations. *System, 32*, 553–575. doi:10.1016/j.system.2004.09.012.

Sykes, J., Oskoz, A., & Thorne, S. (2008). Web 2.0 synthetic immersive environments and mobile resources for language education. *CALICO Journal, 25*(3), 528–546.

Ware, P., Kern, R., & Warschauer, M. (2013). The development of digital literacies. In Manchón, R., & Matsuda, P. K. (Eds.), *Handbook of second and foreign language writing*. New York: De Gruyter Mouton.

Ware, P., & Warschauer, M. (2005). Hybrid literacy texts and practices in technology-intensive environments. *International Journal of Educational Research*. doi:10.1016/j.ijer.2006.07.008.

Warschauer, M. (1997). Computer-mediated collaborative learning: Theory and practice. *Modern Language Journal, 81*(4), 470–481. doi:10.1111/j.1540-4781.1997.tb05514.x.

Warschauer, M. (1999). *Electronic literacies: Language, culture, and power in online education*. Mahwah, NJ: Lawrence Erlbaum Associates.

Warschauer, M. (2006). *Laptops and literacy: Learning in the wireless classroom*. New York: Teachers College Press.

Warschauer, M. (2011). *Learning in the cloud: How and (why) to transform schools with digital media*. New York: Teachers College Press.

Warschauer, M., Knobel, M., & Stone, L. (2004). Technology and equity in schooling: Deconstructing the digital divide. *Educational Policy, 18*, 562–588. doi:10.1177/0895904804266469.

Warschauer, M., & Ware, P. (2008). Learning, change, and power: Competing frames of technology and literacy. In Coiro, J., Knobel, M., Lankshear, C., & Leu, J. (Eds.), *Handbook of research on new literacies* (pp. 215–240). New York: Lawrence Erlbaum.

Zhao, Y., & Lai, C. (2008). Technology and second language learning: Promises and problems. In Parker, L. L. (Ed.), *Technology-mediated learning environments for young English learners: Connections in and out of school*. Mahwah, NJ: Lawrence Erlbaum Associates.

Zheng, B., & Warschauer, M. (2012). *Blogging to learn: Participation and literacy among linguistically diverse fifth-grade students*. Paper presented at the 2012 American Educational Research Association Annual Meeting. Vancouver, Canada.

Section 5
Writing and Identity

If technology is influencing the way people write, what does this mean for how students and teachers perceive themselves as writers and writing instructors? Having a writerly identity is important, but what does it mean to have a writerly identity in an online space? Similarly, when teachers use technology to teach writing in the classroom, what does this mean for not only their pedagogical approaches, but also about their belief structures about writing instruction.

The first two chapters in this section explore the writerly identities of young adults. Hines, Conner-Zachocki, and Rupert report the findings from a case study of one student Shane. Shane used digital media and writing to enact three specific identity performances: Shane the comedian, Shane the artist, and Shane the subversive. This chapter has specific implications for how new literacies can be used in "authentic" ways and the issues and tensions that may arise when new literacies are used in ways that conflict with students' social identities. In the second chapter, Stewart examines the Facebook writing of four Latina/o immigrant youth. Facebook provided opportunities for them to practice and use the English language in an authentic manner and engage in code switching in which they wove English and Spanish together. Findings highlight the divide between the youth's in-school writing and their writing on Facebook that they used to express their Latina/o identities.

In the last chapter of this section, Hicks presents a case study of one teacher and her development as a teacher of digital writing during her involvement in the National Writing Project. The teacher became immersed in digital writing, using Google Docs, creating a digital story, and creating a digital portfolio highlighting her digital writing. Hicks found the teacher's experiences led to substantive changes in her pedagogical practices and her work as a teacher leader.

This section features chapters that provide insight into how digital writing influences people's writerly identities.

Chapter 18
"The More I Write...The More my Mind Evolves into Something Outstanding":
Composing Identities with Social Media Tools

Mary Beth Hines
Indiana University – Bloomington, USA

Jennifer M. Conner-Zachocki
Indiana University – Columbus, USA

Becky Rupert
Graduation High School, USA

ABSTRACT

This chapter draws from a one-year qualitative investigation of a ninth-grade English classroom in a new technology-rich high school. The study explores the question, What identities did students compose as they alternately resisted and embraced the use of digital media in the writing classroom? Presenting a case study of one student, Shane, the chapter traces the ways in which he responded to the teacher's invitations to use digital media, thereby discursively crafting particular identity performances in on-site and online communities. Analysis identifies a number of tensions specific to the use of authentic audiences and purposes in the 21st century digital writing classroom and reveals three identity performance categories: Shane the comedian, Shane the subversive, and Shane the artist. In analyzing the ways in which social networking tools, literacy practices, and identity performances converge in the classroom, the chapter challenges dominant pedagogical assumptions about using new technologies in the schools to engage learners.

DOI: 10.4018/978-1-4666-4341-3.ch018

INTRODUCTION

Since you're here, why don't we take an adventure into my mind? But I hope you're ready, because it's one crazy, crazy place in there. - Shane, Literacy in Our Lives Video Project

With this introduction, Shane, a ninth-grade student in a new technology-rich high school, summoned his classmates to view a video he made to fulfill the first major project in his English class, the *Literacy in Our Lives* project. Becky, Shane's teacher, asked students to develop videos, both as a way to introduce themselves to one another and to document the literacy practices they used in their everyday lives both in and out of school. In so doing, Becky hoped not only to sensitize students to the ways in which they already were proficient readers and writers of text, but also to signal that reading and writing in this classroom community, and across the school, meant using digital media and developing the 21st century literacy practices needed for postsecondary education and the workplace of the future (National Council of Teachers of English, 2008). In asking students to share their videos with each other in an online forum, she hoped to form a classroom community that functioned equally effectively in online and on-site contexts.

But just as Becky had specific goals and a particular audience in mind for the project, so too did Shane. He crafted his introduction to the video to prepare the audience for "an adventure," thereby heralding his own arrival in this classroom community and school, staking his claim for attention. In preparing his peers to watch the video and to foray into his mind, "a crazy, crazy, place," he braced viewers to expect the unexpected, creating anticipation that Shane's video would be both different from the others and entertaining. He was right on both counts. While his classmates typically pursued a literal approach to this literacy project, documenting their favorite books, movies, and songs, Shane took the assignment to a

new level by writing an original script complete with a montage of goofy images accompanied by old, corny songs. He created a spoof of the creative—yet tortured—artist stereotype, with the voice-over of a stern taskmaster insisting upon obedience to school rules while the camera documented Shane breaking them. He declared himself a serious gamer and pretended to throw a laptop on the floor, overcome by feigned anger when his online opponent insulted him. He included a clip in which he was standing on a street corner with white loose-leaf paper in his hands, yelling at passing cars, "Buy my writing! Buy my writing! Doesn't anyone want to buy my writing?"

We do not know if Shane made any money pitching his words that day, but we do know he garnered the class's attention, his teacher's, and ours. This chapter features a case study of Shane, drawn from a one-year qualitative case study of a ninth-grade English classroom in a new technology-rich high school, exploring the research question: What identities did students compose as they alternately resisted and embraced the use of digital media in the writing classroom? This chapter traces the ways in which Shane responded to Becky's invitations to use digital media while discursively crafting particular identity performances in on-site and online communities. The next section explains why we selected Shane and his teacher, Becky, for this study.

CASE STUDY PARTICIPANT SELECTION

We relied upon purposive sampling techniques to select our focal student and teacher because we wanted to understand how teachers and students used digital media to compose texts and identities. We wanted to work with an exemplary teacher who valued writing and new technologies in the classroom, and we wanted to focus on students who were highly invested in writing and technology and at least somewhat social so that we could trace the relationships among writing, technology, and student identities. Becky was widely recognized as an excellent teacher, for she was a National Board Certified English Teacher, one of the first in the state. Becky was widely known in her district as a teacher-leader in developing innovative uses of digital media, and prior to our study, she had been an invited member of a multi-year funded project exploring the uses of new technologies in English classes. Because she taught at a new, technology-rich school in her district, we knew that she would infuse digital media into class activities routinely, providing us with abundant opportunities to explore issues, processes, and products related to using new technologies in the English classroom. She was also among a select group of National Writing Project (NWP) teachers invited to participate in the NWP task force commissioned to develop frameworks for assessing multimodal products, i.e., texts that used visual, graphic and audio elements as well as linguistic signs. In short, she was a widely respected English teacher known both locally and nationally for her progressive uses of technology and for her expertise as an English teacher.

After several weeks in Becky's ninth-grade class, we selected Shane as one of our case study students. Because we thought that a very social person who was also a committed writer and technology user would teach us the most about how student identities were mediated by the discursive and digital, we focused on Shane. His *Literacy in Our Lives* video convinced us that he was definitely social, and a serious writer and technology user to boot. Despite his obvious investments in writing and technology, Shane had contradictory reactions to Becky's invitations to write, and we wanted to understand why. Moreover, his work across various social networking media demonstrated inconsistency in quality and quantity, and his engagement in class waxed and waned as well. At times he enthusiastically immersed himself in writing projects, and at other times he grumbled. We wanted to understand Shane's behaviors of engagement and resistance. We believed that Shane could provide us a window into understanding why a strong writer who relished the limelight would subvert his teacher's efforts to share work on social networking sites, especially when those efforts occurred within the context of a school with a technology mission. Moreover, we wanted to understand the identities Shane constructed through his multimodal and linguistic texts, and how those identities were mediated by discourse and varied across social contexts. In the next section, we situate our study against the backdrop of current literacy research and theory.

NEW LITERACY STUDIES AND COMPOSITION PEDAGOGIES

Digital technology practices pervade virtually every aspect of contemporary daily life—how individuals outside of school learn, communicate, reflect on, produce, consume, create identities, and share knowledge in routine matters (J. P. Gee, 2012). Researchers use the term *New Literacy Studies* (Coiro, Knobel, Lankshear, & Leu, 2008; Hull & Schultz, 2002; Lankshear & Knobel, 2006; New Media Consortium, 2005) to refer to the expanded and multiple practices and ways of knowing associated with digital media (Gee, 2009; Mills, 2010). From this perspective scholars emphasize a shift from static, decontextualized notions of literacy to broader views that understand communication as an array of dynamic social practices situated in a variety of contexts, and those contexts shape and limit possible meanings. Scholars use the term *multiliteracies* to emphasize that what counts as literacy varies and is always situated (Kress, 2003).

Just as the conception of literacy has expanded with New Literacy Studies, so too has the notion of text. Text from this perspective is constituted not only by linguistic signs, but also by audio, graphic and multi-media elements. In order to produce and to decipher multimodal texts, individuals must recruit semiotic resources and the cultural meaning-making possibilities available to them (Kress & van Leeuwen, 2001). Producing and interpreting such texts involves global as well as local texts, resources, audiences, and purposes (Gee, 2007; Lankshear & Knobel, 2006; Lewis & Fabos, 2005; Street, 2003), reinforcing the notion of multiliteracies.

Within a New Literacy framework, the teaching and learning of writing requires not only broader conceptions of text and literacy, but also more complex renderings of composing processes in the stages of writing (i.e., brainstorming, drafting, revising, editing, and publication). Hicks argues that the digital writing classroom is built upon the same five principles as the writing workshop: student choice, revision, author's craft, publication and assessment, but "through a digital lens" (Hicks, 2009, p. vii). However, incorporating visual and audio elements, a writer is no longer limited to producing print texts. From a new literacies perspective, he argues, writers can, for instance, use technological resources in all stages of the composing process, whether gathering data through RSS feeds, Google, Facebook, or brainstorming ideas and drafting collaboratively using Google Docs.

Besides offering new resources for writing, new media makes available social networking options that enable writers to have actual audiences, instant audiences, and multiple audiences, providing authentic contexts for sharing drafts and finished texts. Digital media researchers (Jenkins, 2004; Thomas, 2006) have supported the argument that students posting in authentic, online venues gain valuable literacy skills.

Writers in the digital workshop can assess the demands of the rhetorical situation with virtual and face-to-face audiences, strategizing voice, content, and style in relation to the multiple audiences of their work. Those audiences enable teachers to sidestep the age-old problem of writing for an audience of one, the teacher. Composition teachers and researchers argue (Kahn, 2009) that writing for authentic audiences motivates students to care about the final product. In sum, by using information and communication technologies, teachers can enrich a writer's standard repertoire for all stages of the writing process, and writers can work in an authentic, nonlinear and recursive fashion, utilizing the stages of writing processes as they see fit, rather than in a lockstep, mandated sequence. New technologies serve to reinforce key principles in writing instruction: writing for *authentic* audiences and *actual* purposes, writing for an *array* of audiences and purposes, writing with the demands of the rhetorical situation—the purpose, audience, and context—intentionally governing content and style, and writing with nonlinear and recursive stages determined by the writer, not the teacher.

The emphasis on technology in literacy classrooms can also be found in the National Council of Teachers of English (NCTE) definition of 21st century literacies (National Council of Teachers of English, 2008). At the heart of the 21st Century Literacies statement is recognition that information and communication technologies are vital to English classrooms. The February 2013 version declares that:

Active, successful participants in this 21st century global society must be able to...develop proficiency and fluency with the tools of technology; build intentional cross-cultural connections and relationships with others so to pose and solve problems collaboratively and strengthen independent thought; design and share information for global communities to meet a variety of purposes; manage, analyze, and synthesize multiple streams of simultaneous information; create, critique, analyze, and evaluate multimedia texts; attend to the ethical responsibilities required by these complex environments (National Council of Teachers of English, 2008, 2013).

As the policy encourages use of technology and emphasizes multiple literacies and multimodal texts, it resonates with New Literacy Studies principles and declares priorities for the profession. The NCTE policy statement invites and challenges us to rethink our goals in literacy education (National Council of Teachers of English, 2008). No longer limited by the geo-physical confines of institutional spaces, with increased access to information, knowledge, and networking, students in 21st century learning contexts work within learning ecologies to connect the local with the global (Brofenbrenner & Evans, 2000; Nardi & O'Day, 1999; Walters & Kop, 2009). The 21st Century Literacies Position Statement challenges teachers to utilize the practices and processes that students will need in postsecondary education and the workplace.

Researchers also argue that bringing the out-of-school digital media practices into schools reaps benefits for learners. For instance, the argument goes, teachers can use new media to engage learners resistant to traditional literacy class work (Ito et al., 2009). Also, when students use social networking practices to communicate with various audiences and purposes, they strengthen their reading and writing skills. Cultivating digital media and 21st century literacy skills in classrooms can cultivate new modes of participation that can change the teacher-centered patterns of classroom discourse cited in the research (Applebee, 1993; Cazden, 1988). Proficiency in information and communication technology may not only enhance student engagement with school-based literacy practices, but also prepare students for successful participation in postsecondary education, gaining the 21st century literacies they need for school, citizenship, and the workplace.

Situating our study within a New Literacy Studies framework informed by 21st century literacies and contemporary composition pedagogy, we can explore the ways in which texts, literacies, and identities are constructed and interpreted with social networking technologies. While this section has suggested how literacies, texts, and digital composition processes resonate within New Literacy Studies, the next section explores perspectives on identity that are salient to the study.

IDENTITIES

Because this chapter focuses upon how a student performs identities as he produces and interprets text, it is important not only to define *text* and *literacies*, but also to define *identity performances*. Poststructuralists, feminists, postmodernists, and other scholars in cultural studies have rejected the idea of a singular, monolithic subject with a stable identity (Alcoff, Hames-Garcia, Mohanty, & Moya, 2006; Blommaert, 2005; Moya, 2002), instead arguing that individuals assume various identities that change as social contexts change, and therefore are "performatively constituted" (Butler, 1990, p. 25). That is, we perform different identities within different socially defined spaces that are imbued with cultural norms, power relations, and ideological forces, and lead to varying expectations for different players in different roles (Holland, Lachiotte, Skinner, & Cain, 1998). This allows for a "performance approach to identities, which focuses on identity as a form of socially meaningful practice" (Blommaert, 2005, p. 208).

Gee argues that identity is socially constructed. "Being recognized as a certain 'kind of person,' in a given context," is the key to identity, but individuals have "multiple identities" constructed by "their performances in society" (Gee, 2000b, p. 99). Particular identities are constituted in specific social situations, according to Gee, and each identity issues from one or more of the following four categories:

1. **The Nature Perspective:** The individual's biological traits determine "the kind of person" one is (Gee, 2000b, p. 102), for example, the identity of being a twin.

2. **The Institutional Perspective:** An identity that is sanctioned or authorized by a role or position in an institution that one holds, for example, the identity of a university professor.

3. **The Discursive Perspective:** A quality of the individual constructed through and contingent upon communication with others, for example, possessing charisma.

4. **The Affinity Perspective:** Traits revealed in one's discursive practices that show an individual's allegiance to, access to, and participation in a group with shared interests, for example, engaging in online discussions about one's passion for a specific athletic activity.

Gee's framework gives us an understanding of how identities can be seen as dynamic, discursive, socially situated performances that mediate and are mediated by literacy practices.

When the identity performances of youths using digital media are discussed in theory and research, the notion of "digital natives" is frequently invoked. Prensky (2001) argues that technology has become essential to young people's lives and identities, and that their dependence on digital technologies for entertainment, socializing, and information gathering and sharing makes them distinct from older generations, the "digital immigrants" (2001, p. 4). Prensky's argument resonates with a growing body of scholars who have attempted to document the distinct technological needs and expectations of emerging generations of young people (Bennett, Maton, & Kervin, 2008; Hawkins & Oblinge, 2006; Jenkins, Purushotma, Clinton, Weigel, & Robison, 2006).

DATA COLLECTION AND ANALYSIS

Shane's case study is drawn from a yearlong qualitative case study of an English classroom in a new technology-rich high school during the 2010/2011 school year, exploring the research question: What identities did students compose as they alternately resisted and embraced the use of digital media in the writing classroom?

There were five categories of data included in this larger study. A member of our research team videotaped 24 hours of small group and large group discussion during the six-week unit, which constituted our first set of data. Our second data set included the Twitter feed from all fifty students in the class. Each student was assigned a character from *The Things They Carried* (O'Brien, 1990), a book about the experiences of American soldiers in Vietnam. Each was asked to tweet in character at different points throughout the novel. The Twitter feed was the result of approximately four hours of in-class tweeting produced over the course of the unit. Twenty-five poems written in pairs by all fifty students were also included in the data set. Towards the end of the unit, students wrote poems about the experiences of the soldiers in *The Things They Carried*. Students were required to incorporate some of their own and/or their classmates' tweets into their poems. The fan fiction projects completed independently by all fifty students constituted our fourth data set. Students were invited to write fan fiction pieces in which they created potential prequels or sequels to *The Things They Carried*. Finally, we collected Ning postings from all fifty students in the class. The class Ning was used as a site where students responded to reflective prompts that Becky posted. Students also used the Ning to post their fan fiction projects and poems, and provide feedback to one another in response to these pieces of writing. Students posted an average of two times each week on the Ning.

For Shane's case study and this chapter, we relied on the following data, a subset of the data set for the larger study:

- Shane's tweets.
- Shane's poem.
- Shane's fan fiction project.
- Classmates' Ning postings in response to Shane's work.

- Shane's Ning postings and reflections.
- The thirty-eight minutes of classroom video footage in which Shane appears.
- The video project described in the introduction for the *Literacy in Our Lives* unit at the beginning of the year. While most students posted their videos on the Ning, Shane posted his on YouTube.
- A twenty-minute interview with Becky in which she shares her impressions of and experiences with Shane.

Our data analysis involved using qualitative coding procedures informed by grounded theory (Charmaz, 2006; Strauss, 1987; Strauss & Corbin, 1998). We began by engaging in open coding in order to conceptualize and label our data. We used writing "incidents" (Charmaz, 2006, p. 53) as the unit of analysis for our initial coding; we coded Shane's poem, fan fiction piece, each of Shane's individual tweets and Ning postings, and each Ning posting written by one of his classmates in response to Shane's work as single incidents. Shane developed his *Literacy in our Lives* video with eight discrete episodes, each with a different storyline, setting, and focus. Each episode was coded as a distinct incident. We also coded the transcript of the combined thirty-eight minutes of classroom video footage in which Shane appears and is engaged in conversations with classmates. Each of Shane's contributions on the video was coded as a single incident.

Our initial open coding aimed to capture the various identities that Shane performed in response to the Becky's writing invitations. When possible, we used in vivo codes (Charmaz, 2006) taken directly from Shane's own discourse. Following our initial open coding, we engaged in the process of selecting and identifying core categories, systematically relating them to other categories. Categories were determined inductively using the constant comparative method (Charmaz, 2006; Glaser & Strauss, 1967). Interpretative memos written by the researchers and the use of our "team meetings as memos" (Strauss, 1987, p. 130) helped

with both the identification of categories' properties as well as the need to integrate categories with other categories (Charmaz, 2006; Glaser, 1998). The research team ultimately identified three categories to describe the various identities that Shane performed: (a) Shane the comedian, (b) Shane the subversive, and (c) Shane the artist. Below we describe the ways in which each of these identities is performed within (and against) specific pieces and modes of writing.

Shane the Comedian

Shane the comedian might be best illustrated by his *Literacy in our Lives* video project in which Shane reveals insights about himself as a writer. As the video unfolds, viewers quickly realize that the script he has written to guide his video narrative about himself as a writer is completely tongue-in-cheek. At one point, for example, Shane speaks directly to the camera and introduces himself as a "gamer" who likes to "use his... writing to communicate with people [his online opponents] to see how they react to things." In the next scene, we see Shane sitting at his laptop pretending to be in the throes of an intense battle with an online opponent, when he stops suddenly, pretending to have read an offensive message sent to him by his challenger, to which he responds, "What? Oh, *I'm* the noob? No *you're* the noob, kid!"—employing a term that, according to urbandictionary.com, refers to a gamer who uses "cheap tactics." Pretending to be insulted by a critical assault upon his character, Shane feigns indignation, his ego injured, all to produce humor.

Shane's identity as a wit with a somewhat mordant sense of humor would be, according to Gee's identity framework (2001), a discourse identity—one that relies on acknowledgement and endorsement of others, as Shane himself cannot achieve such an identity on his own. By definition, a discourse identity necessitates that others recognize and sanction that identity. Shane capitalizes on the social networking tools that Becky has incorporated into the unit to help him establish and sustain this identity. He also employs his comedic identity to help him negotiate another – that of Shane the subversive.

Shane the Subversive

Shane the subversive is often enacted by Shane the comedian. As he works to achieve the status of class clown, he engages his wit to forge an identity of one who can undermine while apparently engaging in school literacy practices. This can be illustrated by a segment of Shane's *Literacy in our Lives* video project. In this segment, Shane appears to be writing in a notebook and greets the viewer by saying, "Oh, hello. I didn't see you there. I was just doing some serious writing on the American Revolutionary War… This is my best work yet." In this excerpt Shane parodies the "serious" academic writer investigating a "serious" intellectual topic, the Revolutionary War. However, he is mocking writing assignments on boring school topics, such as the Revolutionary War, when he says dryly, "my best work yet." In so doing, Shane positions himself as a comedian and subversive in the class, one who will complete assignments, but on his own terms. As a subversive, he taps an audience of those alienated from school, those who have felt disengaged from and bored with school writing, and those who would rebuke rather than embrace identities as academics.

Shane's use of parody to achieve subversion resurfaces in the unit on *The Things They Carried* as well. One of Becky's goals for the unit, developing empathy for the experiences of those in war, was cultivated by inviting students to assume the persona of characters in the book, walking in their shoes as they read. Using Twitter, each student/character was to write to other student/characters, responding as events in the text unfolded. Shane tweeted as Norman Bowker, a soldier in *The Things They Carried*. (See Figure 1) Unlike Norman Bowker, Shane amuses himself and others by inserting a series of one-liners into the conversation. He uses tweets to shock and amuse readers: "BURN THE VILLAGE PEOPLE!!!"

Figure 1. Shane's tweets from the perspective of a character in the things they carried

This comment does not reflect Norman Bowker's sympathies, but does represent Shane's attempt to invoke humor by taking an idea to its extreme. He pushes the idea of a soldier's commitments to serve his country to the level of absurdity, issuing an endorsement for slaughtering innocent people that can only be perceived as ridiculous. Shane pushes the boundaries to produce humor by adding sexual innuendoes as well. "I carry std's, just kidding…or am I?" Norman Bowker, a very private person, would not be inclined to discuss this topic, sexually transmitted diseases, or his status as a carrier, in a public forum. Nonetheless, Shane can't resist the opportunity to entertain himself and his peers with inappropriate comments, and his next tweet ups the ante on inappropriate dialogue by suggesting masturbation: "I like my thumb… It's my precious…begins to moan."

Shane's tweets suggest the work of a creative spirit seeking to entertain his peers with a series of parodies of soldiers—over-the-top one-liners, off-color and out of character for Norman Bowker, his assigned character. Nonetheless, he invokes the thumb, villages burning, Jimmy's fox hole and dead soldiers in his Twitter feed, legitimately referencing the text even as he subverts the Twitter activity, ostensibly complying with the assignment. Shane's identity performances in the Twitter activity resonate with those of his video, his literacy practices leveraged for the roles of subversive and comedian.

Shane does not always employ comedy to communicate subversion, however. He did take an oppositional approach at times. For example, in one of Shane's Ning prompts, Becky asked students to reflect on the ways that Becky used Twitter in class for the character role play. In response, he unapologetically and candidly stated, "I don't play those games." Shane's resistance to tweeting was fueled, at least in part, by his frustration with the assignment. Reflecting on the Twitter activity in the class Ning, Shane said:

I think [tweeting in character] a waste of time, and we shouldn't do it. I have learned how Twitter is basically useless within these situations. It will not be taken seriously, and I do not blame anyone for doing so. It would have been better to write short stories in the mind of what we thought would have been our character. I will never know why the class thought it was a good idea to use Twitter.

Shane elaborated that the distinguishing features of Twitter—140 letters per message—and of the assignment—responding as a character, rather than a reader—were too constraining, producing artificial discourse that couldn't be taken "seriously." As a result, Shane took the liberty of using the Twitter activity to reinforce his subversive identity.

Shane used his writing on the Ning, in Twitter, and in his video to perform resistance to many of the attributes ascribed to that of the typical "good student" who complies with the teacher's wishes and expectations. In so doing, Shane refused what Gee calls the institutional identity, one available to Shane by the "laws, rules, traditions, or principles" of school (Gee, 2000a, p. 7).

Shane the Artist

Shane the artist is best illustrated through his work on his fan fiction project and poetry assignment. Shane's fan fiction piece was five pages single-spaced, more than twice as long as any other fan fiction piece created by his classmates. The text was also remarkably rich in details with a raw intensity that, while unpolished and a bit awkward at times, showed his promise as a writer and his ability to empathize with the military:

The sounds of blade meeting skin and bone was so clear, if you closed your eyes you could see what was happening like an echo of sound to a bat showing the way. Our squad and enemy's squad were only half their numbers when this collision began. In just seconds of the collision the path was blood soaked, no longer a light brown dirt color it's now a dirty dark blood trail.

Shane's use of vivid imagery renders a graphic image of death involving all of the reader's senses: "The sounds of blades meeting skin and bone" compels readers to hear the sounds and view the violence of battle, "this collision," producing a "blood-soaked" path, "dirty" and "dark," with the vestiges of battle. Although Shane's piece was twice as long as most others, it drew feedback from 25 of his classmates when posted on the Ning. Only one student's project attracted more feedback, drawing comments from 28 students. Shane's classmates responded to his fan fiction project with overwhelming praise:

- This is awesome. i [sic] always love your stories, shane [sic]. there [sic] my favorite. please [sic] be a writer when you grow up.
- if [sic] you do not become an author i'm [sic] going to punch you in the face [sic] you do just as good writing as some of the books that im [sic] reading now and they were written by old people [sic] i [sic] think you should try to write as much as possible [sic]

Student responses suggest that Shane has made a name for himself as a writer early on, i.e., "I always love your stories," and "If you don't become an author, I am going to punch you in the face."

As Gee says, his peers "recognized" (2000, p.99) him as a writer, and Shane was clearly pleased to receive the accolades: "Thank you! Every time I hear things such as what you said it inspires me to write even more." This dialogic episode illustrates what Gee refers to as "discourse-identity," that is, traits rendered only because of and through dialogue (2000, p.101). Shane stands as the artist because his peers valued his work, their praise convincing him that he was, indeed, a serious and talented writer.

Once students finished the Twitter activity, they worked collaboratively to create a poem in response to *The Things They Carried*. While the poem that Shane and a classmate composed clearly provided Shane with an opportunity to enact his creative artist identity, he also used it to engage his subversive talents. Although the poetry assignment required students to incorporate their own and their classmates' tweets from the Twitter activity, Shane's poem, entitled "I Fall Forever," did not comply with these instructions. The following excerpt reveals the poem's somber tone:

- After war there's never a good story to come back with.
- You don't value life any more nor any less.
- The home you expected to come back to has been burned.
- You only have a new perspective upon death.
- You realize how it surrounds you and how futile you are in its gaze.

The poem represents a serious attempt at capturing the feelings of the soldiers as they return from war; and this text, as well as the fan fiction text, embody those sentiments. When asked to comment on the class Ning about his favorite part of *The Things They Carried* unit, Shane explained:

The main thing I loved overall was the poetry section of this project… The main thing I love to do is write [sic] and especially poetry at the moment. When I'm able to be creative, it seems like the perfect project to me. I would love to have more creative writing projects like this in the future… The more I write it seems as though the more creative I become and the more my mind evolves into something outstanding.

Shane, the artist, revels in sharing his work with others, not just to have an authentic audience, but also to relish the accolades that the audience can bring. Having received numerous compliments from classmates on his fan fiction project on the Ning, Shane responded to his admiring fans with gratitude. Throughout the unit, when extended writing invitations by Becky that he considered suitable for a serious writer, such as the fan fiction project and the poetry assignment, Shane thrived on his fandom, relying heavily on their feedback for motivation and inspiration. As with his comedic identity, Shane used social networking tools to discursively construct an identity as the artist, a gifted writer.

DISCUSSION

Shane's case study traces the ways in which social networking tools, literacy practices, and identity performances converge in the classroom, challenging dominant pedagogical assumptions about using new technologies in the schools to engage learners. The prevailing logic is that students who are digital natives are proficient using new media tools for literacy practices outside of schools; so if teachers bring those tools into the classroom, then those students will become engaged with school literacy practices, and the problem of failing students will be largely resolved. Shane's case helps clarify the fallacy of this thinking. This line of reasoning assumes that literacy practices are defined by the practices themselves and not altered by the contexts in which they are used. Prensky (2001) would likely consider Shane to be a digital native, given that he self-identifies as a gamer, posts videos on YouTube, and ostensibly engages in the types of digitally mediated leisure activities that we associate with the "iKid Generation" (Stevens, 2012). However, when invited to tweet within the context of a class assignment, the identities he performs in his writing are not those that one would associate with the tweets of a digital native. The identities that a tweeter performs when tweeting, for example, are not dictated by the online space – Twitter.com – but rather by the context in which he or she is tweeting (i.e., a class assignment). The social norms of leisure tweeting (e.g., expressing one's opinions in a way that allows for strong identity performances) were in direct conflict with the ways in which Twitter was appropriated in Becky's classroom, where a strict adherence to the assignment guidelines would have disallowed any self-expression or strong identity performances of one's own. Shane, of course, found a way to challenge those constraints and registered his lack of engagement with the Twitter assignment even as he ostensibly completed it, reinforcing his identity as a subversive and comedian.

As K-12 educators clamor to find meaningful ways to engage student in digital literacies (Downes & Bishop, 2012; Prensky, 2010), a number of experts warn against attempting to motivate students simply through the introduction of conspicuously "trendy" forms of new literacies in formal institutions (Lankshear & Knoebel, 2004). In fact, research suggests that young people do not necessarily want to use technology in institutional settings such as schools in the same manner as they do at home (Lohnes & Kizer, 2007). As Tapscott and Williams (2008) assert, young people's "appetite for authenticity means that they are resistant to ill-considered attempts by older generations to 'speak their lingo" (p. 54). Shane's refusal to tweet in character serves as a testimonial to this point.

"Authentically" appropriating literacy practices into new spaces defined by very different historical, social, and cultural norms (i.e., schools) seems like a paradox. Consider fan fiction writing, for example. Fan fiction, or any kind of fandom,

for that matter, by definition must materialize from the fans themselves. It is a social practice that is not bound by external rules, but rather governed by internal appeals (Jenkins, 2008). Those who engage in fan fiction are members of what Gee refers to as "affinity groups" (Gee, 2001, 2007). In such groups, "people are committed through their immersion in practice [and are] recruited as resources for the group, *not as identities that transcend the affinity group itself*" (Gee, 2007, p. 207, emphasis added). Within these parameters, a fan fiction writing invitation that is governed by "external rules," in which students are positioned as "fans" of a text that was chosen for them, and that, as with Shane, could be used as a way to showcase one's talents, ostensibly for the purposes of forging an identity as a writer that "transcends" those of the other participants, are not the same practices in which members of fanfiction.net (an online site where millions of fan fiction writers produce and consume fan fiction) engage.

This raises another question: How can educators appropriate digital tools and practices into their classrooms in ways that are neither inauthentic nor incongruous with the cultural norms of the native spaces of those practices and the social identities of their students? Teachers are being challenged to find ways to support their students in developing 21st century literacies that are essential for succeeding in a digital world (International Reading Association, 2009; National Council of Teachers of English, 2008). According to numerous scholars (Gee, 1999; Helsper & Eynon, 2009; Jenkins et al., 2006), these literacies are not natural by-products of the ways in which most "digital natives," students, are using digital technologies outside of schools. How, then, can teachers appropriate digital practices for their classrooms in ways that don't sabotage their authenticity and that don't lead students to feel frustrated and alienated? These are the issues that Shane and his multiple identity performances challenge us to consider as we conceptualize what it means to compose in 21st century classrooms.

REFERENCES

Alcoff, L., Hames-Garcia, M., Mohanty, S., & Moya, P. (Eds.). (2006). *Identity politics reconsidered*. New York: Palgrave/Macmillan.

Applebee, A. (1993). *Literature in the secondary school: Studies of curriculum and instruction in the United States*. Urbana, IL: National Council of Teachers of English.

Bennett, S., Maton, K., & Kervin, L. (2008). The 'digital natives' debate: A critical review of the evidence. *British Journal of Educational Technology*, *39*(5), 775–786. doi:10.1111/j.1467-8535.2007.00793.x.

Blommaert, J. (2005). *Discourse: A critical introduction*. Cambridge, UK: Cambridge University Press. doi:10.1017/CBO9780511610295.

Brofenbrenner, U., & Evans, G. W. (2000). Developmental science in the 21st century: Emerging questions, theoretical models, research designs, and empirical findings. *Social Development*, *9*, 115–125. doi:10.1111/1467-9507.00114.

Butler, J. (1990). *Gender trouble: Feminism and the subservion of identity*. New York: Routledge.

Cazden, C. (1988). *Classroom discourse: The language of teaching and learning*. Portsmouth, NH: Heinemann.

Charmaz, K. (2006). *Constructing grounded theory: A practice guide through qualitative analysis*. London: Sage.

Coiro, J., Knobel, M., Lankshear, C., & Leu, D. (Eds.). (2008). *The handbook of research on new literacies*. Mahwah, NJ: Erlbaum.

Downes, J. M., & Bishop, P. (2012). Educators engage digital natives and learn from their experiences with technology. *Middle School Journal*, *43*(5), 6–15.

Gee, J. (1999). *The new literacy studies and the social turn*. Retrieved from http://www.schools.ash.org.au/litWeb/page300.html

Gee, J. (2000a). *Identity as an analysis lens for research in education*. Retrieved from http://www.jamespaulgee.com/node/18

Gee, J. (2000b). Identity as an analytic lens for reserach in education. *Review of Research in Education*, *55*, 99–125.

Gee, J. (2007a). *What video games have to teach us about learning and literacy*. New York: Palgrave Macmillan.

Gee, J. P. (2001). Identity as an analytic lens for research in education. In Secada, W. G. (Ed.), *Review of research in education* (*Vol. 25*, pp. 99–125). Washington, DC: American Education Research Association.

Gee, J. P. (2007b). *Good video games + good learning: Collected essays on video games, learning and literacy*. New York: Peter Lang.

Gee, J. P. (2009). Digital media and learning as an emerging field, part I: How we got here. *International Journal of Learning and Media*, *1*(2), 13–23. doi:10.1162/ijlm.2009.0011.

Gee, J. P. (2012). *Social linguistics and literacies: Ideology in discourses* (4th ed.). New York: Routledge.

Glaser, B. (1998). *Doing grounded theory: Issues and discussions*. Mill Valley, CA: The Sociology Press.

Glaser, B., & Strauss, A. (1967). *The discovery of grounded theory: Strategies for qualitative research*. Chicago: Aldine.

Hawkins, B. L., & Oblinge, D. G. (2006). The myth about the digital divide. *EDUCAUSE Review*, *41*(4), 12–13.

Helsper, E., & Eynon, R. (2009). Digital natives: where is the evidence? *British Educational Research Journal, 28*(6), 751–771.

Hicks, T. (2009). *The digital writing workshop.* Portsmouth, NH: Heinemann.

Holland, D., Lachiotte, W., Skinner, D., & Cain, C. (1998). *Identity and agency in cultural worlds.* Cambridge, MA: Harvard University Press.

Hull, G., & Schultz, K. (Eds.). (2002). *School's out! Bridging out-of-school literacies with classroom practice.* New York: Teachers College Press.

International Reading Association. (2009). *New literacies and 21st-century technologies: A position statement of the international reading association.* Retrieved December 20, 2011, from http://www.reading.org/General/AboutIRA/PositionStatements/21stCenturyLiteracies.aspx

Ito, M., Baumer, S., & Bittanti, M. boyd, d., Cody, R., Herr-Stephenson, B., ... Tripp, L. (2009). *Hanging out, messing around, and geeking out: Kids living and learning with new media.* Cambridge, MA: MIT Press.

Jenkins, H. (2004). Why Heather can write. *Technology Review.* Retrieved from http://www.technologyreview.com/news/402471/why-heather-can-write/

Jenkins, H. (2008). *How fan fiction can teach us a new way to read Moby Dick (part one).* Retrieved from http://henryjenkins.org/2008/08/how_fan_fiction_can_teach_us_a.html

Jenkins, H., Purushotma, R., Clinton, K., Weigel, M., & Robison, A. J. (2006). *Confronting the challenges of participatory culture: Media education for the 21st century.* Chicago: MacArthur Foundation.

Kahn, E. (2009). Making writing instruction authentic. *English Journal, 98*(5), 15–17.

Kress, G. (2003). *Literacy in the new media age.* London: Routledge. doi:10.4324/9780203164754.

Kress, G., & van Leeuwen, T. (2001). *Multimodal discourse: The modes and media of contemporary communication.* London: Arnold.

Lankshear, C., & Knobel, M. (2006). *New literacies: Changing knowledge and classroom learning* (2nd ed.). Philadelphia: Open University Press.

Lankshear, C., & Knoebel, M. (2004). *From flogging to blogging via wifi.* Paper presented at the American Educational Research Association. San Diego, CA.

Lewis, C., & Fabos, B. (2005). Instant messaging, literacies, and social identities. *Reading Research Quarterly, 40*(4), 470–501. doi:10.1598/RRQ.40.4.5.

Lohnes, S., & Kizer, C. (2007). Questioning assumptions about students expectations for technology in college classrooms. *Innovate, 3*(5), 1–6.

Mills, K. A. (2010). A review of the digital turn in the new literacy studies. *Review of Educational Research, 80*(2), 246–271. doi:10.3102/0034654310364401.

Moya, P. M. L. (2002). *Learning from experience: Minority identities, multicultural struggles.* Berkeley, CA: University of California Press.

Nardi, B., & O'Day, V. (1999). *Information ecologies: Using technology with heart.* Cambridge, MA: MIT Press.

National Council of Teachers of English. (2008). *21st century literacies.* Retrieved from http://www.ncte.org/governance/literacies

National Council of Teachers of English. (2013). *NCTE framework for 21st century curriculum and assessment.* Retrieved March 1, 2013, from http://www.ncte.org/library/NCTEFiles/Resources/Positions/Framework_21stCent_Curr_Assessment.pdf

New Media Consortium. (2005). *A global imperative: The report of the 21st century literacy summit.* Retrieved from http://www.nmc.org/pdf/Global_Imperative.pdf

O'Brien, T. (1990). *The things they carried.* Boston: Houghton Mifflin Harcourt.

Prensky, M. (2001). Digital natives, digial immigrants. *Horizon, 9,* 1–6. doi:10.1108/10748120110424816.

Prensky, M. (2010). *Teaching digital natives: Partnering for real learning.* Thousand Oaks, CA: Corwin Press.

Stevens, H. (2012, September 15). Bringing up the iKid generation. *The Chicago Tribune.* Retrieved from http://articles.chicagotribune.com/2012-09-15/features/sc-cons-0913-savvy-shopper-kid-tech-20120915_1_ipad-apps-empty-calories-devices

Strauss, A. L. (1987). *Qualitative analysis for social scientists.* Cambridge, UK: University Press. doi:10.1017/CBO9780511557842.

Strauss, A. L., & Corbin, J. (1998). *Basics of qualitative research* (2nd ed.). Newbury Park, CA: Sage.

Street, B. (2003). What's new in new literacy studies? *Current Issues in Comparative Education, 5*(2), 1–14.

Tapscott, D., & Williams, A. (2008). *Wikinomics: How mass collaboration changes everything.* New York: Portfolio.

Thomas, A. (2006). Fan fiction online: Engagement, critical response and affective play through writing. *Australian Journal of Language & Literacy, 29*(3), 226–239.

Walters, P., & Kop, R. (2009). Heidegger, digital technology, and postmodern education: From being in cyberspace to meeting on MySpace. *Bulletin of Science, Technology & Society, 29*(4), 278–286. doi:10.1177/0270467609336305.

Chapter 19

"What Up" and "TQM":
English Learners Writing on Facebook to Acquire English and Express Their Latina/o Identities

Mary Amanda Stewart
Texas Woman's University, USA

ABSTRACT

Previous scholarship demonstrates that immigrant students are using digital technologies for unique purposes in their out-of-school writing. This study explores the writing on Facebook of four Latina/o immigrant youth who are English Learners. The findings show that the participants write on Facebook to further their English acquisition and express their Latina/o identities in ways not accessible to them in school. Their purposes for writing demonstrate there is much academic potential in leveraging social networking for in-school writing instruction for immigrant students.

INTRODUCTION

Alejandra is an 11th grade Intermediate English Learner in her third semester in a U.S. school. Since the time she started her Facebook page 17 months ago, she has posted 91 times. Her writing varies from English and Spanish codes, phrases, and sentences. She regularly posts "what up" to her friends using the newly learned words in English followed by "tqm" (te quiero mucho/*I love you a lot*), using a Spanish code to express love. Most of her writing occurs on Facebook, not for school assignments. Researchers have stated that we must begin to bridge students' in- and out-of-school writing in order to improve our in-school instruc-

tion (Alvermann, 2009; Moje, 2002), particularly regarding the growth of technology students use outside of school (Hornberger, 2007; Warriner, 2007). Furthermore, there is a gap of knowledge in second language writing research regarding adolescents in the U.S. and what they are writing outside of school (Harklau, 2011). Literacy researchers and educators need to understand what Alejandra and other immigrant youth are writing and for what purposes so that we might adapt our second language writing instruction to account for new technologies these students use outside of school such as Facebook.

Facebook is a social networking site which has been defined as "an online site that presents a platform used by individuals [and] focuses on building and reflecting social relations in accor-

DOI: 10.4018/978-1-4666-4341-3.ch019

dance with interests and/or activities" (Aydin, 2012, p. 1093). One in 12 people of the entire world's population use Facebook (Siegle, 2011) and it reached its milestone of over one billion users in September 2012. How, what, and the frequency in which we write is being revolutionized by this phenomenon.

Although Facebook was created for Ivy League college students, it has quickly spread to other populations. According to a 2012 Pew Research study in the U.S., 72% of Hispanics use Facebook, more than any other race, and 71% of people with a household income of $30,000 or less compromise the largest percentage of users by income (Brenner, 2012). Rapidly increasing Facebook use is facilitating new literacies and social practices for everyone, but has not adequately been studied with immigrant youth (Harklau, 2011; Warschauer, 2009), particularly Latinos (Sánchez & Salazar, 2012). Interestingly, the dynamics of this social networking site are helping immigrant youth facilitate a transnational space that meets unique needs in their lives created by the act of immigration. Therefore, this study specifically investigates the writing of Latina/o immigrant youth on Facebook. The questions used to guide this study are: 1) What are the participants writing on Facebook?; 2) How is second language acquisition occurring through their Facebook writing?; 3) How does their writing express their Latina/o identities?; and 4) What implications does this have for writing instruction for immigrant youth?

THEORETICAL FRAMEWORK AND LITERATURE REVIEW

The scholarship employed to frame this study draws from out-of-school writing influenced by the New Literacy Studies, research of digital writing by immigrant youth, and studies that illustrate social networking sites used for educational purposes.

Out-of-School Writing

Many scholars in the field of literacy contend that students' out-of-school writing practices should inform in-school writing instruction (Alvermann, 2009; Hull & Schultz, 2002; Moje, 2002). Discussions of out-of-school literacies (Hull & Schultz, 2001; Street, 2000) often cite the seminal work of Scribner and Cole (1981) and their comparison of literacy of the Vai people in Liberia. Among their specific investigations was the Vai's original writing system not used in school as well as their Qur'anic religious literacy. Scribner and Cole's findings show that different literacies are associated with specialized forms of thinking; for example, Qur'anic literacy improved memory tasks whereas Vai script improved phonological discrimination. This study allowed for a broader definition of literacy, stating that literacy "is not simply knowing how to read and write a particular script, but applying this knowledge for specific purposes in specific contexts of use" (p. 237). Scribner and Cole's (1981) research with the Vai people illustrate the power in studying literacies that are multiple, contextualized, and not associated with the dominant definition of literacy that prevails in school settings.

The New Literacy Studies (NLS) also provides a relevant theoretical foundation to this study of adolescent English learners' out-of-school writing. The NLS is based on Street's (1995) ideological model of reading which states that literacy is not a neutral process, but is always embedded in power relations. Furthermore, it is neither an individual act nor a discreet skill, discrediting the view that literacy is singular. Since literacy and language are always linked to various cultural and social practices, there is not one single literacy to master, but rather multiple literacies that are meaningful within their sociocultural traditions. Therefore, grounded in the framework provided by Street (1995) and Scriber and Cole (1981), the present study aligns with other studies of students' out-of-school literacies to better understand how these practices could connect to academic literacy taught in school.

Building off of the New Literacy Studies, prominent researchers and theorists from different countries have begun a dialogue about the need to view literacy in light of the dynamic nature of technology, complex local diversity, and increasing global connectedness (New London Group, 1996). Similarly, the editors of the *Handbook of Adolescent Literacy Research* (Christenbury, Bomer, & Smagorinsky, 2009) call for imagination and courage from literacy researchers to investigate how nonmainstream youth are using literacy outside of school. They believe this will provide all students a better education, paving the way for a more just society. For them, understanding marginalized youth's out-of-school literacies in order to provide them a more equitable education is a crucial issue of social justice today. Alvermann (2009) echoes their exhortation, stating that the field of adolescent literacy is in need of more research within the framework of the New Literacy Studies, research that moves beyond the in-school reading and writing practices of youth, and includes the many ways they use literacy outside of school.

Immigrant Adolescents' Digital Writing

Social networking sites uniquely allow users to maintain relationships between family and friends across borders, making it a valuable new tool to immigrant youth, particularly newcomers such as the students in this study. These sites also provide a safe space to try on different identities in a new culture. The purposes of these spaces touch on key issues of transnationalism with which immigrant adolescents are already negotiating due to the act of immigration (Suárez-Orozco, Suárez-Orozco, & Todorova, 2008). With the dynamic growth of the Internet to virtually everybody's fingertips through greater accessibility of Smartphones,

immigrant youth have a new venue in which they can negotiate their identities, build and maintain transnational relationships, and stay connected to their (or their parents') home country.

A mixed-methods study of 262 foreign-born American high school students (Lam & Rosario-Ramos, 2009) showed that these youth inhabit transnational spaces outside of school that often take place on the Internet. Through digital networks they were able to develop relationships with people across geopolitical and linguistic borders. The researchers urge educators to consider the transnational resources of these young people and employ them in their literacy education.

Lam's (2000, 2004) studies with Chinese immigrant adolescents illustrate the many purposes that students' out-of-school digital writing had on their identity and language (L1 and L2) development. The first study (2000) shows how a high school senior from Hong Kong felt marginalized in school because he was not a native English-speaker and grew frustrated with his abilities. However, his digital writing allowed him to develop a sense of belonging through using the English language. The English he learned online was not the Standard English taught in school, but contextually bound in adolescent popular culture. Paradoxically, although the school purposed to make him proficient in English, he actually learned more from his online out-of-school writing.

Similarly, in other studies (Black, 2006; Lam, 2004, 2009; McLean, 2010; Yi, 2007, 2010) immigrant adolescents use their online spaces to write in order to develop a specific variety of English and negotiate their specific ethnic, multilingual, multicultural, and transnational identities. These students learned how to cross genres, languages, and digital platforms through writing. Yi (2007) explains why this area of writing research with immigrant students is important:

Exploring the kinds of voluntary, out-of-school writing practices that students engage in and the motivating aspects of those practices is especially important to contributing to the understanding of biliterate students...as writers because such studies may help us take into account the full range of activities within their composing world and not just those surrounding academic writing in the L2 (p. 25).

Additionally, McGinnis and colleagues (2007) investigated how three transnational youth of Bengali, Colombian, and Jewish descent used social networking to reflect their cultural pride, narrate their own identities, and show group loyalty. Specifically, these youth used multiple modalities available to them through social networking to demonstrate their pride in their own cultural heritage. They used music, poetry, pictures, and other writing to express their loyalties to certain cultural practices and their opinions regarding global issues. The authors urge educators to understand how transnational immigrant students are expressing themselves through their multimodal writing that is now most frequently taking place on social networking sites.

Social Networking Sites in Education

Although it is well-documented that most youth in the U.S. use the social networking site of Facebook, and that it is a phenomenon quickly spreading across the globe (Junco, 2012), most studies to date address college students' use of Facebook for academic purposes (Reid, 2011; Skerrett, 2010). Studies at the college level show that when students' Facebook practices are understood and systematically used in the classroom, learning is enhanced. Skerrett (2010) demonstrated how using the venue of Facebook to analyze literature allowed college students to create a unique third space that was neither solely school nor home. She claims that "people's identities and relationships to their literary practices are fundamentally altered as they move into the third space" (p. 81). Through this exercise students thought critically through issues in popular culture such as the most

common terms through which we define ourselves and which are emphasized in social networking: gender, age, and relationship status.

Also at the college level, Reid (2011) used Facebook to create a safe space for her students to practice academic discourse and shift the traditional power relationships in a class. She claims that Facebook is a "literacy practice [which] creates a space for critical practices in relation to writing" (p. 61). Other studies illustrate how college students have created social capital (Steinfield, Ellison, & Lampe, 2008) and a sense of community in the classroom (Reich, 2010), all through Facebook. DePew's (2011) study of graduate students' use of Facebook to further their second language writing is particularly relevant to the present study. These students' L2 writing was facilitated and furthered by the multimodalities they could use to communicate in English through Facebook. Furthermore, this study exemplifies how the students' developmental writing classes emphasized their deficits in English, whereas their Facebook writing demonstrated the same students as competent writers in English who were capable of communicating in sophisticated and complex manners. The literature does note that there are inherent issues in using social networking sites in the academic classroom (DePew, 2011; Selwyn, 2009), but educators would be remiss to not explore how to tap into the limitless possibilities of social networking for educational purposes, much as the business world has successfully accomplished for its advancement (Siegle, 2011).

In conclusion, the literature shows that:

1. There *is* value in bridging youth's in- and out-of-school writing.
2. Immigrant youth *do* use online spaces for various purposes in their writing.
3. Social networking has been used successfully to further academic achievement at the college level.

Consequently, this study purposefully studies the out-of-school Facebook writing of four Latina/o immigrant adolescents who are English Learners in order to consider how that writing might be mobilized for academic learning.

METHODOLOGY AND DATA SOURCES

The present study answers the research questions by constructing thick descriptions (Geertz, 1973) of the participants' Facebook writing. Using Bogdan and Bilken's (2007) idea of phenomenological research, I "attempt[ed] to understand the meaning of events and interactions of ordinary people in particular situations" (p. 25). Specifically, I studied what was already naturally occurring to understand how, what, and why the participants are writing on Facebook without making any purposeful interventions.

A collective case study approach (Stake, 1995) consisting of four participants was used to understand the particular phenomenon under investigation. The four participants were selected from an English as a Second Language (ESL) class based on the similarity of their age, culture, and time in the U.S. After volunteering in their ESL class, I explained that I wanted to understand the full range of their literacies that they did not use for academic purposes. Once the study began and

I learned they were all active Facebook users, they invited me to become their "friend" on Facebook so I could view their pages.

The participants in this study are four high school newcomers from El Salvador, Guatemala, and Mexico. All of the students attended at least five mainstream classes in their high school that comprises 2,000 students who are primarily native English-speakers. Nevertheless, the participants indicated that they did not talk to these students because they were scared to speak in English. They virtually had no contact with the best language teachers they were surrounded by on a daily basis. This was a great impediment for effective second language acquisition to occur in school.

All of the Spanish-speaking participants were classified as English Learners. Using the state's assessment for second language English writing, Celia, Valeria, and Miguel were in the Beginner category, and Alejandra received the Intermediate rating. The ratings continue to Advanced and then Advanced High which is needed to no longer receive language support services. Their ESL teacher expressed that the writing portion of the state-mandated tests required for graduation was by far the greatest challenge for them receiving a high school diploma. Thus, the English acquisition occurring through Facebook writing was and is extremely important to their future success. Table 1 denotes basic information about the participants.

Table 1. Participants

Name	Age	Country of Origin	Time in U.S. as of January 2012	Grade in School	Level of English Writing Determined by a State Assessment
Valeria	19	El Salvador	20 months	Sophomore	Beginner
Alejandra (Valeria's sister)	17	El Salvador	20 months	Junior	Intermediate
Celia	17	Mexico	18 months	Junior	Beginner
Miguel	20	Guatemala	9 months	Junior	Beginner
*All names are pseudonyms approved by the participants.					

Data Collection

After obtaining the proper consent, I collected data from January through May 2012. The data I collected consists of text, images, and audio from the participants' Facebook pages and between five and eight 30-minute interviews with each participant. I analyzed their Facebook pages which included their message wall, information page, photo albums, and posts they made on other people's pages. Since this was not a stagnant document, but in constant change from the participants themselves as well as others, I analyzed the documents continuously over the data collection period. I included all data from the time the students created their Facebook pages one to two years prior in the analysis as well. Table 2 gives the number of Facebook posts included in my data analysis for each participant.

By becoming the students' "friend" on Facebook, I had access to every part of their site, except for private messages they could send others. However, most, if not all, of their private conversations still took place on a forum available to all of their "friends."

I followed a constructivist approach to grounded theory interviews (Charmaz, 2003) which facilitated the participants' ability to create their own meaning of their social networking. Although I am not from the same culture as the students, I speak Spanish as a second language and conducted the interviews primarily in their L1, Spanish. During these interviews I walked through their Facebook pages with them and asked about what they had posted, why they choose the language it was posted in, and what the visual and audio meant to them. I also asked about all of their Facebook friends: if they knew them from the U.S. or their home countries, and how they maintained and developed relationships through the social networking site.

Analytic Approach

I copied all of their Facebook data and transcribed each interview into documents to upload into a computer software program for coding. Using a grounded-theory approach (Glaser & Strauss, 1968), I used inductive coding to describe the themes that emerged from the data during the analysis process. I first coded the data with a specific title that denoted the literacy and its purpose. Examples from this step are "composing a post in English to communicate to an English-speaker" and "posting a picture to demonstrate pride in one's country." This allowed me to compare the data acquired from one participant with another. I continually adjusted the limitations and definitions of each code to account for the full meaning of the data.

After I coded each piece of data, I used my coding to inform subsequent data collection, particularly interview directions. For instance, as I realized Alejandra was attempting to use codes

Table 2. Quantity of Facebook data analyzed

Participant	Date Participant Started Page	All Posts by the Participant as of May 2012	All Posts to the Participant by Others as of May 2012	Number of Facebook Friends as of May 2012
Valeria	January 2011	543	965	241
Alejandra	December 2010	91	364	79
Celia	August 2011	28	58	69
Miguel	May 2011	9	27	83
*Posts include pictures, Internet links, videos, chain messages, and personally written messages and comments.				
*All participants started their Facebook page within months of their arrival to the U.S.				

in English (i.e. "lol" and "omg") on her Facebook page, I asked her how she learned them, why she used them, and if she thought her Facebook friends understood the message. I also asked Celia if she understood the English codes Alejandra regularly posted on her Facebook wall.

RESULTS AND DISCUSSION

The students' Facebook writing contrasted strikingly to their in-school writing. Therefore, in order to better understand the significance of the participants' out-of-school writing on Facebook, I will first share what their in-school writing looked like so comparisons can be made.

In-School Writing

Through 14 classroom observations in the students' 90-minute ESL classes and helping them with their assignments in all content areas, the in-school and academic-related writing I witnessed generally took the form of copying. They copied exact phrases from a history textbook in order to answer homework questions. They copied character names and vocabulary words from novels in order to answer short comprehension questions. Much of their in-class writing also consisted of learning how to write an academic essay for the state exams developed for native English-speakers. In these instances, they merely copied what the teacher wrote on the board and then copied a line from the book excerpt they were assigned to critique. In my time with them, the largest amount of writing I observed them doing was a one-page summary of a chapter from their health textbook regarding the importance of exercise. Valeria spent two entire hours copying sentences from her health textbook onto notebook paper in order to complete the assignment. She stared blankly at the book, copied, erased, and then repeated the series, all with intermittent breaks to make changes to the music she was listening to through her cell phone or talk to a friend.

Through my observations, I did not detect the presence of any authentic writing assignments where students wrote using their own words. Even when I encouraged them to not copy a line from a book, but write the answer in their own words, they did not want to do it for fear of being wrong. They knew their words were "incorrect" whereas the book's or teacher's words were "right." I believe this in-school writing was not as effective for acquiring English as their authentic writing on Facebook.

As demonstrated in another study with high school English learners (de la Piedra, 2010), the school's instruction primarily focused on passing the state's high stakes tests. This correlates with Au's (2011) research that demonstrates the higher the stakes of the tests, the greater the curriculum is focused on teaching to the test. The interview excerpt below illustrates this point as I spoke with Celia about what she was learning in her two ESL classes.

Mandy: So in your class with Mrs. Perez, are you still doing TAKS, the TAKS packet?

Celia: Sí. [Yes.]

Mandy: ¿Todos los días? [Every day?]

Celia: Ayyyy, sí. Muy aburrido. Difícil. [Uhhhh, yes. Very boring. Difficult.]

Mandy: ¿Pero antes no estaban haciendo los paquetes de TAKS, no? [But before you were not doing the TAKS packets in class, right?]

Celia: No. Antes, no. [No. Before, no.]

Mandy: ¿Estaban haciendo cosas más activas, no? [You were doing more active things, right?]

Celia: Sí. Ahorita por eso está muy aburrido porque sólo TAKS, TAKS! Ayyy! [Yes. Right now because of that, it's very boring because we only do TAKS, TAKS! Uhhhh!]

Mandy: ¿Cada dia? [Every day?]

Celia: Sí. [Yes.]

Mandy: ¿Por toda la clase? [For all of the class (90 minutes)?]

Celia: Sí porque miércoles hay los TAKS. Sólo de inglés, pero en abril, todos. [Yes because the TAKS are on Wedesnday. Only the English, but in April, everything.]

As you can see, I began the conversation in English because the students had expressed a strong desire to practice English with me, the only "americana" they spoke to outside of work. Immediately, though, Celia answered in Spanish, determining the language we would use for the conversation. The "TAKS packet" we referred to is a thick compilation of standardized practice tests for the reading and writing portion of the state test referred to as "TAKS." The participants took the same test as other native-speakers which explains why Celia thought it was so difficult-she had lived in the U.S. for less than two years. Later in the conversation I asked Celia if she thought the packets helped her learn English, something she desperately wanted to do. She replied: "El inglés, no. No más lo que tienes que hacer [en el examen.]" [English, no. Just what you have to do (on the exam.)]

Facebook Writing

The participants' Facebook writing fulfilled very unique needs for them that were not equally met in any other area of their lives. This multilingual and multimodal writing was composed to people in their home countries, family across the U.S., other immigrant students, and English-speakers they knew through after school jobs. I will focus on the areas of their writing that allowed them to acquire English and express their Latina/o identities. (The participants' exact writing will appear in quotations, and if in Spanish, an English translation will be in the accompanying brackets.)

Acquire English

The participants recognized that they needed to learn English very quickly in order to pass the state tests and were eager for opportunities for authentic practice. They found a space to do this on Facebook that their school environment did not facilitate. The findings demonstrate that they were acquiring English as they wrote on Facebook by: 1) composing a post entirely in English, 2) using codes in English, 3) responding to a friend's post using English words, and 4) code-switching.

Composing a Post in English

Of the four writing activities that occurred on the participants' Facebook pages in English, composing a post in English was the least common. Creating a post exposes oneself more than responding to another's post or entering into an ongoing conversation. All of the students expressed that this was a difficult task in English, so they rarely felt confident enough to do it.

Celia had very few posts on her page compared to Alejandra and Valeria who had been in the U.S. for about the same length of time. (See Table 2) She did, however, check her Facebook page daily to see what other people had posted. When I asked her why she did not hardly post anything on her Facebook wall despite the fact that her friends did, she responded: "Es que quiero escribir en inglés, pero no puedo." [It's because I want to write in English but I can't.] She wanted to show her friends back in Mexico that she was successful in the U.S. To illustrate this point, she told me the person she admired the most was a cousin who emigrated at fifteen, the same age as Celia when she came, learned English, graduated from college, and became an architect in the U.S. She looked up to him as a role model and wanted to have the same success he has had in the new country. She greatly wanted her friends and family in Mexico to think she was on her way to equal success. Although her few posts were short, they showed others that she was learning English. She was proving that she would be another success story from her small Mexican town. Upon returning from a trip to Mexico, she wrote, "Hoo was beautiful in mexico." After speaking to her, I believe the "Hoo" was supposed to be "How" for her statement to say "How beautiful was Mexico!" This sounds slightly awkward in English, but is a direct translation of how one would commonly express the same sentiment in Spanish.

Miguel was just beginning his second semester in U.S. schools during data collection and was at the beginning stages of acquiring English. Though brief, Miguel also posted a phrase in pure English to caption a picture of a circuit he had made: "My project of electronics:)". His writing was also very understandable, yet not like that of a fluent English-speaker. Like Celia, he used the same word order and sentence structure that would be used in Spanish. Someone fluent in English would write "My electronic's project"; however, I think Miguel was directly translating the phrase from Spanish to English. This is a naturally occurring phase of second language acquisition (Krashen, 1994), and in order for the students to build fluency, they need these opportunities to write in English, regardless of its grammatical accuracy.

Alejandra had the most advanced writing skills in English, but her English-only posts were usually short phrases accompanied by a symbol that denoted a face such as "Whats up miguel>3". Even Alejandra, who could effectively communicate in English, was too scared to initiate oral communication with native English-speakers in her high school. After being in the same school for nearly 4 semesters, she never initiated any conversation in English with other students. Therefore, although her English posts were short, they were very important in helping her build confidence to approach others with a greeting in English. During one interview I asked her: "Why do you choose to write in English so much on facebook?" She responded: "Because I want to learn. I want to practice."

These posts by the participants were an intricate part of their overall English acquisition as Facebook provided them a safe space to "learn" and "practice" by trying out phrases in their L2.

Using Codes in English

All of the participants were very proud to be Spanish-speaking Latina/os, but also greatly wanted to be a part of the American youth culture. Through their Facebook writing, they did this by using English codes, shortened representations of words and expressions. Using these codes made them feel more competent in their new linguistic and cultural environments. Valeria, Celia, and Miguel all learned their English codes from Alejandra who told me when she saw them posted by other people on Facebook, she asked her co-workers what they meant. She ended nearly every post with a code. For example, she responded to a series of messages, "thaks josseline >omg, gracias javi>>33 que alago loll". She regularly used "omg" which stands for "oh my god" and "lol" which represents "laughing out loud." She sometimes added an extra letter to the code "lol", posting "loll". This is rare with native English-speaking youth. It is possible that she was applying the rule for the common Spanish code, "tqm" (te quiero much/*I love you a lot*), where one writes "tqmmmmm" to express even more love. Applying rules from one's L1 to the L2 is an expected and important step of second language acquisition (Krashen, 1994).

Because all of the participants recognized that Alejandra had the most knowledge of English codes, they asked her to post messages to them using these codes on their Facebook pages. One of these messages Alejandra posted to Celia was: "Hola Celia!!!!!!!omg". In an interview I asked Celia if she knew what "omg" meant. She thought it might be a code in Spanish. Her response was "omg? Hola, mi amiga?" [omg? Hello, my friend?] When I explained to her that it was actually a code in English she began using it on her own Facebook page. The next week she posted "omg tomorrow i have test." This also evidences Celia's desire to post messages visible to her friends back in Mexico that demonstrated that she was successful in her American high school, writing in English and even using an English code.

Responding to a Friend's Post Using English Words

Of the four participants, Valeria had the least amount of English acquisition. In the entire semester I worked with her, she spoke hardly any English to me and I never heard her speak in English to other students. Although she greatly wanted to be able to communicate in English, it was extremely difficult for her. She was very shy and introverted in person, but had a very active social networking life managed through her Smartphone. Facebook provided a place for her to use the English words and phrases she was learning. She had composed 543 posts by the end of the study during only 17 months of having a Facebook account. Some of the phrases she wrote in response to someone's posts were "i love," "me too," and "I am sorry tami." Writing short English phrases allowed her to use the language she had learned. Because her school work was beyond her English language level of comprehensible input (Krashen, 1994), she rarely understood her assignments and copied words from her books for anything she needed to turn in. However, on Facebook she could use language in authentic and comprehensible situations, an activity that was lacking from her schooling experiences.

Celia, Alejandra, and Miguel posted similar brief comments in English to their friends with the most frequent being "what up". They were not concerned about spelling or grammar, but only communication, allowing them to gain more fluency in their English writing. Some of their English responses to others' posts are: "ok is fine...don't worry...", "Cute!))) i miss you...", and "Mmmmmmmm prety".

Code-Switching

Code-switching is the use of more than one language in a phrase and is often used systematically with bilinguals and second-language learners. These newcomers often wove English and Span-ish together in their writing on Facebook which was not something they could do in school. Code-switching in their writing allowed them to focus on fluency in their English acquisition and continue to use as much English as they could. In many situations they did not have all of the needed L2 vocabulary to fully express themselves, but could use at least some L2 vocabulary when aided with the L1.

Code-switching in their writing also allowed them to express their transnational identities. Although they lived in the U.S. and attended an English-only school, they were Spanish-speaking Latina/os who encountered both languages on a daily basis. All of them often used both languages in their posts: "Yeap thats true>333 tas preciosa" [you are precious], ">yo tambien i love you!!!" [me too], and "Thank you primo>" [cousin]. They also posted side-by-side bilingual greetings such as "HAPPY VALENTINE DAY !, FELIZ DIA DEL AMOR Y DE LA AMISTAD."

Even though the participants were still relatively new in their English acquisition, they began to use English words in the midst of writing lengthy phrases in Spanish. For example, they used a few English words at the end of these phrases: "Aunque lo dudes jazmin si estrano a my mom so much." [Although you doubt it jazmin I love my mom so much], and "Jajajajanaj no te burles de mi! *_*>3 loll pero esta buena la picture" [Hahahaha don't make fun of me! *_*>3 loll but it's a good picture]. When I asked them about this, they said they had begun to use a few English words by accident in their writing. In these instances, it was more natural for them to write the word in the L2, demonstrating their growing English acquisition.

In the same vein as the student in Lam's (2000) study used online pen pals to acquire English, these students acquired English through Facebook because of how it facilitated their L2 writing differently than their school environment. In this safe, online space they were not required to post complete sentences, but were able to post individual words, codes, or short phrases that better reflected their stage of second language acquisition. They were able to focus on fluency over accuracy which concurs with their English language levels: Beginner and Intermediate.

Express Latina/o Identities

These students also wrote on Facebook to express their Latina/o identities by writing in Spanish, a language not used in their English-only school environment. In addition to the language choices available to them to express themselves, they also used visual images, nontraditional spellings, and codes in Spanish to demonstrate their identities as Latin American youth. As evident in this interview excerpt with Celia, these students were all very proud of their cultural identities.

Yo soy mexicana….porque como nací en México, y viví toda mi vida en México sin conocer aquí nada. Ya me vine cuando ya estaba grande. Bueno, 15 años. Ya conocí todo como es México y nunca voy a olvidar como es. [I am Mexican…. because like I was born in Mexico and I lived all of my life in Mexico without coming here or anything. I came when I was already big. Well, 15-years-old. I already knew everything about Mexico and I will never forget how it is.]

Lewis and Antillana (2009) remind us that identity is central to research regarding adolescents' literacy practices. The participants' identities are the concepts they have of themselves, how they want others to view them, and who they choose to be as they portray themselves to others. However, nonmainstream students such as these, "don't necessarily fit the dominant mold" (p. 310). They were newcomer Latina/o immigrants who attended a school full of "americanos." Facebook provided them a space to express, nurture, and negotiate their identities as Latina/o youth that in-school writing did not.

Language

Although they sometimes struggled understanding all of the English codes they desired to use, as demonstrated by Celia's misunderstanding of "omg," they competently used Spanish codes in their Facebook writing. They were very eager to make sure I understood the meaning behind the codes which can be used to include and exclude individuals from group membership. Unlike the students, I am not a Latina/o youth, but a White, native English-speaking adult woman. I usually have no difficulty reading in Spanish, but struggled to comprehend some of their messages to each other on Facebook. There were many codes that I could not fully comprehend and needed the students to explain them to me. For example, the participants wrote "tqm" or "tkm" for "te quiero mucho" [I love you a lot,] "xf" for "por favor" [please,] and "xk" for "porque" [because.]

They easily wrote to their friends in Spanish using a combination of whole words, symbols, abbreviations, and codes. Table 3 demonstrates this in the phrase: "ANI,,,,, estan muy lindas tus fotogr,,,,, y te ves muy linda cuidate si T.K.M NENA ♥"

Valeria often encountered content and assignments in her classes that were beyond her level of English acquisition. Since she always had her cell phone with her, she would retreat from the frustrating school environment to write in Spanish on Facebook. This is a post she made on Facebook one day during class: "Que aburrida estoy en esta clase. Esque solo estamo leyendo y leer casi no me gusta." [I'm so bored in this class. It's because we're just reading and I don't really like to read.] Of all the participants, Valeria struggled the most with English and her ESL teacher expressed concern that she might also struggle with Spanish literacy. On Facebook,

Table 3. Analysis of Spanish phrase written by a participant

Actual Writing	ANI	,,,,,	estan muy lindas tus fotogr	,,,,,	Y te ves muy linda	cuidate	si	T.K.M	NENA	♥
Explanation or Translation	Shortened form of the recipient's name	Pause	Your pictures are very pretty	Pause	And you look very pretty	Take care	yes	love you a lot	Babe	Love
Further Explanation			Abbreviation: "fotogr" for "fotografías"					T =Te K = Que M=Mucho		

however, Valeria demonstrated sophisticated use of the Spanish language as she wove words and codes together to convey meaning. This is one message to a friend: "me pasa tu numero de cell x msj xf". [send me your cell phone number so I can send you a message please.] The "x" represents "por" [so that,] "msj" represents "mensaje" [message,] and "xf" represents "por favor" [please.]

In the realm of Facebook writing, Valeria flourished and posted regularly. She wrote with confidence and ease. I label her Spanish writing sophisticated because she mixed codes and whole words together in rule-governed patterns to communicate her message. This form of writing would not be considered academic; however, if we choose to take an asset-view of Valeria's writing, we must see that it still possesses sophistication. This contrasts strikingly to her in-school writing that mainly consisted of copying from a book, erasing, and recopying with little comprehension.

Visuals

The participants' writing in Spanish was often accompanied by a picture that further expressed their Latina/o identities. Miguel did not initiate many posts on his Facebook page, but those that he did make contained these captions along with a picture of himself in a Guatemalan soccer jersey: "Soy puro guatemalteco" [I'm pure Guatemalan,] "Soy puro chaplin," [Chaplin is a term for someone from Guatemala.] and "Soy 100% cremas." [Cremas refers to a Guatemalan soccer team called "Comunicaciones."]

Alejandra chose a picture of the words "El Salvador" in flames for her profile picture. Additionally, she and her sister, Valeria, posted many pictures of variations of El Salvador's flag on their pages. These included the flag in the shape of a heart, with a cartoon inspired Latina juxtaposed over it, and their own photographs placed inside the flag. They also posted a picture that emphasized the importance of soccer in their country. Underneath the image of a soccer field and fans dressed in blue and while, the colors of El Salvador's flag, were the words "El Savador HOY! un solo corazón, una sola pasión" [El Salvador TODAY! only one heart, only one passion]. Celia also expressed her identity as a "mexicana" in her post of the Mexican flag waving in the air. The accompanying text read: "cuantos likes a nuestra bandera??" [how many likes for our flag?]

Music was a central part of the students' lives as they listened to Spanish music or watched Latin American music videos on their phones during class and as they walked through the hallway. On Facebook, all four of them posted pictures of popular Latin American music artists under their "likes" section of their Facebook information page and also posted music videos on their walls. These images pictured the Latin American artists with a specific style of sunglasses, clothing, and body language. Miguel's posts of himself were very similar to the pictures of these artists as he expressed his Latino identity by his sunglasses, baggy soccer jersey, and body language that accompanied his writing.

Through Facebook, these youth demonstrated and maintained their identities as a "guatemalteco," a "mexicana," and "salvadoreñas." They are Latina/o youth who cannot be separated from their cultural identities despite living in a new country, learning a new language, and sitting in classrooms full of "americanos." Even while in class, engaging in Standard English writing (copying), they took breaks to go to their phones and send their culturally-expressive multimodal messages.

IMPLICATIONS FOR RESEARCH AND PRACTICE

The findings concur with previous scholarship that demonstrate the learning potential of teaching writing through digital technologies such as social networking, particularly for immigrant students. First, these students were using Facebook to further their second language acquisition much as other immigrant students have used online writing (DePew, 2011; Lam, 2000, 2004; McGinnis, et al., 2007; McLean, 2010; Yi, 2007). There is a great need for more second language writing research at the high school level to examine how adolescents could use social networking to acquire English more effectively in the classroom. Facebook provides English learners a safe environment to use their L2 to engage in conversations, something that they often do not feel comfortable doing face-to-face. The authenticity of language use, informality, and low-stress environment make social networking a prime space for second language writing to flourish, particularly for beginner and intermediate language learners who need to focus on fluency. This suggests that educators could use safe social networking platforms in school in order for students to connect to each other, practice communicating in English, or share their opinions in a class discussion. Using digital spaces to engage students in conversation could potentially lead to more cross-cultural verbal

exchanges in the classroom, an element that was missing from these students' school experiences.

Second, the way the participants expressed their Latina/o identities through writing in Spanish on Facebook shows the need to have their identities seen, heard, and validated by the mainstream school. Future research should address what policy and instructional changes schools could adopt that would allow immigrant students, English Learners or not, to nurture their cultural identities in the academic environment. We need to understand what effect this might have on students' motivation, sense of belonging, test scores, and graduation rates. If schools were a place where immigrant youth were encouraged and taught to negotiate, share, and publically discuss their identities, how might that affect their motivation to learn English, ability to overcome obstacles, and engagement in academic work? These students often felt incompetent and overwhelmed in their English-only environments. They were also bored in class and did not perceive the instruction to be relevant to their lives. Classrooms should become spaces where students' cultural identities are recognized, validated, and shared as part of in-school learning.

Lastly, through writing on Facebook the newcomers in the study were able to begin the sophisticated process of "transcultural repositioning" (Guerra, 2007) as they learned how to negotiate interactions with other people from different countries, language backgrounds, and cultures. Their developing multilingualism is illustrated as they not only posted messages in English and Spanish, but they also used codes in both languages to communicate with their friends. Furthermore, their multilingual writing can also be considered multimodal with the inclusion of visual elements. Social networking sites provide immigrant students a transnational space where multilingual and multimodal writing can flourish as they learn how to strategically position themselves in different cultural environments that often collide within online spaces. Unfortunately, the participants' in-school writing was monolingual, monoliterate, monocultural and monomodal. Writing instruction should embrace the full linguistic repertoires of immigrant students and give them the opportunity to write in multiple languages and registers for different audiences while using a variety of modalities. Educators need to help immigrant students learn how to negotiate the use of the various tools in their writing toolkits to accomplish different purposes.

CONCLUSION

Immigrant students today have new opportunities due to the influx of Facebook across the globe. They can more easily acquire English through writing and express themselves on this one site. Because social networking is one of the most economical ways to maintain relationships with their friends and family back home, they are already using it prolifically. Whereas their writing on Facebook does not resemble traditional writing assignments used in the academic environment, neglecting to recognize these writing practices is a loss for writing education. We need to continue to research how immigrant students are using social networking in their writing and build upon that knowledge in the classroom. In our increasingly globalized society, the possibilities are limitless on how we might capitalize on the growing trend of social networking to teach writing more effectively for the 21st century.

REFERENCES

Alvermann, D. E. (2009). Sociocultural constructions of adolescence and young people's literacies. In Christenbury, L., Bomer, R., & Smagorinsky, P. (Eds.), *Handbook of adolescent literacy research* (p. xii). New York: The Guilford Press.

Au, W. (2011). Teaching under the new Taylorism: High-stakes testing and the standardization of the 21st century curriculum. *Journal of Curriculum Studies*, *43*(1), 25–45. doi:10.1080/00220272.2010.521261.

Aydin, S. (2012). A review of research on Facebook as an educational environment. *Educational Technology Research and Development*, *60*(6), 1093–1106. doi:10.1007/s11423-012-9260-7.

Black, R. W. (2006). Language, culture, and identity in online fanfiction. *E-learning*, *3*(2), 170–184. doi:10.2304/elea.2006.3.2.170.

Bogdan, R., & Biklen, S. K. (2007). *Qualitative research for education: An introduction to theories and methods* (5th ed.). Boston, MA: Pearson.

Brenner, J. (2012). *Pew internet: Social networking (full detail)*. Retrieved from http://pewInternet.org/Commentary/2012/March/Pew-Internet-Social-Networking-full-detail.aspx

Charmaz, K. (2003). Qualitative interviewing and grounded theory analysis. In Holstein, J. A., & Gubrium, J. F. (Eds.), *Inside interviewing: New lenses, new concerns* (pp. 311–330). Thousand Oaks, CA: Sage Publications.

Christenbury, L., Bomer, R., & Smagorinsky, P. (2009). Introduction. In Christenbury, L., Bomer, R., & Smagorinsky, P. (Eds.), *Handbook of adolescent literacy research* (pp. 3–13). New York: The Guilford Press.

de la Piedra, M. T. (2010). Adolescent worlds and literacy practices on the United States-Mexico border. *Journal of Adolescent & Adult Literacy, 53*(7), 575–584. doi:10.1598/JAAL.53.7.5.

DePew, K. E. (2011). Social media at academia's periphery: Studying multilingual developmental writers' Facebook composing strategies. *Reading Matrix: An International Online Journal, 11*(1), 54–75.

Geertz, C. (1973). *The interpretation of cultures: Selected essays.* New York: Basic Books.

Guerra, J. (2007). Out of the valley: Transcultural repositioning as a rhetorical practice in ethnographic research and other aspects of everyday life. In Lewis, C., Enciso, P., & Moje, E. B. (Eds.), *Reframing sociocultural research on literacy: Identity, agency, and power* (pp. 137–162). Mahwah, NJ: Lawrence Erlbaum Associates.

Harklau, L. (2011). Commentary: Adolescent L2 writing research as an emerging field. *Journal of Second Language Writing, 20*, 227–230. doi:10.1016/j.jslw.2011.05.003.

Hornberger, N. H. (2007). Biliteracy, transnationalism, multimodality, and identity: Trajectories across time and space. *Linguistics and Education, 18*(3-4), 325–334. doi:10.1016/j.linged.2007.10.001.

Hull, G. A., & Schultz, K. (2001). Literacy and learning out of school: A review of theory and research. *Review of Educational Research, 71*(4), 575–611. doi:10.3102/00346543071004575.

Hull, G. A., & Schultz, K. (2002). *School's out: Bridging out-of-school literacies with classroom practice.* New York: Teachers College Press.

Junco, R. (2012). The relationship between frequency of Facebook use, participation in Facebook activities, and student engagement. *Computers & Education, 58*(1), 162–171. doi:10.1016/j.compedu.2011.08.004.

Krashen, S. (1994). Bilingual education and second language acquisition theory. In Leyba, C. F. (Ed.), *Schooling language minority students: A theoretical framework* (2nd ed., pp. 47–75). Los Angeles, CA: Evaluation, Dissemination and Assessment Center, School of Education, California State University, Los Angeles.

Lam, W. S. E. (2000). L2 literacy and the design of the self: A case study of a teenager writing on the Internet. *TESOL Quarterly, 34*(3), 457–482. doi:10.2307/3587739.

Lam, W. S. E. (2004). Second language socialization in a bilingual chat room: Global and local considerations. *Language Learning & Technology, 8*(3), 44–65.

Lam, W. S. E. (2009). Multiliteracies on instant messaging in negotiating local, translocal, and transnational affiliations: A case of an adolescent immigrant. *Reading Research Quarterly, 44*(4), 377–397. doi:10.1598/RRQ.44.4.5.

Lam, W. S. E., & Rosario-Ramos, E. (2009). Multilingual literacies in transnational digitally mediated contexts: An exploratory study of immigrant teens in the United States. *Language and Education, 23*(2), 171–190. doi:10.1080/09500780802152929.

Lewis, C., & Del Valle, A. (2009). Literacy and identity: Implications for research and practice. In Christenbury, L., Bomer, R., & Smagorinsky, P. (Eds.), *Handbook of adolescent literacy research* (pp. 307–322). New York: The Guilford Press.

McGinnis, T., Goodstein-Stolzenberg, A., & Saliani, E. C. (2007). ''indnpride'': Online spaces of transnational youth as sites of creative and sophisticated literacy and identity work. *Linguistics and Education, 18*(3-4), 283–304. doi:10.1016/j.linged.2007.07.006.

McLean, C. A. (2010). A space called home: An immigrant adolescent's digital literacy practices. *Journal of Adolescent & Adult Literacy, 54*(1), 13–22. doi:10.1598/JAAL.54.1.2.

Moje, E. B. (2002). Re-framing adolescent literacy research for new times: Studying youth as a resource. *Reading Research and Instruction, 41*(3), 211–228. doi:10.1080/19388070209558367.

New London Group. (1996). A pedagogy of multiliteracies: Designing social futures. *Harvard Educational Review, 66*(1), 60–92.

Reich, S. M. (2010). Adolescents' sense of community on MySpace and Facebook: A mixed-methods approach. *Journal of Community Psychology, 38*(6), 688–705. doi:10.1002/jcop.20389.

Reid, J. (2011). We don't Twitter, we Facebook: An alternative pedagogical space that enables critical practices in relation to writing. *English Teaching: Practice and Critique, 10*(1), 58–80.

Sánchez, P., & Salazar, M. (2012). Transnational computer use in urban Latino immigrant communities: Implications for schooling. *Urban Education, 47*(1), 90–116. doi:10.1177/0042085911427740.

Scribner, S., & Cole, M. (1981). *The psychology of literacy*. Cambridge, MA: Harvard University Press.

Selwyn, N. (2009). Faceworking: Exploring students' education-related use of Facebook. *Learning, Media and Technology, 34*(2), 157–174. doi:10.1080/17439880902923622.

Siegle, D. (2011). Facing Facebook: A guide for nonteens. *Gifted Child Today, 34*(2), 14–19.

Skerrett, A. (2010). Lolita, Facebook, and the third space of literacy teacher education. *Educational Studies: Journal of the American Educational Studies Association, 46*(1), 67–84.

Stake, R. E. (1995). *The art of case study research*. Thousand Oaks, CA: Sage Publications.

Steinfield, C., Ellison, N. B., & Lampe, C. (2008). Social capital, self-esteem, and use of online social network sites: A longitudinal analysis. *Journal of Applied Developmental Psychology, 29*(6), 434–445. doi:10.1016/j.appdev.2008.07.002.

Street, B. (1995). *Social literacies: Critical approaches to literacy in development, ethnography, and education*. London: Longman.

Street, B. (2000). Literacy events and literacy practices: Theory and practice in the new literacy studies. In Martin-Jones, M., & Jones, K. (Eds.), *Multilingual literacies: Reading and writing different worlds* (pp. 17–29). Philadelphia: John Benjamin.

Suárez-Orozco, C., Suárez-Orozco, M. M., & Todorova, I. (2008). *Learning a new land: Immigrant students in American society*. Cambridge, MA: Belknap Press of Harvard University Press.

Warriner, D. S. (2007). Transnational literacies: Immigration, language learning, and identity. *Linguistics and Education, 18*(3-4), 201–214. doi:10.1016/j.linged.2007.10.003.

Warschauer, M. (2009). Digital literacy studies: Progress and prospects. In Baynham, M., & Prinsloo, M. (Eds.), *The future of literacy studies* (pp. 123–140). New York: Palgrave Macmillan.

Yi, Y. (2007). Engaging literacy: A biliterate student's composing practices beyond school. *Journal of Second Language Writing, 16*(1), 23–39. doi:10.1016/j.jslw.2007.03.001.

Yi, Y. (2010). Adolescent multilingual writers' transitions across in- and out-of-school writing contexts. *Journal of Second Language Writing, 19*(1), 17–32. doi:10.1016/j.jslw.2009.10.001.

KEY TERMS AND DEFINITIONS

Codes: Abbreviations for words and phrases often used in digital writing.

Code Switching: Using more than one language in a phrase, sentence, or dialogue.

English Learner: (EL) Someone who is in the process of acquiring the English language as an L2 who has not yet reached native-like fluency.

Immigrant Youth: The term immigrant youth in the chapter refers to youth with at least one immigrant parent. These students have been referred to as "children of immigration" to denote how their lives are directly affected by the act of immigration (Suárez-Orozco & Suárez-Orozco, 2001). This broad term encompasses youth who were and were not born in the country they live in.

L1: First or maternal language.

L2: Any language other than one's first language.

Newcomer: Students who are recent arrivals in their new country.

Social Networking Site: An online space where individuals can connect to other people by sharing information through writing, visuals, and audio.

Transcultural Repositioning: Negotiating interactions with other people from different countries, language backgrounds, and cultures by positioning oneself in a way to have the most power in a given situation.

Transnationalism: The crossing of geographic, linguistic, and cultural borders either physically, digitally, or socially.

Chapter 20
Adding the "Digital Layer":
Examining One Teacher's Growth as a Digital Writer Through an NWP Summer Institute and Beyond

Troy Hicks
Central Michigan University, USA

ABSTRACT

Opportunities for teachers to engage in professional development that leads to substantive change in their instructional practice are few, yet the National Writing Project (NWP) provides one such "transformational" experience through their summer institutes (Whitney, 2008). Also, despite recent moves in the field of English education to integrate digital writing into teacher education and K-12 schools (NWP, et al., 2010), professional development models that support teachers' "technological pedagogical content knowledge" (Mishra & Koehler, 2008) related to teaching digital writing are few. This case study documents the experience of one teacher who participated in an NWP summer institute with the author, himself a teacher educator and site director interested in technology and writing. Relying on evidence from her 2010 summer experience, subsequent work with the writing project, and an interview from the winter of 2013, the author argues that an integrative, immersive model of teaching and learning digital writing in the summer institute led to substantive changes in her classroom practice and work as a teacher leader. Implications for teacher educators, researchers, and educational policy are discussed.

INTRODUCTION

In order to create substantive change in a teacher's practice, professional development must be inquiry-driven, responsive, and ask teachers to take risks with their own learning (e.g. Cochran-Smith & Lytle, 2009; Darling-Hammond, 2010; Goswami, Lewis, Rutherford, & Waff, 2009; Lieberman & Wood, 2003). This is especially true

when the risk involved requires teachers to use technology in some substantive manner, often in a way that pushes back against their own comfort level or existing skills (e.g. Collins & Halverson, 2009; Cuban, 2001; Zhao & Frank, 2003). Inviting teachers to become more proficient at using technology to teach writing, then, involves at least two factors: first, changing their perspective on what it means to *teach writing*, and then changing their perspective on what it means to *teach writing with technology*.

DOI: 10.4018/978-1-4666-4341-3.ch020

One model of such transformational change for teaching writing involves the invitational summer institutes of the National Writing Project (NWP). As an occasion for teachers to bring their own knowledge, experience, and questions into conversation with a wide variety of colleagues, the Summer Institute (SI) acts as a space for what many call "transformational" change as teachers are able to overcome anxiety about writing, share personal writing, offer feedback in writing groups, and simply give one's self the permission to write (Lieberman & Wood, 2003; Whitney, 2008). Year after year, over 90% of teachers "rate the overall quality and value of NWP institutes highly" (Stokes, 2011, p. ii).

Still, while Whitney (2008) claims that the teachers from the SI "presumably set out to live their lives in new ways" based on their experience, she also cautions that:

[T]he changes these teachers made are more about ways of knowing and seeing than about enacting new courses of action— surely it is possible that one could drastically change actions without changing meaning perspectives at all, and conversely, a titanic shift in perspective may not translate into many visible changes at all... (p. 175)

Discovering what changes have occurred in a teacher's practice is not a one-time event, taken by a survey at the end, even if that event is as transformational as a writing project SI. Instead, in order to understand how a teacher has changed, it requires that we build sustained relationships over time. Thus, my research with teachers aims to solve the riddle of whether or not transformations in the SI are sustained, addressing the first factor above.

And, while instructional technology has not always been at the core of the writing project SI experience, the NWP has, over the past decade especially, made a strong case for the importance of teaching digital writing—writing that is composed with a computer, tablet, smart phone, or similar device and designed for reading, listening, viewing, and/or interacting through such a device. This line of work around digital writing addresses the second factor noted above and has emerged from intersections in the fields of composition and rhetoric, new literacies, and technology-rich professional development. Through a variety of initiatives, some of which I have been directly involved, I have seen first-hand how the NWP has taken seriously the many calls over the first decade of the twenty-first century to teach digital writing. For instance, the book *Teaching the New Writing* has extended the work of many existing NWP teachers to think explicitly about how to teach writing with technology (Herrington, Hodgson, & Moran, 2009). *Because Digital Writing Matters* asks and sets out to answer questions such as 1) what does it mean to write digitally, 2) to create spaces for digital writing in our schools, and 3) to extend assessment practices that account for the complexities of writing in a digital world (National Writing, DeVoss, Eidman-Aadahl, & Hicks, 2010)? More recently, NWP has garnered support from the John D. and Catherine T. MacArthur Foundation, to create the "Digital Is..." Website which "gathers resources, collections, reflections, and stories about what it means to teach writing in our digital, interconnected world" (National Writing Project, n.d.-a).

Still, teaching digital writing creates a strong tension that many educators feel in relation to covering a set amount of curriculum in preparing their students for high-stakes tests, coupled with a lack of access to technology (Turner & Hicks, 2012). To put a finer point on it, many teachers find that striking the balance between knowing what they are "supposed" to teach is clearly at odds with what they understand about expanding notions of literacy in general, as well as what they understand about the integration of technology into the classroom. Yet, the NWP and its teachers are showing that there are some key principles related to teaching with technology, two of which are particularly are instructive:

- "The best uses of technology involve students actively in subject-matter-based practices that are tied to learning goals."
- "Teachers who use technology skillfully to teach their content areas are able to re-engage and motivate struggling students" (Inverness Research, 2009, p. 1 PDF).

This involves a careful investment in teacher leaders. Building capacity in people, not in simply keeping up with the latest gadgets, Web applications, or technology-trends allows teachers to make substantive change. In order for them to become teachers of digital writing, quite simply, we have to ask them to be teachers of digital writing. Thus, my research aims to take up the second factor noted above in relation to teaching writing with technology.

And, it is in this line of thinking where I situate myself as director of our local writing project site, the Chippewa River Writing Project (CRWP) at Central Michigan University (CMU), and as the researcher documenting a case study of one of our CRWP teachers, Delia King, a second grade teacher with 30 years of experience in the classroom. This chapter analyzes King's experience and how she experienced transformation in relation to digital writing not only *in* the summer institute, but *beyond* it. To demonstrate this change, I will explore Whitney's framework for teacher transformation in the summer institute, and add components from another framework—Technological Pedagogical Content Knowledge (TPACK)—leading to an analysis of King's work in our 2010 summer institute, her work over the past two-and-a-half years, and sharing her insights from an interview in the winter of 2013. Specifically, building from the experiences she had in our 2010 SI, I will argue that her interest in and capacity for teaching digital writing have both

increased, contributing to her lasting and substantive "transformation" as a result of participating in our SI. Moreover, I will demonstrate how she now adds what she calls the "digital layer" to the work she does in her own classroom as well as in her school and the broader professional community.

CONTEXT FOR CRWP

Begun in the summer of 2009, CRWP adheres to the NWP model of "teachers teaching teachers," and we have hosted three invitational summer institutes for a total of 40 teachers in the past four years. One of the NWP requirements is to host the SI over the course of four to five weeks, inviting teachers to work both as writers and as teachers of writing through various writing activities, teaching demonstrations, and writing response groups. One additional goal of our site given my research interests and the goals of our leadership team is to maintain an intentional, albeit critical, stance on the use of digital writing. To that end, we often refer to ourselves internally as a "digital writing project," and we consider the many ways in which we can thoughtfully and creatively engage our colleagues in technology-rich literacy experiences. A core tenet of the NWP philosophy guides our work: teachers themselves are agents of reform (National Writing Project, n.d.-b). As the NWP has always asked, how might we invite teachers to become better teachers of writing by asking them to be writers themselves? At the same time, I extend this line of thinking to ask: how might we also invite teachers to become better teachers of digital writing by asking them to be digital writers as well?

Research on the teaching of writing shows that teachers who explicitly model writing for and respond directly to students can have a substantial effect on their students' performance (Graham & Perin, 2007; National Council of Teachers of English, 2008). Moreover, technology is poised to play a significant role in writing instruction, if given the chance. Even the Common Core Standards themselves offer one small, yet crucial, way for teachers to integrate technology. Quoting from the sixth grade writing standards, which has language similar to standards in other grade levels, students are expected to "[u]se technology, including the Internet, to produce and publish writing as well as to interact and collaborate with others" (Common Core State Standards Initiative, n.d.). In short, teaching writing with technology matters, and teacher educators are wise to address this pressing need in our methods courses and in the professional development experiences we create.

Delving just a bit deeper into my perspective as a teacher educator and researcher, I make no apologies for working as a participant action researcher, a stance I will elaborate upon in the methodology section below. I often co-author, present conference sessions, and lead workshops with teachers. I genuinely want to understand how—as a writing scholar and teacher educator—I can work to address complicated matters when writing teachers continually seem to be disenfranchised and technology is used in reductive ways. To examine whether or not the work that I do with CRWP and the numerous teachers who are involved has some lasting impact, I relying here on two frameworks.

THEORETICAL FRAMEWORKS: TEACHER TRANSFORMATION AND TPACK

Whitney (2008) describes the factors that contribute to the "transformation" that so many teachers who participate in NWP have experienced. In her study of seven teacher participants over the course of one summer institute, Whitney describes both the "contributing processes" that open teachers up to the possibility of transformation as well as the "major phases" that occur through the course of the summer institute that make that transformation possible (176-7). There are more components to her model that outline the importance of the teacher learning community in the SI, yet for purposes of analyzing King's experience, I will look closely at what Whitney describes as "contributing processes" and "major phases" (see Table 1). Since I am examining King's teaching practice from the summer institute up to the present, I will rely on Whitney's final three phases to frame my analysis: trying new roles, building competence and confidence and living in the new frame.

Along with the NWP model articulated by Whitney, I also draw from Mishra and Koehler's "Technological Pedagogical Content Knowledge" (TPACK) to frame my thinking. TPACK has become a popular tool for thinking about technology and teacher education, and it helps to generatively complicate our understanding what good teaching with technology should look like. TPACK's strength as a framework is, in fact, its flexibility

Table 1. Components of teacher transformation from Whitney (2008)

Contributing processes	Major Phases
• Anxiety about writing • Giving self permission to write and/or share • Sharing and receiving feedback while in the writing group • Trying new roles in writing • Acquiring knowledge, skills, and language	• "Triggering" – described as teacher's dissatisfaction with part of his/her professional life • Accepting the invitation to write and share writing • Self-examination • Re-framing of perspectives • Resolving to reorient • Trying new roles • Building competence and confidence • Living in the new frame

to apply to different contexts and situations for teacher education and professional development. Mishra and Koehler elaborate on different components of TPACK such as "technology knowledge" and "pedagogical knowledge." In particular, because of the various changes that surround digital writing—ideas that include changes in broader social practices and technological tools, as well as the interactions that occur between teachers and students in classrooms—I am interested in their definition of "technological pedagogical knowledge":

Technological pedagogical knowledge (TP or TPK), then, is an understanding of how teaching and learning changes when particular technologies are used. This includes knowing the pedagogical affordances and constraints of a range of technological tools as they relate to disciplinarily and developmentally appropriate pedagogical designs and strategies (Mishra & Koehler, 2008, p. 9).

For teachers to use technologies in critical, creative ways, then their understanding of any given tool must go beyond simple transfer and into a more substantive change around the teaching practice.

For instance, to connect TPK to a specific technology I will discuss more below, I will describe the use of Google Docs. In effect, Google Docs serves as a cloud-based word processor, much leaner than Microsoft Word and available through any network connected device including tablets and smartphones. Indeed, Google Docs becomes a new social and technical space for the composing process. Or, at least it potentially can function in that manner, if a teacher takes advantage of it to invite the new "pedagogical designs and strategies" that Mishra and Koehler describe. Because of the easy possibilities by allowing for (and, indeed, inviting) simultaneous collaborative writing and editing, teachers interested in digital writing, must

understand Google Docs from the perspective of TPK, and make appropriate instructional choices for their students as digital writers.

To enact the goals of having participants in our CRWP SI achieve TPK, there are five main ways that we integrate digital writing into our summer institute experiences. For King, this process began during our orientation day in May of 2010 when we created writer's profile pages on our wiki site. As the SI began, we started creating a variety of additional pieces of writing, incorporating the following digital writing components:

- Using Google Docs for personal writing to be shared in writing groups.
- Using Google Docs for our responses to one another's teaching demonstrations.
- Sharing a teaching demo by putting resources on a wiki page.
- Creating a digital story with a program such as iMovie, Windows Movie Maker, or Photostory.
- Reading and responding to professional texts using various technologies such as podcasts and Prezi.

In the end, each participant created a digital portfolio, highlighting all the work that he or she had completed over the summer. Below, I will argue that the approaches outlined above modeled what Mishra and Koehler describe as effective "pedagogical designs and strategies" were what helped participants, including King, see digital writing as a topic worthy of deeper study. A brief description of my research method for this particular inquiry—a case study of Delia King as a participant in 2010 and changes in her teaching practice since that summer—will further outline my thinking on this process. Using Whitney's final three phases and Mishra and Koehler's description of TPK, I will show how these five digital writing activities in the summer institute have resulted in substantive changes in King's teaching practice.

METHODOLOGY

Throughout my research career, I've been interested in the ways that teachers come to understand digital writing through their work as writers themselves, as well as by understanding the ways that they incorporate digital writing into their classrooms (Autrey et al., 2005; Hicks et al., 2007; Reed & Hicks, 2009). As a participatory action researcher, I recognize that my role as a university faculty member and teacher educator is not to simply observe phenomena in classrooms, or to create randomized, controlled trials to test out educational interventions. Instead, adhering to many of the tenets of participatory action research (Kemmis & McTaggart, 2000), I value a critical and collaborative approach to understanding how we teach writing; I invite teachers into the process of research, and focus on sustained learning, together, over time.

Moreover, I recognize my position as a teacher educator vis-à-vis the teachers with whom I work; understanding the power dynamics that are present, I work diligently to position myself as a coach and collaborator. I am a co-teacher first, a researcher second. From my position as a participatory action researcher, I find that my perspective on the entire research process is somewhat different than if I approached as an objective outsider. To the extent that I report stories of teachers, my hope is that these cases contribute something to the broader field of English education. I make my agenda clear from the first day I meet participants, inviting them to join the on-going inquiry related to CRWP by signing an IRB consent form and framing their own inquiry questions.

Moreover, I am open to different possibilities for analysis and reflection. Like Dyson and Genishi who offer insights into the process of building and analyzing case studies, I believe that:

[I]nterpretive research is reflexive: researchers data gathering, analysis, and indeed, eventual write-up of others' experiences are mediated by their own lives... (Dyson & Genishi, 2005, p. 81).

As the director of a writing project, I recognize that my own professional interest in teacher education and digital writing will guide the ways in which I structure the workshop experience, as well as my analysis of it. Knowing this as a bias, I openly report here that I am not approaching King's particular case with the purpose of coding and analyzing for generalizable results; instead, my purpose is to document King's experiences with digital writing from the SI as a teacher researcher would; in a sense, I have the luxury to follow up on my student nearly three years hence to discover what it is she has done with the knowledge gained from my course.

Thus, for the purposes of this chapter, I argue that King's case can offer us as teacher educators a new way to think about immersive, technology-rich professional development related to writing, reading, and literacy more broadly. Using three Whitney's components of transformation and Mishra and Koehler's understanding of technological pedagogical knowledge, I now present and analyze artifacts from King's experience in the 2010 SI and subsequent CRWP activities in which she has participated, leading up to an interview that I conducted with her in February 2013.

DATA

My relationship with Delia King began when she first applied to the SI in the spring of 2010. The following paragraphs are used, with her permission, from a letter she wrote to me describing her interest:

During the summer institute I would like to discover the joy of writing. I write in front of my class and, of course, they think I am an expert writer, but I do not write for me. There are times that I think I should have my own personal writer's notebook and put ideas in it, but I have yet to start this. I don't take or make the time to write for myself. I would like to write a comprehensive writing curriculum for second grade that has a time-line of instruction as well as lesson plans for specific writing craft lessons. But most of all, I want to discover a passion for writing because I do have a passion for teaching it...

Additionally, I would like to be part of this project because of a promise that I made to myself. In graduate classes, many younger teachers complained about veteran teachers that were set in their way of teaching. I vowed that I would not become a part of that veteran teacher stereotype. Who am I to think that I know all there is to know about teaching? Times are changing, new research is being conducted on how students learn, and I need to stay current in the field of education and technology...(King, Personal Correspondence, March 18, 2010)

Demonstrating her interest in improving her teaching, even near the end of her career, King wanted to avoid the "veteran teacher stereotype" and take on the challenge of writing and learning in the summer institute. In this selection from her application letter, I find it important to note a few phrases: "I don't take or make the time to write for myself," "want to discover a passion for writing," and "I need to stay current in the field of education and technology." These types of "triggers," as Whitney names them, suggest that King was ready and willing to embrace the possibilities of change in the SI. Also, she was referred to the SI by two 2009 SI participants, so she also had some idea about the technologies we would be using throughout the summer, and indicated that she was ready to learn new ideas.

2010 Summer Institute

Along with a number of conversations throughout the summer as a result of our participation in the same writing group, and because I was her coach for the teaching demonstration, I was able to develop a strong relationship with King. Through the summer, she worked on a variety of pieces that she posted to her digital portfolio (http://chippewariverwp.wikispaces.com/SI_2010_Delia_King). There are a few important features of Delia's writer's profile to note. First, the picture and introductory text shows how we had all of our teachers create a brief overview of themselves as writers. Below that, Delia has listed all of her assignments from the summer institute, some posted as links within the wiki, some as links outside, some as documents and, lastly, an embedded podcast audio file. The profile pages served as a "home page" for each participant to organize his or her materials written during the summer institute and as a means to present a final digital portfolio.

- Four personal writing pieces include two stories, one poem, and one digital story.
- Items from her teaching demonstration on the "ABC's of Nonfiction" including her outline, handouts, a rubric, and her reflection.
- Two book reviews, one as a letter to her principal and one as a podcast for colleagues.
- A literature of five other professional books.
- An addition poem, "How to be a Writer," written for an audience of students.
- A portfolio cover sheet and a final reflection.

Part of her final reflective letter reveals what King felt the experience of the summer institute had brought her:

Being in the role of learner, has been an eye-opening experience, one that I hope will guide my teaching. I have felt so uncomfortable and inadequate in my writing abilities these last four-weeks, yet I have shared. It has been difficult to read my pieces and have them out there for others to hear when I did not think of myself as a writer. My writing group helped me to gain confidence in my ability; offering positive feedback and suggestions that indeed improved my pieces...

When I go back into my classroom, I need to remember the feelings I had as a learner. How it felt to feel unsure. How it felt to have to share something that was personal. How being a shy, private person feels when other classmates are extroverts and confident in their ability. I have always tried to build a safe classroom environment, the importance was magnified for me this summer. I am thankful that CRWP was that safe and challenging environment that I needed...

King, as an example of one teacher who arrived at the SI with some anxiety, and departed with newfound confidence, is much like the teachers Whitney describes, a transformation I will describe in more detail in the implications section below. Before that, I share what King reported on a variety of activities that she has participated in since the 2010 SI.

Interim Activities (2010-2013)

In the months following her initial participation in the SI, King continued to learn and grow as a professional with her CRWP colleagues. Beginning in the spring of 2011, she began preparing professional development sessions related to narrative, informational, and opinion writing for elementary students. She also helped coordinate our 2011 youth writing camp, led sessions at both our 2012 and 2013 annual conference, and led professional development in her school under the auspices of CRWP. She is currently working as a teacher leader in our 2012-13 grant project, the CRWP "Content Literacy Collaborative," where she acts as a liaison for her team of three additional colleagues from her elementary school as they perform research around the idea of creating confident and creative writers across subject areas.

In her reflections on the school-based professional development, King continues to work on the balance between teaching writing and teaching digital writing to her colleagues. For instance, in one reflection she noted the fact that many of her colleagues were still having trouble logging in to Google docs, having forgotten their username or password. In another, she noted how she was trying to strike a balance in the presentation style between herself and one other CRWP teacher who was leading the session. These types of reflections show how she was, indeed, feeling more competent and confident leading her to "live within the new frame," as Whitney describes it. Despite her stated interest in helping her students and colleagues learn about digital writing, she understands that there are other elements at play in the way she teaches and leads professional development.

Mid-Winter 2013

The third set of data from, February of 2013, resulted from a one-hour phone call with King who, on the verge of retirement, was still making active changes in her classroom and participating in our current CRWP grant focused on content area literacy. Before our interview, I asked her to reflect on how the technological pedagogical knowledge she gained from specific activities in the SI have led to substantive changes in 1) her classroom practice, 2) her work as a teacher leader in her own school, and 3) as a teacher consultant participating in a broader professional development context. While it is difficult to trace a one-to-one correlation from her experiences in the SI to exactly what she is doing today, I did encourage her throughout the interview to keep connecting back to these particular digital writing experiences, all forms of technological pedagogical knowledge. Findings here are aligned to the final three components of Whitney's framework, suggesting that King did, in fact, "transform" her teaching as a result of participating in the SI experience (see Table 2).

At the end of the interview, I asked King to reflect on what is important to her now based on the experience she initially had in the Summer Institute, and to pertinent quotes from this end portion of our conversation stand out:

Table 2. Components of King's continued transformation as a teacher of digital writing

TPK Activity from SI	Resulting in "trying new roles"	Resulting in "building competence and confidence"	Resulting in "living in the new frame"
Using Google docs for personal and professional writing	• Continues to use Google Docs to collaborate with CRWP colleagues, especially during our advanced institutes • Because of their age, having second grade students use Google Docs is not appropriate	• Also, she and her colleagues used Google Docs for investigating CCSS model lessons and creating rubrics for CCSS writing genres • King introduced colleagues on her staff to Google Docs, using it for "writing into the day" during the district PD she led	• Still, since King's classroom has a computer and LCD projector, she uses Google Docs as a tool to gather ideas, model the writing process, and revise writing • She also uses it as a "live" document for notetaking and collaboration during the various PD sessions she has run
Creating a teaching demonstration and sharing it on a wiki page	• King created multiple wiki pages for her classroom, for parents, for second grade team • Used to share student writing and digital writing as well as to house a collection of mini-lessons	• Gained confidence to present to adults using the wiki as the basis (not just slide show) • Modeled mini lessons for elementary teachers at district level	• Returns often to the CRWP wiki, using the pages she's already made as templates for other PD sessions • Providing teachers time to explore the wiki during PD session
Composing a digital story with script, images, and music	• Has students create digital stories including "I am" poems and informational reports • Only using Photostory (easier for kids; it is what's on computers)	• Noticing connections between non-fiction text features and visual element	• Gave a "tech tip" session on digital storytelling after school with another CRWP teacher • Working with another second grade teacher to use digital stories with her students, too
Reading and responding to professional texts	• Asked tech person to put Photostory and Audacity on the school server • Does create simple, voice only podcasts with her students	• Working with two other second grade colleagues (both much younger) to try podcasting with students	• Additionally, she reports now using Kidblogs and Glogster • Building her credibility as a professional; having expert knowledge about technology (both from reading and experience) to share with other teachers in PD settings

The kids that I have taught over the past three years since the summer institute have really benefitted because they have had a digital layer to their writing that I wouldn't have added to my instruction otherwise.

Being at the summer institute has pushed me as a professional to be a teacher of teachers and I didn't have that confidence before to be a teacher of teachers. I've taught for awhile, and even though I was scared to try the digital piece, I jumped in and found that it was rewarding, both for myself as a writer and for the kids that I teach. (King, Personal Interview, February 18, 2013)

Taken in sum, learning to teach writing, let alone learning to teach digital writing, requires a great deal of time, effort, and patience. Participating in an SI of the National Writing Project site offers teachers a chance to do what Whitney calls "living in the new frame" (p. 175). Her study concludes that teachers who participate in such institutes are more confident based on their "serious inquiry into and adjustment of ways of thinking about teaching, learning, writing, and life" (p. 178).

Given the role that digital writing occupied in my goals as the site director and as a teacher educator, part of the change that I hoped to spark centered specifically on participants learning about digital writing, both as digital writers themselves and as teachers of digital writing. To elaborate on Whitney's components of the transformation, and to connect back to the idea of Mishra and Koehler's technological pedagogical knowledge, two particular points are salient:

- **Trying new roles in writing:** King, like all participants in the Summer Institute, was able to choose a number of different genres, purposes, and audiences for her writing and was able to do so through explicit instruction in scaffolding related to the use of digital writing tools such as wikis, Google Docs, and digital storytelling.
- **Acquiring knowledge, skills, and language:** Moreover, as a way to further understand the importance of digital writing and to be able to transfer her knowledge into other contexts, King (and again, all participants) received significant support through the course readings, opportunities for collaboration, and assignments that help them develop technical skills as well as a new vocabulary about the teaching of digital writing.

One of those questions that Whitney raised had to do with whether the transformation would be ongoing and substantive. King's case suggests that, for some teachers, the SI does lead to lasting change. I am cautious here as a qualitative researcher not to draw a generalizable conclusion, and will admit freely that of the 16 teachers who participated in that summer institute, they are four that I have not spoken to since the last day we spent together in 2010. Still, there are a number of implications that I draw from this case study that are relevant in this collection on teacher education, technology, and writing.

IMPLICATIONS

King's experience—so far as it connects to Whitney's framework for teacher transformation and as a result of the technological pedagogical knowledge that she gained in the CRWP SI—demonstrates that she has, indeed, moved beyond being a stereotypical veteran teacher. Her ability to adapt to new perspectives about literacy, to understand the possibilities (and limitations) of various technologies, and to adapt her newfound skills and attitudes into her teaching context indicate that she has made substantive change in her teaching practice. She now considers herself a teacher of teachers and uses digital writing with her second grade students, building level colleagues, and in wider professional development conversations. In an age of increased teacher accountability, King's experience as one teacher, in one particular "digital writing project," invites us to think about a number of implications for teacher educators as we prepare future teachers, pursue new lines of research, and make recommendations for educational policy.

First, as we think about how to prepare future teachers, I return to a piece of scholarship that I co-authored nearly a decade ago. In 2005, Jeff Grabill and I argued that "we need to engage preservice and inservice teachers in the same critical and rhetorical types of technology-rich literacy activities that we would ask them to design for their own students" (Grabill & Hicks, 2005, p. 307). Given that King reported her own lack of confidence in teaching writing and teaching writing with technology after having 30 years of experience, I wonder how well English educators, curriculum directors, literacy coaches, and teachers leaders are doing in designing technology-rich literacy experiences. Or, to be blunt, have we really changed all that much in the first decade of the 21st century? And, if we haven't, could the model of activities that I include in the CRWP SI serve as one such possibility for change?

Second, as I have argued elsewhere and throughout this chapter, since teacher educators are compelled by the very nature of their positions at universities to also act as researchers, then participatory action research is a valid model for our inquiry. Having worked with King—and dozens of other passionate, dedicated, and creative teachers like her—I understand that their stories are sorely lacking from the conversation about education and educational reform in this country. Rather than introducing an "intervention" into a random classroom and looking to see what effects that might have on students' test performance, I choose to spend my time collaborating with teachers. The types of substantive changes that King has made it her teaching practices, as well as her growth as a teacher leader lead me to no other conclusion than the fact that we must use our position in the university as a bully pulpit to raise the voices of teachers.

Finally, in terms of educational policy, we need to recognize and understand the positions of educational corporations as they define "digital learning," and what that definition will need to in terms of subsequent reforms that are thrust upon teachers and students. For instance, a group that coordinates the annual "Digital Learning Day," the Alliance for Excellent Education, defines digital learning as:

Digital learning is any instructional practice that is effectively using technology to strengthen the student learning experience. Digital learning encompasses a wide spectrum of tools and practices, including online and formative assessments, increased focus and quality of teaching resources, reevaluating the use of time, online content and courses, applications of technology in classrooms and school buildings, adaptive software for students with special needs, learning platforms, participation in professional communities of practice, access to high-level and challenging content and instruction, and many other advancements technology provides to teaching and learning (Alliance For Excellent Education, 2013).

Or, to put a sarcastic spin on it from the point of view of many new educational corporations and billionaire businessman who have much to gain in terms of profit, digital learning will lead to the need for fewer teachers, their bloated salaries and benefits, and the educational opportunities that are provided in classrooms. Instead, content can be delivered anytime, anywhere without critical and creative approach that a teacher like Delia King brings to her craft. If King's example, as a teacher on the verge of retirement, is any motivation at all and if we are serious about the work of teaching writing to the next generation of teachers so that they may share a broader vision with their own students and communities, then we need to put the "digital layer" into our teaching methods courses and research agendas immediately. My hope is that the model of integrating digital writing into a sustained professional development experience such as a summer institute provides one such vision for doing so.

REFERENCES

Alliance for Excellent Education. (2013). D*igital learning day: Digital learning definition*. Retrieved March 7, 2013, from http://digitallearningday.org/about-us/digital-learning-definition/

Autrey, T. M., O'Berry Edington, C., Hicks, T., Kabodian, A., Lerg, N., & Luft-Gardner, R. et al. (2005). More than just a web site: Representing teacher research through digital portfolios. *English Journal, 95*, 65–70.

Cochran-Smith, M., & Lytle, S. L. (2009). *Inquiry as stance: Practitioner research in the next generation*. New York: Teachers College Press.

Collins, A., & Halverson, R. (2009). *Rethinking education in the age of technology: The digital revolution and schooling in America*. New York: Teachers College Press.

Common Core State Standards Initiative. (n.d.). *Common core state standards initiative | English language arts standards | writing | grade 6*. Retrieved February 18, 2012, from http://www.corestandards.org/the-standards/english-language-arts-standards/writing-6-12/grade-6/

Cuban, L. (2001). *Oversold and underused: Computers in the classroom*. Cambridge, MA: Harvard University Press.

Darling-Hammond, L. (2010). *The flat world and education: How America's commitment to equity will determine our future*. New York: Teachers College Press.

Dyson, A. H., & Genishi, C. (2005). *On the case: Approaches to language and literacy research*. New York: Teachers College Press.

Goswami, D., Lewis, C., Rutherford, M., & Waff, D. (2009). *On teacher inquiry: Approaches to language and literacy research*. New York: Teachers College Press.

Grabill, J., & Hicks, T. (2005). Multiliteracies meet methods: The case for digital writing in English education. *English Education*. Retrieved from http://condor.cmich.edu/cdm/singleitem/collection/p1610-01coll1/id/239

Graham, S., & Perin, D. (2007). *Writing next: Effective strategies to improve writing of adolescents in middle and high schools*. Retrieved from http://www.all4ed.org/files/WritingNext.pdf

Herrington, A., Hodgson, K., & Moran, C. (2009). *Teaching the new writing: Technology, change, and assessment in the 21st-century classroom*. New York: Teachers College Press.

Hicks, T., Russo, A., Autrey, T., Gardner, R., Kabodian, A., & Edington, C. (2007). Rethinking the purposes and processes for designing digital portfolios. *Journal of Adult and Adolescent Literacy, 50*, 450–458. doi:10.1598/JAAL.50.6.3.

Inverness Research. (2009). *Keeping the promise of the 21st century: Bringing classroom teaching into the digital age - National writing project*. Retrieved February 18, 2012, from http://www.nwp.org/cs/public/print/resource/2865

Kemmis, S., & McTaggart, R. (2000). Participatory action research. In Denzin, N. K., & Lincoln, Y. S. (Eds.), *Handbook of qualitative research* (2nd ed., pp. 336–396). Thousand Oaks, CA: Sage Publications.

Lieberman, A., & Wood, D. (2003). *Inside the national writing project: Connecting network learning and classroom teaching*. New York: Teachers College Press.

Mishra, P., & Koehler, M. J. (2008). Introducing technological pedagogical content knowledge. In *Proceedings of the Annual Meeting of the American Educational Research Association* (pp. 1–16). Retrieved from http://www.msuedtech-sandbox.com/2010RouenY2/Readings/wk1d2_mishra&koehler.pdf

National Council of Teachers of English. (2008). *Writing now: A policy research brief*. Retrieved from http://www.ncte.org/collections/adolescentliteracy

National Writing. P., DeVoss, D., Eidman-Aadahl, E., & Hicks, T. (2010). Because digital writing matters: Improving student writing in online and multimedia environments. San Francisco, CA: Jossey-Bass.

National Writing Project. (n.d.a). *What is digital is? NWP digital is*. Retrieved February 18, 2012, from http://digitalis.nwp.org/about

National Writing Project. (n.d.b). *About NWP - National writing project*. Retrieved February 18, 2012, from http://www.nwp.org/cs/public/print/doc/about.csp

Reed, D., & Hicks, T. (2009). From the front of the classroom to the ears of the world: Podcasting as an extension of speech class. In Herrington, A., Hodgson, K., & Moran, C. (Eds.), *Teaching the New Writing: Technology, Change, and Assessment in the 21st Century Classroom* (pp. 124–139). New York: Teachers College Press/ National Writing Project.

Stokes, L. (2011). *The enduring quality and value of the national writing project's teacher development institutes: Teachers' assessments of NWP contributions to their classroom practice and development as leaders.* Retrieved from http://www.inverness-research.org/reports/2011-11-Rpt-NWP-NWP-Survey-TeacherInst-Final.pdf

Turner, K. H., & Hicks, T. (2012). That's not writing: Exploring the intersection of digital writing, community literacy, and social justice. *Community Literacy Journal, 6*(1), 55–78. doi:10.1353/clj.2012.0000.

Whitney, A. (2008). Teacher transformation in the national writing project. *Research in the Teaching of English, 43*(2), 144–187.

Zhao, Y., & Frank, K. A. (2003). Factors affecting technology uses in schools: An ecological perspective. *American Educational Research Journal, 40*, 807–840. doi:10.3102/00028312040004807.

Compilation of References

Abrami, P. C., & Barrett, H. C. (2005). Directions for research and development on electronic portfolio. *Canadian Journal of Learning and Technology, 31*(3). Retrieved from http://cjlt.csj.ualberta.ca/index.php/cjlt/article/view/92/86.

Abrams, Z. I. (2001). Computer-mediated communication and group journals: Expanding the repertoire of participant roles. *System, 29*(4), 489–503. doi:10.1016/S0346-251X(01)00041-0.

Adams, R. (2012). Revised list drops FSU, FAMU from 25 most dangerous campuses. *WCTV.TV.* Retrieved from http://www.wctv.tv

Agosto, D. E. (2002). Bounded rationality and satisficing in young people's web-based decision-making. *Journal of the American Society for Information Science and Technology, 53*, 16–27. doi:10.1002/asi.10024.

Alamargot, D., & Chanquoy, L. (2001). General introduction: A definition of writing and a presentation of the main models. In Alamargot & Chanquoy (Eds.), Through the models of writing: With commentaries by Ronald T. Kellogg & John R. Hayes (pp. 1-29). Amsterdam: Kluwer Academic Publishers.

Alamargot, D., Chesnet, D., Dansac, C., & Ros, C. (2006). Eye and pen: A new device for studying reading during writing. *Behavior Research Methods, 38*(2), 287–299. doi:10.3758/BF03192780 PMID:16956105.

Alcoff, L., Hames-Garcia, M., Mohanty, S., & Moya, P. (Eds.). (2006). *Identity politics reconsidered.* New York: Palgrave/Macmillan.

Alexander, P., Graham, S., & Harris, K. (1998). A perspective on strategy research: progress and prospects. *Educational Psychology Review, 10*, 129–154. doi:10.1023/A:1022185502996.

Alliance for Excellent Education. (2013). D*igital learning day: Digital learning definition.* Retrieved March 7, 2013, from http://digitallearningday.org/about-us/digital-learning-definition/

Allington, R. L. (2002). You can't learn much from books you can't read. *Educational Leadership, 60*(3), 16–19.

Almasi, J. F. (1995). The nature of fourth graders' socio-cognitive conflicts in peer-led and teacher-led discussions of literature. *Reading Research Quarterly, 30*(3), 314–351. doi:10.2307/747620.

Altobello, R. (2007). Concentration and contemplation: A lesson in learning to learn. *Journal of Transformative Education, 5*(4), 354–371. doi:10.1177/1541344607312549.

Alvermann, D. E. (2002). *Adolescents and literacies in a digital world.* New York: Peter Lang.

Alvermann, D. E. (2008). Why bother theorizing adolescents' online literacies for classroom practice and research? *Journal of Adolescent & Adult Literacy, 52*(1), 8–19. doi:10.1598/JAAL.52.1.2.

Alvermann, D. E. (2009). Sociocultural constructions of adolescence and young people's literacies. In Christenbury, L., Bomer, R., & Smagorinsky, P. (Eds.), *Handbook of adolescent literacy research* (p. xii). New York: The Guilford Press.

Alvermann, D. E., & Hagood, M. C. (2000). Fandom and critical media literacy. *Journal of Adolescent & Adult Literacy, 43*, 436–446.

Alvermann, D. E., Marshall, J. D., McLean, C. A., Huddleston, A. P., Joaquin, J., & Bishop, J. (2012). Adolescents' web-based literacies, identity construction, and skill development. *Literacy Research and Instruction, 51*(3), 179–195. doi:10.1080/19388071.2010.523135.

Amadieu, F., Tricot, A., & Mariné, C. (2009). Prior knowledge in learning from a non-linear electronic document: Disorientation and coherence of the reading sequences. *Computers in Human Behavior, 25*(2), 381–388. doi:10.1016/j.chb.2008.12.017.

Anderson, J. Q., & Rainie, L. (2008). *The future of the internet III*. Washington, DC: Pew Internet and American Life Project. Retrieved December 15, 2010 from http://www.pewInternet.org/pdfs/PIP_FutureInternet3.pdf

Andrews, R., & Smith, A. (2011). *Developing writers: Teaching and learning in the digital age.* New York: Open University Press.

Appadurai, A. (1996). *Modernity at large: Cultural dimensions of globalization.* Minneapolis, MN: University of Minnesota Press.

Applebee, A. (1993). *Literature in the secondary school: Studies of curriculum and instruction in the United States.* Urbana, IL: National Council of Teachers of English.

Applebee, A. N., & Langer, J. A. (2009). EJ extra: What is happening in the teaching of writing? *English Journal, 98*(5), 18–28.

Applebee, A. N., & Langer, J. A. (2011). A snapshot of writing instruction in middle schools and high schools. *English Journal, 100*(6), 14–27.

Applebee, A. N., Langer, J. A., Nystrand, M., & Gamoran, A. (2003). Discussion-based approaches to developing understanding: Classroom instruction and student performance in middle and high school English. *American Educational Research Journal, 40*(3), 685–730. doi:10.3102/00028312040003685.

Applebee, A., & Langer, J. (2009). What is happening in the teaching of writing? *English Journal, 98*(5), 18–28.

Archer, L., Deweiit, J., Osborne, J., Dillon, J., Willis, B., & Wong, B. (2010). "Doing" science versus "being" a scientist: Examining 10/11-year-old schoolchildren's constructions of science through the lens of identity. *Science Education, 94*, 617–639. doi:10.1002/sce.20399.

Armbruster, B. B., Anderson, T. H., & Ostertag, J. (1989). Teaching text structure to improve reading and writing. *The Reading Teacher, 43*(2), 130–137.

Atwell, N. (1998). *In the middle: New understandings about writing, reading, and learning.* Portsmouth, NH: Boynton/Cook Publishers, Inc..

Autrey, T. M., O'Berry Edington, C., Hicks, T., Kabodian, A., Lerg, N., & Luft-Gardner, R. et al. (2005). More than just a web site: Representing teacher research through digital portfolios. *English Journal, 95*, 65–70.

Au, W. (2011). Teaching under the new Taylorism: High-stakes testing and the standardization of the 21st century curriculum. *Journal of Curriculum Studies, 43*(1), 25–45. doi:10.1080/00220272.2010.521261.

Aydin, S. (2012). A review of research on Facebook as an educational environment. *Educational Technology Research and Development, 60*(6), 1093–1106. doi:10.1007/s11423-012-9260-7.

Azmitia, M. (1988). Peer interaction and problem solving: When are two heads better than one? *Child Development, 59*(1), 87–96. doi:10.2307/1130391.

Baker, E., Rozendal, M., & Whitenack, J. (2000). Audience awareness in a technology-rich elementary classroom. *Journal of Literacy Research, 32*(3), 395–419. doi:10.1080/10862960009548086.

Bakhtin, M. M. (1981). *The dialogic imagination. Four essays by M. M. Bakhtin. (M. Holquist* (Emerson, C., & Holquist, M. (Trans. Eds.)). Austin, TX: University of Texas Press.

Ball, J. (2011). How meditation can give our kids an academic edge. *Huffpost Living.* Retrieved from www.huffingtonpost.com

Barab, S., & Squire, K. (2004). Design-based research: Putting a stake in the ground. *Journal of the Learning Sciences, 13*, 1–14. doi:10.1207/s15327809jls1301_1.

Barbeiro, L. F. (2010). What happens when I write? Pupils' writing about writing. *Reading and Writing, 24*(7), 813–834. doi:10.1007/s11145-010-9226-2.

Baron, N. S. (2008). *Always on: Language in an online and mobile world.* New York, NY: Oxford University Press.

Barrett, H. C. (2007). Researching electronic portfolios and learner engagement: The REFLECT initiative. *Journal of Adolescent & Adult Literacy, 50*, 436–449. doi:10.1598/JAAL.50.6.2.

Barron, B. (2000). Achieving coordination in collaborative problem-solving groups. *Journal of the Learning Sciences, 9*(4), 403–426. doi:10.1207/S15327809JLS0904_2.

Barrouillet, P., & Camos, V. (2007). The time-based resource sharing model of working memory. In Osaka, N., Logie, R. H., & D'Esposito, M. (Eds.), *The cognitive neuroscience of working memory* (pp. 59–80). Oxford, UK: Oxford University Press. doi:10.1093/acprof:oso/9780198570394.003.0004.

Bartholomae, D. (1995). Writing with teachers: A conversation with Peter Elbow. *College Composition and Communication, 46*(1), 62–71. doi:10.2307/358870.

Barton, D. (1994). *Literacy: An introduction to the ecology of written language.* Oxford, UK: Blackwell.

Barton, D. (2001). Literacy in everyday contexts. In Snow, C., & Verhoeven, L. (Eds.), *Literacy and motivation* (pp. 23–37). Mahwah, NJ: Lawrence Erlbaum Associates.

Barton, D., & Hamilton, M. (1998). *Local literacies: Reading and writing in one community.* London: Routledge. doi:10.4324/9780203448885.

Barton, D., Hamilton, M., & Ivanic, R. (Eds.). (2000). *Situated literacies: Reading and writing in context.* London: Routledge.

Beach, R., Campano, G., Edmiston, B., & Borgmann, M. (2010). *Literacy tools in the classroom: Teaching through critical inquiry, grades 5-12.* New York: Teachers College Press/National Writing Project.

Beach, R., Hull, G., & O'Brien, D. (2011). Transforming English language arts in a web 2.0 world. In D. Lapp & D. Fisher (Eds.), Handbook of research on teaching the English language arts (3rd Ed). IRA & NCTE.

Beach, R. (2012). Digital literacies: Constructing digital learning commons in the literacy classroom. *Journal of Adolescent & Adult Literacy, 55*(5), 448–451. doi:10.1002/JAAL.00054.

Beach, R., & Friedrich, T. (2006). Response to writing. In MacArthur, C. A., Graham, S., & Fitzgerald, J. (Eds.), *Handbook of writing research* (pp. 222–234). New York, NY: Guilford Publications.

Beach, R., & Myers, J. (2001). *Inquiry-based English instruction: Engaging students in life and literature.* New York: Teachers College Press.

Beason, L. (1993). Feedback and revision in writing across the curriculum classes. *Research in the Teaching of English, 27,* 395–422.

Beck, I. L., McKeown, M. G., & Kucan, L. (2002). *Bringing words to life: Robust vocabulary instruction.* New York: Guilford Press.

Bélisle, C. (2005). Academic use of online encyclopedias. In P. Kommers & G. Richards (Eds.), *Proceedings of World Conference on Educational Multimedia, Hypermedia and Telecommunications 2005* (pp. 4548-4552). Chesapeake, VA: AACE. Retrieved from http://www.editlib.org/p/20794

Bennett, S., Maton, K., & Kervin, L. (2008). The 'digital natives' debate: A critical review of the evidence. *British Journal of Educational Technology, 39*(5), 775–786. doi:10.1111/j.1467-8535.2007.00793.x.

Benwell, B., & Stokoe, E. (2006). *Discourse and identity.* Edinburgh, UK: Edinburgh University Press.

Bereiter, C., & Scardamalia, M. (1987). *The psychology of written composition.* Hillsdale, NJ: Lawrence Erlbaum Associates.

Berkenkotter, C. (1981). Understanding a writer's awareness of audience. *College Composition and Communication, 32*(4), 388–391. doi:10.2307/356601.

Berninger, V. W., & Richards, T. L. (2002). *Brain literacy for educators and psychologists.* Boston, MA: Academic Press.

Bezemer, J., & Kress, G. (2008). Writing in multimodal texts: A social semiotic account of designs for learning. *Written Communication, 25*(2), 166–195. doi:10.1177/0741088307313177.

Biancarosa, G., & Griffiths, G. G. (2012). Technology tools to support reading in the digital age. *The Future of Children, 22*(2), 139–160. doi:10.1353/foc.2012.0014 PMID:23057135.

Biber, D., & Finegan, E. (1997). Diachronic relations among speech-based and written registers in English. In Nevalainen, T., & Kahlas-Tarkka, L. (Eds.), *To explain the present: Studies in the changing English language in honour of Matti Rissanen* (pp. 253–276). Helsinki: Société Néophilologique.

Biggs, J. B., & Tang, C. (2011). *Teaching for quality learning at university*. Maidenhead, UK: McGraw-Hill Education.

Bintz, W. P. (2012). Using parody to read and write original poetry. *English Journal, 101*(5), 72–79.

Birkerts, S. (1994). *The Gutenberg elegies: The fate of reading in an electronic age*. Boston: Faber & Faber.

Black, R. W. (2005). Online fanfiction: What technology and popular culture can teach us about writing and literacy instruction. *New Horizons for Learning Online Journal, 11*(2).

Blackburn, M., & Clark, C. (Eds.). (2007). *Literacy research for political action and social change*. New York: Peter Lang Publishing, Inc..

Blackmon, S. (2007). (Cyber)conspiracy theories? African-American students in the computerized writing environment. In P. Takayoshi & P. Sullivan's (Eds.), Labor, writing technologies, and the shaping of composition in the academy: New directions in computers and composition (pp. 153-166). New York: Hampton Press.

Black, P., & Wiliam, D. (1998). Assessment and classroom learning. *Assessment in Education, 5*(1), 7–74. doi:10.1080/0969595980050102.

Black, P., & Wiliam, D. (2009). Developing the theory of formative assessment. *Educational Assessment, Evaluation and Accountability, 21*(1), 5–31. doi:10.1007/s11092-008-9068-5.

Black, R. (2008). *Adolescents and online fan fiction*. New York: Peter Lang.

Black, R. (2009). Online fan fiction, global identities, and imagination. *Research in the Teaching of English, 43*(4), 397–425.

Black, R. W. (2005). Access and affiliation: The literacy and composition practices of English-language learners in an online fanfiction community. *Journal of Adolescent & Adult Literacy, 49*(2), 118–128. doi:10.1598/JAAL.49.2.4.

Black, R. W. (2006). Language, culture, and identity in online fanfiction. *E-learning, 3*(2), 170–184. doi:10.2304/elea.2006.3.2.170.

Black, R. W. (2009). Online fanfiction, global identities, and imagination. *Research in the Teaching of English, 43*(4), 397–425.

Blau, S. (1983). Invisible writing: Investigating cognitive processes in composition. *College Composition and Communication, 34*(3), 297–312. doi:10.2307/358261.

Bleha, T. (2005). *Down to the wire*. Retrieved September 25, 2012, from http://www.foreignaffairs. org/20050501 faessay84311–p0/thomas-bleha/down-to-the-wire.htm

Bloch, J. (2007). Abdullah's blogging: A generation 1.5 student enters the blogosphere. *Language Learning & Technology, 11*(2), 128–141.

Blommaert, J. (2005). *Discourse: A critical introduction*. Cambridge, UK: Cambridge University Press. doi:10.1017/CBO9780511610295.

Bloome, D. (1985). Reading as a social process. *Language Arts, 62*(2), 134–142.

Bogdan, R., & Biklen, S. (1992). *Qualitative research for education: An introduction to theories and methods* (2nd ed.). Boston: Allyn and Bacon.

Bogdan, R., & Biklen, S. (2006). *Qualitative research for education: An introduction to theory and methods* (5th ed.). Boston: Allyn & Bacon.

Bogdan, R., & Biklen, S. K. (2007). *Qualitative research for education: An introduction to theories and methods* (5th ed.). Boston, MA: Pearson.

Boling, E., Castek, J., Zawilinski, L., Barton, K., & Nierlich, T. (2008). Collaborative literacy: Blogs and internet projects. *The Reading Teacher, 61*, 504–506. doi:10.1598/RT.61.6.10.

Bomer, R., & Bomer, K. (2001). *For a better world: Reading and writing for social action*. Portsmouth, NH: Heinemann.

Bomer, R., & Laman, T. (2004). Positioning in a primary writing workshop: Joint action in the discursive production of writing subjects. *Research in the Teaching of English, 38*(4), 420–466.

Booth, D. (2006). *Reading doesn't matter anymore: Shattering the myths of literacy*. Portland, ME: Stenhouse.

Boscolo, P., Ariasi, N., Del Favero, L., & Ballarin, C. (2011). Interest in an expository text: How does it flow from reading to writing? *Learning and Instruction, 21*, 467–480. doi:10.1016/j.learninstruc.2010.07.009.

Bovée, C., & Thill, J. (2009). *Business essentials* (4th ed.). Hoboken, NJ: Prentice Hall.

Bowers-Campbell, J. (2011). Take it out of class: Exploring virtual literature circles. *Journal of Adolescent & Adult Literacy, 54*(8), 557–567. doi:10.1598/JAAL.54.8.1.

Boyatzis, R. E. (1998). *Transforming qualitative information: Thematic analysis and code development*. Thousand Oaks, CA: Sage Publications.

Boyne, J. (2006). *The boy in the striped pajamas*. London: David Fickling Books.

Braaksma, M., Rijlaarsdam, G., van den Bergh, H., & van Hout-Wolters, B. (2004). Observational learning and its effects on the orchestration of writing processes. *Cognition and Instruction, 22*, 1–36. doi:10.1207/s1532690Xci2201_1.

Braasch, J. L. G., Lawless, K. A., Goldman, S. R., Manning, F. H., Gomez, K. W., & MacLeod, S. M. (2009). Evaluating search results: An empirical analysis of middle school students' use of source attributes to select useful sources. *Journal of Educational Computing Research, 41*(1), 63–82. doi:10.2190/EC.41.1.c.

Bradley, B. A., & Reinking, D. (2011). Revisiting the connection between research and practice using design research and formative experiments. In Duke, N., & Mallette, M. (Eds.), *Literacy research methodologies* (2nd ed., pp. 188–212). New York: Guilford Press.

Bradley, M. E., Thom, L. R., Hayes, J., & Hay, C. (2008). Ask and you will receive: How question type influences quantity and quality of online discussions. *British Journal of Educational Technology, 39*(5), 888–900. doi:10.1111/j.1467-8535.2007.00804.x.

Brammer, C., & Rees, M. (2007). Peer review from the students' perspective: Invaluable of invalid? *Composition Studies, 35*(2), 71–85.

Bransford, J., Brown, A., & Cocking, R. (2000). *How people learn: Brain, mind, experience, and school*. Washington, DC: National Academy Press.

Bråten, I., & Helge, I. S. (2010). When law students read multiple documents about global warming: Examining the role of topic-specific beliefs about the nature of knowledge and knowing. *Instructional Science, 38*(6), 635-657. doi: http://dx.doi.org/10.1007/s11251-008-9091-4

Breetvelt, I., van den Bergh, H., & Rijlaarsdam, G. (1994). Relations between writing processes and text quality: When and how? *Cognition and Instruction, 12*, 103–123. doi:10.1207/s1532690xci1202_2.

Brem, S. K., Russell, J., & Weems, L. (2001). Science on the web: Student evaluations of scientific arguments. *Discourse Processes, 32*(2&3), 191–213. doi: doi:10.1080/0163853X.2001.9651598.

Brenner, J. (2012). *Pew internet: Social networking (full detail)*. Retrieved from http://pewInternet.org/Commentary/2012/March/Pew-Internet-Social-Networking-full-detail.aspx

Brick, B., & Holmes, J. (2008). Using screen capture software for student feedback: Towards a methodology. In *Proceedings of the IADIS International Conference on Cognition & Exploratory Learning In Digital Age*, (p. 339). IADIS.

Britsch, S. (2005). But what did they learn? Clearing third spaces in virtual dialogues with children. *Journal of Early Childhood Literacy, 5*(2), 99–130. doi:10.1177/1468798405054581.

Britton, J. (1969/1990). *Language, the learner, and the school* (4th ed.). Portsmouth, NH: Boynton-Cook.

Britton, J. (1970). *Language and learning*. New York: Penguin.

Britton, J. (1972). *Writing to learn and learning to write*. Washington, DC: National Council of Teachers of English.

Brofenbrenner, U., & Evans, G. W. (2000). Developmental science in the 21st century: Emerging questions, theoretical models, research designs, and empirical findings. *Social Development, 9*, 115–125. doi:10.1111/1467-9507.00114.

Brophy, J. (1981). Teacher praise: A functional analysis. *Review of Educational Research*, (1): 5. doi:10.3102/00346543051001005.

Brown, A. L. (1992). Design experiments: Theoretical and methodological challenges in creating complex programs in classroom settings. *Journal of the Learning Sciences*, *2*(2), 141–178. doi:10.1207/s15327809jls0202_2.

Brown, H. D. (1987). *Principles of language learning and teaching*. New York: Longman.

Brown, J., Collins, A., & Duguid, P. (1989). Situated cognition and the culture of learning. *Education Researcher*, *18*(1), 32–42. doi:10.3102/0013189X018001032.

Bruce, D. L. (2009). Writing with visual images: Examining the video composition processes of high school students. *Research in the Teaching of English*, *43*(4), 426–450.

Bruffee, K. A. (1985). *A short course in writing: Practical rhetoric for teaching composition through collaborative learning* (3rd ed.). Boston: Little.

Brummett, B. (2010). *Techniques of close reading*. Thousand Oaks, CA: Sage.

Bruner, J. (1962). Introduction to L. S. Vygotsky. In Hanfmann, E., & Vakar, G. (Trans. Eds.) *Thought and language* (pp. v–x). Cambridge, MA: MIT Press.

Bruner, J. (1986). *Actual minds, possible worlds*. Cambridge, MA: Harvard University Press.

Bruning, R., & Horn, C. (2000). Developing motivation to write. *Educational Psychologist*, *35*, 25–37. doi:10.1207/S15326985EP3501_4.

Bryant, K. (2004). *For me, for my mother, and for those who keep secrets. As I roc the mic* (pp. 43–46). Indianapolis, IN: Xlibris Corporation.

Bryant, K., & McKee, J. (Eds.). (2010). *Power to the pen: Finding agency through argument*. Boston: Bedford/St. Martin's.

Buchanan, M. (2002). *Nexus: Small worlds and the groundbreaking science of networks*. New York: W. W. Norton and Company.

Burstein, J., Chodorow, M., & Leacock, C. (2004). Automated essay evaluation: The criterion online writing system. *AI Magazine*, *25*, 27–36.

Butler, J. (1990). *Gender trouble: Feminism and the subservion of identity*. New York: Routledge.

Cahill, K., & Chalut, R. (2009). Optimal results: What libraries need to know about Google and search engine optimization. *The Reference Librarian*, *50*(3), 234–247. doi:10.1080/02763870902961969.

Calkins, L. M. C. (1986). *The art of teaching writing*. Portsmouth, NH: Heinemann.

Calvo, P., & Gomila, A. (Eds.). (2008). *Handbook of cognitive science: An embodied approach*. Amsterdam: Elsevier.

Campano, G. (2007). *Immigrant students and literacy: Reading, writing, and remembering*. New York: Teachers College Press.

Carey, L., Flower, L., Hayes, J., Schriver, K., & Haas, C. (1989). *Differences in writers' initial task representations*. Pittsburgh, PA: Carnegie-Mellon University.

Carico, K. M., Logan, D., & Labbo, L. D. (2004). A generation in cyberspace: Engaging readers through online discussions. *Language Arts*, *81*(4), 293–302.

Carmichael, S., & Alden, P. (2006). The advantages of using electronic processes for commenting on and exchanging the written work of students with learning disabilities and/or AD/HD. *Composition Studies*, *34*(2), 43–57.

Carpenter, S., Pashler, H., Wixted, J., & Vul, E. (2008). The effects of tests on learning and forgetting. *Memory & Cognition*, *36*, 438–448. doi:10.3758/MC.36.2.438 PMID:18426072.

Carr, N. (2008). Is Google making us stupid? What the Internet is doing to our brains. *The Atlantic*. Retrieved from http://www.theatlantic.com

Carrington, V., & Robinson, M. (2009). Introduction: Contentious technologies. In Carrington, V., & Robinson, M. (Eds.), *Digital literacies: Social learning and classroom practices* (pp. 1–9). London: Sage Publications.

Carvalho, J. (2002). Developing audience awareness in writing. *Journal of Research in Reading, 25*(3), 271–282. doi:10.1111/1467-9817.00175.

Castek, J. (2008). *How do 4th and 5th grade students acquire the new literacies of online reading comprehension? Exploring the contexts that facilitate learning.* (Unpublished doctoral dissertation). University of Connecticut, New Haven, CT.

Castek, J., Leu, D. J. Jr, Coiro, J., Gort, M., Henry, L. A., & Lima, C. (2007). Developing new literacies among multilingual learners in the elementary grades. In Parker, L. (Ed.), *Technology-mediated learning environments for young English learners: Connections In and out of school* (pp. 111–153). Mahwah, NJ: Lawrence Erlbaum Associates.

Cazden, C. (1988). *Classroom discourse: The language of teaching and learning.* Portsmouth, NH: Heinemann.

Cazden, C. B. (1986). Classroom discourse. In Wittrock, M. C. (Ed.), *Handbook of research on teaching* (3rd ed., pp. 432–463). New York: Macmillan.

Cazden, C. B. (1997). Foreword. In Paratore, J. R., & McCormack, R. L. (Eds.), *Peer talk in the classroom: Learning from research* (p. v). Newark, DE: International Reading Association.

Cazden, C. B. (2001). *Discourse: The language of teaching and learning.* Portsmouth, NH: Heinemann.

Chafe, W. L. (1980). The deployment of consciousness in the production of a narrative. In Chafe, W. L. (Ed.), *The pear stories: Cognitive, cultural, and linguistic aspects of narrative production.* Norwood, NY: Ablex Publishing Corporation.

Chafe, W., & Tannen, D. (1987). The relation between written and spoken language. *Annual Review of Anthropology*, 383–407. doi:10.1146/annurev.an.16.100187.002123.

Chall, J. S. (1996). *Stages of reading development.* Fort Worth, TX: Harcourt Brace.

Chandler, D. (1995). *The act of writing: A media theory approach.* (Doctoral dissertation). University of Wales, Wales, UK. Retrieved from http://www.aber.ac.uk/media/Documents/act/act.html

Chang, M.-W., Ratinov, L., & Roth, D. (2007). Guiding semi-supervision with constraint driven learning. In *Proceedings of the Annual Meeting of the Association of Computational Linguistics,* (pp. 280-287). Retrieved from http://acl.ldc.upenn.edu/P/P07/P07-1036.pdf

Chang, H.-H. (2004). Understanding computerized adaptive testing: From Robbins-Monro to Lord and beyond. In Kaplan, D. (Ed.), *The SAGE handbook of quantitative methodology for the social sciences* (pp. 117–133). London: Sage Publications. doi:10.4135/9781412986311.n7.

Chapelle, C. A. (2003). *English language learning and technology: Lectures on applied linguistics in the age of information and communication technology.* Amsterdam: John Benjamins Pub..

Chapman, M. (2006). Research in writing, preschool through elementary, 1983-2003. *L1 Educational Studies in Language and Literature, 6*(2), 7-27.

Charmaz, K. (2003). Qualitative interviewing and grounded theory analysis. In Holstein, J. A., & Gubrium, J. F. (Eds.), *Inside interviewing: New lenses, new concerns* (pp. 311–330). Thousand Oaks, CA: Sage Publications.

Charmaz, K. (2006). *Constructing grounded theory: A practice guide through qualitative analysis.* London: Sage.

Charsky, D. (2010). From edutainment to serious games: A change in the use of game characteristics. *Games and Culture, 5*(2), 177–198. doi:10.1177/1555412009354727.

Chawkin, K. (2012). *Meditation in the classroom: An antidote to stress.* Retrieved from http://www.nestress-freeschool.org

Chen, C.-F. E., & Cheng, W.-Y. E. (2008). Beyond the design of automated writing evaluation: Pedagogical practices and perceived learning effectiveness In EFL writing classes. *Language Learning & Technology, 12*(3), 94–112.

Cherny, L. (1999). *Conversation and community: Chat in a virtual world.* Stanford, CA: CSLI Publications.

Cheville, J. (2004). Automated scoring technologies and the rising influence of error. *English Journal, 93*(4), 47–52. doi:10.2307/4128980.

Chiappe, P., Glaeser, B., & Ferko, D. (2007). Speech perception, vocabulary, and the development of reading skills in English among Korean-and English-speaking children. *Journal of Educational Psychology, 99*(1), 154–166. doi:10.1037/0022-0663.99.1.154.

Cho, K., & MacArthur, C. (2010). Student revision with peer and expert reviewing. *Learning and Instruction, 20,* 328–338. doi:10.1016/j.learninstruc.2009.08.006.

Cho, K., & Schunn, C. D. (2007). Scaffolding writing and rewriting in the discipline. *Computers & Education, 48,* 409–426. doi:10.1016/j.compedu.2005.02.004.

Cho, K., Schunn, C. D., & Charney, D. (2006). Commenting on writing: Typology and perceived helpfulness of comments from novice peer reviewers and subject matter experts. *Written Communication, 23,* 260–294. doi:10.1177/0741088306289261.

Chomsky, N. (1970). Reading, writing, and phonology. *Harvard Educational Review, 40*(2), 287–309.

Chow, P., & Cummins, J. (2003). Valuing multilingual and multicultural approaches to learning. In *Multilingual education in practice: Using diversity as a resource* (pp. 32–61). Academic Press.

Christenbury, L., Bomer, R., & Smagorinsky, P. (2009). Introduction. In Christenbury, L., Bomer, R., & Smagorinsky, P. (Eds.), *Handbook of adolescent literacy research* (pp. 3–13). New York: The Guilford Press.

Christensen, L. (2009). *Teaching for joy and justice: Reimagining the language arts classroom.* Milwaukee, WI: Rethinking Schools, Ltd..

Christianakis, M. (2010). I don't need your help! Peer status, race, and gender during peer writing interactions. *Journal of Literacy Research, 42*(4), 418–458. doi:10.1080/1086296X.2010.525202.

Chun, D. M. (1994). Using computer networking to facilitate the acquisition of interactive competence. *System, 22*(1), 17–31. doi:10.1016/0346-251X(94)90037-X.

Chuo, T.-W. (2007). The effects of the WebQuest writing instruction program on EFL learners' writing performance, writing apprehension, and perception. *TESL-EJ, 11*(3).

Cisneros, S. (1984). *The house on mango street.* New York: Random House, Inc..

Clark, I. (2003). Process. In I. Clark's (Ed.), Concepts in composition: Theories and practice in the teaching of writing (pp. 1-29). Hoboken, NJ: Lawrence Erlbaum Associates.

Clarke, M. (2009). The discursive construction of interpersonal relations in an online community of practice. *Journal of Pragmatics, 41*(11), 2333–2344. doi:10.1016/j.pragma.2009.04.001.

Clark, R. (1983). Reconsidering research on learning from media. *Review of Educational Research, 53,* 445–459. doi:10.3102/00346543053004445.

Classen, C. (2012). *The deepest sense: A cultural history of touch.* Urbana, IL: University of Illinois Press.

Cochran-Smith, M., & Lytle, S. L. (2009). *Inquiry as stance: Practitioner research in the next generation.* New York: Teachers College Press.

Cohen, M., & Riel, M. (1989). The effect of distal audiences on students' writing. *American Educational Research Journal, 26,* 143–159. doi:10.3102/00028312026002143.

Coiro, J., & Dobler, E. (2007). Exploring the online reading comprehension strategies used by sixth-grade skilled readers to search for and locate information on the internet. *Reading Research Quarterly, 42,* 214–257. doi:10.1598/RRQ.42.2.2.

Coiro, J., Knobel, M., Lankshear, C., & Leu, D. (2008). Central issues in new literacies and new literacies research. In Coiro, J., Knobel, M., Lankshear, C., & Leu, D. (Eds.), *Handbook of research on new literacies* (pp. 1–21). New York, NY: Taylor & Francis Group.

Coiro, J., Knobel, M., Lankshear, C., & Leu, D. (Eds.). (2008). *Handbook of research on new literacies.* Mahwah, NJ: Lawrence Erlbaum Associates.

Coker, D., & Lewis, W. E. (2008). Beyond writing next: A discussion of writing research and instructional uncertainty. *Harvard Educational Review, 78*(1), 231–250.

Collins, A., & Gentner, D. (1980). A framework for a cognitive theory of writing. *Cognitive Processes in Writing,* 51-72.

Collins, A. (1991). Cognitive apprenticeship and instructional technology. In Idol, L., & Jones, B. F. (Eds.), *Educational values and cognitive instruction: Implication for reform* (pp. 121–138). Hillsdale, NJ: Lawrence Erlbaum Associates.

Collins, A., & Brown, J. S. (1988). The computer as a tool for learning through reflection. In Mandl, H., & Lesgold, A. (Eds.), *Learning issues for intelligent tutoring systems* (pp. 1–18). New York: Springer-Verlag. doi:10.1007/978-1-4684-6350-7_1.

Collins, A., Brown, J. S., & Holum, A. (1991). Cognitive apprenticeship: Making thinking visible. *American Educator, 15*(3), 6–11, 38–46.

Collins, A., Brown, J. S., & Newman, S. E. (1989). Cognitive apprenticeship: Teaching the craft of reading, writing, and mathematics. In Resnick, L. B. (Ed.), *Knowing, learning, and instruction: Essays in honor of Robert Glaser* (pp. 453–494). Hillsdale, NJ: Lawrence Erlbaum Associates.

Collins, A., & Halverson, R. (2009). *Rethinking education in the age of technology: The digital revolution and schooling in America*. New York: Teachers College Press.

Comer, D. K., & Hammer, B. (2008). *Surveying the efficacy of digital response: Pedagogical imperatives, faculty approaches, and student feedback*. Academic Press.

Common Core State Standards Initiative. (2010). Common core state standards for English language arts & literacy in history/social studies, science, and technical subjects. Washington, DC: National Governors Association Center for Best Practices and the Council of Chief State School Officers. Retrieved from www.corestandards.org/assets/CCSSI_ELA%20Standards.pdf

Cook-Sather, A. (2002). Authorizing students' perspectives: Toward trust, dialogue, and change in education. *Educational Researcher, 31*(4), 3–14. doi:10.3102/0013189X031004003.

Cope, B., & Alantzis, M. (2009b). Ubiquitous learning: An agenda for educational transformation. In Cope, B., & Kalantzis, M. (Eds.), *Ubiquitous learning*. Champaign, IL: University of Illinois Press.

Cope, B., & Kalantzis, M. (1993). *The powers of literacy: A genre approach to teaching writing*. Pittsburg, PA: University of Pittsburgh Press.

Cope, B., & Kalantzis, M. (2000). *Multiliteracies: literacy learning and the design of social futures*. London: Routledge.

Cope, B., & Kalantzis, M. (2009a). Multiliteracies: New literacies, new learning. *Pedagogies: An International Journal, 4*, 164–195.

Cope, B., & Kalantzis, M. (2010). New media, new learning. In Cole, D. R., & Pulllen, D. L. (Eds.), *Multiliteracies in motion: Current theory and practice*. New York, NY: Routledge.

Cope, B., & Kalantzis, M. (Eds.). (2000). *Multiliteracies*. London: Routledge.

Cope, B., Kalantzis, M., & Magee, L. (2011). *Towards a semantic web: Connecting knowledge in academic research*. Cambridge, UK: Woodhead Publishing. doi:10.1533/9781780631745.

Cope, B., Kalantzis, M., McCarthey, S., Vojak, C., & Kline, S. (2011). Technology-mediated writing assessments: Principles and processes. *Computers and Composition, 28*, 29–96. doi:10.1016/j.compcom.2011.04.007.

Corbin, J. M., & Strauss, A. L. (2008). *Basics of qualitative research: Techniques and procedures for developing grounded theory*. Thousand Oaks, CA: Sage.

Corden, R. (2007). Developing reading and writing connections: The impact of explicit instruction of literary devices on the quality of children's narrative writing. *Journal of Research in Childhood Education, 21*(3), 269–289. doi:10.1080/02568540709594594.

Corrigan, J. (2010). Improving writing with wiki discussion forums. *Principal Leadership, 11*(3), 44–47.

Coxhead, A. (2000). A new academic word list. *TESOL Quarterly, 34*(2), 213–238. doi:10.2307/3587951.

Crank, V. (2002). Asynchronous electronic peer response in a hybrid basic writing classroom. *Teaching English in the Two-Year College, 30*(2), 146–155.

Creme, P., & Lea, M. (2007). *Writing at university*. Maidenhead, UK: McGraw-Hill Education.

Creswell, J. (2003). *Research design: Qualitative, quantitative, and mixed methods approaches* (2nd ed.). New York: Sage Publications.

Creswell, J. W. (2007). *Research design: Qualitative, quantitative, and mixed methods approaches* (3rd ed.). Thousand Oaks, CA: Sage.

Crystal, D. (2001). *Language and the internet.* New York, NY: Cambridge University Press. doi:10.1017/CBO9781139164771.

Crystal, D. (2008). *Txtng: The gr8 db8.* New York, NY: Oxford University Press.

Csikszentmihalyi, M. (1990). *Flow: The psychology of optimal experience.* New York: Harper & Row.

Cuban, L. (2001). *Oversold and underused: Computers in the classroom.* Cambridge, MA: Harvard University Press.

Cuban, L., Kirkpatrick, H., & Peck, C. (2001). High access and low use of technologies in high school classrooms: Explaining an apparent paradox. *American Educational Research Journal, 38*(4), 813–834. doi:10.3102/00028312038004813.

Cummins, J. (2008). Technology, literacy, and young second language learners: Designing educational futures. In Parker, L. L. (Ed.), *Technology-mediated learning environments for young English learners: Connections in and out of school* (pp. 61–98). New York: Lawrence Erlbaum Associates.

Cummins, J., Brown, K., & Sayers, D. (2007). *Literacy, technology, and diversity: Teaching for success in changing times.* Boston, MA: Allyn and Bacon.

Cummins, J., & Sayers, D. (1995). *Brave new schools: Challenging cultural illiteracy through global learning networks.* New York: St. Martin's Press.

Cunningham, A. E., & Stanovich, K. E. (1990). Early spelling acquisition: Writing beats the computer. *Journal of Educational Psychology, 82,* 159–162. doi:10.1037/0022-0663.82.1.159.

Curwood, J. H. (2011). iPoetry: Creating space for new literacies in the English curriculum. *Journal of Adolescent & Adult Literacy, 55*(2), 110–120. doi:10.1002/JAAL.00014.

Curwood, J. S. (2013a). *The Hunger Games*: Literature, literacy, and online affinity spaces. *Language Arts, 90*(6), 417-427.

Curwood, J. S. (2013b). Fan fiction, remix culture, and *The Potter Games.* In Frankel, V. E. (Ed.), *Teaching with Harry Potter* (pp. 81–92). Jefferson, NC: McFarland.

Curwood, J. S., Magnifico, A. M., & Lammers, J. C. (2013). Writing in the wild: Writers' motivation in fan-based affinity spaces. *Journal of Adolescent & Adult Literacy, 56*(8), 677-685. doi:10.1002/JAAL.192.

Cutler, L., & Graham, S. (2008). Primary grade writing instruction: A national survey. *Journal of Educational Psychology, 100,* 907–919. doi:10.1037/a0012656.

Cynthia, L. S. (n.d). Three voices on literacy, technology, and humanistic perspective. *Computers and Composition,* (pp. 12309-310). doi:10.1016/S8755-4615(05)80069-6

Daiute, C. (1986). Physical and cognitive factors in revising: Insights from studies with computers. *Research in the Teaching of English, 20,* 141–159.

Daiute, C. (2000). Writing and communication technologies. In Indrisano, R., & Squire, J. R. (Eds.), *Perspectives on writing: Research, theory, and practice* (pp. 251–276). Newark, DE: International Reading Association.

Daiute, C., & Dalton, B. (1993). Collaboration between children learning to write: Can novices be masters? *Cognition and Instruction, 10*(4), 281–333. doi:10.1207/s1532690xci1004_1.

Dalton, B., & Proctor, C. P. (2008). The changing landscape of text and comprehension in the age of the new literacies. In Coiro, J., Knobel, M., Lankshear, C., & Leu, D. J. (Eds.), *Handbook of research on new literacies* (pp. 297–324). Mahwah, NJ: Lawrence Erlbaum Associates.

Daniels, H. (2002). *Literature circles: Voice and choice in book clubs and reading groups* (2nd ed.). Portland, ME: Stenhouse.

Danticat, E. (2010). *Create dangerously: The immigrant artist at work.* New York: Vintage Books.

Darling-Hammond, L. (2010). *The flat world and education: How America's commitment to equity will determine our future.* New York: Teachers College Press.

Davidson, C. N., & Goldberg, D. T. (2009). *The future of learning institutions in a digital age.* Cambridge, MA: MIT Press.

Davies, J., & Merchant, G. (2007). Looking from the inside out: Academic blogging as new literacy. In Lankshear, C., & Knobel, M. (Eds.), *A new literacies sampler* (pp. 167–197). New York: Peter Lang.

Davis, A. (2005). Co-authoring identity: Digital storytelling in an urban middle school. *Technology Humanities Education Narrative, 1.* Retrieved from http://thenjournal.org/feature/61/

Davis, B. H., & Brewer, J. (1997). *Electronic discourse: Linguistic individuals in virtual space.* Albany, NY: State University of New York Press.

de la Paz, S., & Graham, S. (2002). Explicitly teaching strategies, skills, and knowledge: Writing instruction in middle school classrooms. *Journal of Educational Psychology, 94,* 687–698. doi:10.1037/0022-0663.94.4.687.

de la Piedra, M. T. (2010). Adolescent worlds and literacy practices on the United States-Mexico border. *Journal of Adolescent & Adult Literacy, 53*(7), 575–584. doi:10.1598/JAAL.53.7.5.

Dean, D. (2006). *Strategic writing: The writing process and beyond in the secondary English classroom.* Urbana, IL: NCTE.

Deane, P., Odendahl, N., Quinlan, T., Fowles, M., Welsh, C., & Bivens-Tatum, J. (2008). *Cognitive models of writing: writing proficiency as a complex integrated skill* (Research Report No. RR-08-55). Princeton, NJ: Educational Testing Service.

Degenhardt, M. (2006). Camtasia and catmovie: Two digital tools for observing, documenting and analyzing writing processes of university students. In Van Waes Luuk, L. Mariëlle, & M. Neuwirth (Eds.), Writing and digital media: Studies in writing (pp. 180–186). Amsterdam: Elsevier.

Delpit, L. D. (1998). The silenced dialogue: Power and pedagogy in educaitng other people's children. *Harvard Educational Review, 58*(3), 280–298.

Delpit, L., & Dowdy, J. K. (Eds.). (2002/2008). *The skin that we speak.* New York: New Press.

Deng, L., & Yuen, A. (2011). Towards a framework for educational affordances of blogs. *Computers & Education, 56*(2), 441–451. doi:10.1016/j.compedu.2010.09.005.

Dennes, V. P. (2005). From message posting to learning dialogues: Factors affecting learner participation in asynchronous discussion. *Distance Education, 26*(1), 127–148. doi:10.1080/01587910500081376.

Denton, D. (2012). Improving the quality of evidence-based writing entries in electronic portfolios. *International Journal of ePortfolio, 2,* 187-197. Retrieved from http://www.theijep.com/pdf/IJEP76.pdf

Deoksoon, K. (2011). Incorporating podcasting and blogging into a core task for ESOL teacher candidates. *Computers & Education, 56*(1), 632–641.

DePew, K. E. (2011). Social media at academia's periphery: Studying multilingual developmental writers' Facebook composing strategies. *Reading Matrix: An International Online Journal, 11*(1), 54–75.

Design-Based Research Collective. (2003). Design-based research: An emerging paradigm for educational inquiry. *Educational Researcher, 32*(1), 5–8. doi:10.3102/0013189X032001005.

DiCamillo, K. (2006). *The miraculous journey of Edward Tulane.* Somerville, MA: Candlewick Press.

Dilthey, W. (1977). *Descriptive psychology and historical understanding* (Zaner, R. M., & Heiges, K. L., Trans.). The Hague, The Netherlands: Nijhoff. (Original work published 1911).

Dipardo, A. (1996). Stimulated recall in research writing: An antidote to I don't know, it was fine. In Smagorinsky, P. (Ed.), *Speaking about writing: Reflections on research methodology* (pp. 163–181). Thousand Oaks, CA: Sage Publications.

Dixon, J., & Durrheim, K. (2000). Displacing place-identity: A discursive approach to locating self and other. *The British Journal of Social Psychology, 39*(1), 27–44. doi:10.1348/014466600164318 PMID:10774526.

Dodge, A. M., Husain, N., & Duke, N. K. (2011). Connected kids? K-2 children's use and understanding of the internet. *Language Arts, 89*(2), 86–98.

Dondlinger, M. (2007). Educational video game design: a review of the literature. *Journal of Applied Educational Technology, 4*, 21–31.

Doneman, M. (1997). Multimediating. In Lankshear, C., Bigum, C., & Durant, C. (Eds.), *Digital Rhetorics: Literacies and technologies in education–current practices and future directions* (*Vol. 3*, pp. 131–148). Brisbane, Australia: QUT/DEETYA.

Downes, J. M., & Bishop, P. (2012). Educators engage digital natives and learn from their experiences with technology. *Middle School Journal, 43*(5), 6–15.

Downes, S. (2004). Educational blogging. *EDUCAUSE Review, 39*(5), 14–21. Retrieved from http://www.educause.edu/pub/er/erm04/erm0450.asp.

Dredger, K., Woods, D., Beach, C., & Sagstetter, V. (2010). Engage me: Using new literacies to create third space classrooms that engage student writers. *Journal of Media Literacy Education, 2*(2), 85–101.

Duke, N. K., & Pearson, P. D. (2008). Effective practices for developing reading comprehension. *Journal of education, 189*(1), 107.

Duncum, P. (2004). Visual culture isn't just visual: Multiliteracy, multimodality and meaning. *Studies in Art Education*, 252–264.

Dwyer, B. (2010). *Scaffolding internet reading: A study of a disadvantaged school community in Ireland.* (Unpublished doctoral dissertation). University of Nottingham, Nottingham, UK.

Dwyer, B. (2012). *Reading today: Election statement for the international reading association board of directors.* Retrieved February 20, 2013 from http://www.reading.org/General/Publications/blog/BlogSinglePost/reading-today-online/2012/11/19/candidates-for-the-2013-ira-board-election

Dwyer, B. (2013). Developing online reading comprehension: Changes, challenges and consequences. In Hall, K., Cremin, T., Comber, B., & Moll, L. (Eds.), *International handbook of research in children's literacy, learning and culture.* London: Wiley-Blackwell. doi:10.1002/9781118323342.ch25.

Dymock, S. (2005). Teaching expository text structure awareness. *The Reading Teacher, 59*, 177–182. doi:10.1598/RT.59.2.7.

Dymoke, S., & Hughes, J. (2009). Using a poetry wiki: How can the medium support pre-service teachers of English in their professional learning about writing poetry and teaching poetry writing in a digital age? *English Teaching: Practice and Critique, 8*(3), 91–106.

Dyson, A. H. (2006). On saying it right (write), Fix-its in the foundations of learning to write. *Research in the Teaching of English, 41*(1), 8–42.

Dyson, A. H., & Genishi, C. (2005). *On the case: Approaches to language and literacy research.* New York: Teachers College Press.

Dyson, A., & Genishi, C. (2005). *On the case: Approaches to language and literacy research.* New York, NY: Teachers College Press.

Dysthe, O. (1996). The multivoiced classroom: Interactions of writing and classroom discourse. *Written Communication, 13*(3), 385–425. doi:10.1177/0741088396013003004.

Eades, C. (2002). A working model of pedagogical triangulation: A holistic approach to peer-revision workshops. *Teaching English in the Two-Year College, 30*(1), 60–67.

Ede, L., & Lunsford, A. (1984). Audience addressed/audience invoked: The role of audience in composition theory and pedagogy. *College Composition and Communication, 35*(2), 155–171. doi:10.2307/358093.

Efimova, L., & de Moor, A. (2005). Beyond personal webpublishing: An exploratory study of conversational blogging practices. In *Proceedings of the Hawaii International Conference on System Sciences* (HICSS-38). Manoa, Australia: IEEE Computer Society Press. Retrieved from http://blog.mathemagenic.com/2004/09/15.html#a1353

Elbow, P. (1973). *Writing without teachers.* New York: Oxford University Press.

Elbow, P. (1981). *Writing with power: Techniques for mastering the writing process.* New York: Oxford University Press.

Elbow, P. (1987). Closing my eyes as I speak: An argument for ignoring audience. *College English*, *49*(1), 50–69. doi:10.2307/377789.

Elder, C., Knoch, U., Barkhuizen, G., & von Randow, J. (2005). Individual feedback to enhance rater training: Does it work? *Language Assessment Quarterly*, *2*, 175–196. doi:10.1207/s15434311laq0203_1.

Eldred, J. C., & Fortune, R. (1992). Exploring the implications of metaphors for computer networks and hypermedia. In Hawisher, G. E., & LeBlanc, P. (Eds.), *Re-imagining computers and composition: Teaching and research in the virtual age* (pp. 58–73). Portsmouth, NH: Boyton.

Elliot, S. M., & Mikulas, C. (2004). *The impact of MY Access!TM use on student writing performance: A technology overview and four studies.* Paper presented at the Annual Meeting of the American Educational Research Association. San Diego, CA.

Ellis, M. J. (2011). Peer feedback on writing: Is on-line actually better than on-paper? *Journal of Academic Language & Learning*, *5*(1), 88–99.

Emig, J. (1971). *The composing processes of twelfth graders.* Urbana, IL: National Council of Teachers of English.

Emig, J. (2001). Embodied learning. *English Education*, *33*(4), 271–280.

Enhancing Education Through Technology Act. (2001). Retrieved from http://www2.ed.gov/policy/elsec/leg/esea02/pg34.html

Epstein, M. L., Lazarus, A. D., Calvano, T. B., Matthews, K. A., Hendel, R. A., Epstein, B. B., & Brosvic, G. M. (2002). Immediate feedback assessment technique promotes learning and corrects inaccurate first responses. *The Psychological Record*, *52*(2), 187.

Ericcson, A., Krampe, R., & Tesch-Romer, C. (1993). The role of deliberate practice in the acquisition of expert performance. *Psychological Review*, *100*, 363–406. doi:10.1037/0033-295X.100.3.363.

Erickson, F. (1986). Qualitative methods in research on teaching. In Wittrock, M. (Ed.), *Handbook of research on teaching* (3rd ed., pp. 119–161). New York, NY: Macmillan.

Erickson, F., & Schultz, J. (1977). When is a context? Some issues and methods in the analysis of social competence. *Quarterly Newsletter of the Institute for Comparative Human Development*, *1*(2), 5–10.

Ericsson, P. F., & Haswell, R. (Eds.). (2006). *Machine scoring of human essays: Truth and consequences.* Provo, UT: Utah State University Press.

Erikson, E. (1968). *Identity: Youth and crisis.* New York: Norton.

Erikson, F. (1975). Gatekeeping and the melting pot: Interaction in counseling encounters. *Harvard Educational Review*, *45*, 224–229.

Erkens, G., Kanselaar, G., Prangsma, M., & Jaspers, J. (2003). Computer support for collaborative and argumentative writing. In *Powerful learning environments: Unravelling basic components and dimensions* (pp. 159–177). Academic Press.

Estes, T. (2007). Constructing the syllabus: Devising a framework for helping students learn to think like historians. *The History Teacher*, *40*(2), 183–201.

Eva Lam, W. S., & Warriner, D. (2012). Transnationalism and literacy: Investigating the mobility of people, languages, texts, and practices in contexts of migration. *Reading Research Quarterly*, *47*(2), 191–215.

Evans, E., & Po, J. (2006). A break in the transition: Examining students' responses to digital texts. *Computers and Composition*, *24*, 56–73. doi:10.1016/j.compcom.2006.12.003.

Eyman, D. et al. (2011). Computers and composition 20/20: A conversation piece, or what some very smart people have to say about the future. *Computers and Composition*, *28*, 327–346. doi:10.1016/j.compcom.2011.09.004.

Farmer, J. (2004). Communication dynamics: Discussion boards, weblogs and the development of communities of inquiry in online learning environments. In R. Atkinson, C. McBeath, D. Jonas-Dwyer, & R. Phillips (Eds.), *Beyond the comfort zone: Proceedings of the 21st ASCILITE Conference* (pp. 274-283). Perth, Australia: Australasian Society for Computers in Learning in Tertiary Education.

Fellner, T., & Apple, M. (2006). Developing writing fluency and lexical complexity with blogs. *The JALT/CALL Journal, 2*(1), 15-26.

Ferenstein, G. (2012, Aug. 1). Study: Texting iz destroying student grammar. *Tech Crunch*. Retrieved from http://techcrunch.com/2012/08/01/study-texting-iz-destroying-student-grammar/

Ferrara, K., Brunner, H., & Whittemore, G. (1991). Interactive written discourse as an emergent register. *Written Communication, 8*(1), 8–34. doi:10.1177/0741088391008001002.

Ferris, D. R., & Hedgecock, J. C. (2005). *Teaching ESL composition: Purpose, process, and practice*. Mahwah, NJ: Erlbaum Associates, Inc..

Fiedler, S. (2003). Personal webpublishing as a reflective conversational tool for selforganized learning. In Burg, T. D. (Ed.), *BlogTalks* (pp. 190–216). Vienna, Austria: Academic Press.

Firestone, W. A. (1993). Alternative arguments for generalizing from data as applied to qualitative research. *Educational Researcher, 22*(4), 16–23. doi:10.3102/0013189X022004016.

Fisher, D., & Frey, N. (2013). Reading and reasoning: Fostering comprehension across multiple texts. *Engaging the Adolescent Learner*. Retrieved from http://www.reading.org/Libraries/members-only/fisherfreyjan2013.pdf

Fisher, D., Frey, N., & Lapp, D. (2012). *Teaching students to read like detectives: Comprehending, analyzing, and discussing texts*. Bloomington, IN: Solution Tree Press.

Fish, S. (1980). *Is there a text in this class?* Cambridge, MA: Harvard University Press.

Fitzgerald, J., & Shanahan, T. (2000). Reading and writing relations and their development. *Educational Psychologist, 35*(1), 39–50. doi:10.1207/S15326985EP3501_5.

Fletcher, R., & Portaluppi, J. (2001). *Writing workshop: The essential guide*. Portsmouth, NH: Heinemann.

Flores, M. (1990). Computer conferencing: Composing a feminist community of writers. In Handa, C. (Ed.), *Computers and community* (pp. 106–117). Portsmouth, NH: Boynton/Cook Heinemann.

Flower, L. (1994). *The construction of negotiated meaning: a social cognitive theory of writing*. Carbondale, IL: Southern Illinois University Press.

Flower, L. S., & Hayes, J. R. (1984). Images, plans, and prose: The representation of meaning in writing. *Written Communication, 1*, 120–160. doi:10.1177/0741088384001001006.

Flower, L., & Hayes, J. (1981). A cognitive process theory of writing. *College Composition and Communication, 32*, 365–387. doi:10.2307/356600.

Flower, L., & Hayes, J. R. (1977). Problem-solving strategies and the writing process. *College English, 39*, 449–461. doi:10.2307/375768.

Flower, L., & Hayes, J. R. (1980). The cognition of discovery: Defining a rhetorical problem. *College Composition and Communication, 31*(1), 21–23. doi:10.2307/356630.

Flower, L., & Hayes, J. R. (1980). The dynamics of composing: Making plans and juggling constraints. In Gregg, L. W., & Steinberg, E. R. (Eds.), *Cognitive processes in writing* (pp. 31–50). Hillsdale, NJ: Erlbaum.

Flower, L., & Hayes, J. R. (2006). A cognitive process theory of writing. In Villanueva, V. (Ed.), *Cross-talk in composition theory: A reader* (2nd ed., pp. 273–297). Urbana, IL: NCTE.

Flower, L., Hayes, J. R., Carey, L., Schriver, K., & Stratman, J. (1986). Detection, diagnosis, and the strategies of revision. *College Composition and Communication, 37*(1), 16–55. doi:10.2307/357381.

Fodor, J. A., & Bever, T. G. (1965). The psychological reality of linguistic segments. *Journal of Verbal Learning and Verbal Behavior, 4*, 414–420. doi:10.1016/S0022-5371(65)80081-0.

Fogassi, L., & Gallese, V. (2004). Action as a binding key to multisensory integration. In Calvert, G. A., Spence, C., & Stein, B. E. (Eds.), *The handbook of multisensory processes* (pp. 425–441). Cambridge, MA: MIT Press.

Forte, A., & Bruckman, A. (2010). Writing, citing, and participatory media: Wikis as learning environments in the high school classroom. *International Journal of Learning and Media, 1*(4), 23–44. doi:10.1162/ijlm_a_00033.

Fox, S., Anderson, J. Q., & Rainie, L. (2005). *The future of the internet*. Washington, DC: Pew Internet and American Life Project. Retrieved September 29, 2010, from http://www.pewInternet.org/pdfs/PIP_Future_of_Internet.pdf

Frank, L. A. (1992). Writing to be read: Young writers' ability to demonstrate audience awareness when evaluated by their readers. *Research in the Teaching of English, 26*(3), 277–298.

Frank, T., & Wall, D. (1996). *Finding your writer's voice: A guide to creative fiction*. New York: St. Martin's Griffin.

Freedman, S. W. (1992). Outside-in and inside-out: Peer response groups in two ninth-grade classes. *Research in the Teaching of English, 26*, 71–107.

Freiermuth, M. R. (2002). Internet chat: collaborating and learning via e-conversations. *TESOL Journal, 11*(3), 36–40.

Freire, P. (1970). *Pedagogy of the oppressed*. New York: Continuum.

Freire, P., & Macedo, D. (1987). *Literacy: Reading the word and the world*. Greenwood, CT: Praeger.

Fridell, M., & Lovelace, T. (2008). Creating a digital world: Five steps to engage students in multicultural learning. *The International Journal of Learning, 15*(3), 179–183.

Friedman, T. L. (2005). *The world is flat: The globalised world in the twenty-first century*. London, UK: Penguin.

Friedman, T. L. (2006). *The world is flat: A brief history of the twenty-first century*. New York: Farrar, Strauss, & Giroux.

Gail, E. H. (n.d). Research update: Writing and word processing. *Computers and Composition, 57*-27. doi:10.1016/8755-4615(88)80002-1

Galbraith, D. (1999). Writing as a knowledge-constituting process. *Knowing what to write: Conceptual processes in text production, 4*, 139-164.

Galbraith, D. (1996). Self-monitoring, discovery through writing and individual differences in drafting strategy. In Rijlaarsdam, G., van den Bergh, H., & Couzijn, M. (Eds.), *Theories, Models and Methodology in Writing Research* (pp. 121–141). Amsterdam: Amsterdam University Press.

Galda, L. (2010). First thing first: Why good books and time to respond to them matter. *New England Reading Association Journal, 46*(1), 1–7.

Gallehr, D. (1994). Wait and the writing will come: Meditation and the composing process. In Brand, A., & Grave, R. (Eds.), *Presence of mind: Writing and the domain beyond the cognitive* (pp. 21–30). Portsmouth, NH: Boynton/Cook.

Gambrell, L. B. (1996). What research reveals about discussion. In Gambrell, L. B., & Almasi, J. F. (Eds.), *Lively discussion! Fostering engaged reading* (pp. 25–38). Newark, DE: International Reading Association.

Gardner, T. (n.d.). *Literary parodies: Exploring a writer's style through imitation*. Retrieved from http://www.readwritethink.org/classroom-resources/lesson-plans/literary-parodies-exploring-writer-839.html

Garrison, D. R., & Cleveland-Innes, M. (2005). Facilitating cognitive presence in online learning: Interaction is not enough. *American Journal of Distance Education, 19*(3), 133–148. doi:10.1207/s15389286ajde1903_2.

Garrod, S. (1992, April). Reconciling the psychological with the linguistic in accounts of text comprehension. Paper presented at the NORDTEXT Symposium. Espoo, Finland.

Gee, J. (1999). *The new literacy studies and the social turn*. Retrieved from http://www.schools.ash.org.au/litWeb/page300.html

Gee, J. (2000a). *Identity as an analysis lens for research in education*. Retrieved from http://www.jamespaulgee.com/node/18

Gee, J. (1996). *Social linguistics and literacies: Ideology in Discourses* (2nd ed.). London: Taylor & Francis.

Gee, J. (2000b). Identity as an analytic lens for reserach in education. *Review of Research in Education, 55*, 99–125.

Gee, J. (2004). Learning by design: Games as learning machines. *Interactive Educational Multimedia, 8*, 15–23.

Gee, J. (2007a). *What video games have to teach us about learning and literacy*. New York: Palgrave Macmillan.

Gee, J. P. (1999). *An introduction to discourse analysis: Theory and method*. New York: Routledge.

Gee, J. P. (2000). Discourse and sociocultural studies in reading. In Kamil, M. L., Mosenthal, P. B., Pearson, P. D., & Barr, R. (Eds.), *Handbook of Reading Research* (*Vol. 3*, pp. 195–207). Mahwah, NJ: Lawrence Erlbaum.

Gee, J. P. (2001). Identity as an analytic lens for research in education. In Secada, W. G. (Ed.), *Review of research in education* (*Vol. 25*, pp. 99–125). Washington, DC: American Education Research Association.

Gee, J. P. (2003). *What video games have to teach us about learning and literacy*. New York: Palgrave MacMillan. doi:10.1145/950566.950595.

Gee, J. P. (2004). *Situated language and learning: A critique of traditional schooling*. New York: Routledge.

Gee, J. P. (2005). Meaning making, communities of practice, and analytical toolkits. *Journal of Sociolinguistics*, *9*(4), 590–594. doi:10.1111/j.1360-6441.2005.00308.x.

Gee, J. P. (2007b). *Good video games + good learning: Collected essays on video games, learning and literacy*. New York: Peter Lang.

Gee, J. P. (2008). *Social linguistics and literacies: Ideology in discourses* (3rd ed.). New York: Taylor and Francis.

Gee, J. P. (2009). Digital media and learning as an emerging field, part I: How we got here. *International Journal of Learning and Media*, *1*(2), 13–23. doi:10.1162/ijlm.2009.0011.

Gee, J. P. (2012). *Social linguistics and literacies: Ideology in discourses* (4th ed.). New York: Routledge.

Gee, J., & Hayes, E. (2011). *Language and learning in the digital age*. New York: Routledge.

Geertz, C. (1973). *The interpretation of cultures: Selected essays*. New York: Basic Books.

Gelbwasser, M. (2011). Running a classroom blog. *Instructor*, *120*(4), 76–77.

Gere, A. R. (1987). *Writing groups: History, theory, and implications*. Carbondale, IL: Southern Illinois University Press.

Gere, A., & Abbott, R. D. (1985). Talking about writing: The language of writing groups. *Research in the Teaching of English*, *19*(4), 362–385.

Geva, E., Yaghoub-Zadeh, Z., & Schuster, B. (2000). Understanding individual differences in word recognition skills of ESL children. *Annals of Dyslexia*, *50*(1), 121–154. doi:10.1007/s11881-000-0020-8 PMID:20563783.

Gibson, J. J. (1979). *The ecological approach to visual perception*. Boston: Houghton Mifflin.

Gibson, W. (1950). Authors, speakers, readers, and mock readers. *College English*, *11*(5), 265–269. doi:10.2307/585994.

Gilbert, J., & Graham, S. (2010). Teaching writing to elementary students in grades 4-6: A national survey. *The Elementary School Journal*, *110*(4), 494–518. doi:10.1086/651193.

Giles, J. (2005). Internet encyclopaedias go head to head. *Nature*, *438*(7070), 900–901. doi:10.1038/438900a PMID:16355180.

Gil, L., Bråten, I., Vidal-Abarca, E., & Strømsø, H. I. (2010). Summary versus argument tasks when working with multiple documents: Which is better for whom? *Contemporary Educational Psychology*, *35*(3), 157–173. doi:10.1016/j.cedpsych.2009.11.002.

Gilles, C., & Pierce, K. M. (2003). Making room for talk: Examining the historical implications of talk in learning. *English Education*, *36*(1), 56–79.

Glaser, B. (1998). *Doing grounded theory: Issues and discussions*. Mill Valley, CA: The Sociology Press.

Glaser, B., & Strauss, A. (1967). *The discovery of grounded theory: Strategies for qualitative research*. Chicago: Aldine.

Glenberg, A. M. (2008). Embodiment for education. In Calvo, P., & Gomila, A. (Eds.), *Handbook of cognitive science: An embodied approach* (pp. 355–372). Amsterdam: Elsevier. doi:10.1016/B978-0-08-046616-3.00018-9.

Glenberg, A. M., Jaworski, B., Rischal, M., & Levin, J. (2007). What brains are for: Action, meaning, and reading comprehension. In McNamara, D. S. (Ed.), *Reading comprehension strategies: Theories, interventions, and technologies* (pp. 221–240). New York: Lawrence Erlbaum Ass.

Glogowski, K. (2008). *Tracing the emergence of a blogging/writing community: Critical transformations in a grade eight classroom.* (Doctoral dissertation). Retrieved from ProQuest Dissertations and Theses database (Order No. 978-0-494-44706-2).

Goddard, A. (2011). Type you soon! A stylistic approach to language use in a virtual learning environment. *Language and Literature, 20,* 184–200. doi:10.1177/0963947011413561.

Goffman, E. (1981). *Forms of talk.* Philadelphia: University of Pennsylvania Press.

Goldberg, A., Russell, M., & Cook, A. (2003). The effect of computers on student writing: A metaanalysis of studies from 1992 to 2002. *Journal of Technology, Learning, and Assessment, 2*(1). Retrieved December 20, 2012 from http://www.jtla.org

Goldberg, A., Russell, M., & Cook, A. (2004). The effect of computers on student writing: A meta-analysis of studies from 1992 to 2002. *Journal of Technology, Learning, and assessment, 2*(1), 3–51.

Goldberg, N. (2005). *Writing down the bones: Freeing the writer within.* Boston: Shambhala.

Goldin, I. M., & Ashley, K. D. (2012). Eliciting formative assessment in peer review. *Journal of Writing Research, 4*(2), 203–237.

Goldin, I. M., Ashley, K. D., & Schunn, C. D. (2012). Redesigning educational peer review interactions using computer tools: An introduction. *Journal of Writing Research, 4*(2), 111–119.

Goldstein, E. (2009). Is it time to unplug? Technology and overconnection. *Psych Central.* Retrieved from http://blogs.psychcentral.com/mindfulness

González, N., Moll, L., & Amanti, C. (2005). *Funds of knowledge: Theorizing practices in households, communities, and classrooms.* Mahwah, NJ: Lawrence Erlbaum Associates.

Goswami, D., Lewis, C., Rutherford, M., & Waff, D. (2009). *On teacher inquiry: Approaches to language and literacy research.* New York: Teachers College Press.

Grabill, J., & Hicks, T. (2005). Multiliteracies meet methods: The case for digital writing in English education. *English Education.* Retrieved from http://condor.cmich.edu/cdm/singleitem/collection/p1610-01coll1/id/239

Graff, G., & Birkenstein, C. (2007). *They say, I say: The moves that matter in persuasive writing.* New York: W.W. Norton.

Graham, S., & Perin, D. (2007). *Writing next: Effective strategies to improve writing of adolescents in middle and high schools.* Retrieved from http://www.all4ed.org/files/WritingNext.pdf

Graham, S., Fitzgerald, J., & MacArthur, C. A. (2007). *Best practices in writing instruction.* New York: Guilford Press.

Graham, S., & Harris, K. R. (2007). Best practices in teaching planning. In MacArthur, C. A., Graham, S., & Fitzgerald, J. (Eds.), *Best practices in writing instruction* (pp. 119–140). New York: Guilford.

Graham, S., Harris, K. R., Fink-Chorzempa, B., & MacArthur, C. (2003). Primary grade teachers' instructional adaptations for struggling writers: A national survey. *Journal of Educational Psychology, 95,* 279–292. doi:10.1037/0022-0663.95.2.279.

Graham, S., Harris, K., & Mason, L. (2005). Improving the writing performance, knowledge, and self-efficacy of struggling young writers: The effects of self-regulated strategy development. *Contemporary Educational Psychology, 30,* 207–241. doi:10.1016/j.cedpsych.2004.08.001.

Graham, S., McKeown, D., Kiuhara, S., & Harris, K. R. (2012). A meta-analysis of writing instruction for students in the elementary grades. *Journal of Educational Psychology, 104*(4), 879–896. doi:10.1037/a0029185.

Graham, S., & Perin, D. (2007). A meta-analysis of writing instruction for adolescent students. *Journal of Educational Psychology, 99,* 445–476. doi:10.1037/0022-0663.99.3.445.

Graham, S., & Perin, D. (2007a). What we know, what we still need to know: Teaching adolescents to write. *Scientific Studies of Reading, 11*(4), 37–41. doi:10.1080/10888430701530664.

Graham, S., & Perin, D. (2007b). *Writing next: Effective strategies to improve writing of adolescents in middle and high schools*. New York, NY: Carnegie Corporation.

Gravemeijer, K., & Cobb, P. (2006). Design research from a learning design perspective. In J. van den akker, K. Gravemeijer, S. McKenney, & N. Nieveen (Eds.), Educational design research (pp. 17-51). New York: Routledge.

Graves, D. H. (1975). An examination of the writing process of seven year old children. *Research in the Teaching of English, 9,* 227–242.

Graves, D. H. (1994). *A fresh look at writing*. Portsmouth, NH: Heinemann.

Greenberg, J. B. (1989). *Funds of knowledge: Historical constitution, social distribution, and transmission.* Paper presented at the annual meeting of the Society for Applied Anthropology. Santa Fe, NM.

Greenhow, C., & Gleason, B. (2012). Twitteracy: Tweeting as a new literacy practice. *The Educational Forum, 76*(4), 464–478. doi:10.1080/00131725.2012.709032.

Greenhow, C., Robelia, B., & Hughes, J. (2009). Web 2.0 and classroom research: What path should we take now? *Educational Researcher, 38*(4), 246–259. doi:10.3102/0013189X09336671.

Green, J. L. (1983). Research on teaching as a linguistic process: A state of the art. In Gordon, E. W. (Ed.), *Review of research in education*. Washington, DC: American Educational Research Association. doi:10.2307/1167138.

Grejda, G. F., & Hannafin, M. J. (1992). Effects of word-processing on 6th graders' holistic writing and revisions. *The Journal of Educational Research, 85,* 144–149. doi:10.1080/00220671.1992.9944430.

Griffin, M. (2003). Using critical incidents to promote and assess reflective thinking in preservice teachers. *Reflective Practice, 4,* 207–220. doi:10.1080/14623940308274.

Grimes, D., & Warschauer, M. (2008). Learning with laptops: A multi-method case study. *Journal of Educational Computing Research, 38*(3), 305–332. doi:10.2190/EC.38.3.d.

Grimes, D., & Warschauer, M. (2010). Utility in a fallible tool: A multi-site case study of automated writing evaluation. *Journal of Technology, Learning, and Assessment, 8,* 4–43.

Grim, V., Pace, D., & Shopkow, L. (2004). Learning to use evidence in the study of history. *New Directions for Teaching and Learning, 98,* 57–65. doi:10.1002/tl.147.

Grisham, D. L., & Wolsey, T. D. (2006). Recentering the middle school classroom as a vibrant learning community: Students, literacy, and technology intersect. *Journal of Adolescent & Adult Literacy, 49*(8), 648–660. doi:10.1598/JAAL.49.8.2.

Groenke, S. L. (2007). Collaborative dialogue in a synchronous CMC environment? A look at one beginning English teacher's strategies. *Journal of Computing in Teacher Education, 24*(2), 41–47.

Gruber, S., Sweany, M. F., & Hawisher, G. E. (1996). *Computers and the teaching of writing in American higher education, 1979-1994: A history*. Norwood, NJ: Ablex Pub..

Guerra, J. (2007). Out of the valley: Transcultural repositioning as a rhetorical practice in ethnographic research and other aspects of everyday life. In Lewis, C., Enciso, P., & Moje, E. B. (Eds.), *Reframing sociocultural research on literacy: Identity, agency, and power* (pp. 137–162). Mahwah, NJ: Lawrence Erlbaum Associates.

Guerra, J. (2008). Writing for transcultural citizenship: A cultural ecology model. *Language Arts, 85*(4), 296–304.

Guiard, Y. (1987). Asymmetric division of labor in human skilled bimanual action: The kinematic chain as a model. *Journal of Motor Behavior, 19,* 486–517. PMID:15136274.

Gunawardena, C. N., Hermans, M. B., Sanchez, D., Richmond, C., Bohley, M., & Tuttle, R. (2009). A theoretical framework for building online communities of practice with social networking tools. *Educational Media International, 46*(1), 3–16. doi:10.1080/09523980802588626.

Gutierrez, K., & Stone, L. D. (2000). Synchronic and diachronic dimensions of social practice: An emerging methodology for cultural-historical perspectives on literacy learning. In Lee, C. D., & Smagorinsky, P. (Eds.), *Vygotskian perspectives on literacy research: Constructing meaning through collaborative inquiry* (pp. 150–164). New York: Cambridge University Press.

Haas, C. (1996). *Writing technology: Studies on the materiality of literacy*. Mahwah, NJ: L. Erlbaum Associates.

Haas, C., Takayoshi, P., Carr, B., Hudson, K., & Pollock, R. (2011). Young people's everyday literacies: The language features of instant messaging. *Research in the Teaching of English, 45*, 378–404.

Habgood, J., & Ainsworth, S. (2011). Motivating children to learn effectively: exploring the value of intrinsic integration in educational games. *Journal of the Learning Sciences, 20*, 169–206. doi:10.1080/10508406.2010.508029.

Hagood, M. (2003). New media and online literacies: No age left behind. *Reading Research Quarterly, 38*(3), 387–392.

Hairston, M. (1978). *A contemporary rhetoric* (2nd ed.). Boston, MA: Houghton Miffin.

Hairston, M. (1982). The winds of change: Thomas Kuhn and the revolution in the teaching of writing. *College Composition and Communication, 33*(1), 76–88. doi:10.2307/357846.

Hall, T., Strangman, N., & Meyer, A. (2003). *Differentiated instruction and implications for UDL implementation*. Wakefield, MA: National Center on Accessing the General Curriculum. Retrieved August 7th 2012 from http://aim.cast.org/learn/historyarchive/backgroundpapers/differentiated_instruction_udl

Halliday, M. (1980). Three aspects of children's language development: Learning language, learning through language, learning about language? In Goodman, Y., Haussler, M., & Strickland, D. (Eds.), *Oral and written language development research: Impact on the schools I* (pp. 7–20). Urbana, IL: NCTE and IRA.

Halverson, R., & Shapiro, R. B. (2012). *Technologies for education and technologies for learners: How information technologies are (and should be) changing schools* (WCER Working Paper No. 2012-6). Madison, WI: Wisconsin Center for Education Research, University of Wisconsin-Madison.

Hamp-Lyons, L. (2007). Worrying about rating. *Assessing Writing, 12*, 1–9. doi:10.1016/j.asw.2007.05.002.

Hancock, M. R. (1993). Exploring the making-making process though the content of literature response journals. *Research in the Teaching of English, 27*(4), 335–368.

Hancock, M. R. (2008). The status of reader response research: Sustaining the reader's voice in challenging times. In Lehr, S. (Ed.), *Shattering the looking glass: Challenge, risk, and controversy in children's literature* (pp. 97–116). Norwood, MA: Christopher-Gordon.

Hanh, T. (1991). *Peace is every step: The path of mindfulness in everyday life. New York: Bantam Books. hooks, b. (1994). Teaching to transgress: Education as the practice of freedom*. New York: Routledge.

Hansen, J., & Kissel, B. (2010). K-12 students as writers: Research to practice. D. Lapp & D. Fisher (Eds.), The handbook of research on teaching the English language arts (3rd ed.), (pp. 271-277). New York: Routledge.

Hansen, J. (1998). *When learners evaluate*. Portsmouth, NH: Heinemann.

Hargittai, E. (2002). Second-level digital divide: Differences in people's online skills. *First Monday, 7*(4). doi:10.5210/fm.v7i4.942.

Harklau, L. (2011). Commentary: Adolescent L2 writing research as an emerging field. *Journal of Second Language Writing, 20*, 227–230. doi:10.1016/j.jslw.2011.05.003.

Harris, J., Mishra, P., & Koehler, M. (2009). Teachers' technological pedagogical content knowledge and learning activity types: Curriculum-based technology integration reframed. *Journal of Research on Technology in Education, 41*(4), 393–416.

Harrison, C. (2008). Researching technology and literacy: Thirteen ways of looking at a blackboard. In Coiro, J., Knobel, M., Lankshear, C., & Leu, D. J. (Eds.), *Handbook of research on new literacies* (pp. 1283–1293). Mahwah, NJ: Lawrence Erlbaum Associates.

Hart, C. (1998). *Doing a literature review: Releasing the social science research imagination.* Thousand Oaks, CA: Sage.

Hattie, J., & Temperley, H. (2007). The power of feedback. *Review of Educational Research*, *77*, 81–112. doi:10.3102/003465430298487.

Hatwell, Y., Streri, A., & Gentaz, E. (Eds.). (2003). *Touching for knowing.* Amsterdam: John Benjamins.

Hawisher, G. E. (1986). Studies in word processing. *Computers and Composition*, *4*(4), 6–31. doi:10.1016/S8755-4615(86)80003-2.

Hawisher, G. E. (1989). Computers and writing: where's the research? *English Journal*, 7889–7891.

Hawkins, B. L., & Oblinge, D. G. (2006). The myth about the digital divide. *EDUCAUSE Review*, *41*(4), 12–13.

Hayes, J. R., & Flower, L. S. (1980). Identifying the organization of writing processes. *Cognitive Processes in Writing*, 3-30.

Hayes, J. R., & Chenoweth, N. A. (2006). Is working memory involved in the transcribing and editing of texts? *Written Communication*, *23*(2), 135–149. doi:10.1177/0741088306286283.

Hayes, J. R., & Flower, L. S. (1986). Writing research and the writer. *The American Psychologist*, *41*(10), 1106. doi:10.1037/0003-066X.41.10.1106.

Healy, A., Schneider, V., & Bourne, L. (2012). Empirically valid principles of training. In Healy, A., & Bourne, L. (Eds.), *Training cognition: Optimizing efficiency, durability, and generalizability* (pp. 13–39). New York: Psychology Press.

Heath, M. (2005). Are you ready to go digital? The pros and cons of electronic portfolio development. *Library Media Connection*, *23*, 66–70.

Heath, S. B. (1983). *Ways with words: Language, life, and work in communities and classrooms.* New York: Cambridge University Press.

Hegelheimer, V. (2006). Helping ESL writers through a multimodal, corpus-based, online grammar resource. *CALICO Journal*, *24*(1), 5–32.

Heller, R. (2010). In praise of amateurism: A friendly critique of Moje's "call for change" in secondary literacy. *Journal of Adolescent & Adult Literacy*, *54*(4), 267–273. doi:10.1598/JAAL.54.4.4.

Helsper, E., & Eynon, R. (2009). Digital natives: where is the evidence? *British Educational Research Journal*, *28*(6), 751–771.

Hendricks, C. C. (2001). Teaching causal reasoning through cognitive apprenticeship: What are results from situated learning? *The Journal of Educational Research*, *94*(5), 302–311. doi:10.1080/00220670109598766.

Hennessey, S. (1993). Situated cognition and cognitive apprenticeship: Implications for classroom learning. *Studies in Science Education*, *22*, 1–41. doi:10.1080/03057269308560019.

Herrington, A., Hodgson, K., & Moran, C. (Eds.). (2009). *Teaching the new writing: Technology, change, and assessment in the 21st-century classroom.* New York: Teachers College Press/National Writing Project.

Herrington, J., & Oliver, R. (2000). An instructional design framework for authentic learning environments. *Educational Technology Research and Development*, *48*(3), 23–48. doi:10.1007/BF02319856.

Hewett, B. L. (2000). Characteristics of interactive oral and computer-mediated peer group talk and its influence on revision. *Computers and Composition*, *17*, 265–288. doi:10.1016/S8755-4615(00)00035-9.

Hew, K. F., & Cheung, W. S. (2003). Evaluating the participation and quality of thinking of pre-service teachers in an asynchronous online discussion environment: Part 1. *International Journal of Instructional Media*, *30*(3), 247–262.

Hicks, T. (2009). *The digital writing workshop.* Portsmouth, NH: Heinemann.

Hicks, T., Russo, A., Autrey, T., Gardner, R., Kabodian, A., & Edington, C. (2007). Rethinking the purposes and processes for designing digital portfolios. *Journal of Adult and Adolescent Literacy, 50*, 450–458. doi:10.1598/JAAL.50.6.3.

Hidi, S., Berndorff, D., & Ainley, M. (2002). Children's argument writing, interest and self-efficacy: An intervention study. *Learning and Instruction, 12*, 429–446. doi:10.1016/S0959-4752(01)00009-3.

Higgins, R., Hartley, P., & Skelton, A. (2002). The conscientious consumer: Reconsidering the role of assessment feedback in student learning. *Studies in Higher Education, 27*(1), 53. doi:10.1080/03075070120099368.

Hillocks, G. (1984). What works in teaching composition: A meta-analysis of experimental treatment studies. *American Journal of Education, 93*(1), 133–170. doi:10.1086/443789.

Hillocks, G. Jr. (1986). *Research on written composition: New directions for teaching*. Urbana, IL: NCTE.

Hoadley, C. M. (2004). Methodological alignment in design-based research. *Educational Psychologist, 39*, 203–212. doi:10.1207/s15326985ep3904_2.

Holland, D., Lachiotte, W., Skinner, D., & Cain, C. (1998). *Identity and agency in cultural worlds*. Cambridge, MA: Harvard University Press.

Holliway, D. R. (2004). Through the eyes of my reader: A strategy for improving audience perspective in children's descriptive writing. *Journal of Research in Childhood Education, 18*(4), 334–349. doi:10.1080/02568540409595045.

Holliway, D. R., & McCutchen, D. (2004). Audience perspective in young writers' composing and revising. In Allal, L., Chanquoy, L., & Largy, P. (Eds.), *Revision: Cognitive and instructional processes* (pp. 87–101). Norwell, MA: Kluwer. doi:10.1007/978-94-007-1048-1_6.

Honan, E. (2009). Mapping discourses in teachers' talk about using digital texts in classrooms. *Discourse: Studies in the Cultural Politics of Education, 31*(2), 179–193. doi:10.1080/01596301003679701.

Honeycutt, L. (2001). Comparing e-mail and synchronous conferencing in online peer response. *Written Communication, 18*, 26. doi:10.1177/0741088301018001002.

Honeyford, M. (2013). Critical projects of Latino cultural citizenship: Literacy and immigrant activism. *Pedagogies: An International Journal, 8*(1), 60–76.

Honeyford, M. (2013). The simultaneity of experience: Cultural identity, magical realism, and the artefactual in digital storytelling. *Literacy*. doi:10.1111/j.1741-4369.2012.00675.x.

Hongyan, M., Yong Lu, E., Turner, S., & Guofang, W. (2007). An empirical investigation of digital cheating and plagiarism among middle school students. *American Secondary Education, 35*(2), 69–82.

Hornberger, N. H. (2007). Biliteracy, transnationalism, multimodality, and identity: Trajectories across time and space. *Linguistics and Education, 18*(3-4), 325–334. doi:10.1016/j.linged.2007.10.001.

Howard, C. (2012, February 14). The Gr8 Deb8 of teen Txting: Text messaging ruining the English language? *World Now*. Retrieved from http://www.khq.com/story/16937099/the-gr8-deb8-of-teen-txting-text-messaging-ruining-the-english-language

Howard, T. W. (2010). *Design to thrive: Creating social networks and online communities that last*. Burlington, MA: Morgan Kauffman.

Hsieh, Y. H., & Tsai, C. C. (2012). The effect of moderator's facilitative strategies on online synchronous discussions. *Computers in Human Behavior, 28*(5), 1708–1716. doi:10.1016/j.chb.2012.04.010.

Huang, H.-J. (2006). Promoting multicultural awareness through electronic communication. *International Electronic Journal for Leadership in Learning, 10*(7).

Huffaker, D. (2005). The educated blogger: Using weblogs to promote literacy in the classroom. *AACE Journal, 13*(2), 91–98.

Hughes, L. (1940). Salvation. In Fine Clouse, B. (Ed.), *Patterns for a purpose: A rhetorical reader* (pp. 203–204). Boston: McGraw.

Hughes, T. P. (2004). *Human-built world: How to think about technology and culture.* Chicago: University of Chicago Press.

Hull, G. A., & Stornaiuolo, A. (2010). Literate arts in a global world: Reframing social networking as cosmopolitan practice. *Journal of Adolescent & Adult Literacy, 54*(2), 85–97. doi:10.1598/JAAL.54.2.1.

Hull, G., & Nelson, M. E. (2005). Locating the semiotic power of multimodality. *Written Communication, 22,* 224–261. doi:10.1177/0741088304274170.

Hull, G., & Schultz, K. (2001). Literacy and learning out of school: A review of theory and research. *Review of Educational Research, 71*(4), 575–611. doi:10.3102/00346543071004575.

Hull, G., & Schultz, K. (2002). Connecting schools with out-of-school worlds: Insights from recent research on literacy in non-school settings. In Hull, G., & Schultz, K. (Eds.), *School's out! Bridging out-of-school literacies with classroom practice.* New York: Teachers College Press.

Hull, G., & Schultz, K. (2002). *School's out: Bridging out-of-school literacies with classroom practice.* New York, NY: Teachers College Press.

Hungerford-Kresser, H., Wiggins, J., & Amaro-Jimenez, C. (2012). Learning from our mistakes: What matters when incorporating blogging in the content area literacy classroom. *Journal of Adolescent & Adult Literacy, 55*(4), 326–335. doi:10.1002/JAAL.00039.

Hunicke, R., LeBlanc, M., & Zubek, R. (2004). MDA: A formal approach to game design and game research. In *Proceedings of the Challenges in Games AI Workshop, 19ᵗʰ National Conference on Artificial Intelligence* (pp. 1-5). San Jose, CA: AAAI Press.

Huot, B. (1990). The literature of direct writing assessment: Major concerns and prevailing trends. *Review of Educational Research, 60,* 237–263. doi:10.3102/00346543060002237.

Hutchins, E. (1995). *Cognition in the wild.* Cambridge, MA: MIT University Press.

Hutchison, A., & Reinking, D. (2011). Teachers' perceptions of integrating information and communication technologies into literacy instruction: A national survey in the U.S. *Reading Research Quarterly, 46*(4), 308–329.

Hyland, F. (2000). ESL writers and feedback: giving more autonomy to students. *Language Teaching Research, 4*(1), 33–54.

Hynd, C. R. (1999). Teaching students to think critically using multiple texts in history. *Journal of Adolescent & Adult Literacy, 42*(6), 428–436.

Ice, P., Curtis, R., Phillips, P., & Wells, J. (2007). Using asynchronous audio feedback to enhance teaching presence and students' sense of community. *Journal of Asynchronous Learning Networks, 11*(2), 3–25.

Ife, F. (2012). Powerful writing: Promoting a political writing community of students. *English Journal, 101*(4), 64–69.

International Reading Association. (2009). *New literacies and 21st-century technologies: A position statement of the international reading association.* Retrieved December 20, 2011, from http://www.reading.org/General/AboutIRA/PositionStatements/21stCenturyLiteracies.aspx

Inverness Research. (2009). *Keeping the promise of the 21st century: Bringing classroom teaching into the digital age - National writing project.* Retrieved February 18, 2012, from http://www.nwp.org/cs/public/print/resource/2865

Ito, M., Baumer, S., & Bittani, M. boyd, d., Cody, R., Herr-Stephenson, B., et al. (2009). Hanging out, messing around, and geeking out: Kids living and learning with new media. Cambridge, MA: MIT Press/MacArthur Foundation.

Jacobs, G. E. (2008). We learn what we do: Developing a repertoire of writing practices in an instant messaging world. *Journal of Adolescent & Adult Literacy, 52*(3), 203–211. doi:10.1598/JAAL.52.3.3.

Janks, H. (2010). *Literacy and power.* New York: Routledge.

Jarvella, R. J. (1971). Syntactic processing of connected speech. *Journal of Verbal Learning and Verbal Behavior, 10,* 409–416. doi:10.1016/S0022-5371(71)80040-3.

Jenkins, H. (2004). Why Heather can write. *Technology Review.* Retrieved from http://www.technologyreview.com/news/402471/why-heather-can-write/

Jenkins, H. (2006). *Confronting the challenges of participatory culture: Media education for the 21ˢᵗ century.* White paper for the Mac Arthur Foundation. Retrieved September, 1, 2011 from www.digitallearningmacfound. org

Jenkins, H. (2008). *How fan fiction can teach us a new way to read Moby Dick (part one).* Retrieved from http://henryjenkins.org/2008/08/how_fan_fiction_can_teach_us_a.html

Jenkins, H., Clinton, K., Purushotma, R., Robison, A. J., & Weigel, M. (2009). *Confronting the challenges of participatory culture: Media education for the 21ˢᵗ century.* Retrieved April 5, 2012 from http://digitallearning.macfound.org/site/c.enJLKQNlFiG/b.2029291/k.97E5/Occasional_Papers.htm

Jenkins, H. (1992). *Textual poachers: Television, fans, and participatory culture.* New York: Routledge.

Jenkins, H. (2006). *Fans, bloggers, and gamers: Media consumers in a digital age.* New York: New York University Press.

Jewitt, C. (2005). Multimodality, reading, and writing for the 21st century. *Discourse: Studies in the cultural politics of education, 26*(3), 315-331.

Jewitt, C., Bezemer, J., Jones, K., & Kress, G. (2009). Changing English? The impact of technology and policy on a school subject in the 21ˢᵗ century. *English Teaching: Practice and Critique, 8*(3), 8-20. Retrieved from http://education.waikato.ac.nz/research/files/etpc/files/2009v8n3art1.pdf

Jewitt, C. (2008). Multimodality and literacy in school classrooms. *Review of Research in Education, 32*(1), 241–267. doi:10.3102/0091732X07310586.

Jin, L., & Zhu, W. (2010). Dynamic motives in ESL computer-mediated peer response. *Computers and Composition, 27*(4), 284–303. doi:10.1016/j.compcom.2010.09.001.

Johnson, D. (2010). Teaching with authors' blogs: Connections, collaborations, creativity. *Journal of Adolescent & Adult Literacy, 54*(3), 172–180. doi:10.1598/JAAL.54.3.2.

Johnson, R. B., & Onwuegbuzie, A. J. (2004). Mixed methods research: A research paradigm whose time has come. *Educational Researcher, 33*(7), 14–26. doi:10.3102/0013189X033007014.

Jones, R. H., Garralda, A., Li, D., & Lock, G. (2006). Interactional dynamics in on-line and face-to-face peer-tutoring sessions for second language writers. *Journal of Second Language Writing, 15*, 1–23. doi:10.1016/j.jslw.2005.12.001.

Junco, R. (2012). The relationship between frequency of Facebook use, participation in Facebook activities, and student engagement. *Computers & Education, 58*(1), 162–171. doi:10.1016/j.compedu.2011.08.004.

Juzwik, M. M., Nystrand, M., Kelly, S., & Sherry, M. B. (2008). Oral narrative genres as dialogic resources for classroom literature study: A contextualized case study of conversational narrative discussion. *American Educational Research Journal, 45*(4), 1111–1154. doi:10.3102/0002831208321444.

Juzwik, M. M., & Sherry, M. B. (2007). Expressive language and the art of English teaching: Theorizing the relationship between literature and oral narrative. *English Education, 39*(3), 226–259.

Juzwik, M., Curcic, S., Wolbers, K., Moxley, K., Dimling, L., & Shankland, R. (2006). Writing into the 21ˢᵗ century: An overview of research on writing, 1999-2004. *Written Communication, 23*, 451–476. doi:10.1177/0741088306291619.

Kabat-Zinn, J. (1991). *Full catastrophe living: Using the wisdom of your body and mind to face stress, pain, and illness.* New York: Dell Publishing.

Kafai, Y., Peppler, K., & Chapman, R. (Eds.). (2009). *The computer clubhouse: Constructionism and creativity in youth communities.* New York: Teachers College Press.

Kahn, E. (2009). Making writing instruction authentic. *English Journal, 98*(5), 15–17.

Kalantzis, M., & Cope, W. (2012). *Literacies.* New York: Cambridge University Press. doi:10.1017/CBO9781139196581.

Karchmer-Klein, R., & Shinas, V. H. (2012). Guiding principles for supporting new literacies in your classroom. *The Reading Teacher*, *65*(5), 288–293. doi:10.1002/TRTR.01044.

Karegianes, M., Pascarella, E., & Pflaum, S. (1980). The effects of peer editing on the writing proficiency of low-achieving tenth grade students. *The Journal of Educational Research*, *73*(4), 203–207.

Karolides, N. J. (Ed.). (2000). *Reader response in secondary and college classrooms*. Mahwah, NJ: Lawrence Erlbaum Associates.

Kellogg, R. (2001). Competition for working memory among writing processes. *The American Journal of Psychology*, *114*, 175–191. doi:10.2307/1423513 PMID:11430147.

Kellogg, R. (2008). Training writing skills: a cognitive development perspective. *Journal of Writing Research*, *1*, 1–26.

Kellogg, R. T. (2006). Professional writing expertise. In Ericsson, K. A., Charness, N., Feltovich, P. J., & Hoffman, R. R. (Eds.), *The Cambridge handbook of expertise and expert performance* (pp. 389–402). New York, NY: Cambridge University Press. doi:10.1017/CBO9780511816796.022.

Kellogg, R. T., Whiteford, A. P., & Quinlan, T. (2010). Does automated feedback help students learn to write? *Journal of Educational Computing Research*, *42*(2), 173–196. doi:10.2190/EC.42.2.c.

Kellogg, R., & Whiteford, A. (2009). Training advanced writing skills: the case for deliberate practice. *Educational Psychologist*, *44*, 250–266. doi:10.1080/00461520903213600.

Kells, M. (2007). Writing across communities: Deliberation and the discursive possibilities of WAC. *Reflections: The SoL Journal*, 87–108.

Kelly, T., Gray, V., & Minges, M. (2003). *Broadband Korea: Internet case study*. Geneva, Switzerland: International Telecommunications Union.

Kemmis, S., & McTaggart, R. (2000). Participatory action research. In Denzin, N. K., & Lincoln, Y. S. (Eds.), *Handbook of qualitative research* (2nd ed., pp. 336–396). Thousand Oaks, CA: Sage Publications.

Kemp, N., & Bushnell, C. (2011). Children's text messaging: Abbreviations, input methods and links with literacy. *Journal of Computer Assisted Learning*, *27*, 18–27. doi:10.1111/j.1365-2729.2010.00400.x.

Kessler, G., & Bikowski, D. (2010). Developing collaborative autonomous learning abilities in computer mediated language learning: Attention to meaning among students in wiki space. *Computer Assisted Language Learning*, *23*(1), 41–58. doi:10.1080/09588220903467335.

Kiili, C., Laurinen, L., & Marttunen, M. (2008). Students evaluating Internet sources: From versatile evaluators to uncritical readers. *Journal of Educational Computing Research*, *39*(1), 75–95. doi:10.2190/EC.39.1.e.

Kimber, K., & Wyatt-Smith, C. (2006). Using and creating knowledge with new technologies: A case for students-as-designers. *Learning, Media and Technology*, *31*(1), 19–34. doi:10.1080/17439880500515440.

Kinneavy, J. L. (1971). *A theory of discourse: The aims of discourse*. New York, NY: W. W. Norton.

Kintsch, E., Caccamise, D., Franzke, M., Johnson, N., & Dooley, S. (2007). Summary street ®: computer-guided summary writing. In T. K. Landauer, D. M., McNamara, S. Dennis, & W. Kintsch (Eds.), Latent Semantic Analysis (pp. 263-277). Mahwah, NJ: Erlbaum.

Klein, P. D. (1999). Reopening inquiry into cognitive processes in writing-to-learn. *Educational Psychology Review*, *11*, 203–270. doi:10.1023/A:1021913217147.

Klenowski, V., Askew, S., & Carnell, E. (2006). Portfolios for learning, assessment and professional development in higher education. *Assessment & Evaluation in Higher Education*, *31*, 267–286. doi:10.1080/02602930500352816.

Kline, S., Letofsky, K., & Woodard, R. L. (2013). Democratizing classroom discourse: The challenge for online writing environments. *E-Learning and Digital Media*, *10*(4).

Kling, R. (2000). Learning about information technologies and social change: The contribution of social informatics. *The Information Society, 16*(3), 217–232. doi:10.1080/01972240050133661.

Koehler, M. J., & Mishra, P. (2008). Introducing TPACK. In AACTE Committee on Innovation & Technology (Eds.), Handbook of technological pedagogical content knowledge for educators (pp. 3–29). New York: Routledge.

Kos, R., & Maslowski, C. (2001). Second graders perceptions of what is important in writing. *The Elementary School Journal, 101*(5), 567–578. doi:10.1086/499688.

Kozlowski, S., & Hattrup, K. (1992). A disagreement about within-group agreement: Disentangling issues of consistency vs consensus. *The Journal of Applied Psychology, 77*(2), 161–167. doi:10.1037/0021-9010.77.2.161.

Krashen, S. (1994). Bilingual education and second language acquisition theory. In Leyba, C. F. (Ed.), *Schooling language minority students: A theoretical framework* (2nd ed., pp. 47–75). Los Angeles, CA: Evaluation, Dissemination and Assessment Center, School of Education, California State University, Los Angeles.

Kress, G. (2003). *Literacy in the new media age.* New York: Routledge. doi:10.4324/9780203164754.

Kress, G., & van Leeuwen, T. (2001). *Multimodal discourse: The modes and media of contemporary communication.* London: Arnold.

Kucan, L., & Beck, I. L. (1997). Thinking aloud and reading comprehension research: Inquiry, instruction and social interaction. *Review of Educational Research, 67*(3), 271–279. doi:10.3102/00346543067003271.

Kucer, S. B. (2005). *Dimensions of literacy: A conceptual base for teaching reading and writing in school settings* (2nd ed.). Mahwah, NJ: Lawrence Erlbaum.

Kuiper, E., & Volman, M. (2008). The web as a source of information for K-12 education. In Coiro, J., Knobel, M., Lankshear, C., & Leu, D. J. (Eds.), *Handbook of research on new literacies* (pp. 267–296). Mahwah, NJ: Erlbaum.

Labbo, L., & Reinking, D. (1999). Negotiating the multiple realities of technology in literacy research and instruction. *Reading Research Quarterly, 34*(4), 478–492. doi:10.1598/RRQ.34.4.5.

Lakoff, G., & Johnson, M. (1980). *Metaphors we live by.* Chicago: University of Chicago Press.

Lammers, J. C. (2013). Fan girls as teachers: Examining pedagogic discourse in an online fan site. *Learning, Media and Technology.* doi:10.1080/17439884.2013.764895 PMID:23459677.

Lammers, J. C., Curwood, J. S., & Magnifico, A. M. (2012). Toward an affinity space methodology: Considerations for literacy research. *English Teaching: Practice and Critique, 11*(2), 44–58.

Lamonica, C. (2010). *What are the benefits of blogging in the elementary classroom?* (Master's thesis). Retrieved from http://reflectivepractitioner.pbworks.com/f/Lamonica+Capstone+Paper.pdf

Lam, W. S. E. (2000). L2 literacy and the design of the self: A case study of a teenager writing on the internet. *TESOL Quarterly, 34*, 457–482. doi:10.2307/3587739.

Lam, W. S. E. (2004). Second language socialization in a bilingual chat room: Global and local considerations. *Language Learning & Technology, 8*(3), 44–65.

Lam, W. S. E. (2009). Multiliteracies on instant messaging in negotiating local, translocal, and transnational affiliations: A case of an adolescent immigrant. *Reading Research Quarterly, 44*(4), 377–397. doi:10.1598/RRQ.44.4.5.

Lam, W. S. E., & Rosario-Ramos, E. (2009). Multilingual literacies in transnational digitally mediated contexts: An exploratory study of immigrant teens in the United States. *Language and Education, 23*(2), 171–190. doi:10.1080/09500780802152929.

Langer, J. A., & National Research Center on English Learning and Achievement. (1999). *Beating the odds: Teaching middle and high school students to read and write well.* Retrieved May 6, 2012 from http://www.albany.edu/cela/reports.html#L

Langer, J. A., & National Research Center on English Learning and Achievement. (2000). *Guidelines for teaching middle and high school students to read and write well: Six features of effective instruction.* Retrieved May 6, 2012 from http://www.albany.edu/cela/reports.html#L

Langer, J. (2001). Beating the odds: Teaching middle and high school students to read and write well. *American Educational Research Journal*, *38*(4), 837–880. doi:10.3102/00028312038004837.

Langer, J., & Flihan, S. (2000). Writing and reading relationships: Constructive tasks. In Indrisano, R., & Squire, J. R. (Eds.), *Writing: Research/Theory/Practice*. Newark, DE: International Reading Association.

Lankshear, C., & Knoebel, M. (2004). *From flogging to blogging via wifi*. Paper presented at the American Educational Research Association. San Diego, CA.

Lankshear, C., & Knobel, M. (2003). *New literacies: Changing knowledge and classroom learning*. Philadelphia, PA: Open University Press.

Lankshear, C., & Knobel, M. (2006). *New literacies: Changing knowledge and classroom learning* (2nd ed.). Philadelphia: Open University Press.

Lankshear, C., & Knobel, M. (2011). *The new literacies: Everyday practices and social learning*. Berkshire, UK: Open University Press.

Lapp, D., Fisher, D., & Wolsey, T. D. (2009). *Literacy growth for every child: Differentiated small-group instruction K-6*. New York: Guilford Publishers.

Lapp, D., Shea, A., & Wolsey, T. D. (2010/2011). Blogging and audience awareness. *Journal of Education*, *191*(1), 33–44.

Larson, L. C. (2009). Reader response meets new literacies: Empowering readers in online learning communities. *The Reading Teacher*, *62*(8), 638–648. doi:10.1598/RT.62.8.2.

Larson, L. C. (2010). Digital readers: The next chapter in e-book reading and response. *The Reading Teacher*, *64*(1), 15–22. doi:10.1598/RT.64.1.2.

Larson, L. C. (2012). It's time to turn the digital page: Preservice teachers explore e-book reading. *Journal of Adolescent & Adult Literacy*, *56*(4), 280–290. doi:10.1002/JAAL.00141.

Lave, J., & Wenger, E. (1991). *Situated learning: Legitimate peripheral participation*. Cambridge, UK: Cambridge University Press. doi:10.1017/CBO9780511815355.

Lawrence, S., & Sommers, E. (1996). From the park bench to the (writing) workshop table: Encouraging collaboration among inexperienced writers. *Teaching English in the Two-Year College*, *23*(2), 101–110.

Leander, K. M. (2007). You won't be needing your laptops today: Wired bodies in the wireless classroom. In Knobel, M., & Lankshear, C. (Eds.), *A new literacies sampler* (pp. 25–48). New York: Peter Lang.

LeBlanc, P. (1988). How to get the words just right: A reappraisal of word processing and revision. *Computers and Composition*, *5*(3), 29–42.

LeBlanc, P. (1992). Letter from the guest editor. *Computers and Composition*, *10*(1), 3–7. doi:10.1016/S8755-4615(06)80012-5.

Lee, D., & Swales, J. (2006). A corpus-based EAP course for NNS doctoral students: Moving from available specialized corpora to self-compiled corpora. *English for Specific Purposes*, *25*, 56–75. doi:10.1016/j.esp.2005.02.010.

Lee, L. (2011a). Blogging: Promoting learner autonomy and intercultural competence through study abroad. *Language Learning & Technology*, *15*(3), 87–109.

Lee, L. (2011b). Focus on form through peer feedback in a Spanish-American telecollaborative exchange. *Language Awareness*, *20*(4), 343–357. doi:10.1080/09658416.2011.592589.

Leijten, M., & Van Waes, L. (2006). Inputlog: New perspectives on the logging of on-line writing. In Sullivan, K. P. H., & Lindgren, E. (Eds.), *Computer keystroke logging and writing: Methods and applications* (pp. 73–94). Amsterdam: Elsevier.

Lenhart, A. (2005). *Unstable texts: An ethnographic look at how bloggers and their audience negotiate self-presentation, authenticity, and norm formation*. (Unpublished master's thesis). Georgetown University, Washington, DC.

Lenhart, A., Arafeh, S., Smith, A., & Macgill, A. R. (2008). *Writing, technology and teens*. Retrieved from http://www.pewInternet.org/PPF/r/247/report_display.asp

Lenhart, A., Madden, M., Smith, A., Purcell, K., Zickuhr, K., & Rainie, L. (2011). Teens, kindness and cruelty on social network sites: How American teens navigate the new world of digital citizenship. [Electronic version]. *Pew Internet & American Life Project.* Retrieved February 5, 2013 from http://www.pewInternet.org/Reports/2011/Teens-and-social-media.aspx

Lenski, S. D. (1998). Strategic knowledge when reading in order to write. *Reading Psychology, 19*(3), 287–315. doi:10.1080/0270271980190303.

Lesaux, N. K., Lipka, O., & Siegel, L. S. (2006). Investigating cognitive and linguistic abilities that influence the reading comprehension skills of children from diverse linguistic backgrounds. *Reading and Writing, 19*(1), 99–131. doi:10.1007/s11145-005-4713-6.

Leu, D. J., Castek, J., Hartman, D., Coiro, J., Henry, L., Kulikowich, J., & Lyver, S. (2005). *Evaluating the development of scientific knowledge and new forms of reading comprehension during online learning.* Paper presented to the North Central Regional Educational Laboratory/Learning Point Associates.

Leu, D. J., Kinzer, C. K., Coiro, J., & Cammack, D. (2004). Toward a theory of new literacies emerging from the Internet and other information and communication technologies. In R.B. Ruddell & N. Unrau (Eds.), *Theoretical Models and Processes of Reading* (5th ed), (1568-1611). Newark, DE: International Reading Association. Retrieved October 15, 2008 from http://www.readingonline.org/newliteracies/lit_index.asp?HREF=/newliteracies /leu

Leu, D. J., Zawilinski, L., Castek, J., Benerjee, M., Housand, B., Liu, Y., & O'Neil, M. (2007). *What is new about the new literacies of online reading comprehension?* Retrieved from http://www.newliteracies.uconn.edu/pub_files/What_is_new_about_new_literacies_of_online_reading

Leu, D. J. (2000). Literacy and technology: Deictic consequences for literacy education in an information age. In Kamil, M. L., Mosenthal, P., Barr, R., & Pearson, P. D. (Eds.), *Handbook of reading research (Vol. III,* pp. 743–770). Mahwah, NJ: Erlbaum.

Leu, D. J., Kinzer, C. K., Coiro, J., & Cammack, D. (2004). Towards a theory of new literacies emerging from the internet and other information and communication technologies. In Ruddell, R. B., & Unrau, N. (Eds.), *Theoretical models and processes of reading* (5th ed., pp. 1570–1613). International Reading Association.

Leu, D. J., Kinzer, C. K., Coiro, J., Castek, J., & Henry, L. A. (2013). New literacies and the new literacies of online reading comprehension: A dual level theory. In Unrau, N., & Alvermann, D. (Eds.), *Theoretical models and processes of reading* (6th ed.). Newark, DE: International Reading Association. doi:10.1598/0710.42.

Leu, D. J., McVerry, J. G., O'Byrne, W. I., Kiili, C., Zawilinski, L., & Everett-Cacopardo, H. et al. (2011). The new literacies of online reading comprehension: Expanding the literacy and learning curriculum. *Journal of Adolescent & Adult Literacy, 55,* 5–14.

Leu, D. J., O'Byrne, W. I., Zawilinski, L., McVerry, J. G., & Everett-Cacopardo, H. (2009). Expanding the new literacies conversation. *Educational Researcher, 38*(4), 264–269. doi:10.3102/0013189X09336676.

Leu, D., Coiro, J., Castek, J., Hartman, D., Henry, L., & Reinking, D. (2008). Research on instruction and assessment in the new literacies of online reading comprehension. In Collins Block, C., & Parris, S. (Eds.), *Comprehension instruction: Research-based best practices* (pp. 321–346). New York: Guilford Press.

Lewis, C., & Del Valle, A. (2009). Literacy and identity: Implications for research and practice. In Christenbury, L., Bomer, R., & Smagorinsky, P. (Eds.), *Handbook of adolescent literacy research* (pp. 307–322). New York: The Guilford Press.

Lewis, C., Enciso, P., & Moje, E. (2007). *Reframing sociocultural research on literacy: Identity, agency, and power.* Mahwah, NJ: Lawrence Erlbaum Associates, Inc..

Lewis, C., & Fabos, B. (2005). Instant messaging, literacies, and social identities. *Reading Research Quarterly, 40*(4), 470–501. doi:10.1598/RRQ.40.4.5.

Lewis, D. (1969). *Convention: A philosophical study.* Cambridge, MA: Harvard University Press.

Li, D. (2005). *Why do you blog: A uses and gratification inquiry into bloggers' motivations.* (Unpublished master's thesis). Marquette University, Milwaukee, WI.

Li, M., & Zhu, W. (2011). Patterns of computer-mediated interaction in small writing groups using wikis. *Computer Assisted Language Learning.* Retrieved Nov. 20, 2012, from http://www.tandfonline.com/doi/abs/10.1080/09588221.2011.631142

Lichtmann, M. (2005). *The teacher's way: Teaching and the contemplative life.* New York: Paulist Press.

Lieberman, A., & Wood, D. (2003). *Inside the national writing project: Connecting network learning and classroom teaching.* New York: Teachers College Press.

Li, M. (2012). Use of Wikis in second/foreign language classes: A literature review. *CALL-EJ, 13*(1), 17–35.

Lincoln, Y. S., & Guba, E. G. (1985). *Naturalistic inquiry.* Beverly Hills, CA: Sage.

Ling, R., & Baron, N. S. (2007). Messaging and IM: Linguistic comparison of American college data. *Journal of Language and Social Psychology, 26*(3), 291–298. doi:10.1177/0261927X06303480.

Liu, X., & LaRose, R. (2008). The impact of perceived audiences on blogging. Paper presented the meeting of the National Communication Association. San Diego, CA.

Livingstone, S. (2004). Media literacy and the challenge of new information and communication technologies. *Communication Review, 1*(7), 3–14. doi:10.1080/10714420490280152.

Lohnes, S., & Kizer, C. (2007). Questioning assumptions about students expectations for technology in college classrooms. *Innovate, 3*(5), 1–6.

Longcamp, M., Boucard, C., Gilhodes, J.-C., Anton, J.-L., Roth, M., Nazarian, B., & Velay, J.-L. (2008). Learning through hand- or typewriting influences visual recognition of new graphic shapes: Behavioral and functional imaging evidence. *Journal of Cognitive Neuroscience, 20*(5), 802–815. doi:10.1162/jocn.2008.20504 PMID:18201124.

Longcamp, M., Boucard, C., Gilhodes, J.-C., & Velay, J.-L. (2006). Remembering the orientation of newly learned characters depends on the associated writing knowledge: A comparison between handwriting and typing. *Human Movement Science, 25*(4-5), 646–656. doi:10.1016/j.humov.2006.07.007 PMID:17011660.

Longcamp, M., Zerbato-Poudou, M.-T., & Velay, J.-L. (2005). The influence of writing practice on letter recognition in preschool children: A comparison between handwriting and typing. *Acta Psychologica, 119*(1), 67–79. doi:10.1016/j.actpsy.2004.10.019 PMID:15823243.

Long, R. C. (1980). Writer-audience relationships: Analysis or invention? *College Composition and Communication, 31*, 221–226. doi:10.2307/356377.

Lorde, A. (1977). Poetry is not a luxury. In *Essays and speeches by Audre Lorde* (pp. 36–39). Thousand Oaks, CA: Crossing Press.

Loughran, J., & Corrigan, D. (1995). Teaching portfolios: A strategy for developing learning and teaching in pre-service education. *Teaching and Teacher Education, 11*, 565–577. doi:10.1016/0742-051X(95)00012-9.

Luehmann, A., & MacBride, R. (2009). Classroom blogging in the service of student-centered pedagogy: Two high school teachers use of blogs. *Technology Humanities Education Narrative, 6.* Retrieved from http://thenjournal.org/feature/175/

Luke, A. (1994). *The social construction of literacy in the classroom.* Melbourne, Australia: Macmillan.

Luke, A. (2000). Critical literacy in Australia: A matter of context and standpoint. *Journal of Adolescent & Adult Literacy, 43*(5), 448–461.

Luke, A. (2008). *Introduction. Literacy and education: Understanding the new literacy studies in the classroom* (pp. x–xiv). Thousand Oaks, CA: Sage.

Luke, C. (2003). Pedagogy, connectivity, multimodality, and interdisciplinarity. *Reading Research Quarterly, 38*(3), 297–314.

Lu, M. L. (1990). Writing as repositioning. *Journal of Education, 172*, 18–21.

Lundin, R. W. (2008). Teaching with wikis: Toward a networked pedagogy. *Computers and Composition, 25,* 432–448. doi:10.1016/j.compcom.2008.06.001.

Lunsford, A. (2004). Toward a mestiza rhetoric: Gloria Anzaldúa on composition and postcoloniality. In A. Lunsford & L. Ouzgane's (Eds.), Crossing borderlands: Composition and postcoloniality studies (pp. 33-66). Pittsburgh, PA: University of Pittsburgh Press.

Lunsford, A., & Ede, L. (2009). Among the audience: On audience in an age of new literacies. In Weiser, M. E., Fehler, B. M., & González, A. M. (Eds.), *Engaging audience: Writing in an age of new literacies* (pp. 42–73). Urbana, IL: NCTE.

Lyman, F. (1987). Think-pair-share: An expanding teaching technique. *MAA-CIE Cooperative News, 1*(1-2).

Mabrito, M. (1991). Electronic mail as a vehicle for peer response. *Written Communication, 8,* 509–532. doi:10.1177/0741088391008004004.

Mack, M. (2012). Meditation in schools. *Wildmind Buddhist Meditation.* Retrieved from http://www.wildmind.org/

Macrorie, K. (1970). *Telling writing.* Rochelle Park, NJ: Hayden.

Magnifico, A. M., & Halverson, E. R. (2012). Bidirectional artifact analysis: A method for analyzing creative processes. In J. van Aalst, K. Thompson, M.J. Jacobson, & P. Reimann (Eds.), *The future of learning: Proceedings of the 10th International Conference of the Learning Sciences,* (Vol. 2, pp. 276-280). Sydney, Australia: International Society of the Learning Sciences.

Magnifico, A. M., Kline, S., Woodard, R. L., Letofsky, K., Carlin-Menter, S., McCarthey, S., & Cope, B. (2013). *A formative investigation of peer response and revisions in an online writing environment.*

Magnifico, A. M. (2010). Writing for whom: Cognition, motivation, and a writer's audience. *Educational Psychologist, 45*(3), 167–184. doi:10.1080/00461520.2010.493470.

Mahiri, J. (2011). *Digital tools in urban schools: Mediating a remix of learning.* Ann Arbor, MI: University of Michigan Press. doi:10.3998/toi.10329379.0001.001.

Mahiri, J. (Ed.). (2004). *What they don't learn in school: Literacy in the lives of urban youth.* New York: Peter Lang.

Mak, B., & Coniam, D. (2008). Using wikis to enhance and develop writing skills among secondary school students in Hong Kong. *System, 36,* 437–455. doi:10.1016/j.system.2008.02.004.

Malloy, J., Castek, J., & Leu, D. J. (2010). Silent reading and online reading comprehension. In Hiebert, E., & Reutzel, R. (Eds.), *Revisiting silent reading* (pp. 221–240). Newark, DE: International Reading Association.

Maloch, B. (2002). Scaffolding student talk: One teacher's role in literature discussion groups. *Reading Research and Instruction, 42,* 1–29.

Malone, T., & Lepper, M. (1987). Making learning fun: a taxonomy of intrinsic motivations of learning. In R. Snow & M. Farr (Eds.), Aptitude, learning, and instruction: Vol. 3: Cognition and affective process analyses (pp. 223-253). Hillsdale, NJ: Lawrence Erlbaum.

Mangen, A., & Schilhab, T. S. S. (2012). An embodied view of reading: Theoretical considerations, empirical findings, and educational implications. In S. Matre & A. Skaftun (Eds.), Skriv! Les! (pp. 285-300). Trondheim, Norway: Akademika forlag.

Mangen, A., Anda, L. G., Oxborough, G. H. O., & Brønnick, K. (submitted). *Handwriting versus typewriting: Effect of writing modality on word recall and recognition.* Submitted to Memory & Cognition.

Mangen, A., & Velay, J.-L. (2010). Digitizing literacy: Reflections on the haptics of writing. In Zadeh, M. H. (Ed.), *Advances in Haptics* (pp. 385–402). Vienna, Austria: IN-TECH Web. doi:10.5772/8710.

Mangen, A., & Velay, J.-L. (2013). Cognitive implications of digital media. In Ryan, M.-L., Emerson, L., & Robertson, B. (Eds.), *The Johns Hopkins guide to new media and digital textuality.* Baltimore, MD: Johns Hopkins University Press.

Maples, J. (2010). The digital divide: One middle school teacher attempts to connect with his students in online literature discussions. *The Language and Literacy Spectrum, 20,* 25–39.

Markel, S. L. (2001). Technology and education online discussion forums: It's in the response. *Online Journal of Distance Learning Administration, 4*(2).

Markham, A. N. (2003). *Images of internet: Tool, place, way of being*. Paper presented at the Fourth Annual Conference of the Association of Internet Researchers. Toronto, Canada.

Mary Lourdes, S. (n.d). Camtasia in the classroom: Student attitudes and preferences for video commentary or microsoft word comments during the revision process. *Computers and Composition*, 291-22. doi:10.1016/j.compcom.2011.12.001

Matsumura, S., & Hann, G. (2004). Computer anxiety and students' preferred feedback methods in EFL writing. *Modern Language Journal, 88*, 403–415. doi:10.1111/j.0026-7902.2004.00237.x.

Maybin, J. (2000). The new literacy studies: Context, intertextuality and discourse. In Barton, D., Hamilton, M., & Ivanic, R. (Eds.), *Situated literacies: Reading and writing in context* (pp. 197–209). London: Routledge.

Mayer, R. E. (2009). *Multi-media learning* (2nd ed.). New York: Cambridge University Press. doi:10.1017/CBO9780511811678.

McCarthey, S. (2008). The impact of no child left behind on teachers' writing instruction. *Written Communication, 25*, 462–505. doi:10.1177/0741088308322554.

McCarthey, S. J., Magnifico, A. M., Woodard, R. L., & Kline, S. (2013). Situating technology-facilitated feedback and revision: The case of Tom. In Pytash, K., & Ferdig, R. (Eds.), *Exploring technology for writing and writing Instruction*. Hershey, PA: IGI Global.

McCullough, M. (1996). *Abstracting craft: The practiced digital hand*. Cambridge, MA: MIT Press.

McCutchen, D. (2000). Knowledge, processing, and working memory: Implications for a theory of writing. *Instructional Science, 37*, 375–401.

McEneaney, J. E. (2006). Agent-based literacy theory. *Reading Research Quarterly, 41*(3), 352–371. doi:10.1598/RRQ.41.3.3.

McGarrell, H., & Verbeem, J. (2007). Motivating revision of drafts through formative feedback. *ELT Journal, 61*, 228–236. doi:10.1093/elt/ccm030.

McGinnis, T., Goodstein-Stolzenberg, A., & Saliani, E. C. (2007). ''indnpride'': Online spaces of transnational youth as sites of creative and sophisticated literacy and identity work. *Linguistics and Education, 18*(3-4), 283–304. doi:10.1016/j.linged.2007.07.006.

McGrail, E., & Davis, A. (2011). The influence of classroom blogging on elementary student writing. *Journal of Research in Childhood Education, 25*(4), 415-437. Doi: http://dx.doi.org/10.1080/02568543.2011.605205

McGrail, E., & Davis, A. (2013). Blogversing with fifth graders: The intersection of blogging, conversations, and writing. In Young, C. A., & Kajder, S. (Eds.), *Research in English language arts and technology* (pp. 265–290). Charlotte, NC: Information Age Publishing.

McKeown, M., Beck, I., & Blake, R. G. (2009). Rethinking reading comprehension instruction: A comparison of instruction for strategies and content approaches. *Reading Research Quarterly, 44*(3), 218–253. doi:10.1598/RRQ.44.3.1.

McLean, C. (2012). The author's I: Adolescents mediating selfhood through writing. *Pedagogies: An International Journal, 7*(3), 229–245.

McLean, C. A. (2010). A space called home: An immigrant adolescent's digital literacy practices. *Journal of Adolescent & Adult Literacy, 54*(1), 13–22. doi:10.1598/JAAL.54.1.2.

McNamara, D., Jackson, G., & Graesser, A. (2009). Intelligent tutoring and games (iTaG). In H. Lane, A. Ogan, & V. Shute (Eds.), *Proceedings of the Workshop on Intelligent Educational Games at the 14th Annual Conference on Artificial Intelligence in Education* (pp. 1-10). Brighton, UK: AIED.

McNamara, D., Raine, R., Roscoe, R., Crossley, S., Jackson, G., & Dai, J. … Graesser, A. (2012). The writing-pal: Natural language algorithms to support intelligent tutoring on writing strategies. In P. McCarthy & C. Boonthum-Denecke (Eds.), Applied natural language processing and content analysis: Identification, investigation, and resolution (pp. 298-311). Hershey, PA: IGI Global.

McNamara, D., Crossley, S., & Roscoe, R. (2012). Natural language processing in an intelligent writing strategy tutoring system. *Behavior Research Methods*. doi: doi:10.3758/s13428-012-0258-1 PMID:23055164.

McWilliams, J., Hickey, D., Hines, M., Conner, J., & Bishop, S. (2011). Using collaborative writing tools for literary analysis: Twitter, fan fiction and the crucible in the secondary English classroom. *Journal of Media Literacy Education*, 2(3), 238–245.

Means, B., Toyama, Y., Murphy, R., Bakia, M., & Jones, K. (2010). *Evaluation of evidence-based practices in online learning: A meta-analysis and review of online learning studies. Technical Report*. Washington, DC: U.S. Department of Education.

Merchant, G. (2005). Electronic involvement: Identify performance in children's informal digital writing. *Discourse: Studies in the Cultural Politics of Education*, 26, 301–314. doi:10.1080/01596300500199940.

Meredith, H., Coyle, V., & Newman, D. (2011). Digital media's role in adolescent recreational and academic reading. In M. Koehler & P. Mishra (Eds.), *Proceedings of Society for Information Technology & Teacher Education International Conference 2011* (pp. 3736-3741). Chesapeake, VA: AACE. Retrieved from http://www.editlib.org/p/36908

Merriam, S. (1998). *Qualitative research and case study applications in education*. San Francisco, CA: Jossey-Bass.

Merry, S., & Orsmond, P. (2008). *Students' attitudes to and usage of academic feedback provided via audio files*. Retrieved from http://www.bioscience.heacademy.ac.uk/journal/vol11/beej-11-3.aspx

Miles, M. B., & Huberman, A. M. (1994). *Qualitative data analysis: An expanded sourcebook* (2nd ed.). Thousand Oaks, CA: Sage.

Miller, C., Purcell, K., & Rainie, L. (2012). Reading habits in different communities. *Pew Internet and American Life Project*. Retrieved from http://libraries.pewInternet.org/2012/12/20/reading-habits-in-different-communities/

Miller, C., & Shepherd, D. (2009). Blogging as social action: A genre analysis of the weblog. In Miller, S. (Ed.), *The Norton book of composition studies* (pp. 1450–1473). New York: W.W. Norton & Company, Inc..

Mills, K. A. (2010). A review of the digital turn in the new literacy studies. *Review of Educational Research*, 80(2), 246–271. doi:10.3102/0034654310364401.

Mills, K. A., & Chandra, V. (2011). Microblogging as a literacy practice for educational communities. *Journal of Adolescent & Adult Literacy*, 55(1), 35–45.

Miltsakaki, E., & Troutt, A. (2007). Read-X: Automatic evaluation of reading difficulty of web text. In T. Bastiaens & S. Carliner (Eds.), *Proceedings of World Conference on E-Learning in Corporate, Government, Healthcare, and Higher Education 2007* (pp. 7280-7286). Chesapeake, VA: AACE. Retrieved from http://www.editlib.org/p/26932

Mirel, B., & Wright, Z. (2009). Heuristic evaluations of bioinformatics tools: A development case. In *Proceedings of the 13th International Conference on Human Computer Interaction* (HCII-09) (LNCS), (vol. 5610, pp. 329-338). Berlin: Springer.

Mishra, P., & Koehler, M. J. (2008). Introducing technological pedagogical content knowledge. In *Proceedings of the Annual Meeting of the American Educational Research Association* (pp. 1–16). Retrieved from http://www.msuedtechsandbox.com/2010RouenY2/Readings/wk1d2_mishra&koehler.pdf

Mishra, P., & Koehler, M. J. (2006). Technological pedagogical content knowledge: A new framework for teacher knowledge. *Teachers College Record*, 108(6), 1017–1054. doi:10.1111/j.1467-9620.2006.00684.x.

Mitchell, R., & Taylor, M. (1979). The integrating perspective: An audience-response model for writing. *College English*, 41(3), 247–271. doi:10.2307/376441.

Moffett, J. (1982). Writing, inner speech, and meditation. *College English*, 44(3), 231–246. doi:10.2307/377011.

Moffett, J. (1983). *Teaching the universe of discourse*. Portsmouth, NH: Heinemann.

Moje, E. B. (2002). Re-framing adolescent literacy research for new times: Studying youth as a resource. *Reading Research and Instruction*, *41*(3), 211–228. doi:10.1080/19388070209558367.

Moje, E. B. (2007). Developing socially just subject-matter instruction: A review of the literature on disciplinary literacy teaching. *Review of Research in Education*, *31*, 1–44. doi:10.3102/0091732X07300046.

Moje, E. B. (2009). Standpoints: A call for new research on new and multi-literacies. *Research in the Teaching of English*, *43*(4), 348–362.

Moje, E. B., & Luke, A. (2009). Literacy and identity: Examining the metaphors in history and contemporary research. *Reading Research Quarterly*, *44*(4), 415–437. dx.doi.org/10.1598/RRQ.44.4.7 doi:10.1598/RRQ.44.4.7.

Moje, E. B., & Shepardson, D. P. (1998). Social interactions and children's changing understanding of electric circuits: Exploring unequal power relations in peer-led learning groups. In Guzzetti, B., & Hynd, C. (Eds.), *Perspectives on conceptual change: Multiple ways to understand knowing and learning in a complex world* (pp. 225–234). Mahwah, NJ: Erlbaum.

Moore, M., & Karabenick, S. (1992). The effects of computer communications on the reading and writing performance of fifth-grade students. *Computers in Human Behavior*, *8*(1), 27–38. doi:10.1016/0747-5632(92)90017-9.

Moran, P. P., & Greenberg, B. (2008). Peer revision: Helping students to develop a meta-editor. *Ohio Journal of English Language Arts*, *48*(1), 33–39.

Moreno, R. (2004). Decreasing cognitive load for novice students: effects of explanatory versus corrective feedback in discovery-based multimedia. *Instructional Science: An International Journal of Learning and Cognition*, *32*(1-2), 99–113.

Moss, P. (1994). Can there be validity without reliability? *Educational Research*, *23*, 5–12.

Moxley, J. (2012). *My reviewers*. Tampa, FL: University of South Florida.

Moya, P. M. L. (2002). *Learning from experience: Minority identities, multicultural struggles*. Berkeley, CA: University of California Press.

Moya, P. M. L. (2006). What's identity got to do with it? Mobilizing identities in the multicultural classroom. In Alcoff, L. M., Hames-Garcia, M., Mohanty, S. P., & Moya, P. M. L. (Eds.), *Identity politics reconsidered* (pp. 96–117). New York: Palgrave Macmillan.

Murray, D. (1968). *A writer teaches writing: A practical method of teaching composition*. Boston: Houghton Mifflin.

Murray, D. M. (1972). Teach writing as a process not product. *The Leaflet*, *71*(3), 11–14.

Murray, D. M. (1999). *Write to learn*. New York: Harcourt Brace College Pub..

Myhill, D., & Fisher, R. (2010). Editorial: Writing development: Cognitive, sociocultural, linguistic perspectives. *Journal of Research in Reading*, *33*(1), 1–3. doi:10.1111/j.1467-9817.2009.01428.x.

Napier, J. (1993). *Hands*. Princeton, NJ: Princeton University Press.

Nardi, B., & O'Day, V. (1999). *Information ecologies: Using technology with heart*. Cambridge, MA: MIT Press.

National Center for Education Statistics. (2012a). *The nation's report card: Mathematics 2011 (NCES 2012–458)*. Washington, DC: Institute of Education Sciences, U.S. Department of Education.

National Center for Education Statistics. (2012b). *The nation's report card: Reading 2011 (NCES 2012–457)*. Washington, DC: Institute of Education Sciences, U.S. Department of Education.

National Center for Education Statistics. (2012c). *The nation's report card: Science 2011 (NCES 2012–465)*. Washington, DC: Institute of Education Sciences, U.S. Department of Education.

National Center for Education Statistics. (2012d). *The nation's report card: Writing 2011 (NCES 2012–470)*. Washington, DC: Institute of Education Sciences, U.S. Department of Education.

National Commission on Writing. (2003). *The neglected R: The need for a writing revolution.* Retrieved January 2, 2011 from http://www.host-collegeboard.com/advocacy/writing/publications.html

National Council for Teachers of English (NCTE). (2013). *Context for NCTE's 21st century framework.* Retrieved February, 22,2013 from http://www.ncte.org/positions/statements/21stcentframework

National Council of Teachers of English. (2008). *21st century literacies.* Retrieved from http://www.ncte.org/governance/literacies

National Council of Teachers of English. (2008). *Writing now: A policy research brief.* Retrieved from http://www.ncte.org/collections/adolescentliteracy

National Council of Teachers of English. (2009). *Writing between the lines and everywhere else.* Urbana, IL: NCTE.

National Council of Teachers of English. (2013). *NCTE framework for 21st century curriculum and assessment.* Retrieved March 1, 2013, from http://www.ncte.org/library/NCTEFiles/Resources/Positions/Framework_21stCent_Curr_Assessment.pdf

National Governors Association Center for Best Practices & Council of State School Officers. (2010). *Common core state standards for English language arts & literacy in history/ social studies, science, and technical subjects.* Washington, DC: Authors. Retrieved January 13, 2013, from http://corestandards.org/assets/CCSSI_ELA%20 Standards.pdf

National Governors Association Center for Best Practices (NGA Center) & Council of Chief State School Officers. (CCSSO). (2010). Common core state standards. Washington, DC: National Governors Association Center for Best Practices, Council of Chief State School Officers.

National Governors Association Center for Best Practices, Council of Chief State School Officers. (2010). *Common core state standards.* Washington, DC: National Governors Association Center for Best Practices, Council of Chief State School Officers.

National Writing Project. (n.d.b). *About NWP - National writing project.* Retrieved February 18, 2012, from http://www.nwp.org/cs/public/print/doc/about.csp

National Writing. P., DeVoss, D., Eidman-Aadahl, E., & Hicks, T. (2010). Because digital writing matters: Improving student writing in online and multimedia environments. San Francisco, CA: Jossey-Bass.

Neilsen, J. (2012). F-shaped pattern for reading web-content. *The Neilsen Norman Group.* Retrieved from http://www.nngroup.com/articles/f-shaped-pattern-reading-Web-content/

Nelson, M. M., & Schunn, C. D. (2009). The nature of feedback: how different types of peer feedback affect writing performance. *Instructional Science: An International Journal of the Learning Sciences, 37*(4), 375–401. doi:10.1007/s11251-008-9053-x.

New London Group. (1996). A pedagogy of multiliteracies: Designing social futures. *Harvard Educational Review, 66*(1), 60–92.

New Media Consortium. (2005). *A global imperative: The report of the 21st century literacy summit.* Retrieved from http://www.nmc.org/pdf/Global_Imperative.pdf

Newkirk, T. (2012). *The art of slow reading.* Portsmouth, NH: Heinemann.

Newman, D. R., Johnson, C., Webb, B., & Cochrane, C. (1997). Evaluating the quality of learning in computer supported cooperative learning. *Journal of the American Society for Information Science American Society for Information Science, 48,* 484–495. doi:10.1002/(SICI)1097-4571(199706)48:6<484::AID-ASI2>3.0.CO;2-Q.

Newman, K., Samimy, K., & Romstedt, K. (2010). Developing a training program for secondary teachers of English language learners in Ohio. *Theory into Practice, 49*(2), 152–161. doi:10.1080/00405841003641535.

Nickerson, R. S. (2005). Technology and cognition amplification. In Sternberg, R. J., & Preiss, D. (Eds.), *Intelligence and technology: The impact of tools on the nature and development of human abilities* (pp. 3–27). Mahwah, NJ: Lawrence Erlbaum Ass.

Nielsen, J. (1992). Finding usability problems through heuristic evaluation. In *Proceedings ACM CHI'92 Conference* (pp. 373-380). ACM.

Nielsen, J. (1994a). Enhancing the explanatory power of usability heuristics. In *Proceedings of ACM CHI'94 Conference* (pp. 152-158). ACM.

Nielsen, J. (1994b). Heuristic evaluation. In Nielsen & Mack (Eds.), Usability Inspection Methods. New York: John Wiley & Sons.

Nielsen, J., & Molich, R. (1990). Heuristic evaluation of user interfaces. In *Proceedings of the ACM CHI'90 Conference* (pp. 249-256). ACM.

Nielsen. (2011). *State of the media: U.S. digital consumer report, Q3-Q4 2011.* Retrieved from http://www.nielsen.com/us/en/insights/reports-downloads/2012/us-digital-consumer-report.html

Nieto, S. (2010). *The light in their eyes: Creating multicultural learning communities.* New York: Teachers College Press.

Niguidula, D. (2005). Documenting learning with digital portfolios. *Educational Leadership, 63,* 44–47.

Niiya, M., Warschauer, M., & Zheng, B. (2013). Emerging literacies in digital media and L2 secondary writing. In de Oliveira, L. C., & Silva, T. (Eds.), *L2 writing in secondary classroom: Student experiences, academic issues, and teacher education.* New York: Routledge.

Noë, A. (2004). *Action in perception.* Cambridge, MA: MIT Press.

Nystrand, M. (1986). *The structure of written communication: Studies in reciprocity between readers and writers.* Orlando, FL: Academic Press.

Nystrand, M. (1997). *Opening dialogue: Understanding the dynamics of language and learning in the English classroom.* New York: Teachers College Press.

Nystrand, M. (2006). Classroom discourse and reading comprehension. *Research in the Teaching of English, 40,* 392–412.

Nystrand, M., Gamoran, A., & Carbonaro, W. (1998). *Toward an ecology of learning: The case of classroom discourse and its effects on writing in high school English and social studies.* Albany, NY: National Research Center on English Learning & Achievement.

Nystrand, M., Gamoran, A., Kachur, R., & Prendergast, C. (Eds.). (1997). *Opening dialogue: Understanding the dynamics of language and learning in the English classroom.* New York, NY: Teachers College Press.

O'Byrne, W. I. (2009). *Facilitating critical thinking skills through content creation.* Paper presented at the 58th Annual National Reading Conference. Albuquerque, NM.

O'Byrne, W. I. (2012). *Facilitating critical evaluation skills through content creation: Empowering adolescents as readers and writers of online information.* (Unpublished doctoral dissertation). University of Connecticut, Storrs, CT.

O'Donnell, M. (2005). *Blogging as pedagogic practice: Artefact and ecology.* Paper presented at the Blog Talk Downunder Conference. Sydney, Australia. Retrieved from http://incsub.org/blogtalk/?page_id=66

O'Reilley, M. (1998). *Radical presence: Teaching as a contemplative practice.* Boynton/Cook Publishers.

Oblinger, D. (2006). *Learning spaces (Vol. 2).* Washington, DC: Educause.

O'Brien, T. (1990). *The things they carried.* Boston: Houghton Mifflin Harcourt.

Ochs, E. (1979). Planned and unplanned discourse. In Givón, T. (Ed.), *Syntax and semantics: Discourse and syntax* (pp. 51–80). New York: Academic.

Office of Educational Technology. (2010). *Transforming American education: Learning powered by technology: National educational technology plan 2010.* Washington, DC: US Department of Education.

Olsen, N. S. (2011). Coding ATC incident data using HFACS: Inter-coder consensus. *Safety Science, 49,* 1365–1370. doi:10.1016/j.ssci.2011.05.007.

Olson, D. (1977). From utterance to text: The bias of language in speech and writing. *Harvard Educational Review, 47,* 257–281.

Ong, W. (1975). The writer's audience is always a fiThe w. *Publications of the Modern Language Association of America, 90*(1), 9–21.

Ong, W. J. (1979). The writer's audience is always a fiction. *PMLA, 90*(1), 9–21. doi:10.2307/461344.

O'Regan, J. K., & Noë, A. (2001). A sensorimotor account of vision and visual consciousness. *The Behavioral and Brain Sciences*, *24*(5), 939–973. doi:10.1017/S0140525X01000115 PMID:12239892.

Pace, J. L. (2007). Understanding authority in classrooms: A review of theory, ideology, and research. *Review of Educational Research*, *77*(1), 4–27. doi:10.3102/003465430298489.

Pahl, K. (2012). A reason to write: Exploring writing epistemologies in two contexts. *Pedagogies: An International Journal*, *7*(3), 209–228.

Pahl, K., & Rowsell, J. (2005). *Literacy and education: Understanding the new literacy studies in the classroom.* London, UK: Paul Chapman Publishing.

Pahl, K., & Rowsell, J. (2008). *Literacy and education: Understanding the new literacy studies in the classroom.* Thousand Oaks, CA: Sage.

Pajares, F. (2003). Self-efficacy beliefs, motivation, and achievement in writing: A review of the literature. *Reading & Writing Quarterly*, *19*, 139–158. doi:10.1080/10573560308222.

Palincsar, A. S., & Brown, A. L. (1984). Reciprocal teaching of comprehension-fostering and monitoring activities. *Cognition and Instruction*, *1*(2), 117–175. doi:10.1207/s1532690xci0102_1.

Palincsar, A. S., Brown, A. L., & Campione, J. C. (1993). First-grade dialogues for knowledge acquisition and use. In Forman, E. A., Minick, N., & Stone, C. A. (Eds.), *Contexts for learning: Sociocultural dynamics in children's development* (pp. 43–57). New York, NY: Oxford University Press.

Palmer, P. (1983). *To know as we are known: Education as a spiritual journey.* New York: HarperOne.

Parisi, L., & Crosby, B. (2012). *Making connections with blogging: Authentic learning for today's classrooms.* Eugene, OR: Society for Integration of Technology in Education.

Park, Y., Warschauer, M., Farkas, G., & Collins, P. (2012). The effects of visual-syntactic text formatting on adolescents' academic development. Manuscript submitted for publication.

Parker, J. (1971). What is poverty? In Fine Clouse, B. (Ed.), *Patterns for a purpose: A rhetorical reader* (pp. 546–549). Boston: McGraw.

Park, J. Y. (2012). Re-imaging reader-response in middle and secondary schools: Early adolescent girls' critical and communal reader responses to the young adult novel *Speak. Children's Literature in Education*, *43*, 191–212. doi:10.1007/s10583-012-9164-5.

Partnership for Assessment of Readiness for College and Careers (PARCC). (2012). Structure of the model content frameworks for ELA/literacy. *Achieve, Inc.* Retrieved from http://www.parcconline.org/mcf/english-language-artsliteracy/structure-model-content-frameworks-elaliteracy

Patton, M. Q. (2002). *Qualitative research and evaluation methods* (3rd ed.). Thousand Oaks, CA: Sage.

Pearsall, P. (1998). *The heart's code: Tapping the wisdom and the power of our heart energy.* New York: Broadway Books.

Pearson, P. D. (2009). The roots of reading comprehension instruction. In Israel, S. E., & Duffy, G. G. (Eds.), *Handbook of research on reading comprehension* (pp. 3–31). New York: Routledge.

Pennington, M. (2004). Electronic media in second language writing: An overview of tools and research findings. In Fotos, S., & Browne, C. M. (Eds.), *New perspectives on CALL for second language classrooms* (pp. 69–92). Mahwah, NJ: Erlbaum Associates Inc..

Penrod, D. (2005). *Composition in convergence: The impact of new media on writing assessment.* Mahwah, NJ: Lawrence Erlbaum.

Penrod, D. (2007). *Using blogs to enhance literacy: The next 21st-century learning.* Lanham, MD: Rowman & Littlefield Education Publishers.

Pfister, F.R. & Petrik. (1980). A heuristic model for creating a writer's audience. *College Composition and Communication*, *31*, 213–220. doi:10.2307/356376.

Piazza, C. L., & Siebert, C. F. (2008). Development and validation of a writing disposition scale for elementary and middle school students. *The Journal of Educational Research*, *101*(5), 275–285. doi:10.3200/JOER.101.5.275-286.

Piper, A. (2012). *Book was there: Reading in electronic times.* Chicago: University of Chicago Press. doi:10.7208/chicago/9780226922898.001.0001.

Plant, E., Ericcson, K., Hill, L., & Asberg, K. (2005). Why study time does not predict grade point average across college students: implications of deliberate practice for academic performance. *Contemporary Educational Psychology, 30*, 96–116. doi:10.1016/j.cedpsych.2004.06.001.

Plester, B., Wood, C., & Bell, V. (2008). Txt msg n school literacy: Does texting and knowledge of text abbreviations adversely affect children's literacy attainment. *Literacy, 42*, 137–144. doi:10.1111/j.1741-4369.2008.00489.x.

Plester, B., Wood, C., & Joshi, P. (2009). Exploring the relationship between children's knowledge of text message abbreviations and school literacy outcomes. *The British Journal of Developmental Psychology, 27*, 145–161. doi:10.1348/026151008X320507 PMID:19972666.

Porter, J. E. (1996). Audience. In Enos, T. (Ed.), *Encyclopedia of rhetoric and composition: Communication from ancient times to the information age* (p. 43). New York: Routledge.

Powell, D., & Dixon, M. (2011). Does SMS text messaging help or harm adults' knowledge of standard spelling? *Journal of Computer Assisted Learning, 27*, 58–66. doi:10.1111/j.1365-2729.2010.00403.x.

Pratt, M. L. (1991). Arts of the contact zone. *Profession, 91*, 33–40.

Prensky, M. (2001). Digital natives, digial immigrants. *Horizon, 9*, 1–6. doi:10.1108/10748120110424816.

Prensky, M. (2010). *Teaching digital natives: Partnering for real learning.* Thousand Oaks, CA: Corwin Press.

Pressley, M. (2005). *Reading instruction that works: The case for balanced teaching* (3rd ed.). New York, NY: Guilford.

Prestidge, S. (2012). The beliefs behind the teacher that influences their ICT practices. *Computers & Education, 58*(1), 449–458. doi:10.1016/j.compedu.2011.08.028.

Prior, P. (2004). Tracing processes: How texts come into being. In Bazerman & Prior (Eds.), What writing does and how it does it: An introduction to analyzing texts and textual practices (pp. 167-200). Mahwah, NJ: Lawrence Erlbaum Associates.

Protopsaltis, A. (2008). Reading strategies in hypertexts and factors influencing hyperlink selection. *Journal of Educational Multimedia and Hypermedia, 17*(2), 191–213.

Purcell, K., Rainie, L., Heaps, A., Buchanan, J., Friedrich, L., Jacklin, A., et al. (2012). How teens do research in the digital world. *Pew Internet and American Life Project.* Retrieved from http://pewInternet.org/Reports/2012/Student-Research.aspx

Purcell-Gates, V., Duke, N. K., & Martineau, J. A. (2007). Learning to read and write genre-specific text: Roles of authentic experience and explicit teaching. *Reading Research Quarterly, 42*(1), 8–45. doi:10.1598/RRQ.42.1.1.

Purdy, J. P. (2009). When the tenets of composition go public: A study of writing in wikipedia. *College Composition and Communication, 61*(2), 351–373.

Putney, L. A. G., Green, J., Dixon, C., Durán, C., & Yeager, B. (2000). Consequential progressions: Exploring collective-individual development in a bilingual classroom. In Lee, C. D., & Smagorinsky, P. (Eds.), *Vygotskian perspectives on literacy research: Constructing meaning through collaborative inquiry* (pp. 86–126). New York: Cambridge University Press.

Quick, J., Atkinson, R., & Lin, L. (2012). Empirical taxonomies of gameplay enjoyment: Personality and video game preference. *International Journal of Game-Based Learning, 2*, 11–31. doi:10.4018/ijgbl.2012070102.

Rainie, L., & Duggan, M. (2012). E-book reading jumps: Print book reading declines. *Pew Internet and American Life Project.* Retrieved from http://libraries.pewInternet.org/files/legacy-pdf/PIP_Reading%20and%20ebooks.pdf

RAND Reading Study Group (RRSG). (2002). *Reading for understanding: Toward a research and development program in reading comprehension.* Pittsburgh, PA: Office of Educational Research and Improvement.

Rand, A. (2010). Mediating at the student-Wikipedia intersection. *Journal of Library Administration, 50*(7/8), 923–932. doi:10.1080/01930826.2010.488994.

Ransdell, S., Levy, C. M., & Kellogg, R. T. (2002). The structure of writing processes as revealed by secondray task demands. L1—Educational Studies in Language and Literature, 2(2), 141-163.

Raphael, T. E., Florio-Ruane, S., George, M., Hasty, N. L., & Highfield, K. (2004). *Book club plus! A literacy framework for the primary grades*. Lawrence, MA: Small Planet Communications.

Reardon, M. (2005). *China to trump U.S. in broadband subscribers*. Retrieved Sep. 21, 2012, from http://news.zdnet.com/2100-6005_22-5695591.html

Reed, D., & Hicks, T. (2009). From the front of the classroom to the ears of the world: Podcasting as an extension of speech class. In Herrington, A., Hodgson, K., & Moran, C. (Eds.), *Teaching the New Writing: Technology, Change, and Assessment in the 21st Century Classroom* (pp. 124–139). New York: Teachers College Press/National Writing Project.

Reich, S. M. (2010). Adolescents' sense of community on MySpace and Facebook: A mixed-methods approach. *Journal of Community Psychology*, *38*(6), 688–705. doi:10.1002/jcop.20389.

Reid, J. (2011). We don't Twitter, we Facebook: An alternative pedagogical space that enables critical practices in relation to writing. *English Teaching: Practice and Critique*, *10*(1), 58–80.

Reinhardt, J., & Zander, V. (2011). Social networking in an intensive English program classroom: A language socialization perspective. *CALICO Journal*, *28*(2), 326–344.

Reinking, D. (1997). Me and my hypertext: A multiple digression analysis of technology and literacy (sic). *Reading Online*. Retrieved from http://www.readingonline.org/articles/art_index.asp?HREF=/articles/hypertext/index.html

Reinking, D. (1998). Synthesizing technological transformations of literacy in a post-typographical world. In Reinking, D., McKenna, M. C., Labbo, L. D., & Kieffer, R. D. (Eds.), *Handbook of literacy and technology: Transformations in a post-typographic world* (pp. xi–xxx). Mahwah, NJ: Lawrence Erlbaum.

Reinking, D. (2008). Thoughts on the Lewis and Fabos article on instant messaging. In Coiro, J., Knobel, M., Lankshear, C., & Leu, D. J. (Eds.), *Handbook of research on new literacies* (pp. 1175–1187). Mahwah, NJ: Erlbaum.

Reinking, D. (2009). Valuing reading, writing, and books in a post-typographic world. In Nord, D., & Rubin, J. (Eds.), *The history of the book in American* (pp. 485–502). Cambridge, UK: American Antiquarian Society and Cambridge University Press.

Reinking, D., & Bradley, B. A. (2008). *Formative and design experiments: Approaches to language and literacy research*. New York: Teachers College Press.

Reinking, D., Labbo, L. D., & McKenna, M. C. (2000). From assimilation to accommodation: A developmental framework for integrating digital technologies into literacy research and instruction. *Journal of Research in Reading*, *23*(2), 110–122. doi:10.1111/1467-9817.00108.

Reitman, W. R. (1964). Heuristic decision procedures open constraints and the structure of ill-defined problems. In Shelly, M. W., & Bryan, G. L. (Eds.), *Human Judgments and Optimality*. New York: John Wiley & Sons, Inc..

Reynolds, N., Bizzell, P., & Herzberg, B. (Eds.). (2004). *The Bedford bibliography for teaching of writing* (6th ed.). Boston: Bedford/St. Martin's.

Rhodes, J. A., & Robnolt, V. J. (2009). Digital literacies in the classroom. In Christenbury, L., Bomar, R., & Smagorinsky, P. (Eds.), *Handbook of Adolescent Literacy Research* (pp. 153–169). New York: Guilford Press.

Rice, K. L. (2006). A comprehensive look at distance education in the K-12 context. *Journal of Research on Technology in Education*, *38*(4), 425.

Rideout, V. J., Foehr, U. G., & Roberts, D. F. (2010). *Generation M2: Media in the lives of 8- to 18-year olds*. Menlo. Park, CA: Henry J. Kaiser Family Foundation.

Rijlaarsdam, G., Van den Bergh, H., Couzijn, M., Janssen, T., Braaksma, M., & Tillema, M. et al. (2012). Writing. In Anderman, E., Winne, P. H., Alexander, P. A., & Corno, L. (Eds.), *Handbook of educational psychology* (pp. 189–227). New York, NY: Routledge.

Risko, V. J., Roller, C. M., Cummins, C., Bean, R. M., Block, C. C., & Anders, P. L. et al. (2008). A critical analysis of research on reading teacher education. *Reading Research Quarterly*, *43*, 252–288. doi:10.1598/RRQ.43.3.3.

Ritchel, M. (2010). Digital devices deprive brain of needed downtime. *New York Times*. Retrieved from http://www.newyorktimes.com

Roberts, K. L. (2012). The linguistic demands of the common core state standards for reading and writing informational text in the primary grades. *Seminars in Speech and Language, 33*(2), 146–159. doi:10.1055/s-0032-1310314 PMID:22538710.

Robinson, E., & Robinson, S. (2003). *What does it mean-discourse, text, culture: An introduction*. Sydney, Australia: McGraw-Hill.

Rogoff, B. (1990). *Apprenticeship in thinking: Cognitive development in social context*. New York, NY: Oxford University Press.

Rohrer, D., & Pashler, H. (2010). Recent research on human learning challenges conventional instructional strategies. *Educational Researcher, 39*, 406–412. doi:10.3102/0013189X10374770.

Romano, T. (2000). *Blending genre, altering style*. Portsmouth, NH: Boynton/Cook.

Roscoe, R., Varner, L., & Weston, J., Crossley, & McNamara, D. (2013). The writing pal intelligent tutoring system: Usability testing and development. *Computers and Composition*.

Rose, L. T., Daley, S. G., & Rose, D. H. (2011). Let the questions be your guide: MBE as interdisciplinary science. *Mind, Brain, and Education, 5*(4), 153–162. doi:10.1111/j.1751-228X.2011.01123.x.

Rosenblatt, L. M. (1938). *Literature as exploration*. New York: Appleton-Century-Croft.

Rosenblatt, L. M. (1978). *The reader, the text, the poem: The transactional theory of the literary work*. Carbondale, IL: Southern Illinois University Press.

Rosenblatt, L. M. (2005). *Making meaning with texts: Selected essays*. Portsmouth, NH: Heinemann.

Rowsell, J. (2009). My life on Facebook: Assessing the art of online social networking. In Burke, A., & Hammett, R. F. (Eds.), *Assessing new literacies: Perspectives from the classroom* (pp. 95–112). New York, NY: Peter Lang Publishing.

Rudner, L., Garcia, V., & Welch, C. (2006). An evaluation of the IntelliMetric essay scoring system. *Journal of Technology, Learning, and Assessment, 4*(4), 3–21.

Ruiz, R. (1988). Orientations in language planning. In McKay, S. L., & Wong, S. C. (Eds.), *Language diversity: Problem or resource?* (pp. 3–25). New York: Newbury House.

Rushkoff, D. (2010). *Program or be programmed: Ten commands for a digital age*. Berkeley, CA: Soft Skull Press.

Russell, M., & Abrams, L. (2004). Instructional effects of computers for writing: The effect of state testing programs. *Teachers College Record, 106*(6), 1332–1357. doi:10.1111/j.1467-9620.2004.00381.x.

Ryan, R., Rigby, C., & Przybylski, A. (2006). The motivational pull of video games: A self-determination theory approach. *Motivation and Emotion, 30*, 347–363. doi:10.1007/s11031-006-9051-8.

Salaberry, M. R. (2001). The use of technology for second language learning and teaching: A retrospective. *Modern Language Journal, 85*(1), 39–56. doi:10.1111/0026-7902.00096.

Saldaña, J. (2009). *The coding manual for qualitative researchers*. Thousand Oaks, CA: Sage.

Saltzman, A. (2013). *Association for mindfulness in education*. Retrieved from www.mindfuleducation.org

Samuels, L. (2006). *The effectiveness of web conferencing technology in student-teacher conferencing in the writing classroom: A study of first-year student writers*. (Unpublished master's thesis). North Carolina State University, Raleigh, NC.

Samuels, B. M. (2009). Can the differences between education and neuroscience be overcome by mind, brain, and education? *Mind, Brain, and Education, 3*(1), 45–55. doi:10.1111/j.1751-228X.2008.01052.x.

Sánchez, P., & Salazar, M. (2012). Transnational computer use in urban Latino immigrant communities: Implications for schooling. *Urban Education, 47*(1), 90–116. doi:10.1177/0042085911427740.

Sawyer, R. K. (2006). The Cambridge handbook of the learning sciences. New York: Cambridge.

Scarcella, R. (2003). *Accelerating academic English: A focus on English language learners.* Oakland, CA: Regents of the University of California.

Scardamalia, M., & Bereiter, C. (1983). Child as co-investigator: Helping children gain insight into their own mental processes. In Paris, S., Olson, G., & Stevenson, H. (Eds.), *Learning and motivation in the classroom* (pp. 83–107). Hillsdale, NJ: Lawrence Erlbaum Associates.

Scardamalia, M., & Bereiter, C. (1985). Fostering the development of self-regulation in children's knowledge processing. In Chipman, S. F., Segal, J. W., & Glaser, R. (Eds.), *Thinking and learning skills: Research and open questions* (pp. 563–577). Hillsdale, NJ: Lawrence Erlbaum Associates.

Scardamalia, M., & Bereiter, C. (1994). Computer support for knowledge-building communities. *Journal of the Learning Sciences, 3*(3), 265–283. doi:10.1207/s15327809jls0303_3.

Scardamalia, M., Bereiter, C., & Steinbach, R. (1984). Teachability of reflective processes in written composition. *Cognitive Science, 8*(2), 173–190. doi:10.1207/s15516709cog0802_4.

Scheidt, L. (2006). Adolescent diary weblogs and the unseen audience. In Buckingham, D., & Rebekah, W. (Eds.), *Digital generations: Children, young people and new media.* London: Lawrence Erlbaum.

Schellens, T., & Valcke, M. (2005). Collaborative learning in asynchronous discussion groups: What about the impact on cognitive processing? *Computers in Human Behavior, 21*(6), 957–975. doi:10.1016/j.chb.2004.02.025.

Schiller, S. (1999). Spirituality in pedagogy: A field of possibilities. *JAEPL, 5*, 57–68.

Schleppegrell, M., Greer, S., & Taylor, S. (2008). Literacy in history: Language and meaning. *Australian Journal of Language and Literacy, 31*(2), 174–187.

Schmoker, M. (2007). Reading, writing, and thinking for all. *Educational Leadership, 64*(7), 63–66.

Schoeberlein, D., & Sheth, S. (2009). *Mindful teaching and teaching mindfulness: A guide for anyone who teaches anything.* Boston: Wisdom Publications.

Schultz, J. (2000). Computers and collaborative writing in the foreign language curriculum. In Warschauer, M., & Kern, R. (Eds.), *Network-based language teaching: Concepts and practice.* Cambridge, UK: Cambridge University Press. doi:10.1017/CBO9781139524735.008.

Schwan, S., Garsoffky, B., & Hesse, F. (2000). Do film cuts facilitate the perceptual and cognitive organization of activity sequences? *Memory & Cognition, 28*, 214–223. doi:10.3758/BF03213801 PMID:10790977.

Schwartz, F., & White, K. (2000). Making sense of it all: Giving and getting online course feedback. In White, K. W., & Weight, B. H. (Eds.), *The online teaching guide: A handbook of attitudes, strategies, and techniques for the virtual classroom* (pp. 57–72). Boston: Allyn and Bacon.

Scribner, S., & Cole, M. (1981). *The psychology of literacy.* Cambridge, MA: Harvard University Press.

Selfe, C.L., & Wahlstrom, B.J. (1979). *Beyond bandaids and bactine: Computer-assisted instruction and revision.* (ERIC Reproduction Service Document N. 232182).

Selfe, C. L. (1990). Technology in the English classroom: Computers through the lens of feminist theory. In Handa, C. (Ed.), *Computers and community* (pp. 118–139). Portsmouth, NH: Boynton/Cook Heinemann.

Selfe, C. L., & Wahlstrom, B. J. (1983). The benevolent beast: Computer-assisted instruction for the teacher of writing. *Writing Instructor, 2*(4), 192–193.

Selwyn, N. (2009). Faceworking: Exploring students' education-related use of Facebook. *Learning, Media and Technology, 34*(2), 157–174. doi:10.1080/17439880902923622.

Serafini, F. (2011). Expanding perspectives for comprehending visual images in multimodal texts. *Journal of Adolescent & Adult Literacy, 54*(5), 342–350. doi:10.1598/JAAL.54.5.4.

Shaffer, D. W. (2006). *How computer games help children learn.* New York, NY: Palgrave Macmillan. doi:10.1057/9780230601994.

Shanahan, T. (2006). Relations among oral language, reading, and writing development. In MacArthur, C. A., Graham, S., & Fitzgerald, J. (Eds.), *Handbook of writing research* (pp. 171–183). New York, NY: Guilford Press.

Shapiro, A. L. (2000). *The control revolution how the internet is putting individuals in charge and changing the world we know*. PublicAffairs.

Shapiro, L. A. (2010). *Embodied cognition*. New York: Routledge.

Shaughnessy, M. P. (1977). *Errors and expectations: A guide for the teacher of basic writing*. Oxford, UK: Oxford University Press.

Sheppard, J. (2009). The rhetorical work of multimedia production practices: It's more than just technical skill. *Computers and Composition, 26*(2), 122–131. doi:10.1016/j.compcom.2009.02.004.

Shermis, M., & Burstein, J. (2003). *Automated essay scoring: A cross-disciplinary perspective*. Mahwah, NJ: Erlbaum.

Short, K. G., Harste, J. C., & Burke, C. (1996). *Creating classrooms for authors and inquirers* (2nd ed.). Portsmouth, NH: Heinemann.

Shute, V. (2008). Focus on formative feedback. *Review of Educational Research, 78*, 153–189. doi:10.3102/0034654307313795.

Shute, V., Rieber, L., & Van Eck, R. (2011). Games… and… learning. In Reiser, R., & Dempsey, J. (Eds.), *Trends and issues in instructional design and technology* (3rd ed., pp. 321–332). Upper Saddle River, NJ: Pearson Education Inc..

Siegel, F., & Warnock, S. (2006). Using video capture software for asynchronous A/V writing feedback. *CCCC 2006 Review*. Retrieved from http://wac.colostate.edu/atd/reviews/cccc2006/c24.cfm

Siegel, D. (2007). *The mindful brain: Reflection and attunement in the cultivation of well-being*. New York: W.W. Norton.

Siegle, D. (2011). Facing Facebook: A guide for nonteens. *Gifted Child Today, 34*(2), 14–19.

Simmons, J. (2003). Responders are taught, not born. *Journal of Adolescent & Adult Literacy, 46*, 684–693.

Simon, H. A. (1973). The structure of ill-structured problems. *Artificial Intelligence, 4*, 181–201. doi:10.1016/0004-3702(73)90011-8.

Sinclair, J., & Coulthard, M. (1975). *Towards an analysis of discourse*. Oxford, UK: Oxford University Press.

Singel, D., & Sundar, S. S. (2012). Texting, techspeak, and tweens: The relationship between text messaging and English grammar skills. *New Media & Society, 14*, 1304–1320. doi:10.1177/1461444812442927.

Skerrett, A. (2010). Lolita, Facebook, and the third space of literacy teacher education. *Educational Studies: Journal of the American Educational Studies Association, 46*(1), 67–84.

Smith, B., & Gorsuch, G. (2004). Synchronous computer mediated communication captured by usability lab technologies: New interpretations. *System, 32*, 553–575. doi:10.1016/j.system.2004.09.012.

Smith, F. (1983). Reading like a writer. *Language Arts, 60*, 558–567.

Smith, F. (1988). *Joining the literacy club: Further essays into education*. Portsmouth, NH: Heinemann.

Smith, K., & Tillema, H. (2003). Clarifying different types of portfolio use. *Assessment & Evaluation in Higher Education, 28*, 625–648. doi:10.1080/0260293 032000130252.

Smoker, T. J., Murphy, C. E., & Rockwell, A. K. (2009). *Comparing memory for handwriting versus typing*. Paper presented at the Human Factors and Ergonomics Society Annual Meeting. New York, NY.

Snipes, V., Ellis, W., & Thomas, J. (2006). Are HBCUs up to speed technologically? One case study. *Journal of Black Studies, 36*, 382–395. doi:10.1177/0021934705278782.

Soames, C. (2012). Most popular search engines – UK, US and worldwide. *Smart Insights*. Retrieved from http://www.smartinsights.com/search-engine-optimisation-seo/multilingual-seo/search-engine-popularity-statistics/

Sommers, E. (1993). *Student-centered, not teacher-abandoned: Peer response groups that work*. Retrieved from ERIC database.

Sommers, N. (1982). Responding to student writing. *College Composition and Communication, 33*, 148–156. doi:10.2307/357622.

Soter, A. O., Wilkinson, I. A., Murphy, P. K., Rudge, L., Reninger, K., & Edwards, M. (2008). What the discourse tells us: Talk and indicators of high-level comprehension. *International Journal of Educational Research, 47*, 372–391. doi:10.1016/j.ijer.2009.01.001.

Sotillo, S. M. (2000). Discourse functions and syntactic complexity in synchronous and asynchronous communication. *Language Learning & Technology, 4*(1), 82–119.

Spillane, J. P. (2012). Data in practice: Conceptualizing data-based decision-making phenomena. *American Journal of Education, 118*(2), 113–141. doi:10.1086/663283.

Spiro, R. (2004). Principled pluralism for adaptive flexibility in teaching and learning to read. In Ruddell, R. B., & Unrau, N. (Eds.), *Theoretical models and processes of reading* (5th ed., pp. 654–659). Newark, DE: International Reading Association.

Spiro, R. C., Coulson, R. L., Feltovich, P. J., & Anderson, D. K. (2004). Cognitive flexibility theory: Advanced knowledge acquisition in ill-structured domains. In Ruddell, R. B., & Unrau, N. (Eds.), *Theoretical models and processes of reading* (5th ed., pp. 640–653). Newark, DE: International Reading Association.

Spiro, R. J., Feltovich, P. J., & Coulson, R. L. (1996). Two epistemic world-views: Prefigurative schemas and learning in complex domains. *Applied Cognitive Psychology, 10*, 51–61. doi:10.1002/(SICI)1099-0720(199611)10:7<51::AID-ACP437>3.0.CO;2-F.

St. Augustine. (398). *Confessions.*

Stake, R. E. (1995). *The art of case study research.* Thousand Oaks, CA: Sage Publications.

Stanley, L. (2004). The epistolarium: On theorizing letters and correspondences. *Auto/Biography, 12*, 201–235. doi:10.1191/0967550704ab014oa.

Stannard, R. (2007). Using screen capture software in student feedback. *The Higher Education Academy.* Retrieved from http://www.english.heacademy.ac.uk/explore/publications/casestudies/technology/camtasia.php

Stannard, R. (2008). Screen capture software for feedback in language education. In *Proceedings of the Second International Wireless Ready Symposium.* Retrieved from http://wirelessready.nucba.ac.jp/Stannard.pdf

Starkey, L. (2010). Teachers' pedagogical reasoning and action in the digital age. *Teachers and Teaching: Theory and Practice, 16*(2), 233–244. doi:10.1080/13540600903478433.

Stefanone, M., & Jang, C. (2008). Writing for friends and family: The interpersonal nature of blogs. *Journal of Computer-Mediated Communication, 13*, 123–140. doi:10.1111/j.1083-6101.2007.00389.x.

Steinfield, C., Ellison, N. B., & Lampe, C. (2008). Social capital, self-esteem, and use of online social network sites: A longitudinal analysis. *Journal of Applied Developmental Psychology, 29*(6), 434–445. doi:10.1016/j.appdev.2008.07.002.

Steinkuehler, C., Black, R., & Clinton, K. (2005). Researching literacy as tool, place, and way of being. *Reading Research Quarterly, 40*(1), 7–12.

Stevens, H. (2012, September 15). Bringing up the iKid generation. *The Chicago Tribune.* Retrieved from http://articles.chicagotribune.com/2012-09-15/features/sc-cons-0913-savvy-shopper-kid-tech-20120915_1_ipad-apps-empty-calories-devices

Stewart, T. (1997). *Intellectual capital: The new wealth of organizations.* New York: Doubleday.

Still, B. (2006). Talking to students embedded voice commenting as a tool for critiquing student writing. *Journal of Business and Technical Communication, 20*(4), 460–475. doi:10.1177/1050651906290270.

Stokes, L. (2011). *The enduring quality and value of the national writing project's teacher development institutes: Teachers' assessments of NWP contributions to their classroom practice and development as leaders.* Retrieved from http://www.inverness-research.org/reports/2011-11-Rpt-NWP-NWP-Survey-TeacherInst-Final.pdf

Stolle, E. (2008). Teachers, literacy, & technology: Tensions, com- plexities, conceptualizations & practice. In Y. Kim, V. Risko, D. Compton, D. Dickinson, M. Hundley, R. Jimenez, K. Leander, & D. Wells-Rowe (Eds.), *57th Yearbook of the National Reading Conference* (pp. 56–69). Oak Creek, WI: National Reading Conference.

Strasma, K. (2009). Spotlighting: Peer-response in digitally supported first-year writing courses. *Teaching English in the Two-Year College, 37*(2), 153–160.

Strauss, A. L. (1987). *Qualitative analysis for social scientists*. Cambridge, UK: University Press. doi:10.1017/CBO9780511557842.

Strauss, A. L., & Corbin, J. (1998). *Basics of qualitative research* (2nd ed.). Newbury Park, CA: Sage.

Street, B. (2003). What's "new" in new literacy studies? Critical approaches to literacy in theory and practice. *Current Issues in Comparative Education, 5*(2).

Street, B. (1984). *Literacy in theory and practice*. Cambridge, UK: Cambridge University Press.

Street, B. (1995). *Social literacies: Critical approaches to literacy in development, ethnography, and education*. London: Longman.

Street, B. (1998). New literacies in theory and practice: What are the implications for language in education? *Linguistics and Education, 10*(1), 1–24. doi:10.1016/S0898-5898(99)80103-X.

Street, B. (2000). Literacy events and literacy practices: Theory and practice in the new literacy studies. In Martin-Jones, M., & Jones, K. (Eds.), *Multilingual literacies: Reading and writing different worlds* (pp. 17–29). Philadelphia: John Benjamin.

Street, B. (2003). What's new in new literacy studies? *Current Issues in Comparative Education, 5*(2), 1–14.

Street, B. V. (1999). Literacy and social change: The significance of social context in the development of literacy programmes. In Wagner, D. A. (Ed.), *Future of literacy in a changing world* (pp. 55–72). Cresskill, NJ: Hampton Press.

Strömqvist, S., Holmqvist, K., Johansson, V., Karlsson, H., & Wengelin, Å. (2006). What keystroke logging can reveal about writing. In Sullivan, K. P. H., & Lindgren, E. (Eds.), *Computer keystroke logging and writing: Methods and applications*. Amsterdam: Elsevier.

Styslinger, M. E. (1998). Some milk, a song, and a set of keys: Students respond to peer revision. *Teaching & Change, 5*(2), 116–138.

Styslinger, M. E. (2008). Gendered performances during peer revision. *Literacy Research and Instruction, 47*(3), 211–228. doi:10.1080/19388070802062815.

Suárez-Orozco, C., Suárez-Orozco, M. M., & Todorova, I. (2008). *Learning a new land: Immigrant students in American society*. Cambridge, MA: Belknap Press of Harvard University Press.

Suhor, C. (2002). Contemplative reading—The experience, the idea, the applications. *English Journal, 91*(4), 28–32. doi:10.2307/822453.

Sullivan, N., & Pratt, E. (1996). A comparative study of two ESL writing environments: A computer-assisted classroom and a traditional oral classroom. *System, 24*, 491–501. doi:10.1016/S0346-251X(96)00044-9.

Sutherland-Smith, W. (2002). Integrating online discussion in an Australian intensive English language course. *TESOL Journal, 11*(3), 31–35.

Sutherland-Smith, W. (2002). Weaving the literacy web: Changes in reading from page to screen. *The Reading Teacher, 55*(7), 662–669.

Suttie, J. (2009). Mindfulness and meditation in schools for stress management. *Greater Good Magazine*. Retrieved from http://greatergood.berkeley.edu/

Swanson, K., & Legutko, R. (2008). The effect of book blogging on the motivation of 3rd-grade students. *Online Submission*, 1-8.

Swenson, J., Young, C. A., McGrail, E., Rozema, R., & Whitin, P. (2006). Extending the conversation: New technologies, new literacies, and English education. *English Education, 38*(4), 351–369.

Sykes, J., Oskoz, A., & Thorne, S. (2008). Web 2.0 synthetic immersive environments and mobile resources for language education. *CALICO Journal, 25*(3), 528–546.

Tagliamonte, S. A., & Denis, D. (2008). Linguistic ruin? LOL! Instant messaging and teen language. *American Speech, 83*(1), 3–34. doi:10.1215/00031283-2008-001.

Tallis, R. (2003). *The hand: A philosophical inquiry into human being*. Edinburgh, UK: Edinburgh University Press.

Tannen, D. (1982). *Spoken and written language: Exploring orality and literacy*. ABLEX Publishing Corporation.

Tapscott, D., & Williams, A. (2008). *Wikinomics: How mass collaboration changes everything*. New York: Portfolio.

Taylor, D. B. (2012). Multiliteracies: Moving from theory to practice in teacher education. In A. B. Polly, Mims, & K. Persichitte (Eds.), Creating Technology-Rich Teacher Education Programs: Key Issues (pp. 266-287). Hershey, PA: IGI Global.

Tearle, P. (2003). ICT implementation: What makes the difference? *British Journal of Educational Technology*, *34*(5), 567–583. doi:10.1046/j.0007-1013.2003.00351.x.

Tewissen, F., Lingnau, A., Hoppe, U., Mannhaupt, G., & Nischk, D. (2001). Collaborative writing in a computer-integrated classroom for early learning. In P. Dillenbourg, A. Eurelings, & K. Hakkarainen (Eds.), *Proceedings of the European Conference on Computer-Supported Collaborative Learning* (Euro- CSCL 2001), (pp. 593-600). Maastricht, The Netherlands: Euro-CSCL.

The New London Group. (1996). A pedagogy of multiliteracies: Designing social futures. *Harvard Educational Review*, *66*(1), 60–92.

The New London Group. (2000). A pedagogy of multiliteracies designing social futures. In Cope, B., & Kalantzis, M. (Eds.), *Multiliteracies: Literacy learning and the design of social futures* (pp. 9–37). London: Routledge.

Thomas, A. (2006). Fan fiction online: Engagement, critical response and affective play through writing. *Australian Journal of Language & Literacy*, *29*(3), 226–239.

Thurlow, C. (2006). From statistical panic to moral panic: The metadiscursive construction and popular exaggeration of new media language in the print media. *Journal of Computer-Mediated Communication*, *11*, 667–701. doi:10.1111/j.1083-6101.2006.00031.x.

Tierney, R. J., & Shanahan, T. (1991). Research on the reading-writing relationship--Interactions, transactions, and outcomes. In Barr, R., Kamil, M., Mosenthal, P., & Pearson, P. D. (Eds.), *Handbook of reading research* (pp. 246–280). New York, NY: Longman.

Tobin, L. (2001). Process pedagogy. In Tate, G., Rupiper, A., & Schick, K. (Eds.), *A guide to composition pedagogies* (pp. 1–18). New York: Oxford UP.

Tomlinson, E. (2009). Gender and peer response. *Teaching English in the Two-Year College*, *37*(2), 139–152.

Tompkins, G. E. (1997). *Literacy for the 21st century: A balanced approach*. Upper Saddle River, NJ: Prentice Hall.

Toulmin, S. (2003). *The uses of argument, updated edition*. New York: Cambridge University Press. doi:10.1017/CBO9780511840005.

Tsai, H. F., & Wilkinson, I. A. (2010). *Why should discussion affect reading comprehension? An analysis of theoretical frameworks*. Paper presented at the Annual Meeting of the American Educational Research Association. Denver, CO.

Tseng, M. C. (2010). Subjective and objective evaluation of hypertext reading performance: In-depth analysis of contributing factors. *Journal of Educational Multimedia and Hypermedia*, *19*(2), 221–232. Retrieved from http://www.editlib.org/p/33201.

Turner, K. H. (2013). The challenge of acceptance: Digitalk and language as conformity and resistance. In Spielhagen & Schwarz (Eds.), Adolescence in the 21st Century: Constants and Challenge. Information Age.

Turner, K. H. (2010). Digitalk: A new literacy for a digital generation. *Phi Delta Kappan*, *92*(1), 41–46.

Turner, K. H. (2011). Digitalk: Community, convention, and self-expression. In Rowsell, J., & Abrams, S. A. (Eds.), *Rethinking Identity and Literacy Education in the 21st Century* (pp. 263–282). New York: Teachers College Record Yearbook.

Turner, K. H., Abrams, S., Katic, E., & Donovan, M. J. (2013). Digitalk: The what and the why of adolescent digital language. *Journal of Literacy Research*.

Turner, K. H., & Hicks, T. (2012). That's not writing: Exploring the intersection of digital writing, community literacy, and social justice. *Community Literacy Journal*, *6*(1), 55–78. doi:10.1353/clj.2012.0000.

Tuzi, F. (2004). The impact of e-feedback on the revisions of L2 writers in an academic writing course. *Computers and Composition: An International Journal for Teachers of Writing*, *21*(2), 217–235. doi:10.1016/j.compcom.2004.02.003.

Tyner, K. (1998). *Literacy in the digital world: Teaching and learning in the age of information*. Mahweh, NJ: Erlbaum.

United States Department of Education. (2010). *Transforming American education: Learning powered by technology*. Washington, DC: US Department of Education. Retrieved from http://www.ed.gov/sites/default/files/netp2010.pdf

Unsworth, L. (2001). *Teaching multiliteracies across the curriculum: Changing contexts of text and image in classroom practice*. Buckingham, UK: Open University Press.

van den Akker, J., Gravemeijer, K., McKenney, S., & Nieveen, N. (2007). Introducing educational design research. In van den Akker, J., Gravemeijer, K., McKenney, S., & Nieveen, N. (Eds.), *Educational design research* (pp. 3–7). New York: Routledge.

Van den Bergh, H., Rijlaarsdam, G., Janssen, T., Braaksma, M., Weijen, D., & Tillema, M. (2009). Process execution of writing and reading: Considering text quality, learner and task characteristics. Quality Research in Literacy and Science Education, 399-425.

Van den Branden, K. (2000). Does negotiation of meaning promote reading comprehension? A study of multilingual primary school classes. *Reading Research Quarterly, 35*, 426–443. doi:10.1598/RRQ.35.3.6.

van der Hoeven, J. (1997). *Children's composing: A study into the relationships between writing processes, text quality, and cognitive and linguistic skills* (Vol. 12). Atlanta, GA: Rodopi.

van der Linden, W. J., & Twente Univ. (2000). *Optimal stratification of item pools in a stratified computerized adaptive testing*. Research Report. Twente, The Netherlands: Twente University.

van Galen, G. P. (1991). Handwriting: Issues for a psychomotor theory. *Human Movement Science, 10*, 165–191. doi:10.1016/0167-9457(91)90003-G.

Varela, F. J., Thompson, E., & Rosch, E. (1991). *The embodied mind: Cognitive science and human experience*. Cambridge, MA: MIT Press.

Vasquez, O. A. (2006). Cross-national explorations of sociocultural research on learning. *Review of Research in Education, 30*, 33–64. doi:10.3102/0091732X030001033.

Vasudevan, L., Schultz, K., & Bateman, J. (2010). Rethinking composing in a digital age: Authoring literate identities through multimodal storytelling. *Written Communication, 27*, 442–468. doi:10.1177/0741088310378217.

Vaughn, S., Schumm, J. S., & Gordon, J. (1992). Early spelling acquisition: Does writing really beat the computer? *Learning Disability Quarterly, 15*, 223–228. doi:10.2307/1510245.

Velay, J.-L., & Longcamp, M. (2012). Handwriting versus typewriting: Behavioural and cerebral consequences in letter recognition. In M. Torrance, D. Alamargot, M. Castelló, F. Ganier, O. Kruse, A. Mangen, L. Tolchinsky, & L. van Waes (Eds.), Learning to write effectively: Current trends in European research (pp. 371-373). Emerald Group Publishing Limited.

Vie, S. (2008). Digital divide 2.0: 'Generation M' and online social networking sites in the composition classroom. *Computers and Composition, 25*(1), 9–23. doi:10.1016/j.compcom.2007.09.004.

Vogel, C. (2011, February). CSAP and ACT bootcamp: Using the Liveink reading format. Paper presented at the Colorado Council International Reading Council Annual Conference. Denver, CO.

Vogel, C. A. (2002). A program evaluation of the live ink format. (Unpublished dissertation). University of Denver College of Education, Denver, CO.

Vygotsky, L. S. (1978). *Mind and society: The development of higher psychological processes*. Cambridge, MA: Harvard University Press.

Vygotsky, L. S. (1986). *Thought and language*. Cambridge, MA: MIT Press.

Wade, A., Abrami, P. C., & Sclater, J. (2005). An electronic portfolio to support learning. *Canadian Journal of Learning and Technology, 31*(3). Retrieved from http://cjlt.csj.ualberta.ca/index.php/cjlt/article/view/94/88.

Wade, S. E., & Fauske, J. R. (2004). Dialogue online: Prospective teachers' discourse strategies in computer-mediate discussions. *Reading Research Quarterly, 39*(2), 134–160. doi:10.1598/RRQ.39.2.1.

Wake, D. G., & Modla, V. B. (2012). Using wikis with teacher candidates: Promoting collaborative practice and contextual analysis. *Journal of Research on Technology in Education, 44*(3), 243–265.

Walker, R., & Vogel, C. (2005, June). Live ink: Brain-based text formatting raises standardized test scores. Paper presented at the National Educational Computing Conference. Philadelphia, PA.

Walker, R., Gordon, A. S., Schloss, P., Fletcher, C. R., Vogel, C., & Walker, S. (2007). Visual-syntactic text formatting: Theoretical basis and empirical evidence for impact on human reading. Paper presented at the IEEE Professional Communication Conference. Seattle, WA.

Walker, A. (2006). Introduction. In *We are the ones we have been waiting for: Inner light in a time of darkness*. New York: The New Press.

Walker, S., Schloss, P., Fletcher, C. R., Vogel, C. A., & Walker, R. (2005). Visual-syntactic text formatting: A new method to enhance online reading. *Reading Online, 8*(6).

Wall, K., Higgins, S., Miller, J., & Packard, N. (2006). Developing digital portfolios: Investigating how digital portfolios can facilitate pupil talk about learning. *Technology, Pedagogy and Education, 15*, 261–273. doi:10.1080/14759390600923535.

Walters, P., & Kop, R. (2009). Heidegger, digital technology, and postmodern education: From being in cyberspace to meeting on MySpace. *Bulletin of Science, Technology & Society, 29*(4), 278–286. doi:10.1177/0270467609336305.

Walther, J. B., & D'Addario, K. P. (2001). The impacts of emoticons on message interpretation in computer-mediated communication. *Social Science Computer Review, 19*(3), 324–347. doi:10.1177/089443930101900307.

Wang, Q., & Woo, H. L. (2006). Comparing asynchronous online discussions and face-to-face discussions in a classroom setting. *British Journal of Educational Technology, 38*(2), 272–286. doi:10.1111/j.1467-8535.2006.00621.x.

Ward, M., Peters, G., & Shelley, K. (2010). Student and faculty perceptions of the quality of online learning experiences. *International Review of Research in Open and Distance Learning, 11*(3), 57–77.

Ware, P., Kern, R., & Warschauer, M. (2013). The development of digital literacies. In Manchón, R., & Matsuda, P. K. (Eds.), *Handbook of second and foreign language writing*. New York: De Gruyter Mouton.

Ware, P., & Warschauer, M. (2005). Hybrid literacy texts and practices in technology-intensive environments. *International Journal of Educational Research*. doi:10.1016/j.ijer.2006.07.008.

Warriner, D. S. (2007). Transnational literacies: Immigration, language learning, and identity. *Linguistics and Education, 18*(3-4), 201–214. doi:10.1016/j.linged.2007.10.003.

Warschauer, M. (1997). Computer-mediated collaborative learning: Theory and practice. *Modern Language Journal, 81*(4), 470–481. doi:10.1111/j.1540-4781.1997.tb05514.x.

Warschauer, M. (1999). *Electronic literacies: Language, culture, and power in online education*. Mahwah, NJ: Lawrence Erlbaum Associates.

Warschauer, M. (2000). The changing global economy and the future of English teaching. *TESOL Quarterly, 34*(3), 511–535. doi:10.2307/3587741.

Warschauer, M. (2006). *Laptops and literacy: Learning in the wireless classroom*. New York: Teachers College Press.

Warschauer, M. (2007). Technology and writing. In Davison, C., & Cummins, J. (Eds.), *The international handbook of English language teaching* (pp. 907–912). Norwell, MA: Springer. doi:10.1007/978-0-387-46301-8_60.

Warschauer, M. (2009). Digital literacy studies: Progress and prospects. In Baynham, M., & Prinsloo, M. (Eds.), *The future of literacy studies* (pp. 123–140). New York: Palgrave Macmillan.

Warschauer, M. (2011). *Learning in the cloud: How and (why) to transform schools with digital media*. New York: Teachers College Press.

Warschauer, M., & Grimes, D. (2008). Automated writing assessment in the classroom. *Pedagogies. International Journal (Toronto, Ont.), 3*, 22–36.

Warschauer, M., Knobel, M., & Stone, L. (2004). Technology and equity in schooling: Deconstructing the digital divide. *Educational Policy, 18*, 562–588. doi:10.1177/0895904804266469.

Warschauer, M., & Ware, P. (2008). Learning, change, and power: Competing frames of technology and literacy. In Coiro, J., Knobel, M., Lankshear, C., & Leu, J. (Eds.), *Handbook of research on new literacies* (pp. 215–240). New York: Lawrence Erlbaum.

Waters, N. L. (2007). Why you can't cite Wikipedia in my class. *Communications of the ACM, 50*(9), 15–17. doi:10.1145/1284621.1284635.

Weigle, S. (1994). Effects of training on raters of ESL compositions. *Language Testing, 11*, 197–223. doi:10.1177/026553229401100206.

Wells, G. (2007). Semiotic mediation, dialogue and the construction of knowledge. *Human Development, 50*(5), 244–274. doi:10.1159/000106414.

Wenger, E. C. (1998). *Communities of practice: Learning, meaning and identity*. New York, NY: Cambridge University Press.

Whitaker, D., Berninger, V., Johnston, J., & Swanson, H. L. (1994). Intraindividual differences in levels of language in intermediate grade writers: Implications for the translating process. *Learning and Individual Differences, 6*, 107–130. doi:10.1016/1041-6080(94)90016-7.

Whitehead, A. N. (1929). *The aims of education and other essays*. New York: Macmillan.

Whitney, A. (2008). Teacher transformation in the national writing project. *Research in the Teaching of English, 43*(2), 144–187.

Wieder, B. (2011). *Publishers struggle to get professors to use latest e-textbook features*. Retrieved from http://chronicle.com.ezproxy.lib.usf.edu/blogs/wiredcampus/publishers-struggle-to-get-professors-to-use-latest-e-textbook-features/29683

Wikipedia. (n.d.). *Blogging*. Retrieved November 30, 2012, from http://www.wikipedia.org

Wilkenson, I. A. G., & Son, E. H. (2011). A dialogic turn in research on learning and teaching to comprehend. In Kamil, M. L., Pearson, P. D., Moje, E. B., & Afflerbach, P. P. (Eds.), *Handbook of Reading Research* (*Vol. 4*, pp. 359–387). New York: Routledge.

Williams, B. T. (2005). Leading double lives: Literacy and technology in and out of school. *Journal of Adolescent & Adult Literacy, 48*(8), 702–706. doi:10.1598/JAAL.48.8.7.

Wilson, C., & Coyne, K. (2001). Tracking usability issues: To bug or not to bug? *Interaction, 8*, 15–19. doi:10.1145/369825.369828.

Wilson, F. R. (1998). *The hand: How its use shapes the brain, language, and human culture*. New York: Pantheon Books.

Wilson, N., Zygouris-Coe, V., Cardullo, V., & Fong, J. L. (2013). Pedagogical frameworks of e-reader technologies in education. In Keengwe, J. (Ed.), *Pedagogical applications and social effects of mobile technology integration* (pp. 1–24). Hershey, PA: IGI Global. doi:10.4018/978-1-4666-2985-1.ch001.

Wolfe, C., Britt, M., Petrovic, M., Albrecht, M., & Kopp, K. (2009). The efficacy of a web-based counterargument tutor. *Behavior Research Methods, 41*, 691–698. doi:10.3758/BRM.41.3.691 PMID:19587180.

Wolf, M. J. P. (2000). *Abstracting reality: Art, communication, and cognition in the digital age*. Lanham, MD: University Press of America.

Wolf, M. K., Crosson, A. C., & Resnick, L. B. (2005). Classroom talk for rigorous reading comprehension instruction. *Reading Psychology, 26*(1), 27–53. doi:10.1080/02702710490897518.

Wolsey, T. D., & Grisham, D. L. (2012). *Transforming writing instruction in the digital age: Techniques for grades* 5-12. New York: The Guilford Press.

Wolsey, T. D., Grisham, D. L., & Hiebert, E. H. (2012). What is text complexity? *Teacher Development Series*. Retrieved from http://textproject.org/tds

Wolsey, T. D. (2010). Complexity in student writing: The relationship between the task and vocabulary uptake. *Literacy Research and Instruction, 49*(2), 194–208. doi:10.1080/19388070902947360.

Wolsey, T. D., Lapp, D., & Fisher, D. (2012). Students' and teachers' perceptions: An inquiry into academic writing. *Journal of Adolescent & Adult Literacy, 55*(8), 714–724. doi:10.1002/JAAL.00086.

Wong, R. M., & Hew, K. F. (2010). The impact of blogging and scaffolding on primary school pupils' narrative writing: A case study. *International Journal of Web-Based Learning and Teaching Technologies, 5*(2), 1–17. doi:10.4018/jwltt.2010040101.

Woodard, R. L., Magnifico, A. M., & McCarthey S. J. (2013). Supporting teacher metacognition about formative assessment in online writing environments. *E-Learning and Digital Media, 10*(4).

Wood, C., Jackson, E., Hart, L., Plester, B., & Wilde, L. (2011). The effect of text messaging on 9- and 10-year-old children's reading, spelling, and phonological processing skills. *Journal of Computer Assisted Learning, 27*, 28–36. doi:10.1111/j.1365-2729.2010.00398.x.

Wouters, P., Paas, F., & van Merriënboer, J. J. G. (2008). How to optimize learning from animated models: A review of guidelines based on cognitive load. *Review of Educational Research, 78*, 645–675. doi:10.3102/0034654308320320.

Wrede, O. (2003, May). *Weblogs and discourse: Weblogs as a transformational technology for higher education and academic research*. Paper presented at the Blogtalk Conference. Vienna, Austria. Retrieved from http://wrede.interfacedesign.org/articles/Weblogs-and-discourse

Xie, K., DeBacker, T. K., & Ferguson, C. (2006). Extending the traditional classroom through online discussion: The role of student motivation. *Journal of Educational Computing Research, 34*(1), 67–89. doi:10.2190/7BAK-EGAH-3MH1-K7C6.

Yagelski, R. P. (2009). A thousand writers writing: Seeking change through the radical practice of writing as a way of being. *English Education, 42*(1), 6–28.

Yancey, K. B. (2009). *Writing in the 21st century: A report from the national council of teachers of English*. Urbana, IL: NCTE. Retrieved from http://www.ncte.org/library/NCTEFiles/Press/Yancey_final.pdf

Yancey, K. B. (2004). Definition, intersection, and difference – Mapping the landscape of voice. In Yancey, K. B. (Ed.), *Voices on voice: Perspectives, definitions, inquiry (vii – xxiv)*. Urbana, IL: National Council of Teachers of English.

Yancey, K. B. (2009). 2008 NCTE presidential address: The impulse to compose and the age of composition. *Research in the Teaching of English, 43*(3), 316–338.

Yelland, N. (1999). Reconceptualising schooling with technology for the 21st century: Images and reflections. *Information Technology in Childhood Education Annual*, (1): 39–59.

Yin, R. K. (2003). *Case study research: Design and methods* (3rd ed.). Thousand Oaks, CA: Sage Publications.

Yin, R. K. (2009). *Case study research: Design and methods* (4th ed.). Thousand Oaks, CA: Sage.

Yi, Y. (2007). Engaging literacy: A biliterate student's composing practices beyond school. *Journal of Second Language Writing, 16*(1), 23–39. doi:10.1016/j.jslw.2007.03.001.

Yi, Y. (2010). Adolescent multilingual writers' transitions across in- and out-of-school writing contexts. *Journal of Second Language Writing, 19*(1), 17–32. doi:10.1016/j.jslw.2009.10.001.

Young, M., Slota, S., Cutter, A., Jalette, G., Mullin, G., & Lai, B. et al. (2012). Our princess is in another castle: A review of trends in serious gaming for education. *Review of Educational Research, 82*, 61–89. doi:10.3102/0034654312436980.

Zammit, K. P. (2011). Connecting multiliteracies and engagement of students from low socio-economic backgrounds: Using Bernstein's pedagogic discourse as a bridge. *Language and Education, 25*(3), 203–220. doi:10.1080/09500782.2011.560945.

Zammit, K., & Downes, T. (2002). New learning environments and the multiliterate individual: A framework for educators. *Australian Journal of Language and Literacy, 25*(2), 24–36.

Zawilinski, L. (2009). Hot blogging: A framework for blogging to promote higher order thinking. *The Reading Teacher, 62*(8), 650–661. doi:10.1598/RT.62.8.3.

Zhang, J. (2007). Conditional covariance theory and detection for polytomous items. *Psychometrika, 72*, 69–91. doi:10.1007/s11336-004-1257-7.

Zhao, Y., & Frank, K. A. (2003). Factors affecting technology uses in schools: An ecological perspective. *American Educational Research Journal, 40*, 807–840. doi:10.3102/00028312040004807.

Zhao, Y., & Lai, C. (2008). Technology and second language learning: Promises and problems. In Parker, L. L. (Ed.), *Technology-mediated learning environments for young English learners: Connections in and out of school.* Mahwah, NJ: Lawrence Erlbaum Associates.

Zheng, B., & Warschauer, M. (2012). *Blogging to learn: Participation and literacy among linguistically diverse fifth-grade students.* Paper presented at the 2012 American Educational Research Association Annual Meeting. Vancouver, Canada.

Zickhur, K., & Smith, A. (2012). Digital differences. *Pew Internet and American Life Project.* Retrieved from http://www.pewInternet.org

Zubizarreta, J. (2004). *The learning portfolio: Reflective practice for improving student learning.* San Francisco, CA: Jossey-Bass.

About the Contributors

Kristine E. Pytash is an assistant professor in Teaching, Learning, and Curriculum Studies at Kent State University's College of Education, Health, and Human Services, where she co-directs the secondary Integrated Language Arts teacher preparation program. Prior to obtaining her Ph.D. in curriculum and instruction with a concentration on literacy education, she was a high school English teacher. Her research focuses on disciplinary writing, writing instruction in juvenile detention facilities, and the literacy practices of youth in alternative schools and juvenile detention facilities. Her recent work has appeared in the *Journal of Adolescent & Adult Literacy, English Journal, Voices from the Middle*, and *Middle School Journal*. She has reviewed for *Voices from the Middle* and the *British Journal of Educational Technology*.

Richard E. Ferdig is the Summit Professor of Learning Technologies and Professor of Instructional Technology at Kent State University. He works within the Research Center for Educational Technology and also the School of Lifespan Development and Educational Sciences. He earned his Ph.D. in Educational Psychology from Michigan State University. He has served as researcher and instructor at Michigan State University, the University of Florida, the Wyzsza Szkola Pedagogiczna (Krakow, Poland), and the Università degli studi di Modena e Reggio Emilia (Italy). At Kent State University, his research, teaching, and service focus on combining cutting-edge technologies with current pedagogic theory to create innovative learning environments. His research interests include online education, educational games and simulations, and what he labels a deeper psychology of technology. In addition to publishing and presenting nationally and internationally, Ferdig has also been funded to study the impact of emerging technologies such as K-12 Virtual Schools. Rick is the Editor-in-Chief of the *International Journal of Gaming and Computer Mediated Simulations*, the Associate Editor-in-Chief of the *Journal of Technology and Teacher Education*, and currently serves as a Consulting Editor for the Development Editorial Board of *Educational Technology Research and Development* and on the Review Panel of the *British Journal of Educational Technology*.

* * *

Russell D. Brandon is a graduate student in Department of Psychology and the Learning Sciences Institute at Arizona State University. He is pursuing doctoral research in the area of Cognitive Science. His research interests focus upon the use of games and game features (e.g., narrative, customizable avatars, and competition) to increase the efficacy of instructional technologies and influence learning and enjoyment in educational games. This work also considers the effects of task framing and students' expectations of enjoyment and learning. Other interests include the influence of prior knowledge and ability on learning in educational games, and how students' broader perceptions of work and play affect their experience with instructional technologies.

Kendra N. Bryant, Ph.D., is currently an assistant professor of English at Florida A&M University where she teaches First Year Composition and Improving Writing. She spent four years teaching high school English prior to moving into postsecondary education. Kendra is twice published in Deborah Plant's (Ed.) *"The Inside Light": New Critical Essays on Zora Neale Hurston*, 2010, and is the 2012 recipient of the College Language Association's Margaret Walker Memorial Prize in poetry. In addition to contemplative education, her interests lie in womanist theory, spiritual memoir, creative nonfiction, civil rights rhetoric, hip-hop, and poetry.

Penelope Collins is an Associate Professor in the School of Education at the University of California, Irvine. Her research examines the development of language and literacy skills for children from linguistically diverse backgrounds, and the early identification of children at-risk for reading difficulties. Currently, she is involved in ongoing projects on effective instructional interventions to promote academic success for English learners in elementary, middle, and secondary school. In addition to her scholarly research, Dr. Collins co-authored the Institute for Education Sciences' guide for practitioners and administrators, *Effective Literacy and Language Instruction for English Learners in the Elementary Grades, An IES Practice Guide*, and the curricular program for struggling readers in elementary and middle school, *California Gateways: Mastering the California Standards*. Dr. Collins' international work includes writing reports on student performance on early grade reading in Zambia and Yemen for the United States Agency for International Development.

Jamie Colwell is an assistant professor of literacy at Old Dominion University in Norfolk, Virginia. Her research focuses on adolescent and disciplinary literacy and using digital technology in literacy instruction. Dr. Colwell primarily employs qualitative and formative experiment research methodologies in her research. Her research is set in middle schools and in teacher education, working with educators to integrate disciplinary and digital literacy instruction into content area curricula. She also works closely with public libraries to integrate online platforms of learning to enhance summer reading programs for adolescents. Dr. Colwell's teaching is in content area literacy at both the undergraduate and graduate levels.

Jennifer M. Conner-Zachocki is Assistant Professor of Language Education and Coordinator of Literacy Education in the Division of Education at Indiana University, Columbus, in Columbus, Indiana. She teaches language-related courses for pre-service and in-service teachers, including those that emphasize at their curricular core issues of critical literacy, sociolinguistics, and digital literacies. Her current research is situated in New Literacies Studies and the impact of digital writing and social networking tools on the understandings and identities of pre-service and in-service teachers and their students. A second strand of research considers the potential of action research (teacher research) for supporting pre-service teachers' understandings of literacy as a complex social practice, and of literacy instruction as apprenticing students into the discourses and social practices of literate communities.

Jen Scott Curwood is a lecturer in English education and media studies at the University of Sydney, where she is a lead researcher in the Sciences and Technologies of Learning Network and affiliated with the Centre for Research on Computer-Supported Learning and Cognition. Her research focuses on adolescent literacy, technology, and teacher professional development. A former high school English teacher, Jen holds a Ph.D. from the University of Wisconsin – Madison; her recent work has appeared in the *Journal of Adolescent & Adult Literacy, E-Learning and Digital Media, International Journal of Learning and Media, English Teaching: Practice and Critique, The Reading Teacher*, and *Literacy*.

Bernadette Dwyer lectures in St. Patrick's College, Dublin City University, Ireland, where she teaches courses in literacy studies at undergraduate and post graduate levels. She is also involved in a range of continuing professional development courses with teachers, both nationally and internationally. Bernadette completed her doctoral studies in 2010 at the University of Nottingham, UK. Dr. Dwyer's current research focuses on the development of new literacies, particularly online reading comprehension processes, digital tools that support the development of reading and writing, and supporting struggling readers in an online environment. Bernadette has presented at national and international conferences and has authored numerous reports, chapters, and articles. She is a member of the Board of Directors of the International Reading Association (2013-2016).

Douglas Fisher, Ph.D., is Professor of Language and Literacy Education in the Department of Teacher Education at San Diego State University and a classroom teacher at Health Sciences High & Middle College. He is a member of the California Reading Hall of Fame and is the recipient of several awards including the International Reading Association Celebrate Literacy Award, the Farmer award for excellence in writing from the National Council of Teachers of English, and the Christa McAuliffe award for excellence in teacher education. He has published numerous articles and books on school-wide approaches to improving student achievement, reading, and literacy, differentiated instruction, assessment, and curriculum design. He is a board member of the Literacy Research Association and co-editor of NCTE's middle level journal, *Voices from the Middle*. He is highly sought after for his dynamic and engaging professional development workshops.

Troy Hicks is an associate professor of English at Central Michigan University and focuses his work on the teaching of writing, literacy and technology, and teacher education and professional development. A former middle school teacher, he collaborates with K–12 colleagues and explores how they implement newer literacies in their classrooms. Hicks directs CMU's Chippewa River Writing Project, a site of the National Writing Project, and he frequently conducts professional development workshops related to writing and technology. Also, Hicks is author of the *The Digital Writing Workshop* (Heinemann, 2009) and a co-author of *Because Digital Writing Matters* (Jossey-Bass, 2010) as well as numerous journal articles. In March 2011, Hicks was honored with CMU's Provost's Award for junior faculty who have demonstrated outstanding achievement in research and creative activity. Most importantly, he is the father of six digital natives and is always learning something new about writing and technology from them.

Jennifer Higgs is a doctoral student of Language, Literacy, and Culture in the Graduate School of Education at UC Berkeley, with a designated emphasis in new media. Her research, which focuses on the integration of digital tools in secondary English classrooms and the impact of digital cultures on literacy practices and pedagogical approaches, is informed and inspired by her experiences as a middle and high school English teacher.

Mary Beth Hines is Chair of the Literacy, Culture, and Language Education Department at Indiana University, Bloomington. She has taught composition classes at the high school and college levels. She has taught teacher education courses on writing to pre-service and in-service English teachers. She has published a number of journal articles and book chapters on research that focuses on the intersection of literacy and social justice. She is currently conducting a qualitative study of English teachers and their students using digital media to explore social justice, focusing on the ways that students enact and resist engagement in discussions of social justice issues.

Michelle Honeyford is an Assistant Professor in Language and Literacy in the Faculty of Education at the University of Manitoba. Her research interests focus on understanding how learning is mediated by students' cultural identities and how ways of knowing and learning privileged in schools can be expanded to include and represent diverse youth more effectively, particularly through new media, multiliteracies, and critical inquiry. These interests are framed by her commitment to equity and her belief that literacy is a powerful tool for civic engagement and social justice. Dr. Honeyford received her Ph.D. in Literacy, Culture, and Language Education from Indiana University, Bloomington.

Sarah-Beth Hopton is a Ph.D. student studying Rhetoric & Technical Communications at the University of South Florida in Tampa, Florida. She holds two Master's degrees from Mercy College and Lancaster University in English Literature and Creative Nonfiction. She is a graduate of the Journalism program at Florida Southern College, and has worked at the state and national levels of government as a reporter and aide. Her research interests include online curriculum development, big data, and social justice, but the common thread is technology. She is particularly interested in how technology enhances access, participation, and political change. Her dissertation is tentatively titled, "Evidence of Things Not Seen: A Critical and Network Analysis of Congressional Testimony on Agent Orange."

Sarah Hunt-Barron is an assistant professor of education at Converse College in Spartanburg, SC. Her research interests include using digital technology in writing and literacy and the development of teachers of writing. Dr. Hunt-Barron conducts her research primarily with middle and high school teachers and students. The director of the middle level education and gifted education programs at Converse College, she works with educators to integrate writing and digital literacy instruction across the curriculum. Dr. Hunt-Barron is also actively involved with the Upstate Writing Project, a site of the National Writing Project.

Jin Kyoung Hwang is a Ph.D. student in Education at University of California, Irvine. Her research interests include understanding (a) first and second language and literacy development and (b) academic language development among adolescent students. Her ongoing work includes examining how different subgroups of language minority learners write academic texts in comparison to their native-English-speaking peers. She is also investigating the relation between students' English language proficiency status and their responsiveness to an academic vocabulary intervention. As she progresses through the graduate program, Jin Kyoung hopes to make contributions to the field by developing her research skills and deepening her knowledge around language minority learners and their language and literacy development. As a mother of a 30-month-old toddler, Jin Kyoung enjoys spending time with her son and watching him grow up way too quickly.

Brian Kissel is an Associate Professor of Reading and Elementary Education at the University of North Carolina at Charlotte. He conducts research in writing development, writing pedagogy, and digital literacy. He teaches courses in Elementary Language Arts, K-12 Writing Development and Instruction, and Multiliteracies.

Sonia Kline is a doctoral candidate in Curriculum and Instruction at the University of Illinois at Urbana-Champaign. She formerly taught K-8 children, and worked as a technology curriculum manager in schools in Canterbury, Budapest, and New York. Her research interests evolve from points where issues of literacy, learning, and technology converge.

Jayne C. Lammers is an assistant professor in Teaching and Curriculum at the University of Rochester's Warner School of Education, where she directs the English education teacher preparation program. Her research focuses on adolescents' literacy learning, particularly in online affinity spaces, and aims to shape classroom practice in ways that motivate and prepare young people for 21st century futures. Jayne is a former secondary English/Reading teacher who earned her Ph.D. from Arizona State University. Her recent work has appeared in *Learning, Media, and Technology*, *English Teaching: Practice and Critique*, and *Journal of Adolescent & Adult Literacy*.

Diane Lapp, EdD, Distinguished Professor of Education in the Department of Teacher Education at San Diego State University (SDSU), has taught in elementary and middle schools. She is currently also an English/literacy teacher and instructional coach at Health Sciences High and Middle College (HSHMC) in San Diego, CA. Her major areas of research and instruction regard issues related to struggling readers and writers, their families, and their teachers. Coeditor of *Voices From The Middle*, published by National Council of Teachers of English (NCTE), Dr. Lapp has authored, coauthored and edited numerous articles, columns, texts, handbooks and children's materials on reading, language arts, and instructional issues. She has also chaired and co-chaired several International Reading Association (IRA) and Literacy Research Association (LRA) Committees. Her many educational awards include being named as the Outstanding Teacher Educator and Faculty Member in the Department of Teacher Education at SDSU, the Distinguished Research Lecturer from SDSU's Graduate Division of Research, IRA's 1996 Outstanding Teacher Educator of the Year, and IRA's 2011 John Manning Award recipient for her work in public schools. Dr. Lapp is also a member of both the California and the International Reading, Halls of Fame. Dr. Lapp has co-authored three recent texts that relate to the CCSS, two related columns for IRA, and has conducted many workshops addressing topics related to the CCSS.

Lotta Larson earned a Ph.D. in 2007 and is currently an Associate Professor at Kansas State University, where she teaches courses in the areas of literacy, leadership, and instructional technologies. She advises doctoral students and reading specialists. Dr. Larson's research examines affordances of digital reading devices and electronic texts in K-12 classrooms as a means to differentiating instruction, supporting comprehension, and increasing motivation and engagement. Dr. Larson is a frequent presenter at both national and international conferences and her research has been published in multiple journals including *The Reading Teacher* and *Journal of Adolescent & Adult Literacy*.

Alicia Marie Magnifico is a learning scientist and an IES postdoctoral fellow in the College of Education at the University of Illinois at Urbana-Champaign. Her research interests focus on adolescents' in-school and out-of-school writing and literacies, participation in digital media sites, and critique practices. She has investigated such topics in classrooms, extracurricular writing spaces, and online affinity spaces. A former secondary school teacher, Alecia holds a Ph.D. from the University of Wisconsin-Madison. Recently, her work has appeared in such venues as *E-learning and Digital Media*, *Educational Psychologist*, and the *Journal of Adolescent & Adult Literacy*.

Anne Mangen, Ph.D., is post-doctoral researcher at Oslo and Akershus University College, Norway, and associate professor in literacy and reading research at The Reading Centre, University of Stavanger, Norway. Research interests include the impact of digital technology on reading and writing, and she is particularly interested in cross-disciplinary approaches to reading and writing focusing on the multisensory, embodied aspects involved in handwriting vs. typewriting, and in reading print vs. reading on screens.

She is currently doing research on how medium-specific specific affordances of hand-held transportable reading devices such as surf tablets (e.g., iPads), and e-readers (e.g., Kindle, Kobo) impact cognitive and emotional/experiential aspects of reading different kinds of texts for different purposes (e.g., study reading of expository/informational texts; recreational reading of literary texts). Additional research area: physiological, psychological, phenomenological, and educational (social/cultural, pedagogical) implications of replacing handwriting with typewriting.

Sarah McCarthey is a professor in the department of Curriculum and Instruction at the University of Illinois at Urbana-Champaign. Her main research interests focus on understanding the impact of professional development on teachers' writing instruction, philosophies of writing, assessment methods, and perceptions of professional development.

Ewa McGrail, Ph.D., is an Associate Professor of Language and Literacy at Georgia State University. Dr. McGrail is the winner (with Anne Davis) of the *Journal of Research in Childhood Education* Distinguished Education Research Article Award for 2011 and the recipient of the *National Leadership Fellowship Award Program* from the Conference on English Education (CEE), National Council of Teachers of English, and the Society for Information Technology and Teacher Education (SITE). In her research, she examines the literacy and technology connection; teacher education, professional development and technology; and copyright and media literacy in and out of the classroom. She also explores innovation and newer technology applications for research.

J. Patrick McGrail, Ph.D., is an Assistant Professor of Communication at Jacksonville State University. He teaches theoretics and production in television. Before this, he was Assistant Professor of Communications at Penn State/Altoona, where he taught a broad range of courses in news and entertainment. His research interests include media law and policy, objectivity and narratives in journalism, and international broadcasting, especially that in Great Britain. Prior to his career in academia, Dr. McGrail worked in television as an actor, announcer, and anchor. He also has a keen interest in music production, and holds a number of musical copyrights.

Danielle McNamara is a Professor in the Department of Psychology and Senior Learning Scientist in the Learning Sciences Institute at Arizona State University. She earned her PhD in Cognitive Psychology from the University of Colorado, Boulder. Her work involves the theoretical study of cognitive processes as well as the application of cognitive principles to educational practice. Her research ranges a variety of topics including text comprehension, writing strategies, building tutoring technologies, and developing natural language algorithms. Current instructional and analytical technologies include Coh-Metrix, Common Core TERA, iSTART, iSTART-ME, and Writing Pal. Dr. McNamara's research has been supported by the Institute of Education Sciences, National Science Foundation, McDonnell Foundation, and the Gates Foundation.

Catherine Miller is a doctoral student of Human Development and Cognition in the Graduate School of Education at UC Berkeley, with a focus on reading comprehension, technology, and teacher knowledge. She is currently the managing editor and instructional designer for an online vocabulary project with Pearson Education. Her previous work includes writing, editing, and designing digital curriculum for K-12 schools for the Pearson Foundation.

W. Ian O'Byrne is an Assistant Professor of Educational Technologies at the University of New Haven. Ian is the coordinator of the Instructional Technology and Digital Media Literacy program at the University of New Haven. He is currently a member of AERA, NCTE, and currently serves on the Policy and Legislative Committee for LRA, and the Technology, Communication, and Literacy committee for IRA. Ian has been involved in initiatives in school districts ranging from online and hybrid coursework, integrating technology in the classroom, ePortfolio systems, and supporting marginalized students in literacy practices. His research examines the literacy practices of individuals as they read, write, and communicate in online spaces. Additionally, he is interested in assessment and psychometric properties of these measurements as we move online.

Youngmin Park is a Ph.D. student in Education at the University of California, Irvine, specializing in Language, Literacy, and Technology. Previously a high school teacher and teacher trainer in Korea, she has published and presented on topics related to English teaching and learning in English as a Foreign Language environments. As a recipient of a fellowship from Korean Ministry of Education, she is using her studies at UCI to advance practical knowledge that she brings from her previous posts. Her research focuses on the use of digital media for English language learning, especially adolescent reading instruction. She is currently participating in research on Visual Syntactic Text Formatting (VSTF) to investigate the effectiveness of digital scaffolding in reading development.

P. David Pearson is a professor of Language and Literacy and Human Development in the Graduate School of Education at UC Berkeley, where he conducts research on reading curriculum, pedagogy, and policy practices in K-12 educational settings. His most recent work focuses on a research and development project in which reading, writing, and language serve as tools to promote the acquisition of knowledge and inquiry skills in science.

S. Michael Putman is an Associate Professor in the Department of Reading and Elementary Education at the University of North Carolina at Charlotte. He has taught courses in pedagogy, action research, and literacy in both face-to-face and online formats. His research interests include digital literacy, efficacy, and motivation. He has published works in each of these interests in various outlets, including the *International Journal of Teaching and Learning in Higher Education* and *The Reading Teacher.*

Rod D. Roscoe is an Assistant Research Professor in the Learning Sciences Institute at Arizona State University. He earned his PhD in Cognitive Psychology from the University of Pittsburgh. His research interests include learning and feedback within computer-based learning environments, educational games, learning strategies and self-regulated learning, and peer tutoring. Previous studies have examined the benefits of explaining, questioning, and self-monitoring in peer tutoring, both with human peers and computer-simulated peers. More recent research has investigated how intelligent tutoring systems and automated feedback can be designed to facilitate students' writing strategy acquisition, writing proficiency, and engagement.

Rebecca Rupert is a 9th- and 10th-grade language arts teacher at Monroe County Community School Corporation in Bloomington, Indiana; a Hoosier Writing Project teacher consultant; and a National Board certified teacher.

Erica L. Snow is a graduate student in the Department of Psychology and the Learning Sciences Institute at Arizona State University. She is pursuing doctoral research in the area of Cognitive Science. Her current research explores the interplay of students' learning outcomes, learning behaviors, and individual differences within intelligent tutoring systems and educational games. Ms. Snow is particularly interested in how methodologies from artificial intelligence, educational data mining, and learning analytics can be applied to discover patterns in students' logged interactions with computer-based learning environments.

Mary Amanda (Mandy) Stewart began her career teaching new adolescent immigrants and continues to be passionate about providing a more equitable education for that population of brilliant youth. In 2012, she received a Ph. D. from the Literacy and Language Studies program at the University of North Texas and received the Outstanding Dissertation Award from Phi Delta Kappa International. She is an Assistant Professor of Bilingual and English and a Second Language Education at Texas Woman's University where she pursues her research agenda of understanding adolescent immigrants' out-of-school literacies to create more relevant curriculum and teaching methods that build upon their unique strengths. Dr. Stewart strongly believes that *all* students' multilingual, multiliterate, multicultural, and multimodal skills should be valued in our educational system for the benefit of all of society.

Katie Stover is an Assistant Professor in the Education Department at Furman University in Greenville, SC. She holds a Ph.D. in Curriculum and Instruction in Urban Literacy from the University of North Carolina at Charlotte. Prior to the completion of her doctorate, Katie was a literacy coach, elementary school teacher, and an instructor in the Reading and Elementary Education Department at the University of North Carolina at Charlotte. She has authored a number of publications in the field of literacy in journals such as *The Reading Teacher*, *The Middle School Journal*, and *The Journal of Early Childhood Research*. Katie's research interests include critical literacy, writing for social justice, digital literacy, and teacher education.

Kristen Hawley Turner, PhD, is a faculty member in the Fordham University Graduate School of Education. She teaches in the Adolescence education MST and Contemporary Learning and Interdisciplinary Research PhD programs. Her research looks broadly at the intersections between technology and writing, and she focuses on teaching writing and digital literacy to adolescents. A former high school English and social studies teacher, she is an active member of the National Council of Teachers of English, and she serves as a Teacher Consultant for the National Writing Project.

Charles A. Vogel is an instructor in secondary social sciences and communications for Eagle County School, RE 50–J. He has thirty-eight years of classroom experience. Dr. Vogel earned his B.A. from Western State College, Gunnison Colorado, his M.A. in Curriculum and Instruction from New Mexico State University, Las Cruses, and his PhD from the University of Denver in Curriculum and Instruction. His dissertation topic was a *Program Evaluation of the Liveink Reading Format*. Dr. Vogel was the "Outstanding Educator of the Year, 1991-92" awarded by the Colorado Council for the Social Studies. He continues to research and develop methods in literacy instruction, specializing in the use of VSTF reading and writing formats, utilizing computer technology.

Mark Warchauer is Professor of Education and Informatics at the University of California, Irvine, and Associate Dean of UCI's School of Education. He has previously taught or conducted research in Russia, the Czech Republic, Egypt, and Japan. He is the founding editor of *Language Learning & Technology* journal. His most recent book is *Learning in the Cloud: How (and Why) to Transform Schools with Digital Media* (Teachers College Press, 2011). With funding from the National Science Foundation, Spencer Foundation, Haynes Foundation, and Google Research, he is currently investigating the use of digital tools to promote improved literacy and learning among diverse K-12 students.

Thomas DeVere Wolsey, Ed.D., is specialization coordinator for the literacy graduate degree programs for teachers at Walden University. He worked in public schools for twenty years teaching English and social studies. Currently, his publications appear in *The Journal of Educational Administration*, *The Journal of Adolescent and Adult Literacy*, *The Journal of Literacy Research and Instruction*, and others. His books are published by Guilford Publishing, Holcomb-Hathaway, and Allyn & Bacon/Pearson. Dr. Wolsey is interested in how school spaces affect learning, how technology changes and intersects literacy instruction, and how writing in the disciplines is best taught.

Rebecca Woodard is a doctoral candidate in Curriculum and Instruction at the University of Illinois at Urbana-Champaign. She is a former elementary and middle school literacy teacher, with interests in the social and cultural processes of teaching literacy, including out-of-school literacies, digital literacies, literate identities, and language ideologies.

Soobin Yim is a doctoral student in the School of Education at the University of California, Irvine, with a specialization in Language, Literacy, and Technology. She formerly worked as a language-testing researcher in South Korea and earned her Master's in Language and Literacy at the Harvard Graduate School of Education. Her primary research interest includes second language writing, Computer-Assisted Language Learning (CALL), language assessment, and academic language development.

Index

CPSIA information can be obtained at www.ICGtesting.com
Printed in the USA
BVOW020512120713

325729BV00007B/49/P

9 781466 643413